175 Best Jobs Not Behind a Desk

Part of JIST's Best Jobs™ Series

Michael Farr and Laurence Shatkin, Ph.D.

Also in JIST's *Best Jobs* Series

- *Best Jobs for the 21st Century*
- *200 Best Jobs for College Graduates*
- *300 Best Jobs Without a Four-Year Degree*
- *250 Best Jobs Through Apprenticeships*
- *50 Best Jobs for Your Personality*
- *40 Best Fields for Your Career*
- *225 Best Jobs for Baby Boomers*
- *250 Best-Paying Jobs*
- *150 Best Jobs for Your Skills*

JIST Works

America's Career Publisher

175 Best Jobs Not Behind a Desk

© 2007 by JIST Publishing, Inc.

Published by JIST Works, an imprint of JIST Publishing, Inc.
8902 Otis Avenue
Indianapolis, IN 46216-1033

Phone: 1-800-648-JIST   Fax: 1-800-JIST-FAX
E-mail: info@jist.com   Web site: www.jist.com

Some Other Books by the Authors

Michael Farr

The Quick Resume & Cover Letter Book

Getting the Job You Really Want

The Very Quick Job Search

Overnight Career Choice

Laurence Shatkin

90-Minute College Major Matcher

Quantity discounts are available for JIST products. Have future editions of JIST books automatically delivered to you on publication through our convenient standing order program. Please call 1-800-648-JIST or visit www.jist.com for a free catalog and more information.

Visit www.jist.com for information on JIST, free job search information, book excerpts, and ordering information on our many products. For free information on 14,000 job titles, visit www.careeroink.com.

Acquisitions Editor: Susan Pines
Development Editor: Stephanie Koutek
Cover and Interior Designer: Aleata Howard
Cover Illustration: © 2007 Jupiter Images Corporation
Interior Layout: Aleata Howard
Proofreaders: Paula Lowell, Jeanne Clark
Indexer: Kelly D. Henthorne

Printed in the United States of America

12 11 10 09 08 07   9 8 7 6 5 4 3 2 1

Library of Congress Cataloging-in-Publication Data

Farr, J. Michael.
    175 best jobs not behind a desk / Michael Farr and Laurence Shatkin.
        p. cm. -- (JIST's best jobs series)
    Includes index.
    ISBN 978-1-59357-441-3 (alk. paper)
    1. Vocational guidance--United States. 2. Job descriptions--United States.
    3. Exercise--United States. I. Shatkin, Laurence. II. Title. III. Title:
    One hundred seventy-five.
    HF5382.5.U5F364 2007
    331.7020973--dc22

                                                    2007000651

ISBN 978-1-59357-441-3

This Is a Big Book, But It Is Very Easy to Use

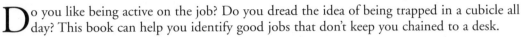

Do you like being active on the job? Do you dread the idea of being trapped in a cubicle all day? This book can help you identify good jobs that don't keep you chained to a desk.

Today's information-based economy depends heavily on office workers. But this book lists lots of good jobs that let you be active and get out of the office. The jobs on the lists are selected and ordered to emphasize those with the highest earnings and the highest demand for workers. Specialized lists arrange these jobs by the level of education or training required and by interest fields. You can also see lists of jobs that have high percentages of part-time or self-employed workers.

Every job is described in detail later in the book, so you can explore the jobs that interest you the most. You'll learn the major work tasks, all the important skills, educational programs, and many other informative facts.

Using this book, you'll be surprised how quickly you'll get new ideas for careers that can keep you active and can suit you in many other ways.

Some Things You Can Do with This Book

- Identify active jobs that don't require you to get additional training or education.
- Develop long-term career plans that may require additional training, education, or experience.
- Explore and select a training or educational program that relates to a career objective suited to your energy level.
- Prepare for interviews by learning how to connect your work preferences to your career goal.

These are a few of the many ways you can use this book. We hope you find it as interesting to browse as we did to put together. We have tried to make it easy to use and as interesting as occupational information can be.

When you are done with this book, pass it along or tell someone else about it. We wish you well in your career and in your life.

(continued)

(continued)

Credits and Acknowledgments: While the authors created this book, it is based on the work of many others. The occupational information is based on data obtained from the U.S. Department of Labor and the U.S. Census Bureau. These sources provide the most authoritative occupational information available. The job titles and their related descriptions are from the O*NET database, which was developed by researchers and developers under the direction of the U.S. Department of Labor. They, in turn, were assisted by thousands of employers who provided details on the nature of work in the many thousands of job samplings used in the database's development. We used the most recent version of the O*NET database, release 10.0. We appreciate and thank the staff of the U.S. Department of Labor for their efforts and expertise in providing such a rich source of data.

Table of Contents

Summary of Major Sections

Introduction. A short overview to help you better understand and use the book. *Starts on page 1.*

Part I. The Best Jobs Lists: Jobs Not Behind a Desk. Very useful for exploring career options! The first group of lists presents the 175 best high-activity jobs overall. These jobs are selected to have a high level of activity; have a low level of sitting; and be outstanding in terms of earnings, job growth, and job openings. Another series of lists gives the 50 best-paying high-activity jobs, the 50 fastest-growing high-activity jobs, and the 50 high-activity jobs with the most openings. More-specialized lists follow, presenting the 50 most active jobs, the 50 jobs that spend the most time outdoors, the 50 high-activity jobs that require the least physical strength, the 50 jobs that require the most physical strength, and the 50 jobs that require fast motion or reaction time. You can also see lists of the best jobs that have a high concentration of certain kinds of workers (for example, workers in certain age brackets, part-time workers, or female workers) and lists with the jobs organized by level of education or training and by interest area. The column starting at right presents all the list titles. *Starts on page 13.*

Part II. Descriptions of the Best Jobs Not Behind a Desk. Provides complete descriptions of the jobs that appear on the lists in Part I. Each description contains information on work tasks, skills, education and training required, earnings, projected growth, job duties, level of activity, related knowledge and courses, working conditions, and many other details. *Starts on page 101.*

Appendix A. The GOE Interest Areas and Work Groups. This appendix lists the GOE Interest Areas and Work Groups. *Starts on page 399.*

Appendix B. Skills Referenced in This Book. This appendix defines the skills listed in the job descriptions. *Starts on page 405.*

Detailed Table of Contents

Introduction

Not everybody will want to read this introduction. You may want to skip this background information and go directly to Part I, which lists the best jobs not behind a desk.

But if you want to understand how (and why) we put this book together, where the information comes from, and what makes a job "best," this introduction can answer a lot of questions.

Why Seek an Active Job?

Maybe you have an antsy personality. Something about you is not satisfied with sitting in one place all day. Perhaps you prefer a fast pace or love the outdoors.

Maybe you favor an active job because you are aware that it would be better for your health. Researchers have linked desk jobs to increased incidence of back pain, eyestrain, obesity, and even colon cancer. One Australian study found that men who sit at their desks for more than six hours per day were almost twice as likely to be obese as men who sit for less than 45 minutes. An American study found that women who worked at a sedentary job for 14 years gained 20 pounds more than women who worked in the least sedentary jobs.

Whatever your reason is for seeking active work, that kind of job is harder to find than it used to be. The shift to an information-based economy has meant a constant increase in the proportion of workers who manipulate data for a living—and who therefore spend most of the workday sitting at a desk. Researchers have estimated that the percentage of workers in physically demanding jobs decreased from about 20 percent in 1950 to less than 8 percent in 1996. Even in offices, people are probably doing less physical work than they used to do in the days when desk workers cranked mimeograph machines, hand-collated documents, whacked staplers, carried memos from one room to another, and typed (and re-typed) on manual typewriters.

Fortunately, there are still plenty of high-activity jobs for people who prefer them. And these are not just menial jobs that are likely to be phased out as soon as someone invents the right kind of robot to do them. Many active jobs have good earnings and are expected to have good job opportunities. They allow you to use your brains as well as your muscles and involve the kinds of people and problems that can keep you interested in your work.

That's where this book can help you. We identified 175 jobs that have a high level of physical activity; a low amount of sitting; and a good combination of earnings, job growth, and job openings. So browse the lists in Part I to find high-energy jobs that match your interests, your age group, your work preferences (e.g., for self-employment), your plans for education or training, or your personality type. Then read the job descriptions in Part II to get more detailed facts and narrow down your choices.

Where the Information Came From

The information we used in creating this book came mostly from databases created by the U.S. Department of Labor:

- We started with the job information included in the Department of Labor's O*NET (Occupational Information Network) database, which is now the primary source of detailed information on occupations. The Labor Department updates the O*NET on a regular basis, and we used the most recent one available—O*NET release 10. Data from the O*NET allowed us to determine the level of activity of jobs, among other topics.

- We linked the information from the O*NET to several other kinds of data that the U.S. Bureau of Labor Statistics collects: on earnings, projected growth, number of openings, part-time workers, and self-employed workers. For data on these topics, the BLS uses a slightly different set of job titles than the O*NET uses, so we had to match similar titles. In a few cases, we could not obtain data about every one of these topics for every occupation. Nevertheless, the information we report here is the most reliable data we could obtain.

- We used the Classification of Instructional Programs, a system developed by the U.S. Department of Education, to cross-reference the education or training programs related to each job.

Of course, information in a database format can be boring and even confusing, so we did many things to help make the data useful and present it to you in a form that is easy to understand.

How the Best Jobs Not Behind a Desk Were Selected

Here is the procedure we followed to select the 175 jobs we included in the lists in this book:

1. We began with the 949 job titles in the O*NET database. Of these, 741 have the full range of information—economic topics, work tasks, skills, and work conditions—needed for a reasonably complete description in this book. We eliminated 11 jobs that are expected to employ fewer than 500 workers per year and to shrink rather than grow in workforce size—and that therefore cannot be considered best jobs.

2. Next we eliminated 54 jobs with annual median earnings of less than $20,000. These jobs are held by roughly the lowest 25 percent of wage-earners. Some high-activity jobs that were eliminated were Lifeguards, Ski Patrol, and Other Recreational Protective Service Workers; Forest and Conservation Workers; Veterinary Assistants and Laboratory Animal Caretakers; and Bartenders. Although these jobs are physically active and some employ a lot of workers, their low pay makes them unlikely to be of interest to the readers of this book. Admittedly, some of the jobs that appear in this book—such as Septic Tank Servicers and Sewer Pipe Cleaners—may not appeal to you for other reasons, but we'll leave it to you to decide how you feel about other aspects of jobs.

3. We combined several O*NET jobs because information on job openings is available only at a higher level of aggregation. For example, we combined three inspecting jobs in the field of transportation because the Department of Labor reports the job openings only for a combined occupation called Transportation Inspectors. The list at this point included 578 jobs.

4. For each job, we looked at two measures in the O*NET database that indicate level of physical activity. One is a work activity measure called Performing General Physical Activities. It is defined as "Performing physical activities that require considerable use of your arms and legs and moving your whole body, such as climbing, lifting, balancing, walking, stooping, and handling of materials." Every job has a rating between 0 and 7 on this measure. The other measure is a physical work condition called Spending Time Sitting, which represents how much the job requires sitting. (Despite the name, it is not strictly a measure of time, so in this book we refer to it simply as "Sitting.") This measure also uses a rating scale between 0 and 7, so we subtracted each job's rating from 7 to determine the amount to which the job does not involve sitting. We then took the average of these two work activity measures to get an overall score indicating the level of physical activity—i.e., how much the job is not behind a desk.

5. We ordered all 578 jobs by this physical activity score, from highest to lowest, and then cut this list in half by removing the least-active half of the jobs and keeping the most-active half.

6. We ranked the 289 remaining high-activity jobs three times, based on these major criteria: median annual earnings, projected growth through 2014, and number of job openings projected per year.

7. We then added the three numerical rankings for each job to calculate its overall score.

8. To emphasize jobs that tend to pay more, are likely to grow more rapidly, and have more job openings, we selected the 175 job titles with the best total numerical scores.

For example, the job with the best combined score for earnings, growth, and number of job openings is Registered Nurses, so this job is listed first even though it is not the best-paying job (which is Oral and Maxillofacial Surgeons), the fastest-growing job (which is Medical Assistants), or the job with the most openings (which is Laborers and Freight, Stock, and Material Movers, Hand).

Why This Book Has More Than 175 Jobs

We didn't think you would mind that this book actually provides information on more than 175 jobs. We combined several jobs to create the lists in Part I, as mentioned earlier, but in Part II we describe these jobs separately. This means that although we used 175 job titles to construct the lists, Part II actually has a total of 194 job descriptions.

Understand the Limits of the Data in This Book

In this book we use the most reliable and up-to-date information available on earnings, projected growth, number of openings, and other topics. The earnings data came from the U.S. Department of Labor's Bureau of Labor Statistics. As you look at the figures, keep in mind that they are estimates. They give you a general idea about the number of workers employed, annual earnings, rate of job growth, and annual job openings.

Understand that a problem with such data is that it describes an average. Just as there is no precisely average person, there is no such thing as a statistically average example of a particular job. We say this because data, while helpful, can also be misleading.

Take, for example, the yearly earnings information in this book. This is highly reliable data obtained from a very large U.S. working population sample by the Bureau of Labor Statistics. It tells us the average annual pay received as of May 2005 by people in various job titles (actually, it is the median annual pay, which means that half earned more and half less).

This sounds great, except that half of all people in that occupation earned less than that amount. For example, people who are new to the occupation or with only a few years of work experience often earn much less than the average amount. People who live in rural areas or who work for smaller employers typically earn less than those who do similar work in cities (where the cost of living is higher) or for bigger employers. People in certain areas of the country earn less than those in others.

Also keep in mind that the figures for job growth and number of openings are projections by labor economists—their best guesses about what we can expect between now and 2014. They are not guarantees. A major economic downturn, war, or technological breakthrough could change the actual outcome.

Finally, don't forget that the job market consists of both job openings and job-*seekers*. The figures on job growth and openings don't tell you how many people will be competing with you to be hired. The Department of Labor does not publish figures on the supply of job candidates, so we are unable to tell you about the level of competition you can expect. Competition is an important issue that you should research for any tentative career goal. The *Occupational Outlook Handbook* provides informative statements for many occupations. You should speak to people who educate or train tomorrow's workers; they probably have a good idea of how many graduates find rewarding employment and how quickly. People in the workforce also can provide insights into this issue. Use your critical thinking skills to evaluate what people tell you. For example, educators or trainers may be trying to recruit you, whereas people in the workforce may be trying to discourage you from competing. Get a variety of opinions to balance out possible biases.

So, in reviewing the information in this book, please understand the limitations of the data. You need to use common sense in career decision making as in most other things in life. We hope that, using that approach, you find the information helpful and interesting.

The Data Complexities

For those of you who like details, we present some of the complexities inherent in our sources of information and what we did to make sense of them here. You don't need to know this to use the book, so jump to the next section of the Introduction if you are bored with details.

Earnings, Growth, and Number of Openings

We include information on earnings, projected growth, and number of job openings for each job throughout this book.

Earnings

The employment security agency of each state gathers information on earnings for various jobs and forwards it to the U.S. Bureau of Labor Statistics. This information is organized in standardized ways by a BLS program called Occupational Employment Statistics, or OES. To keep the earnings for the various jobs and regions comparable, the OES screens out certain types of earnings and includes others, so the OES earnings we use in this book represent straight-time gross pay exclusive of premium pay. More specifically, the OES earnings include the job's base rate; cost-of-living allowances; guaranteed pay; hazardous-duty pay; incentive pay, including commissions and production bonuses; on-call pay; and tips but do not include back pay, jury duty pay, overtime pay, severance pay, shift differentials, nonproduction bonuses, or tuition reimbursements. Also, self-employed workers are not included in the estimates, and they can be a significant segment in certain occupations. When data on annual earnings for an occupation is highly unreliable, OES does not report a figure, which meant that we reluctantly had to exclude from this book a few occupations such as Musicians and Singers. The median earnings for all workers in all occupations were $29,430 in May 2005. The 175 jobs in this book were chosen partly on the basis of good earnings, so their average is a respectable $35,258.

The data from the OES survey is reported under a system of job titles called the Standard Occupational Classification system, or SOC. These are the job titles we use in the lists in Part I, but in Part II we cross-reference these titles to O*NET job titles so we can provide O*NET-derived information on many useful topics. In some cases, an SOC title cross-references to more than one O*NET job title. For example, the SOC title Carpenters, which we use in Part I, is linked to two jobs described in Part II: Construction Carpenters and Rough Carpenters. Because earnings data is available only for the combined job title Carpenters, in Part II you will find the same earnings figure, $35,580, reported for both kinds of carpenters. In reality there probably is a difference in what the two kinds of carpenters earn, but this is the best information that is available.

Projected Growth and Number of Job Openings

This information comes from the Office of Occupational Statistics and Employment Projections, a program within the Bureau of Labor Statistics that develops information about projected trends in the nation's labor market for the next ten years. The most recent projections available cover the years from 2004 to 2014. The projections are based on information about people moving into and out of occupations. The BLS uses data from various sources in projecting the growth and number of openings for each job title—some data comes from the Census Bureau's Current Population Survey and some comes from an OES survey. The projections assume that there will be no major war, depression, or other economic upheaval.

Like the earnings figures, the figures on projected growth and job openings are reported according to the SOC classification, so again you will find that some of the SOC jobs that we use in Part I crosswalk to more than one O*NET job in Part II. To continue the example we used earlier, SOC reports growth (13.8 percent) and openings (210,000) for one occupation called Carpenters, but in Part II of this book we report these figures separately for the occupation Construction Carpenters and for the occupation Rough Carpenters. When you see Construction Carpenters with 13.8 percent projected growth and 210,000 projected job openings and Rough Carpenters with the same two numbers, you should realize that the 13.8-percent rate of projected growth represents the *average* of these two occupations—one may actually experience higher growth than the other—and that these two occupations will *share* the 210,000 projected openings.

While salary figures are fairly straightforward, you may not know what to make of job-growth figures. For example, is projected growth of 15 percent good or bad? You should keep in mind that the average (mean) growth projected for all occupations by the Bureau of Labor Statistics is 13.0 percent. One-quarter of the SOC occupations have a growth projection of 3.2 percent or lower. Growth of 11.6 percent is the median, meaning that half of the occupations have more, half less. Only one-quarter of the occupations have growth projected at more than 17.4 percent.

You're probably already aware that more of the job growth in our economy is happening for office jobs than for high-activity jobs. Therefore, even though the jobs in this book were selected as "best" partly on the basis of job growth, their mean growth is 13.9 percent, which is only slightly higher than the mean for all jobs. Among these 175 jobs, the job ranked 132nd by projected growth has a figure of 8.9 percent, the jobs ranked 87th and 88th (the median) have a projected growth of 14.3 percent, and the job ranked 44th has a projected growth of 18.4 percent.

The news about job openings for active jobs is similar to the news about job growth: slightly better than the national average for all occupations. The Bureau of Labor Statistics projects an average of about 35,000 job openings per year for each of the 750 occupations that it studies, and for each of the 175 occupations included in this book, the average is not quite 38,000 openings. The job ranked 44th for job openings has a figure of 33,000 annual openings, the jobs ranked 87th and 88th (the median) have 10,000 openings projected, and the job ranked 132nd has 4,000 openings projected.

Perhaps you're wondering why we present figures on both job growth *and* number of openings. Aren't these two ways of saying the same thing? Actually, you need to know both. Consider the occupation Athletic Trainers, which is projected to grow at the outstanding rate of 29.3 percent. There should be lots of opportunities in such a fast-growing job, right? Not exactly. This is a tiny occupation, with only about 15,000 people currently employed, so even though it is growing rapidly, it will not create many new jobs (about 1,000 per year). Now consider Laborers and Freight, Stock, and Material Movers, Hand. This occupation is growing at the lukewarm rate of 10.2 percent, held back by automation and foreign competition. Nevertheless, this is a huge occupation that employs more than 2.4 million workers, so even though its growth rate is unimpressive, it is expected to take on 671,000 new workers each year as existing workers retire, die, or move on to other jobs. That's why we base our selection of the best jobs on both of these economic indicators and why you should pay attention to both when you scan our lists of best jobs.

How This Book Is Organized

The information in this book about best active jobs moves from the general to the highly specific.

Part I. The Best Jobs Lists: Jobs Not Behind a Desk

For many people, the 70 lists in Part I are the most interesting section of the book. Here you can see titles of the 175 high-energy jobs that have the best combination of high salaries, fast growth, and plentiful job openings. You can see which jobs are best in terms of each of these factors combined or considered separately. Additional lists highlight jobs with a high percentage of female, male, part-time, and self-employed workers. Look in the Table of Contents for a complete list of lists. Although there are a lot of lists, they are not difficult to understand because they have clear titles and are organized into groupings of related lists.

Depending on your situation, some of the jobs lists in Part I will interest you more than others. For example, if you are young, you may be interested in the best-paying active jobs that employ high percentages of people age 16–24. Other lists show jobs within interest groupings, personality types, levels of education, or other ways that you might find helpful in exploring your career options.

Whatever your situation, we suggest you use the lists that make sense for you to help explore career options. Following are the names of each group of lists along with short comments on each group. You will find additional information in a brief introduction provided at the beginning of each group of lists in Part I.

Best Jobs Overall Not Behind a Desk: Jobs with the Highest Pay, Fastest Growth, and Most Openings

Four lists are in this group, and they are the ones that most people want to see first. The first list presents the top 175 high-activity job titles in order of their combined scores for earnings, growth, and number of job openings. Three more lists in this group are extracted from the 175 best and present the 50 jobs with the highest earnings, the 50 jobs projected to grow most rapidly, and the 50 jobs with the most openings.

Best Jobs Not Behind a Desk with Particular Physical Demands and Work Conditions

These five lists are subsets of the 175 best, selected to highlight particular physical demands and work conditions. One list shows the 50 most active of the high-activity jobs. One list shows the 50 jobs whose workers spend the most time outdoors. One list identifies the 50 jobs that require the least amount of physical strength even though they are active. Another list—aimed at people who really want to work up a sweat—identifies the 50 jobs that require the *greatest* amount of physical strength. In addition, a list of the 50 fastest-moving jobs features those that require rapid movement and reaction time.

Bonus List: Metropolitan Areas with the Highest Percentages of the Best Jobs Not Behind a Desk

Unlike the other lists, this one doesn't contain jobs. Instead, it identifies the 50 metropolitan areas with the highest concentrations of people employed in the 175 best jobs. If you relocate to one of these areas, you may have better chances of finding a good high-energy job.

Best Jobs Not Behind a Desk with High Percentages of Workers Age 16–24, Workers Age 55 and Over, Part-Time Workers, Self-Employed Workers, Women, and Men

This group of lists presents interesting information for a variety of types of people based on data from the U.S. Census Bureau. The lists are arranged into groups for workers age 16–24, workers 55 and older, part-time workers, self-employed workers, women, and men. We created five lists for each group, basing the last four on the information in the first list:

- The jobs not behind a desk having the highest percentage of people of each type
- The 25 jobs with the highest combined scores for earnings, growth, and number of openings
- The 25 jobs with the highest earnings

- The 25 jobs with the highest growth rates
- The 25 jobs with the largest number of openings

Best Jobs Not Behind a Desk Listed by Levels of Education, Training, and Experience

We created separate lists for each level of education, training, and experience as defined by the U.S. Department of Labor. We put each of the top 175 job titles into one of the lists based on the kind of preparation required for entry. Jobs within these lists are presented in order of their total combined scores for earnings, growth, and number of openings. The lists include high-activity jobs in these groupings:

- Short-term on-the-job training
- Moderate-term on-the-job training
- Long-term on-the-job training
- Work experience in a related job
- Postsecondary vocational training
- Associate degree
- Bachelor's degree
- Work experience plus degree
- Master's degree
- Doctoral degree
- First professional degree

Best Jobs Not Behind a Desk Listed by Interests

These lists organize the 175 best jobs into groups based on interests. Within each list, jobs are presented in order of their total scores for earnings, growth, and number of openings. Here are the 16 interest areas used in these lists: Agriculture and Natural Resources; Architecture and Construction; Arts and Communication; Business and Administration; Education and Training; Finance and Insurance; Government and Public Administration; Health Science; Hospitality, Tourism, and Recreation; Human Service; Information Technology; Law and Public Safety; Manufacturing; Retail and Wholesale Sales and Service; Scientific Research, Engineering, and Mathematics; and Transportation, Distribution, and Logistics. These interest areas are based on the U.S. Department of Education career clusters.

Best Jobs Not Behind a Desk Listed by Personality Types

These lists organize the 175 best jobs into six personality types described in the introduction to the lists: Realistic, Investigative, Artistic, Social, Enterprising, and Conventional. The jobs within each list are presented in order of their total scores for earnings, growth, and number of openings.

Part II: Descriptions of the Best Jobs Not Behind a Desk

This part contains 194 job descriptions and covers each of the 175 best jobs not behind a desk, using a format that is informative yet compact and easy to read. The descriptions contain statistics such as earnings and projected percent of growth; ratings of physical activity, sitting, and time outdoors; lists such as major skills and work tasks; and key descriptors such as personality type and interest field. Because the jobs in this section are arranged in alphabetical order, you can easily find a job that you've identified from Part I and that you want to learn more about.

In some cases, a job title in Part I cross-references to two or more job titles in Part II. For example, if you look up Nuclear Technicians in Part II, you'll find a note telling you to look at the descriptions for Nuclear Equipment Operation Technicians and Nuclear Monitoring Technicians. That's why there are 194 descriptions in Part II rather than 175.

We used the most current information from a variety of government sources to create the descriptions. Although we've tried to make the descriptions easy to understand, the sample that follows—with an explanation of each of its parts—may help you better understand and use the descriptions.

Here are some details on each of the major parts of the job descriptions you will find in Part II:

- **Job Title:** This is the job title for the job as defined by the U.S. Department of Labor and used in its O*NET database.

- **Data Elements:** The information comes from various U.S. Department of Labor and Census Bureau databases, as explained elsewhere in this Introduction.

- **Summary Description and Tasks:** The bold sentence provides a summary description of the occupation. It is followed by a listing of tasks that are generally performed by people who work in this job. This information comes from the O*NET database but where necessary has been edited to avoid exceeding 2,200 characters.

- **Level of Activity:** We provide three ratings that indicate how active the job is—in terms of General Physical Activity, Sitting, and Outdoors. The ratings use a scale in which 0 is the lowest level and 100 is the highest. These ratings are not percentages and represent the level of each kind of activity, not the amount of time spent.

- **Skills:** For each job, we included the skills whose level-of-performance scores exceeded the average for all jobs by the greatest amount and whose ratings on the importance scale were not very low. We included as many as six such skills for each job, and we ranked them by the extent to which their rating exceeds the average.

- **GOE Information:** This information cross-references the Guide for Occupational Exploration (or the GOE), a system developed by the U.S. Department of Labor that organizes jobs based on interests. We use the groups from the *New Guide for*

Occupational Exploration, Fourth Edition, as published by JIST. That book uses a set of interest areas based on the 16 career clusters developed by the U.S. Department of Education and used in a variety of career information systems. Here we include the major Interest Area the job fits into, its more-specific Work Group, and a list of related O*NET job titles that are in this same GOE Work Group. This information will help you identify other job titles that have similar interests or require similar skills, but note that not all jobs in a work group have an equal level of physical activity. You can find a list of the GOE Interest Areas and Work Groups in the appendix.

⊚ **Personality Type:** The O*NET database assigns each job to its most closely related personality type. Our job descriptions include the name of the related personality type as well as a brief definition of this personality type.

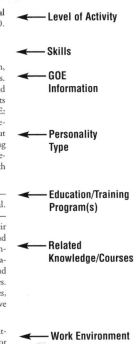

Job Title ⟶

Athletes and Sports Competitors

Data Elements ⟶

⊚ Education/Training Required: Long-term on-the-job training

⊚ Annual Earnings: $39,930

⊚ Growth: 21.1%

⊚ Annual Job Openings: 6,000

⊚ Self-Employed: 24.5%

⊚ Part-Time: 47.6%

Summary Description and Tasks ⟶

Compete in athletic events. Lead teams by serving as captains. Receive instructions from coaches and other sports staff prior to events and discuss their performance afterwards. Participate in athletic events and competitive sports according to established rules and regulations. Maintain optimum physical fitness levels by training regularly, following nutrition plans, and consulting with health professionals. Exercise and practice under the direction of athletic trainers or professional coaches in order to develop skills, improve physical condition, and prepare for competitions. Attend scheduled practice and training sessions. Assess performance following athletic competition, identifying strengths and weaknesses and making adjustments to improve future performance. Maintain equipment used in a particular sport. Represent teams or professional sports clubs, performing such activities as meeting with members of the media, making speeches, or participating in charity events.

LEVEL OF ACTIVITY (out of 100)—General Physical Activity: 91.4. Sitting: 40.0. Outdoors: 54.3. ⟵ **Level of Activity**

SKILLS—Monitoring. ⟵ **Skills**

GOE—**Interest Area:** 09. Hospitality, Tourism, and Recreation. **Work Group:** 09.06. Sports. **Other Jobs in This Work Group:** Coaches and Scouts; Umpires, Referees, and Other Sports Officials. ⟵ **GOE Information** **PERSONALITY TYPE:** Enterprising. Enterprising occupations frequently involve starting up and carrying out projects. These occupations can involve leading people and making many decisions. They sometimes require risk taking and often deal with business. ⟵ **Personality Type**

EDUCATION/TRAINING PROGRAM(S)—Health and Physical Education, General. ⟵ **Education/Training Program(s)** **RELATED KNOWLEDGE/COURSES**—**Biology:** Plant and animal organisms and their tissues, cells, functions, interdependencies, and interactions with each other and the environment. **Medicine and Dentistry:** The information and techniques needed to diagnose and treat human injuries, diseases, and deformities. This includes symptoms, treatment alternatives, drug properties and interactions, and preventive health-care measures. ⟵ **Related Knowledge/Courses**

WORK ENVIRONMENT—More often outdoors than indoors; minor burns, cuts, bites, or stings; standing; walking and running; bending or twisting the body. ⟵ **Work Environment**

⊚ **Education/Training Program(s):** This part of the job description provides the name of the educational or training program or programs for the job. It will help you identify sources of formal or informal training for a job that interests you. To get this information, we adapted a crosswalk created by the National Center for O*NET Development to connect information in the Classification of Instructional Programs (CIP) to the O*NET job titles we use in this book. We made various changes to connect the O*NET job titles to the education or training programs related to them and also modified the names of some education and training programs so they would be more easily understood. In 10 cases, we abbreviated the listing of related programs for the sake of space; such entries end with "others."

⊚ **Related Knowledge/Courses:** This entry can help you understand the most important knowledge areas that are required for a job and the types of courses or programs you will likely need to take to prepare for it. We used information in the Department of Labor's O*NET database for this entry. For each job, we identified any knowledge area with a rating that was higher than the average rating for that knowledge area for all jobs; then we listed them in descending order.

⊚ **Work Environment:** We included any work condition with a rating that exceeds the midpoint of the rating scale. The order does not indicate their frequency on the job. Consider whether you like these conditions and whether any of these conditions would make you uncomfortable. Keep in mind that when hazards are present (for example, contaminants), protective equipment and procedures are provided to keep you safe.

Getting all the information we used in the job descriptions was not a simple process, and it is not always perfect. Even so, we used the best and most recent sources of data we could find, and we think that our efforts will be helpful to many people.

PART I

The Best Jobs Lists: Jobs Not Behind a Desk

Different people have different ideas about what makes a job a good one, but the fact that you're reading this book indicates that you care about the level of physical activity on the job. Most people also want to have a good level of pay and a good likelihood of being employed, so we also used economic factors in creating the lists that follow. In several lists we added other factors that various people deem important in making a career choice. The result is a set of lists that make for interesting browsing and can start you thinking about jobs you may not have previously considered.

Remember that these lists are only starting places in the process of career exploration. If a job interests you, research it thoroughly before making any commitments.

Best Jobs Overall: Jobs Not Behind a Desk with the Highest Pay, Fastest Growth, and Most Openings

The four lists that follow are the most important lists in this book. The first list presents the high-energy jobs with the highest combined scores for pay, growth, and number of openings. These are very appealing lists because they represent jobs with the very highest quantifiable measures from our labor market. The 175 jobs in the first list are the basis for all the job lists in Part I and are described in detail in Part II.

The three additional sets of lists present 50 jobs with the highest scores on each of three measures: annual earnings, projected percentage growth, and largest number of openings.

The 175 Best Jobs Overall Not Behind a Desk

This is the list that most people want to see first. You can see the jobs that have the highest overall combined ratings for earnings, projected growth, and number of openings. (The section in the Introduction on "How the Best Jobs Not Behind a Desk Were Selected" explains in detail how we rated jobs to assemble this list.)

You'll notice a wide variety of jobs on the list. For example, although the top 10 jobs are heavily dominated by the healthcare field, among the top 50 you'll also find jobs in education, law enforcement, construction, and transportation. Some of the jobs on the list are supervisory or managerial, demonstrating that not all bosses are chained to a desk.

A look at the list will clarify how we ordered the jobs. Registered Nurses was the occupation with the best total score, and it is on the top of the list. The other occupations follow in descending order based on their total scores. Many jobs had tied scores and were simply listed one after another, so there are often only very small or even no differences between the scores of jobs that are near each other on the list. All other jobs lists in this book use these jobs as their source list. You can find descriptions for each of these jobs in Part II, beginning on page 101. If a job appeals to you, or if you're not sure what it is, find it alphabetically in Part II and read the description.

The 175 Best Jobs Overall Not Behind a Desk

Job	Annual Earnings	Percent Growth	Annual Openings
1. Registered Nurses	$54,670	29.4%	229,000
2. Physical Therapists	$63,080	36.7%	13,000
3. Physician Assistants	$72,030	49.6%	10,000
4. Elementary School Teachers, Except Special Education	$44,040	18.2%	203,000
5. Radiologic Technologists and Technicians	$45,950	23.2%	17,000
6. Kindergarten Teachers, Except Special Education	$42,230	22.4%	28,000
7. Occupational Therapists	$56,860	33.6%	7,000
8. Secondary School Teachers, Except Special and Vocational Education	$46,060	14.4%	107,000
9. Police and Sheriff's Patrol Officers	$46,290	15.5%	47,000
10. Veterinarians	$68,910	17.4%	8,000
11. Plumbers, Pipefitters, and Steamfitters	$42,160	15.7%	61,000
12. Heating, Air Conditioning, and Refrigeration Mechanics and Installers	$37,040	19.0%	33,000
13. Construction Managers	$72,260	10.4%	28,000
14. Licensed Practical and Licensed Vocational Nurses	$35,230	17.1%	84,000
15. Middle School Teachers, Except Special and Vocational Education	$44,640	13.7%	83,000
16. Detectives and Criminal Investigators	$55,790	16.3%	9,000
17. First-Line Supervisors/Managers of Mechanics, Installers, and Repairers	$51,980	12.4%	33,000
18. First-Line Supervisors/Managers of Construction Trades and Extraction Workers	$51,970	10.9%	57,000
19. Respiratory Therapists	$45,140	28.4%	7,000
20. First-Line Supervisors/Managers of Police and Detectives	$65,570	15.5%	9,000

The 175 Best Jobs Overall Not Behind a Desk

Job	Annual Earnings	Percent Growth	Annual Openings
21. Self-Enrichment Education Teachers	$32,360	25.3%	74,000
22. Chiropractors	$67,200	22.4%	4,000
23. Physical Therapist Assistants	$39,490	44.2%	7,000
24. First-Line Supervisors/Managers of Fire Fighting and Prevention Workers	$60,840	21.1%	4,000
25. Surgical Technologists	$34,830	29.5%	12,000
26. Education Administrators, Preschool and Child Care Center/Program	$37,010	27.9%	9,000
27. Electricians	$42,790	11.8%	68,000
28. Carpenters	$35,580	13.8%	210,000
29. Construction and Building Inspectors	$44,720	22.3%	6,000
30. Flight Attendants	$46,680	16.3%	7,000
31. Food Service Managers	$41,340	11.5%	61,000
32. Automotive Service Technicians and Mechanics	$33,050	15.7%	93,000
33. Tile and Marble Setters	$36,530	22.9%	9,000
34. First-Line Supervisors/Managers of Landscaping, Lawn Service, and Groundskeeping Workers	$36,320	17.8%	14,000
35. Hazardous Materials Removal Workers	$33,690	31.2%	11,000
36. Truck Drivers, Heavy and Tractor-Trailer	$34,280	12.9%	274,000
37. Bus and Truck Mechanics and Diesel Engine Specialists	$36,620	14.4%	32,000
38. Cardiovascular Technologists and Technicians	$40,420	32.6%	5,000
39. Aircraft Mechanics and Service Technicians	$47,310	13.4%	11,000
40. Railroad Conductors and Yardmasters	$54,040	20.3%	3,000
41. Structural Iron and Steel Workers	$40,580	15.0%	13,000
42. Athletes and Sports Competitors	$39,930	21.1%	6,000
43. Medical Assistants	$25,350	52.1%	93,000
44. Highway Maintenance Workers	$30,250	23.3%	27,000
45. Nuclear Medicine Technologists	$59,670	21.5%	2,000
46. Roofers	$31,230	16.8%	38,000
47. Gaming Supervisors	$40,300	16.3%	8,000
48. Maintenance and Repair Workers, General	$31,210	15.2%	154,000
49. Telecommunications Line Installers and Repairers	$42,410	10.8%	23,000
50. Sheet Metal Workers	$36,390	12.2%	50,000
51. Brickmasons and Blockmasons	$41,860	12.0%	17,000
52. Cement Masons and Concrete Finishers	$32,030	15.9%	32,000
53. Operating Engineers and Other Construction Equipment Operators	$35,830	11.6%	37,000

(continued)

(continued)

The 175 Best Jobs Overall Not Behind a Desk

Job	Annual Earnings	Percent Growth	Annual Openings
54. First-Line Supervisors/Managers of Production and Operating Workers	$46,140	2.7%	89,000
55. Radiation Therapists	$62,340	26.3%	1,000
56. First-Line Supervisors/Managers of Housekeeping and Janitorial Workers	$30,330	19.0%	21,000
57. Fitness Trainers and Aerobics Instructors	$25,840	27.1%	50,000
58. Gaming Managers	$59,940	22.6%	1,000
59. Coaches and Scouts	$25,990	20.4%	63,000
60. First-Line Supervisors/Managers of Food Preparation and Serving Workers	$26,050	16.6%	187,000
61. Surveyors	$45,860	15.9%	4,000
62. Vocational Education Teachers, Secondary School	$47,090	9.1%	10,000
63. Elevator Installers and Repairers	$59,190	14.8%	3,000
64. Occupational Therapist Assistants	$39,750	34.1%	2,000
65. Preschool Teachers, Except Special Education	$21,990	33.1%	77,000
66. Emergency Medical Technicians and Paramedics	$26,080	27.3%	21,000
67. Painters, Construction and Maintenance	$30,800	12.6%	102,000
68. Nursing Aides, Orderlies, and Attendants	$21,440	22.3%	307,000
69. Environmental Science and Protection Technicians, Including Health	$36,260	16.3%	6,000
70. Industrial Production Managers	$75,580	0.8%	13,000
71. Electrical and Electronics Repairers, Commercial and Industrial Equipment	$44,120	9.7%	8,000
72. Water and Liquid Waste Treatment Plant and System Operators	$34,930	16.2%	6,000
73. Painters, Transportation Equipment	$34,840	14.1%	10,000
74. Automotive Body and Related Repairers	$34,810	10.3%	18,000
75. Mobile Heavy Equipment Mechanics, Except Engines	$39,410	8.8%	14,000
76. First-Line Supervisors/Managers of Helpers, Laborers, and Material Movers, Hand	$39,000	8.1%	15,000
77. Truck Drivers, Light or Delivery Services	$24,790	15.7%	169,000
78. Landscaping and Groundskeeping Workers	$20,670	19.5%	243,000
79. Mechanical Engineering Technicians	$44,830	12.3%	5,000
80. Correctional Officers and Jailers	$34,090	6.7%	54,000
81. Drywall and Ceiling Tile Installers	$34,740	9.0%	17,000
82. Electrical Power-Line Installers and Repairers	$50,150	2.5%	11,000
83. Camera Operators, Television, Video, and Motion Picture	$41,610	14.2%	4,000
84. Glaziers	$33,530	14.2%	9,000

The 175 Best Jobs Overall Not Behind a Desk

Job	Annual Earnings	Percent Growth	Annual Openings
85. Chemists	$57,890	7.3%	5,000
86. Postal Service Mail Carriers	$46,330	0.0%	19,000
87. Telecommunications Equipment Installers and Repairers, Except Line Installers	$50,620	−4.9%	21,000
88. Medical Equipment Repairers	$39,570	14.8%	4,000
89. Oral and Maxillofacial Surgeons	$145,600	more than 16.2%	fewer than 500
90. First-Line Supervisors/Managers of Retail Sales Workers	$32,840	3.8%	229,000
91. Reinforcing Iron and Rebar Workers	$34,910	14.1%	6,000
92. Audio and Video Equipment Technicians	$32,940	18.1%	5,000
93. Orthotists and Prosthetists	$53,760	18.0%	fewer than 500
94. Machinists	$34,350	4.3%	33,000
95. Tree Trimmers and Pruners	$27,920	16.5%	11,000
96. Motorboat Mechanics	$32,780	15.1%	7,000
97. Nuclear Technicians	$61,120	13.7%	1,000
98. Choreographers	$32,950	16.8%	4,000
99. Geoscientists, Except Hydrologists and Geographers	$71,640	8.3%	2,000
100. Recreation Workers	$20,110	17.3%	69,000
101. Transportation Inspectors	$49,490	11.4%	2,000
102. Audio-Visual Collections Specialists	$40,260	18.6%	1,000
103. Curators	$45,240	15.7%	1,000
104. Helpers—Installation, Maintenance, and Repair Workers	$21,230	16.4%	41,000
105. Paving, Surfacing, and Tamping Equipment Operators	$30,320	15.6%	7,000
106. Carpet Installers	$33,550	8.4%	11,000
107. Crossing Guards	$20,050	19.7%	26,000
108. Hairdressers, Hairstylists, and Cosmetologists	$20,610	16.1%	59,000
109. Welders, Cutters, Solderers, and Brazers	$30,990	5.0%	52,000
110. Athletic Trainers	$34,260	29.3%	1,000
111. Industrial Truck and Tractor Operators	$27,080	7.9%	114,000
112. Zoologists and Wildlife Biologists	$52,050	13.0%	1,000
113. Embalmers	$36,960	15.6%	2,000
114. Ship Engineers	$52,780	12.7%	1,000
115. Helpers—Pipelayers, Plumbers, Pipefitters, and Steamfitters	$22,820	16.6%	17,000
116. Locksmiths and Safe Repairers	$30,880	16.1%	5,000
117. Medical Equipment Preparers	$24,880	20.0%	8,000
118. Millwrights	$44,780	5.9%	5,000
119. Septic Tank Servicers and Sewer Pipe Cleaners	$30,440	21.8%	3,000

(continued)

(continued)

The 175 Best Jobs Overall Not Behind a Desk

Job	Annual Earnings	Percent Growth	Annual Openings
120. Bakers	$21,520	15.2%	37,000
121. Refuse and Recyclable Material Collectors	$28,460	8.9%	31,000
122. Aircraft Structure, Surfaces, Rigging, and Systems Assemblers	$43,990	7.8%	4,000
123. Boilermakers	$48,050	8.7%	2,000
124. Avionics Technicians	$46,630	9.1%	2,000
125. Photographers	$26,100	12.3%	23,000
126. Supervisors, Farming, Fishing, and Forestry Workers	$36,030	3.6%	11,000
127. Recreational Vehicle Service Technicians	$30,480	19.5%	3,000
128. Chemical Technicians	$38,500	4.4%	7,000
129. Industrial Machinery Mechanics	$39,740	−0.2%	13,000
130. Excavating and Loading Machine and Dragline Operators	$32,380	8.0%	11,000
131. Funeral Directors	$47,630	6.7%	3,000
132. Gas Plant Operators	$51,920	7.7%	2,000
133. Security Guards	$20,760	12.6%	230,000
134. Conservation Scientists	$53,350	6.3%	2,000
135. Riggers	$37,010	13.9%	2,000
136. Construction Laborers	$25,410	5.9%	245,000
137. Helpers—Brickmasons, Blockmasons, Stonemasons, and Tile and Marble Setters	$24,600	14.9%	14,000
138. Helpers—Carpenters	$21,990	14.5%	24,000
139. Control and Valve Installers and Repairers, Except Mechanical Door	$44,120	4.9%	4,000
140. Stationary Engineers and Boiler Operators	$44,600	3.4%	5,000
141. Farmers and Ranchers	$34,140	−14.5%	96,000
142. Pesticide Handlers, Sprayers, and Applicators, Vegetation	$26,120	16.6%	6,000
143. Driver/Sales Workers	$20,120	13.8%	72,000
144. Tapers	$39,870	5.9%	5,000
145. Laborers and Freight, Stock, and Material Movers, Hand	$20,610	10.2%	671,000
146. Printing Machine Operators	$30,730	2.9%	26,000
147. Pest Control Workers	$27,170	18.4%	4,000
148. Petroleum Pump System Operators, Refinery Operators, and Gaugers	$51,060	−8.6%	6,000
149. Motorcycle Mechanics	$29,450	13.7%	6,000
150. Plasterers and Stucco Masons	$33,440	8.2%	6,000
151. Outdoor Power Equipment and Other Small Engine Mechanics	$25,810	14.0%	10,000
152. Museum Technicians and Conservators	$34,090	14.1%	2,000
153. Physical Therapist Aides	$21,510	34.4%	5,000

The 175 Best Jobs Overall Not Behind a Desk

Job	Annual Earnings	Percent Growth	Annual Openings
154. Tool and Die Makers	$43,580	–2.6%	7,000
155. Postal Service Clerks	$48,310	0.0%	4,000
156. Chemical Plant and System Operators	$46,710	–17.7%	8,000
157. Slaughterers and Meat Packers	$21,220	13.8%	22,000
158. Stonemasons	$34,640	13.0%	2,000
159. Fish and Game Wardens	$42,850	10.5%	1,000
160. Butchers and Meat Cutters	$26,590	7.9%	20,000
161. Floor Layers, Except Carpet, Wood, and Hard Tiles	$33,010	10.2%	4,000
162. Set and Exhibit Designers	$37,390	9.3%	2,000
163. Umpires, Referees, and Other Sports Officials	$21,610	19.0%	6,000
164. Bailiffs	$33,800	13.2%	2,000
165. Structural Metal Fabricators and Fitters	$30,290	2.9%	18,000
166. Paper Goods Machine Setters, Operators, and Tenders	$31,160	2.4%	15,000
167. Foresters	$48,670	6.7%	1,000
168. Pipelayers	$28,760	9.9%	7,000
169. Transit and Railroad Police	$48,850	9.2%	fewer than 500
170. Costume Attendants	$25,360	23.4%	2,000
171. Earth Drillers, Except Oil and Gas	$33,770	7.9%	4,000
172. Electrical and Electronics Repairers, Powerhouse, Substation, and Relay	$54,970	–0.4%	2,000
173. Animal Trainers	$24,800	20.3%	3,000
174. Helpers—Production Workers	$20,390	7.9%	107,000
175. Animal Control Workers	$26,780	14.4%	4,000

The 50 Best-Paying Jobs Not Behind a Desk

On the following list you'll find the 50 best-paying jobs that met our criteria for this book. This is a popular list, for obvious reasons.

It shouldn't be a big surprise to learn that most of the highest-paying jobs require advanced levels of education, training, and experience. For example, most of the top 20 jobs require either a professional degree, a technical degree, or work experience to qualify for a management-level position. Although the top 20 jobs may not appeal to you for a variety of reasons, you are likely to find others that will among the top 50 jobs with the highest earnings.

Keep in mind that the earnings reflect the national average for all workers in the occupation. This is an important consideration because starting pay in the job is usually a lot less than the pay that workers can earn with several years of experience. Earnings also vary significantly by region of the country, so actual pay in your area could be substantially different.

The 50 Best-Paying Jobs Not Behind a Desk

Job	Annual Earnings
1. Oral and Maxillofacial Surgeons	more than $145,600
2. Industrial Production Managers	$75,580
3. Construction Managers	$72,260
4. Physician Assistants	$72,030
5. Geoscientists, Except Hydrologists and Geographers	$71,640
6. Veterinarians	$68,910
7. Chiropractors	$67,200
8. First-Line Supervisors/Managers of Police and Detectives	$65,570
9. Physical Therapists	$63,080
10. Radiation Therapists	$62,340
11. Nuclear Technicians	$61,120
12. First-Line Supervisors/Managers of Fire Fighting and Prevention Workers	$60,840
13. Gaming Managers	$59,940
14. Nuclear Medicine Technologists	$59,670
15. Elevator Installers and Repairers	$59,190
16. Chemists	$57,890
17. Occupational Therapists	$56,860
18. Detectives and Criminal Investigators	$55,790
19. Electrical and Electronics Repairers, Powerhouse, Substation, and Relay	$54,970
20. Registered Nurses	$54,670
21. Railroad Conductors and Yardmasters	$54,040
22. Orthotists and Prosthetists	$53,760
23. Conservation Scientists	$53,350
24. Ship Engineers	$52,780
25. Zoologists and Wildlife Biologists	$52,050
26. First-Line Supervisors/Managers of Mechanics, Installers, and Repairers	$51,980
27. First-Line Supervisors/Managers of Construction Trades and Extraction Workers	$51,970
28. Gas Plant Operators	$51,920
29. Petroleum Pump System Operators, Refinery Operators, and Gaugers	$51,060
30. Telecommunications Equipment Installers and Repairers, Except Line Installers	$50,620
31. Electrical Power-Line Installers and Repairers	$50,150
32. Transportation Inspectors	$49,490
33. Transit and Railroad Police	$48,850
34. Foresters	$48,670
35. Postal Service Clerks	$48,310
36. Boilermakers	$48,050
37. Funeral Directors	$47,630
38. Aircraft Mechanics and Service Technicians	$47,310

The 50 Best-Paying Jobs Not Behind a Desk

Job	Annual Earnings
39. Vocational Education Teachers, Secondary School	$47,090
40. Chemical Plant and System Operators	$46,710
41. Flight Attendants	$46,680
42. Avionics Technicians	$46,630
43. Postal Service Mail Carriers	$46,330
44. Police and Sheriff's Patrol Officers	$46,290
45. First-Line Supervisors/Managers of Production and Operating Workers	$46,140
46. Secondary School Teachers, Except Special and Vocational Education	$46,060
47. Radiologic Technologists and Technicians	$45,950
48. Surveyors	$45,860
49. Curators	$45,240
50. Respiratory Therapists	$45,140

The 50 Fastest-Growing Jobs Not Behind a Desk

From the list of the 175 best active jobs, this list shows the 50 jobs that are projected to have the highest percentage increase in the numbers of people employed through 2014.

Jobs in the healthcare fields heavily dominate the top 20 fastest-growing jobs, but none of these jobs requires a professional degree. In fact, four of the top five are "assistant" jobs that require a bachelor's degree or less education. You can find a wide range of rapidly growing jobs in a variety of fields and at different levels of training and education among the list of the 50 fastest-growing jobs.

The 50 Fastest-Growing Jobs Not Behind a Desk

Job	Percent Growth
1. Medical Assistants	52.1%
2. Physician Assistants	49.6%
3. Physical Therapist Assistants	44.2%
4. Physical Therapists	36.7%
5. Physical Therapist Aides	34.4%
6. Occupational Therapist Assistants	34.1%
7. Occupational Therapists	33.6%
8. Preschool Teachers, Except Special Education	33.1%
9. Cardiovascular Technologists and Technicians	32.6%
10. Hazardous Materials Removal Workers	31.2%
11. Surgical Technologists	29.5%

(continued)

(continued)

The 50 Fastest-Growing Jobs Not Behind a Desk

Job	Percent Growth
12. Registered Nurses	29.4%
13. Athletic Trainers	29.3%
14. Respiratory Therapists	28.4%
15. Education Administrators, Preschool and Child Care Center/Program	27.9%
16. Emergency Medical Technicians and Paramedics	27.3%
17. Fitness Trainers and Aerobics Instructors	27.1%
18. Radiation Therapists	26.3%
19. Self-Enrichment Education Teachers	25.3%
20. Costume Attendants	23.4%
21. Highway Maintenance Workers	23.3%
22. Radiologic Technologists and Technicians	23.2%
23. Tile and Marble Setters	22.9%
24. Gaming Managers	22.6%
25. Chiropractors	22.4%
26. Kindergarten Teachers, Except Special Education	22.4%
27. Construction and Building Inspectors	22.3%
28. Nursing Aides, Orderlies, and Attendants	22.3%
29. Septic Tank Servicers and Sewer Pipe Cleaners	21.8%
30. Nuclear Medicine Technologists	21.5%
31. Athletes and Sports Competitors	21.1%
32. First-Line Supervisors/Managers of Fire Fighting and Prevention Workers	21.1%
33. Coaches and Scouts	20.4%
34. Animal Trainers	20.3%
35. Railroad Conductors and Yardmasters	20.3%
36. Medical Equipment Preparers	20.0%
37. Crossing Guards	19.7%
38. Landscaping and Groundskeeping Workers	19.5%
39. Recreational Vehicle Service Technicians	19.5%
40. First-Line Supervisors/Managers of Housekeeping and Janitorial Workers	19.0%
41. Heating, Air Conditioning, and Refrigeration Mechanics and Installers	19.0%
42. Umpires, Referees, and Other Sports Officials	19.0%
43. Audio-Visual Collections Specialists	18.6%
44. Pest Control Workers	18.4%
45. Elementary School Teachers, Except Special Education	18.2%
46. Audio and Video Equipment Technicians	18.1%
47. Orthotists and Prosthetists	18.0%

The 50 Fastest-Growing Jobs Not Behind a Desk

Job	Percent Growth
48. First-Line Supervisors/Managers of Landscaping, Lawn Service, and Groundskeeping Workers	17.8%
49. Veterinarians	17.4%
50. Recreation Workers	17.3%

The 50 Jobs Not Behind a Desk with the Most Openings

From the list of best jobs not behind a desk, this list shows the 50 jobs that are projected to have the largest number of job openings per year through 2014.

Jobs with many openings present several advantages that may be attractive to you. Because there are many openings, these jobs can be easier to obtain, particularly for those just entering the job market. These jobs may also offer more opportunities to move from one employer to another with relative ease. Though some of these jobs have average or below-average pay, some also pay quite well and can provide good long-term career opportunities or the ability to move up to more responsible roles. This list is especially noteworthy because of the great variety of jobs included; unlike the previous two lists, it is not dominated by jobs in the healthcare field.

The 50 Jobs Not Behind a Desk with the Most Openings

Job	Annual Openings
1. Laborers and Freight, Stock, and Material Movers, Hand	671,000
2. Nursing Aides, Orderlies, and Attendants	307,000
3. Truck Drivers, Heavy and Tractor-Trailer	274,000
4. Construction Laborers	245,000
5. Landscaping and Groundskeeping Workers	243,000
6. Security Guards	230,000
7. First-Line Supervisors/Managers of Retail Sales Workers	229,000
8. Registered Nurses	229,000
9. Carpenters	210,000
10. Elementary School Teachers, Except Special Education	203,000
11. First-Line Supervisors/Managers of Food Preparation and Serving Workers	187,000
12. Truck Drivers, Light or Delivery Services	169,000
13. Maintenance and Repair Workers, General	154,000
14. Industrial Truck and Tractor Operators	114,000
15. Helpers—Production Workers	107,000
16. Secondary School Teachers, Except Special and Vocational Education	107,000

(continued)

(continued)

The 50 Jobs Not Behind a Desk with the Most Openings

Job	Annual Openings
17. Painters, Construction and Maintenance	102,000
18. Farmers and Ranchers	96,000
19. Automotive Service Technicians and Mechanics	93,000
20. Medical Assistants	93,000
21. First-Line Supervisors/Managers of Production and Operating Workers	89,000
22. Licensed Practical and Licensed Vocational Nurses	84,000
23. Middle School Teachers, Except Special and Vocational Education	83,000
24. Preschool Teachers, Except Special Education	77,000
25. Self-Enrichment Education Teachers	74,000
26. Driver/Sales Workers	72,000
27. Recreation Workers	69,000
28. Electricians	68,000
29. Coaches and Scouts	63,000
30. Food Service Managers	61,000
31. Plumbers, Pipefitters, and Steamfitters	61,000
32. Hairdressers, Hairstylists, and Cosmetologists	59,000
33. First-Line Supervisors/Managers of Construction Trades and Extraction Workers	57,000
34. Correctional Officers and Jailers	54,000
35. Welders, Cutters, Solderers, and Brazers	52,000
36. Fitness Trainers and Aerobics Instructors	50,000
37. Sheet Metal Workers	50,000
38. Police and Sheriff's Patrol Officers	47,000
39. Helpers—Installation, Maintenance, and Repair Workers	41,000
40. Roofers	38,000
41. Bakers	37,000
42. Operating Engineers and Other Construction Equipment Operators	37,000
43. First-Line Supervisors/Managers of Mechanics, Installers, and Repairers	33,000
44. Heating, Air Conditioning, and Refrigeration Mechanics and Installers	33,000
45. Machinists	33,000
46. Bus and Truck Mechanics and Diesel Engine Specialists	32,000
47. Cement Masons and Concrete Finishers	32,000
48. Refuse and Recyclable Material Collectors	31,000
49. Construction Managers	28,000
50. Kindergarten Teachers, Except Special Education	28,000

Best Jobs with Particular Physical Demands and Work Conditions

Because you don't want to spend your workdays like Dilbert, trapped in a cubicle, we thought you would be interested in jobs that involve particular types of physical activity or work conditions. The lists that follow consist of subsets of the 175 best jobs and are selected to highlight certain conditions that you might prefer—or prefer to avoid.

The 50 Most Active Jobs

The 175 best jobs all rank high on Performing General Physical Activities and low on Sitting. We created the following list by identifying the 50 jobs with the *most* outstanding scores when these two measures are averaged. The jobs are ordered with the most active at the top, and you can see why we consider them highly active: For each job we show the O*NET ratings of the job for Performing General Physical Activities and Sitting. The rating is based on a scale where 0 represents the lowest level of the activity and 100 the highest.

Job	Rating for Performing General Physical Activities	Rating for Sitting
The 50 Most Active Jobs		
1. Stonemasons	91.0	18.9
2. Umpires, Referees, and Other Sports Officials	81.6	16.7
3. Tree Trimmers and Pruners	80.9	22.9
4. Carpet Installers	80.3	23.4
5. Plasterers and Stucco Masons	79.1	22.6
6. Tile and Marble Setters	81.0	24.9
7. Electricians	76.3	21.4
8. Structural Iron and Steel Workers	85.7	31.0
9. Electrical Power-Line Installers and Repairers	83.7	29.1
10. Sheet Metal Workers	76.3	22.3
11. Carpenters	73.9	20.6
12. Brickmasons and Blockmasons	70.1	17.3
13. Athletes and Sports Competitors	91.4	40.0
14. Fitness Trainers and Aerobics Instructors	75.6	24.6
15. Heating, Air Conditioning, and Refrigeration Mechanics and Installers	77.5	26.6
16. Millwrights	73.7	23.1
17. Animal Trainers	77.9	28.7
18. First-Line Supervisors/Managers of Fire Fighting and Prevention Workers	81.3	32.9

(continued)

(continued)

The 50 Most Active Jobs

Job	Rating for Performing General Physical Activities	Rating for Sitting
19. Telecommunications Line Installers and Repairers	76.1	28.6
20. Floor Layers, Except Carpet, Wood, and Hard Tiles	70.3	22.9
21. Recreational Vehicle Service Technicians	73.3	26.1
22. Transit and Railroad Police	84.1	37.9
23. Coaches and Scouts	82.0	36.7
24. Slaughterers and Meat Packers	73.7	28.6
25. Maintenance and Repair Workers, General	69.7	24.7
26. Helpers—Carpenters	74.0	29.6
27. Laborers and Freight, Stock, and Material Movers, Hand	72.0	27.7
28. Butchers and Meat Cutters	60.7	17.0
29. Pipelayers	74.3	31.4
30. Painters, Transportation Equipment	63.3	21.1
31. Physical Therapist Assistants	73.3	31.6
32. Cement Masons and Concrete Finishers	65.4	24.3
33. Printing Machine Operators	62.0	21.3
34. Postal Service Mail Carriers	83.3	42.9
35. Roofers	71.4	31.4
36. Motorcycle Mechanics	67.1	27.1
37. Construction Laborers	71.4	31.4
38. Helpers—Pipelayers, Plumbers, Pipefitters, and Steamfitters	64.9	26.6
39. Helpers—Brickmasons, Blockmasons, Stonemasons, and Tile and Marble Setters	68.6	31.4
40. Boilermakers	61.9	25.0
41. Bus and Truck Mechanics and Diesel Engine Specialists	65.1	28.7
42. First-Line Supervisors/Managers of Retail Sales Workers	59.0	23.4
43. Automotive Service Technicians and Mechanics	58.9	23.5
44. Emergency Medical Technicians and Paramedics	70.0	36.0
45. Mobile Heavy Equipment Mechanics, Except Engines	61.6	27.6
46. Physical Therapists	63.9	29.9
47. Painters, Construction and Maintenance	59.4	25.7
48. Machinists	58.3	24.7
49. Tapers	61.9	28.6
50. Drywall and Ceiling Tile Installers	59.6	26.9

The 50 Most Outdoorsy Jobs

Many people want to do more than just get out from behind a desk; they want to get out of the *building* and work in the fresh air. For these people, we created the following list, which highlights those jobs that allow workers to spend the most time outdoors. The O*NET uses four measures to indicate the amount of work activity done outdoors: Outdoors, Exposed to Weather; Outdoors, Under Cover; In an Open Vehicle or Equipment; and In an Enclosed Vehicle or Equipment. For each of the 175 best jobs, we calculated the average of these four measures and then ordered all the jobs by this combined measure. The 50 top-ranked jobs are listed here, and we represent the average rating on the four measures as a number on a scale in which 0 is the lowest and 100 is the highest.

The 50 Most Outdoorsy Jobs	
Job	Average Rating for Amount of Work Done Outdoors
1. Crossing Guards	71.4
2. Roofers	71.4
3. Tree Trimmers and Pruners	71.4
4. Excavating and Loading Machine and Dragline Operators	70.0
5. Pipelayers	68.6
6. Pesticide Handlers, Sprayers, and Applicators, Vegetation	65.7
7. Septic Tank Servicers and Sewer Pipe Cleaners	65.7
8. Earth Drillers, Except Oil and Gas	63.1
9. Construction Laborers	62.9
10. Farmers and Ranchers	62.9
11. Postal Service Mail Carriers	62.9
12. Truck Drivers, Light or Delivery Services	62.9
13. First-Line Supervisors/Managers of Landscaping, Lawn Service, and Groundskeeping Workers	60.0
14. Hazardous Materials Removal Workers	60.0
15. Bus and Truck Mechanics and Diesel Engine Specialists	59.4
16. Helpers—Brickmasons, Blockmasons, Stonemasons, and Tile and Marble Setters	57.1
17. Telecommunications Line Installers and Repairers	57.1
18. Recreational Vehicle Service Technicians	57.0
19. Supervisors, Farming, Fishing, and Forestry Workers	56.8
20. Fish and Game Wardens	56.4
21. Structural Iron and Steel Workers	54.7
22. Athletes and Sports Competitors	54.3
23. First-Line Supervisors/Managers of Construction Trades and Extraction Workers	54.3
24. Riggers	54.3

(continued)

(continued)

The 50 Most Outdoorsy Jobs

Job	Average Rating for Amount of Work Done Outdoors
25. Operating Engineers and Other Construction Equipment Operators	54.1
26. Cement Masons and Concrete Finishers	54.0
27. Highway Maintenance Workers	53.9
28. Paving, Surfacing, and Tamping Equipment Operators	53.6
29. Reinforcing Iron and Rebar Workers	53.6
30. Water and Liquid Waste Treatment Plant and System Operators	53.0
31. Landscaping and Groundskeeping Workers	52.9
32. Control and Valve Installers and Repairers, Except Mechanical Door	52.4
33. First-Line Supervisors/Managers of Police and Detectives	51.1
34. Pest Control Workers	51.0
35. Refuse and Recyclable Material Collectors	50.9
36. Mobile Heavy Equipment Mechanics, Except Engines	50.2
37. Electrical Power-Line Installers and Repairers	50.0
38. First-Line Supervisors/Managers of Fire Fighting and Prevention Workers	49.5
39. Transit and Railroad Police	49.4
40. Truck Drivers, Heavy and Tractor-Trailer	48.8
41. Animal Control Workers	48.5
42. Helpers—Pipelayers, Plumbers, Pipefitters, and Steamfitters	48.2
43. Helpers—Carpenters	47.9
44. Police and Sheriff's Patrol Officers	47.9
45. Emergency Medical Technicians and Paramedics	47.4
46. Heating, Air Conditioning, and Refrigeration Mechanics and Installers	47.0
47. Locksmiths and Safe Repairers	46.9
48. Detectives and Criminal Investigators	46.7
49. Plumbers, Pipefitters, and Steamfitters	46.1
50. Aircraft Structure, Surfaces, Rigging, and Systems Assemblers	45.7

The 50 Lowest-Strength High-Activity Jobs

Maybe you want to do active work but not strenuous work. In that case, you may be interested in the following list, which highlights the jobs that have high activity but do not demand a lot of strength. To create this list, we brought together four measures of physical strength that the O*NET uses to rate jobs: Static Strength, Explosive Strength, Dynamic Strength, and Trunk Strength. For each of the 175 best jobs not behind a desk, we computed the average of these four measures and used that combined score to rank all the jobs. The following list identifies the top 50 jobs we found—in other words, the high-activity jobs that require the *least* amount of strength. For each job, we show the average rating for the four measures of strength, represented on a scale from 0 (lowest) to 100 (highest).

The 50 Lowest-Strength High-Activity Jobs

Job	Average Rating for Strength
1. Crossing Guards	5.7
2. Geoscientists, Except Hydrologists and Geographers	9.0
3. Chemists	9.4
4. Construction Managers	11.2
5. Chemical Technicians	11.2
6. Zoologists and Wildlife Biologists	11.6
7. Audio-Visual Collections Specialists	13.4
8. Physician Assistants	13.4
9. Environmental Science and Protection Technicians, Including Health	14.8
10. First-Line Supervisors/Managers of Food Preparation and Serving Workers	14.8
11. Gas Plant Operators	15.4
12. Bakers	15.7
13. Medical Assistants	16.1
14. First-Line Supervisors/Managers of Housekeeping and Janitorial Workers	16.1
15. Middle School Teachers, Except Special and Vocational Education	17.0
16. Elementary School Teachers, Except Special Education	17.4
17. Funeral Directors	17.4
18. Paper Goods Machine Setters, Operators, and Tenders	17.9
19. Secondary School Teachers, Except Special and Vocational Education	17.9
20. Costume Attendants	17.9
21. Industrial Production Managers	17.9
22. Occupational Therapists	18.3
23. Orthotists and Prosthetists	18.3
24. Self-Enrichment Education Teachers	18.3
25. Kindergarten Teachers, Except Special Education	18.4
26. Radiation Therapists	18.4
27. Postal Service Mail Carriers	18.6
28. Education Administrators, Preschool and Child Care Center/Program	18.8
29. Construction and Building Inspectors	19.2
30. Gaming Supervisors	19.3
31. Set and Exhibit Designers	19.6
32. Museum Technicians and Conservators	20.1

(continued)

(continued)

The 50 Lowest-Strength High-Activity Jobs

Job	Average Rating for Strength
33. Nuclear Medicine Technologists	20.1
34. Transportation Inspectors	20.5
35. Preschool Teachers, Except Special Education	20.6
36. Cardiovascular Technologists and Technicians	20.6
37. Hairdressers, Hairstylists, and Cosmetologists	21.0
38. Printing Machine Operators	21.0
39. Recreation Workers	21.0
40. Avionics Technicians	21.5
41. First-Line Supervisors/Managers of Production and Operating Workers	21.5
42. Medical Equipment Preparers	21.9
43. Surveyors	22.3
44. Electrical and Electronics Repairers, Commercial and Industrial Equipment	22.8
45. Conservation Scientists	22.8
46. Locksmiths and Safe Repairers	22.8
47. Nuclear Technicians	22.8
48. Postal Service Clerks	22.9
49. Licensed Practical and Licensed Vocational Nurses	23.3
50. Hazardous Materials Removal Workers	23.6

The 50 Highest-Strength High-Activity Jobs

Some people enjoy working up a sweat on the job and want to feel physically tired at the end of the workday. For them, high activity on the job is not enough; the job must demand that they use physical strength. If you're one of these people, you'll want to peruse the following list. As we did for the previous list, we took the average of four measures of strength—Static Strength, Explosive Strength, Dynamic Strength, and Trunk Strength—and used this average to rank the 175 best jobs by the overall amount of strength required. The following list shows the 50 jobs that required the *greatest* amount of strength, and for each job it gives a figure on the scale from 0 to 100 to indicate the job's average rating on the four measures of strength.

The 50 Highest-Strength High-Activity Jobs

Job	Average Rating for Strength
1. Athletes and Sports Competitors	77.9
2. Structural Iron and Steel Workers	68.4
3. Truck Drivers, Heavy and Tractor-Trailer	54.8
4. Earth Drillers, Except Oil and Gas	53.9
5. Pipelayers	53.6
6. Choreographers	51.4
7. Slaughterers and Meat Packers	49.4
8. Industrial Machinery Mechanics	48.8
9. Construction Laborers	48.6
10. Electricians	47.8
11. Fitness Trainers and Aerobics Instructors	47.4
12. Riggers	47.1
13. Industrial Truck and Tractor Operators	46.5
14. Roofers	46.4
15. Correctional Officers and Jailers	45.6
16. Laborers and Freight, Stock, and Material Movers, Hand	45.5
17. Carpet Installers	45.1
18. Stonemasons	44.7
19. Helpers—Production Workers	43.2
20. Emergency Medical Technicians and Paramedics	42.5
21. First-Line Supervisors/Managers of Police and Detectives	42.5
22. Police and Sheriff's Patrol Officers	42.5
23. Carpenters	41.8
24. Boilermakers	41.4
25. Glaziers	41.4
26. Septic Tank Servicers and Sewer Pipe Cleaners	41.4
27. Helpers—Installation, Maintenance, and Repair Workers	40.7
28. Transit and Railroad Police	40.7
29. Brickmasons and Blockmasons	40.2
30. Physical Therapist Assistants	40.2
31. Tree Trimmers and Pruners	40.0
32. Aircraft Mechanics and Service Technicians	39.5
33. Helpers—Brickmasons, Blockmasons, Stonemasons, and Tile and Marble Setters	39.3
34. Aircraft Structure, Surfaces, Rigging, and Systems Assemblers	38.9
35. Nursing Aides, Orderlies, and Attendants	38.9
36. Farmers and Ranchers	38.6

(continued)

(continued)

The 50 Highest-Strength High-Activity Jobs

Job	Average Rating for Strength
37. Millwrights	38.0
38. Sheet Metal Workers	38.0
39. Plasterers and Stucco Masons	37.5
40. Coaches and Scouts	37.5
41. First-Line Supervisors/Managers of Fire Fighting and Prevention Workers	37.3
42. Tile and Marble Setters	37.2
43. Elevator Installers and Repairers	37.1
44. Reinforcing Iron and Rebar Workers	37.1
45. Helpers—Carpenters	37.1
46. Fish and Game Wardens	37.1
47. Structural Metal Fabricators and Fitters	36.8
48. Automotive Body and Related Repairers	36.6
49. Plumbers, Pipefitters, and Steamfitters	36.4
50. Pesticide Handlers, Sprayers, and Applicators, Vegetation	36.4

The 50 Fastest-Moving Jobs

One measure of activity on the job is how fast you need to move at work. Some people enjoy working in situations where they move quickly and react rapidly to events. For them, we created an overall measure of speed on the job by using the average of three O*NET measures: Reaction Time, Wrist-Finger Speed, and Speed of Limb Movement. We ordered the 175 best jobs according to their score on this combined measure of speed, and we put the top 50 fast-moving jobs on the following list. The score for each job is shown on a scale from 0 to 100.

The 50 Fastest-Moving Jobs

Job	Average Rating for Speed
1. Athletes and Sports Competitors	59.0
2. Truck Drivers, Heavy and Tractor-Trailer	50.3
3. Structural Iron and Steel Workers	46.8
4. Earth Drillers, Except Oil and Gas	46.4
5. Emergency Medical Technicians and Paramedics	46.4
6. Electricians	45.9
7. Riggers	43.8
8. Industrial Machinery Mechanics	43.6

The 50 Fastest-Moving Jobs

Job	Average Rating for Speed
9. Industrial Truck and Tractor Operators	43.5
10. First-Line Supervisors/Managers of Police and Detectives	41.7
11. Automotive Body and Related Repairers	41.1
12. Choreographers	41.0
13. Slaughterers and Meat Packers	40.4
14. Helpers—Installation, Maintenance, and Repair Workers	39.9
15. Photographers	39.3
16. Aircraft Structure, Surfaces, Rigging, and Systems Assemblers	38.4
17. Glaziers	38.1
18. Aircraft Mechanics and Service Technicians	37.8
19. Plasterers and Stucco Masons	37.5
20. Electrical and Electronics Repairers, Powerhouse, Substation, and Relay	37.1
21. Helpers—Production Workers	37.1
22. Railroad Conductors and Yardmasters	37.0
23. Water and Liquid Waste Treatment Plant and System Operators	37.0
24. Chemical Plant and System Operators	36.9
25. Automotive Service Technicians and Mechanics	36.6
26. Carpenters	36.6
27. Police and Sheriff's Patrol Officers	35.7
28. Pipelayers	35.2
29. Control and Valve Installers and Repairers, Except Mechanical Door	35.2
30. Highway Maintenance Workers	35.2
31. Paving, Surfacing, and Tamping Equipment Operators	35.1
32. Stonemasons	35.1
33. Heating, Air Conditioning, and Refrigeration Mechanics and Installers	34.9
34. Electrical Power-Line Installers and Repairers	34.6
35. Helpers—Carpenters	34.6
36. Carpet Installers	34.5
37. Correctional Officers and Jailers	34.5
38. Millwrights	34.0
39. Mobile Heavy Equipment Mechanics, Except Engines	34.0
40. Machinists	33.4
41. Transit and Railroad Police	33.4
42. Crossing Guards	33.3
43. Driver/Sales Workers	33.3
44. Truck Drivers, Light or Delivery Services	33.3

(continued)

(continued)

The 50 Fastest-Moving Jobs

Job	Average Rating for Speed
45. Locksmiths and Safe Repairers	32.8
46. Painters, Transportation Equipment	32.8
47. Sheet Metal Workers	32.8
48. First-Line Supervisors/Managers of Construction Trades and Extraction Workers	32.4
49. Refuse and Recyclable Material Collectors	32.2
50. Butchers and Meat Cutters	31.6

Bonus List: Metropolitan Areas with the Highest Percentages of Workers in the Best Jobs Not Behind a Desk

The following list does not contain jobs. Instead, it lists the 50 metropolitan areas with the highest percentage of people working in the 175 best jobs not behind a desk. If you are considering relocating, you might want to move to one of these areas where good high-energy jobs are concentrated.

You may notice that the list does not include many of the nation's most populous metropolitan areas. The economies of the really big cities tend to be dominated by office jobs. That's not to say that you cannot find an active job in a big city. Almost all of the jobs in this book have many openings in large cities.

The 50 Metropolitan Areas with the Highest Percentages of Workers in the Best Jobs Not Behind a Desk

Metropolitan Area	Percentage of Workers in the 175 Best Jobs Not Behind a Desk
1. Beaumont–Port Arthur, TX	35.0%
2. Houma–Bayou Cane–Thibodaux, LA	34.1%
3. Riverside–San Bernardino–Ontario, CA	33.9%
4. Baton Rouge, LA	33.8%
5. Texarkana–Texarkana, TX–AR	33.4%
6. Toledo, OH	32.8%
7. Evansville, IN–KY	32.6%
8. Youngstown–Warren–Boardman, OH–PA	32.5%
9. Killeen–Temple–Fort Hood, TX	32.3%

The 50 Metropolitan Areas with the Highest Percentages of Workers in the Best Jobs Not Behind a Desk

Metropolitan Area	Percentage of Workers in the 175 Best Jobs Not Behind a Desk
10. Mobile, AL	32.1%
11. Huntington–Ashland, WV–KY–OH	31.9%
12. Vallejo–Fairfield, CA	31.6%
13. Stockton, CA	31.4%
14. Canton–Massillon, OH	31.4%
15. Duluth, MN–WI	31.1%
16. Lancaster, PA	31.1%
17. Jackson, MS	31.0%
18. Decatur, AL	30.8%
19. Florence, SC	30.8%
20. Elkhart–Goshen, IN	30.8%
21. Wheeling, WV–OH	30.7%
22. Lake Charles, LA	30.7%
23. Lebanon, PA	30.6%
24. Augusta–Richmond County, GA–SC	30.6%
25. Roanoke, VA	30.6%
26. Birmingham–Hoover, AL	30.6%
27. Houston–Sugar Land–Baytown, TX	30.6%
28. Charleston, WV	30.6%
29. Sarasota–Bradenton–Venice, FL	30.5%
30. Little Rock–North Little Rock, AR	30.5%
31. Memphis, TN–MS–AR	30.5%
32. Allentown–Bethlehem–Easton, PA–NJ	30.4%
33. Altoona, PA	30.4%
34. Lima, OH	30.2%
35. Longview, TX	30.2%
36. Louisville–Jefferson County, KY–IN	30.2%
37. Johnstown, PA	30.1%
38. Modesto, CA	30.1%
39. El Paso, TX	30.1%
40. Hattiesburg, MS	30.0%
41. Corpus Christi, TX	30.0%
42. Charleston–North Charleston, SC	30.0%

(continued)

(continued)

The 50 Metropolitan Areas with the Highest Percentages of Workers in the Best Jobs Not Behind a Desk

Metropolitan Area	Percentage of Workers in the 175 Best Jobs Not Behind a Desk
43. Scranton–Wilkes-Barre, PA	29.9%
44. Indianapolis–Carmel, IN	29.9%
45. Asheville, NC	29.7%
46. Anniston–Oxford, AL	29.7%
47. Virginia Beach–Norfolk–Newport News, VA–NC	29.7%
48. McAllen–Edinburg–Mission, TX	29.7%
49. Las Vegas–Paradise, NV	29.7%
50. Vineland–Millville–Bridgeton, NJ	29.6%

Best Jobs Lists with High Percentages of Workers Age 16–24, Workers Age 55 and Over, Part-Time Workers, Self-Employed Workers, Women, and Men

We decided it would be interesting to include lists in this section that show what sorts of jobs different types of people are most likely to have. For example, what high-energy jobs have the highest percentage of men or young workers? We're not saying that men or young people should consider these jobs over others, but it is interesting information to know.

In some cases, the lists can give you ideas for jobs to consider that you might otherwise overlook. For example, perhaps women should consider some jobs that traditionally have high percentages of men in them. Or older workers might consider some jobs typically held by young people. Although these are not obvious ways of using these lists, the lists may give you some good ideas on jobs to consider. The lists may also help you identify jobs that work well for others in your situation—for example, jobs with plentiful opportunities for part-time work, if that is something you want to do.

All of the lists in this section were created using a similar process. We began with the 175 best jobs not behind a desk. Next, we sorted those jobs in order of the primary criterion for each set of lists. For example, we sorted the 175 jobs based on the percentage of workers age 16 to 24 from highest to lowest percentage and then selected the jobs with a high percentage (the 51 jobs with a percentage greater than 15 percent). From this initial list of jobs with a high percentage of each type of worker, we created four more-specialized lists:

- 25 Best Jobs Overall (jobs that have the highest combined scores for earnings, growth rate, and number of openings)
- 25 Best-Paying Jobs
- 25 Fastest-Growing Jobs
- 25 Jobs with the Most Openings

Again, each of these four lists includes only jobs that have high percentages of different types of workers. The same basic process was used to create all the lists in this section. The lists are very interesting, and we hope you find them helpful.

Best Jobs Not Behind a Desk with the Highest Percentage of Workers Age 16–24

These jobs have higher percentages (more than 15 percent) of workers between the ages of 16 and 24. Young people are found in all jobs, but those with higher percentages of young people may present more opportunities for initial entry or upward mobility. Many jobs with the highest percentages of young people are those that are learned through on-the-job training, such as construction jobs, but there is a wide variety of jobs in different fields among the top 51.

Best Jobs Not Behind a Desk with the Highest Percentage of Workers Age 16–24

Job	Percent Age 16–24
1. Costume Attendants	52.4%
2. Choreographers	46.9%
3. Helpers—Brickmasons, Blockmasons, Stonemasons, and Tile and Marble Setters	44.7%
4. Helpers—Carpenters	44.7%
5. Helpers—Pipelayers, Plumbers, Pipefitters, and Steamfitters	44.7%
6. Athletes and Sports Competitors	35.3%
7. Coaches and Scouts	35.3%
8. Umpires, Referees, and Other Sports Officials	35.3%
9. Laborers and Freight, Stock, and Material Movers, Hand	31.9%
10. Helpers—Production Workers	31.5%
11. Environmental Science and Protection Technicians, Including Health	30.8%
12. Fitness Trainers and Aerobics Instructors	29.1%
13. Recreation Workers	29.1%
14. Recreational Vehicle Service Technicians	26.7%

(continued)

(continued)

Best Jobs Not Behind a Desk with the Highest Percentage of Workers Age 16–24

Job	Percent Age 16–24
15. Landscaping and Groundskeeping Workers	26.6%
16. Pesticide Handlers, Sprayers, and Applicators, Vegetation	26.6%
17. Tree Trimmers and Pruners	26.6%
18. Motorboat Mechanics	25.9%
19. Motorcycle Mechanics	25.9%
20. Outdoor Power Equipment and Other Small Engine Mechanics	25.9%
21. Helpers—Installation, Maintenance, and Repair Workers	25.8%
22. Surgical Technologists	24.7%
23. First-Line Supervisors/Managers of Food Preparation and Serving Workers	24.3%
24. Construction Laborers	23.7%
25. Animal Control Workers	23.1%
26. Roofers	22.7%
27. Medical Assistants	21.5%
28. Medical Equipment Preparers	21.5%
29. Security Guards	20.6%
30. Drywall and Ceiling Tile Installers	19.5%
31. Tapers	19.5%
32. Emergency Medical Technicians and Paramedics	19.0%
33. Automotive Service Technicians and Mechanics	18.6%
34. Self-Enrichment Education Teachers	18.4%
35. Electrical and Electronics Repairers, Powerhouse, Substation, and Relay	18.2%
36. Photographers	17.8%
37. Locksmiths and Safe Repairers	17.4%
38. Plasterers and Stucco Masons	17.0%
39. Carpet Installers	17.0%
40. Floor Layers, Except Carpet, Wood, and Hard Tiles	17.0%
41. Tile and Marble Setters	17.0%
42. Painters, Construction and Maintenance	16.8%
43. Animal Trainers	16.7%
44. Embalmers	16.7%
45. Nursing Aides, Orderlies, and Attendants	16.6%
46. Butchers and Meat Cutters	15.8%
47. Slaughterers and Meat Packers	15.8%
48. Carpenters	15.7%
49. Physical Therapist Aides	15.5%
50. Physical Therapist Assistants	15.5%
51. Orthotists and Prosthetists	15.5%

The jobs in the following four lists are derived from the preceding list of the active jobs with the highest percentage of workers age 16–24.

Best Jobs Overall Not Behind a Desk with a High Percentage of Workers Age 16–24

Job	Percent Age 16–24	Annual Earnings	Percent Growth	Annual Openings
1. Self-Enrichment Education Teachers	18.4%	$32,360	25.3%	74,000
2. Physical Therapist Assistants	15.5%	$39,490	44.2%	7,000
3. Surgical Technologists	24.7%	$34,830	29.5%	12,000
4. Tile and Marble Setters	17.0%	$36,530	22.9%	9,000
5. Medical Assistants	21.5%	$25,350	52.1%	93,000
6. Athletes and Sports Competitors	35.3%	$39,930	21.1%	6,000
7. Carpenters	15.7%	$35,580	13.8%	210,000
8. Automotive Service Technicians and Mechanics	18.6%	$33,050	15.7%	93,000
9. Fitness Trainers and Aerobics Instructors	29.1%	$25,840	27.1%	50,000
10. Emergency Medical Technicians and Paramedics	19.0%	$26,080	27.3%	21,000
11. Nursing Aides, Orderlies, and Attendants	16.6%	$21,440	22.3%	307,000
12. Roofers	22.7%	$31,230	16.8%	38,000
13. Coaches and Scouts	35.3%	$25,990	20.4%	63,000
14. First-Line Supervisors/Managers of Food Preparation and Serving Workers	24.3%	$26,050	16.6%	187,000
15. Landscaping and Groundskeeping Workers	26.6%	$20,670	19.5%	243,000
16. Environmental Science and Protection Technicians, Including Health	30.8%	$36,260	16.3%	6,000
17. Painters, Construction and Maintenance	16.8%	$30,800	12.6%	102,000
18. Orthotists and Prosthetists	15.5%	$53,760	18.0%	fewer than 500
19. Tree Trimmers and Pruners	26.6%	$27,920	16.5%	11,000
20. Drywall and Ceiling Tile Installers	19.5%	$34,740	9.0%	17,000
21. Choreographers	46.9%	$32,950	16.8%	4,000
22. Motorboat Mechanics	25.9%	$32,780	15.1%	7,000
23. Medical Equipment Preparers	21.5%	$24,880	20.0%	8,000
24. Recreation Workers	29.1%	$20,110	17.3%	69,000
25. Carpet Installers	17.0%	$33,550	8.4%	11,000

Best-Paying Jobs Not Behind a Desk for Workers Age 16–24

Job	Percent Age 16–24	Annual Earnings
1. Electrical and Electronics Repairers, Powerhouse, Substation, and Relay	18.2%	$54,970
2. Orthotists and Prosthetists	15.5%	$53,760
3. Athletes and Sports Competitors	35.3%	$39,930
4. Tapers	19.5%	$39,870
5. Physical Therapist Assistants	15.5%	$39,490
6. Embalmers	16.7%	$36,960
7. Tile and Marble Setters	17.0%	$36,530
8. Environmental Science and Protection Technicians, Including Health	30.8%	$36,260
9. Carpenters	15.7%	$35,580
10. Surgical Technologists	24.7%	$34,830
11. Drywall and Ceiling Tile Installers	19.5%	$34,740
12. Carpet Installers	17.0%	$33,550
13. Plasterers and Stucco Masons	17.0%	$33,440
14. Automotive Service Technicians and Mechanics	18.6%	$33,050
15. Floor Layers, Except Carpet, Wood, and Hard Tiles	17.0%	$33,010
16. Choreographers	46.9%	$32,950
17. Motorboat Mechanics	25.9%	$32,780
18. Self-Enrichment Education Teachers	18.4%	$32,360
19. Roofers	22.7%	$31,230
20. Locksmiths and Safe Repairers	17.4%	$30,880
21. Painters, Construction and Maintenance	16.8%	$30,800
22. Recreational Vehicle Service Technicians	26.7%	$30,480
23. Motorcycle Mechanics	25.9%	$29,450
24. Tree Trimmers and Pruners	26.6%	$27,920
25. Animal Control Workers	23.1%	$26,780

Fastest-Growing Jobs Not Behind a Desk for Workers Age 16–24

Job	Percent Age 16–24	Percent Growth
1. Medical Assistants	21.5%	52.1%
2. Physical Therapist Assistants	15.5%	44.2%
3. Physical Therapist Aides	15.5%	34.4%
4. Surgical Technologists	24.7%	29.5%
5. Emergency Medical Technicians and Paramedics	19.0%	27.3%
6. Fitness Trainers and Aerobics Instructors	29.1%	27.1%

Fastest-Growing Jobs Not Behind a Desk for Workers Age 16–24

Job	Percent Age 16–24	Percent Growth
7. Self-Enrichment Education Teachers	18.4%	25.3%
8. Costume Attendants	52.4%	23.4%
9. Tile and Marble Setters	17.0%	22.9%
10. Nursing Aides, Orderlies, and Attendants	16.6%	22.3%
11. Athletes and Sports Competitors	35.3%	21.1%
12. Coaches and Scouts	35.3%	20.4%
13. Animal Trainers	16.7%	20.3%
14. Medical Equipment Preparers	21.5%	20.0%
15. Landscaping and Groundskeeping Workers	26.6%	19.5%
16. Recreational Vehicle Service Technicians	26.7%	19.5%
17. Umpires, Referees, and Other Sports Officials	35.3%	19.0%
18. Orthotists and Prosthetists	15.5%	18.0%
19. Recreation Workers	29.1%	17.3%
20. Choreographers	46.9%	16.8%
21. Roofers	22.7%	16.8%
22. First-Line Supervisors/Managers of Food Preparation and Serving Workers	24.3%	16.6%
23. Helpers—Pipelayers, Plumbers, Pipefitters, and Steamfitters	44.7%	16.6%
24. Pesticide Handlers, Sprayers, and Applicators, Vegetation	26.6%	16.6%
25. Tree Trimmers and Pruners	26.6%	16.5%

Jobs Not Behind a Desk with the Most Openings for Workers Age 16–24

Job	Percent Age 16–24	Annual Openings
1. Laborers and Freight, Stock, and Material Movers, Hand	31.9%	671,000
2. Nursing Aides, Orderlies, and Attendants	16.6%	307,000
3. Construction Laborers	23.7%	245,000
4. Landscaping and Groundskeeping Workers	26.6%	243,000
5. Security Guards	20.6%	230,000
6. Carpenters	15.7%	210,000
7. First-Line Supervisors/Managers of Food Preparation and Serving Workers	24.3%	187,000
8. Helpers—Production Workers	31.5%	107,000
9. Painters, Construction and Maintenance	16.8%	102,000
10. Automotive Service Technicians and Mechanics	18.6%	93,000
11. Medical Assistants	21.5%	93,000

(continued)

(continued)

Jobs Not Behind a Desk with the Most Openings for Workers Age 16–24

Job	Percent Age 16–24	Annual Openings
12. Self-Enrichment Education Teachers	18.4%	74,000
13. Recreation Workers	29.1%	69,000
14. Coaches and Scouts	35.3%	63,000
15. Fitness Trainers and Aerobics Instructors	29.1%	50,000
16. Helpers—Installation, Maintenance, and Repair Workers	25.8%	41,000
17. Roofers	22.7%	38,000
18. Helpers—Carpenters	44.7%	24,000
19. Photographers	17.8%	23,000
20. Slaughterers and Meat Packers	15.8%	22,000
21. Emergency Medical Technicians and Paramedics	19.0%	21,000
22. Butchers and Meat Cutters	15.8%	20,000
23. Helpers—Pipelayers, Plumbers, Pipefitters, and Steamfitters	44.7%	17,000
24. Drywall and Ceiling Tile Installers	19.5%	17,000
25. Helpers—Brickmasons, Blockmasons, Stonemasons, and Tile and Marble Setters	44.7%	14,000

Best Jobs Not Behind a Desk with a High Percentage of Workers Age 55 and Over

We created the following list by identifying the best jobs not behind a desk that employ more than 15 percent of workers age 55 and over. You may be surprised to note that 59 of the best 175 jobs met this cutoff, whereas only 51 employ the same percentage of people age 16–24. You probably expected that more young people are concentrated into high-activity jobs.

There are a number of reasons for this situation. First of all, we selected our 175 best jobs partly by eliminating all jobs with annual earnings of less than $20,000, and a lot of entry-level jobs with high concentrations of young people were among those removed. In addition, much of the growth in our economy is in office jobs, so a lot of young people who are entering the workforce are steered into those jobs rather than into high-energy jobs. Many of the more active jobs have high concentrations of older workers who established themselves in those careers several decades ago, when those jobs held more promise than they do now. A good example is Farmers and Ranchers. Finally, most of the active jobs with high concentrations of older workers do not require a lot of physical strength; many of them attract older workers who have experience in related jobs that are more physically demanding. For example, many retired police and sheriff's patrol officers find second careers as security guards or detectives and criminal investigators. Construction workers who are tired of the physical demands of the job may become construction and building inspectors. And people from many backgrounds may work as crossing guards in their later years.

Best Jobs Not Behind a Desk with the Highest Percentage of Workers Age 55 and Over

Job	Percent Age 55 and Over
1. Ship Engineers	50.0%
2. Farmers and Ranchers	48.7%
3. Embalmers	41.7%
4. Funeral Directors	40.7%
5. Crossing Guards	38.6%
6. Industrial Machinery Mechanics	31.6%
7. Tool and Die Makers	30.7%
8. Avionics Technicians	27.3%
9. Oral and Maxillofacial Surgeons	26.1%
10. Education Administrators, Preschool and Child Care Center/Program	25.9%
11. Reinforcing Iron and Rebar Workers	25.0%
12. Railroad Conductors and Yardmasters	24.5%
13. Security Guards	24.3%
14. Construction and Building Inspectors	24.2%
15. Helpers—Installation, Maintenance, and Repair Workers	22.6%
16. Veterinarians	22.0%
17. Supervisors, Farming, Fishing, and Forestry Workers	21.5%
18. Audio-Visual Collections Specialists	20.9%
19. Self-Enrichment Education Teachers	19.9%
20. First-Line Supervisors/Managers of Housekeeping and Janitorial Workers	19.9%
21. Curators	19.4%
22. Medical Equipment Repairers	19.4%
23. Museum Technicians and Conservators	19.4%
24. Millwrights	19.2%
25. Postal Service Clerks	19.0%
26. Postal Service Mail Carriers	18.3%
27. Water and Liquid Waste Treatment Plant and System Operators	18.0%
28. Bakers	18.0%
29. Electrical and Electronics Repairers, Commercial and Industrial Equipment	17.9%
30. Maintenance and Repair Workers, General	17.8%
31. Construction Managers	17.6%
32. Secondary School Teachers, Except Special and Vocational Education	17.6%

(continued)

(continued)

Best Jobs Not Behind a Desk with the Highest Percentage of Workers Age 55 and Over

Job	Percent Age 55 and Over
33. Vocational Education Teachers, Secondary School	17.6%
34. Gaming Supervisors	17.6%
35. Driver/Sales Workers	17.4%
36. Truck Drivers, Heavy and Tractor-Trailer	17.4%
37. Truck Drivers, Light or Delivery Services	17.4%
38. Locksmiths and Safe Repairers	17.4%
39. Transportation Inspectors	17.4%
40. Conservation Scientists	17.2%
41. Foresters	17.2%
42. First-Line Supervisors/Managers of Retail Sales Workers	17.2%
43. Surveyors	17.1%
44. Excavating and Loading Machine and Dragline Operators	17.0%
45. First-Line Supervisors/Managers of Mechanics, Installers, and Repairers	16.8%
46. Riggers	16.7%
47. First-Line Supervisors/Managers of Production and Operating Workers	16.6%
48. Elementary School Teachers, Except Special Education	16.5%
49. Middle School Teachers, Except Special and Vocational Education	16.5%
50. Machinists	16.3%
51. Paving, Surfacing, and Tamping Equipment Operators	16.0%
52. Structural Metal Fabricators and Fitters	16.0%
53. Bus and Truck Mechanics and Diesel Engine Specialists	15.9%
54. Refuse and Recyclable Material Collectors	15.9%
55. Licensed Practical and Licensed Vocational Nurses	15.6%
56. Orthotists and Prosthetists	15.5%
57. Athletic Trainers	15.2%
58. Butchers and Meat Cutters	15.1%
59. Slaughterers and Meat Packers	15.1%

The jobs in the following four lists are derived from the preceding list of the active jobs with the highest percentage of workers age 55 and over.

Best Jobs Overall Not Behind a Desk for Workers Age 55 and Over

Job	Percent Age 55 and Over	Annual Earnings	Percent Growth	Annual Openings
1. Elementary School Teachers, Except Special Education	16.5%	$44,040	18.2%	203,000
2. Veterinarians	22.0%	$68,910	17.4%	8,000
3. Secondary School Teachers, Except Special and Vocational Education	17.6%	$46,060	14.4%	107,000
4. Railroad Conductors and Yardmasters	24.5%	$54,040	20.3%	3,000
5. Licensed Practical and Licensed Vocational Nurses	15.6%	$35,230	17.1%	84,000
6. Self-Enrichment Education Teachers	19.9%	$32,360	25.3%	74,000
7. Construction Managers	17.6%	$72,260	10.4%	28,000
8. First-Line Supervisors/Managers of Mechanics, Installers, and Repairers	16.8%	$51,980	12.4%	33,000
9. Construction and Building Inspectors	24.2%	$44,720	22.3%	6,000
10. Education Administrators, Preschool and Child Care Center/Program	25.9%	$37,010	27.9%	9,000
11. Middle School Teachers, Except Special and Vocational Education	16.5%	$44,640	13.7%	83,000
12. Gaming Supervisors	17.6%	$40,300	16.3%	8,000
13. Orthotists and Prosthetists	15.5%	$53,760	18.0%	fewer than 500
14. Oral and Maxillofacial Surgeons	26.1% more than	$145,600	16.2%	fewer than 500
15. Truck Drivers, Heavy and Tractor-Trailer	17.4%	$34,280	12.9%	274,000
16. Maintenance and Repair Workers, General	17.8%	$31,210	15.2%	154,000
17. Truck Drivers, Light or Delivery Services	17.4%	$24,790	15.7%	169,000
18. Bus and Truck Mechanics and Diesel Engine Specialists	15.9%	$36,620	14.4%	32,000
19. First-Line Supervisors/Managers of Housekeeping and Janitorial Workers	19.9%	$30,330	19.0%	21,000
20. Surveyors	17.1%	$45,860	15.9%	4,000
21. First-Line Supervisors/Managers of Production and Operating Workers	16.6%	$46,140	2.7%	89,000
22. Helpers—Installation, Maintenance, and Repair Workers	22.6%	$21,230	16.4%	41,000
23. Vocational Education Teachers, Secondary School	17.6%	$47,090	9.1%	10,000
24. Crossing Guards	38.6%	$20,050	19.7%	26,000
25. Audio-Visual Collections Specialists	20.9%	$40,260	18.6%	1,000

Best-Paying Jobs Not Behind a Desk for Workers Age 55 and Over

Job	Percent Age 55 and Over	Annual Earnings
1. Oral and Maxillofacial Surgeons	26.1%	more than $145,600
2. Construction Managers	17.6%	$72,260
3. Veterinarians	22.0%	$68,910
4. Railroad Conductors and Yardmasters	24.5%	$54,040
5. Orthotists and Prosthetists	15.5%	$53,760
6. Conservation Scientists	17.2%	$53,350
7. Ship Engineers	50.0%	$52,780
8. First-Line Supervisors/Managers of Mechanics, Installers, and Repairers	16.8%	$51,980
9. Transportation Inspectors	17.4%	$49,490
10. Foresters	17.2%	$48,670
11. Postal Service Clerks	19.0%	$48,310
12. Funeral Directors	40.7%	$47,630
13. Vocational Education Teachers, Secondary School	17.6%	$47,090
14. Avionics Technicians	27.3%	$46,630
15. Postal Service Mail Carriers	18.3%	$46,330
16. First-Line Supervisors/Managers of Production and Operating Workers	16.6%	$46,140
17. Secondary School Teachers, Except Special and Vocational Education	17.6%	$46,060
18. Surveyors	17.1%	$45,860
19. Curators	19.4%	$45,240
20. Millwrights	19.2%	$44,780
21. Construction and Building Inspectors	24.2%	$44,720
22. Middle School Teachers, Except Special and Vocational Education	16.5%	$44,640
23. Electrical and Electronics Repairers, Commercial and Industrial Equipment	17.9%	$44,120
24. Elementary School Teachers, Except Special Education	16.5%	$44,040
25. Tool and Die Makers	30.7%	$43,580

Fastest-Growing Jobs Not Behind a Desk for Workers Age 55 and Over

Job	Percent Age 55 and Over	Percent Growth
1. Athletic Trainers	15.2%	29.3%
2. Education Administrators, Preschool and Child Care Center/Program	25.9%	27.9%
3. Self-Enrichment Education Teachers	19.9%	25.3%
4. Construction and Building Inspectors	24.2%	22.3%
5. Railroad Conductors and Yardmasters	24.5%	20.3%
6. Crossing Guards	38.6%	19.7%
7. First-Line Supervisors/Managers of Housekeeping and Janitorial Workers	19.9%	19.0%
8. Audio-Visual Collections Specialists	20.9%	18.6%
9. Elementary School Teachers, Except Special Education	16.5%	18.2%
10. Orthotists and Prosthetists	15.5%	18.0%
11. Veterinarians	22.0%	17.4%
12. Licensed Practical and Licensed Vocational Nurses	15.6%	17.1%
13. Helpers—Installation, Maintenance, and Repair Workers	22.6%	16.4%
14. Gaming Supervisors	17.6%	16.3%
15. Oral and Maxillofacial Surgeons	26.1%	16.2%
16. Water and Liquid Waste Treatment Plant and System Operators	18.0%	16.2%
17. Locksmiths and Safe Repairers	17.4%	16.1%
18. Surveyors	17.1%	15.9%
19. Curators	19.4%	15.7%
20. Truck Drivers, Light or Delivery Services	17.4%	15.7%
21. Embalmers	41.7%	15.6%
22. Paving, Surfacing, and Tamping Equipment Operators	16.0%	15.6%
23. Bakers	18.0%	15.2%
24. Maintenance and Repair Workers, General	17.8%	15.2%
25. Medical Equipment Repairers	19.4%	14.8%

Jobs Not Behind a Desk with the Most Openings for Workers Age 55 and Over

Job	Percent Age 55 and Over	Annual Openings
1. Truck Drivers, Heavy and Tractor-Trailer	17.4%	274,000
2. Security Guards	24.3%	230,000
3. First-Line Supervisors/Managers of Retail Sales Workers	17.2%	229,000
4. Elementary School Teachers, Except Special Education	16.5%	203,000
5. Truck Drivers, Light or Delivery Services	17.4%	169,000
6. Maintenance and Repair Workers, General	17.8%	154,000
7. Secondary School Teachers, Except Special and Vocational Education	17.6%	107,000
8. Farmers and Ranchers	48.7%	96,000
9. First-Line Supervisors/Managers of Production and Operating Workers	16.6%	89,000
10. Licensed Practical and Licensed Vocational Nurses	15.6%	84,000
11. Middle School Teachers, Except Special and Vocational Education	16.5%	83,000
12. Self-Enrichment Education Teachers	19.9%	74,000
13. Driver/Sales Workers	17.4%	72,000
14. Helpers—Installation, Maintenance, and Repair Workers	22.6%	41,000
15. Bakers	18.0%	37,000
16. First-Line Supervisors/Managers of Mechanics, Installers, and Repairers	16.8%	33,000
17. Machinists	16.3%	33,000
18. Bus and Truck Mechanics and Diesel Engine Specialists	15.9%	32,000
19. Refuse and Recyclable Material Collectors	15.9%	31,000
20. Construction Managers	17.6%	28,000
21. Crossing Guards	38.6%	26,000
22. Slaughterers and Meat Packers	15.1%	22,000
23. First-Line Supervisors/Managers of Housekeeping and Janitorial Workers	19.9%	21,000
24. Butchers and Meat Cutters	15.1%	20,000
25. Postal Service Mail Carriers	18.3%	19,000

Best Jobs Not Behind a Desk with a High Percentage of Part-Time Workers

Look over the list of the active jobs with high percentages (more than 20 percent) of part-time workers and you will find some interesting things. For example, five of the top 10 involve the sports, fitness, and recreation industry, which leads one to think that many people working in this industry do so less than full time. But a wide variety of other industries—including education, healthcare, and the arts—are also represented in this list. Some active jobs have high percentages of part-time workers and might deserve to be on this list, but they were eliminated from this book because their earnings are so unpredictable that the Department of Labor reports no average annual earnings figure for them. Dancers and Actors are good examples.

In some cases, people work part time because they want the freedom of time this arrangement can provide, but others may do so because they can't find full-time employment in these jobs. These folks may work in other full- or part-time jobs to make ends meet. Still others work part time in night-shift positions that pay a higher hourly wage than full-time workers earn—an option available to many registered nurses and other skilled healthcare workers. If you want to work part time now or in the future, these lists will help you identify active jobs that are more likely to provide that opportunity. If you want full-time work, the lists may also help you identify high-energy jobs for which such opportunities are more difficult to find. In either case, it's good information to know in advance.

Best Jobs Not Behind a Desk with the Highest Percentage of Part-Time Workers

Job	Percent Part-Time Workers
1. Costume Attendants	56.0%
2. Crossing Guards	53.9%
3. Choreographers	47.7%
4. Athletes and Sports Competitors	47.6%
5. Coaches and Scouts	47.6%
6. Umpires, Referees, and Other Sports Officials	47.6%
7. Self-Enrichment Education Teachers	45.6%
8. Embalmers	44.0%
9. Fitness Trainers and Aerobics Instructors	41.3%
10. Recreation Workers	41.3%
11. Hairdressers, Hairstylists, and Cosmetologists	34.8%
12. Helpers—Installation, Maintenance, and Repair Workers	32.9%
13. Occupational Therapists	29.4%
14. Photographers	28.9%
15. Flight Attendants	28.8%
16. Physical Therapist Aides	28.6%
17. Physical Therapist Assistants	28.6%
18. Nursing Aides, Orderlies, and Attendants	28.0%
19. Camera Operators, Television, Video, and Motion Picture	27.6%
20. Medical Assistants	27.5%
21. Medical Equipment Preparers	27.5%

(continued)

(continued)

Best Jobs Not Behind a Desk with the Highest Percentage of Part-Time Workers

Job	Percent Part-Time Workers
22. Bakers	26.8%
23. Kindergarten Teachers, Except Special Education	25.1%
24. Laborers and Freight, Stock, and Material Movers, Hand	25.1%
25. Preschool Teachers, Except Special Education	25.1%
26. Physical Therapists	24.7%
27. Landscaping and Groundskeeping Workers	24.4%
28. Pesticide Handlers, Sprayers, and Applicators, Vegetation	24.4%
29. Tree Trimmers and Pruners	24.4%
30. Registered Nurses	24.1%
31. Farmers and Ranchers	23.6%
32. Audio-Visual Collections Specialists	23.4%
33. Helpers—Production Workers	23.3%
34. Surgical Technologists	23.2%
35. Animal Trainers	23.1%
36. Environmental Science and Protection Technicians, Including Health	22.7%
37. Nuclear Technicians	22.7%
38. Oral and Maxillofacial Surgeons	22.4%
39. Licensed Practical and Licensed Vocational Nurses	21.9%
40. Set and Exhibit Designers	21.3%
41. Animal Control Workers	21.3%
42. Chiropractors	20.7%

The jobs in the following four lists are derived from the preceding list of the active jobs with the highest percentage of part-time workers.

Best Overall Part-Time Jobs Not Behind a Desk

Job	Percent Part-Time Workers	Annual Earnings	Percent Growth	Annual Openings
1. Registered Nurses	24.1%	$54,670	29.4%	229,000
2. Physical Therapists	24.7%	$63,080	36.7%	13,000
3. Occupational Therapists	29.4%	$56,860	33.6%	7,000
4. Medical Assistants	27.5%	$25,350	52.1%	93,000

Best Overall Part-Time Jobs Not Behind a Desk

Job	Percent Part-Time Workers	Annual Earnings	Percent Growth	Annual Openings
5. Kindergarten Teachers, Except Special Education	25.1%	$42,230	22.4%	28,000
6. Physical Therapist Assistants	28.6%	$39,490	44.2%	7,000
7. Self-Enrichment Education Teachers	45.6%	$32,360	25.3%	74,000
8. Surgical Technologists	23.2%	$34,830	29.5%	12,000
9. Preschool Teachers, Except Special Education	25.1%	$21,990	33.1%	77,000
10. Chiropractors	20.7%	$67,200	22.4%	4,000
11. Licensed Practical and Licensed Vocational Nurses	21.9%	$35,230	17.1%	84,000
12. Fitness Trainers and Aerobics Instructors	41.3%	$25,840	27.1%	50,000
13. Nursing Aides, Orderlies, and Attendants	28.0%	$21,440	22.3%	307,000
14. Athletes and Sports Competitors	47.6%	$39,930	21.1%	6,000
15. Coaches and Scouts	47.6%	$25,990	20.4%	63,000
16. Flight Attendants	28.8%	$46,680	16.3%	7,000
17. Landscaping and Groundskeeping Workers	24.4%	$20,670	19.5%	243,000
18. Farmers and Ranchers	23.6%	$34,140	−14.5%	96,000
19. Physical Therapist Aides	28.6%	$21,510	34.4%	5,000
20. Medical Equipment Preparers	27.5%	$24,880	20.0%	8,000
21. Tree Trimmers and Pruners	24.4%	$27,920	16.5%	11,000
22. Audio-Visual Collections Specialists	23.4%	$40,260	18.6%	1,000
23. Environmental Science and Protection Technicians, Including Health	22.7%	$36,260	16.3%	6,000
24. Oral and Maxillofacial Surgeons	22.4%	more than $145,600	16.2%	fewer than 500
25. Costume Attendants	56.0%	$25,360	23.4%	2,000

Best-Paying Part-Time Jobs Not Behind a Desk

Job	Percent Part-Time Workers	Annual Earnings
1. Oral and Maxillofacial Surgeons	22.4%	more than $145,600
2. Chiropractors	20.7%	$67,200
3. Physical Therapists	24.7%	$63,080
4. Nuclear Technicians	22.7%	$61,120
5. Occupational Therapists	29.4%	$56,860
6. Registered Nurses	24.1%	$54,670
7. Flight Attendants	28.8%	$46,680

(continued)

(continued)

Best-Paying Part-Time Jobs Not Behind a Desk

Job	Percent Part-Time Workers	Annual Earnings
8. Kindergarten Teachers, Except Special Education	25.1%	$42,230
9. Camera Operators, Television, Video, and Motion Picture	27.6%	$41,610
10. Audio-Visual Collections Specialists	23.4%	$40,260
11. Athletes and Sports Competitors	47.6%	$39,930
12. Physical Therapist Assistants	28.6%	$39,490
13. Set and Exhibit Designers	21.3%	$37,390
14. Embalmers	44.0%	$36,960
15. Environmental Science and Protection Technicians, Including Health	22.7%	$36,260
16. Licensed Practical and Licensed Vocational Nurses	21.9%	$35,230
17. Surgical Technologists	23.2%	$34,830
18. Farmers and Ranchers	23.6%	$34,140
19. Choreographers	47.7%	$32,950
20. Self-Enrichment Education Teachers	45.6%	$32,360
21. Tree Trimmers and Pruners	24.4%	$27,920
22. Animal Control Workers	21.3%	$26,780
23. Pesticide Handlers, Sprayers, and Applicators, Vegetation	24.4%	$26,120
24. Photographers	28.9%	$26,100
25. Coaches and Scouts	47.6%	$25,990

Fastest-Growing Part-Time Jobs Not Behind a Desk

Job	Percent Part-Time Workers	Percent Growth
1. Medical Assistants	27.5%	52.1%
2. Physical Therapist Assistants	28.6%	44.2%
3. Physical Therapists	24.7%	36.7%
4. Physical Therapist Aides	28.6%	34.4%
5. Occupational Therapists	29.4%	33.6%
6. Preschool Teachers, Except Special Education	25.1%	33.1%
7. Surgical Technologists	23.2%	29.5%
8. Registered Nurses	24.1%	29.4%
9. Fitness Trainers and Aerobics Instructors	41.3%	27.1%
10. Self-Enrichment Education Teachers	45.6%	25.3%
11. Costume Attendants	56.0%	23.4%

Fastest-Growing Part-Time Jobs Not Behind a Desk

Job	Percent Part-Time Workers	Percent Growth
12. Chiropractors	20.7%	22.4%
13. Kindergarten Teachers, Except Special Education	25.1%	22.4%
14. Nursing Aides, Orderlies, and Attendants	28.0%	22.3%
15. Athletes and Sports Competitors	47.6%	21.1%
16. Coaches and Scouts	47.6%	20.4%
17. Animal Trainers	23.1%	20.3%
18. Medical Equipment Preparers	27.5%	20.0%
19. Crossing Guards	53.9%	19.7%
20. Landscaping and Groundskeeping Workers	24.4%	19.5%
21. Umpires, Referees, and Other Sports Officials	47.6%	19.0%
22. Audio-Visual Collections Specialists	23.4%	18.6%
23. Recreation Workers	41.3%	17.3%
24. Licensed Practical and Licensed Vocational Nurses	21.9%	17.1%
25. Choreographers	47.7%	16.8%

Part-Time Jobs Not Behind a Desk with the Most Openings

Job	Percent Part-Time Workers	Annual Openings
1. Laborers and Freight, Stock, and Material Movers, Hand	25.1%	671,000
2. Nursing Aides, Orderlies, and Attendants	28.0%	307,000
3. Landscaping and Groundskeeping Workers	24.4%	243,000
4. Registered Nurses	24.1%	229,000
5. Helpers—Production Workers	23.3%	107,000
6. Farmers and Ranchers	23.6%	96,000
7. Medical Assistants	27.5%	93,000
8. Licensed Practical and Licensed Vocational Nurses	21.9%	84,000
9. Preschool Teachers, Except Special Education	25.1%	77,000
10. Self-Enrichment Education Teachers	45.6%	74,000
11. Recreation Workers	41.3%	69,000
12. Coaches and Scouts	47.6%	63,000
13. Hairdressers, Hairstylists, and Cosmetologists	34.8%	59,000
14. Fitness Trainers and Aerobics Instructors	41.3%	50,000
15. Helpers—Installation, Maintenance, and Repair Workers	32.9%	41,000

(continued)

(continued)

Part-Time Jobs Not Behind a Desk with the Most Openings

Job	Percent Part-Time Workers	Annual Openings
16. Bakers	26.8%	37,000
17. Kindergarten Teachers, Except Special Education	25.1%	28,000
18. Crossing Guards	53.9%	26,000
19. Photographers	28.9%	23,000
20. Physical Therapists	24.7%	13,000
21. Surgical Technologists	23.2%	12,000
22. Tree Trimmers and Pruners	24.4%	11,000
23. Medical Equipment Preparers	27.5%	8,000
24. Flight Attendants	28.8%	7,000
25. Occupational Therapists	29.4%	7,000

Best Jobs Not Behind a Desk with a High Percentage of Self-Employed Workers

About 8 percent of all working people are self-employed. Although you may think of the self-employed as having similar jobs, they actually work in an enormous range of situations, fields, and work environments that you may not have considered.

Among the self-employed are people who own small or large businesses, as many carpet installers do; professionals such as veterinarians and oral and maxillofacial surgeons; part-time workers; people working on a contract basis for one or more employers; people running home consulting or other businesses; and people in many other situations. They may go to the same worksite every day, as funeral directors do; visit multiple employers during the course of a week; or do most of their work from home. Some work part time, others full time, some as a way to have fun, some so they can spend time with their kids or go to school.

The point is that there is an enormous range of situations, and one of them could make sense for you now or in the future.

The following list contains active jobs in which more than 15 percent of the workers are self-employed.

Best Jobs Not Behind a Desk with the Highest Percentage of Self-Employed Workers

Job	Percent Self-Employed Workers
1. Farmers and Ranchers	100.0%
2. Photographers	58.8%
3. Animal Trainers	58.2%
4. Construction Managers	54.2%
5. Chiropractors	49.2%
6. Carpet Installers	46.4%
7. Floor Layers, Except Carpet, Wood, and Hard Tiles	44.7%
8. Painters, Construction and Maintenance	44.6%
9. Hairdressers, Hairstylists, and Cosmetologists	43.8%
10. First-Line Supervisors/Managers of Landscaping, Lawn Service, and Groundskeeping Workers	42.4%
11. Food Service Managers	40.5%
12. Locksmiths and Safe Repairers	37.6%
13. Carpenters	32.4%
14. First-Line Supervisors/Managers of Retail Sales Workers	31.9%
15. Self-Enrichment Education Teachers	31.1%
16. Gaming Supervisors	29.6%
17. Brickmasons and Blockmasons	28.6%
18. Set and Exhibit Designers	27.6%
19. Umpires, Referees, and Other Sports Officials	24.8%
20. First-Line Supervisors/Managers of Construction Trades and Extraction Workers	24.7%
21. Athletes and Sports Competitors	24.5%
22. Tile and Marble Setters	24.4%
23. Roofers	23.8%
24. Drywall and Ceiling Tile Installers	23.4%
25. Stonemasons	23.1%
26. Tree Trimmers and Pruners	22.2%
27. Coaches and Scouts	21.5%
28. Supervisors, Farming, Fishing, and Forestry Workers	21.3%
29. Camera Operators, Television, Video, and Motion Picture	21.1%
30. Tapers	21.0%
31. Veterinarians	20.7%
32. Landscaping and Groundskeeping Workers	20.5%
33. Funeral Directors	19.7%

(continued)

(continued)

Best Jobs Not Behind a Desk with the Highest Percentage of Self-Employed Workers

Job	Percent Self-Employed Workers
34. Pesticide Handlers, Sprayers, and Applicators, Vegetation	19.6%
35. Outdoor Power Equipment and Other Small Engine Mechanics	19.2%
36. Excavating and Loading Machine and Dragline Operators	19.1%
37. Motorboat Mechanics	18.9%
38. Choreographers	17.7%
39. Automotive Body and Related Repairers	17.6%
40. Medical Equipment Repairers	16.2%
41. Oral and Maxillofacial Surgeons	15.7%
42. Motorcycle Mechanics	15.7%

The jobs in the following four lists are derived from the preceding list of the active jobs with the highest percentage of self-employed workers.

Best Jobs Overall Not Behind a Desk for Self-Employed Workers

Job	Percent Self-Employed Workers	Annual Earnings	Percent Growth	Annual Openings
1. Self-Enrichment Education Teachers	31.1%	$32,360	25.3%	74,000
2. Veterinarians	20.7%	$68,910	17.4%	8,000
3. Chiropractors	49.2%	$67,200	22.4%	4,000
4. Tile and Marble Setters	24.4%	$36,530	22.9%	9,000
5. Athletes and Sports Competitors	24.5%	$39,930	21.1%	6,000
6. First-Line Supervisors/Managers of Landscaping, Lawn Service, and Groundskeeping Workers	42.4%	$36,320	17.8%	14,000
7. Carpenters	32.4%	$35,580	13.8%	210,000
8. Construction Managers	54.2%	$72,260	10.4%	28,000
9. First-Line Supervisors/Managers of Construction Trades and Extraction Workers	24.7%	$51,970	10.9%	57,000
10. Food Service Managers	40.5%	$41,340	11.5%	61,000
11. Coaches and Scouts	21.5%	$25,990	20.4%	63,000
12. Gaming Supervisors	29.6%	$40,300	16.3%	8,000
13. Landscaping and Groundskeeping Workers	20.5%	$20,670	19.5%	243,000

Best Jobs Overall Not Behind a Desk for Self-Employed Workers

Job	Percent Self-Employed Workers	Annual Earnings	Percent Growth	Annual Openings
14. Brickmasons and Blockmasons	28.6%	$41,860	12.0%	17,000
15. Roofers	23.8%	$31,230	16.8%	38,000
16. Oral and Maxillofacial Surgeons	15.7% more than	$145,600	16.2%	fewer than 500
17. Camera Operators, Television, Video, and Motion Picture	21.1%	$41,610	14.2%	4,000
18. Painters, Construction and Maintenance	44.6%	$30,800	12.6%	102,000
19. Automotive Body and Related Repairers	17.6%	$34,810	10.3%	18,000
20. Medical Equipment Repairers	16.2%	$39,570	14.8%	4,000
21. Tree Trimmers and Pruners	22.2%	$27,920	16.5%	11,000
22. First-Line Supervisors/Managers of Retail Sales Workers	31.9%	$32,840	3.8%	229,000
23. Hairdressers, Hairstylists, and Cosmetologists	43.8%	$20,610	16.1%	59,000
24. Choreographers	17.7%	$32,950	16.8%	4,000
25. Drywall and Ceiling Tile Installers	23.4%	$34,740	9.0%	17,000

Best-Paying Jobs Not Behind a Desk for Self-Employed Workers

Job	Percent Self-Employed Workers	Annual Earnings
1. Oral and Maxillofacial Surgeons	15.7% ..more than	$145,600
2. Construction Managers	54.2%	$72,260
3. Veterinarians	20.7%	$68,910
4. Chiropractors	49.2%	$67,200
5. First-Line Supervisors/Managers of Construction Trades and Extraction Workers	24.7%	$51,970
6. Funeral Directors	19.7%	$47,630
7. Brickmasons and Blockmasons	28.6%	$41,860
8. Camera Operators, Television, Video, and Motion Picture	21.1%	$41,610
9. Food Service Managers	40.5%	$41,340
10. Gaming Supervisors	29.6%	$40,300
11. Athletes and Sports Competitors	24.5%	$39,930
12. Tapers	21.0%	$39,870
13. Medical Equipment Repairers	16.2%	$39,570
14. Set and Exhibit Designers	27.6%	$37,390

(continued)

(continued)

Best-Paying Jobs Not Behind a Desk for Self-Employed Workers

Job	Percent Self-Employed Workers	Annual Earnings
15. Tile and Marble Setters	24.4%	$36,530
16. First-Line Supervisors/Managers of Landscaping, Lawn Service, and Groundskeeping Workers	42.4%	$36,320
17. Carpenters	32.4%	$35,580
18. Automotive Body and Related Repairers	17.6%	$34,810
19. Drywall and Ceiling Tile Installers	23.4%	$34,740
20. Stonemasons	23.1%	$34,640
21. Supervisors, Farming, Fishing, and Forestry Workers	21.3%	$34,331
22. Farmers and Ranchers	100.0%	$34,140
23. Carpet Installers	46.4%	$33,550
24. Floor Layers, Except Carpet, Wood, and Hard Tiles	44.7%	$33,010
25. Choreographers	17.7%	$32,950

Fastest-Growing Jobs Not Behind a Desk for Self-Employed Workers

Job	Percent Self-Employed Workers	Percent Growth
1. Self-Enrichment Education Teachers	31.1%	25.3%
2. Tile and Marble Setters	24.4%	22.9%
3. Chiropractors	49.2%	22.4%
4. Athletes and Sports Competitors	24.5%	21.1%
5. Coaches and Scouts	21.5%	20.4%
6. Animal Trainers	58.2%	20.3%
7. Landscaping and Groundskeeping Workers	20.5%	19.5%
8. Umpires, Referees, and Other Sports Officials	24.8%	19.0%
9. First-Line Supervisors/Managers of Landscaping, Lawn Service, and Groundskeeping Workers	42.4%	17.8%
10. Veterinarians	20.7%	17.4%
11. Choreographers	17.7%	16.8%
12. Roofers	23.8%	16.8%
13. Pesticide Handlers, Sprayers, and Applicators, Vegetation	19.6%	16.6%
14. Tree Trimmers and Pruners	22.2%	16.5%

Fastest-Growing Jobs Not Behind a Desk for Self-Employed Workers

Job	Percent Self-Employed Workers	Percent Growth
15. Gaming Supervisors	29.6%	16.3%
16. Oral and Maxillofacial Surgeons	15.7%	16.2%
17. Hairdressers, Hairstylists, and Cosmetologists	43.8%	16.1%
18. Locksmiths and Safe Repairers	37.6%	16.1%
19. Motorboat Mechanics	18.9%	15.1%
20. Medical Equipment Repairers	16.2%	14.8%
21. Camera Operators, Television, Video, and Motion Picture	21.1%	14.2%
22. Outdoor Power Equipment and Other Small Engine Mechanics	19.2%	14.0%
23. Carpenters	32.4%	13.8%
24. Motorcycle Mechanics	15.7%	13.7%
25. Stonemasons	23.1%	13.0%

Jobs Not Behind a Desk with the Most Openings for Self-Employed Workers

Job	Percent Self-Employed Workers	Annual Openings
1. Landscaping and Groundskeeping Workers	20.5%	243,000
2. First-Line Supervisors/Managers of Retail Sales Workers	31.9%	229,000
3. Carpenters	32.4%	210,000
4. Painters, Construction and Maintenance	44.6%	102,000
5. Farmers and Ranchers	100.0%	96,000
6. Self-Enrichment Education Teachers	31.1%	74,000
7. Coaches and Scouts	21.5%	63,000
8. Food Service Managers	40.5%	61,000
9. Hairdressers, Hairstylists, and Cosmetologists	43.8%	59,000
10. First-Line Supervisors/Managers of Construction Trades and Extraction Workers	24.7%	57,000
11. Roofers	23.8%	38,000
12. Construction Managers	54.2%	28,000
13. Photographers	58.8%	23,000
14. Automotive Body and Related Repairers	17.6%	18,000
15. Brickmasons and Blockmasons	28.6%	17,000

(continued)

(continued)

Jobs Not Behind a Desk with the Most Openings for Self-Employed Workers

Job	Percent Self-Employed Workers	Annual Openings
16. Drywall and Ceiling Tile Installers	23.4%	17,000
17. First-Line Supervisors/Managers of Landscaping, Lawn Service, and Groundskeeping Workers	42.4%	14,000
18. Carpet Installers	46.4%	11,000
19. Excavating and Loading Machine and Dragline Operators	19.1%	11,000
20. Supervisors, Farming, Fishing, and Forestry Workers	21.3%	11,000
21. Tree Trimmers and Pruners	22.2%	11,000
22. Outdoor Power Equipment and Other Small Engine Mechanics	19.2%	10,000
23. Tile and Marble Setters	24.4%	9,000
24. Gaming Supervisors	29.6%	8,000
25. Veterinarians	20.7%	8,000

Best Jobs Not Behind a Desk Employing a High Percentage of Women

To create the eight lists that follow, we sorted the 175 best jobs not behind a desk according to the percentages of women and men in the workforce. These are our most controversial lists, and we knew we would create some controversy when we first included the best jobs lists with high percentages (more than 70 percent) of men and women in earlier *Best Jobs* books. But these lists are not meant to restrict women or men from considering job options—our reason for including these lists is exactly the opposite. We hope the lists help people see possibilities that they might not otherwise have considered.

The fact is that jobs with high percentages of women or high percentages of men offer good opportunities for both men and women if they want to do one of these jobs. So we suggest that women browse the lists of active jobs that employ high percentages of men and that men browse the lists of active jobs with high percentages of women. There are jobs among both lists that pay well, and women or men who are interested in them and who have or can obtain the necessary education and training should consider them.

It is interesting to compare the economic measures of the active jobs with the highest percentage of men and of women. In every other book in the *Best Jobs* series where we look at jobs by the sex of the workers, the jobs with high concentrations of men have higher average earnings than the jobs with high concentrations of women. But for the 175 best jobs not behind a desk, *the female-dominated jobs earn more:* an average of $39,763, compared to

$33,358 for the male-dominated jobs. The reason for this discrepancy is the large number of allied health and teaching jobs, especially registered nurses and elementary school teachers, except special education, that pay well and have large workforces. Active female-dominated jobs also offer higher average growth and job openings: 24.3 percent growth and 54,000 openings, compared to 10.7 percent growth and 38,000 openings for the active jobs with the highest percentage of men. Men appear to be having more problems than women in adapting to an economy in which the active jobs are mostly in service industries, especially healthcare. Many women may simply be better prepared for these jobs, possessing more appropriate skills for the jobs that are now growing rapidly and have more job openings.

Best Jobs Not Behind a Desk Employing the Highest Percentage of Women

Job	Percent Women
1. Kindergarten Teachers, Except Special Education	97.7%
2. Preschool Teachers, Except Special Education	97.7%
3. Licensed Practical and Licensed Vocational Nurses	93.4%
4. Occupational Therapists	92.9%
5. Registered Nurses	92.3%
6. Hairdressers, Hairstylists, and Cosmetologists	92.0%
7. Athletic Trainers	89.0%
8. Medical Assistants	89.0%
9. Medical Equipment Preparers	89.0%
10. Orthotists and Prosthetists	89.0%
11. Nursing Aides, Orderlies, and Attendants	88.7%
12. Occupational Therapist Assistants	88.7%
13. Costume Attendants	85.1%
14. Choreographers	84.2%
15. Elementary School Teachers, Except Special Education	82.2%
16. Middle School Teachers, Except Special and Vocational Education	82.2%
17. Surgical Technologists	81.8%
18. Physical Therapist Aides	77.5%
19. Physical Therapist Assistants	77.5%
20. Flight Attendants	74.5%
21. Cardiovascular Technologists and Technicians	72.0%
22. Nuclear Medicine Technologists	72.0%
23. Radiologic Technologists and Technicians	72.0%

The jobs in the following four lists are derived from the preceding list of the active jobs employing the highest percentage of women.

Best Jobs Overall Not Behind a Desk Employing High Percentages of Women

Job	Percent Women	Annual Earnings	Percent Growth	Annual Openings
1. Registered Nurses	92.3%	$54,670	29.4%	229,000
2. Occupational Therapists	92.9%	$56,860	33.6%	7,000
3. Medical Assistants	89.0%	$25,350	52.1%	93,000
4. Physical Therapist Assistants	77.5%	$39,490	44.2%	7,000
5. Elementary School Teachers, Except Special Education	82.2%	$44,040	18.2%	203,000
6. Radiologic Technologists and Technicians	72.0%	$45,950	23.2%	17,000
7. Kindergarten Teachers, Except Special Education	97.7%	$42,230	22.4%	28,000
8. Cardiovascular Technologists and Technicians	72.0%	$40,420	32.6%	5,000
9. Preschool Teachers, Except Special Education	97.7%	$21,990	33.1%	77,000
10. Surgical Technologists	81.8%	$34,830	29.5%	12,000
11. Occupational Therapist Assistants	88.7%	$39,750	34.1%	2,000
12. Nuclear Medicine Technologists	72.0%	$59,670	21.5%	2,000
13. Middle School Teachers, Except Special and Vocational Education	82.2%	$44,640	13.7%	83,000
14. Licensed Practical and Licensed Vocational Nurses	93.4%	$35,230	17.1%	84,000
15. Nursing Aides, Orderlies, and Attendants	88.7%	$21,440	22.3%	307,000
16. Flight Attendants	74.5%	$46,680	16.3%	7,000
17. Physical Therapist Aides	77.5%	$21,510	34.4%	5,000
18. Orthotists and Prosthetists	89.0%	$53,760	18.0%	fewer than 500
19. Athletic Trainers	89.0%	$34,260	29.3%	1,000
20. Costume Attendants	85.1%	$25,360	23.4%	2,000
21. Medical Equipment Preparers	89.0%	$24,880	20.0%	8,000
22. Hairdressers, Hairstylists, and Cosmetologists	92.0%	$20,610	16.1%	59,000
23. Choreographers	84.2%	$32,950	16.8%	4,000

Best-Paying Jobs Not Behind a Desk Employing High Percentages of Women

Job	Percent Women	Annual Earnings
1. Nuclear Medicine Technologists	72.0%	$59,670
2. Occupational Therapists	92.9%	$56,860
3. Registered Nurses	92.3%	$54,670

Best-Paying Jobs Not Behind a Desk Employing High Percentages of Women

Job	Percent Women	Annual Earnings
4. Orthotists and Prosthetists	89.0%	$53,760
5. Flight Attendants	74.5%	$46,680
6. Radiologic Technologists and Technicians	72.0%	$45,950
7. Middle School Teachers, Except Special and Vocational Education	82.2%	$44,640
8. Elementary School Teachers, Except Special Education	82.2%	$44,040
9. Kindergarten Teachers, Except Special Education	97.7%	$42,230
10. Cardiovascular Technologists and Technicians	72.0%	$40,420
11. Occupational Therapist Assistants	88.7%	$39,750
12. Physical Therapist Assistants	77.5%	$39,490
13. Licensed Practical and Licensed Vocational Nurses	93.4%	$35,230
14. Surgical Technologists	81.8%	$34,830
15. Athletic Trainers	89.0%	$34,260
16. Choreographers	84.2%	$32,950
17. Costume Attendants	85.1%	$25,360
18. Medical Assistants	89.0%	$25,350
19. Medical Equipment Preparers	89.0%	$24,880
20. Preschool Teachers, Except Special Education	97.7%	$21,990
21. Physical Therapist Aides	77.5%	$21,510
22. Nursing Aides, Orderlies, and Attendants	88.7%	$21,440
23. Hairdressers, Hairstylists, and Cosmetologists	92.0%	$20,610

Fastest-Growing Jobs Not Behind a Desk Employing High Percentages of Women

Job	Percent Women	Percent Growth
1. Medical Assistants	89.0%	52.1%
2. Physical Therapist Assistants	77.5%	44.2%
3. Physical Therapist Aides	77.5%	34.4%
4. Occupational Therapist Assistants	88.7%	34.1%
5. Occupational Therapists	92.9%	33.6%
6. Preschool Teachers, Except Special Education	97.7%	33.1%
7. Cardiovascular Technologists and Technicians	72.0%	32.6%
8. Surgical Technologists	81.8%	29.5%

(continued)

(continued)

Fastest-Growing Jobs Not Behind a Desk Employing High Percentages of Women

Job	Percent Women	Percent Growth
9. Registered Nurses	92.3%	29.4%
10. Athletic Trainers	89.0%	29.3%
11. Costume Attendants	85.1%	23.4%
12. Radiologic Technologists and Technicians	72.0%	23.2%
13. Kindergarten Teachers, Except Special Education	97.7%	22.4%
14. Nursing Aides, Orderlies, and Attendants	88.7%	22.3%
15. Nuclear Medicine Technologists	72.0%	21.5%
16. Medical Equipment Preparers	89.0%	20.0%
17. Elementary School Teachers, Except Special Education	82.2%	18.2%
18. Orthotists and Prosthetists	89.0%	18.0%
19. Licensed Practical and Licensed Vocational Nurses	93.4%	17.1%
20. Choreographers	84.2%	16.8%
21. Flight Attendants	74.5%	16.3%
22. Hairdressers, Hairstylists, and Cosmetologists	92.0%	16.1%
23. Middle School Teachers, Except Special and Vocational Education	82.2%	13.7%

Jobs Not Behind a Desk with the Most Openings Employing High Percentages of Women

Job	Percent Women	Annual Openings
1. Nursing Aides, Orderlies, and Attendants	88.7%	307,000
2. Registered Nurses	92.3%	229,000
3. Elementary School Teachers, Except Special Education	82.2%	203,000
4. Medical Assistants	89.0%	93,000
5. Licensed Practical and Licensed Vocational Nurses	93.4%	84,000
6. Middle School Teachers, Except Special and Vocational Education	82.2%	83,000
7. Preschool Teachers, Except Special Education	97.7%	77,000
8. Hairdressers, Hairstylists, and Cosmetologists	92.0%	59,000
9. Kindergarten Teachers, Except Special Education	97.7%	28,000
10. Radiologic Technologists and Technicians	72.0%	17,000
11. Surgical Technologists	81.8%	12,000
12. Medical Equipment Preparers	89.0%	8,000

Jobs Not Behind a Desk with the Most Openings Employing High Percentages of Women

Job	Percent Women	Annual Openings
13. Flight Attendants	74.5%	7,000
14. Occupational Therapists	92.9%	7,000
15. Physical Therapist Assistants	77.5%	7,000
16. Cardiovascular Technologists and Technicians	72.0%	5,000
17. Physical Therapist Aides	77.5%	5,000
18. Choreographers	84.2%	4,000
19. Costume Attendants	85.1%	2,000
20. Nuclear Medicine Technologists	72.0%	2,000
21. Occupational Therapist Assistants	88.7%	2,000
22. Athletic Trainers	89.0%	1,000
23. Orthotists and Prosthetists	89.0%	fewer than 500

Best Jobs Not Behind a Desk Employing a High Percentage of Men

If you have not already read the intro to the previous group of lists, best jobs not behind a desk with high percentages of women, consider doing so. Much of the content there applies to these lists as well.

We did not include these groups of lists with the assumption that men should consider active jobs with high percentages of men or that women should consider active jobs with high percentages of women. Instead, these lists are here because we think they are interesting and perhaps helpful in considering nontraditional career options. For example, some men would do very well in and enjoy some of the jobs with high percentages of women but may not have considered them seriously. In a similar way, some women would very much enjoy and do well in some jobs that traditionally have been held by high percentages of men. We hope that these lists help you consider options that you simply did not seriously consider because of gender stereotypes.

In the jobs on the following lists, more than 70 percent of the workers are men. Note that 112 jobs meet this cutoff, whereas only 23 female-dominated jobs do. High-energy jobs, especially those requiring a lot of physical strength, have traditionally been held primarily by men. In fact, every job that appears on the list of the 50 Highest-Strength High-Activity Jobs also appears on the following list. Nevertheless, increasing numbers of women are entering many of these jobs.

Best Jobs Not Behind a Desk Employing the Highest Percentage of Men

Job	Percent Men
1. Excavating and Loading Machine and Dragline Operators	99.8%
2. Bus and Truck Mechanics and Diesel Engine Specialists	99.5%
3. Railroad Conductors and Yardmasters	99.3%
4. Drywall and Ceiling Tile Installers	99.2%
5. Tapers	99.2%
6. Brickmasons and Blockmasons	99.1%
7. Stonemasons	99.1%
8. Mobile Heavy Equipment Mechanics, Except Engines	99.0%
9. Tool and Die Makers	98.9%
10. Pipelayers	98.8%
11. Plumbers, Pipefitters, and Steamfitters	98.8%
12. Earth Drillers, Except Oil and Gas	98.7%
13. Plasterers and Stucco Masons	98.7%
14. Elevator Installers and Repairers	98.6%
15. Heating, Air Conditioning, and Refrigeration Mechanics and Installers	98.6%
16. Ship Engineers	98.5%
17. Control and Valve Installers and Repairers, Except Mechanical Door	98.4%
18. Structural Iron and Steel Workers	98.4%
19. Cement Masons and Concrete Finishers	98.3%
20. Riggers	98.3%
21. Automotive Service Technicians and Mechanics	98.2%
22. Motorboat Mechanics	98.2%
23. Motorcycle Mechanics	98.2%
24. Outdoor Power Equipment and Other Small Engine Mechanics	98.2%
25. Recreational Vehicle Service Technicians	98.2%
26. Automotive Body and Related Repairers	98.1%
27. Carpenters	98.1%
28. Millwrights	98.0%
29. Carpet Installers	97.7%
30. Floor Layers, Except Carpet, Wood, and Hard Tiles	97.7%
31. Tile and Marble Setters	97.7%
32. Reinforcing Iron and Rebar Workers	97.6%
33. Roofers	97.6%
34. Electricians	97.4%
35. Industrial Machinery Mechanics	97.4%
36. Pest Control Workers	97.4%
37. Operating Engineers and Other Construction Equipment Operators	97.3%

Best Jobs Not Behind a Desk Employing the Highest Percentage of Men

Job	Percent Men
38. Paving, Surfacing, and Tamping Equipment Operators	97.3%
39. Surveyors	97.3%
40. First-Line Supervisors/Managers of Construction Trades and Extraction Workers	97.1%
41. Stationary Engineers and Boiler Operators	97.0%
42. Septic Tank Servicers and Sewer Pipe Cleaners	96.9%
43. Boilermakers	96.8%
44. Helpers—Brickmasons, Blockmasons, Stonemasons, and Tile and Marble Setters	96.8%
45. Helpers—Carpenters	96.8%
46. Helpers—Pipelayers, Plumbers, Pipefitters, and Steamfitters	96.8%
47. Electrical Power-Line Installers and Repairers	96.5%
48. Construction Laborers	96.4%
49. Sheet Metal Workers	96.4%
50. Helpers—Installation, Maintenance, and Repair Workers	95.9%
51. Maintenance and Repair Workers, General	95.9%
52. Locksmiths and Safe Repairers	95.8%
53. Glaziers	95.6%
54. Aircraft Mechanics and Service Technicians	95.5%
55. Driver/Sales Workers	95.5%
56. Electrical and Electronics Repairers, Commercial and Industrial Equipment	95.5%
57. Electrical and Electronics Repairers, Powerhouse, Substation, and Relay	95.5%
58. Truck Drivers, Heavy and Tractor-Trailer	95.5%
59. Truck Drivers, Light or Delivery Services	95.5%
60. Highway Maintenance Workers	95.4%
61. Water and Liquid Waste Treatment Plant and System Operators	95.4%
62. First-Line Supervisors/Managers of Mechanics, Installers, and Repairers	94.3%
63. Welders, Cutters, Solderers, and Brazers	94.2%
64. Telecommunications Line Installers and Repairers	94.0%
65. First-Line Supervisors/Managers of Landscaping, Lawn Service, and Groundskeeping Workers	93.8%
66. Construction Managers	93.7%
67. Industrial Truck and Tractor Operators	93.7%
68. Machinists	93.2%
69. Landscaping and Groundskeeping Workers	92.5%
70. Painters, Construction and Maintenance	92.5%
71. Pesticide Handlers, Sprayers, and Applicators, Vegetation	92.5%
72. Tree Trimmers and Pruners	92.5%

(continued)

(continued)

Best Jobs Not Behind a Desk Employing the Highest Percentage of Men

Job	Percent Men
73. Medical Equipment Repairers	92.3%
74. Construction and Building Inspectors	91.5%
75. Refuse and Recyclable Material Collectors	91.3%
76. Hazardous Materials Removal Workers	90.8%
77. First-Line Supervisors/Managers of Fire Fighting and Prevention Workers	87.5%
78. First-Line Supervisors/Managers of Police and Detectives	87.5%
79. Avionics Technicians	86.5%
80. Telecommunications Equipment Installers and Repairers, Except Line Installers	86.5%
81. Audio and Video Equipment Technicians	86.4%
82. Camera Operators, Television, Video, and Motion Picture	86.4%
83. Animal Control Workers	85.7%
84. Fish and Game Wardens	85.7%
85. Police and Sheriff's Patrol Officers	85.7%
86. Transit and Railroad Police	85.7%
87. Painters, Transportation Equipment	85.0%
88. Chemical Plant and System Operators	84.8%
89. Gas Plant Operators	84.8%
90. Petroleum Pump System Operators, Refinery Operators, and Gaugers	84.8%
91. Printing Machine Operators	84.4%
92. Supervisors, Farming, Fishing, and Forestry Workers	84.4%
93. Helpers—Production Workers	83.8%
94. Transportation Inspectors	83.8%
95. Industrial Production Managers	82.8%
96. Laborers and Freight, Stock, and Material Movers, Hand	82.7%
97. First-Line Supervisors/Managers of Helpers, Laborers, and Material Movers, Hand	81.9%
98. Mechanical Engineering Technicians	79.8%
99. First-Line Supervisors/Managers of Production and Operating Workers	79.1%
100. Funeral Directors	78.5%
101. Chiropractors	78.2%
102. Embalmers	78.0%
103. Butchers and Meat Cutters	77.7%
104. Slaughterers and Meat Packers	77.7%
105. Geoscientists, Except Hydrologists and Geographers	77.5%
106. Oral and Maxillofacial Surgeons	77.5%
107. Detectives and Criminal Investigators	76.0%
108. Security Guards	75.3%

Best Jobs Not Behind a Desk Employing the Highest Percentage of Men

Job	Percent Men
109. Farmers and Ranchers	74.4%
110. Chemical Technicians	71.9%
111. Bailiffs	70.9%
112. Correctional Officers and Jailers	70.9%

The jobs in the following four lists are derived from the preceding list of the active jobs employing the highest percentage of men.

Best Jobs Overall Not Behind a Desk Employing High Percentages of Men

Job	Percent Men	Annual Earnings	Percent Growth	Annual Openings
1. Police and Sheriff's Patrol Officers	85.7%	$46,290	15.5%	47,000
2. Plumbers, Pipefitters, and Steamfitters	98.8%	$42,160	15.7%	61,000
3. Heating, Air Conditioning, and Refrigeration Mechanics and Installers	98.6%	$37,040	19.0%	33,000
4. Detectives and Criminal Investigators	76.0%	$55,790	16.3%	9,000
5. Chiropractors	78.2%	$67,200	22.4%	4,000
6. First-Line Supervisors/Managers of Construction Trades and Extraction Workers	97.1%	$51,970	10.9%	57,000
7. First-Line Supervisors/Managers of Fire Fighting and Prevention Workers	87.5%	$60,840	21.1%	4,000
8. First-Line Supervisors/Managers of Mechanics, Installers, and Repairers	94.3%	$51,980	12.4%	33,000
9. First-Line Supervisors/Managers of Police and Detectives	87.5%	$65,570	15.5%	9,000
10. Construction Managers	93.7%	$72,260	10.4%	28,000
11. Construction and Building Inspectors	91.5%	$44,720	22.3%	6,000
12. Carpenters	98.1%	$35,580	13.8%	210,000
13. Railroad Conductors and Yardmasters	99.3%	$54,040	20.3%	3,000
14. First-Line Supervisors/Managers of Landscaping, Lawn Service, and Groundskeeping Workers	93.8%	$36,320	17.8%	14,000
15. Automotive Service Technicians and Mechanics	98.2%	$33,050	15.7%	93,000
16. Electricians	97.4%	$42,790	11.8%	68,000
17. Tile and Marble Setters	97.7%	$36,530	22.9%	9,000
18. Roofers	97.6%	$31,230	16.8%	38,000
19. Bus and Truck Mechanics and Diesel Engine Specialists	99.5%	$36,620	14.4%	32,000

(continued)

(continued)

Best Jobs Overall Not Behind a Desk Employing High Percentages of Men

Job	Percent Men	Annual Earnings	Percent Growth	Annual Openings
20. Landscaping and Groundskeeping Workers	92.5%	$20,670	19.5%	243,000
21. Hazardous Materials Removal Workers	90.8%	$33,690	31.2%	11,000
22. Maintenance and Repair Workers, General	95.9%	$31,210	15.2%	154,000
23. Truck Drivers, Heavy and Tractor-Trailer	95.5%	$34,280	12.9%	274,000
24. Highway Maintenance Workers	95.4%	$30,250	23.3%	27,000
25. Structural Iron and Steel Workers	98.4%	$40,580	15.0%	13,000

Best-Paying Jobs Not Behind a Desk Employing High Percentages of Men

Job	Percent Men	Annual Earnings
1. Oral and Maxillofacial Surgeons	77.5%	more than $146,500
2. Industrial Production Managers	82.8%	$75,580
3. Construction Managers	93.7%	$72,260
4. Geoscientists, Except Hydrologists and Geographers	77.5%	$71,640
5. Chiropractors	78.2%	$67,200
6. First-Line Supervisors/Managers of Police and Detectives	87.5%	$65,570
7. First-Line Supervisors/Managers of Fire Fighting and Prevention Workers	87.5%	$60,840
8. Elevator Installers and Repairers	98.6%	$59,190
9. Detectives and Criminal Investigators	76.0%	$55,790
10. Electrical and Electronics Repairers, Powerhouse, Substation, and Relay	95.5%	$54,970
11. Railroad Conductors and Yardmasters	99.3%	$54,040
12. Ship Engineers	98.5%	$52,780
13. First-Line Supervisors/Managers of Mechanics, Installers, and Repairers	94.3%	$51,980
14. First-Line Supervisors/Managers of Construction Trades and Extraction Workers	97.1%	$51,970
15. Gas Plant Operators	84.8%	$51,920
16. Petroleum Pump System Operators, Refinery Operators, and Gaugers	84.8%	$51,060
17. Telecommunications Equipment Installers and Repairers, Except Line Installers	86.5%	$50,620
18. Electrical Power-Line Installers and Repairers	96.5%	$50,150
19. Transportation Inspectors	83.8%	$49,490

Best-Paying Jobs Not Behind a Desk Employing High Percentages of Men

Job	Percent Men	Annual Earnings
20. Transit and Railroad Police	85.7%	$48,850
21. Boilermakers	96.8%	$48,050
22. Funeral Directors	78.5%	$47,630
23. Aircraft Mechanics and Service Technicians	95.5%	$47,310
24. Chemical Plant and System Operators	84.8%	$46,710
25. Avionics Technicians	86.5%	$46,630

Fastest-Growing Jobs Not Behind a Desk Employing High Percentages of Men

Job	Percent Men	Percent Growth
1. Hazardous Materials Removal Workers	90.8%	31.2%
2. Highway Maintenance Workers	95.4%	23.3%
3. Tile and Marble Setters	97.7%	22.9%
4. Chiropractors	78.2%	22.4%
5. Construction and Building Inspectors	91.5%	22.3%
6. Septic Tank Servicers and Sewer Pipe Cleaners	96.9%	21.8%
7. First-Line Supervisors/Managers of Fire Fighting and Prevention Workers	87.5%	21.1%
8. Railroad Conductors and Yardmasters	99.3%	20.3%
9. Landscaping and Groundskeeping Workers	92.5%	19.5%
10. Recreational Vehicle Service Technicians	98.2%	19.5%
11. Heating, Air Conditioning, and Refrigeration Mechanics and Installers	98.6%	19.0%
12. Pest Control Workers	97.4%	18.4%
13. Audio and Video Equipment Technicians	86.4%	18.1%
14. First-Line Supervisors/Managers of Landscaping, Lawn Service, and Groundskeeping Workers	93.8%	17.8%
15. Roofers	97.6%	16.8%
16. Helpers—Pipelayers, Plumbers, Pipefitters, and Steamfitters	96.8%	16.6%
17. Pesticide Handlers, Sprayers, and Applicators, Vegetation	92.5%	16.6%
18. Tree Trimmers and Pruners	92.5%	16.5%
19. Helpers—Installation, Maintenance, and Repair Workers	95.9%	16.4%
20. Detectives and Criminal Investigators	76.0%	16.3%
21. Oral and Maxillofacial Surgeons	77.5%	16.2%
22. Water and Liquid Waste Treatment Plant and System Operators	95.4%	16.2%

(continued)

(continued)

Fastest-Growing Jobs Not Behind a Desk Employing High Percentages of Men

Job	Percent Men	Percent Growth
23. Locksmiths and Safe Repairers	95.8%	16.1%
24. Cement Masons and Concrete Finishers	98.3%	15.9%
25. Surveyors	97.3%	15.9%

Jobs Not Behind a Desk with the Most Openings Employing High Percentages of Men

Job	Percent Men	Annual Openings
1. Laborers and Freight, Stock, and Material Movers, Hand	82.7%	671,000
2. Truck Drivers, Heavy and Tractor-Trailer	95.5%	274,000
3. Construction Laborers	96.4%	245,000
4. Landscaping and Groundskeeping Workers	92.5%	243,000
5. Security Guards	75.3%	230,000
6. Carpenters	98.1%	210,000
7. Truck Drivers, Light or Delivery Services	95.5%	169,000
8. Maintenance and Repair Workers, General	95.9%	154,000
9. Industrial Truck and Tractor Operators	93.7%	114,000
10. Helpers—Production Workers	83.8%	107,000
11. Painters, Construction and Maintenance	92.5%	102,000
12. Farmers and Ranchers	74.4%	96,000
13. Automotive Service Technicians and Mechanics	98.2%	93,000
14. First-Line Supervisors/Managers of Production and Operating Workers	79.1%	89,000
15. Driver/Sales Workers	95.5%	72,000
16. Electricians	97.4%	68,000
17. Plumbers, Pipefitters, and Steamfitters	98.8%	61,000
18. First-Line Supervisors/Managers of Construction Trades and Extraction Workers	97.1%	57,000
19. Correctional Officers and Jailers	70.9%	54,000
20. Welders, Cutters, Solderers, and Brazers	94.2%	52,000
21. Sheet Metal Workers	96.4%	50,000
22. Police and Sheriff's Patrol Officers	85.7%	47,000

Jobs Not Behind a Desk with the Most Openings Employing High Percentages of Men

Job	Percent Men	Annual Openings
23. Helpers—Installation, Maintenance, and Repair Workers	95.9%	41,000
24. Roofers	97.6%	38,000
25. Operating Engineers and Other Construction Equipment Operators	97.3%	37,000

Best Jobs Not Behind a Desk Sorted by Education or Training Required

The lists in this section organize the 175 best jobs not behind a desk into groups based on the education or training typically required for entry. Unlike in many of the previous sections, here we do not include separate lists for highest pay, growth, or number of openings. Instead, we provide one list that includes all the best active jobs that fit into each of the education levels and ranks them by their total combined score for earnings, growth, and number of openings.

These lists can help you identify a job with higher earnings or upward mobility but with a similar level of education to the job you now hold. For example, you will find jobs within the same level of education that require similar skills, yet one pays significantly better than the other, is projected to grow more rapidly, or has significantly more job openings per year. This information can help you leverage your present skills and experience into jobs that might provide better long-term career opportunities.

You can also use these lists to explore possible job options if you were to get additional training, education, or work experience. For example, you can use these lists to identify high-energy occupations that offer high potential and then look into the education or training required to get the jobs that interest you most.

The lists can also help you when you plan your education. For example, you might be thinking about a construction job but you aren't sure what kind of work you want to do. The lists show that drywall and ceiling tile installers need moderate-term on-the-job training and earn $34,740, while glaziers need long-term on-the-job training but earn an average of $33,530. If you want higher earnings without lengthy training, this information might make a difference in your choice.

The Education Levels

Short-term on-the-job training. It is possible to work in these occupations and achieve an average level of performance within a few days or weeks through on-the-job training.

Moderate-term on-the-job training. Occupations that require this type of training can be performed adequately after a one- to 12-month period of combined on-the-job and informal training. Typically, untrained workers observe experienced workers performing tasks and are gradually moved into progressively more difficult assignments.

Long-term on-the-job training. This training requires more than 12 months of on-the-job training or combined work experience and formal classroom instruction. This includes occupations that use formal apprenticeships for training workers that may take up to four years. It also includes intensive occupation-specific, employer-sponsored training such as police academies. Furthermore, it includes occupations that require natural talent that must be developed over many years.

Work experience in a related occupation. This type of job requires experience in a related occupation. For example, police detectives are selected based on their experience as police patrol officers.

Postsecondary vocational training. This requirement can vary from training that involves a few months but is usually less than one year. In a few instances, there may be as many as four years of training.

Associate degree. This degree usually requires two years of full-time academic work beyond high school.

Bachelor's degree. This degree requires approximately four to five years of full-time academic work beyond high school.

Work experience plus degree. Jobs in this category are often management-related and require some experience in a related nonmanagerial position.

Master's degree. Completion of a master's degree usually requires one to two years of full-time study beyond the bachelor's degree.

Doctoral degree. This degree normally requires two or more years of full-time academic work beyond the bachelor's degree.

First professional degree. This type of degree normally requires a minimum of two years of education beyond the bachelor's degree and frequently requires three years.

Another Warning About the Data

We warned you in the Introduction to use caution in interpreting the data we use, and we want to do it again here. The occupational data we use is the most accurate available anywhere, but it has its limitations. For example, the education or training requirements for entry into a job are those typically required as a minimum—but some people working in those jobs may have considerably more or different credentials. For example, most registered nurses now have a four-year bachelor's degree, although the two-year associate's degree is the minimum level of training the job requires.

In a similar way, you need to be cautious about assuming that more education or training always leads to higher income. It is true that people with jobs that require long-term on-the-job training typically earn more than people with jobs that require short-term on-the-job training. However, some people with short-term on-the-job training do earn more than the average for the highest-paying occupations listed in this book; furthermore, some people with long-term on-the-job training earn much less than the average shown in this book—this is particularly true early in a person's career.

So as you browse the lists that follow, please use them as a way to be encouraged rather than discouraged. Education and training are very important for success in the labor market of the future, but so are ability, drive, initiative, and, yes, luck.

Having said this, we encourage you to get as much education and training as you can. An old saying goes, "The harder you work, the luckier you get." It is just as true now as it ever was.

Best Jobs Not Behind a Desk Requiring Short-Term On-the-Job Training

Job	Annual Earnings	Percent Growth	Annual Openings
1. Nursing Aides, Orderlies, and Attendants	$21,440	22.3%	307,000
2. Truck Drivers, Light or Delivery Services	$24,790	15.7%	169,000
3. Landscaping and Groundskeeping Workers	$20,670	19.5%	243,000
4. Costume Attendants	$25,360	23.4%	2,000
5. Medical Equipment Preparers	$24,880	20.0%	8,000
6. Tree Trimmers and Pruners	$27,920	16.5%	11,000
7. Industrial Truck and Tractor Operators	$27,080	7.9%	114,000
8. Refuse and Recyclable Material Collectors	$28,460	8.9%	31,000
9. Helpers—Pipelayers, Plumbers, Pipefitters, and Steamfitters	$22,820	16.6%	17,000
10. Physical Therapist Aides	$21,510	34.4%	5,000
11. Helpers—Installation, Maintenance, and Repair Workers	$21,230	16.4%	41,000
12. Laborers and Freight, Stock, and Material Movers, Hand	$20,610	10.2%	671,000
13. Postal Service Mail Carriers	$46,330	0.0%	19,000
14. Security Guards	$20,760	12.6%	230,000
15. Helpers—Brickmasons, Blockmasons, Stonemasons, and Tile and Marble Setters	$24,600	14.9%	14,000
16. Helpers—Carpenters	$21,990	14.5%	24,000
17. Riggers	$37,010	13.9%	2,000
18. Crossing Guards	$20,050	19.7%	26,000
19. Postal Service Clerks	$48,310	0.0%	4,000
20. Driver/Sales Workers	$20,120	13.8%	72,000
21. Helpers—Production Workers	$20,390	7.9%	107,000

Best Jobs Not Behind a Desk Requiring Moderate-Term On-the-Job Training

Job	Annual Earnings	Percent Growth	Annual Openings
1. Truck Drivers, Heavy and Tractor-Trailer	$34,280	12.9%	274,000
2. Hazardous Materials Removal Workers	$33,690	31.2%	11,000
3. Roofers	$31,230	16.8%	38,000
4. Sheet Metal Workers	$36,390	12.2%	50,000
5. Maintenance and Repair Workers, General	$31,210	15.2%	154,000
6. Cement Masons and Concrete Finishers	$32,030	15.9%	32,000
7. Operating Engineers and Other Construction Equipment Operators	$35,830	11.6%	37,000
8. Medical Assistants	$25,350	52.1%	93,000
9. Highway Maintenance Workers	$30,250	23.3%	27,000
10. Painters, Transportation Equipment	$34,840	14.1%	10,000
11. Camera Operators, Television, Video, and Motion Picture	$41,610	14.2%	4,000
12. Audio-Visual Collections Specialists	$40,260	18.6%	1,000
13. Correctional Officers and Jailers	$34,090	6.7%	54,000
14. Painters, Construction and Maintenance	$30,800	12.6%	102,000
15. Drywall and Ceiling Tile Installers	$34,740	9.0%	17,000
16. Locksmiths and Safe Repairers	$30,880	16.1%	5,000
17. Carpet Installers	$33,550	8.4%	11,000
18. Paving, Surfacing, and Tamping Equipment Operators	$30,320	15.6%	7,000
19. Control and Valve Installers and Repairers, Except Mechanical Door	$44,120	4.9%	4,000
20. Excavating and Loading Machine and Dragline Operators	$32,380	8.0%	11,000
21. Septic Tank Servicers and Sewer Pipe Cleaners	$30,440	21.8%	3,000
22. Tapers	$39,870	5.9%	5,000
23. Pest Control Workers	$27,170	18.4%	4,000
24. Pesticide Handlers, Sprayers, and Applicators, Vegetation	$26,120	16.6%	6,000
25. Bailiffs	$33,800	13.2%	2,000
26. Construction Laborers	$25,410	5.9%	245,000
27. Floor Layers, Except Carpet, Wood, and Hard Tiles	$33,010	10.2%	4,000
28. Slaughterers and Meat Packers	$21,220	13.8%	22,000
29. Earth Drillers, Except Oil and Gas	$33,770	7.9%	4,000
30. Outdoor Power Equipment and Other Small Engine Mechanics	$25,810	14.0%	10,000
31. Printing Machine Operators	$30,730	2.9%	26,000
32. Animal Control Workers	$26,780	14.4%	4,000
33. Paper Goods Machine Setters, Operators, and Tenders	$31,160	2.4%	15,000
34. Animal Trainers	$24,800	20.3%	3,000
35. Pipelayers	$28,760	9.9%	7,000
36. Structural Metal Fabricators and Fitters	$30,290	2.9%	18,000

Best Jobs Not Behind a Desk Requiring Long-Term On-the-Job Training

Job	Annual Earnings	Percent Growth	Annual Openings
1. Police and Sheriff's Patrol Officers	$46,290	15.5%	47,000
2. Plumbers, Pipefitters, and Steamfitters	$42,160	15.7%	61,000
3. Heating, Air Conditioning, and Refrigeration Mechanics and Installers	$37,040	19.0%	33,000
4. Flight Attendants	$46,680	16.3%	7,000
5. Electricians	$42,790	11.8%	68,000
6. Carpenters	$35,580	13.8%	210,000
7. Tile and Marble Setters	$36,530	22.9%	9,000
8. Coaches and Scouts	$25,990	20.4%	63,000
9. Athletes and Sports Competitors	$39,930	21.1%	6,000
10. Structural Iron and Steel Workers	$40,580	15.0%	13,000
11. Telecommunications Line Installers and Repairers	$42,410	10.8%	23,000
12. Elevator Installers and Repairers	$59,190	14.8%	3,000
13. Brickmasons and Blockmasons	$41,860	12.0%	17,000
14. Telecommunications Equipment Installers and Repairers, Except Line Installers	$50,620	–4.9%	21,000
15. Electrical Power-Line Installers and Repairers	$50,150	2.5%	11,000
16. Water and Liquid Waste Treatment Plant and System Operators	$34,930	16.2%	6,000
17. Bakers	$21,520	15.2%	37,000
18. Glaziers	$33,530	14.2%	9,000
19. Automotive Body and Related Repairers	$34,810	10.3%	18,000
20. Petroleum Pump System Operators, Refinery Operators, and Gaugers	$51,060	–8.6%	6,000
21. Reinforcing Iron and Rebar Workers	$34,910	14.1%	6,000
22. Motorboat Mechanics	$32,780	15.1%	7,000
23. Photographers	$26,100	12.3%	23,000
24. Chemical Plant and System Operators	$46,710	–17.7%	8,000
25. Gas Plant Operators	$51,920	7.7%	2,000
26. Audio and Video Equipment Technicians	$32,940	18.1%	5,000
27. Boilermakers	$48,050	8.7%	2,000
28. Machinists	$34,350	4.3%	33,000
29. Umpires, Referees, and Other Sports Officials	$21,610	19.0%	6,000
30. Farmers and Ranchers	$34,140	–14.5%	96,000
31. Tool and Die Makers	$43,580	–2.6%	7,000
32. Transit and Railroad Police	$48,850	9.2%	fewer than 500
33. Welders, Cutters, Solderers, and Brazers	$30,990	5.0%	52,000
34. Industrial Machinery Mechanics	$39,740	–0.2%	13,000

(continued)

(continued)

Best Jobs Not Behind a Desk Requiring Long-Term On-the-Job Training

Job	Annual Earnings	Percent Growth	Annual Openings
35. Millwrights	$44,780	5.9%	5,000
36. Recreational Vehicle Service Technicians	$30,480	19.5%	3,000
37. Aircraft Structure, Surfaces, Rigging, and Systems Assemblers	$43,990	7.8%	4,000
38. Stationary Engineers and Boiler Operators	$44,600	3.4%	5,000
39. Fish and Game Wardens	$42,850	10.5%	1,000
40. Butchers and Meat Cutters	$26,590	7.9%	20,000
41. Motorcycle Mechanics	$29,450	13.7%	6,000
42. Plasterers and Stucco Masons	$33,440	8.2%	6,000
43. Stonemasons	$34,640	13.0%	2,000

Best Jobs Not Behind a Desk Requiring Work Experience in a Related Occupation

Job	Annual Earnings	Percent Growth	Annual Openings
1. First-Line Supervisors/Managers of Fire Fighting and Prevention Workers	$60,840	21.1%	4,000
2. Self-Enrichment Education Teachers	$32,360	25.3%	74,000
3. First-Line Supervisors/Managers of Police and Detectives	$65,570	15.5%	9,000
4. Gaming Managers	$59,940	22.6%	1,000
5. Detectives and Criminal Investigators	$55,790	16.3%	9,000
6. First-Line Supervisors/Managers of Mechanics, Installers, and Repairers	$51,980	12.4%	33,000
7. Construction and Building Inspectors	$44,720	22.3%	6,000
8. Railroad Conductors and Yardmasters	$54,040	20.3%	3,000
9. First-Line Supervisors/Managers of Construction Trades and Extraction Workers	$51,970	10.9%	57,000
10. First-Line Supervisors/Managers of Food Preparation and Serving Workers	$26,050	16.6%	187,000
11. Food Service Managers	$41,340	11.5%	61,000
12. First-Line Supervisors/Managers of Landscaping, Lawn Service, and Groundskeeping Workers	$36,320	17.8%	14,000
13. First-Line Supervisors/Managers of Production and Operating Workers	$46,140	2.7%	89,000
14. Industrial Production Managers	$75,580	0.8%	13,000

Best Jobs Not Behind a Desk Requiring Work Experience in a Related Occupation

Job	Annual Earnings	Percent Growth	Annual Openings
15. First-Line Supervisors/Managers of Housekeeping and Janitorial Workers	$30,330	19.0%	21,000
16. First-Line Supervisors/Managers of Retail Sales Workers	$32,840	3.8%	229,000
17. Gaming Supervisors	$40,300	16.3%	8,000
18. Choreographers	$32,950	16.8%	4,000
19. First-Line Supervisors/Managers of Helpers, Laborers, and Material Movers, Hand	$39,000	8.1%	15,000
20. Transportation Inspectors	$49,490	11.4%	2,000

Best Jobs Not Behind a Desk Requiring Postsecondary Vocational Training

Job	Annual Earnings	Percent Growth	Annual Openings
1. Licensed Practical and Licensed Vocational Nurses	$35,230	17.1%	84,000
2. Preschool Teachers, Except Special Education	$21,990	33.1%	77,000
3. Automotive Service Technicians and Mechanics	$33,050	15.7%	93,000
4. Surgical Technologists	$34,830	29.5%	12,000
5. Emergency Medical Technicians and Paramedics	$26,080	27.3%	21,000
6. Fitness Trainers and Aerobics Instructors	$25,840	27.1%	50,000
7. Aircraft Mechanics and Service Technicians	$47,310	13.4%	11,000
8. Bus and Truck Mechanics and Diesel Engine Specialists	$36,620	14.4%	32,000
9. Hairdressers, Hairstylists, and Cosmetologists	$20,610	16.1%	59,000
10. Embalmers	$36,960	15.6%	2,000
11. Electrical and Electronics Repairers, Commercial and Industrial Equipment	$44,120	9.7%	8,000
12. Electrical and Electronics Repairers, Powerhouse, Substation, and Relay	$54,970	–0.4%	2,000
13. Mobile Heavy Equipment Mechanics, Except Engines	$39,410	8.8%	14,000
14. Ship Engineers	$52,780	12.7%	1,000
15. Avionics Technicians	$46,630	9.1%	2,000

Best Jobs Not Behind a Desk Requiring an Associate Degree

Job	Annual Earnings	Percent Growth	Annual Openings
1. Registered Nurses	$54,670	29.4%	229,000
2. Radiologic Technologists and Technicians	$45,950	23.2%	17,000
3. Respiratory Therapists	$45,140	28.4%	7,000
4. Physical Therapist Assistants	$39,490	44.2%	7,000
5. Cardiovascular Technologists and Technicians	$40,420	32.6%	5,000
6. Radiation Therapists	$62,340	26.3%	1,000
7. Nuclear Medicine Technologists	$59,670	21.5%	2,000
8. Occupational Therapist Assistants	$39,750	34.1%	2,000
9. Nuclear Technicians	$61,120	13.7%	1,000
10. Mechanical Engineering Technicians	$44,830	12.3%	5,000
11. Funeral Directors	$47,630	6.7%	3,000
12. Environmental Science and Protection Technicians, Including Health	$36,260	16.3%	6,000
13. Chemical Technicians	$38,500	4.4%	7,000
14. Medical Equipment Repairers	$39,570	14.8%	4,000
15. Supervisors, Farming, Fishing, and Forestry Workers	$36,030	3.6%	11,000

Best Jobs Not Behind a Desk Requiring a Bachelor's Degree

Job	Annual Earnings	Percent Growth	Annual Openings
1. Physician Assistants	$72,030	49.6%	10,000
2. Occupational Therapists	$56,860	33.6%	7,000
3. Elementary School Teachers, Except Special Education	$44,040	18.2%	203,000
4. Construction Managers	$72,260	10.4%	28,000
5. Secondary School Teachers, Except Special and Vocational Education	$46,060	14.4%	107,000
6. Kindergarten Teachers, Except Special Education	$42,230	22.4%	28,000
7. Middle School Teachers, Except Special and Vocational Education	$44,640	13.7%	83,000
8. Chemists	$57,890	7.3%	5,000
9. Orthotists and Prosthetists	$53,760	18.0%	fewer than 500
10. Recreation Workers	$20,110	17.3%	69,000
11. Surveyors	$45,860	15.9%	4,000
12. Athletic Trainers	$34,260	29.3%	1,000
13. Conservation Scientists	$53,350	6.3%	2,000
14. Foresters	$48,670	6.7%	1,000
15. Museum Technicians and Conservators	$34,090	14.1%	2,000
16. Set and Exhibit Designers	$37,390	9.3%	2,000

Best Jobs Not Behind a Desk Requiring Work Experience Plus Degree

Job	Annual Earnings	Percent Growth	Annual Openings
1. Vocational Education Teachers, Secondary School	$47,090	9.1%	10,000
2. Education Administrators, Preschool and Child Care Center/Program	$37,010	27.9%	9,000

Best Jobs Not Behind a Desk Requiring a Master's Degree

Job	Annual Earnings	Percent Growth	Annual Openings
1. Physical Therapists	$63,080	36.7%	13,000
2. Geoscientists, Except Hydrologists and Geographers	$71,640	8.3%	2,000
3. Curators	$45,240	15.7%	1,000

Best Jobs Not Behind a Desk Requiring a Doctoral Degree

Job	Annual Earnings	Percent Growth	Annual Openings
1. Zoologists and Wildlife Biologists	$52,050	13.0%	1,000

Best Jobs Not Behind a Desk Requiring a First Professional Degree

Job	Annual Earnings	Percent Growth	Annual Openings
1. Veterinarians	$68,910	17.4%	8,000
2. Chiropractors	$67,200	22.4%	4,000
3. Oral and Maxillofacial Surgeons	more than $145,600	16.2%	fewer than 500

Best Jobs Not Behind a Desk Listed by Interest

This group of lists organizes the 175 best jobs not behind a desk into 16 interest areas. You can use these lists to identify jobs quickly based on your interests. Within each interest area, jobs are listed in order of their combined score on earnings, job growth, and job openings, from highest to lowest.

Find the interest area or areas that appeal to you most and review the high-energy jobs in those areas. When you find jobs you want to explore in more detail, look up their descriptions in Part II. You can also review interest areas where you have had past experience, education, or training to see if other jobs in those areas would meet your current requirements.

As you scan the following lists, you may notice that three interest areas have *no* jobs listed: Finance and Insurance, Human Service, and Information Technology. These interest areas are dominated by sedentary work, and any active jobs they may include do not have sufficient economic rewards to earn a place in this book. But keep in mind that this book is based on averages. If you have the right skills and are really motivated, you may be able to find a high-energy and rewarding position in the financial, human service, or computer industry. That's one reason we describe all 16 interest areas. Another reason is that you can more easily decide on your most important interests in the context of the complete classification scheme.

Note: The 16 interest areas used in these lists are those used in the *New Guide for Occupational Exploration,* Fourth Edition, published by JIST. The original GOE was developed by the U.S. Department of Labor as an intuitive way to assist in career exploration. The 16 interest areas used in the New GOE are based on the 16 career clusters that were developed by the U.S. Department of Education's Office of Vocational and Adult Education around 1999 and that presently are being used by many states to organize their career-oriented programs and career information. Appendix A lists the Interest Areas and their Work Groups.

Descriptions for the 16 Interest Areas

Brief descriptions for the 16 interest areas we use in the lists follow. The descriptions are from the *New Guide for Occupational Exploration,* Fourth Edition. Some of them refer to jobs (as examples) that aren't included in this book.

Also note that we put each of the 175 best jobs into only one interest area list, the one it fit into best. However, many jobs could be included in more than one list, so consider reviewing a variety of these interest areas to find jobs that you might otherwise overlook.

⊚ Agriculture and Natural Resources: *An interest in working with plants, animals, forests, or mineral resources for agriculture, horticulture, conservation, extraction, and other purposes.* You can satisfy this interest by working in farming, landscaping, forestry, fishing, mining, and related fields. You may like doing physical work outdoors, such as on a farm or ranch, in a forest, or on a drilling rig. If you have scientific curiosity, you could study plants and animals or analyze biological or rock samples in a lab. If you have management ability, you could own, operate, or manage a fish hatchery, a landscaping business, or a greenhouse.

⊚ Architecture and Construction: *An interest in designing, assembling, and maintaining components of buildings and other structures.* You may want to be part of the team of architects, drafters, and others who design buildings and render the plans. If construction interests you, you can find fulfillment in the many building projects that are being undertaken at all times. If you like to organize and plan, you can find careers in managing these projects. Or you can play a more direct role in putting up and finishing buildings by doing jobs such as plumbing, carpentry, masonry, painting, or roofing, either as a skilled craftsworker or as a helper. You can prepare the building site by operating heavy equipment or install, maintain, and repair vital building equipment and systems such as electricity and heating.

◉ Arts and Communication: *An interest in creatively expressing feelings or ideas, in communicating news or information, or in performing.* You can satisfy this interest in creative, verbal, or performing activities. For example, if you enjoy literature, perhaps writing or editing would appeal to you. Journalism and public relations are other fields for people who like to use their writing or speaking skills. Do you prefer to work in the performing arts? If so, you could direct or perform in drama, music, or dance. If you especially enjoy the visual arts, you could create paintings, sculpture, or ceramics or design products or visual displays. A flair for technology might lead you to specialize in photography, broadcast production, or dispatching.

◉ Business and Administration: *An interest in making a business organization or function run smoothly.* You can satisfy this interest by working in a position of leadership or by specializing in a function that contributes to the overall effort in a business, a nonprofit organization, or a government agency. If you especially enjoy working with people, you may find fulfillment from working in human resources. An interest in numbers may lead you to consider accounting, finance, budgeting, billing, or financial record-keeping. A job as an administrative assistant may interest you if you like a variety of work in a busy environment. If you are good with details and word processing, you may enjoy a job as a secretary or data entry keyer. Or perhaps you would do well as the manager of a business.

◉ Education and Training: *An interest in helping people learn.* You can satisfy this interest by teaching students, who may be preschoolers, retirees, or any age in between. You may specialize in a particular academic field or work with learners of a particular age, with a particular interest, or with a particular learning problem. Working in a library or museum may give you an opportunity to expand people's understanding of the world.

◉ Finance and Insurance: *An interest in helping businesses and people be assured of a financially secure future.* You can satisfy this interest by working in a financial or insurance business in a leadership or support role. If you like gathering and analyzing information, you may find fulfillment as an insurance adjuster or financial analyst. Or you may deal with information at the clerical level as a banking or insurance clerk or in person-to-person situations providing customer service. Another way to interact with people is to sell financial or insurance services that will meet their needs.

◉ Government and Public Administration: *An interest in helping a government agency serve the needs of the public.* You can satisfy this interest by working in a position of leadership or by specializing in a function that contributes to the role of government. You may help protect the public by working as an inspector or examiner to enforce standards. If you enjoy using clerical skills, you may work as a clerk in a law court or government office. Or perhaps you prefer the top-down perspective of a government executive or urban planner.

◎ Health Science: *An interest in helping people and animals be healthy.* You can satisfy this interest by working in a health care team as a doctor, therapist, or nurse. You might specialize in one of the many different parts of the body (such as the teeth or eyes) or in one of the many different types of care. Or you may want to be a generalist who deals with the whole patient. If you like technology, you might find satisfaction working with X rays or new methods of diagnosis. You might work with healthy people, helping them eat right. If you enjoy working with animals, you might care for them and keep them healthy.

◎ Hospitality, Tourism, and Recreation: *An interest in catering to the personal wishes and needs of others so that they may enjoy a clean environment, good food and drink, comfortable lodging away from home, and recreation.* You can satisfy this interest by providing services for the convenience, care, and pampering of others in hotels, restaurants, airplanes, beauty parlors, and so on. You may want to use your love of cooking as a chef. If you like working with people, you may want to provide personal services by being a travel guide, a flight attendant, a concierge, a hairdresser, or a waiter. You may want to work in cleaning and building services if you like a clean environment. If you enjoy sports or games, you may work for an athletic team or casino.

◎ Human Service: *An interest in improving people's social, mental, emotional, or spiritual well-being.* You can satisfy this interest as a counselor, social worker, or religious worker who helps people sort out their complicated lives or solve personal problems. You may work as a caretaker for very young people or the elderly. Or you may interview people to help identify the social services they need.

◎ Information Technology: *An interest in designing, developing, managing, and supporting information systems.* You can satisfy this interest by working with hardware, software, multimedia, or integrated systems. If you like to use your organizational skills, you might work as an administrator of a system or database. Or you can solve complex problems as a software engineer or systems analyst. If you enjoy getting your hands on the hardware, you might find work servicing computers, peripherals, and information-intense machines such as cash registers and ATMs.

◎ Law and Public Safety: *An interest in upholding people's rights or in protecting people and property by using authority, inspecting, or investigating.* You can satisfy this interest by working in law, law enforcement, fire fighting, the military, and related fields. For example, if you enjoy mental challenge and intrigue, you could investigate crimes or fires for a living. If you enjoy working with verbal skills and research skills, you may want to defend citizens in court or research deeds, wills, and other legal documents. If you want to help people in critical situations, you may want to fight fires, work as a police officer, or become a paramedic. Or, if you want more routine work in public safety, perhaps a job in guarding, patrolling, or inspecting would appeal to you. If you have management ability, you could seek a leadership position in law enforcement and the protective services. Work in the military gives you a chance to use technical and leadership skills while serving your country.

◎ Manufacturing: *An interest in processing materials into intermediate or final products or maintaining and repairing products by using machines or hand tools.* You can satisfy this interest by working in one of many industries that mass-produce goods or by working for a utility that distributes electric power or other resources. You may enjoy manual work, using your hands or hand tools in highly skilled jobs such as assembling engines or electronic equipment. If you enjoy making machines run efficiently or fixing them when they break down, you could seek a job installing or repairing such devices as copiers, aircraft engines, cars, or watches. Perhaps you prefer to set up or operate machines that are used to manufacture products made of food, glass, or paper. You may enjoy cutting and grinding metal and plastic parts to desired shapes and measurements. Or you may want to operate equipment in systems that provide water and process wastewater. You may like inspecting, sorting, counting, or weighing products. Another option is to work with your hands and machinery to move boxes and freight in a warehouse. If leadership appeals to you, you could manage people engaged in production and repair.

◎ Retail and Wholesale Sales and Service: *An interest in bringing others to a particular point of view by personal persuasion and by sales and promotional techniques.* You can satisfy this interest in a variety of jobs that involve persuasion and selling. If you like using your knowledge of science, you may enjoy selling pharmaceutical, medical, or electronic products or services. Real estate offers several kinds of sales jobs as well. If you like speaking on the phone, you could work as a telemarketer. Or you may enjoy selling apparel and other merchandise in a retail setting. If you prefer to help people, you may want a job in customer service.

◎ Scientific Research, Engineering, and Mathematics: *An interest in discovering, collecting, and analyzing information about the natural world; in applying scientific research findings to problems in medicine, the life sciences, human behavior, and the natural sciences; in imagining and manipulating quantitative data; and in applying technology to manufacturing, transportation, and other economic activities.* You can satisfy this interest by working with the knowledge and processes of the sciences. You may enjoy researching and developing new knowledge in mathematics, or perhaps solving problems in the physical, life, or social sciences would appeal to you. You may want to study engineering and help create new machines, processes, and structures. If you want to work with scientific equipment and procedures, you could seek a job in a research or testing laboratory.

◎ Transportation, Distribution, and Logistics: *An interest in operations that move people or materials.* You can satisfy this interest by managing a transportation service, by helping vehicles keep on their assigned schedules and routes, or by driving or piloting a vehicle. If you enjoy taking responsibility, perhaps managing a rail line would appeal to you. If you work well with details and can take pressure on the job, you might consider being an air traffic controller. Or would you rather get out on the highway, on the water, or up in the air? If so, then you could drive a truck from state to state, be employed on a ship, or fly a crop duster over a cornfield. If you prefer to stay closer to home, you could drive a delivery van, taxi, or school bus. You can use your physical strength to load freight and arrange it so it gets to its destination in one piece.

Best Jobs Not Behind a Desk for People Interested in Agriculture and Natural Resources

Job	Annual Earnings	Percent Growth	Annual Openings
1. First-Line Supervisors/Managers of Landscaping, Lawn Service, and Groundskeeping Workers	$36,320	17.8%	14,000
2. First-Line Supervisors/Managers of Construction Trades and Extraction Workers	$51,970	10.9%	57,000
3. Landscaping and Groundskeeping Workers	$20,670	19.5%	243,000
4. Environmental Science and Protection Technicians, Including Health	$36,260	16.3%	6,000
5. Tree Trimmers and Pruners	$27,920	16.5%	11,000
6. Zoologists and Wildlife Biologists	$52,050	13.0%	1,000
7. Excavating and Loading Machine and Dragline Operators	$32,380	8.0%	11,000
8. Farmers and Ranchers	$34,140	–14.5%	96,000
9. Pest Control Workers	$27,170	18.4%	4,000
10. Conservation Scientists	$53,350	6.3%	2,000
11. Pesticide Handlers, Sprayers, and Applicators, Vegetation	$26,120	16.6%	6,000
12. Supervisors, Farming, Fishing, and Forestry Workers	$36,030	3.6%	11,000
13. Foresters	$48,670	6.7%	1,000
14. Earth Drillers, Except Oil and Gas	$33,770	7.9%	4,000

Best Jobs Not Behind a Desk for People Interested in Architecture and Construction

Job	Annual Earnings	Percent Growth	Annual Openings
1. Plumbers, Pipefitters, and Steamfitters	$42,160	15.7%	61,000
2. Heating, Air Conditioning, and Refrigeration Mechanics and Installers	$37,040	19.0%	33,000
3. Electricians	$42,790	11.8%	68,000
4. Carpenters	$35,580	13.8%	210,000
5. Construction Managers	$72,260	10.4%	28,000
6. Roofers	$31,230	16.8%	38,000
7. Tile and Marble Setters	$36,530	22.9%	9,000
8. Maintenance and Repair Workers, General	$31,210	15.2%	154,000
9. Hazardous Materials Removal Workers	$33,690	31.2%	11,000
10. Sheet Metal Workers	$36,390	12.2%	50,000
11. Structural Iron and Steel Workers	$40,580	15.0%	13,000

Best Jobs Not Behind a Desk for People Interested in Architecture and Construction

Job	Annual Earnings	Percent Growth	Annual Openings
12. Cement Masons and Concrete Finishers	$32,030	15.9%	32,000
13. Highway Maintenance Workers	$30,250	23.3%	27,000
14. Surveyors	$45,860	15.9%	4,000
15. Elevator Installers and Repairers	$59,190	14.8%	3,000
16. Telecommunications Line Installers and Repairers	$42,410	10.8%	23,000
17. Brickmasons and Blockmasons	$41,860	12.0%	17,000
18. Operating Engineers and Other Construction Equipment Operators	$35,830	11.6%	37,000
19. Helpers—Installation, Maintenance, and Repair Workers	$21,230	16.4%	41,000
20. Painters, Construction and Maintenance	$30,800	12.6%	102,000
21. Telecommunications Equipment Installers and Repairers, Except Line Installers	$50,620	−4.9%	21,000
22. Helpers—Pipelayers, Plumbers, Pipefitters, and Steamfitters	$22,820	16.6%	17,000
23. Electrical Power-Line Installers and Repairers	$50,150	2.5%	11,000
24. Glaziers	$33,530	14.2%	9,000
25. Reinforcing Iron and Rebar Workers	$34,910	14.1%	6,000
26. Drywall and Ceiling Tile Installers	$34,740	9.0%	17,000
27. Helpers—Carpenters	$21,990	14.5%	24,000
28. Septic Tank Servicers and Sewer Pipe Cleaners	$30,440	21.8%	3,000
29. Riggers	$37,010	13.9%	2,000
30. Construction Laborers	$25,410	5.9%	245,000
31. Helpers—Brickmasons, Blockmasons, Stonemasons, and Tile and Marble Setters	$24,600	14.9%	14,000
32. Paving, Surfacing, and Tamping Equipment Operators	$30,320	15.6%	7,000
33. Boilermakers	$48,050	8.7%	2,000
34. Electrical and Electronics Repairers, Powerhouse, Substation, and Relay	$54,970	−0.4%	2,000
35. Carpet Installers	$33,550	8.4%	11,000
36. Stonemasons	$34,640	13.0%	2,000
37. Tapers	$39,870	5.9%	5,000
38. Floor Layers, Except Carpet, Wood, and Hard Tiles	$33,010	10.2%	4,000
39. Plasterers and Stucco Masons	$33,440	8.2%	6,000
40. Pipelayers	$28,760	9.9%	7,000

Best Jobs Not Behind a Desk for People Interested in Arts and Communication

Job	Annual Earnings	Percent Growth	Annual Openings
1. Audio and Video Equipment Technicians	$32,940	18.1%	5,000
2. Camera Operators, Television, Video, and Motion Picture	$41,610	14.2%	4,000
3. Choreographers	$32,950	16.8%	4,000
4. Photographers	$26,100	12.3%	23,000
5. Costume Attendants	$25,360	23.4%	2,000
6. Set and Exhibit Designers	$37,390	9.3%	2,000

Best Jobs Not Behind a Desk for People Interested in Business and Administration

Job	Annual Earnings	Percent Growth	Annual Openings
1. First-Line Supervisors/Managers of Housekeeping and Janitorial Workers	$30,330	19.0%	21,000
2. Postal Service Clerks	$48,310	0.0%	4,000

Best Jobs Not Behind a Desk for People Interested in Education and Training

Job	Annual Earnings	Percent Growth	Annual Openings
1. Elementary School Teachers, Except Special Education	$44,040	18.2%	203,000
2. Secondary School Teachers, Except Special and Vocational Education	$46,060	14.4%	107,000
3. Preschool Teachers, Except Special Education	$21,990	33.1%	77,000
4. Kindergarten Teachers, Except Special Education	$42,230	22.4%	28,000
5. Middle School Teachers, Except Special and Vocational Education	$44,640	13.7%	83,000
6. Education Administrators, Preschool and Child Care Center/Program	$37,010	27.9%	9,000
7. Self-Enrichment Education Teachers	$32,360	25.3%	74,000
8. Fitness Trainers and Aerobics Instructors	$25,840	27.1%	50,000
9. Vocational Education Teachers, Secondary School	$47,090	9.1%	10,000
10. Curators	$45,240	15.7%	1,000
11. Audio-Visual Collections Specialists	$40,260	18.6%	1,000
12. Museum Technicians and Conservators	$34,090	14.1%	2,000

Best Jobs Not Behind a Desk for People Interested in Government and Public Administration

Job	Annual Earnings	Percent Growth	Annual Openings
1. Construction and Building Inspectors	$44,720	22.3%	6,000
2. Transportation Inspectors	$49,490	11.4%	2,000
3. Fish and Game Wardens	$42,850	10.5%	1,000

Best Jobs Not Behind a Desk for People Interested in Health Science

Job	Annual Earnings	Percent Growth	Annual Openings
1. Physician Assistants	$72,030	49.6%	10,000
2. Physical Therapists	$63,080	36.7%	13,000
3. Registered Nurses	$54,670	29.4%	229,000
4. Medical Assistants	$25,350	52.1%	93,000
5. Occupational Therapists	$56,860	33.6%	7,000
6. Physical Therapist Assistants	$39,490	44.2%	7,000
7. Radiologic Technologists and Technicians	$45,950	23.2%	17,000
8. Veterinarians	$68,910	17.4%	8,000
9. Surgical Technologists	$34,830	29.5%	12,000
10. Cardiovascular Technologists and Technicians	$40,420	32.6%	5,000
11. Chiropractors	$67,200	22.4%	4,000
12. Respiratory Therapists	$45,140	28.4%	7,000
13. Occupational Therapist Assistants	$39,750	34.1%	2,000
14. Radiation Therapists	$62,340	26.3%	1,000
15. Nursing Aides, Orderlies, and Attendants	$21,440	22.3%	307,000
16. Nuclear Medicine Technologists	$59,670	21.5%	2,000
17. Physical Therapist Aides	$21,510	34.4%	5,000
18. Licensed Practical and Licensed Vocational Nurses	$35,230	17.1%	84,000
19. Oral and Maxillofacial Surgeons	more than $145,600	16.2%	fewer than 500
20. Medical Equipment Preparers	$24,880	20.0%	8,000

(continued)

(continued)

Best Jobs Not Behind a Desk for People Interested in Health Science

Job	Annual Earnings	Percent Growth	Annual Openings
21. Athletic Trainers	$34,260	29.3%	1,000
22. Orthotists and Prosthetists	$53,760	18.0%	fewer than 500
23. Animal Trainers	$24,800	20.3%	3,000
24. Embalmers	$36,960	15.6%	2,000

Best Jobs Not Behind a Desk for People Interested in Hospitality, Tourism, and Recreation

Job	Annual Earnings	Percent Growth	Annual Openings
1. Gaming Managers	$59,940	22.6%	1,000
2. Coaches and Scouts	$25,990	20.4%	63,000
3. First-Line Supervisors/Managers of Food Preparation and Serving Workers	$26,050	16.6%	187,000
4. Athletes and Sports Competitors	$39,930	21.1%	6,000
5. Flight Attendants	$46,680	16.3%	7,000
6. Food Service Managers	$41,340	11.5%	61,000
7. Recreation Workers	$20,110	17.3%	69,000
8. Gaming Supervisors	$40,300	16.3%	8,000
9. Umpires, Referees, and Other Sports Officials	$21,610	19.0%	6,000
10. Butchers and Meat Cutters	$26,590	7.9%	20,000
11. Hairdressers, Hairstylists, and Cosmetologists	$20,610	16.1%	59,000

Best Jobs Not Behind a Desk for People Interested in Law and Public Safety

Job	Annual Earnings	Percent Growth	Annual Openings
1. First-Line Supervisors/Managers of Fire Fighting and Prevention Workers	$60,840	21.1%	4,000
2. Detectives and Criminal Investigators	$55,790	16.3%	9,000
3. First-Line Supervisors/Managers of Police and Detectives	$65,570	15.5%	9,000
4. Police and Sheriff's Patrol Officers	$46,290	15.5%	47,000
5. Emergency Medical Technicians and Paramedics	$26,080	27.3%	21,000
6. Crossing Guards	$20,050	19.7%	26,000
7. Correctional Officers and Jailers	$34,090	6.7%	54,000
8. Security Guards	$20,760	12.6%	230,000
9. Animal Control Workers	$26,780	14.4%	4,000
10. Bailiffs	$33,800	13.2%	2,000
11. Transit and Railroad Police	$48,850	9.2%	fewer than 500

Best Jobs Not Behind a Desk for People Interested in Manufacturing

Job	Annual Earnings	Percent Growth	Annual Openings
1. First-Line Supervisors/Managers of Mechanics, Installers, and Repairers	$51,980	12.4%	33,000
2. Automotive Service Technicians and Mechanics	$33,050	15.7%	93,000
3. Bus and Truck Mechanics and Diesel Engine Specialists	$36,620	14.4%	32,000
4. Aircraft Mechanics and Service Technicians	$47,310	13.4%	11,000
5. First-Line Supervisors/Managers of Production and Operating Workers	$46,140	2.7%	89,000
6. Bakers	$21,520	15.2%	37,000
7. Water and Liquid Waste Treatment Plant and System Operators	$34,930	16.2%	6,000
8. Automotive Body and Related Repairers	$34,810	10.3%	18,000
9. Electrical and Electronics Repairers, Commercial and Industrial Equipment	$44,120	9.7%	8,000
10. Painters, Transportation Equipment	$34,840	14.1%	10,000
11. Industrial Production Managers	$75,580	0.8%	13,000
12. First-Line Supervisors/Managers of Helpers, Laborers, and Material Movers, Hand	$39,000	8.1%	15,000
13. Mobile Heavy Equipment Mechanics, Except Engines	$39,410	8.8%	14,000
14. Ship Engineers	$52,780	12.7%	1,000

(continued)

(continued)

Best Jobs Not Behind a Desk for People Interested in Manufacturing

Job	Annual Earnings	Percent Growth	Annual Openings
15. Medical Equipment Repairers	$39,570	14.8%	4,000
16. Motorboat Mechanics	$32,780	15.1%	7,000
17. Industrial Truck and Tractor Operators	$27,080	7.9%	114,000
18. Machinists	$34,350	4.3%	33,000
19. Welders, Cutters, Solderers, and Brazers	$30,990	5.0%	52,000
20. Slaughterers and Meat Packers	$21,220	13.8%	22,000
21. Locksmiths and Safe Repairers	$30,880	16.1%	5,000
22. Avionics Technicians	$46,630	9.1%	2,000
23. Refuse and Recyclable Material Collectors	$28,460	8.9%	31,000
24. Helpers—Production Workers	$20,390	7.9%	107,000
25. Gas Plant Operators	$51,920	7.7%	2,000
26. Millwrights	$44,780	5.9%	5,000
27. Outdoor Power Equipment and Other Small Engine Mechanics	$25,810	14.0%	10,000
28. Recreational Vehicle Service Technicians	$30,480	19.5%	3,000
29. Chemical Plant and System Operators	$46,710	–17.7%	8,000
30. Industrial Machinery Mechanics	$39,740	–0.2%	13,000
31. Petroleum Pump System Operators, Refinery Operators, and Gaugers	$51,060	–8.6%	6,000
32. Aircraft Structure, Surfaces, Rigging, and Systems Assemblers	$43,990	7.8%	4,000
33. Stationary Engineers and Boiler Operators	$44,600	3.4%	5,000
34. Motorcycle Mechanics	$29,450	13.7%	6,000
35. Printing Machine Operators	$30,730	2.9%	26,000
36. Control and Valve Installers and Repairers, Except Mechanical Door	$44,120	4.9%	4,000
37. Paper Goods Machine Setters, Operators, and Tenders	$31,160	2.4%	15,000
38. Structural Metal Fabricators and Fitters	$30,290	2.9%	18,000
39. Tool and Die Makers	$43,580	–2.6%	7,000

Best Jobs Not Behind a Desk for People Interested in Retail and Wholesale Sales and Service

Job	Annual Earnings	Percent Growth	Annual Openings
1. Funeral Directors	$47,630	6.7%	3,000
2. First-Line Supervisors/Managers of Retail Sales Workers	$32,840	3.8%	229,000

Best Jobs Not Behind a Desk for People Interested in Scientific Research, Engineering, and Mathematics

Job	Annual Earnings	Percent Growth	Annual Openings
1. Geoscientists, Except Hydrologists and Geographers	$71,640	8.3%	2,000
2. Mechanical Engineering Technicians	$44,830	12.3%	5,000
3. Nuclear Technicians	$61,120	13.7%	1,000
4. Chemists	$57,890	7.3%	5,000
5. Chemical Technicians	$38,500	4.4%	7,000

Best Jobs Not Behind a Desk for People Interested in Transportation, Distribution, and Logistics

Job	Annual Earnings	Percent Growth	Annual Openings
1. Railroad Conductors and Yardmasters	$54,040	20.3%	3,000
2. Truck Drivers, Heavy and Tractor-Trailer	$34,280	12.9%	274,000
3. Truck Drivers, Light or Delivery Services	$24,790	15.7%	169,000
4. Laborers and Freight, Stock, and Material Movers, Hand	$20,610	10.2%	671,000
5. Driver/Sales Workers	$20,120	13.8%	72,000
6. Postal Service Mail Carriers	$46,330	0.0%	19,000

Best Jobs Not Behind a Desk Listed by Personality Type

These lists organize the 175 best jobs not behind a desk into groups matching six personality types. The personality types are Realistic, Investigative, Artistic, Social, Enterprising, and Conventional. This system was developed by John Holland and is used in the *Self-Directed Search (SDS)* and other career assessment inventories and information systems.

If you have used one of these career inventories or systems, the lists will help you identify jobs that most closely match these personality types. Even if you have not used one of these systems, the concept of personality types and the jobs that are related to them can help you identify active jobs that most closely match the type of person you are.

We've ranked the active jobs within each personality type based on their total combined scores for earnings, growth, and annual job openings. Like the job lists for education levels, there is only one list for each personality type. Note that each job is listed in the one personality type it most closely matches, even though it might also fit into others. Consider reviewing the jobs for more than one personality type so you don't overlook possible jobs that would interest you.

Following are brief descriptions for each of the six personality types used in the lists. Select the two or three descriptions that most closely describe you and then use the lists to identify high-energy jobs that best fit these personality types.

Descriptions of the Six Personality Types

- **Realistic:** These occupations frequently involve work activities that include practical, hands-on problems and solutions. They often deal with plants; animals; and real-world materials like wood, tools, and machinery. Many of the occupations require working outside and do not involve a lot of paperwork or working closely with others.

- **Investigative:** These occupations frequently involve working with ideas and require an extensive amount of thinking. These occupations can involve searching for facts and figuring out problems mentally.

- **Artistic:** These occupations frequently involve working with forms, designs, and patterns. They often require self-expression, and the work can be done without following a clear set of rules.

- **Social:** These occupations frequently involve working with, communicating with, and teaching people. These occupations often involve helping or providing service to others.

- **Enterprising:** These occupations frequently involve starting up and carrying out projects. These occupations can involve leading people and making many decisions. They sometimes require risk taking and often deal with business.

- **Conventional:** These occupations frequently involve following set procedures and routines. These occupations can include working with data and details more than with ideas. Usually there is a clear line of authority to follow.

Best Jobs Not Behind a Desk for People with a Realistic Personality Type

Job	Annual Earnings	Percent Growth	Annual Openings
1. Radiologic Technologists and Technicians	$45,950	23.2%	17,000
2. Plumbers, Pipefitters, and Steamfitters	$42,160	15.7%	61,000
3. Heating, Air Conditioning, and Refrigeration Mechanics and Installers	$37,040	19.0%	33,000
4. First-Line Supervisors/Managers of Fire Fighting and Prevention Workers	$60,840	21.1%	4,000
5. Carpenters	$35,580	13.8%	210,000
6. Electricians	$42,790	11.8%	68,000
7. Railroad Conductors and Yardmasters	$54,040	20.3%	3,000
8. Surgical Technologists	$34,830	29.5%	12,000
9. Automotive Service Technicians and Mechanics	$33,050	15.7%	93,000
10. First-Line Supervisors/Managers of Landscaping, Lawn Service, and Groundskeeping Workers	$36,320	17.8%	14,000

Best Jobs Not Behind a Desk for People with a Realistic Personality Type

Job	Annual Earnings	Percent Growth	Annual Openings
11. Bus and Truck Mechanics and Diesel Engine Specialists	$36,620	14.4%	32,000
12. Tile and Marble Setters	$36,530	22.9%	9,000
13. Roofers	$31,230	16.8%	38,000
14. Truck Drivers, Heavy and Tractor-Trailer	$34,280	12.9%	274,000
15. Maintenance and Repair Workers, General	$31,210	15.2%	154,000
16. Hazardous Materials Removal Workers	$33,690	31.2%	11,000
17. Structural Iron and Steel Workers	$40,580	15.0%	13,000
18. Highway Maintenance Workers	$30,250	23.3%	27,000
19. Sheet Metal Workers	$36,390	12.2%	50,000
20. Landscaping and Groundskeeping Workers	$20,670	19.5%	243,000
21. Cement Masons and Concrete Finishers	$32,030	15.9%	32,000
22. Telecommunications Line Installers and Repairers	$42,410	10.8%	23,000
23. Brickmasons and Blockmasons	$41,860	12.0%	17,000
24. Operating Engineers and Other Construction Equipment Operators	$35,830	11.6%	37,000
25. Truck Drivers, Light or Delivery Services	$24,790	15.7%	169,000
26. Elevator Installers and Repairers	$59,190	14.8%	3,000
27. Water and Liquid Waste Treatment Plant and System Operators	$34,930	16.2%	6,000
28. Painters, Construction and Maintenance	$30,800	12.6%	102,000
29. Helpers—Installation, Maintenance, and Repair Workers	$21,230	16.4%	41,000
30. Telecommunications Equipment Installers and Repairers, Except Line Installers	$50,620	−4.9%	21,000
31. Painters, Transportation Equipment	$34,840	14.1%	10,000
32. Mechanical Engineering Technicians	$44,830	12.3%	5,000
33. Electrical and Electronics Repairers, Commercial and Industrial Equipment	$44,120	9.7%	8,000
34. Nuclear Technicians	$61,120	13.7%	1,000
35. Automotive Body and Related Repairers	$34,810	10.3%	18,000
36. Bakers	$21,520	15.2%	37,000
37. Mobile Heavy Equipment Mechanics, Except Engines	$39,410	8.8%	14,000
38. Medical Equipment Repairers	$39,570	14.8%	4,000
39. Helpers—Pipelayers, Plumbers, Pipefitters, and Steamfitters	$22,820	16.6%	17,000
40. Tree Trimmers and Pruners	$27,920	16.5%	11,000
41. Correctional Officers and Jailers	$34,090	6.7%	54,000
42. Electrical Power-Line Installers and Repairers	$50,150	2.5%	11,000
43. Reinforcing Iron and Rebar Workers	$34,910	14.1%	6,000
44. Ship Engineers	$52,780	12.7%	1,000

(continued)

(continued)

Best Jobs Not Behind a Desk for People with a Realistic Personality Type

Job	Annual Earnings	Percent Growth	Annual Openings
45. Drywall and Ceiling Tile Installers	$34,740	9.0%	17,000
46. Embalmers	$36,960	15.6%	2,000
47. Glaziers	$33,530	14.2%	9,000
48. Motorboat Mechanics	$32,780	15.1%	7,000
49. Medical Equipment Preparers	$24,880	20.0%	8,000
50. Transportation Inspectors	$49,490	11.4%	2,000
51. Helpers—Carpenters	$21,990	14.5%	24,000
52. Laborers and Freight, Stock, and Material Movers, Hand	$20,610	10.2%	671,000
53. Machinists	$34,350	4.3%	33,000
54. Farmers and Ranchers	$34,140	−14.5%	96,000
55. Locksmiths and Safe Repairers	$30,880	16.1%	5,000
56. Paving, Surfacing, and Tamping Equipment Operators	$30,320	15.6%	7,000
57. Industrial Truck and Tractor Operators	$27,080	7.9%	114,000
58. Septic Tank Servicers and Sewer Pipe Cleaners	$30,440	21.8%	3,000
59. Helpers—Brickmasons, Blockmasons, Stonemasons, and Tile and Marble Setters	$24,600	14.9%	14,000
60. Riggers	$37,010	13.9%	2,000
61. Avionics Technicians	$46,630	9.1%	2,000
62. Pesticide Handlers, Sprayers, and Applicators, Vegetation	$26,120	16.6%	6,000
63. Recreational Vehicle Service Technicians	$30,480	19.5%	3,000
64. Boilermakers	$48,050	8.7%	2,000
65. Industrial Machinery Mechanics	$39,740	−0.2%	13,000
66. Welders, Cutters, Solderers, and Brazers	$30,990	5.0%	52,000
67. Chemical Plant and System Operators	$46,710	−17.7%	8,000
68. Petroleum Pump System Operators, Refinery Operators, and Gaugers	$51,060	−8.6%	6,000
69. Slaughterers and Meat Packers	$21,220	13.8%	22,000
70. Construction Laborers	$25,410	5.9%	245,000
71. Gas Plant Operators	$51,920	7.7%	2,000
72. Millwrights	$44,780	5.9%	5,000
73. Pest Control Workers	$27,170	18.4%	4,000
74. Refuse and Recyclable Material Collectors	$28,460	8.9%	31,000
75. Aircraft Structure, Surfaces, Rigging, and Systems Assemblers	$43,990	7.8%	4,000
76. Carpet Installers	$33,550	8.4%	11,000
77. Fish and Game Wardens	$42,850	10.5%	1,000
78. Stationary Engineers and Boiler Operators	$44,600	3.4%	5,000

Best Jobs Not Behind a Desk for People with a Realistic Personality Type

Job	Annual Earnings	Percent Growth	Annual Openings
79. Tool and Die Makers	$43,580	−2.6%	7,000
80. Chemical Technicians	$38,500	4.4%	7,000
81. Outdoor Power Equipment and Other Small Engine Mechanics	$25,810	14.0%	10,000
82. Control and Valve Installers and Repairers, Except Mechanical Door	$44,120	4.9%	4,000
83. Excavating and Loading Machine and Dragline Operators	$32,380	8.0%	11,000
84. Helpers—Production Workers	$20,390	7.9%	107,000
85. Tapers	$39,870	5.9%	5,000
86. Electrical and Electronics Repairers, Powerhouse, Substation, and Relay	$54,970	−0.4%	2,000
87. Stonemasons	$34,640	13.0%	2,000
88. Foresters	$48,670	6.7%	1,000
89. Motorcycle Mechanics	$29,450	13.7%	6,000
90. Printing Machine Operators	$30,730	2.9%	26,000
91. Butchers and Meat Cutters	$26,590	7.9%	20,000
92. Plasterers and Stucco Masons	$33,440	8.2%	6,000
93. Floor Layers, Except Carpet, Wood, and Hard Tiles	$33,010	10.2%	4,000
94. Paper Goods Machine Setters, Operators, and Tenders	$31,160	2.4%	15,000
95. Structural Metal Fabricators and Fitters	$30,290	2.9%	18,000
96. Pipelayers	$28,760	9.9%	7,000
97. Earth Drillers, Except Oil and Gas	$33,770	7.9%	4,000

Best Jobs Not Behind a Desk for People with an Investigative Personality Type

Job	Annual Earnings	Percent Growth	Annual Openings
1. Physician Assistants	$72,030	49.6%	10,000
2. Veterinarians	$68,910	17.4%	8,000
3. Chiropractors	$67,200	22.4%	4,000
4. Respiratory Therapists	$45,140	28.4%	7,000
5. Aircraft Mechanics and Service Technicians	$47,310	13.4%	11,000
6. Cardiovascular Technologists and Technicians	$40,420	32.6%	5,000
7. Nuclear Medicine Technologists	$59,670	21.5%	2,000
8. Oral and Maxillofacial Surgeons	more than $145,600	16.2%	fewer than 500

(continued)

(continued)

Best Jobs Not Behind a Desk for People with an Investigative Personality Type

Job	Annual Earnings	Percent Growth	Annual Openings
9. Geoscientists, Except Hydrologists and Geographers	$71,640	8.3%	2,000
10. Chemists	$57,890	7.3%	5,000
11. Environmental Science and Protection Technicians, Including Health	$36,260	16.3%	6,000
12. Surveyors	$45,860	15.9%	4,000
13. Conservation Scientists	$53,350	6.3%	2,000
14. Zoologists and Wildlife Biologists	$52,050	13.0%	1,000

Best Jobs Not Behind a Desk for People with an Artistic Personality Type

Job	Annual Earnings	Percent Growth	Annual Openings
1. Camera Operators, Television, Video, and Motion Picture	$41,610	14.2%	4,000
2. Choreographers	$32,950	16.8%	4,000
3. Curators	$45,240	15.7%	1,000
4. Costume Attendants	$25,360	23.4%	2,000
5. Museum Technicians and Conservators	$34,090	14.1%	2,000
6. Photographers	$26,100	12.3%	23,000
7. Set and Exhibit Designers	$37,390	9.3%	2,000

Best Jobs Not Behind a Desk for People with a Social Personality Type

Job	Annual Earnings	Percent Growth	Annual Openings
1. Registered Nurses	$54,670	29.4%	229,000
2. Physical Therapists	$63,080	36.7%	13,000
3. Medical Assistants	$25,350	52.1%	93,000
4. Occupational Therapists	$56,860	33.6%	7,000
5. Elementary School Teachers, Except Special Education	$44,040	18.2%	203,000
6. Physical Therapist Assistants	$39,490	44.2%	7,000
7. Secondary School Teachers, Except Special and Vocational Education	$46,060	14.4%	107,000
8. Kindergarten Teachers, Except Special Education	$42,230	22.4%	28,000
9. Preschool Teachers, Except Special Education	$21,990	33.1%	77,000

Best Jobs Not Behind a Desk for People with a Social Personality Type

Job	Annual Earnings	Percent Growth	Annual Openings
10. Occupational Therapist Assistants	$39,750	34.1%	2,000
11. Radiation Therapists	$62,340	26.3%	1,000
12. Self-Enrichment Education Teachers	$32,360	25.3%	74,000
13. Education Administrators, Preschool and Child Care Center/Program	$37,010	27.9%	9,000
14. Middle School Teachers, Except Special and Vocational Education	$44,640	13.7%	83,000
15. Nursing Aides, Orderlies, and Attendants	$21,440	22.3%	307,000
16. Police and Sheriff's Patrol Officers	$46,290	15.5%	47,000
17. Licensed Practical and Licensed Vocational Nurses	$35,230	17.1%	84,000
18. Fitness Trainers and Aerobics Instructors	$25,840	27.1%	50,000
19. Emergency Medical Technicians and Paramedics	$26,080	27.3%	21,000
20. Physical Therapist Aides	$21,510	34.4%	5,000
21. Athletic Trainers	$34,260	29.3%	1,000
22. Vocational Education Teachers, Secondary School	$47,090	9.1%	10,000
23. Orthotists and Prosthetists	$53,760	18.0%	fewer than 500
24. Security Guards	$20,760	12.6%	230,000
25. Recreation Workers	$20,110	17.3%	69,000
26. Crossing Guards	$20,050	19.7%	26,000
27. Animal Trainers	$24,800	20.3%	3,000
28. Animal Control Workers	$26,780	14.4%	4,000
29. Bailiffs	$33,800	13.2%	2,000

Best Jobs Not Behind a Desk for People with an Enterprising Personality Type

Job	Annual Earnings	Percent Growth	Annual Openings
1. First-Line Supervisors/Managers of Food Preparation and Serving Workers	$26,050	16.6%	187,000
2. First-Line Supervisors/Managers of Mechanics, Installers, and Repairers	$51,980	12.4%	33,000
3. Gaming Managers	$59,940	22.6%	1,000
4. Coaches and Scouts	$25,990	20.4%	63,000
5. Construction Managers	$72,260	10.4%	28,000

(continued)

(continued)

Best Jobs Not Behind a Desk for People with an Enterprising Personality Type

Job	Annual Earnings	Percent Growth	Annual Openings
6. First-Line Supervisors/Managers of Construction Trades and Extraction Workers	$51,970	10.9%	57,000
7. First-Line Supervisors/Managers of Police and Detectives	$65,570	15.5%	9,000
8. Food Service Managers	$41,340	11.5%	61,000
9. Athletes and Sports Competitors	$39,930	21.1%	6,000
10. First-Line Supervisors/Managers of Housekeeping and Janitorial Workers	$30,330	19.0%	21,000
11. Flight Attendants	$46,680	16.3%	7,000
12. First-Line Supervisors/Managers of Production and Operating Workers	$46,140	2.7%	89,000
13. First-Line Supervisors/Managers of Retail Sales Workers	$32,840	3.8%	229,000
14. Gaming Supervisors	$40,300	16.3%	8,000
15. Industrial Production Managers	$75,580	0.8%	13,000
16. Driver/Sales Workers	$20,120	13.8%	72,000
17. Hairdressers, Hairstylists, and Cosmetologists	$20,610	16.1%	59,000
18. Umpires, Referees, and Other Sports Officials	$21,610	19.0%	6,000
19. First-Line Supervisors/Managers of Helpers, Laborers, and Material Movers, Hand	$39,000	8.1%	15,000
20. Transit and Railroad Police	$48,850	9.2%	fewer than 500
21. Funeral Directors	$47,630	6.7%	3,000
22. Supervisors, Farming, Fishing, and Forestry Workers	$36,030	3.6%	11,000

Best Jobs Not Behind a Desk for People with a Conventional Personality Type

Job	Annual Earnings	Percent Growth	Annual Openings
1. Detectives and Criminal Investigators	$55,790	16.3%	9,000
2. Construction and Building Inspectors	$44,720	22.3%	6,000
3. Postal Service Mail Carriers	$46,330	0.0%	19,000
4. Postal Service Clerks	$48,310	0.0%	4,000
5. Audio and Video Equipment Technicians	$32,940	18.1%	5,000
6. Audio-Visual Collections Specialists	$40,260	18.6%	1,000

PART II

Descriptions of the Best Jobs Not Behind a Desk

This part provides descriptions for all the jobs included in the lists in Part I. The Introduction gives more details on how to use and interpret the job descriptions, but here is some additional information:

- Job descriptions are arranged in alphabetical order by job title. This approach allows you to find a description quickly if you know its correct title from one of the lists in Part I.

- In some cases, a job title that appears in Part I is linked to two or more different job titles in Part II. For example, if you look for the job title Carpenters, you will find it listed here alphabetically, but a note will tell you to see the descriptions for Construction Carpenters and Rough Carpenters. These job titles are also listed alphabetically, so you can find the descriptions easily.

- If you are using this section to browse for interesting options, we suggest you begin with the Table of Contents. Part I features many interesting lists that will help you identify job titles to explore in more detail. If you have not browsed the lists in Part I, consider spending some time there. The lists are interesting and will help you identify job titles you can find described in the material that follows. The job titles in Part II are also listed in the Table of Contents.

Aircraft Mechanics and Service Technicians

- ◎ Education/Training Required: Postsecondary vocational training
- ◎ Annual Earnings: $47,310
- ◎ Growth: 13.4%
- ◎ Annual Job Openings: 11,000
- ◎ Self-Employed: 3.0%
- ◎ Part-Time: 1.8%

Diagnose, adjust, repair, or overhaul aircraft engines and assemblies, such as hydraulic and pneumatic systems. Read and interpret maintenance manuals, service bulletins, and other specifications to determine the feasibility and method of repairing or replacing malfunctioning or damaged components. Inspect completed work to certify that maintenance meets standards and that aircraft are ready for operation. Maintain repair logs, documenting all preventive and corrective aircraft maintenance. Conduct routine and special inspections as required by regulations. Examine and inspect aircraft components, including landing gear, hydraulic systems, and de-icers, to locate cracks, breaks, leaks, or other problem. Inspect airframes for wear or other defects. Maintain, repair, and rebuild aircraft structures; functional components; and parts such as wings and fuselage, rigging, hydraulic units, oxygen systems, fuel systems, electrical systems, gaskets, and seals. Measure the tension of control cables. Replace or repair worn, defective, or damaged components, using hand tools, gauges, and testing equipment. Measure parts for wear, using

precision instruments. Assemble and install electrical, plumbing, mechanical, hydraulic, and structural components and accessories, using hand tools and power tools. Test operation of engines and other systems, using test equipment such as ignition analyzers, compression checkers, distributor timers, and ammeters. Obtain fuel and oil samples and check them for contamination. Reassemble engines following repair or inspection and re-install engines in aircraft. Read and interpret pilots' descriptions of problems in order to diagnose causes. Modify aircraft structures, space vehicles, systems, or components, following drawings, schematics, charts, engineering orders, and technical publications. Install and align repaired or replacement parts for subsequent riveting or welding, using clamps and wrenches. Locate and mark dimensions and reference lines on defective or replacement parts, using templates, scribes, compasses, and steel rules. Clean, strip, prime, and sand structural surfaces and materials to prepare them for bonding. Service and maintain aircraft and related apparatus by performing activities such as flushing crankcases, cleaning screens, and lubricating moving parts.

LEVEL OF ACTIVITY (out of 100)—General Physical Activity: 62.6. **Sitting:** 36.1. **Outdoors:** 31.5.

SKILLS—Repairing; Equipment Maintenance; Operation Monitoring; Installation; Troubleshooting; Operation and Control; Quality Control Analysis; Complex Problem Solving.

GOE—Interest Area: 13. Manufacturing. **Work Group:** 13.14. Vehicle and Facility Mechanical Work. **Other Jobs in This Work Group:** Aircraft Structure, Surfaces, Rigging, and Systems Assemblers; Automotive Body and Related Repairers; Automotive Glass Installers and Repairers; Automotive Master Mechanics;

Automotive Service Technicians and Mechanics; Automotive Specialty Technicians; Bus and Truck Mechanics and Diesel Engine Specialists; Farm Equipment Mechanics; Fiberglass Laminators and Fabricators; Mobile Heavy Equipment Mechanics, Except Engines; Motorboat Mechanics; Motorcycle Mechanics; Outdoor Power Equipment and Other Small Engine Mechanics; Rail Car Repairers; Recreational Vehicle Service Technicians; Tire Repairers and Changers. **PERSONALITY TYPE:** Investigative. Investigative occupations frequently involve working with ideas and require an extensive amount of thinking. These occupations can involve searching for facts and figuring out problems mentally.

EDUCATION/TRAINING PROGRAM(S)— Agricultural Mechanics and Equipment/ Machine Technology; Aircraft Powerplant Technology/Technician; Airframe Mechanics and Aircraft Maintenance Technology/ Technician. **RELATED KNOWLEDGE/ COURSES—Mechanical Devices:** Machines and tools, including their designs, uses, repair, and maintenance. **Design:** Design techniques, tools, and principles involved in production of precision technical plans, blueprints, drawings, and models. **Physics:** Physical principles and laws and their interrelationships and applications to understanding fluid, material, and atmospheric dynamics and mechanical, electrical, atomic, and subatomic structures and processes. **Chemistry:** The chemical composition, structure, and properties of substances and of the chemical processes and transformations that they undergo. This includes uses of chemicals and their danger signs, production tech-

niques, and disposal methods. **Engineering and Technology:** The practical application of engineering science and technology. This includes applying principles, techniques, procedures, and equipment to the design and production of various goods and services. **Transportation:** Principles and methods for moving people or goods by air, rail, sea, or road, including the relative costs and benefits.

WORK ENVIRONMENT—Noisy; contaminants; cramped work space, awkward positions; standing; using hands on objects, tools, or controls; bending or twisting the body.

Aircraft Structure, Surfaces, Rigging, and Systems Assemblers

- Education/Training Required: Long-term on-the-job training
- Annual Earnings: $43,990
- Growth: 7.8%
- Annual Job Openings: 4,000
- Self-Employed: 0.0%
- Part-Time: 1.7%

Assemble, fit, fasten, and install parts of airplanes, space vehicles, or missiles, such as tails, wings, fuselage, bulkheads, stabilizers, landing gear, rigging and control equipment, or heating

and ventilating systems. Lay out and mark reference points and locations for installation of parts and components, using jigs, templates, and measuring and marking instruments. Fabricate parts needed for assembly and installation, using shop equipment. Clean, oil, and/or coat system components as necessary before assembling and attaching them. Weld tubing and fittings and solder cable ends, using tack-welders, induction brazing chambers, or other equipment. Verify dimensions of cable assemblies and positions of fittings, using measuring instruments. Swage fittings onto cables, using swaging machines. Set up and operate machines and systems to crimp, cut, bend, form, swage, flare, bead, burr, and straighten tubing, according to specifications. Set, align, adjust, and synchronize aircraft armament and rigging and control system components to established tolerances and requirements, using sighting devices and hand tools. Read and interpret blueprints, illustrations, and specifications to determine layouts, sequences of operations, or identities and relationships of parts. Assemble and fit prefabricated parts to form subassemblies. Measure and cut cables and tubing, using master templates, measuring instruments, and cable cutters or saws. Adjust, repair, rework, or replace parts and assemblies to eliminate malfunctions and to ensure proper operation. Join structural assemblies such as wings, tails, and fuselage. Install mechanical linkages and actuators and verify tension of cables, using tensiometers. Inspect and test installed units, parts, systems, and assemblies for fit, alignment, performance, defects, and compliance with standards, using measuring instruments and test equipment. Form loops or splices in cables, using clamps and fittings, or reweave cable strands. Cut, trim, file, bend, and smooth parts and verify sizes and fitting tolerances in order to ensure proper fit and clearance of parts. Attach brackets, hinges, or clips to secure or support components and subassemblies, using bolts, screws, rivets, chemical bonding, or welding. Assemble, install, and connect parts, fittings, and assemblies on aircraft, using layout tools; hand tools; power tools; and fasteners such as bolts, screws, rivets, and clamps.

LEVEL OF ACTIVITY (out of 100)—General Physical Activity: 43.9. **Sitting:** 42.9. **Outdoors:** 45.7.

SKILLS—Installation; Repairing; Equipment Maintenance; Quality Control Analysis; Troubleshooting; Operation and Control; Operation Monitoring; Equipment Selection.

GOE—Interest Area: 13. Manufacturing. **Work Group:** 13.14. Vehicle and Facility Mechanical Work. **Other Jobs in This Work Group:** Aircraft Mechanics and Service Technicians; Automotive Body and Related Repairers; Automotive Glass Installers and Repairers; Automotive Master Mechanics; Automotive Service Technicians and Mechanics; Automotive Specialty Technicians; Bus and Truck Mechanics and Diesel Engine Specialists; Farm Equipment Mechanics; Fiberglass Laminators and Fabricators; Mobile Heavy Equipment Mechanics, Except Engines; Motorboat Mechanics; Motorcycle Mechanics; Outdoor Power Equipment and Other Small Engine Mechanics; Rail Car Repairers; Recreational Vehicle Service Technicians; Tire Repairers and Changers. **PERSONALITY TYPE:** Realistic. Realistic occupations frequently involve work activities that include practical, hands-on problems and solutions. They often deal with plants; animals; and real-world materials like wood, tools, and machinery. Many of the occupations require working outside and do not involve a lot of paperwork or working closely with others.

EDUCATION/TRAINING PROGRAM(S)— Airframe Mechanics and Aircraft Maintenance Technology/Technician; Aircraft Powerplant Technology/Technician; Avionics Maintenance Technology/Technician. **RELATED KNOWLEDGE/COURSES**—**Mechanical Devices:** Machines and tools, including their designs, uses, repair, and maintenance. **Production and Processing:** Raw materials, production processes, quality control, costs, and other techniques for maximizing the effective manufacture and distribution of goods. **Design:** Design techniques, tools, and principles involved in production of precision technical plans, blueprints, drawings, and models. **Building and Construction:** The materials, methods, and tools involved in the construction or repair of houses, buildings, or other structures such as highways and roads. **Engineering and Technology:** The practical application of engineering science and technology. This includes applying principles, techniques, procedures, and equipment to the design and production of various goods and services. **Physics:** Physical principles and laws and their interrelationships and applications to understanding fluid, material, and atmospheric dynamics and mechanical, electrical, atomic, and subatomic structures and processes.

WORK ENVIRONMENT—More often indoors than outdoors; hazardous equipment; standing; kneeling, crouching, stooping, or crawling; using hands on objects, tools, or controls.

Animal Control Workers

- Education/Training Required: Moderate-term on-the-job training
- Annual Earnings: $26,780
- Growth: 14.4%
- Annual Job Openings: 4,000
- Self-Employed: 4.9%
- Part-Time: 21.3%

Handle animals for the purpose of investigations of mistreatment or control of abandoned, dangerous, or unattended animals. Investigate reports of animal attacks or animal cruelty, interviewing witnesses, collecting evidence, and writing reports. Capture and remove stray, uncontrolled, or abused animals from undesirable conditions, using nets, nooses, or tranquilizer darts as necessary. Examine animals for injuries or malnutrition and arrange for any necessary medical treatment. Remove captured animals from animal-control service vehicles and place animals in shelter cages or other enclosures. Euthanize rabid, unclaimed, or severely injured animals. Supply animals with food, water, and personal care. Clean facilities and equipment such as dog pens and animal control trucks. Prepare for prosecutions related to animal treatment and give evidence in court. Contact animal owners to inform them that their pets are at animal holding facilities. Educate the public about animal welfare and animal control laws and regulations. Write reports of activities and maintain files of impoundments and dispositions of animals. Issue warnings or citations in connection with animal-related offenses or contact police to report violations and request arrests. Answer inquiries from the public concerning animal control operations. Examine animal licenses and inspect establishments housing animals for compliance with laws. Organize the adoption of unclaimed animals. Train police officers in dog handling and training techniques for tracking, crowd control, and narcotics and bomb detection.

LEVEL OF ACTIVITY (out of 100)—General Physical Activity: 65.6. **Sitting:** 43.1. **Outdoors:** 48.5.

SKILLS—Negotiation; Active Listening; Writing; Reading Comprehension; Equipment Maintenance; Social Perceptiveness; Service Orientation; Equipment Selection.

GOE—Interest Area: 12. Law and Public Safety. **Work Group:** 12.05. Safety and Security. **Other Jobs in This Work Group:** Crossing Guards; Gaming Surveillance Officers and Gaming Investigators; Lifeguards, Ski Patrol, and Other Recreational Protective Service Workers; Private Detectives and Investigators; Security Guards; Transportation Security Screeners. **PERSONALITY TYPE:** Social. Social occupations frequently involve working with, communicating with, and teaching people. These occupations often involve helping or providing service to others.

EDUCATION/TRAINING PROGRAM(S)—Security and Protective Services, Other. **RELATED KNOWLEDGE/COURSES**—**Public Safety and Security:** Relevant equipment, policies, procedures, and strategies to promote effective local, state, or national security operations for the protection of people, data, property, and institutions. **Law and Government:** Laws, legal codes, court procedures, precedents, government regulations, executive

orders, agency rules, and the democratic political process. **Customer and Personal Service:** Principles and processes for providing customer and personal services. This includes customer needs assessment, meeting quality standards for services, and evaluation of customer satisfaction. **Biology:** Plant and animal organisms and their tissues, cells, functions, interdependencies, and interactions with each other and the environment. **Education and Training:** Principles and methods for curriculum and training design, teaching and instruction for individuals and groups, and the measurement of training effects. **Transportation:** Principles and methods for moving people or goods by air, rail, sea, or road, including the relative costs and benefits.

WORK ENVIRONMENT—More often outdoors than indoors; contaminants; disease or infections; minor burns, cuts, bites, or stings; using hands on objects, tools, or controls.

Animal Trainers

- Education/Training Required: Moderate-term on-the-job training
- Annual Earnings: $24,800
- Growth: 20.3%
- Annual Job Openings: 3,000
- Self-Employed: 58.2%
- Part-Time: 23.1%

Train animals for riding, harness, security, performance, obedience, or assisting persons with disabilities. Accustom animals to human voice and contact and condition animals to respond to commands. **Train animals according to prescribed standards for show or competition. May train animals to carry pack loads or work as part of pack team.** Observe animals' physical conditions in order to detect illness or unhealthy conditions requiring medical care. Cue or signal animals during performances. Administer prescribed medications to animals. Evaluate animals in order to determine their temperaments, abilities, and aptitude for training. Feed and exercise animals and provide other general care such as cleaning and maintaining holding and performance areas. Talk to and interact with animals in order to familiarize them to human voices and contact. Conduct training programs in order to develop and maintain desired animal behaviors for competition, entertainment, obedience, security, riding, and related areas. Keep records documenting animal health, diet, and behavior. Advise animal owners regarding the purchase of specific animals. Instruct jockeys in handling specific horses during races. Train horses or other equines for riding, harness, show, racing, or other work, using knowledge of breed characteristics, training methods, performance standards, and the peculiarities of each animal. Use oral, spur, rein, and/or hand commands in order to condition horses to carry riders or to pull horse-drawn equipment. Place tack or harnesses on horses in order to accustom horses to the feel of equipment. Train dogs in human-assistance or property protection duties. Retrain horses to break bad habits, such as kicking, bolting, and resisting bridling and grooming. Train and rehearse animals according to scripts for motion picture, television, film, stage, or circus performances. Organize and conduct animal shows. Arrange for mating of stallions and mares and assist mares during foaling.

LEVEL OF ACTIVITY (out of 100)—General Physical Activity: 77.9. **Sitting:** 28.7. **Outdoors:** 43.8.

SKILLS—Management of Financial Resources; Persuasion; Instructing; Service Orientation; Learning Strategies; Social Perceptiveness; Monitoring; Management of Material Resources.

GOE—Interest Area: 08. Health Science. **Work Group:** 08.05. Animal Care. **Other Jobs in This Work Group:** Animal Breeders; Nonfarm Animal Caretakers; Veterinarians; Veterinary Assistants and Laboratory Animal Caretakers; Veterinary Technologists and Technicians. **PERSONALITY TYPE:** Social. Social occupations frequently involve working with, communicating with, and teaching people. These occupations often involve helping or providing service to others.

EDUCATION/TRAINING PROGRAM(S)— Animal Training; Equestrian/Equine Studies. **RELATED KNOWLEDGE/COURSES— Sales and Marketing:** Principles and methods for showing, promoting, and selling products or services. This includes marketing strategy and tactics, product demonstration, sales techniques, and sales control systems. **Biology:** Plant and animal organisms and their tissues, cells, functions, interdependencies, and interactions with each other and the environment. **Customer and Personal Service:** Principles and processes for providing customer and personal services. This includes customer needs assessment, meeting quality standards for services, and evaluation of customer satisfaction. **Economics and Accounting:** Economic and accounting principles and practices, the financial markets, banking, and the analysis and reporting of financial data. **Communications and Media:** Media production, communication, and dissemination techniques and methods. This includes alternative ways to inform and entertain via written, oral, and visual media. **Clerical Practices:** Administrative and clerical procedures and systems such as word processing, managing files and records, stenography and transcription, designing forms, and other office procedures and terminology.

WORK ENVIRONMENT—Outdoors; noisy; standing; walking and running; using hands on objects, tools, or controls; repetitive motions.

Athletes and Sports Competitors

- ◉ Education/Training Required: Long-term on-the-job training
- ◉ Annual Earnings: $39,930
- ◉ Growth: 21.1%
- ◉ Annual Job Openings: 6,000
- ◉ Self-Employed: 24.5%
- ◉ Part-Time: 47.6%

Compete in athletic events. Lead teams by serving as captains. Receive instructions from coaches and other sports staff prior to events and discuss their performance afterwards. Participate in athletic events and competitive sports according to established rules and regulations. Maintain optimum physical fitness levels by training regularly, following nutrition plans, and consulting with health professionals. Exercise

and practice under the direction of athletic trainers or professional coaches in order to develop skills, improve physical condition, and prepare for competitions. Attend scheduled practice and training sessions. Assess performance following athletic competition, identifying strengths and weaknesses and making adjustments to improve future performance. Maintain equipment used in a particular sport. Represent teams or professional sports clubs, performing such activities as meeting with members of the media, making speeches, or participating in charity events.

LEVEL OF ACTIVITY (out of 100)—General Physical Activity: 91.4. **Sitting:** 40.0. **Outdoors:** 54.3.

SKILLS—Monitoring.

GOE—Interest Area: 09. Hospitality, Tourism, and Recreation. **Work Group:** 09.06. Sports. **Other Jobs in This Work Group:** Coaches and Scouts; Umpires, Referees, and Other Sports Officials. **PERSONALITY TYPE:** Enterprising. Enterprising occupations frequently involve starting up and carrying out projects. These occupations can involve leading people and making many decisions. They sometimes require risk taking and often deal with business.

EDUCATION/TRAINING PROGRAM(S)—Health and Physical Education, General. **RELATED KNOWLEDGE/COURSES**—**Biology:** Plant and animal organisms and their tissues, cells, functions, interdependencies, and interactions with each other and the environment. **Medicine and Dentistry:** The information and techniques needed to diagnose and treat human injuries, diseases, and deformities. This includes symptoms, treatment alternatives, drug properties and interactions, and preventive health-care measures.

WORK ENVIRONMENT—More often outdoors than indoors; minor burns, cuts, bites, or stings; standing; walking and running; bending or twisting the body.

Athletic Trainers

- Education/Training Required: Bachelor's degree
- Annual Earnings: $34,260
- Growth: 29.3%
- Annual Job Openings: 1,000
- Self-Employed: 4.0%
- Part-Time: 6.5%

Evaluate, advise, and treat athletes to assist recovery from injury, avoid injury, or maintain peak physical fitness. Conduct an initial assessment of an athlete's injury or illness to provide emergency or continued care and to determine whether they should be referred to physicians for definitive diagnosis and treatment. Care for athletic injuries, using physical therapy equipment, techniques, and medication. Evaluate athletes' readiness to play and provide participation clearances when necessary and warranted. Apply protective or injury preventive devices such as tape, bandages, or braces to body parts such as ankles, fingers, or wrists. Assess and report the progress of recovering athletes to coaches and physicians. Collaborate with physicians to develop and implement comprehensive rehabilitation programs for athletic injuries. Advise athletes on the proper use of equipment. Plan and implement comprehensive athletic injury and illness prevention programs. Develop training programs and routines designed to improve athletic performance. Travel with athletic teams to be available at sporting events. Instruct coaches, athletes, parents, medical personnel, and community members in the care and prevention of athletic injuries. Inspect playing fields to locate any items that could injure players. Conduct research and provide instruction on subject matter related to athletic training or sports medicine. Recommend special diets to improve athletes' health, increase their stamina, or alter their weight. Massage body parts to relieve soreness, strains, and bruises. Confer with coaches to select protective equipment. Accompany injured athletes to hospitals. Perform team-support duties such as running errands, maintaining equipment, and stocking supplies. Lead stretching exercises for team members prior to games and practices.

LEVEL OF ACTIVITY (out of 100)—General Physical Activity: 65.0. **Sitting:** 35.0. **Outdoors:** 40.3.

SKILLS—Social Perceptiveness; Management of Material Resources; Science; Time Management; Management of Financial Resources; Management of Personnel Resources; Writing; Service Orientation.

GOE—**Interest Area:** 08. Health Science. **Work Group:** 08.09. Health Protection and Promotion. **Other Jobs in This Work Group:** Dietetic Technicians; Dietitians and Nutritionists; Embalmers. **PERSONALITY TYPE:** Social. Social occupations frequently involve working with, communicating with, and teaching people. These occupations often involve helping or providing service to others.

EDUCATION/TRAINING PROGRAM(S)— Athletic Training/Trainer. **RELATED**

KNOWLEDGE/COURSES—Therapy and Counseling: Principles, methods, and procedures for diagnosis, treatment, and rehabilitation of physical and mental dysfunctions and for career counseling and guidance. Medicine and Dentistry: The information and techniques needed to diagnose and treat human injuries, diseases, and deformities. This includes symptoms, treatment alternatives, drug properties and interactions, and preventive health-care measures. Biology: Plant and animal organisms and their tissues, cells, functions, interdependencies, and interactions with each other and the environment. Psychology: Human behavior and performance; individual differences in ability, personality, and interests; learning and motivation; psychological research methods; and the assessment and treatment of behavioral and affective disorders. Customer and Personal Service: Principles and processes for providing customer and personal services. This includes customer needs assessment, meeting quality standards for services, and evaluation of customer satisfaction. Education and Training: Principles and methods for curriculum and training design, teaching and instruction for individuals and groups, and the measurement of training effects.

WORK ENVIRONMENT—More often indoors than outdoors; very hot or cold; contaminants; disease or infections; standing.

Audio and Video Equipment Technicians

- Education/Training Required: Long-term on-the-job training
- Annual Earnings: $32,940
- Growth: 18.1%
- Annual Job Openings: 5,000
- Self-Employed: 5.9%
- Part-Time: 18.3%

Set up or set up and operate audio and video equipment, including microphones, sound speakers, video screens, projectors, video monitors, recording equipment, connecting wires and cables, sound and mixing boards, and related electronic equipment for concerts, sports events, meetings and conventions, presentations, and news conferences. May also set up and operate associated spotlights and other custom lighting systems. Notify supervisors when major equipment repairs are needed. Monitor incoming and outgoing pictures and sound feeds to ensure quality and notify directors of any possible problems. Mix and regulate sound inputs and feeds or coordinate audio feeds with television pictures. Install, adjust, and operate electronic equipment used to record, edit, and transmit radio and television programs, cable programs, and motion pictures. Design layouts of audio and video equipment and perform upgrades and maintenance. Perform minor repairs and routine cleaning of audio and video equipment. Diagnose and resolve media system problems in classrooms. Switch sources of video input from one camera or studio to another, from film to live programming, or from network to local programming. Meet with directors and senior members of camera crews to discuss assignments and determine filming sequences, camera movements, and picture composition. Construct and position properties, sets, lighting equipment, and other equipment. Compress, digitize, duplicate, and store audio and video data. Obtain, set up, and load videotapes for scheduled productions or broadcasts. Edit videotapes by erasing and removing portions of programs and adding video or sound as required. Direct and coordinate activities of assistants and other personnel during production. Plan and develop pre-production ideas into outlines, scripts, storyboards, and graphics, using own ideas or specifications of assignments. Maintain inventories of audiotapes and videotapes and related supplies. Determine formats, approaches, content, levels, and media to effectively meet objectives within budgetary constraints, utilizing research, knowledge, and training. Record and edit audio material such as movie soundtracks, using audio recording and editing equipment. Inform users of audiotaping and videotaping service policies and procedures. Obtain and preview musical performance programs prior to events to become familiar with the order and approximate times of pieces. Produce rough and finished graphics and graphic designs. Control the lights and sound of events, such as live concerts, before and after performances and during intermissions.

LEVEL OF ACTIVITY (out of 100)—General Physical Activity: 61.3. **Sitting:** 41.7. **Outdoors:** 26.5.

SKILLS—Installation; Operation and Control; Troubleshooting; Equipment Maintenance; Operation Monitoring; Repairing; Technology Design; Systems Analysis.

GOE—Interest Area: 03. Arts and Communication. **Work Group:** 03.09. Media Technology. **Other Jobs in This Work Group:** Broadcast Technicians; Camera Operators, Television, Video, and Motion Picture; Film and Video Editors; Multi-Media Artists and Animators; Photographers; Radio Operators; Sound Engineering Technicians. **PERSONALITY TYPE:** Conventional. Conventional occupations frequently involve following set procedures and routines. These occupations can include working with data and details more than with ideas. Usually there is a clear line of authority to follow.

EDUCATION/TRAINING PROGRAM(S)—Agricultural Communication/Journalism; Photographic and Film/Video Technology/Technician and Assistant; Recording Arts Technology/Technician. **RELATED KNOWLEDGE/COURSES—Computers and Electronics:** Circuit boards; processors; chips; electronic equipment; and computer hardware and software, including applications and programming. **Telecommunications:** Transmission, broadcasting, switching, control, and operation of telecommunications systems. **Engineering and Technology:** The practical application of engineering science and technology. This includes applying principles, techniques, procedures, and equipment to the design and production of various goods and services. **Communications and Media:** Media production, communication, and dissemination techniques and methods. This includes alternative ways to inform and entertain via written, oral, and visual media. **Mechanical Devices:** Machines and tools, including their designs, uses, repair, and maintenance. **Design:** Design techniques, tools, and principles involved in production of precision technical plans, blueprints, drawings, and models.

WORK ENVIRONMENT—Indoors; standing; using hands on objects, tools, or controls.

Audio-Visual Collections Specialists

- ◎ Education/Training Required: Moderate-term on-the-job training
- ◎ Annual Earnings: $40,260
- ◎ Growth: 18.6%
- ◎ Annual Job Openings: 1,000
- ◎ Self-Employed: 3.8%
- ◎ Part-Time: 23.4%

Prepare, plan, and operate audio-visual teaching aids for use in education. May record, catalogue, and file audio-visual materials. Set up, adjust, and operate audio-visual equipment, such as cameras, film and slide projectors, and recording equipment, for meetings, events, classes, seminars, and videoconferences. Offer presentations and workshops on the role of multimedia in effective presentations. Attend conventions and conferences, read trade journals, and communicate with industry insiders to keep abreast of industry developments. Instruct users in the selection, use, and design of audio-visual materials and assist them in the preparation of instructional materials and the rehearsal of presentations. Maintain hardware and software, including computers, scanners, color copiers, and color laser printers. Confer with teachers to select course materials and to determine which training aids are best suited to particular grade levels. Perform simple maintenance tasks such as cleaning monitors and lenses and changing batteries and light bulbs. Develop manuals, texts, workbooks, or related materials for use in conjunction with production materials. Determine formats, approaches, content, levels, and media necessary to meet production objectives effectively and within budgetary constraints. Direct and coordinate activities of assistants and other personnel during production. Acquire, catalog, and maintain collections of audio-visual material such as films, videotapes and audiotapes, photographs, and software programs. Narrate presentations and productions. Construct and position properties, sets, lighting equipment, and other equipment. Develop preproduction ideas and incorporate them into outlines, scripts, storyboards, and graphics. Plan and prepare audio-visual teaching aids and methods for use in school systems. Produce rough and finished graphics and graphic designs. Locate and secure settings, properties, effects, and other production necessities.

LEVEL OF ACTIVITY (out of 100)—General Physical Activity: 49.1. **Sitting:** 47.3. **Outdoors:** 21.8.

SKILLS—Troubleshooting; Installation; Technology Design; Instructing; Equipment Selection; Operations Analysis; Writing; Equipment Maintenance.

GOE—Interest Area: 05. Education and Training. **Work Group:** 05.05. Archival and Museum Services. **Other Jobs in This Work Group:** Archivists; Curators; Museum Technicians and Conservators. **PERSONALITY TYPE:** Conventional. Conventional occupations frequently involve following set procedures and routines. These occupations can include working with data and details more than with ideas. Usually there is a clear line of authority to follow.

EDUCATION/TRAINING PROGRAM(S)—Educational/Instructional Media Design. **RELATED KNOWLEDGE/COURSES—Education and Training:** Principles and methods for curriculum and training design, teaching and instruction for individuals and groups, and the measurement of training effects. **Communications and Media:** Media production, communication, and dissemination techniques and methods. This includes alternative ways to inform and entertain via written, oral, and visual media. **Computers and Electronics:** Circuit boards; processors; chips; electronic equipment; and computer hardware and software, including applications and programming. **Telecommunications:** Transmission, broadcasting, switching, control, and operation of telecommunications systems. **Customer and Personal Service:** Principles and processes for providing customer and personal services. This includes customer needs assessment, meeting quality standards for services, and evaluation of customer satisfaction. **Clerical Practices:** Administrative and clerical procedures and systems such as word processing, managing files and records, stenography and transcription, designing forms, and other office procedures and terminology.

WORK ENVIRONMENT—Indoors; sitting; using hands on objects, tools, or controls.

Automotive Body and Related Repairers

- Education/Training Required: Long-term on-the-job training
- Annual Earnings: $34,810
- Growth: 10.3%
- Annual Job Openings: 18,000
- Self-Employed: 17.6%
- Part-Time: 6.7%

Repair and refinish automotive vehicle bodies and straighten vehicle frames. File, grind, sand, and smooth filled or repaired surfaces, using power tools and hand tools. Sand body areas to be painted and cover bumpers, windows, and trim with masking tape or paper to protect them from the paint. Follow supervisors' instructions as to which parts to restore or replace and how much time the job should take. Remove damaged sections of vehicles, using metal-cutting guns, air grinders, and wrenches, and install replacement parts, using wrenches or welding equipment. Cut and tape plastic separating film to outside repair areas to avoid damaging surrounding surfaces during repair procedure and remove tape and wash surfaces after repairs are complete. Prime and paint repaired surfaces, using paint spray guns and motorized sanders. Inspect repaired vehicles for dimensional accuracy and test-drive them to ensure proper alignment and handling. Mix polyester resins and hardeners to be used in restoring damaged areas. Chain or clamp frames and sections to alignment machines that use hydraulic pressure to align damaged components. Fill small dents that cannot be worked out with plastic or solder. Fit and weld replacement parts into place, using wrenches and welding equipment, and grind down welds to smooth them, using power grinders and other tools. Position dolly blocks against surfaces of dented areas and beat opposite surfaces to remove dents, using hammers. Remove damaged panels and identify the family and properties of the plastic used on a vehicle. Review damage reports, prepare or review repair cost estimates, and plan work to be performed. Remove small pits and dimples in body metal, using pick hammers and punches. Remove upholstery, accessories, electrical window-and-seat-operating equipment, and trim to gain access to vehicle bodies and fenders. Clean work areas, using air hoses, to remove damaged material and discarded fiberglass strips used in repair procedures. Adjust or align headlights, wheels, and brake systems. Apply heat to plastic panels, using hot-air welding guns or immersion in hot water, and press the softened panels back into shape by hand. Soak fiberglass matting in resin mixtures and apply layers of matting over repair areas to specified thicknesses.

LEVEL OF ACTIVITY (out of 100)—General Physical Activity: 49.3. **Sitting:** 26.3. **Outdoors:** 23.3.

SKILLS—Repairing; Installation; Equipment Maintenance; Troubleshooting; Equipment Selection; Management of Financial Resources; Management of Material Resources; Learning Strategies.

GOE—Interest Area: 13. Manufacturing. **Work Group:** 13.14. Vehicle and Facility Mechanical Work. **Other Jobs in This Work Group:** Aircraft Mechanics and Service Technicians; Aircraft Structure, Surfaces, Rigging, and Systems Assemblers; Automotive Glass Installers and Repairers; Automotive Master Mechanics; Automotive Service Technicians and Mechanics; Automotive Specialty Technicians; Bus and Truck Mechanics and Diesel Engine Specialists; Farm Equipment Mechanics; Fiberglass Laminators and Fabricators; Mobile Heavy Equipment Mechanics, Except Engines; Motorboat Mechanics; Motorcycle Mechanics; Outdoor Power Equipment and Other Small Engine Mechanics; Rail Car Repairers; Recreational Vehicle Service Technicians; Tire Repairers and Changers. **PERSONALITY TYPE:** Realistic. Realistic occupations frequently involve work activities that include practical, hands-on problems and solutions. They often deal with plants; animals; and real-world materials like wood, tools, and machinery. Many of the occupations require working outside and do not involve a lot of paperwork or working closely with others.

EDUCATION/TRAINING PROGRAM(S)— Auto Body/Collision and Repair Technology/Technician. **RELATED KNOWLEDGE/COURSES—Mechanical Devices:** Machines and tools, including their designs, uses, repair, and maintenance. **Building and Construction:** The materials, methods, and tools involved in the construction or repair of houses, buildings, or other structures such as highways and roads. **Chemistry:** The chemical composition, structure, and properties of substances and of the chemical processes and transformations that they undergo. This includes uses of chemicals and their danger signs, production techniques, and disposal methods. **Administration and Management:** Business and management principles involved in strategic planning, resource allocation, human resources modeling, leadership technique, production methods, and coordination of people and resources. **Customer and Personal Service:** Principles and processes for providing customer and personal services.

This includes customer needs assessment, meeting quality standards for services, and evaluation of customer satisfaction. **Production and Processing:** Raw materials, production processes, quality control, costs, and other techniques for maximizing the effective manufacture and distribution of goods.

WORK ENVIRONMENT—Noisy; contaminants; hazardous equipment; standing; using hands on objects, tools, or controls; repetitive motions.

Automotive Master Mechanics

This job can be found in the Part I lists under the title Automotive Service Technicians and Mechanics.

◎ Education/Training Required: Postsecondary vocational training

◎ Annual Earnings: $33,050

◎ Growth: 15.7%

◎ Annual Job Openings: 93,000

◎ Self-Employed: 14.8%

◎ Part-Time: 7.0%

The job openings listed here are shared with Automotive Specialty Technicians.

Repair automobiles, trucks, buses, and other vehicles. Master mechanics repair virtually any part on the vehicle or specialize in the transmission system. Examine vehicles to determine extent of damage or malfunctions. Test-drive vehicles and test components and systems, using equipment such as infrared engine analyzers, compression gauges, and computerized diagnostic devices. Repair, reline, replace, and adjust brakes. Review work orders and discuss work with supervisors. Follow checklists to ensure all important parts are examined, including belts, hoses, steering systems, spark plugs, brake and fuel systems, wheel bearings, and other potentially troublesome areas. Plan work procedures, using charts, technical manuals, and experience. Test and adjust repaired systems to meet manufacturers' performance specifications. Confer with customers to obtain descriptions of vehicle problems and to discuss work to be performed and future repair requirements. Perform routine and scheduled maintenance services such as oil changes, lubrications, and tune-ups. Disassemble units and inspect parts for wear, using micrometers, calipers, and gauges. Overhaul or replace carburetors, blowers, generators, distributors, starters, and pumps. Repair and service air conditioning, heating, engine-cooling, and electrical systems. Repair or replace parts such as pistons, rods, gears, valves, and bearings. Tear down, repair, and rebuild faulty assemblies such as power systems, steering systems, and linkages. Rewire ignition systems, lights, and instrument panels. Repair radiator leaks. Install and repair accessories such as radios, heaters, mirrors, and windshield wipers. Repair manual and automatic transmissions. Repair or replace shock absorbers. Align vehicles' front ends. Rebuild parts such as crankshafts and cylinder blocks. Repair damaged automobile bodies. Replace and adjust headlights.

LEVEL OF ACTIVITY (out of 100)—General Physical Activity: 59.3. **Sitting:** 22.0. **Outdoors:** 39.7.

SKILLS—Repairing; Troubleshooting; Installation; Equipment Maintenance; Active Learning; Complex Problem Solving; Operation Monitoring; Equipment Selection.

GOE—**Interest Area:** 13. Manufacturing. **Work Group:** 13.14. Vehicle and Facility Mechanical Work. **Other Jobs in This Work Group:** Aircraft Mechanics and Service Technicians; Aircraft Structure, Surfaces, Rigging, and Systems Assemblers; Automotive Body and Related Repairers; Automotive Glass Installers and Repairers; Automotive Service Technicians and Mechanics; Automotive Specialty Technicians; Bus and Truck Mechanics and Diesel Engine Specialists; Farm Equipment Mechanics; Fiberglass Laminators and Fabricators; Mobile Heavy Equipment Mechanics, Except Engines; Motorboat Mechanics; Motorcycle Mechanics; Outdoor Power Equipment and Other Small Engine Mechanics; Rail Car Repairers; Recreational Vehicle Service Technicians; Tire Repairers and Changers. **PERSONALITY TYPE:** Realistic. Realistic occupations frequently involve work activities that include practical, hands-on problems and solutions. They often deal with plants; animals; and real-world materials like wood, tools, and machinery. Many of the occupations require working outside and do not involve a lot of paperwork or working closely with others.

EDUCATION/TRAINING PROGRAM(S)—Automotive Engineering Technology/Technician; Automobile/Automotive Mechanics Technology/Technician; Medium/Heavy Vehicle and Truck Technology/Technician. **RELATED KNOWLEDGE/COURSES**—**Mechanical Devices:** Machines and tools, including their designs, uses, repair, and maintenance. **Physics:** Physical principles and laws and their interrelationships and applications to understanding fluid, material, and atmospheric dynamics and mechanical, electrical, atomic, and subatomic structures and processes. **Computers and Electronics:** Circuit boards; processors; chips; electronic equipment; and computer hardware and software, including applications and programming. **Engineering and Technology:** The practical application of engineering science and technology. This includes applying principles, techniques, procedures, and equipment to the design and production of various goods and services. **Chemistry:** The chemical composition, structure, and properties of substances and of the chemical processes and transformations that they undergo. This includes uses of chemicals and their danger signs, production techniques, and disposal methods. **Education and Training:** Principles and methods for curriculum and training design, teaching and instruction for individuals and groups, and the measurement of training effects.

WORK ENVIRONMENT—Noisy; contaminants; hazardous equipment; minor burns, cuts, bites, or stings; standing; using hands on objects, tools, or controls.

Automotive Service Technicians and Mechanics

See the descriptions of these jobs:

◉ **Automotive Master Mechanics**

◉ **Automotive Specialty Technicians**

Automotive Specialty Technicians

This job can be found in the Part I lists under the title Automotive Service Technicians and Mechanics.

◉ Education/Training Required: Postsecondary vocational training

◉ Annual Earnings: $33,050

◉ Growth: 15.7%

◉ Annual Job Openings: 93,000

◉ Self-Employed: 14.8%

◉ Part-Time: 7.0%

The job openings listed here are shared with Automotive Master Mechanics.

Repair only one system or component on a vehicle, such as brakes, suspension, or radiator. Examine vehicles, compile estimates of repair costs, and secure customers' approval to perform repairs. Repair, overhaul, and adjust automobile brake systems. Use electronic test equipment to locate and correct malfunctions in fuel, ignition, and emissions control systems. Repair and replace defective ball joint suspensions, brake shoes, and wheel bearings. Inspect and test new vehicles for damage; then record findings so that necessary repairs can be made. Test electronic computer components in automobiles to ensure that they are working properly. Tune automobile engines to ensure proper and efficient functioning. Install and repair air conditioners and service components such as compressors, condensers, and controls. Repair, replace, and adjust defective carburetor parts and gasoline filters. Remove and replace defective mufflers and tailpipes. Repair and replace automobile leaf springs. Rebuild, repair, and test automotive fuel injection units. Align and repair wheels, axles, frames, torsion bars, and steering mechanisms of automobiles, using special alignment equipment and wheel-balancing machines. Repair, install, and adjust hydraulic and electromagnetic automatic lift mechanisms used to raise and lower automobile windows, seats, and tops. Repair and rebuild clutch systems. Convert vehicle fuel systems from gasoline to butane gas operations and repair and service operating butane fuel units.

LEVEL OF ACTIVITY (out of 100)—General Physical Activity: 58.6. **Sitting:** 25.0. **Outdoors:** 47.1.

SKILLS—Repairing; Troubleshooting; Operation Monitoring; Equipment Maintenance; Installation; Equipment Selection; Active Learning; Monitoring.

GOE—Interest Area: 13. Manufacturing. **Work Group:** 13.14. Vehicle and Facility Mechanical Work. **Other Jobs in This Work Group:** Aircraft Mechanics and Service Technicians; Aircraft Structure, Surfaces, Rigging, and Systems Assemblers; Automotive Body and Related

Repairers; Automotive Glass Installers and Repairers; Automotive Master Mechanics; Automotive Service Technicians and Mechanics; Bus and Truck Mechanics and Diesel Engine Specialists; Farm Equipment Mechanics; Fiberglass Laminators and Fabricators; Mobile Heavy Equipment Mechanics, Except Engines; Motorboat Mechanics; Motorcycle Mechanics; Outdoor Power Equipment and Other Small Engine Mechanics; Rail Car Repairers; Recreational Vehicle Service Technicians; Tire Repairers and Changers. **PERSONALITY TYPE:** Realistic. Realistic occupations frequently involve work activities that include practical, hands-on problems and solutions. They often deal with plants; animals; and real-world materials like wood, tools, and machinery. Many of the occupations require working outside and do not involve a lot of paperwork or working closely with others.

EDUCATION/TRAINING PROGRAM(S)— Automotive Engineering Technology/Technician; Vehicle Emissions Inspection and Maintenance Technology/Technician; Alternative Fuel Vehicle Technology/Technician. **RELATED KNOWLEDGE/COURSES— Mechanical Devices:** Machines and tools, including their designs, uses, repair, and maintenance. **Customer and Personal Service:** Principles and processes for providing customer and personal services. This includes customer needs assessment, meeting quality standards for services, and evaluation of customer satisfaction. **Engineering and Technology:** The practical application of engineering science and technology. This includes applying principles, techniques, procedures, and equipment to the design and production of various goods and services. **Physics:** Physical principles and laws and their interrelationships and applications to understanding fluid, material, and atmospheric dynamics and mechanical, electrical, atomic, and subatomic structures and processes. **Administration and Management:** Business and management principles involved in strategic planning, resource allocation, human resources modeling, leadership technique, production methods, and coordination of people and resources. **Sales and Marketing:** Principles and methods for showing, promoting, and selling products or services. This includes marketing strategy and tactics, product demonstration, sales techniques, and sales control systems.

WORK ENVIRONMENT—Contaminants; cramped work space, awkward positions; minor burns, cuts, bites, or stings; standing; using hands on objects, tools, or controls; bending or twisting the body.

Aviation Inspectors

This job can be found in the Part I lists under the title Transportation Inspectors.

- Education/Training Required: Work experience in a related occupation
- Annual Earnings: $49,490
- Growth: 11.4%
- Annual Job Openings: 2,000
- Self-Employed: 1.9%
- Part-Time: 2.3%

The job openings listed here are shared with Freight and Cargo Inspectors and with Transportation Vehicle, Equipment, and Systems Inspectors, Except Aviation.

Inspect aircraft, maintenance procedures, air navigational aids, air traffic controls, and communications equipment to ensure conformance with federal safety regulations. Inspect work of aircraft mechanics performing maintenance, modification, or repair and overhaul of aircraft and aircraft mechanical systems in order to ensure adherence to standards and procedures. Start aircraft and observe gauges, meters, and other instruments to detect evidence of malfunctions. Examine aircraft access plates and doors for security. Examine landing gear; tires; and exteriors of fuselage, wings, and engines for evidence of damage or corrosion and to determine whether repairs are needed. Prepare and maintain detailed repair, inspection, investigation, and certification records and reports. Inspect new, repaired, or modified aircraft to identify damage or defects and to assess airworthiness and conformance to standards, using checklists, hand tools, and test instruments. Examine maintenance records and flight logs to determine if service and maintenance checks and overhauls were performed at prescribed intervals. Recommend replacement, repair, or modification of aircraft equipment. Recommend changes in rules, policies, standards, and regulations, based on knowledge of operating conditions, aircraft improvements, and other factors. Issue pilots' licenses to individuals meeting standards. Investigate air accidents and complaints to determine causes. Observe flight activities of pilots to assess flying skills and to ensure conformance to flight and safety regulations. Conduct flight test programs to test equipment, instruments, and systems under a variety of conditions, using both manual and automatic controls. Approve or deny issuance of certificates of airworthiness. Analyze training programs and conduct oral and written examinations to ensure the competency of persons operating, installing, and repairing aircraft equipment. Schedule and coordinate in-flight testing programs with ground crews and air traffic control to ensure availability of ground tracking, equipment monitoring, and related services.

LEVEL OF ACTIVITY (out of 100)—General Physical Activity: 67.7. **Sitting:** 53.6. **Outdoors:** 39.4.

SKILLS—Systems Analysis; Systems Evaluation; Troubleshooting; Operation Monitoring; Quality Control Analysis; Reading Comprehension; Judgment and Decision Making; Monitoring.

GOE—Interest Area: 07. Government and Public Administration. **Work Group:** 07.03. Regulations Enforcement. **Other Jobs in This Work Group:** Agricultural Inspectors; Compliance Officers, Except Agriculture, Construction, Health and Safety, and Transportation; Construction and Building Inspectors; Environmental Compliance Inspectors; Equal Opportunity Representatives and Officers; Financial Examiners; Fire Inspectors; Fish and Game Wardens; Forest Fire Inspectors and Prevention Specialists; Freight and Cargo Inspectors; Government Property Inspectors and Investigators; Immigration and Customs Inspectors; Licensing Examiners and Inspectors; Nuclear Monitoring Technicians; Occupational Health and Safety Specialists; Occupational Health and Safety Technicians; Tax Examiners, Collectors, and Revenue Agents; Transportation Vehicle, Equipment, and Systems Inspectors, Except Aviation. **PERSONALITY TYPE:** Realistic. Realistic occupations frequently involve work activities that include practical, hands-on problems and solutions. They often deal with plants; animals; and real-world materials like wood, tools, and machinery. Many of the occupations require working outside and do not involve a lot of paperwork or working closely with others.

EDUCATION/TRAINING PROGRAM(S)— Avionics Maintenance Technology/Technician. **RELATED KNOWLEDGE/COURSES— Mechanical Devices:** Machines and tools, including their designs, uses, repair, and maintenance. **Transportation:** Principles and methods for moving people or goods by air, rail, sea, or road, including the relative costs and benefits. **Physics:** Physical principles and laws and their interrelationships and applications to understanding fluid, material, and atmospheric dynamics and mechanical, electrical, atomic, and subatomic structures and processes. **Design:** Design techniques, tools, and principles involved in production of precision technical plans, blueprints, drawings, and models. **Chemistry:** The chemical composition, structure, and properties of substances and of the chemical processes and transformations that they undergo. This includes uses of chemicals and their danger signs, production techniques, and disposal methods. **Law and Government:** Laws, legal codes, court procedures, precedents, government regulations, executive orders, agency rules, and the democratic political process.

WORK ENVIRONMENT—More often indoors than outdoors; noisy; sitting.

Avionics Technicians

- Education/Training Required: Postsecondary vocational training
- Annual Earnings: $46,630
- Growth: 9.1%
- Annual Job Openings: 2,000
- Self-Employed: 0.0%
- Part-Time: 4.9%

Install, inspect, test, adjust, or repair avionics equipment such as radar, radio, navigation, and missile control systems in aircraft or space vehicles. Set up and operate ground support and test equipment to perform functional flight tests of electrical and electronic systems. Test and troubleshoot instruments, components, and assemblies, using circuit testers, oscilloscopes, and voltmeters. Keep records of maintenance and repair work. Coordinate work with that of engineers, technicians, and other aircraft maintenance personnel. Interpret flight test data in order to diagnose malfunctions and systemic performance problems. Install electrical and electronic components, assemblies, and systems in aircraft, using hand tools, power tools, and/or soldering irons. Adjust, repair, or replace malfunctioning components or assemblies, using hand tools and/or soldering irons. Connect components to assemblies such as radio systems, instruments, magnetos, inverters, and in-flight refueling systems, using hand tools and soldering irons. Assemble components such as switches, electrical controls, and junction boxes, using hand tools and soldering irons. Fabricate parts and test aids as required. Lay out installation of aircraft assemblies and systems, following documentation such as blueprints, manuals, and wiring diagrams. Assemble prototypes or models of circuits, instruments, and systems so that they can be used for testing. Operate computer-aided drafting and design applications to design avionics system modifications.

LEVEL OF ACTIVITY (out of 100)—General Physical Activity: 53.7. **Sitting:** 46.6. **Outdoors:** 27.3.

SKILLS—Installation; Repairing; Equipment Maintenance; Troubleshooting; Operation Monitoring; Operation and Control; Quality Control Analysis; Systems Evaluation.

GOE—Interest Area: 13. Manufacturing. **Work Group:** 13.12. Electrical and Electronic Repair. **Other Jobs in This Work Group:** Electric Motor, Power Tool, and Related Repairers; Electrical and Electronics Installers and Repairers, Transportation Equipment; Electrical and Electronics Repairers, Commercial and Industrial Equipment; Electronic Equipment Installers and Repairers, Motor Vehicles; Electronic Home Entertainment Equipment Installers and Repairers; Radio Mechanics. **PERSONALITY TYPE:** Realistic. Realistic occupations frequently involve work activities that include practical, hands-on problems and solutions. They often deal with plants; animals; and real-world materials like wood, tools, and machinery. Many of the occupations require working outside and do not involve a lot of paperwork or working closely with others.

EDUCATION/TRAINING PROGRAM(S)—Airframe Mechanics and Aircraft Maintenance Technology/Technician; Avionics Maintenance Technology/Technician. **RELATED KNOWLEDGE/COURSES—Engineering and Tech-**nology: The practical application of engineering science and technology. This includes applying principles, techniques, procedures, and equipment to the design and production of various goods and services. **Mechanical Devices:** Machines and tools, including their designs, uses, repair, and maintenance. **Computers and Electronics:** Circuit boards; processors; chips; electronic equipment; and computer hardware and software, including applications and programming. **Telecommunications:** Transmission, broadcasting, switching, control, and operation of telecommunications systems. **Production and Processing:** Raw materials, production processes, quality control, costs, and other techniques for maximizing the effective manufacture and distribution of goods. **Design:** Design techniques, tools, and principles involved in production of precision technical plans, blueprints, drawings, and models.

WORK ENVIRONMENT—Indoors; noisy; contaminants; hazardous conditions; sitting; using hands on objects, tools, or controls.

Bailiffs

- Education/Training Required: Moderate-term on-the-job training
- Annual Earnings: $33,800
- Growth: 13.2%
- Annual Job Openings: 2,000
- Self-Employed: 0.0%
- Part-Time: 2.1%

Maintain order in courts of law. Collect and retain unauthorized firearms from persons entering courtroom. Maintain order in courtroom during trial and guard jury from outside contact. Guard lodging of sequestered jury. Provide jury escort to restaurant and other areas outside of courtroom to prevent jury contact with public. Enforce courtroom rules of behavior and warn persons not to smoke or disturb court procedure. Report need for police or medical assistance to sheriff's office. Check courtroom for security and cleanliness and assure availability of sundry supplies for use of judge. Announce entrance of judge. Stop people from entering courtroom while judge charges jury.

LEVEL OF ACTIVITY (out of 100)—General Physical Activity: 50.1. **Sitting:** 44.7. **Outdoors:** 26.1.

SKILLS—Persuasion; Social Perceptiveness; Active Listening; Negotiation.

GOE—Interest Area: 12. Law and Public Safety. **Work Group:** 12.04. Law Enforcement and Public Safety. **Other Jobs in This Work Group:** Correctional Officers and Jailers; Criminal Investigators and Special Agents; Detectives and Criminal Investigators; Fire Investigators; Forensic Science Technicians; Parking Enforcement Workers; Police and Sheriff's Patrol Officers; Police Detectives; Police Identification and Records Officers; Police Patrol Officers; Sheriffs and Deputy Sheriffs; Transit and Railroad Police. **PERSONALITY TYPE:** Social. Social occupations frequently involve working with, communicating with, and teaching people. These occupations often involve helping or providing service to others.

EDUCATION/TRAINING PROGRAM(S)— Criminal Justice/Police Science. **RELATED KNOWLEDGE/COURSES—Public Safety and Security:** Relevant equipment, policies, procedures, and strategies to promote effective local, state, or national security operations for the protection of people, data, property, and institutions. **Law and Government:** Laws, legal codes, court procedures, precedents, government regulations, executive orders, agency rules, and the democratic political process. **Customer and Personal Service:** Principles and processes for providing customer and personal services. This includes customer needs assessment, meeting quality standards for services, and evaluation of customer satisfaction. **Philosophy and Theology:** Different philosophical systems and religions. This includes their basic principles, values, ethics, ways of thinking, customs, and practices and their impact on human culture. **Psychology:** Human behavior and performance; individual differences in ability, personality, and interests; learning and motivation; psychological research methods; and the assessment and treatment of behavioral and affective disorders. **Sociology and Anthropology:** Group behavior and dynamics, societal trends and influences, human migrations, ethnicity, and cultures and their history and origins.

WORK ENVIRONMENT—Indoors; contaminants; disease or infections; sitting.

Bakers

- ◎ Education/Training Required: Long-term on-the-job training
- ◎ Annual Earnings: $21,520
- ◎ Growth: 15.2%
- ◎ Annual Job Openings: 37,000
- ◎ Self-Employed: 8.1%
- ◎ Part-Time: 26.8%

Mix and bake ingredients according to recipes to produce breads, rolls, cookies, cakes, pies, pastries, or other baked goods. Operate slicing and wrapping machines. Observe color of products being baked and adjust oven temperatures, humidity, and conveyor speeds accordingly. Place dough in pans, in molds, or on sheets and bake in production ovens or on grills. Roll, knead, cut, and shape dough to form sweet rolls, pie crusts, tarts, cookies, and other products. Set oven temperatures and place items into hot ovens for baking. Set time and speed controls for mixing machines, blending machines, or steam kettles so that ingredients will be mixed or cooked according to instructions. Check the quality of raw materials to ensure that standards and specifications are met. Develop new recipes for baked goods. Order and receive supplies and equipment. Prepare and maintain inventory and production records. Direct and coordinate bakery deliveries. Measure and weigh flour and other ingredients to prepare batters, doughs, fillings, and icings, using scales and graduated containers. Combine measured ingredients in bowls of mixing, blending, or cooking machinery. Apply glazes, icings, or other toppings to baked goods, using spatulas or brushes. Adapt the quantity of ingredients to match the amount of items to be baked. Check equipment to ensure that it meets health and safety regulations and perform maintenance or cleaning as necessary. Decorate baked goods such as cakes and pastries.

LEVEL OF ACTIVITY (out of 100)—General Physical Activity: 40.4. **Sitting:** 31.4. **Outdoors:** 14.3.

SKILLS—None met the criteria.

GOE—Interest Area: 13. Manufacturing. **Work Group:** 13.03. Production Work, Assorted Materials Processing. **Other Jobs in This Work Group:** Cementing and Gluing Machine Operators and Tenders; Chemical Equipment Operators and Tenders; Cleaning, Washing, and Metal Pickling Equipment Operators and Tenders; Coating, Painting, and Spraying Machine Setters, Operators, and Tenders; Cooling and Freezing Equipment Operators and Tenders; Cutting and Slicing Machine Setters, Operators, and Tenders; Extruding and Forming Machine Setters, Operators, and Tenders, Synthetic and Glass Fibers; Extruding, Forming, Pressing, and Compacting Machine Setters, Operators, and Tenders; Food and Tobacco Roasting, Baking, and Drying Machine Operators and Tenders; Food Batchmakers; Food Cooking Machine Operators and Tenders; Furnace, Kiln, Oven, Drier, and Kettle Operators and Tenders; Heat Treating Equipment Setters, Operators, and Tenders, Metal and Plastic; Helpers—Production Workers; Meat, Poultry, and Fish Cutters and Trimmers; Metal-Refining Furnace Operators and Tenders; Mixing and Blending Machine Setters, Operators, and Tenders; Packaging and Filling Machine Operators and Tenders; Plating and Coating Machine Setters, Operators, and Tenders, Metal and Plastic; Pourers and Casters, Metal; Sawing Machine Setters, Operators, and

Tenders, Wood; Separating, Filtering, Clarifying, Precipitating, and Still Machine Setters, Operators, and Tenders; Sewing Machine Operators; Shoe Machine Operators and Tenders; Slaughterers and Meat Packers; Team Assemblers; Textile Bleaching and Dyeing Machine Operators and Tenders; Tire Builders; Woodworking Machine Setters, Operators, and Tenders, Except Sawing. **PERSONALITY TYPE:** Realistic. Realistic occupations frequently involve work activities that include practical, hands-on problems and solutions. They often deal with plants; animals; and real-world materials like wood, tools, and machinery. Many of the occupations require working outside and do not involve a lot of paperwork or working closely with others.

EDUCATION/TRAINING PROGRAM(S)— Baking and Pastry Arts/Baker/Pastry Chef. **RELATED KNOWLEDGE/COURSES— Production and Processing:** Raw materials, production processes, quality control, costs, and other techniques for maximizing the effective manufacture and distribution of goods. **Food Production:** Techniques and equipment for planting, growing, and harvesting food products (both plant and animal) for consumption, including storage/handling techniques.

WORK ENVIRONMENT—Indoors; minor burns, cuts, bites, or stings; standing; using hands on objects, tools, or controls.

Boilermakers

- Education/Training Required: Long-term on-the-job training
- Annual Earnings: $48,050
- Growth: 8.7%
- Annual Job Openings: 2,000
- Self-Employed: 0.0%
- Part-Time: No data available

Construct, assemble, maintain, and repair stationary steam boilers and boiler house auxiliaries. Align structures or plate sections to assemble boiler frame tanks or vats, following blueprints. Work involves use of hand and power tools, plumb bobs, levels, wedges, dogs, or turnbuckles. Assist in testing assembled vessels. Direct cleaning of boilers and boiler furnaces. Inspect and repair boiler fittings, such as safety valves, regulators, automatic-control mechanisms, water columns, and auxiliary machines. Repair or replace defective pressure vessel parts, such as safety valves and regulators, using torches, jacks, caulking hammers, power saws, threading dies, welding equipment, and metalworking machinery. Shape and fabricate parts, such as stacks, uptakes, and chutes, in order to adapt pressure vessels, heat exchangers, and piping to premises, using heavy-metalworking machines such as brakes, rolls, and drill presses. Clean pressure vessel equipment, using scrapers, wire brushes, and cleaning solvents. Attach rigging and signal crane or hoist operators to lift heavy frame and plate sections and other parts into place. Assemble large vessels in an on-site fabrication shop prior to installation in order to ensure proper fit. Study blueprints to determine locations, relationships, and dimensions of parts. Straighten or reshape bent pressure vessel plates and structure parts, using hammers, jacks, and torches. Shape seams, joints, and irregular edges of pressure vessel sections and structural parts in order to attain specified fit of parts, using cutting torches, hammers, files, and metalworking machines. Locate and mark reference points for columns or plates on boiler foundations, following blueprints and using straightedges, squares, transits, and measuring instruments. Lay out plate, sheet steel, or other heavy metal and locate and mark bending and cutting lines, using protractors, compasses, and drawing instruments or templates. Install refractory bricks and other heat-resistant materials in fireboxes of pressure vessels. Install manholes, handholes, taps, tubes, valves, gauges, and feedwater connections in drums of water tube boilers, using hand tools. Inspect assembled vessels and individual components, such as tubes, fittings, valves, controls, and auxiliary mechanisms, to locate any defects. Examine boilers, pressure vessels, tanks, and vats to locate defects such as leaks, weak spots, and defective sections so that they can be repaired. Bolt or arc-weld pressure vessel structures and parts together, using wrenches and welding equipment. Bell, bead with power hammers, or weld pressure vessel tube ends in order to ensure leakproof joints.

LEVEL OF ACTIVITY (out of 100)—General Physical Activity: 61.9. **Sitting:** 25.0. **Outdoors:** 39.3.

SKILLS—Installation; Repairing; Equipment Maintenance; Quality Control Analysis; Troubleshooting; Systems Analysis; Operation Monitoring; Operation and Control.

GOE—Interest Area: 02. Architecture and Construction. **Work Group:** 02.04. Construction Crafts. **Other Jobs in This Work Group:** Brickmasons and Blockmasons; Carpet Installers; Cement Masons and Concrete Finishers; Commercial Divers; Construction Carpenters; Crane and Tower Operators; Drywall and Ceiling Tile Installers; Electricians; Fence Erectors; Floor Layers, Except Carpet, Wood, and Hard Tiles; Floor Sanders and Finishers; Glaziers; Hazardous Materials Removal Workers; Insulation Workers, Floor, Ceiling, and Wall; Insulation Workers, Mechanical; Manufactured Building and Mobile Home Installers; Operating Engineers and Other Construction Equipment Operators; Painters, Construction and Maintenance; Paperhangers; Paving, Surfacing, and Tamping Equipment Operators; Pile-Driver Operators; Pipe Fitters and Steamfitters; Pipelayers; Plasterers and Stucco Masons; Plumbers; Plumbers, Pipefitters, and Steamfitters; Rail-Track Laying and Maintenance Equipment Operators; Refractory Materials Repairers, Except Brickmasons; Reinforcing Iron and Rebar Workers; Riggers; Roofers; Rough Carpenters; Security and Fire Alarm Systems Installers; Segmental Pavers; Sheet Metal Workers; Stone Cutters and Carvers, Manufacturing; Stonemasons; Structural Iron and Steel Workers; Tapers; Terrazzo Workers and Finishers; Tile and Marble Setters. **PERSONALITY TYPE:** Realistic. Realistic occupations frequently involve work activities that include practical, hands-on problems and solutions. They often deal with plants; animals; and real-world materials like wood, tools, and machinery. Many of the occupations require working outside and do not involve a lot of paperwork or working closely with others.

EDUCATION/TRAINING PROGRAM(S)—Boilermaking/Boilermaker. **RELATED KNOWLEDGE/COURSES**—**Mechanical Devices:** Machines and tools, including their designs, uses, repair, and maintenance. **Building and Construction:** The materials, methods, and tools involved in the construction or repair of houses, buildings, or other structures such as highways and roads. **Engineering and Technology:** The practical application of engineering science and technology. This includes applying principles, techniques, procedures, and equipment to the design and production of various goods and services. **Physics:** Physical principles and laws and their interrelationships and applications to understanding fluid, material, and atmospheric dynamics and mechanical, electrical, atomic, and subatomic structures and processes. **Design:** Design techniques, tools, and principles involved in production of precision technical plans, blueprints, drawings, and models. **Public Safety and Security:** Relevant equipment, policies, procedures, and strategies to promote effective local, state, or national security operations for the protection of people, data, property, and institutions.

WORK ENVIRONMENT—Indoors; noisy; hazardous equipment; minor burns, cuts, bites, or stings; standing; using hands on objects, tools, or controls.

Brickmasons and Blockmasons

- Education/Training Required: Long-term on-the-job training
- Annual Earnings: $41,860
- Growth: 12.0%
- Annual Job Openings: 17,000
- Self-Employed: 28.6%
- Part-Time: No data available

Lay and bind building materials, such as brick, structural tile, concrete block, cinder block, glass block, and terra-cotta block, with mortar and other substances to construct or repair walls, partitions, arches, sewers, and other structures. Construct corners by fastening in plumb position a corner pole or building a corner pyramid of bricks and filling in between the corners using a line from corner to corner to guide each course, or layer, of brick. Measure distance from reference points and mark guidelines to lay out work, using plumb bobs and levels. Fasten or fuse brick or other building material to structure with wire clamps, anchor holes, torch, or cement. Calculate angles and courses and determine vertical and horizontal alignment of courses. Break or cut bricks, tiles, or blocks to size, using trowel edge, hammer, or power saw. Remove excess mortar with trowels and hand tools and finish mortar joints with jointing tools for a sealed, uniform appearance. Interpret blueprints and drawings to determine specifications and to calculate the materials required. Apply and smooth mortar or other mixture over work surface. Mix specified amounts of sand, clay, dirt, or mortar powder with water to form refractory mixtures. Examine brickwork or structure to determine need for repair. Clean working surface to remove scale, dust, soot, or chips of brick and mortar, using broom, wire brush, or scraper. Lay and align bricks, blocks, or tiles to build or repair structures or high-temperature equipment, such as cupola, kilns, ovens, or furnaces. Remove burned or damaged brick or mortar, using sledgehammer, crowbar, chipping gun, or chisel. Spray or spread refractory material over brickwork to protect against deterioration.

LEVEL OF ACTIVITY (out of 100)—General Physical Activity: 70.1. **Sitting:** 17.3. **Outdoors:** 39.8.

SKILLS—Equipment Maintenance; Mathematics; Installation; Management of Financial Resources; Coordination; Repairing; Technology Design; Instructing.

GOE—Interest Area: 02. Architecture and Construction. **Work Group:** 02.04. Construction Crafts. **Other Jobs in This Work Group:** Boilermakers; Carpet Installers; Cement Masons and Concrete Finishers; Commercial Divers; Construction Carpenters; Crane and Tower Operators; Drywall and Ceiling Tile Installers; Electricians; Fence Erectors; Floor Layers, Except Carpet, Wood, and Hard Tiles; Floor Sanders and Finishers; Glaziers; Hazardous Materials Removal Workers; Insulation Workers, Floor, Ceiling, and Wall; Insulation Workers, Mechanical; Manufactured Building and Mobile Home Installers; Operating Engineers and Other Construction Equipment Operators; Painters, Construction and Maintenance; Paperhangers; Paving, Surfacing, and Tamping Equipment Operators; Pile-Driver Operators; Pipe Fitters and Steamfitters; Pipelayers; Plasterers and Stucco Masons; Plumbers; Plumbers, Pipefitters, and Steamfitters; Rail-Track Laying and Maintenance Equipment Operators; Refractory Materials Repairers, Except Brickmasons; Reinforcing Iron and Rebar Workers; Riggers; Roofers; Rough Carpenters; Security and Fire Alarm Systems Installers; Segmental Pavers; Sheet Metal Workers; Stone Cutters and Carvers, Manufacturing; Stonemasons; Structural Iron and Steel Workers; Tapers; Terrazzo Workers and Finishers; Tile and Marble Setters. **PERSONALITY TYPE:** Realistic. Realistic occupations frequently involve work activities that include practical, hands-on problems and solutions. They often deal with plants; animals; and real-world materials like wood, tools, and machinery. Many of the occupations require working outside and do not involve a lot of paperwork or working closely with others.

EDUCATION/TRAINING PROGRAM(S)—Mason/Masonry. **RELATED KNOWLEDGE/COURSES—Building and Construction:** The materials, methods, and tools involved in the construction or repair of houses, buildings, or other structures such as highways and roads. **Design:** Design techniques, tools, and principles involved in production of precision technical plans, blueprints, drawings, and models. **Production and Processing:** Raw materials, production processes, quality control, costs, and other techniques for maximizing the effective manufacture and distribution of goods. **Public**

Safety and Security: Relevant equipment, policies, procedures, and strategies to promote effective local, state, or national security operations for the protection of people, data, property, and institutions. **Mechanical Devices:** Machines and tools, including their designs, uses, repair, and maintenance. **Mathematics:** Arithmetic, algebra, geometry, calculus, and statistics and their applications.

WORK ENVIRONMENT—Outdoors; very hot or cold; hazardous equipment; standing; using hands on objects, tools, or controls; bending or twisting the body.

Bus and Truck Mechanics and Diesel Engine Specialists

- ◎ Education/Training Required: Postsecondary vocational training
- ◎ Annual Earnings: $36,620
- ◎ Growth: 14.4%
- ◎ Annual Job Openings: 32,000
- ◎ Self-Employed: 5.3%
- ◎ Part-Time: 2.8%

Diagnose, adjust, repair, or overhaul trucks, buses, and all types of diesel engines. Includes mechanics working primarily with automobile diesel engines. Use hand tools such as screwdrivers, pliers, wrenches, pressure gauges, and precision instruments, as well as power tools such as pneumatic wrenches, lathes, welding equipment, and jacks and hoists. Inspect brake systems, steering mechanisms, wheel bearings, and other important parts to ensure that they are in proper operating condition. Perform routine maintenance such as changing oil, checking batteries, and lubricating equipment and machinery. Adjust and reline brakes, align wheels, tighten bolts and screws, and reassemble equipment. Raise trucks, buses, and heavy parts or equipment, using hydraulic jacks or hoists. Test-drive trucks and buses to diagnose malfunctions or to ensure that they are working properly. Inspect, test, and listen to defective equipment to diagnose malfunctions, using test instruments such as handheld computers, motor analyzers, chassis charts, and pressure gauges. Examine and adjust protective guards, loose bolts, and specified safety devices. Inspect and verify dimensions and clearances of parts to ensure conformance to factory specifications. Specialize in repairing and maintaining parts of the engine, such as fuel injection systems. Attach test instruments to equipment and read dials and gauges to diagnose malfunctions. Rewire ignition systems, lights, and instrument panels. Recondition and replace parts, pistons, bearings, gears, and valves. Repair and adjust seats, doors, and windows and install and repair accessories. Inspect, repair, and maintain automotive and mechanical equipment and machinery such as pumps and compressors. Disassemble and overhaul internal combustion engines, pumps, generators, transmissions, clutches, and differential units. Rebuild gas or diesel engines. Align front ends and suspension systems. Operate valve-grinding machines to grind and reset valves.

LEVEL OF ACTIVITY (out of 100)—General Physical Activity: 65.1. **Sitting:** 28.7. **Outdoors:** 59.4.

SKILLS—Repairing; Equipment Maintenance; Troubleshooting; Installation; Science; Technology Design; Equipment Selection; Learning Strategies.

GOE—**Interest Area:** 13. Manufacturing. **Work Group:** 13.14. Vehicle and Facility Mechanical Work. **Other Jobs in This Work Group:** Aircraft Mechanics and Service Technicians; Aircraft Structure, Surfaces, Rigging, and Systems Assemblers; Automotive Body and Related Repairers; Automotive Glass Installers and Repairers; Automotive Master Mechanics; Automotive Service Technicians and Mechanics; Automotive Specialty Technicians; Farm Equipment Mechanics; Fiberglass Laminators and Fabricators; Mobile Heavy Equipment Mechanics, Except Engines; Motorboat Mechanics; Motorcycle Mechanics; Outdoor Power Equipment and Other Small Engine Mechanics; Rail Car Repairers; Recreational Vehicle Service Technicians; Tire Repairers and Changers. **PERSONALITY TYPE:** Realistic. Realistic occupations frequently involve work activities that include practical, hands-on problems and solutions. They often deal with plants; animals; and real-world materials like wood, tools, and machinery. Many of the occupations require working outside and do not involve a lot of paperwork or working closely with others.

EDUCATION/TRAINING PROGRAM(S)— Diesel Mechanics Technology/Technician; Medium/Heavy Vehicle and Truck Technology/ Technician. **RELATED KNOWLEDGE/ COURSES—Mechanical Devices:** Machines and tools, including their designs, uses, repair, and maintenance. **Transportation:** Principles and methods for moving people or goods by air, rail, sea, or road, including the relative costs and benefits. **Public Safety and Security:** Relevant equipment, policies, procedures, and strategies to promote effective local, state, or national security operations for the protection of people, data, property, and institutions. **Physics:** Physical principles and laws and their interrelationships and applications to understanding fluid, material, and atmospheric dynamics and mechanical, electrical, atomic, and subatomic structures and processes. **Engineering and Technology:** The practical application of engineering science and technology. This includes applying principles, techniques, procedures, and equipment to the design and production of various goods and services. **Law and Government:** Laws, legal codes, court procedures, precedents, government regulations, executive orders, agency rules, and the democratic political process.

WORK ENVIRONMENT—Noisy; very bright or dim lighting; contaminants; hazardous equipment; minor burns, cuts, bites, or stings; using hands on objects, tools, or controls.

Butchers and Meat Cutters

- Education/Training Required: Long-term on-the-job training
- Annual Earnings: $26,590
- Growth: 7.9%
- Annual Job Openings: 20,000
- Self-Employed: 1.4%
- Part-Time: 10.5%

Cut, trim, or prepare consumer-sized portions of meat for use or sale in retail establishments. Wrap, weigh, label, and price cuts of meat. Prepare and place meat cuts and products in display counter so they will appear attractive and catch the shopper's eye. Prepare special cuts of meat ordered by customers. Cut, trim, bone, tie, and grind meats, such as beef, pork, poultry, and fish, to prepare meat in cooking form. Receive, inspect, and store meat upon delivery to ensure meat quality. Shape, lace, and tie roasts, using boning knife, skewer, and twine. Estimate requirements and order or requisition meat supplies to maintain inventories. Supervise other butchers or meat cutters. Record quantity of meat received and issued to cooks and/or keep records of meat sales. Negotiate with representatives from supply companies to determine order details. Cure, smoke, tenderize, and preserve meat. Total sales and collect money from customers.

LEVEL OF ACTIVITY (out of 100)—General Physical Activity: 60.7. **Sitting:** 17.0. **Outdoors:** 16.8.

SKILLS—Equipment Maintenance.

GOE—Interest Area: 09. Hospitality, Tourism, and Recreation. **Work Group:** 09.04. Food and Beverage Preparation. **Other Jobs in This Work Group:** Chefs and Head Cooks; Cooks, Fast Food; Cooks, Institution and Cafeteria; Cooks, Private Household; Cooks, Restaurant; Cooks, Short Order; Dishwashers; Food Preparation Workers. **PERSONALITY TYPE:** Realistic. Realistic occupations frequently involve work activities that include practical, hands-on problems and solutions. They often deal with plants; animals; and real-world materials like wood, tools, and machinery. Many of the occupations require working outside and do not involve a lot of paperwork or working closely with others.

EDUCATION/TRAINING PROGRAM(S)—Meat Cutting/Meat Cutter. **RELATED KNOWLEDGE/COURSES—Food Production:** Techniques and equipment for planting, growing, and harvesting food products (both plant and animal) for consumption, including storage/handling techniques. **Production and Processing:** Raw materials, production processes, quality control, costs, and other techniques for maximizing the effective manufacture and distribution of goods. **Mechanical Devices:** Machines and tools, including their designs, uses, repair, and maintenance. **Sales and Marketing:** Principles and methods for showing, promoting, and selling products or services. This includes marketing strategy and tactics, product demonstration, sales techniques, and sales control systems. **Customer and Personal Service:** Principles and processes for providing customer and personal services. This includes customer needs assessment, meeting quality standards for services, and evaluation of customer satisfaction.

WORK ENVIRONMENT—Indoors; very hot or cold; hazardous equipment; standing; using hands on objects, tools, or controls; repetitive motions.

Camera Operators, Television, Video, and Motion Picture

- ⦿ Education/Training Required: Moderate-term on-the-job training
- ⦿ Annual Earnings: $41,610
- ⦿ Growth: 14.2%
- ⦿ Annual Job Openings: 4,000
- ⦿ Self-Employed: 21.1%
- ⦿ Part-Time: 27.6%

Operate television, video, or motion picture camera to photograph images or scenes for various purposes, such as TV broadcasts, advertising, video production, or motion pictures. Operate television or motion picture cameras to record scenes for television broadcasts, advertising, or motion pictures. Compose and frame each shot, applying the technical aspects of light, lenses, film, filters, and camera settings to achieve the effects sought by directors. Operate zoom lenses, changing images according to specifications and rehearsal instructions. Use cameras in any of several different camera mounts such as stationary, track-mounted, or crane-mounted. Test, clean, and maintain equipment to ensure proper working condition. Adjust positions and controls of cameras, printers, and related equipment to change focus, exposure, and lighting. Gather and edit raw footage on location to send to television affiliates for broadcast, using electronic news-gathering or film-production equipment. Confer with directors, sound and lighting technicians, electricians, and other crew members to discuss assignments and

determine filming sequences, desired effects, camera movements, and lighting requirements. Observe sets or locations for potential problems and to determine filming and lighting requirements. Instruct camera operators regarding camera setups, angles, distances, movement, and variables and cues for starting and stopping filming. Select and assemble cameras, accessories, equipment, and film stock to be used during filming, using knowledge of filming techniques, requirements, and computations. Label and record contents of exposed film and note details on report forms. Read charts and compute ratios to determine variables such as lighting, shutter angles, filter factors, and camera distances. Set up cameras, optical printers, and related equipment to produce photographs and special effects. View films to resolve problems of exposure control, subject and camera movement, changes in subject distance, and related variables. Reload camera magazines with fresh raw film stock. Read and analyze work orders and specifications to determine locations of subject material, work procedures, sequences of operations, and machine setups. Receive raw film stock and maintain film inventories.

LEVEL OF ACTIVITY (out of 100)—General Physical Activity: 61.7. **Sitting:** 38.1. **Outdoors:** 39.1.

SKILLS—Operation Monitoring; Equipment Maintenance; Operation and Control; Troubleshooting; Active Listening; Coordination; Equipment Selection; Time Management.

GOE—Interest Area: 03. Arts and Communication. **Work Group:** 03.09. Media Technology. **Other Jobs in This Work Group:** Audio and Video Equipment Technicians; Broadcast Technicians; Film and Video Editors; Multi-Media Artists and Animators; Photographers; Radio Operators; Sound Engineering Technicians. **PERSONALITY**

TYPE: Artistic. Artistic occupations frequently involve working with forms, designs, and patterns. They often require self-expression, and the work can be done without following a clear set of rules.

EDUCATION/TRAINING PROGRAM(S)— Radio and Television Broadcasting Technology/Technician; Audiovisual Communications Technologies/Technicians, Other; Cinematography and Film/Video Production. **RELATED KNOWLEDGE/COURSES—** **Communications and Media:** Media production, communication, and dissemination techniques and methods. This includes alternative ways to inform and entertain via written, oral, and visual media. **Telecommunications:** Transmission, broadcasting, switching, control, and operation of telecommunications systems. **Computers and Electronics:** Circuit boards; processors; chips; electronic equipment; and computer hardware and software, including applications and programming. **Engineering and Technology:** The practical application of engineering science and technology. This includes applying principles, techniques, procedures, and equipment to the design and production of various goods and services. **Customer and Personal Service:** Principles and processes for providing customer and personal services. This includes customer needs assessment, meeting quality standards for services, and evaluation of customer satisfaction. **Education and Training:** Principles and methods for curriculum and training design, teaching and instruction for individuals and groups, and the measurement of training effects.

WORK ENVIRONMENT—More often indoors than outdoors; very bright or dim lighting; standing; using hands on objects, tools, or controls.

Cardiovascular Technologists and Technicians

- Education/Training Required: Associate degree
- Annual Earnings: $40,420
- Growth: 32.6%
- Annual Job Openings: 5,000
- Self-Employed: 0.4%
- Part-Time: 17.2%

Conduct tests on pulmonary or cardiovascular systems of patients for diagnostic purposes. May conduct or assist in electrocardiograms, cardiac catheterizations, pulmonary-functions, lung capacity, and similar tests. Monitor patients' blood pressure and heart rate, using electrocardiogram (EKG) equipment, during diagnostic and therapeutic procedures to notify the physician if something appears wrong. Monitor patients' comfort and safety during tests, alerting physicians to abnormalities or changes in patient responses. Explain testing procedures to patient to obtain cooperation and reduce anxiety. Prepare reports of diagnostic procedures for interpretation by physician. Observe gauges, recorder, and video screens of data analysis system during imaging of cardiovascular system. Conduct electrocardiogram (EKG), phonocardiogram, echocardiogram, stress testing, or other cardiovascular tests to record patients' cardiac activity, using specialized electronic test equipment, recording devices, and laboratory instruments. Obtain and record patient identification, medical history, or test results. Prepare and position patients for testing. Attach electrodes to the patients' chests, arms, and legs; connect electrodes to leads from the electrocardiogram (EKG) machine; and operate the EKG machine to obtain a reading. Adjust equipment and controls according to physicians' orders or established protocol. Check, test, and maintain cardiology equipment, making minor repairs when necessary, to ensure proper operation. Supervise and train other cardiology technologists and students. Assist physicians in diagnosis and treatment of cardiac and peripheral vascular treatments; for example, assisting with balloon angioplasties to treat blood vessel blockages. Operate diagnostic imaging equipment to produce contrast-enhanced radiographs of heart and cardiovascular system. Inject contrast medium into patients' blood vessels. Observe ultrasound display screen and listen to signals to record vascular information such as blood pressure, limb volume changes, oxygen saturation, and cerebral circulation. Assess cardiac physiology and calculate valve areas from blood flow velocity measurements. Compare measurements of heart wall thickness and chamber sizes to standard norms to identify abnormalities. Activate fluoroscope and camera to produce images used to guide catheter through cardiovascular system.

LEVEL OF ACTIVITY (out of 100)—General Physical Activity: 49.3. **Sitting:** 35.7. **Outdoors:** 14.9.

SKILLS—Operation Monitoring; Equipment Maintenance; Instructing; Science; Service Orientation; Active Learning; Equipment Selection; Management of Material Resources.

GOE—Interest Area: 08. Health Science. **Work Group:** 08.06. Medical Technology. **Other Jobs in This Work Group:** Biological Technicians; Diagnostic Medical Sonographers; Medical and Clinical Laboratory Technicians; Medical and Clinical Laboratory Technologists; Medical Equipment Preparers; Medical Records and Health Information Technicians; Nuclear Medicine Technologists; Opticians, Dispensing; Orthotists and Prosthetists; Radiologic Technicians; Radiologic Technologists; Radiologic Technologists and Technicians. **PERSONALITY TYPE:** Investigative. Investigative occupations frequently involve working with ideas and require an extensive amount of thinking. These occupations can involve searching for facts and figuring out problems mentally.

EDUCATION/TRAINING PROGRAM(S)—Cardiovascular Technology/Technologist; Electrocardiograph Technology/Technician; Perfusion Technology/Perfusionist; Cardiopulmonary Technology/Technologist. **RELATED KNOWLEDGE/COURSES—Medicine and Dentistry:** The information and techniques needed to diagnose and treat human injuries, diseases, and deformities. This includes symptoms, treatment alternatives, drug properties and interactions, and preventive health-care measures. **Customer and Personal Service:** Principles and processes for providing customer and personal services. This includes customer needs assessment, meeting quality standards for services, and evaluation of customer satisfaction. **Psychology:** Human behavior and performance; individual differences in ability, personality, and interests; learning and motivation; psychological research methods; and the assessment and treatment of behavioral and affective disorders. **Physics:** Physical principles and laws and their interrelationships and applications to understanding fluid, material, and atmospheric dynamics and mechanical, electrical, atomic, and subatomic structures and processes. **Biology:** Plant and animal organisms and their tissues, cells, functions, interdependencies, and interactions with each other and the environment. **Therapy and Counseling:** Principles, methods, and procedures for diagnosis, treatment, and rehabilitation of physical and mental dysfunctions and for career counseling and guidance.

WORK ENVIRONMENT—Indoors; radiation; disease or infections; standing; walking and running; using hands on objects, tools, or controls.

Carpenters

See the descriptions of these jobs:

- **Construction Carpenters**
- **Rough Carpenters**

Carpet Installers

- Education/Training Required: Moderate-term on-the-job training
- Annual Earnings: $33,550
- Growth: 8.4%
- Annual Job Openings: 11,000
- Self-Employed: 46.4%
- Part-Time: 12.3%

Lay and install carpet from rolls or blocks on floors. Install padding and trim flooring materials. Join edges of carpet and seam edges where necessary by sewing or by using tape with glue and heated carpet iron. Cut and trim carpet to fit along wall edges, openings, and projections, finishing the edges with a wall trimmer. Roll out, measure, mark, and cut carpeting to size with a carpet knife, following floor sketches and allowing extra carpet for final fitting. Inspect the surface to be covered to determine its condition and correct any imperfections that might show through carpet or cause carpet to wear unevenly. Plan the layout of the carpet, allowing for expected traffic patterns and placing seams for best appearance and longest wear. Stretch carpet to align with walls and ensure a smooth surface and press carpet in place over tack strips or use staples, tape, tacks, or glue to hold carpet in place. Take measurements and study floor sketches to calculate the area to be carpeted and the amount of material needed. Cut carpet padding to size and install padding, following prescribed method. Install carpet on some floors using adhesive, following prescribed method. Nail tack strips around area to be carpeted or use old strips to attach edges of new carpet. Fasten metal treads across door openings or where carpet meets flooring to hold carpet in place. Measure, cut, and install tackless strips along the baseboard or wall. Draw building diagrams and record dimensions. Move furniture from area to be carpeted and remove old carpet and padding. Cut and bind material.

LEVEL OF ACTIVITY (out of 100)—General Physical Activity: 80.3. **Sitting:** 23.4. **Outdoors:** 36.1.

SKILLS—Installation; Equipment Selection; Repairing; Management of Personnel Resources; Mathematics; Equipment Maintenance; Coordination; Complex Problem Solving.

GOE—**Interest Area:** 02. Architecture and Construction. **Work Group:** 02.04. Construction Crafts. **Other Jobs in This Work Group:** Boilermakers; Brickmasons and Blockmasons; Cement Masons and Concrete Finishers; Commercial Divers; Construction Carpenters; Crane and Tower Operators; Drywall and Ceiling Tile Installers; Electricians; Fence Erectors; Floor Layers, Except Carpet, Wood, and Hard Tiles; Floor Sanders and Finishers; Glaziers; Hazardous Materials Removal Workers; Insulation Workers, Floor, Ceiling, and Wall; Insulation Workers, Mechanical; Manufactured Building and Mobile Home Installers; Operating Engineers and Other Construction Equipment Operators; Painters, Construction and Maintenance; Paperhangers; Paving, Surfacing, and Tamping Equipment Operators; Pile-Driver Operators; Pipe Fitters and Steamfitters; Pipelayers; Plasterers and Stucco Masons; Plumbers; Plumbers, Pipefitters, and Steamfitters; Rail-Track Laying and Maintenance Equipment Operators; Refractory Materials Repairers, Except Brickmasons; Reinforcing Iron and Rebar Workers; Riggers; Roofers; Rough Carpenters; Security and Fire Alarm Systems Installers; Segmental Pavers; Sheet Metal Workers; Stone Cutters and Carvers, Manufacturing; Stonemasons; Structural Iron and Steel Workers; Tapers; Terrazzo Workers and Finishers; Tile and Marble Setters. **PERSONALITY TYPE:** Realistic. Realistic occupations frequently involve work activities that include practical, hands-on problems and solutions. They often deal with plants; animals; and real-world materials like wood, tools, and machinery.

Many of the occupations require working outside and do not involve a lot of paperwork or working closely with others.

EDUCATION/TRAINING PROGRAM(S)—Construction Trades, Other. **RELATED KNOWLEDGE/COURSES—Building and Construction:** The materials, methods, and tools involved in the construction or repair of houses, buildings, or other structures such as highways and roads. **Public Safety and Security:** Relevant equipment, policies, procedures, and strategies to promote effective local, state, or national security operations for the protection of people, data, property, and institutions. **Sales and Marketing:** Principles and methods for showing, promoting, and selling products or services. This includes marketing strategy and tactics, product demonstration, sales techniques, and sales control systems. **Transportation:** Principles and methods for moving people or goods by air, rail, sea, or road, including the relative costs and benefits. **Design:** Design techniques, tools, and principles involved in production of precision technical plans, blueprints, drawings, and models. **Mechanical Devices:** Machines and tools, including their designs, uses, repair, and maintenance.

WORK ENVIRONMENT—Minor burns, cuts, bites, or stings; standing; walking and running; kneeling, crouching, stooping, or crawling; using hands on objects, tools, or controls; bending or twisting the body.

Cement Masons and Concrete Finishers

- Education/Training Required: Moderate-term on-the-job training
- Annual Earnings: $32,030
- Growth: 15.9%
- Annual Job Openings: 32,000
- Self-Employed: 3.1%
- Part-Time: 8.5%

Smooth and finish surfaces of poured concrete, such as floors, walks, sidewalks, roads, or curbs, using a variety of hand and power tools. Align forms for sidewalks, curbs, or gutters; patch voids; use saws to cut expansion joints. Check the forms that hold the concrete to see that they are properly constructed. Set the forms that hold concrete to the desired pitch and depth and align them. Spread, level, and smooth concrete, using rake, shovel, hand or power trowel, hand or power screed, and float. Mold expansion joints and edges, using edging tools, jointers, and straightedge. Monitor how the wind, heat, or cold affect the curing of the concrete throughout the entire process. Signal truck driver to position truck to facilitate pouring concrete and move chute to direct concrete on forms. Produce rough concrete surface, using broom. Operate power vibrator to compact concrete. Direct the casting of the concrete and supervise laborers who use shovels or special tools to spread it. Mix cement, sand, and water to produce concrete, grout, or slurry, using hoe, trowel, tamper, scraper, or concrete-mixing machine. Cut out damaged areas, drill holes for reinforcing rods, and position reinforcing rods to repair concrete, using power saw and drill. Wet surface to prepare for bonding, fill holes and cracks with grout or slurry, and smooth, using trowel. Wet concrete surface and rub with stone to smooth surface and obtain specified finish. Clean chipped area, using wire brush, and feel and observe surface to determine if it is rough or uneven. Apply hardening and sealing compounds to cure surface of concrete and waterproof or restore surface. Chip, scrape, and grind high spots, ridges, and rough projections to finish concrete, using pneumatic chisels, power grinders, or hand tools. Spread roofing paper on surface of foundation and spread concrete onto roofing paper with trowel to form terrazzo base. Build wooden molds and clamp molds around area to be repaired, using hand tools. Sprinkle colored marble or stone chips, powdered steel, or coloring powder over surface to produce prescribed finish. Cut metal division strips and press them into terrazzo base so that top edges form desired design or pattern. Fabricate concrete beams, columns, and panels. Waterproof or restore concrete surfaces, using appropriate compounds.

LEVEL OF ACTIVITY (out of 100)—General Physical Activity: 65.4. **Sitting:** 24.3. **Outdoors:** 54.0.

SKILLS—Mathematics; Installation; Repairing; Equipment Maintenance; Coordination; Equipment Selection; Persuasion; Active Learning.

GOE—Interest Area: 02. Architecture and Construction. **Work Group:** 02.04. Construction Crafts. **Other Jobs in This Work Group:** Boilermakers; Brickmasons and Blockmasons; Carpet Installers; Commercial Divers; Construction Carpenters; Crane and Tower Operators; Drywall and Ceiling Tile Installers; Electricians; Fence Erectors; Floor Layers, Except Carpet, Wood, and Hard Tiles; Floor Sanders and Finishers; Glaziers;

Hazardous Materials Removal Workers; Insulation Workers, Floor, Ceiling, and Wall; Insulation Workers, Mechanical; Manufactured Building and Mobile Home Installers; Operating Engineers and Other Construction Equipment Operators; Painters, Construction and Maintenance; Paperhangers; Paving, Surfacing, and Tamping Equipment Operators; Pile-Driver Operators; Pipe Fitters and Steamfitters; Pipelayers; Plasterers and Stucco Masons; Plumbers; Plumbers, Pipefitters, and Steamfitters; Rail-Track Laying and Maintenance Equipment Operators; Refractory Materials Repairers, Except Brickmasons; Reinforcing Iron and Rebar Workers; Riggers; Roofers; Rough Carpenters; Security and Fire Alarm Systems Installers; Segmental Pavers; Sheet Metal Workers; Stone Cutters and Carvers, Manufacturing; Stonemasons; Structural Iron and Steel Workers; Tapers; Terrazzo Workers and Finishers; Tile and Marble Setters. **PERSONALITY TYPE:** Realistic. Realistic occupations frequently involve work activities that include practical, hands-on problems and solutions. They often deal with plants; animals; and real-world materials like wood, tools, and machinery. Many of the occupations require working outside and do not involve a lot of paperwork or working closely with others.

EDUCATION/TRAINING PROGRAM(S)— Concrete Finishing/Concrete Finisher. **RELATED KNOWLEDGE/COURSES—Building and Construction:** The materials, methods, and tools involved in the construction or repair of houses, buildings, or other structures such as highways and roads. **Foreign Language:** The structure and content of a foreign (non-English) language, including the meaning and spelling of words, rules of composition and grammar, and pronunciation. **Mechanical Devices:** Machines

and tools, including their designs, uses, repair, and maintenance. **Design:** Design techniques, tools, and principles involved in production of precision technical plans, blueprints, drawings, and models. **Administration and Management:** Business and management principles involved in strategic planning, resource allocation, human resources modeling, leadership technique, production methods, and coordination of people and resources. **Engineering and Technology:** The practical application of engineering science and technology. This includes applying principles, techniques, procedures, and equipment to the design and production of various goods and services.

WORK ENVIRONMENT—Outdoors; noisy; hazardous equipment; standing; using hands on objects, tools, or controls; bending or twisting the body.

Chemical Plant and System Operators

- ◎ Education/Training Required: Long-term on-the-job training
- ◎ Annual Earnings: $46,710
- ◎ Growth: –17.7%
- ◎ Annual Job Openings: 8,000
- ◎ Self-Employed: 0.1%
- ◎ Part-Time: 0.8%

Control or operate an entire chemical process or system of machines. Move control settings to make necessary adjustments on equipment units affecting speeds of chemical reactions, quality, and yields. Monitor recording instruments, flowmeters, panel lights, and other indicators and listen for warning signals in order to verify conformity of process conditions. Control or operate chemical processes or systems of machines, using panelboards, control boards, or semi-automatic equipment. Record operating data such as process conditions, test results, and instrument readings. Confer with technical and supervisory personnel to report or resolve conditions affecting safety, efficiency, and product quality. Draw samples of products and conduct quality control tests in order to monitor processing and to ensure that standards are met. Regulate or shut down equipment during emergency situations, as directed by supervisory personnel. Start pumps to wash and rinse reactor vessels; to exhaust gases and vapors; to regulate the flow of oil, steam, air, and perfume to towers; and to add products to converter or blending vessels. Interpret chemical reactions visible through sight glasses or on television monitors and review laboratory test reports for process adjustments. Patrol work areas to ensure that solutions in tanks and troughs are not in danger of overflowing. Notify maintenance, stationary-engineering, and other auxiliary personnel to correct equipment malfunctions and to adjust power, steam, water, or air supplies. Direct workers engaged in operating machinery that regulates the flow of materials and products. Inspect operating units such as towers, soap-spray storage tanks, scrubbers, collectors, and driers to ensure that all are functioning and to maintain maximum efficiency. Turn valves to regulate flow of products or byproducts through agitator tanks, storage drums, or neutralizer tanks. Calculate material requirements or yields according to formulas. Gauge tank levels, using calibrated rods. Repair and replace damaged equipment. Defrost frozen valves, using steam hoses. Supervise the cleaning of towers, strainers, and spray tips.

LEVEL OF ACTIVITY (out of 100)—General Physical Activity: 74.0. **Sitting:** 42.0. **Outdoors:** 43.9.

SKILLS—Operation Monitoring; Operation and Control; Troubleshooting; Equipment Maintenance; Systems Analysis; Science; Operations Analysis; Repairing.

GOE—**Interest Area:** 13. Manufacturing. **Work Group:** 13.16. Utility Operation and Energy Distribution. **Other Jobs in This Work Group:** Gas Compressor and Gas Pumping Station Operators; Gas Plant Operators; Nuclear Power Reactor Operators; Petroleum Pump System Operators, Refinery Operators, and Gaugers; Power Distributors and Dispatchers; Power Plant Operators; Ship Engineers; Stationary Engineers and Boiler Operators; Water and Liquid Waste Treatment Plant and System Operators. **PERSONALITY TYPE:** Realistic. Realistic occupations frequently involve work activities that include practical, hands-on problems and solutions. They often deal with plants; animals; and real-world materials like wood, tools, and machinery. Many of the occupations require working outside and do not involve a lot of paperwork or working closely with others.

EDUCATION/TRAINING PROGRAM(S)—Chemical Technology/Technician. **RELATED KNOWLEDGE/COURSES**—**Production and Processing:** Raw materials, production processes, quality control, costs, and other techniques for maximizing the effective manufacture and distribution of goods. **Chemistry:** The chemical composition, structure, and properties of substances and of the chemical processes and transformations that they undergo. This includes uses of chemicals and their danger signs, production techniques, and disposal methods. **Mechanical Devices:** Machines and tools, including their designs, uses, repair, and maintenance. **Physics:** Physical principles and laws and their interrelationships and applications to understanding fluid, material, and atmospheric dynamics and mechanical, electrical, atomic, and subatomic structures and processes. **Engineering and Technology:** The practical application of engineering science and technology. This includes applying principles, techniques, procedures, and equipment to the design and production of various goods and services. **Public Safety and Security:** Relevant equipment, policies, procedures, and strategies to promote effective local, state, or national security operations for the protection of people, data, property, and institutions.

WORK ENVIRONMENT—More often indoors than outdoors; noisy; very hot or cold; contaminants; hazardous conditions.

Chemical Technicians

◎ Education/Training Required: Associate degree

◎ Annual Earnings: $38,500

◎ Growth: 4.4%

◎ Annual Job Openings: 7,000

◎ Self-Employed: 0.0%

◎ Part-Time: 5.6%

Conduct chemical and physical laboratory tests to assist scientists in making qualitative and quantitative analyses of solids, liquids, and gaseous materials for purposes such as research and development of new products or processes; quality control; maintenance of environmental standards; and other work involving experimental, theoretical, or practical application of chemistry and related sciences. Monitor product quality to ensure compliance to standards and specifications. Set up and conduct chemical experiments, tests, and analyses, using techniques such as chromatography, spectroscopy, physical and chemical separation techniques, and microscopy. Conduct chemical and physical laboratory tests to assist scientists in making qualitative and quantitative analyses of solids, liquids, and gaseous materials. Compile and interpret results of tests and analyses. Provide technical support and assistance to chemists and engineers. Prepare chemical solutions for products and processes, following standardized formulas, or create experimental formulas. Maintain, clean, and sterilize laboratory instruments and equipment. Write technical reports or prepare graphs and charts to document experimental results. Order and inventory materials to maintain supplies. Develop and conduct programs of sampling and analysis to maintain quality standards of raw materials, chemical intermediates, and products. Direct or monitor other workers producing chemical products. Operate experimental pilot plants, assisting with experimental design. Develop new chemical engineering processes or production techniques. Design and fabricate experimental apparatus to develop new products and processes.

LEVEL OF ACTIVITY (out of 100)—General Physical Activity: 42.9. **Sitting:** 34.4. **Outdoors:** 19.1.

SKILLS—Operation Monitoring; Science; Quality Control Analysis; Equipment Maintenance; Operation and Control; Repairing; Troubleshooting; Mathematics.

GOE—**Interest Area:** 15. Scientific Research, Engineering, and Mathematics. **Work Group:** 15.05. Physical Science Laboratory Technology. **Other Jobs in This Work Group:** Nuclear Equipment Operation Technicians; Nuclear Technicians. **PERSONALITY TYPE:** Realistic. Realistic occupations frequently involve work activities that include practical, hands-on problems and solutions. They often deal with plants; animals; and real-world materials like wood, tools, and machinery. Many of the occupations require working outside and do not involve a lot of paperwork or working closely with others.

EDUCATION/TRAINING PROGRAM(S)— Food Science; Chemical Technology/ Technician. **RELATED KNOWLEDGE/ COURSES—Chemistry:** The chemical composition, structure, and properties of substances and of the chemical processes and transformations that they undergo. This includes uses of chemicals and their danger signs, production techniques, and disposal methods. **Mechanical Devices:** Machines and tools, including their designs, uses, repair, and maintenance. **Computers and Electronics:** Circuit boards; processors; chips; electronic equipment; and computer hardware and software, including applications and programming. **Mathematics:** Arithmetic, algebra, geometry, calculus, and statistics and their applications. **Engineering and Technology:** The practical application of engineering science and technology. This includes applying principles, techniques, procedures, and equipment to the design and production of various goods and services. **Clerical Practices:** Administrative and clerical procedures and systems such as word processing, managing files and records, stenography and transcription, designing forms, and other office procedures and terminology.

WORK ENVIRONMENT—Indoors; noisy; contaminants; hazardous conditions; standing.

Chemists

- Education/Training Required: Bachelor's degree
- Annual Earnings: $57,890
- Growth: 7.3%
- Annual Job Openings: 5,000
- Self-Employed: 0.4%
- Part-Time: 6.6%

Conduct qualitative and quantitative chemical analyses or chemical experiments in laboratories for quality or process control or to develop new products or knowledge. Analyze organic and inorganic compounds to determine chemical and physical properties, composition, structure, relationships, and reactions, utilizing chromatography, spectroscopy, and spectrophotometry techniques. Develop, improve, and customize products, equipment, formulas, processes, and analytical methods. Compile and analyze test information to determine process or equipment operating efficiency and to diagnose malfunctions. Confer with scientists and engineers to conduct analyses of research projects, interpret test results, or develop nonstandard tests. Direct, coordinate, and advise personnel in test procedures for analyzing components and physical properties of materials. Induce changes in composition of substances by introducing heat, light, energy, and chemical catalysts for quantitative and qualitative analysis. Write technical papers and reports and prepare standards and specifications for processes, facilities, products, or tests. Study effects of various methods of processing, preserving, and packaging on composition and properties of foods. Prepare test solutions, compounds, and reagents for laboratory personnel to conduct test.

LEVEL OF ACTIVITY (out of 100)—General Physical Activity: 40.4. **Sitting:** 39.3. **Outdoors:** 20.1.

SKILLS—Science; Quality Control Analysis; Technology Design; Operation Monitoring; Management of Financial Resources; Equipment Selection; Management of Material Resources; Systems Evaluation.

GOE—Interest Area: 15. Scientific Research, Engineering, and Mathematics. **Work Group:** 15.02. Physical Sciences. **Other Jobs in This Work Group:** Astronomers; Atmospheric and Space Scientists; Geographers; Geoscientists, Except Hydrologists and Geographers; Hydrologists; Materials Scientists; Physicists. **PERSONALITY TYPE:** Investigative. Investigative occupations frequently involve working with ideas and require an extensive amount of thinking. These occupations can involve searching for facts and figuring out problems mentally.

EDUCATION/TRAINING PROGRAM(S)— Chemistry, General; Analytical Chemistry; Inorganic Chemistry; Organic Chemistry; Physical and Theoretical Chemistry; Polymer Chemistry; Chemical Physics; Chemistry, Other. **RELATED KNOWLEDGE/COURSES—Chemistry:** The chemical composition, structure, and properties of substances and of the chemical processes and transformations that they undergo. This includes uses of chemicals and their danger signs, production techniques, and disposal methods. **Mathematics:**

Arithmetic, algebra, geometry, calculus, and statistics and their applications. **Engineering and Technology:** The practical application of engineering science and technology. This includes applying principles, techniques, procedures, and equipment to the design and production of various goods and services. **Production and Processing:** Raw materials, production processes, quality control, costs, and other techniques for maximizing the effective manufacture and distribution of goods. **Computers and Electronics:** Circuit boards; processors; chips; electronic equipment; and computer hardware and software, including applications and programming. **Education and Training:** Principles and methods for curriculum and training design, teaching and instruction for individuals and groups, and the measurement of training effects.

WORK ENVIRONMENT—Indoors; contaminants; hazardous conditions; standing.

Chiropractors

- Education/Training Required: First professional degree
- Annual Earnings: $67,200
- Growth: 22.4%
- Annual Job Openings: 4,000
- Self-Employed: 49.2%
- Part-Time: 20.7%

Adjust spinal column and other articulations of the body to correct abnormalities of the human body believed to be caused by interference with the nervous system. Examine patient to determine nature and extent of disorder. Manipulate spine or other involved area. May utilize supplementary measures, such as exercise, rest, water, light, heat, and nutritional therapy. Perform a series of manual adjustments to the spine, or other articulations of the body, to correct the musculoskeletal system. Evaluate the functioning of the neuromuscularskeletal system and the spine, using systems of chiropractic diagnosis. Diagnose health problems by reviewing patients' health and medical histories; questioning, observing, and examining patients; and interpreting X rays. Maintain accurate case histories of patients. Advise patients about recommended courses of treatment. Obtain and record patients' medical histories. Analyze X rays to locate the sources of patients' difficulties and to rule out fractures or diseases as sources of problems. Counsel patients about nutrition, exercise, sleeping habits, stress management, and other matters. Arrange for diagnostic X rays to be taken. Consult with and refer patients to appropriate health practitioners when necessary. Suggest and apply the use of supports such as straps, tapes, bandages, and braces if necessary.

LEVEL OF ACTIVITY (out of 100)—General Physical Activity: 59.3. **Sitting:** 32.0. **Outdoors:** 15.0.

SKILLS—Social Perceptiveness; Science; Management of Financial Resources; Persuasion; Service Orientation; Reading Comprehension; Monitoring; Critical Thinking.

GOE—Interest Area: 08. Health Science. **Work Group:** 08.04. Health Specialties. **Other Jobs in This Work Group:** Optometrists; Podiatrists. **PERSONALITY TYPE:** Investigative. Investigative occupations frequently involve working with ideas and require an extensive amount of thinking. These occupations can involve searching for facts and figuring out problems mentally.

EDUCATION/TRAINING PROGRAM(S)— Chiropractic (DC). **RELATED KNOWL-EDGE/COURSES—Medicine and Dentistry:** The information and techniques needed to diagnose and treat human injuries, diseases, and deformities. This includes symptoms, treatment alternatives, drug properties and interactions, and preventive health-care measures. **Therapy and Counseling:** Principles, methods, and procedures for diagnosis, treatment, and rehabilitation of physical and mental dysfunctions and for career counseling and guidance. **Biology:** Plant and animal organisms and their tissues, cells, functions, interdependencies, and interactions with each other and the environment. **Psychology:** Human behavior and performance; individual differences in ability, personality, and interests; learning and motivation; psychological research methods; and the assessment and treatment of behavioral and affective disorders. **Sales and Marketing:** Principles and methods for showing, promoting, and selling products or services. This includes marketing strategy and tactics, product demonstration, sales techniques, and sales control systems. **Customer and Personal Service:** Principles and processes for providing customer and personal services. This includes customer needs assessment, meeting quality standards for services, and evaluation of customer satisfaction.

WORK ENVIRONMENT—Indoors; disease or infections; standing; using hands on objects, tools, or controls; bending or twisting the body; repetitive motions.

Choreographers

- ◎ Education/Training Required: Work experience in a related occupation
- ◎ Annual Earnings: $32,950
- ◎ Growth: 16.8%
- ◎ Annual Job Openings: 4,000
- ◎ Self-Employed: 17.7%
- ◎ Part-Time: 47.7%

Create and teach dance. May direct and stage presentations. Coordinate production music with music directors. Audition performers for one or more dance parts. Record dance movements and their technical aspects, using a technical understanding of the patterns and formations of choreography. Choose the music, sound effects, or spoken narrative to accompany a dance. Direct and stage dance presentations for various forms of entertainment. Manage dance schools or assist in their management. Seek influences from other art forms such as theatre, the visual arts, and architecture. Teach students, dancers, and other performers about rhythm and interpretive movement. Train, exercise, and attend dance classes to maintain high levels of technical proficiency, physical ability, and physical fitness. Advise dancers on how to stand and move properly, teaching correct dance techniques to help prevent injuries. Design sets, lighting, costumes, and other artistic elements of productions in collaboration with cast members. Re-stage traditional dances and works in dance companies' repertoires, developing new interpretations. Assess students' dancing abilities to determine where improvement or change is needed. Experiment with different types of dancers, steps, dances, and placements, testing ideas informally to get feedback from dancers. Direct rehearsals to instruct dancers in how to use dance steps and in techniques to achieve desired effects. Design dances for individual dancers, dance companies, musical theatre, opera, fashion shows, film, television productions, and special events and for dancers ranging from beginners to professionals. Read and study story lines and musical scores to determine how to translate ideas and moods into dance movements. Develop ideas for creating dances, keeping notes and sketches to record influences.

LEVEL OF ACTIVITY (out of 100)—General Physical Activity: 65.7. **Sitting:** 42.9. **Outdoors:** 28.6.

SKILLS—Instructing.

GOE—Interest Area: 03. Arts and Communication. **Work Group:** 03.08. Dance. **Other Jobs in This Work Group:** Dancers. **PERSONALITY TYPE:** Artistic. Artistic occupations frequently involve working with forms, designs, and patterns. They often require self-expression, and the work can be done without following a clear set of rules.

EDUCATION/TRAINING PROGRAM(S)— Dance, General; Dance, Other. **RELATED KNOWLEDGE/COURSES—Fine Arts:** The theory and techniques required to compose, produce, and perform works of music, dance, visual arts, drama, and sculpture. **Communications and Media:** Media production, communication, and dissemination techniques and methods. This includes alternative ways to inform and entertain via written, oral, and visual media. **Personnel and Human Resources:** Principles and procedures for personnel recruitment, selection, training, compensation and benefits, labor relations and

C

negotiation, and personnel information systems. **Education and Training:** Principles and methods for curriculum and training design, teaching and instruction for individuals and groups, and the measurement of training effects.

WORK ENVIRONMENT—Indoors; standing; walking and running; keeping or regaining balance; bending or twisting the body; repetitive motions.

Coaches and Scouts

- Education/Training Required: Long-term on-the-job training
- Annual Earnings: $25,990
- Growth: 20.4%
- Annual Job Openings: 63,000
- Self-Employed: 21.5%
- Part-Time: 47.6%

Instruct or coach groups or individuals in the fundamentals of sports. Demonstrate techniques and methods of participation. May evaluate athletes' strengths and weaknesses as possible recruits or to improve the athletes' technique to prepare them for competition. Those required to hold teaching degrees should be reported in the appropriate teaching category. Plan, organize, and conduct practice sessions. Provide training direction, encouragement, and motivation in order to prepare athletes for games, competitive events, and/or tours. Identify and recruit potential athletes, arranging and offering incentives such as athletic scholarships. Plan strategies and choose team members for individual games and/or sports seasons. Plan

and direct physical conditioning programs that will enable athletes to achieve maximum performance. Adjust coaching techniques based on the strengths and weaknesses of athletes. File scouting reports that detail player assessments, provide recommendations on athlete recruitment, and identify locations and individuals to be targeted for future recruitment efforts. Keep records of athlete, team, and opposing team performance. Instruct individuals or groups in sports rules; game strategies; and performance principles such as specific ways of moving the body, hands, and/or feet in order to achieve desired results. Analyze the strengths and weaknesses of opposing teams in order to develop game strategies. Evaluate athletes' skills and review performance records in order to determine their fitness and potential in a particular area of athletics. Keep abreast of changing rules, techniques, technologies, and philosophies relevant to their sport. Monitor athletes' use of equipment in order to ensure safe and proper use. Explain and enforce safety rules and regulations. Develop and arrange competition schedules and programs. Serve as organizer, leader, instructor, or referee for outdoor and indoor games, such as volleyball, football, and soccer. Explain and demonstrate the use of sports and training equipment, such as trampolines or weights. Perform activities that support a team or a specific sport, such as meeting with media representatives and appearing at fundraising events. Arrange and conduct sports-related activities, such as training camps, skill-improvement courses, clinics, and/or pre-season tryouts. Select, acquire, store, and issue equipment and other materials as necessary. Negotiate with professional athletes or their representatives in order to obtain services and arrange contracts.

LEVEL OF ACTIVITY (out of 100)—General **Physical Activity:** 82.0. **Sitting:** 36.7. **Outdoors:** 34.0.

SKILLS—Social Perceptiveness; Management of Personnel Resources; Persuasion; Instructing; Negotiation; Management of Financial Resources; Time Management; Learning Strategies.

GOE—**Interest Area:** 09. Hospitality, Tourism, and Recreation. **Work Group:** 09.06. Sports. **Other Jobs in This Work Group:** Athletes and Sports Competitors; Umpires, Referees, and Other Sports Officials. **PERSONALITY TYPE:** Enterprising. Enterprising occupations frequently involve starting up and carrying out projects. These occupations can involve leading people and making many decisions. They sometimes require risk taking and often deal with business.

EDUCATION/TRAINING PROGRAM(S)— Physical Education Teaching and Coaching; Health and Physical Education, General; Sport and Fitness Administration/Management. **RELATED KNOWLEDGE/COURSES**— **Psychology:** Human behavior and performance; individual differences in ability, personality, and interests; learning and motivation; psychological research methods; and the assessment and treatment of behavioral and affective disorders. **Education and Training:** Principles and methods for curriculum and training design, teaching and instruction for individuals and groups, and the measurement of training effects. **Sales and Marketing:** Principles and methods for showing, promoting, and selling products or services. This includes marketing strategy and tactics, product demonstration, sales techniques, and sales control systems. **Therapy and Counseling:** Principles, methods, and procedures for diagnosis, treatment, and rehabilitation of physical and mental dysfunctions and for career counseling and guidance. **Personnel and Human Resources:** Principles and procedures for personnel recruitment, selection, training, compensation and benefits, labor relations and negotiation, and personnel information systems. **Sociology and Anthropology:** Group behavior and dynamics, societal trends and influences, human migrations, ethnicity, and cultures and their history and origins.

WORK ENVIRONMENT—More often indoors than outdoors; noisy; standing; walking and running.

Conservation Scientists

See the descriptions of these jobs:

- **Park Naturalists**
- **Range Managers**
- **Soil and Water Conservationists**

Construction and Building Inspectors

- Education/Training Required: Work experience in a related occupation
- Annual Earnings: $44,720
- Growth: 22.3%
- Annual Job Openings: 6,000
- Self-Employed: 10.2%
- Part-Time: 7.8%

Inspect structures, using engineering skills to determine structural soundness and compliance with specifications, building codes, and other regulations. Inspections may be general in nature or may be limited to a specific area, such as electrical systems or plumbing. Use survey instruments; metering devices; tape measures; and test equipment, such as concrete strength measurers, to perform inspections. Inspect bridges, dams, highways, buildings, wiring, plumbing, electrical circuits, sewers, heating systems, and foundations during and after construction for structural quality, general safety, and conformance to specifications and codes. Maintain daily logs and supplement inspection records with photographs. Review and interpret plans, blueprints, site layouts, specifications, and construction methods to ensure compliance to legal requirements and safety regulations. Inspect and monitor construction sites to ensure adherence to safety standards, building codes, and specifications. Measure dimensions and verify level, alignment, and elevation of structures and fixtures to ensure compliance to building plans and codes. Issue violation notices and stop-work orders, conferring with owners, violators, and authorities to explain regulations and recommend rectifications. Issue permits for construction, relocation, demolition, and occupancy. Approve and sign plans that meet required specifications. Compute estimates of work completed or of needed renovations or upgrades and approve payment for contractors. Monitor installation of plumbing, wiring, equipment, and appliances to ensure that installation is performed properly and is in compliance with applicable regulations. Examine lifting and conveying devices, such as elevators, escalators, moving sidewalks, lifts and hoists, inclined railways, ski lifts, and amusement rides, to ensure safety and proper functioning. Train, direct and supervise other construction inspectors. Evaluate premises for cleanliness, including proper garbage disposal and lack of vermin infestation.

LEVEL OF ACTIVITY (out of 100)—General Physical Activity: 47.0. **Sitting:** 37.9. **Outdoors:** 41.5.

SKILLS—Mathematics; Persuasion; Time Management; Reading Comprehension; Quality Control Analysis; Active Learning; Active Listening; Negotiation.

GOE—Interest Area: 07. Government and Public Administration. **Work Group:** 07.03. Regulations Enforcement. **Other Jobs in This Work Group:** Agricultural Inspectors; Aviation Inspectors; Compliance Officers, Except Agriculture, Construction, Health and Safety, and Transportation; Environmental Compliance Inspectors; Equal Opportunity Representatives and Officers; Financial Examiners; Fire Inspectors; Fish and Game Wardens; Forest Fire Inspectors and Prevention Specialists; Freight and Cargo Inspectors; Government Property Inspectors and Investigators; Immigration and Customs Inspectors; Licensing Examiners and Inspectors; Nuclear Monitoring Technicians; Occupational Health and Safety Specialists; Occupational Health and Safety Technicians; Tax Examiners, Collectors, and Revenue Agents; Transportation Vehicle, Equipment, and Systems Inspectors, Except Aviation. **PERSONALITY TYPE:** Conventional. Conventional occupations frequently involve following set procedures and routines. These occupations can include working with data and details more than with ideas. Usually there is a clear line of authority to follow.

EDUCATION/TRAINING PROGRAM(S)— Building/Home/Construction Inspection/Inspector. **RELATED KNOWLEDGE/COURSES— Building and Construction:** The materials, methods, and tools involved in the construction or repair of houses, buildings, or other structures such as highways and roads. **Design:** Design techniques, tools, and principles involved in production of precision technical plans, blueprints, drawings, and models. **Engineering and Technology:** The practical application of engineering science and technology. This includes applying principles, techniques, procedures, and equipment to the design and production of various goods and services. **Public Safety and Security:** Relevant equipment, policies, procedures, and strategies to promote effective local, state, or national security operations for the protection of people, data, property, and institutions. **Mechanical Devices:** Machines and tools, including their designs, uses, repair, and maintenance. **Customer and Personal Service:** Principles and processes for providing customer and personal services. This includes customer needs assessment, meeting quality standards for services, and evaluation of customer satisfaction.

WORK ENVIRONMENT—More often outdoors than indoors; noisy; contaminants; hazardous equipment; standing.

Construction Carpenters

This job can be found in the Part I lists under the title Carpenters.

- Education/Training Required: Long-term on-the-job training
- Annual Earnings: $35,580
- Growth: 13.8%
- Annual Job Openings: 210,000
- Self-Employed: 32.4%
- Part-Time: 8.2%

The job openings listed here are shared with Rough Carpenters.

Construct, erect, install, and repair structures and fixtures of wood, plywood, and wallboard, using carpenter's hand tools and power tools. Measure and mark cutting lines on materials, using ruler, pencil, chalk, and marking gauge. Follow established safety rules and regulations and maintain a safe and clean environment. Verify trueness of structure, using plumb bob and level. Shape or cut materials to specified measurements, using hand tools, machines, or power saw. Study specifications in blueprints, sketches, or building plans to prepare project layout and determine dimensions and materials required. Assemble and fasten materials to make framework or props, using hand tools and wood screws, nails, dowel pins, or glue. Build or repair cabinets, doors, frameworks, floors, and other wooden fixtures used in buildings, using woodworking machines, carpenter's hand tools, and power tools. Erect scaffolding and ladders for assembling structures above ground level. Remove damaged or defective parts or sections of structures and repair or replace, using hand tools. Install structures and fixtures, such as windows, frames, floorings, and trim, or hardware, using carpenter's hand and power tools. Select and order lumber and other required materials. Maintain records, document actions, and present written progress reports. Finish surfaces of woodwork or wallboard in houses and buildings, using paint, hand tools, and paneling. Prepare cost estimates for clients or employers. Arrange for subcontractors to deal with special areas such as heating and electrical wiring work. Inspect ceiling or floor tile, wall coverings, siding, glass, or woodwork to detect broken or damaged structures. Work with or remove hazardous material. Construct forms and chutes for pouring concrete. Cover subfloors with building paper to keep out moisture and lay hardwood, parquet, and wood-strip-block floors by nailing floors to subfloor or cementing them to mastic or asphalt base. Fill cracks and other defects in plaster or plasterboard and sand patch, using patching plaster, trowel, and sanding tool. Perform minor plumbing, welding, or concrete mixing work. Apply shock-absorbing, sound-deadening, and decorative paneling to ceilings and walls.

LEVEL OF ACTIVITY (out of 100)—General Physical Activity: 74.9. **Sitting:** 16.0. **Outdoors:** 41.8.

SKILLS—Management of Personnel Resources; Management of Financial Resources; Management of Material Resources; Equipment Maintenance; Repairing; Quality Control Analysis; Installation; Mathematics.

GOE—Interest Area: 02. Architecture and Construction. **Work Group:** 02.04. Construction Crafts. **Other Jobs in This Work Group:** Boilermakers; Brickmasons and Blockmasons; Carpet Installers; Cement Masons and Concrete Finishers; Commercial Divers; Crane and Tower Operators; Drywall and Ceiling Tile Installers; Electricians; Fence Erectors; Floor Layers, Except Carpet, Wood, and Hard Tiles; Floor Sanders and Finishers; Glaziers; Hazardous Materials Removal Workers; Insulation Workers, Floor, Ceiling, and Wall; Insulation Workers, Mechanical; Manufactured Building and Mobile Home Installers; Operating Engineers and Other Construction Equipment Operators; Painters, Construction and Maintenance; Paperhangers; Paving, Surfacing, and Tamping Equipment Operators; Pile-Driver Operators; Pipe Fitters and Steamfitters; Pipelayers; Plasterers and Stucco Masons; Plumbers; Plumbers, Pipefitters, and Steamfitters; Rail-Track Laying and Maintenance Equipment Operators; Refractory Materials Repairers, Except Brickmasons; Reinforcing Iron and Rebar Workers; Riggers; Roofers; Rough Carpenters; Security and Fire Alarm Systems Installers; Segmental Pavers; Sheet Metal Workers; Stone Cutters and Carvers, Manufacturing; Stonemasons; Structural Iron and Steel Workers; Tapers; Terrazzo Workers and Finishers; Tile and Marble Setters. **PERSONALITY TYPE:** Realistic.

Realistic occupations frequently involve work activities that include practical, hands-on problems and solutions. They often deal with plants; animals; and real-world materials like wood, tools, and machinery. Many of the occupations require working outside and do not involve a lot of paperwork or working closely with others.

EDUCATION/TRAINING PROGRAM(S)—Carpentry/Carpenter. **RELATED KNOWLEDGE/COURSES—Building and Construction:** The materials, methods, and tools involved in the construction or repair of houses, buildings, or other structures such as highways and roads. **Design:** Design techniques, tools, and principles involved in production of precision technical plans, blueprints, drawings, and models. **Production and Processing:** Raw materials, production processes, quality control, costs, and other techniques for maximizing the effective manufacture and distribution of goods. **Mechanical Devices:** Machines and tools, including their designs, uses, repair, and maintenance. **Engineering and Technology:** The practical application of engineering science and technology. This includes applying principles, techniques, procedures, and equipment to the design and production of various goods and services. **Public Safety and Security:** Relevant equipment, policies, procedures, and strategies to promote effective local, state, or national security operations for the protection of people, data, property, and institutions.

WORK ENVIRONMENT—Outdoors; noisy; hazardous equipment; standing; walking and running; using hands on objects, tools, or controls.

Construction Laborers

- Education/Training Required: Moderate-term on-the-job training
- Annual Earnings: $25,410
- Growth: 5.9%
- Annual Job Openings: 245,000
- Self-Employed: 12.9%
- Part-Time: 12.8%

Perform tasks involving physical labor at building, highway, and heavy construction projects, tunnel and shaft excavations, and demolition sites. May operate hand and power tools of all types: air hammers, earth tampers, cement mixers, small mechanical hoists, surveying and measuring equipment, and a variety of other equipment and instruments. May clean and prepare sites; dig trenches; set braces to support the sides of excavations; erect scaffolding; clean up rubble and debris; and remove asbestos, lead, and other hazardous waste materials. May assist other craft workers. Install sewer, water, and storm drain pipes, using pipe-laying machinery and laser guidance equipment. Position, join, align, and seal structural components, such as concrete wall sections and pipes. Apply caulking compounds by hand or using caulking guns. Build and position forms for pouring concrete and dismantle forms after use, using saws, hammers, nails, or bolts. Clean and prepare construction sites to eliminate possible hazards. Control traffic passing near, in, and around work zones. Dig ditches or trenches, backfill excavations, and compact and level earth to grade specifications, using picks, shovels, pneumatic tampers, and rakes. Erect and disassemble scaffolding, shoring, braces, traffic barricades, ramps, and other temporary structures. Grind, scrape, sand, or polish surfaces such as concrete, marble, terrazzo, or wood flooring, using abrasive tools or machines. Load, unload, and identify building materials, machinery, and tools and distribute them to the appropriate locations according to project plans and specifications. Measure, mark, and record openings and distances to lay out areas where construction work will be performed. Mix ingredients to create compounds for covering or cleaning surfaces. Mop, brush, or spread paints, cleaning solutions, or other compounds over surfaces to clean them or to provide protection. Place, consolidate, and protect case-in-place concrete or masonry structures. Lubricate, clean, and repair machinery, equipment, and tools. Shovel cement and other materials into portable cement mixers; mix, pour, and spread concrete. Signal equipment operators to facilitate alignment, movement, and adjustment of machinery, equipment, and materials. Smooth and finish freshly poured cement or concrete, using floats, trowels, screeds, or powered cement-finishing tools. Spray materials such as water, sand, steam, vinyl, paint, or stucco through hoses to clean, coat, or seal surfaces. Tend machines that pump concrete, grout, cement, sand, plaster, or stucco through spray guns for application to ceilings and walls. Tend pumps, compressors, and generators to provide power for tools, machinery, and equipment or to heat and move materials such as asphalt.

LEVEL OF ACTIVITY (out of 100)—General Physical Activity: 71.4. **Sitting:** 31.4. **Outdoors:** 62.9.

SKILLS—Equipment Maintenance.

GOE—Interest Area: 02. Architecture and Construction. **Work Group:** 02.06. Construction Support/Labor. **Other Jobs in This Work Group:** Helpers—Brickmasons, Blockmasons, Stonemasons, and Tile and Marble Setters; Helpers—Carpenters; Helpers—Electricians; Helpers—Installation, Maintenance, and Repair Workers; Helpers—Painters, Paperhangers, Plasterers, and Stucco Masons; Helpers—Pipelayers, Plumbers, Pipefitters, and Steamfitters; Helpers—Roofers; Highway Maintenance Workers; Septic Tank Servicers and Sewer Pipe Cleaners. **PERSONALITY TYPE:** Realistic. Realistic occupations frequently involve work activities that include practical, hands-on problems and solutions. They often deal with plants; animals; and real-world materials like wood, tools, and machinery. Many of the occupations require working outside and do not involve a lot of paperwork or working closely with others.

EDUCATION/TRAINING PROGRAM(S)— Construction Trades, Other. **RELATED KNOWLEDGE/COURSES—Building and Construction:** The materials, methods, and tools involved in the construction or repair of houses, buildings, or other structures such as highways and roads. **Mechanical Devices:** Machines and tools, including their designs, uses, repair, and maintenance. **Engineering and Technology:** The practical application of engineering science and technology. This includes applying principles, techniques, procedures, and equipment to the design and production of various goods and services. **Production and Processing:** Raw materials, production processes, quality control, costs, and other techniques for maximizing the effective manufacture and distribution of goods.

WORK ENVIRONMENT—Outdoors; noisy; contaminants; hazardous equipment; standing; using hands on objects, tools, or controls.

Construction Managers

- Education/Training Required: Bachelor's degree
- Annual Earnings: $72,260
- Growth: 10.4%
- Annual Job Openings: 28,000
- Self-Employed: 54.2%
- Part-Time: 5.4%

Plan, direct, coordinate, or budget, usually through subordinate supervisory personnel, activities concerned with the construction and maintenance of structures, facilities, and systems. Participate in the conceptual development of a construction project and oversee its organization, scheduling, and implementation. Confer with supervisory personnel, owners, contractors, and design professionals to discuss and resolve matters such as work procedures, complaints, and construction problems. Plan, organize, and direct activities concerned with the construction and maintenance of structures, facilities, and systems. Schedule the project in logical steps and budget time required to meet deadlines. Determine labor requirements and dispatch workers to construction sites. Inspect and review projects to monitor compliance with building and safety codes and other regulations.

Prepare contracts and negotiate revisions, changes, and additions to contractual agreements with architects, consultants, clients, suppliers, and subcontractors. Interpret and explain plans and contract terms to administrative staff, workers, and clients, representing the owner or developer. Obtain all necessary permits and licenses. Direct and supervise workers. Study job specifications to determine appropriate construction methods. Select, contract, and oversee workers who complete specific pieces of the project, such as painting or plumbing. Requisition supplies and materials to complete construction projects. Prepare and submit budget estimates and progress and cost tracking reports. Take actions to deal with the results of delays, bad weather, or emergencies at construction site. Develop and implement quality control programs. Investigate damage, accidents, or delays at construction sites to ensure that proper procedures are being carried out. Evaluate construction methods and determine cost-effectiveness of plans, using computers. Direct acquisition of land for construction projects.

LEVEL OF ACTIVITY (out of 100)—**General Physical Activity:** 50.3. **Sitting:** 43.7. **Outdoors:** 35.7.

SKILLS—Repairing; Installation; Troubleshooting; Management of Material Resources; Coordination; Management of Financial Resources; Negotiation; Mathematics.

GOE—**Interest Area:** 02. Architecture and Construction. **Work Group:** 02.01. Managerial Work in Architecture and Construction. **Other Jobs in This Work Group:** No other jobs in this group. **PERSONALITY TYPE:** Enterprising. Enterprising occupations frequently involve starting up and carrying out projects. These occupations can involve leading people and making many decisions. They sometimes require risk taking and often deal with business.

EDUCATION/TRAINING PROGRAM(S)— Construction Engineering Technology/Technician; Business/Commerce, General; Business Administration and Management, General; Operations Management and Supervision; Construction Management. **RELATED KNOWLEDGE/COURSES—Building and Construction:** The materials, methods, and tools involved in the construction or repair of houses, buildings, or other structures such as highways and roads. **Design:** Design techniques, tools, and principles involved in production of precision technical plans, blueprints, drawings, and models. **Mechanical Devices:** Machines and tools, including their designs, uses, repair, and maintenance. **Administration and Management:** Business and management principles involved in strategic planning, resource allocation, human resources modeling, leadership technique, production methods, and coordination of people and resources. **Public Safety and Security:** Relevant equipment, policies, procedures, and strategies to promote effective local, state, or national security operations for the protection of people, data, property, and institutions. **Sales and Marketing:** Principles and methods for showing, promoting, and selling products or services. This includes marketing strategy and tactics, product demonstration, sales techniques, and sales control systems.

WORK ENVIRONMENT—Indoors; noisy; sitting.

Control and Valve Installers and Repairers, Except Mechanical Door

- Education/Training Required: Moderate-term on-the-job training
- Annual Earnings: $44,120
- Growth: 4.9%
- Annual Job Openings: 4,000
- Self-Employed: 0.0%
- Part-Time: No data available

Install, repair, and maintain mechanical regulating and controlling devices, such as electric meters, gas regulators, thermostats, safety and flow valves, and other mechanical governors. Operate power-driven foot pedals to raise and/or lower regulators into and out of water tanks. Disconnect and/or remove defective or unauthorized meters, using hand tools. Dip valves and regulators in molten lead to prevent leakage and paint valves, fittings, and other devices, using spray guns. Cut seats to receive new orifices, tap inspection ports, and perform other repairs in order to salvage usable materials, using hand tools and machine tools. Connect hoses from provers to meter inlets and outlets and raise prover bells until prover gauges register zero. Clean plant growth, scale, paint, soil, and/or rust from meter housings, using wire brushes, scrapers, buffers, sandblasters, and/or cleaning compounds. Attach pressurized meters to fixtures that submerge them in water and observe meters for leaks. Turn valves to allow measured amounts of air or gas to pass through meters at specified flow rates. Clamp regulator units into vises on stages above water tanks and attach compressed air hoses to intake ports. Recondition displacement-type gas meters and governors, fabricating, machining, and/or modifying parts needed for repairs. Record maintenance information, including test results, material usage, and repairs made. Reassemble repaired equipment and solder top, front, and back case panels in place, using soldering guns, power tools, and hand tools. Turn meters on or off to establish or close service. Recommend and write up specifications for changes in hardware, such as house wiring. Vary air pressure flowing into regulators and turn handles to assess functioning of valves and pistons. Collect money due on delinquent accounts. Investigate instances of illegal tapping into service lines. Report hazardous field situations and damaged or missing meters. Trace and tag meters or house lines. Repair leaks in valve seats or bellows of automotive heater thermostats, using soft solder, flux, and acetylene torches. Record meter readings and installation data on meter cards, work orders, or field service orders or enter data into hand-held computers. Mount and install meters and other electric equipment such as time clocks, transformers, and circuit breakers, using electricians' hand tools.

LEVEL OF ACTIVITY (out of 100)—General Physical Activity: 42.9. **Sitting:** 34.3. **Outdoors:** 52.4.

SKILLS—Repairing; Installation; Equipment Maintenance; Quality Control Analysis; Troubleshooting; Operation and Control; Operation Monitoring.

GOE—Interest Area: 13. Manufacturing. **Work Group:** 13.13. Machinery Repair. **Other Jobs in This Work Group:** Bicycle Repairers; Home Appliance Repairers; Industrial Machinery Mechanics; Locksmiths and Safe Repairers; Maintenance Workers, Machinery; Mechanical Door Repairers; Millwrights; Signal and Track Switch Repairers. **PERSONALITY TYPE:** Realistic. Realistic occupations frequently involve work activities that include practical, hands-on problems and solutions. They often deal with plants; animals; and real-world materials like wood, tools, and machinery. Many of the occupations require working outside and do not involve a lot of paperwork or working closely with others.

EDUCATION/TRAINING PROGRAM(S)— Instrumentation Technology/Technician. **RELATED KNOWLEDGE/COURSES— Mechanical Devices:** Machines and tools, including their designs, uses, repair, and maintenance. **Engineering and Technology:** The practical application of engineering science and technology. This includes applying principles, techniques, procedures, and equipment to the design and production of various goods and services.

WORK ENVIRONMENT—Outdoors; hazardous conditions; hazardous equipment; minor burns, cuts, bites, or stings; standing; using hands on objects, tools, or controls.

Correctional Officers and Jailers

- Education/Training Required: Moderate-term on-the-job training
- Annual Earnings: $34,090
- Growth: 6.7%
- Annual Job Openings: 54,000
- Self-Employed: 0.0%
- Part-Time: 2.1%

Guard inmates in penal or rehabilitative institution in accordance with established regulations and procedures. May guard prisoners in transit between jail, courtroom, prison, or other point. Includes deputy sheriffs and police who spend the majority of their time guarding prisoners in correctional institutions. Monitor conduct of prisoners, according to established policies, regulations, and procedures, in order to prevent escape or violence. Inspect conditions of locks, window bars, grills, doors, and gates at correctional facilities in order to ensure that they will prevent escapes. Search prisoners, cells, and vehicles for weapons, valuables, or drugs. Guard facility entrances to screen visitors. Search for and recapture escapees. Inspect mail for the presence of contraband. Take prisoners into custody and escort to locations within and outside of facility, such as visiting room, courtroom, or airport. Record information such as prisoner identification, charges, and incidences of inmate disturbance. Use weapons, handcuffs, and physical force to maintain discipline and order among prisoners. Conduct fire, safety, and sanitation inspections. Provide to supervisors oral and written reports of the quality and quantity of work performed by inmates, inmate disturbances and rule violations, and unusual occurrences. Settle disputes between inmates. Drive passenger vehicles and trucks used to transport inmates to other institutions, courtrooms, hospitals, and work sites. Arrange daily schedules for prisoners, including library visits, work assignments, family visits, and counseling appointments. Assign duties to inmates, providing instructions as needed. Issue clothing, tools, and other authorized items to inmates. Serve meals and distribute commissary items to prisoners. Investigate crimes that have occurred within an institution or assist police in their investigations of crimes and inmates. Maintain records of prisoners' identification and charges. Supervise and coordinate work of other correctional service officers. Sponsor inmate recreational activities, such as newspapers and self-help groups.

LEVEL OF ACTIVITY (out of 100)—General Physical Activity: 62.7. **Sitting:** 37.0. **Outdoors:** 36.1.

SKILLS—Social Perceptiveness; Persuasion; Negotiation; Speaking; Writing; Monitoring; Active Listening; Critical Thinking.

GOE—Interest Area: 12. Law and Public Safety. **Work Group:** 12.04. Law Enforcement and Public Safety. **Other Jobs in This Work Group:** Bailiffs; Criminal Investigators and Special Agents; Detectives and Criminal Investigators; Fire Investigators; Forensic Science Technicians; Parking Enforcement Workers; Police and Sheriff's Patrol Officers; Police Detectives; Police Identification and Records Officers; Police Patrol Officers; Sheriffs and Deputy Sheriffs; Transit and Railroad Police. **PERSONALITY TYPE:** Realistic. Realistic occupations frequently involve work activities that include practical, hands-on problems and solutions. They often deal with plants; animals; and real-world materials like wood, tools, and machinery. Many of the occupations require working outside and do not involve a lot of paperwork or working closely with others.

EDUCATION/TRAINING PROGRAM(S)—Corrections; Juvenile Corrections; Corrections and Criminal Justice, Other. **RELATED KNOWLEDGE/COURSES—Psychology:** Human behavior and performance; individual differences in ability, personality, and interests; learning and motivation; psychological research methods; and the assessment and treatment of behavioral and affective disorders. **Public Safety and Security:** Relevant equipment, policies, procedures, and strategies to promote effective local, state, or national security operations for the protection of people, data, property, and institutions. **Law and Government:** Laws, legal codes, court procedures, precedents, government regulations, executive orders, agency rules, and the democratic political process. **Philosophy and Theology:** Different philosophical systems and religions. This includes their basic principles, values, ethics, ways of thinking, customs, and practices and their impact on human culture. **Sociology and Anthropology:** Group behavior and dynamics, societal trends and influences, human migrations, ethnicity, and cultures and their history and origins. **Therapy and Counseling:** Principles, methods, and procedures for diagnosis, treatment, and rehabilitation of physical and mental dysfunctions and for career counseling and guidance.

WORK ENVIRONMENT—More often indoors than outdoors; noisy; contaminants; disease or infections; standing.

Costume Attendants

- Education/Training Required: Short-term on-the-job training
- Annual Earnings: $25,360
- Growth: 23.4%
- Annual Job Openings: 2,000
- Self-Employed: 0.9%
- Part-Time: 56.0%

Select, fit, and take care of costumes for cast members and aid entertainers. Distribute costumes and related equipment and keep records of item status. Arrange costumes in order of use to facilitate quick-change procedures for performances. Return borrowed or rented items when productions are complete and return other items to storage. Clean and press costumes before and after performances and perform any minor repairs. Assign lockers to employees and maintain locker rooms, dressing rooms, wig rooms, and costume storage and laundry areas. Provide assistance to cast members in wearing costumes or assign cast dressers to assist specific cast members with costume changes. Design and construct costumes or send them to tailors for construction, major repairs, or alterations. Purchase, rent, or requisition costumes and other wardrobe necessities. Check the appearance of costumes on-stage and under lights in order to determine whether desired effects are being achieved. Inventory stock in order to determine types and conditions of available costuming. Collaborate with production designers, costume designers, and other production staff in order to discuss and execute costume design details. Monitor, maintain, and secure inventories of costumes, wigs, and makeup, providing keys or access to assigned directors, costume designers, and wardrobe mistresses/masters. Create worksheets for dressing lists, show notes, and costume checks. Direct the work of wardrobe crews during dress rehearsals and performances. Examine costume fit on cast members and sketch or write notes for alterations. Review scripts or other production information in order to determine a story's locale and period, as well as the number of characters and required costumes. Recommend vendors and monitor their work. Study books, pictures, and examples of period clothing in order to determine styles worn during specific periods in history. Provide managers with budget recommendations and take responsibility for budgetary line items related to costumes, storage, and makeup needs. Participate in the hiring, training, scheduling, and supervision of alteration workers. Care for non-clothing items such as flags, table skirts, and draperies.

LEVEL OF ACTIVITY (out of 100)—General Physical Activity: 47.4. **Sitting:** 33.9. **Outdoors:** 16.3.

SKILLS—Management of Financial Resources; Coordination; Operations Analysis; Negotiation; Social Perceptiveness; Service Orientation; Instructing; Active Listening; Persuasion.

GOE—Interest Area: 03. Arts and Communication. **Work Group:** 03.06. Drama.

Other Jobs in This Work Group: Actors; Directors—Stage, Motion Pictures, Television, and Radio; Makeup Artists, Theatrical and Performance; Public Address System and Other Announcers; Radio and Television Announcers. **PERSONALITY TYPE:** Artistic. Artistic occupations frequently involve working with forms, designs, and patterns. They often require self-expression, and the work can be done without following a clear set of rules.

EDUCATION/TRAINING PROGRAM(S)— Apparel and Textiles, Other. **RELATED KNOWLEDGE/COURSES—Fine Arts:** The theory and techniques required to compose, produce, and perform works of music, dance, visual arts, drama, and sculpture. **Customer and Personal Service:** Principles and processes for providing customer and personal services. This includes customer needs assessment, meeting quality standards for services, and evaluation of customer satisfaction. **Sociology and Anthropology:** Group behavior and dynamics, societal trends and influences, human migrations, ethnicity, and cultures and their history and origins. **Psychology:** Human behavior and performance; individual differences in ability, personality, and interests; learning and motivation; psychological research methods; and the assessment and treatment of behavioral and affective disorders.

WORK ENVIRONMENT—Indoors; contaminants; standing; walking and running; using hands on objects, tools, or controls.

Criminal Investigators and Special Agents

This job can be found in the Part I lists under the title Detectives and Criminal Investigators.

- ☉ Education/Training Required: Work experience in a related occupation
- ☉ Annual Earnings: $55,790
- ☉ Growth: 16.3%
- ☉ Annual Job Openings: 9,000
- ☉ Self-Employed: 0.0%
- ☉ Part-Time: 2.5%

The job openings listed here are shared with Immigration and Customs Inspectors; Police Detectives; and Police Identification and Records Officers.

Investigate alleged or suspected criminal violations of federal, state, or local laws to determine if evidence is sufficient to recommend prosecution. Record evidence and documents, using equipment such as cameras and photocopy machines. Obtain and verify evidence by interviewing and observing suspects and witnesses or by analyzing records. Examine records in order to locate links in chains of evidence or information. Prepare reports that detail investigation findings. Determine scope, timing, and direction of investigations. Collaborate with other offices and agencies in order to exchange information and coordinate activities. Testify before grand juries concerning criminal activity investigations. Analyze evidence in laboratories or in the field. Investigate organized crime, public corruption, financial crime, copyright infringement, civil rights violations, bank robbery, extortion, kidnapping, and other violations of federal or state statutes. Identify case issues and evidence needed, based on analysis of charges, complaints, or allegations of law violations. Obtain and use search and arrest warrants. Serve subpoenas or other official papers. Collaborate with other authorities on activities such as surveillance, transcription, and research. Develop relationships with informants in order to obtain information related to cases. Search for and collect evidence such as fingerprints, using investigative equipment. Collect and record physical information about arrested suspects, including fingerprints, height and weight measurements, and photographs. Compare crime scene fingerprints with those from suspects or fingerprint files to identify perpetrators, using computers. Administer counter-terrorism and counter-narcotics reward programs. Provide protection for individuals such as government leaders, political candidates, and visiting foreign dignitaries. Perform undercover assignments and maintain surveillance, including monitoring authorized wiretaps. Manage security programs designed to protect personnel, facilities, and information. Issue security clearances.

LEVEL OF ACTIVITY (out of 100)—General Physical Activity: 61.0. **Sitting:** 42.1. **Outdoors:** 44.9.

SKILLS—Negotiation; Programming; Service Orientation; Judgment and Decision Making; Operations Analysis; Persuasion; Complex Problem Solving; Social Perceptiveness.

GOE—Interest Area: 12. Law and Public Safety. **Work Group:** 12.04. Law Enforcement and Public Safety. **Other Jobs in This Work Group:** Bailiffs; Correctional Officers and Jailers; Detectives and Criminal Investigators; Fire Investigators; Forensic Science Technicians; Parking Enforcement Workers; Police and

Sheriff's Patrol Officers; Police Detectives; Police Identification and Records Officers; Police Patrol Officers; Sheriffs and Deputy Sheriffs; Transit and Railroad Police. **PERSONALITY TYPE: Enterprising.** Enterprising occupations frequently involve starting up and carrying out projects. These occupations can involve leading people and making many decisions. They sometimes require risk taking and often deal with business.

EDUCATION/TRAINING PROGRAM(S)— Criminal Justice/Police Science; Criminalistics and Criminal Science. **RELATED KNOWLEDGE/COURSES—Law and Government:** Laws, legal codes, court procedures, precedents, government regulations, executive orders, agency rules, and the democratic political process. **Psychology:** Human behavior and performance; individual differences in ability, personality, and interests; learning and motivation; psychological research methods; and the assessment and treatment of behavioral and affective disorders. **Public Safety and Security:** Relevant equipment, policies, procedures, and strategies to promote effective local, state, or national security operations for the protection of people, data, property, and institutions. **Geography:** Principles and methods for describing the features of land, sea, and air masses, including their physical characteristics; locations; interrelationships; and distribution of plant, animal, and human life. **Clerical Practices:** Administrative and clerical procedures and systems such as word processing, managing files and records, stenography and transcription, designing forms, and other office procedures and terminology. **Sociology and Anthropology:** Group behavior and dynamics, societal trends and influences, human migrations, ethnicity, and cultures and their history and origins.

WORK ENVIRONMENT—More often outdoors than indoors; noisy; very hot or cold; standing.

Crossing Guards

- ⊚ Education/Training Required: Short-term on-the-job training
- ⊚ Annual Earnings: $20,050
- ⊚ Growth: 19.7%
- ⊚ Annual Job Openings: 26,000
- ⊚ Self-Employed: 0.0%
- ⊚ Part-Time: 53.9%

Guide or control vehicular or pedestrian traffic at such places as streets, schools, railroad crossings, or construction sites. Direct or escort pedestrians across streets, stopping traffic as necessary. Guide or control vehicular or pedestrian traffic at such places as street and railroad crossings and construction sites. Learn the location and purpose of street traffic signs within assigned patrol areas. Communicate traffic and crossing rules and other information to students and adults. Inform drivers of detour routes through construction sites. Stop speeding vehicles to warn drivers of traffic laws. Monitor traffic flow to locate safe gaps through which pedestrians can cross streets. Activate railroad warning signal lights, lower crossing gates until trains pass, and raise gates when crossings are clear. Discuss traffic routing plans and control point locations with superiors. Distribute traffic control signs and markers at designated points. Record license numbers of vehicles disregarding traffic signals and report infractions to appropriate authorities. Report unsafe behavior of children to school officials. Direct traffic movement or warn of hazards, using signs, flags, lanterns, and hand signals.

LEVEL OF ACTIVITY (out of 100)—General Physical Activity: 40.0. **Sitting:** 22.9. **Outdoors:** 71.4.

SKILLS—None met the criteria.

GOE—Interest Area: 12. Law and Public Safety. **Work Group:** 12.05. Safety and Security. **Other Jobs in This Work Group:** Animal Control Workers; Gaming Surveillance Officers and Gaming Investigators; Lifeguards, Ski Patrol, and Other Recreational Protective Service Workers; Private Detectives and Investigators; Security Guards; Transportation Security Screeners. **PERSONALITY TYPE:** Social. Social occupations frequently involve working with, communicating with, and teaching people. These occupations often involve helping or providing service to others.

EDUCATION/TRAINING PROGRAM(S)— Security and Protective Services, Other. **RELATED KNOWLEDGE/COURSES— Public Safety and Security:** Relevant equipment, policies, procedures, and strategies to promote effective local, state, or national security operations for the protection of people, data, property, and institutions. **Law and Government:** Laws, legal codes, court procedures, precedents, government regulations, executive orders, agency rules, and the democratic political process.

WORK ENVIRONMENT—Outdoors; contaminants; standing; walking and running; using hands on objects, tools, or controls; repetitive motions.

Curators

- Education/Training Required: Master's degree
- Annual Earnings: $45,240
- Growth: 15.7%
- Annual Job Openings: 1,000
- Self-Employed: 6.4%
- Part-Time: 23.4%

Administer affairs of museum and conduct research programs. Direct instructional, research, and public service activities of institution. Plan and organize the acquisition, storage, and exhibition of collections and related materials, including the selection of exhibition themes and designs. Develop and maintain an institution's registration, cataloging, and basic record-keeping systems, using computer databases. Provide information from the institution's holdings to other curators and to the public. Inspect premises to assess the need for repairs and to ensure that climate and pest-control issues are addressed. Train and supervise curatorial, fiscal, technical, research, and clerical staff, as well as volunteers or interns. Negotiate and authorize purchase, sale, exchange, or loan of collections. Plan and conduct special research projects in area of interest or expertise. Conduct or organize tours, workshops, and instructional sessions to acquaint individuals with an institution's facilities and materials. Confer with the board of directors to formulate and interpret policies, to determine budget requirements, and to plan overall operations. Attend meetings, conventions, and civic events to promote use of institution's services, to seek financing, and to maintain

C

community alliances. Schedule events and organize details, including refreshment, entertainment, decorations, and the collection of any fees. Write and review grant proposals, journal articles, institutional reports, and publicity materials. Study, examine, and test acquisitions to authenticate their origin, composition, and history and to assess their current value. Arrange insurance coverage for objects on loan or for special exhibits and recommend changes in coverage for the entire collection. Establish specifications for reproductions and oversee their manufacture or select items from commercially available replica sources.

LEVEL OF ACTIVITY (out of 100)—General Physical Activity: 63.1. **Sitting:** 44.3. **Outdoors:** 23.6.

SKILLS—Management of Financial Resources; Management of Personnel Resources; Writing; Time Management; Persuasion; Speaking; Negotiation; Service Orientation.

GOE—Interest Area: 05. Education and Training. **Work Group:** 05.05. Archival and Museum Services. **Other Jobs in This Work Group:** Archivists; Audio-Visual Collections Specialists; Museum Technicians and Conservators. **PERSONALITY TYPE:** Artistic. Artistic occupations frequently involve working with forms, designs, and patterns. They often require self-expression, and the work can be done without following a clear set of rules.

EDUCATION/TRAINING PROGRAM(S)—Museology/Museum Studies; Art History, Criticism, and Conservation; Public/Applied History and Archival Administration. **RELATED KNOWLEDGE/COURSES—Fine Arts:** The theory and techniques required to compose, produce, and perform works of music, dance, visual arts, drama, and sculpture. **History and Archeology:** Historical events and their causes, indicators, and effects on civilizations and cultures. **Clerical Practices:** Administrative and clerical procedures and systems such as word processing, managing files and records, stenography and transcription, designing forms, and other office procedures and terminology. **Philosophy and Theology:** Different philosophical systems and religions. This includes their basic principles, values, ethics, ways of thinking, customs, and practices and their impact on human culture. **Sociology and Anthropology:** Group behavior and dynamics, societal trends and influences, human migrations, ethnicity, and cultures and their history and origins. **Geography:** Principles and methods for describing the features of land, sea, and air masses, including their physical characteristics; locations; interrelationships; and distribution of plant, animal, and human life.

WORK ENVIRONMENT—Indoors; sitting.

Detectives and Criminal Investigators

See the descriptions of these jobs:

- **Criminal Investigators and Special Agents**
- **Immigration and Customs Inspectors**
- **Police Detectives**
- **Police Identification and Records Officers**

Driver/Sales Workers

- ◉ Education/Training Required:
  Short-term on-the-job training
- ◉ Annual Earnings: $20,120
- ◉ Growth: 13.8%
- ◉ Annual Job Openings: 72,000
- ◉ Self-Employed: 8.8%
- ◉ Part-Time: 9.1%

Drive truck or other vehicle over established routes or within an established territory and sell goods such as food products, including restaurant take-out items, or pick up and deliver items such as laundry. May also take orders and collect payments. Includes newspaper delivery drivers. Collect money from customers, make change, and record transactions on customer receipts. Listen to and resolve customers' complaints regarding products or services. Inform regular customers of new products or services and price changes. Write customer orders and sales contracts according to company guidelines. Drive trucks in order to deliver such items as food, medical supplies, or newspapers. Collect coins from vending machines, refill machines, and remove aged merchandise. Call on prospective customers to explain company services and to solicit new business. Record sales or delivery information on daily sales or delivery record. Review lists of dealers, customers, or station drops and load trucks. Arrange merchandise and sales promotion displays or issue sales promotion materials to customers. Maintain trucks and food-dispensing equipment and clean inside of machines that dispense food or beverages. Sell food specialties, such as sandwiches and beverages, to office workers and patrons of sports events.

LEVEL OF ACTIVITY (out of 100)—General Physical Activity: 48.1. **Sitting:** 44.4. **Outdoors:** 44.1.

SKILLS—Social Perceptiveness; Speaking.

GOE—Interest Area: 16. Transportation, Distribution, and Logistics. **Work Group:** 16.06. Other Services Requiring Driving. **Other Jobs in This Work Group:** Ambulance Drivers and Attendants, Except Emergency Medical Technicians; Bus Drivers, School; Bus Drivers, Transit and Intercity; Couriers and Messengers; Parking Lot Attendants; Postal Service Mail Carriers; Taxi Drivers and Chauffeurs. **PERSONALITY TYPE:** Enterprising. Enterprising occupations frequently involve starting up and carrying out projects. These occupations can involve leading people and making many decisions. They sometimes require risk taking and often deal with business.

EDUCATION/TRAINING PROGRAM(S)— Retailing and Retail Operations. **RELATED KNOWLEDGE/COURSES—Transportation:** Principles and methods for moving people or goods by air, rail, sea, or road, including the relative costs and benefits. **Sales and Marketing:** Principles and methods for showing, promoting, and selling products or services. This includes marketing strategy and tactics, product demonstration, sales techniques, and sales control systems. **Customer and Personal Service:** Principles and processes for providing customer and personal services. This includes customer needs assessment, meeting quality standards for services, and evaluation of customer satisfaction. **Public Safety and Security:** Relevant equipment, policies, procedures, and strategies to promote effective local, state, or national security operations for the protection of people, data, property, and institutions.

WORK ENVIRONMENT—More often outdoors than indoors; very hot or cold; sitting; using hands on objects, tools, or controls; repetitive motions.

Drywall and Ceiling Tile Installers

- Education/Training Required: Moderate-term on-the-job training
- Annual Earnings: $34,740
- Growth: 9.0%
- Annual Job Openings: 17,000
- Self-Employed: 23.4%
- Part-Time: 8.0%

Apply plasterboard or other wallboard to ceilings or interior walls of buildings. Apply or mount acoustical tiles or blocks or strips or sheets of shock-absorbing materials to ceilings and walls of buildings to reduce or reflect sound. Materials may be of decorative quality. Includes lathers who fasten wooden, metal, or rockboard lath to walls, ceilings, or partitions of buildings to provide support base for plaster, fire-proofing, or acoustical material. Fasten metal or rockboard lath to the structural framework of walls, ceilings, and partitions of buildings, using nails, screws, staples, or wire-ties. Apply cement to backs of tiles and press tiles into place, aligning them with layout marks or joints of previously laid tile. Apply or mount acoustical tile or blocks or strips or sheets of shock-absorbing materials to ceilings and walls of buildings to reduce reflection of sound or to decorate rooms. Assemble and install metal framing and decorative trim for windows, doorways, and vents. Cut and screw together metal channels to make floor and ceiling frames, according to plans for the location of rooms and hallways. Cut metal or wood framing and trim to size, using cutting tools. Measure and cut openings in panels or tiles for electrical outlets, windows, vents, and plumbing and other fixtures, using keyhole saws or other cutting tools. Fit and fasten wallboard or drywall into position on wood or metal frameworks, using glue, nails, or screws. Hang dry lines (stretched string) to wall moldings in order to guide positioning of main runners. Hang drywall panels on metal frameworks of walls and ceilings in offices, schools, and other large buildings, using lifts or hoists to adjust panel heights when necessary. Inspect furrings, mechanical mountings, and masonry surface for plumbness and level, using spirit or water levels. Install horizontal and vertical metal or wooden studs to frames so that wallboard can be attached to interior walls. Measure and mark surfaces to lay out work according to blueprints and drawings, using tape measures, straightedges or squares, and marking devices. Nail channels or wood furring strips to surfaces to provide mounting for tile. Read blueprints and other specifications to determine methods of installation, work procedures, and material and tool requirements. Scribe and cut edges of tile to fit walls where wall molding is not specified. Seal joints between ceiling tiles and walls. Cut fixture and border tiles to size, using keyhole saws, and insert them into surrounding frameworks. Suspend angle iron grids and channel irons from ceilings, using wire.

LEVEL OF ACTIVITY (out of 100)—General Physical Activity: 59.6. **Sitting:** 26.9. **Outdoors:** 25.7.

SKILLS—Installation.

GOE—Interest Area: 02. Architecture and Construction. **Work Group:** 02.04. Construction Crafts. **Other Jobs in This Work Group:** Boilermakers; Brickmasons and Blockmasons; Carpet Installers; Cement Masons and Concrete Finishers; Commercial Divers; Construction Carpenters; Crane and Tower Operators; Electricians; Fence Erectors; Floor Layers, Except Carpet, Wood, and Hard Tiles; Floor Sanders and Finishers; Glaziers; Hazardous Materials Removal Workers; Insulation Workers, Floor, Ceiling, and Wall; Insulation Workers, Mechanical; Manufactured Building and Mobile Home Installers; Operating Engineers and Other Construction Equipment Operators; Painters, Construction and Maintenance; Paperhangers; Paving, Surfacing, and Tamping Equipment Operators; Pile-Driver Operators; Pipe Fitters and Steamfitters; Pipelayers; Plasterers and Stucco Masons; Plumbers; Plumbers, Pipefitters, and Steamfitters; Rail-Track Laying and Maintenance Equipment Operators; Refractory Materials Repairers, Except Brickmasons; Reinforcing Iron and Rebar Workers; Riggers; Roofers; Rough Carpenters; Security and Fire Alarm Systems Installers; Segmental Pavers; Sheet Metal Workers; Stone Cutters and Carvers, Manufacturing; Stonemasons; Structural Iron and Steel Workers; Tapers; Terrazzo Workers and Finishers; Tile and Marble Setters. **PERSONALITY TYPE:** Realistic. Realistic occupations frequently involve work activities that include practical, hands-on problems and solutions. They often deal with plants; animals; and real-world materials like wood, tools, and machinery. Many of the occupations require working outside and do not involve a lot of paperwork or working closely with others.

EDUCATION/TRAINING PROGRAM(S)—Drywall Installation/Drywaller. **RELATED KNOWLEDGE/COURSES—Building and Construction:** The materials, methods, and tools involved in the construction or repair of houses, buildings, or other structures such as highways and roads. **Design:** Design techniques, tools, and principles involved in production of precision technical plans, blueprints, drawings, and models. **Engineering and Technology:** The practical application of engineering science and technology. This includes applying principles, techniques, procedures, and equipment to the design and production of various goods and services.

WORK ENVIRONMENT—Indoors; contaminants; hazardous equipment; minor burns, cuts, bites, or stings; standing; using hands on objects, tools, or controls.

Earth Drillers, Except Oil and Gas

- Education/Training Required: Moderate-term on-the-job training
- Annual Earnings: $33,770
- Growth: 7.9%
- Annual Job Openings: 4,000
- Self-Employed: 10.5%
- Part-Time: 0.5%

Operate a variety of drills—such as rotary, churn, and pneumatic—to tap sub-surface water and salt deposits, to remove core samples during mineral exploration or soil testing, and to facilitate the use of explosives in mining or construction. May use explosives. Includes horizontal and earth boring machine operators. Fabricate well casings. Perform routine maintenance and upgrade work on machines and equipment, such as replacing parts, building up drill bits, and lubricating machinery. Verify depths and alignments of boring positions. Withdraw drill rods from holes and extract core samples. Drive trucks, tractors, or truck-mounted drills to and from work sites. Document geological formations encountered during work. Perform pumping tests to assess well performance. Record drilling progress and geological data. Operate hoists to lift power-line poles into position. Review client requirements and proposed locations for drilling operations to determine feasibility and to determine cost estimates. Retrieve lost equipment from bore holes, using retrieval tools and equipment. Start, stop, and control drilling speed of machines and insertion of casings into holes. Disinfect, reconstruct, and redevelop contaminated wells and water pumping systems and clean and disinfect new wells in preparation for use. Design well pumping systems. Drill or bore holes in rock for blasting, grouting, anchoring, or building foundations. Select the appropriate drill for the job, using knowledge of rock or soil conditions. Assemble and position machines, augers, casing pipes, and other equipment, using hand and power tools. Drive or guide truck-mounted equipment into position, level and stabilize rigs, and extend telescoping derricks. Inspect core samples to determine nature of strata or take samples to laboratories for analysis. Monitor drilling operations, checking gauges and listening to equipment to assess drilling conditions and to determine the need to adjust drilling or alter equipment. Observe electronic graph recorders and flow meters that monitor the water used to flush debris from holes. Operate controls to stabilize machines and to position and align drills. Operate water-well drilling rigs and other equipment to drill, bore, and dig for water wells or for environmental assessment purposes. Place and install screens, casings, pumps, and other well fixtures in order to develop wells. Pour water into wells or pump water or slush into wells to cool drill bits and to remove drillings.

LEVEL OF ACTIVITY (out of 100)—General Physical Activity: 58.3. **Sitting:** 34.6. **Outdoors:** 63.1.

SKILLS—Operation Monitoring; Operation and Control; Equipment Maintenance.

GOE—Interest Area: 01. Agriculture and Natural Resources. **Work Group:** 01.08. Mining and Drilling. **Other Jobs in This Work Group:** Continuous Mining Machine Operators; Derrick Operators, Oil and Gas; Excavating and Loading Machine and Dragline Operators; Explosives Workers, Ordnance Handling Experts, and Blasters; Helpers—Extraction Workers; Loading Machine Operators, Underground Mining; Mine Cutting and Channeling Machine Operators; Rock Splitters, Quarry; Roof Bolters, Mining; Rotary Drill Operators, Oil and Gas; Roustabouts, Oil and Gas; Service Unit Operators, Oil, Gas, and Mining; Shuttle Car Operators; Wellhead Pumpers. **PERSONALITY TYPE:** Realistic. Realistic occupations frequently involve work activities that include practical, hands-on problems and solutions. They often deal with plants; animals; and real-world materials like wood, tools, and machinery. Many of the occupations require working outside and do not involve a lot of paperwork or working closely with others.

EDUCATION/TRAINING PROGRAM(S)— Construction/Heavy Equipment/Earthmoving Equipment Operation; Well Drilling/Driller. **RELATED KNOWLEDGE/COURSES— Mechanical Devices:** Machines and tools, including their designs, uses, repair, and maintenance. **Transportation:** Principles and methods for moving people or goods by air, rail, sea, or road, including the relative costs and benefits. **Physics:** Physical principles and laws and their interrelationships and applications to understanding fluid, material, and atmospheric dynamics and mechanical, electrical, atomic, and subatomic structures and processes. **Engineering and Technology:** The practical application of engineering science and technology. This includes applying principles, techniques, procedures, and equipment to the design and production of various goods and services.

WORK ENVIRONMENT—Outdoors; noisy; contaminants; hazardous equipment; standing; using hands on objects, tools, or controls.

Education Administrators, Preschool and Child Care Center/Program

- Education/Training Required: Work experience plus degree
- Annual Earnings: $37,010
- Growth: 27.9%
- Annual Job Openings: 9,000
- Self-Employed: 3.2%
- Part-Time: 9.3%

Plan, direct, or coordinate the academic and nonacademic activities of preschool and child care centers or programs. Confer with parents and staff to discuss educational activities and policies and students' behavioral or learning problems. Prepare and maintain attendance, activity, planning, accounting, or personnel reports and records for officials and agencies or direct preparation and maintenance activities. Set educational standards and goals and help establish policies, procedures, and programs to carry them out. Monitor students' progress and provide students and teachers with assistance in resolving any problems. Determine allocations of funds for staff, supplies, materials, and equipment and authorize purchases. Recruit, hire, train, and evaluate primary and supplemental staff and recommend personnel actions for programs and services. Direct and coordinate activities of teachers or administrators at daycare centers, schools, public agencies, or institutions.

Plan, direct, and monitor instructional methods and content of educational, vocational, or student activity programs. Review and interpret government codes and develop procedures to meet codes and to ensure facility safety, security, and maintenance. Determine the scope of educational program offerings and prepare drafts of program schedules and descriptions to estimate staffing and facility requirements. Review and evaluate new and current programs to determine their efficiency; effectiveness; and compliance with state, local, and federal regulations and recommend any necessary modifications. Teach classes or courses or provide direct care to children. Prepare and submit budget requests or grant proposals to solicit program funding. Write articles, manuals, and other publications and assist in the distribution of promotional literature about programs and facilities. Collect and analyze survey data, regulatory information, and demographic and employment trends to forecast enrollment patterns and the need for curriculum changes. Inform businesses, community groups, and governmental agencies about educational needs, available programs, and program policies. Organize and direct committees of specialists, volunteers, and staff to provide technical and advisory assistance for programs.

LEVEL OF ACTIVITY (out of 100)—General Physical Activity: 44.3. **Sitting:** 40.3. **Outdoors:** 30.0.

SKILLS—Management of Personnel Resources; Management of Financial Resources; Learning Strategies; Management of Material Resources; Social Perceptiveness; Monitoring; Negotiation; Persuasion.

GOE—Interest Area: 05. Education and Training. **Work Group:** 05.01. Managerial Work in Education. **Other Jobs in This Work Group:** Education Administrators, Elementary and Secondary School; Education Administrators, Postsecondary; Instructional Coordinators. **PERSONALITY TYPE:** Social. Social occupations frequently involve working with, communicating with, and teaching people. These occupations often involve helping or providing service to others.

EDUCATION/TRAINING PROGRAM(S)— Educational Leadership and Administration, General; Educational, Instructional, and Curriculum Supervision; Elementary and Middle School Administration/Principalship; Educational Administration and Supervision, Other. **RELATED KNOWLEDGE/COURSES—Education and Training:** Principles and methods for curriculum and training design, teaching and instruction for individuals and groups, and the measurement of training effects. **Personnel and Human Resources:** Principles and procedures for personnel recruitment, selection, training, compensation and benefits, labor relations and negotiation, and personnel information systems. **Clerical Practices:** Administrative and clerical procedures and systems such as word processing, managing files and records, stenography and transcription, designing forms, and other office procedures and terminology. **Philosophy and Theology:** Different philosophical systems and religions. This includes their basic principles, values, ethics, ways of thinking, customs, and practices and their impact on human culture. **Customer and Personal Service:** Principles and processes for providing customer and personal services. This includes customer needs assessment, meeting quality standards for services, and evaluation of customer satisfaction. **Therapy and Counseling:** Principles, methods, and procedures for diagnosis, treatment, and rehabilitation of physical and mental dysfunctions and for career counseling and guidance.

WORK ENVIRONMENT—Indoors; standing.

Electrical and Electronics Repairers, Commercial and Industrial Equipment

- ◉ Education/Training Required: Postsecondary vocational training
- ◉ Annual Earnings: $44,120
- ◉ Growth: 9.7%
- ◉ Annual Job Openings: 8,000
- ◉ Self-Employed: 0.0%
- ◉ Part-Time: 5.5%

Repair, test, adjust, or install electronic equipment, such as industrial controls, transmitters, and antennas. Perform scheduled preventive maintenance tasks, such as checking, cleaning, and repairing equipment, to detect and prevent problems. Examine work orders and converse with equipment operators to detect equipment problems and to ascertain whether mechanical or human errors contributed to the problems. Operate equipment to demonstrate proper use and to analyze malfunctions. Set up and test industrial equipment to ensure that it functions properly. Test faulty equipment to diagnose malfunctions, using test equipment and software and applying knowledge of the functional operation of electronic units and systems. Repair and adjust equipment, machines, and defective components, replacing worn parts such as gaskets and seals in watertight electrical equipment. Calibrate testing instruments and installed or repaired equipment to prescribed specifications. Advise management regarding customer satisfaction, product performance, and suggestions for product improvements. Study blueprints, schematics, manuals, and other specifications to determine installation procedures. Inspect components of industrial equipment for accurate assembly and installation and for defects such as loose connections and frayed wires. Maintain equipment logs that record performance problems, repairs, calibrations, and tests. Coordinate efforts with other workers involved in installing and maintaining equipment or components. Maintain inventory of spare parts. Consult with customers, supervisors, and engineers to plan layout of equipment and to resolve problems in system operation and maintenance. Install repaired equipment in various settings, such as industrial or military establishments. Send defective units to the manufacturer or to a specialized repair shop for repair. Determine feasibility of using standardized equipment and develop specifications for equipment required to perform additional functions. Enter information into computer to copy program or to draw, modify, or store schematics, applying knowledge of software package used. Sign overhaul documents for equipment replaced or repaired. Develop or modify industrial electronic devices, circuits, and equipment according to available specifications.

LEVEL OF ACTIVITY (out of 100)—General Physical Activity: 44.0. **Sitting:** 36.3. **Outdoors:** 30.8.

SKILLS—Installation; Repairing; Operation Monitoring; Troubleshooting; Equipment Maintenance; Operation and Control; Systems Analysis; Science.

GOE—**Interest Area:** 13. Manufacturing. **Work Group:** 13.12. Electrical and Electronic Repair. **Other Jobs in This Work Group:** Avionics Technicians; Electric Motor, Power Tool, and Related Repairers; Electrical and Electronics Installers and Repairers, Transportation Equipment; Electronic Equipment Installers and Repairers, Motor Vehicles; Electronic Home Entertainment Equipment Installers and Repairers; Radio Mechanics. **PERSONALITY TYPE:** Realistic. Realistic occupations frequently involve work activities that include practical, hands-on problems and solutions. They often deal with plants; animals; and real-world materials like wood, tools, and machinery. Many of the occupations require working outside and do not involve a lot of paperwork or working closely with others.

EDUCATION/TRAINING PROGRAM(S)—Computer Installation and Repair Technology/Technician; Industrial Electronics Technology/Technician. **RELATED KNOWLEDGE/COURSES**—**Mechanical Devices:** Machines and tools, including their designs, uses, repair, and maintenance. **Computers and Electronics:** Circuit boards; processors; chips; electronic equipment; and computer hardware and software, including applications and programming. **Telecommunications:** Transmission, broadcasting, switching, control, and operation of telecommunications systems. **Engineering and Technology:** The practical application of engineering science and technology. This includes applying principles, techniques, procedures, and equipment to the design and production of various goods and services.

WORK ENVIRONMENT—Indoors; noisy; cramped work space, awkward positions; hazardous conditions; standing; using hands on objects, tools, or controls.

Electrical and Electronics Repairers, Powerhouse, Substation, and Relay

- ⊚ Education/Training Required: Postsecondary vocational training
- ⊚ Annual Earnings: $54,970
- ⊚ Growth: –0.4%
- ⊚ Annual Job Openings: 2,000
- ⊚ Self-Employed: 0.0%
- ⊚ Part-Time: 5.5%

Inspect, test, repair, or maintain electrical equipment in generating stations, substations, and in-service relays. Test oil in circuit breakers and transformers for dielectric strength, refilling oil periodically. Schedule and supervise the construction and testing of special devices and the implementation of unique monitoring or control systems. Set forms and pour concrete footings for installation of heavy equipment. Schedule and supervise splicing or termination of cables in color-code order. Analyze test data to diagnose malfunctions, to determine performance characteristics of systems, and to evaluate effects of system modifications. Prepare and maintain records detailing tests, repairs, and maintenance. Construct, test, maintain, and repair substation relay and control systems. Maintain inventories of spare parts for all equipment, requisitioning parts as necessary. Disconnect voltage regulators, bolts, and screws and connect replacement regulators to high-voltage lines. Run signal quality and connectivity tests for individual cables and record results. Test insulators and bushings of equipment by inducing voltage across insulation, testing current, and calculating insulation loss. Repair, replace, and clean equipment and components such as circuit breakers, brushes, and commutators. Open and close switches to isolate defective relays; then perform adjustments or repairs. Inspect and test equipment and circuits to identify malfunctions or defects, using wiring diagrams and testing devices such as ohmmeters, voltmeters, or ammeters. Consult manuals, schematics, wiring diagrams, and engineering personnel to troubleshoot and solve equipment problems and to determine optimum equipment functioning. Notify facility personnel of equipment shutdowns.

LEVEL OF ACTIVITY (out of 100)—General Physical Activity: 54.7. **Sitting:** 40.0. **Outdoors:** 42.9.

SKILLS—Repairing; Equipment Maintenance; Installation; Science; Operation Monitoring; Troubleshooting; Quality Control Analysis; Equipment Selection.

GOE—Interest Area: 02. Architecture and Construction. **Work Group:** 02.05. Systems and Equipment Installation, Maintenance, and Repair. **Other Jobs in This Work Group:** Electrical Power-Line Installers and Repairers; Elevator Installers and Repairers; Heating and Air Conditioning Mechanics and Installers; Maintenance and Repair Workers, General; Refrigeration Mechanics and Installers; Telecommunications Equipment Installers and Repairers, Except Line Installers; Telecommunications Line Installers and Repairers. **PERSONALITY TYPE:** Realistic. Realistic occupations frequently involve work activities that include practical, hands-on problems and solutions. They often deal with plants; animals; and real-world materials like wood, tools, and machinery. Many of the occupations require working outside and do not involve a lot of paperwork or working closely with others.

EDUCATION/TRAINING PROGRAM(S)— Mechanic and Repair Technologies/Technicians, Other. **RELATED KNOWLEDGE/COURSES—Computers and Electronics:** Circuit boards; processors; chips; electronic equipment; and computer hardware and software, including applications and programming. **Mechanical Devices:** Machines and tools, including their designs, uses, repair, and maintenance. **Physics:** Physical principles and laws and their interrelationships and applications to understanding fluid, material, and atmospheric dynamics and mechanical, electrical, atomic, and subatomic structures and processes. **Engineering and Technology:** The practical application of engineering science and technology. This includes applying principles, techniques, procedures, and equipment to the design and production of various goods and services. **Mathematics:** Arithmetic, algebra, geometry, calculus, and statistics and their applications.

WORK ENVIRONMENT—Indoors; hazardous conditions; standing; using hands on objects, tools, or controls.

Electrical Power-Line Installers and Repairers

- ◉ Education/Training Required: Long-term on-the-job training
- ◉ Annual Earnings: $50,150
- ◉ Growth: 2.5%
- ◉ Annual Job Openings: 11,000
- ◉ Self-Employed: 2.3%
- ◉ Part-Time: 0.9%

Install or repair cables or wires used in electrical power or distribution systems. May erect poles and light- or heavy-duty transmission towers. Adhere to safety practices and procedures, such as checking equipment regularly and erecting barriers around work areas. Open switches or attach grounding devices in order to remove electrical hazards from disturbed or fallen lines or to facilitate repairs. Climb poles or use truck-mounted buckets to access equipment. Place insulating or fireproofing materials over conductors and joints. Install, maintain, and repair electrical distribution and transmission systems, including conduits; cables; wires; and related equipment such as transformers, circuit breakers, and switches. Identify defective sectionalizing devices, circuit breakers, fuses, voltage regulators, transformers, switches, relays, or wiring, using wiring diagrams and electrical-testing instruments. Drive vehicles equipped with tools and materials to job sites. Coordinate work assignment preparation and completion with other workers. String wire conductors and cables between poles, towers, trenches, pylons, and buildings, setting lines in place and using winch-es to adjust tension. Inspect and test power lines and auxiliary equipment to locate and identify problems, using reading and testing instruments. Test conductors, according to electrical diagrams and specifications, to identify corresponding conductors and to prevent incorrect connections. Replace damaged poles with new poles and straighten the poles. Install watt-hour meters and connect service drops between power lines and consumers' facilities. Attach crossarms, insulators, and auxiliary equipment to poles prior to installing them. Travel in trucks, helicopters, and airplanes to inspect lines for freedom from obstruction and adequacy of insulation. Dig holes, using augers, and set poles, using cranes and power equipment. Trim trees that could be hazardous to the functioning of cables or wires. Splice or solder cables together or to overhead transmission lines, customer service lines, or street light lines, using hand tools, epoxies, or specialized equipment. Cut and peel lead sheathing and insulation from defective or newly installed cables and conduits prior to splicing.

LEVEL OF ACTIVITY (out of 100)—General Physical Activity: 83.7. **Sitting:** 29.1. **Outdoors:** 50.0.

SKILLS—Repairing; Installation; Equipment Maintenance; Operation Monitoring; Troubleshooting; Operation and Control; Equipment Selection; Systems Analysis.

GOE—Interest Area: 02. Architecture and Construction. **Work Group:** 02.05. Systems and Equipment Installation, Maintenance, and Repair. **Other Jobs in This Work Group:** Electrical and Electronics Repairers, Powerhouse, Substation, and Relay; Elevator Installers and Repairers; Heating and Air Conditioning Mechanics and Installers; Maintenance and Repair Workers, General;

Refrigeration Mechanics and Installers; Telecommunications Equipment Installers and Repairers, Except Line Installers; Telecommunications Line Installers and Repairers. **PERSONALITY TYPE:** Realistic. Realistic occupations frequently involve work activities that include practical, hands-on problems and solutions. They often deal with plants; animals; and real-world materials like wood, tools, and machinery. Many of the occupations require working outside and do not involve a lot of paperwork or working closely with others.

EDUCATION/TRAINING PROGRAM(S)— Electrical and Power Transmission Installation/Installer, General; Lineworker; Electrical and Power Transmission Installers, Other. **RELATED KNOWLEDGE/COURSES—Building and Construction:** The materials, methods, and tools involved in the construction or repair of houses, buildings, or other structures such as highways and roads. **Customer and Personal Service:** Principles and processes for providing customer and personal services. This includes customer needs assessment, meeting quality standards for services, and evaluation of customer satisfaction. **Mechanical Devices:** Machines and tools, including their designs, uses, repair, and maintenance. **Engineering and Technology:** The practical application of engineering science and technology. This includes applying principles, techniques, procedures, and equipment to the design and production of various goods and services. **Transportation:** Principles and methods for moving people or goods by air, rail, sea, or road, including the relative costs and benefits. **Design:** Design techniques, tools, and principles involved in production of precision technical plans, blueprints, drawings, and models.

WORK ENVIRONMENT—Outdoors; very hot or cold; high places; hazardous conditions; hazardous equipment; using hands on objects, tools, or controls.

Electricians

- Education/Training Required: Long-term on-the-job training
- Annual Earnings: $42,790
- Growth: 11.8%
- Annual Job Openings: 68,000
- Self-Employed: 9.5%
- Part-Time: 3.3%

Install, maintain, and repair electrical wiring, equipment, and fixtures. Ensure that work is in accordance with relevant codes. May install or service street lights, intercom systems, or electrical control systems. Assemble, install, test, and maintain electrical or electronic wiring, equipment, appliances, apparatus, and fixtures, using hand tools and power tools. Diagnose malfunctioning systems, apparatus, and components, using test equipment and hand tools, to locate the cause of a breakdown and correct the problem. Connect wires to circuit breakers, transformers, or other components. Inspect electrical systems, equipment, and components to identify hazards, defects, and the need for adjustment or repair and to ensure compliance with codes. Advise management on whether continued operation of equipment could be hazardous. Test electrical systems and continuity of circuits in electrical wiring, equipment, and fixtures, using testing devices such as ohmmeters, voltmeters, and oscilloscopes, to ensure compatibility and safety of system. Maintain current electrician's license or identification card to meet governmental regulations. Plan layout and installation of electrical wiring, equipment, and fixtures based on job specifications and local codes. Direct and train workers to install, maintain, or repair electrical wiring, equipment, and fixtures. Prepare sketches or follow blueprints to determine the location of wiring and equipment and to ensure conformance to building and safety codes. Use a variety of tools and equipment such as power construction equipment; measuring devices; power tools; and testing equipment, including oscilloscopes, ammeters, and test lamps. Install ground leads and connect power cables to equipment such as motors. Perform business management duties such as maintaining records and files, preparing reports, and ordering supplies and equipment. Repair or replace wiring, equipment, and fixtures, using hand tools and power tools. Work from ladders, scaffolds, and roofs to install, maintain, or repair electrical wiring, equipment, and fixtures. Place conduit, pipes, or tubing inside designated partitions, walls, or other concealed areas and pull insulated wires or cables through the conduit to complete circuits between boxes. Construct and fabricate parts, using hand tools and specifications.

LEVEL OF ACTIVITY (out of 100)—General Physical Activity: 76.3. **Sitting:** 21.4. **Outdoors:** 43.0.

SKILLS—Installation; Repairing; Equipment Maintenance; Troubleshooting; Technology Design; Operation and Control; Operation Monitoring; Equipment Selection.

GOE—Interest Area: 02. Architecture and Construction. **Work Group:** 02.04. Construction Crafts. **Other Jobs in This Work Group:** Boilermakers; Brickmasons and Blockmasons; Carpet Installers; Cement Masons and Concrete Finishers; Commercial Divers; Construction Carpenters; Crane and Tower Operators; Drywall and Ceiling Tile Installers; Fence Erectors; Floor Layers, Except Carpet, Wood, and Hard Tiles; Floor Sanders and Finishers; Glaziers; Hazardous Materials Removal Workers; Insulation Workers, Floor, Ceiling, and Wall; Insulation Workers, Mechanical; Manufactured Building and Mobile Home Installers; Operating Engineers and Other Construction Equipment Operators; Painters, Construction and Maintenance; Paperhangers; Paving, Surfacing, and Tamping Equipment Operators; Pile-Driver Operators; Pipe Fitters and Steamfitters; Pipelayers; Plasterers and Stucco Masons; Plumbers; Plumbers, Pipefitters, and Steamfitters; Rail-Track Laying and Maintenance Equipment Operators; Refractory Materials Repairers, Except Brickmasons; Reinforcing Iron and Rebar Workers; Riggers; Roofers; Rough Carpenters; Security and Fire Alarm Systems Installers; Segmental Pavers; Sheet Metal Workers; Stone Cutters and Carvers, Manufacturing; Stonemasons; Structural Iron and Steel Workers; Tapers; Terrazzo Workers and Finishers; Tile and Marble Setters. **PERSONALITY TYPE:** Realistic. Realistic occupations frequently involve work activities that include practical, hands-on problems and solutions. They often deal with plants; animals; and real-world materials like wood, tools, and machinery. Many of the occupations require working outside and do not involve a lot of paperwork or working closely with others.

EDUCATION/TRAINING PROGRAM(S)—Electrician. **RELATED KNOWLEDGE/COURSES—Building and Construction:** The materials, methods, and tools involved in the construction or repair of houses, buildings, or other structures such as highways and roads. **Mechanical Devices:** Machines and tools, including their designs, uses, repair, and maintenance. **Design:** Design techniques, tools, and principles involved in production of precision technical plans, blueprints, drawings, and models. **Production and Processing:** Raw materials, production processes, quality control, costs, and other techniques for maximizing the effective manufacture and distribution of goods. **Physics:** Physical principles and laws and their interrelationships and applications to understanding fluid, material, and atmospheric dynamics and mechanical, electrical, atomic, and subatomic structures and processes. **Administration and Management:** Business and management principles involved in strategic planning, resource allocation, human resources modeling, leadership technique, production methods, and coordination of people and resources.

WORK ENVIRONMENT—Outdoors; noisy; minor burns, cuts, bites, or stings; standing; walking and running; using hands on objects, tools, or controls.

Elementary School Teachers, Except Special Education

- Education/Training Required: Bachelor's degree
- Annual Earnings: $44,040
- Growth: 18.2%
- Annual Job Openings: 203,000
- Self-Employed: 0.0%
- Part-Time: 12.6%

Teach pupils in public or private schools at the elementary level basic academic, social, and other formative skills. Establish and enforce rules for behavior and procedures for maintaining order among the students for whom they are responsible. Observe and evaluate students' performance, behavior, social development, and physical health. Prepare materials and classrooms for class activities. Adapt teaching methods and instructional materials to meet students' varying needs and interests. Plan and conduct activities for a balanced program of instruction, demonstration, and work time that provides students with opportunities to observe, question, and investigate. Instruct students individually and in groups, using various teaching methods such as lectures, discussions, and demonstrations. Establish clear objectives for all lessons, units, and projects and communicate those objectives to students. Assign and grade class work and homework. Read books to entire classes or small groups. Prepare, administer, and grade tests and assignments in order to evaluate students' progress. Confer with parents or guardians, teachers, counselors, and administrators in order to resolve students' behavioral and academic problems. Meet with parents and guardians to discuss their children's progress and to determine their priorities for their children and their resource needs. Prepare students for later grades by encouraging them to explore learning opportunities and to persevere with challenging tasks. Maintain accurate and complete student records as required by laws, district policies, and administrative regulations. Guide and counsel students with adjustment and/or academic problems or special academic interests. Prepare and implement remedial programs for students requiring extra help. Prepare objectives and outlines for courses of study, following curriculum guidelines or requirements of states and schools. Provide a variety of materials and resources for children to explore, manipulate, and use, both in learning activities and in imaginative play. Enforce administration policies and rules governing students. Confer with other staff members to plan and schedule lessons promoting learning, following approved curricula.

LEVEL OF ACTIVITY (out of 100)—General Physical Activity: 34.0. Sitting: 30.6. Outdoors: 20.4.

SKILLS—Instructing; Learning Strategies; Monitoring; Social Perceptiveness; Persuasion; Speaking; Service Orientation; Time Management.

GOE—Interest Area: 05. Education and Training. Work Group: 05.02. Preschool, Elementary, and Secondary Teaching and Instructing. Other Jobs in This Work Group: Kindergarten Teachers, Except Special Education; Middle School Teachers, Except Special and Vocational Education; Preschool Teachers, Except Special Education; Secondary School Teachers, Except Special and Vocational Education; Special Education Teachers, Middle School; Special Education Teachers, Preschool, Kindergarten, and Elementary School; Special Education Teachers, Secondary School; Teacher Assistants; Vocational Education Teachers, Middle School; Vocational Education Teachers, Secondary School. **PERSONALITY TYPE:** Social. Social occupations frequently involve working with, communicating with, and teaching people. These occupations often involve helping or providing service to others.

EDUCATION/TRAINING PROGRAM(S)— Elementary Education and Teaching; Teacher Education, Multiple Levels; Montessori Teacher Education. **RELATED KNOWLEDGE/ COURSES—Geography:** Principles and methods for describing the features of land, sea, and air masses, including their physical characteristics; locations; interrelationships; and distribution of plant, animal, and human life. **History and Archeology:** Historical events and their causes, indicators, and effects on civilizations and cultures. **Education and Training:** Principles and methods for curriculum and training design, teaching and instruction for individuals and groups, and the measurement of training effects. **Sociology and Anthropology:** Group behavior and dynamics, societal trends and influences, human migrations, ethnicity, and cultures and their history and origins. **Therapy and Counseling:** Principles, methods, and procedures for diagnosis, treatment, and rehabilitation of physical and mental dysfunctions and for career counseling and guidance. **Psychology:** Human behavior and performance; individual differences in ability, personality, and interests; learning and motivation; psychological research methods; and the assessment and treatment of behavioral and affective disorders.

WORK ENVIRONMENT—Indoors; noisy; disease or infections; standing.

Elevator Installers and Repairers

- Education/Training Required: Long-term on-the-job training
- Annual Earnings: $59,190
- Growth: 14.8%
- Annual Job Openings: 3,000
- Self-Employed: 0.4%
- Part-Time: No data available

Assemble, install, repair, or maintain electric or hydraulic freight or passenger elevators, escalators, or dumbwaiters. Connect electrical wiring to control panels and electric motors. Connect car frames to counterweights, using steel cables. Check that safety regulations and building codes are met and complete service reports verifying conformance to standards. Bolt or weld steel rails to the walls of shafts to guide elevators, working from scaffolding or platforms. Assemble, install, repair, and maintain elevators, escalators, moving sidewalks, and dumbwaiters, using hand and power tools and testing devices such as test lamps, ammeters, and voltmeters. Cut prefabricated sections of framework, rails, and other components to specified dimensions. Adjust safety controls; counterweights; door mechanisms; and components such as valves, ratchets, seals, and brake linings. Locate malfunctions in brakes, motors, switches, and signal and control systems, using test equipment. Assemble electrically powered stairs, steel frameworks, and tracks and install associated motors and electrical wiring. Disassemble defective units and repair or replace parts such as locks, gears, cables, and electric wiring. Inspect wiring connections, control panel hookups, door installations, and alignments and clearances of cars and hoistways to ensure that equipment will operate properly. Install outer doors and door frames at elevator entrances on each floor of a structure. Assemble elevator cars, installing each car's platform, walls, and doors. Maintain log books that detail all repairs and checks performed. Operate elevators to determine power demands and test power consumption to detect overload factors. Read and interpret blueprints to determine the layout of system components, frameworks, and foundations and to select installation equipment. Test newly installed equipment to ensure that it meets specifications, such as stopping at floors for set amounts of time. Participate in additional training to keep skills up to date. Install electrical wires and controls by attaching conduit along shaft walls from floor to floor and then pulling plastic-covered wires through the conduit. Attach guide shoes and rollers to minimize the lateral motion of cars as they travel through shafts.

LEVEL OF ACTIVITY (out of 100)—General Physical Activity: 59.4. **Sitting:** 28.6. **Outdoors:** 25.0.

SKILLS—Installation; Repairing; Equipment Maintenance; Troubleshooting; Quality Control Analysis; Operation Monitoring; Systems Analysis; Operation and Control.

GOE—Interest Area: 02. Architecture and Construction. **Work Group:** 02.05. Systems and Equipment Installation, Maintenance, and Repair. **Other Jobs in This Work Group:** Electrical and Electronics Repairers,

Powerhouse, Substation, and Relay; Electrical Power-Line Installers and Repairers; Heating and Air Conditioning Mechanics and Installers; Maintenance and Repair Workers, General; Refrigeration Mechanics and Installers; Telecommunications Equipment Installers and Repairers, Except Line Installers; Telecommunications Line Installers and Repairers. **PERSONALITY TYPE:** Realistic. Realistic occupations frequently involve work activities that include practical, hands-on problems and solutions. They often deal with plants; animals; and real-world materials like wood, tools, and machinery. Many of the occupations require working outside and do not involve a lot of paperwork or working closely with others.

EDUCATION/TRAINING PROGRAM(S)— Industrial Mechanics and Maintenance Technology. **RELATED KNOWLEDGE/ COURSES—Building and Construction:** The materials, methods, and tools involved in the construction or repair of houses, buildings, or other structures such as highways and roads. **Mechanical Devices:** Machines and tools, including their designs, uses, repair, and maintenance. **Engineering and Technology:** The practical application of engineering science and technology. This includes applying principles, techniques, procedures, and equipment to the design and production of various goods and services. **Physics:** Physical principles and laws and their interrelationships and applications to understanding fluid, material, and atmospheric dynamics and mechanical, electrical, atomic, and subatomic structures and processes. **Public Safety and Security:** Relevant equipment, policies, procedures, and strategies to promote effective local, state, or national security operations for the protection of people, data, property, and institutions.

WORK ENVIRONMENT—Indoors; hazardous conditions; hazardous equipment; minor burns, cuts, bites, or stings; standing; using hands on objects, tools, or controls.

Embalmers

- Education/Training Required: Postsecondary vocational training
- Annual Earnings: $36,960
- Growth: 15.6%
- Annual Job Openings: 2,000
- Self-Employed: 0.0%
- Part-Time: 44.0%

Prepare bodies for interment in conformity with legal requirements. Conform to laws of health and sanitation and ensure that legal requirements concerning embalming are met. Apply cosmetics to impart lifelike appearance to the deceased. Incise stomach and abdominal walls and probe internal organs, using trocar, to withdraw blood and waste matter from organs. Close incisions, using needles and sutures. Reshape or reconstruct disfigured or maimed bodies when necessary, using derma-surgery techniques and materials such as clay, cotton, plaster of paris, and wax. Make incisions in arms or thighs and drain blood from circulatory system and replace it with embalming fluid, using pump. Dress bodies and place them in caskets. Join lips, using needles and thread or wire. Conduct interviews to arrange for the preparation of obituary notices, to assist with the selection of caskets or urns, and to determine the location and time of burials or cremations. Perform the duties of funeral directors, including coordinating funeral activities. Attach trocar to pump-tube, start pump, and repeat probing to force embalming fluid into organs. Perform special procedures necessary for remains that are to be transported to other states or overseas or where death was caused by infectious disease. Maintain records such as itemized lists of clothing or valuables delivered with body and names of persons embalmed. Insert convex celluloid or cotton between eyeballs and eyelids to prevent slipping and sinking of eyelids. Wash and dry bodies, using germicidal soap and towels or hot air dryers. Arrange for transporting the deceased to another state for interment. Supervise funeral attendants and other funeral home staff. Pack body orifices with cotton saturated with embalming fluid to prevent escape of gases or waste matter. Assist with placing caskets in hearses and organize cemetery processions. Serve as pallbearers, attend visiting rooms, and provide other assistance to the bereaved. Direct casket and floral display placement and arrange guest seating. Arrange funeral home equipment and perform general maintenance. Assist coroners at death scenes or at autopsies, file police reports, and testify at inquests or in court if employed by a coroner.

LEVEL OF ACTIVITY (out of 100)—General Physical Activity: 58.1. **Sitting:** 34.7. **Outdoors:** 40.6.

SKILLS—Service Orientation; Science; Management of Financial Resources; Social Perceptiveness; Management of Material Resources; Equipment Maintenance; Management of Personnel Resources; Operation Monitoring.

GOE—Interest Area: 08. Health Science. **Work Group:** 08.09. Health Protection and Promo-tion. **Other Jobs in This Work Group:** Athletic Trainers; Dietetic Technicians; Dietitians and Nutritionists. **PERSONALITY TYPE:** Realistic. Realistic occupations frequently involve work activities that include practical, hands-on problems and solutions. They often deal with plants; animals; and real-world materials like wood, tools, and machinery. Many of the occupations require working outside and do not involve a lot of paperwork or working closely with others.

EDUCATION/TRAINING PROGRAM(S)— Funeral Service and Mortuary Science, General; Mortuary Science and Embalming/Embalmer. **RELATED KNOWLEDGE/COURSES—** **Chemistry:** The chemical composition, structure, and properties of substances and of the chemical processes and transformations that they undergo. This includes uses of chemicals and their danger signs, production techniques, and disposal methods. **Biology:** Plant and animal organisms and their tissues, cells, functions, interdependencies, and interactions with each other and the environment. **Customer and Personal Service:** Principles and processes for providing customer and personal services. This includes customer needs assessment, meeting quality standards for services, and evaluation of customer satisfaction. **Philosophy and Theology:** Different philosophical systems and religions. This includes their basic principles, values, ethics, ways of thinking, customs, and practices and their impact on human culture. **Therapy and Counseling:** Principles, methods, and procedures for diagnosis, treatment, and rehabilitation of physical and mental dysfunctions and for career counseling and guidance. **Medicine and Dentistry:** The information and techniques needed to diagnose and treat human injuries, diseases, and deformities. This includes symptoms, treatment alternatives, drug proper-

E

ties and interactions, and preventive health-care measures.

WORK ENVIRONMENT—Indoors; contaminants; disease or infections; hazardous conditions; standing; using hands on objects, tools, or controls.

Emergency Medical Technicians and Paramedics

- Education/Training Required: Postsecondary vocational training
- Annual Earnings: $26,080
- Growth: 27.3%
- Annual Job Openings: 21,000
- Self-Employed: 0.1%
- Part-Time: 10.6%

Assess injuries, administer emergency medical care, and extricate trapped individuals. Transport injured or sick persons to medical facilities. Administer first-aid treatment and life-support care to sick or injured persons in pre-hospital setting. Operate equipment such as electrocardiograms (EKGs), external defibrillators, and bag-valve mask resuscitators in advanced life-support environments. Assess nature and extent of illness or injury to establish and prioritize medical procedures. Maintain vehicles and medical and communication equipment and replenish first-aid equipment and supplies. Observe, record, and report to physician the patient's condition or injury, the treatment provided, and reactions to drugs and treatment. Perform emergency diagnostic and treatment procedures, such as stomach suction, airway management, or heart monitoring, during ambulance ride. Administer drugs, orally or by injection, and perform intravenous procedures under a physician's direction. Comfort and reassure patients. Coordinate work with other emergency medical team members and police and fire department personnel. Communicate with dispatchers and treatment center personnel to provide information about situation, to arrange reception of victims, and to receive instructions for further treatment. Immobilize patient for placement on stretcher and ambulance transport, using backboard or other spinal immobilization device. Decontaminate ambulance interior following treatment of patient with infectious disease and report case to proper authorities. Drive mobile intensive care unit to specified location, following instructions from emergency medical dispatcher. Coordinate with treatment center personnel to obtain patients' vital statistics and medical history, to determine the circumstances of the emergency, and to administer emergency treatment.

LEVEL OF ACTIVITY (out of 100)—General Physical Activity: 70.0. **Sitting:** 36.0. **Outdoors:** 47.4.

SKILLS—Equipment Maintenance; Service Orientation; Social Perceptiveness; Operation Monitoring; Coordination; Operation and Control; Instructing; Equipment Selection.

GOE—Interest Area: 12. Law and Public Safety. **Work Group:** 12.06. Emergency Responding. **Other Jobs in This Work Group:** Fire Fighters; Forest Fire Fighters; Municipal Fire Fighters. **PERSONALITY TYPE:** Social. Social occupations frequently involve working with, communicating with, and teaching people. These occupations often involve helping or providing service to others.

EDUCATION/TRAINING PROGRAM(S)— Emergency Care Attendant (EMT Ambulance); Emergency Medical Technology/Technician (EMT Paramedic). **RELATED KNOWL-EDGE/COURSES**—**Medicine and Dentistry:** The information and techniques needed to diagnose and treat human injuries, diseases, and deformities. This includes symptoms, treatment alternatives, drug properties and interactions, and preventive health-care measures. **Customer and Personal Service:** Principles and processes for providing customer and personal services. This includes customer needs assessment, meeting quality standards for services, and evaluation of customer satisfaction. **Therapy and Counseling:** Principles, methods, and procedures for diagnosis, treatment, and rehabilitation of physical and mental dysfunctions and for career counseling and guidance. **Chemistry:** The chemical composition, structure, and properties of substances and of the chemical processes and transformations that they undergo. This includes uses of chemicals and their danger signs, production techniques, and disposal methods. **Psychology:** Human behavior and performance; individual differences in ability, personality, and interests; learning and motivation; psychological research methods; and the assessment and treatment of behavioral and affective disorders. **Biology:** Plant and animal organisms and their tissues, cells, functions, interdependencies, and interactions with each other and the environment.

WORK ENVIRONMENT—Outdoors; noisy; very bright or dim lighting; contaminants; cramped work space, awkward positions; disease or infections.

Environmental Science and Protection Technicians, Including Health

- Education/Training Required: Associate degree
- Annual Earnings: $36,260
- Growth: 16.3%
- Annual Job Openings: 6,000
- Self-Employed: 1.4%
- Part-Time: 22.7%

Perform laboratory and field tests to monitor the environment and investigate sources of pollution, including those that affect health. Under direction of an environmental scientist or specialist, may collect samples of gases, soil, water, and other materials for testing and take corrective actions as assigned. Record test data and prepare reports, summaries, and charts that interpret test results. Collect samples of gases, soils, water, industrial wastewater, and asbestos products to conduct tests on pollutant levels and identify sources of pollution. Respond to and investigate hazardous conditions or spills or outbreaks of disease or food poisoning, collecting samples for analysis. Provide information and technical and program assistance to government representatives, employers, and the general public on the issues of public health, environmental protection, or workplace safety. Calibrate microscopes and test instruments. Make recommendations to control or eliminate unsafe conditions at workplaces or public facilities. Inspect sanitary conditions at public facilities. Prepare samples or photomicrographs for testing and analysis. Calculate amount of pollutant in samples or compute air pollution or gas flow in industrial processes, using chemical and mathematical formulas. Initiate procedures to close down or fine establishments violating environmental or health regulations. Determine amounts and kinds of chemicals to use in destroying harmful organisms and removing impurities from purification systems. Discuss test results and analyses with customers. Maintain files such as hazardous waste databases, chemical usage data, personnel exposure information, and diagrams showing equipment locations. Perform statistical analysis of environmental data. Set up equipment or stations to monitor and collect pollutants from sites such as smokestacks, manufacturing plants, or mechanical equipment. Distribute permits, closure plans, and cleanup plans. Inspect workplaces to ensure the absence of health and safety hazards such as high noise levels, radiation, or potential lighting hazards. Weigh, analyze, and measure collected sample particles, such as lead, coal dust, or rock, to determine concentration of pollutants. Examine and analyze material for presence and concentration of contaminants such as asbestos, using variety of microscopes. Develop testing procedures or direct activities of workers in laboratory.

LEVEL OF ACTIVITY (out of 100)—General Physical Activity: 58.1. **Sitting:** 45.3. **Outdoors:** 42.5.

SKILLS—Science; Persuasion; Active Learning; Troubleshooting; Mathematics; Reading Comprehension; Quality Control Analysis; Operation Monitoring.

GOE—Interest Area: 01. Agriculture and Natural Resources. **Work Group:** 01.03. Resource Technologies for Plants, Animals, and the Environment. **Other Jobs in This Work Group:** Agricultural and Food Science Technicians; Agricultural Technicians; Food Science Technicians; Food Scientists and Technologists; Geological and Petroleum Technicians; Geological Sample Test Technicians; Geophysical Data Technicians. **PERSONALITY TYPE:** Investigative. Investigative occupations frequently involve working with ideas and require an extensive amount of thinking. These occupations can involve searching for facts and figuring out problems mentally.

EDUCATION/TRAINING PROGRAM(S)— Environmental Studies; Environmental Science; Physical Science Technologies/Technicians, Other; Science Technologies/Technicians, Other. **RELATED KNOWLEDGE/COURSES—Biology:** Plant and animal organisms and their tissues, cells, functions, interdependencies, and interactions with each other and the environment. **Engineering and Technology:** The practical application of engineering science and technology. This includes applying principles, techniques, procedures, and equipment to the design and production of various goods and services. **Chemistry:** The chemical composition, structure, and properties of substances and of the chemical processes and transformations that they undergo. This includes uses of chemicals and their danger signs, production techniques, and disposal methods. **Building and Construction:** The materials, methods, and tools involved in the construction or repair of houses, buildings, or other structures such as highways and roads. **Physics:** Physical principles and laws and their interrelationships and applications to understanding fluid, material, and atmospheric dynamics and mechanical, electrical, atomic, and subatomic structures and processes. **Design:** Design techniques, tools, and principles involved in production of precision technical plans, blueprints, drawings, and models.

WORK ENVIRONMENT—More often indoors than outdoors; noisy; very hot or cold; contaminants; sitting.

Excavating and Loading Machine and Dragline Operators

- Education/Training Required: Moderate-term on-the-job training
- Annual Earnings: $32,380
- Growth: 8.0%
- Annual Job Openings: 11,000
- Self-Employed: 19.1%
- Part-Time: 3.6%

Operate or tend machinery equipped with scoops, shovels, or buckets to excavate and load loose materials. Operate machinery to perform activities such as backfilling excavations, vibrating or breaking rock or concrete, and making winter roads. Perform manual labor to prepare or finish sites, such as shoveling materials by hand. Lubricate, adjust, and repair machinery and replace parts such as gears, bearings, and bucket teeth. Drive machines to work sites. Direct ground workers engaged in activities such as moving stakes or markers or changing positions of towers. Receive written or oral instructions regarding material movement or excavation. Set up and inspect equipment prior to operation. Move materials over short distances, such as around a construction site, factory, or warehouse. Move levers, depress foot pedals, and turn dials to operate power machinery such as power shovels, stripping shovels, scraper loaders, or backhoes. Measure and verify levels of rock or gravel, bases, and other excavated material. Direct workers engaged in placing blocks and outriggers in order to prevent capsizing of machines when lifting heavy loads. Become familiar with digging plans, machine capabilities and limitations, and efficient and safe digging procedures in a given application. Adjust dig face angles for varying overburden depths and set lengths. Create and maintain inclines and ramps; handle slides, mud, and pit cleanings and maintenance. Observe hand signals, grade stakes, and other markings when operating machines so that work can be performed to specifications.

LEVEL OF ACTIVITY (out of 100)—General Physical Activity: 52.1. **Sitting:** 52.6. **Outdoors:** 70.0.

SKILLS—Operation and Control; Operation Monitoring.

GOE—Interest Area: 01. Agriculture and Natural Resources. **Work Group:** 01.08. Mining and Drilling. **Other Jobs in This Work Group:** Continuous Mining Machine Operators; Derrick Operators, Oil and Gas; Earth Drillers, Except Oil and Gas; Explosives Workers, Ordnance Handling Experts, and Blasters; Helpers—Extraction Workers; Loading Machine Operators, Underground Mining; Mine Cutting and Channeling Machine Operators; Rock Splitters, Quarry; Roof Bolters, Mining; Rotary Drill Operators, Oil and Gas; Roustabouts, Oil and Gas; Service Unit Operators, Oil, Gas, and Mining; Shuttle Car Operators; Wellhead Pumpers. **PERSONALI-**

TY TYPE: Realistic. Realistic occupations frequently involve work activities that include practical, hands-on problems and solutions. They often deal with plants; animals; and real-world materials like wood, tools, and machinery. Many of the occupations require working outside and do not involve a lot of paperwork or working closely with others.

EDUCATION/TRAINING PROGRAM(S)—Construction/Heavy Equipment/Earthmoving Equipment Operation. RELATED KNOWLEDGE/COURSES—Mechanical Devices: Machines and tools, including their designs, uses, repair, and maintenance. Building and Construction: The materials, methods, and tools involved in the construction or repair of houses, buildings, or other structures such as highways and roads.

WORK ENVIRONMENT—Outdoors; noisy; whole-body vibration; hazardous equipment; sitting; using hands on objects, tools, or controls.

Farmers and Ranchers

- Education/Training Required: Long-term on-the-job training
- Annual Earnings: $34,140
- Growth: –14.5%
- Annual Job Openings: 96,000
- Self-Employed: 100.0%
- Part-Time: 23.6%

On an ownership or rental basis, operate farms, ranches, greenhouses, nurseries, timber tracts, or other agricultural production establishments that produce crops, horticultural specialties, livestock, poultry, finfish, shellfish, or animal specialties. May plant, cultivate, harvest, perform post-harvest activities for, and market crops and livestock; may hire, train, and supervise farm workers or supervise a farm labor contractor; may prepare cost, production, and other records. May maintain and operate machinery and perform physical work. Monitor crops as they grow in order to ensure that they are growing properly and are free from diseases and contaminants. Select animals for market and provide transportation of livestock to market. Select and purchase supplies and equipment such as seed, fertilizers, and farm machinery. Remove lower-quality or older animals from herds and purchase other livestock to replace culled animals. Purchase and store livestock feed. Plan crop activities based on factors such as crop maturity and weather conditions. Negotiate and arrange with buyers for the sale, storage, and shipment of crops. Determine types and quantities of crops or livestock to be raised, according to factors such as market conditions, federal program availability, and soil conditions. Milk cows, using milking machinery. Maintain pastures or grazing lands to ensure that animals have enough feed, employing pasture-conservation measures such as arranging rotational grazing. Install and shift irrigation systems to irrigate fields evenly or according to crop need. Harvest crops and collect specialty products such as royal jelly, wax, pollen, and honey from bee colonies. Evaluate product marketing alternatives and then promote and market farm products, acting as the sales agent for livestock and crops. Assist in animal births and care for newborn livestock. Breed and raise stock such as cattle, poultry, and honeybees, using recognized breeding practices to ensure continued improvement in stock. Clean and disinfect buildings and yards and remove manure. Clean and sanitize milking equipment, storage tanks, collection cups, and cows' udders or ensure that procedures are followed to maintain sanitary conditions for handling of milk. Clean, grade, and package crops for marketing. Control the spread of disease and parasites in herds by using vaccination and medication and by separating sick animals. Destroy diseased or superfluous crops. Perform crop production duties such as planning, tilling, planting, fertilizing, cultivating, spraying, and harvesting. Set up and operate farm machinery to cultivate, harvest, and haul crops.

LEVEL OF ACTIVITY (out of 100)—General Physical Activity: 64.3. **Sitting:** 37.1. **Outdoors:** 62.9.

SKILLS—Management of Financial Resources; Installation; Operation and Control; Management of Material Resources; Management of Personnel Resources; Equipment Selection; Equipment Maintenance; Repairing.

GOE—Interest Area: 01. Agriculture and Natural Resources. **Work Group:** 01.01. Managerial Work in Agriculture and Natural Resources. **Other Jobs in This Work Group:** Aquacultural Managers; Crop and Livestock Managers; Farm Labor Contractors; Farm, Ranch, and Other Agricultural Managers; First-Line Supervisors/Managers of Agricultural Crop and Horticultural Workers; First-Line Supervisors/Managers of Animal Husbandry and Animal Care Workers; First-Line Supervisors/Managers of Aquacultural Workers; First-Line Supervisors/Managers of Construction Trades and Extraction Workers; First-Line Supervisors/Managers of Farming, Fishing, and Forestry Workers; First-Line Supervisors/Managers of Landscaping, Lawn Service, and Groundskeeping Workers; First-Line Supervisors/Managers of Logging Workers; Nursery and Greenhouse Managers; Park Naturalists; Purchasing Agents and Buyers, Farm Products. **PERSONALITY TYPE:** Realistic. Realistic occupations frequently involve work activities that include practical, hands-on problems and solutions. They often deal with plants; animals; and real-world materials like wood, tools, and machinery. Many of the occupations require working outside and do not involve a lot of paperwork or working closely with others.

EDUCATION/TRAINING PROGRAM(S)— Agricultural Business and Management, General; Agribusiness/Agricultural Business Operations; Farm/Farm and Ranch Management; Agricultural Production Operations, General; Animal/Livestock Husbandry and Production; Aquaculture; Crop Production; Dairy Husbandry and Production; Agricultural Production Operations, Other; Ornamental Horticulture; Greenhouse Operations and Management; others. **RELATED KNOWLEDGE/COURSES—Food Production:** Techniques and equipment for planting, growing, and harvesting food products (both plant and animal) for consumption, including storage/handling techniques. **Economics and Accounting:** Economic and accounting principles and practices, the financial markets, banking, and the analysis and reporting of financial data. **Personnel and Human Resources:** Principles and procedures for personnel recruitment, selection, training, compensation and benefits, labor relations and negotiation, and personnel information systems. **Production and Processing:** Raw materials, production processes, quality control, costs, and other techniques for maximizing the effective manufacture and distribution of goods. **Biology:** Plant and animal organisms and their tissues, cells, functions, interdependencies, and interactions with each other and the environment. **Sales and Marketing:** Principles and methods for showing, promoting, and selling products or services. This includes marketing strategy and tactics, product demonstration, sales techniques, and sales control systems.

WORK ENVIRONMENT—Outdoors; contaminants; hazardous equipment; minor burns, cuts, bites, or stings; standing; using hands on objects, tools, or controls.

First-Line Supervisors/Managers of Agricultural Crop and Horticultural Workers

This job can be found in the Part I lists under the title Supervisors, Farming, Fishing, and Forestry Workers.

- Education/Training Required: Associate degree
- Annual Earnings: $36,030
- Growth: 3.6%
- Annual Job Openings: 11,000
- Self-Employed: 17.1%
- Part-Time: 9.9%

The job openings listed here are shared with Farm Labor Contractors; First-Line Supervisors/Managers of Animal Husbandry and Animal Care Workers; First-Line Supervisors/Managers of Aquacultural Workers; and First-Line Supervisors/Managers of Logging Workers.

Directly supervise and coordinate activities of agricultural crop or horticultural workers. Confer with managers to evaluate weather and soil conditions; to develop plans and procedures; and to discuss issues such as changes in fertilizers, herbicides, or cultivating techniques. Estimate labor requirements for jobs and plan work schedules accordingly. Inspect crops, fields, and plant stock to determine conditions and need for cultivating, spraying, weeding, or harvesting. Issue equipment such as farm implements, machinery, ladders, or containers to workers and collect equipment when work is complete. Observe workers to detect inefficient and unsafe work procedures or to identify problems, initiating corrective action as necessary. Read inventory records, customer orders, and shipping schedules to determine required activities. Assign duties such as cultivation, irrigation, and harvesting of crops or plants; product packaging and grading; and equipment maintenance. Investigate grievances and settle disputes to maintain harmony among workers. Drive and operate farm machinery such as trucks, tractors, or self-propelled harvesters in order to transport workers and supplies or to cultivate and harvest fields. Prepare and maintain time and payroll reports, as well as details of personnel actions such as performance evaluations, hires, promotions, and disciplinary actions. Prepare reports regarding farm conditions, crop yields, machinery breakdowns, or labor problems. Requisition and purchase supplies such as insecticides, machine parts or lubricants, and tools. Calculate and monitor budgets for maintenance and development of collections, grounds, and infrastructure. Monitor and oversee construction projects such as horticultural buildings and irrigation systems. Perform hardscape activities, including installation and repair of irrigation systems, resurfacing and grading of paths, rockwork, or erosion control. Perform the same horticultural or agricultural duties as subordinates. Review employees' work to evaluate quality and quantity. Inspect facilities to determine maintenance needs. Recruit, hire, and discharge workers. Train workers in techniques such as planting, harvesting, weeding, and insect identification and in the use of safety measures.

LEVEL OF ACTIVITY (out of 100)—General Physical Activity: 47.1. **Sitting:** 41.4. **Outdoors:** 55.7.

SKILLS—Management of Personnel Resources; Management of Material Resources; Systems Analysis; Systems Evaluation; Equipment Maintenance; Operation Monitoring; Coordination; Science.

GOE—Interest Area: 01. Agriculture and Natural Resources. **Work Group:** 01.01. Managerial Work in Agriculture and Natural Resources. **Other Jobs in This Work Group:** Aquacultural Managers; Crop and Livestock Managers; Farm Labor Contractors; Farm, Ranch, and Other Agricultural Managers; Farmers and Ranchers; First-Line Supervisors/Managers of Animal Husbandry and Animal Care Workers; First-Line Supervisors/Managers of Aquacultural Workers; First-Line Supervisors/Managers of Construction Trades and Extraction Workers; First-Line Supervisors/Managers of Farming, Fishing, and Forestry Workers; First-Line Supervisors/Managers of Landscaping, Lawn Service, and Groundskeeping Workers; First-Line Supervisors/Managers of Logging Workers; Nursery and Greenhouse Managers; Park Naturalists; Purchasing Agents and Buyers, Farm Products. **PERSONALITY TYPE:** Realistic. Realistic occupations frequently involve work activities that include practical, hands-on problems and solutions. They often deal with plants; animals; and real-world materials like wood, tools, and machinery. Many of the occupations require working outside and do not involve a lot of paperwork or working closely with others.

EDUCATION/TRAINING PROGRAM(S)— Farm/Farm and Ranch Management; Agricultural Business and Management, Other; Agricultural Production Operations, General; Crop Production; Agricultural Production Operations, Other; Plant Sciences, General; Agronomy and Crop Science; Range Science and Management; Agriculture, Agriculture Operations, and Related Sciences, Other. **RELATED KNOWLEDGE/COURSES**— **Food Production:** Techniques and equipment for planting, growing, and harvesting food products (both plant and animal) for consumption, including storage/handling techniques. **Biology:** Plant and animal organisms and their tissues, cells, functions, interdependencies, and interactions with each other and the environment. **Personnel and Human Resources:** Principles and procedures for personnel recruitment, selection, training, compensation and benefits, labor relations and negotiation, and personnel information systems. **Administration and Management:** Business and management principles involved in strategic planning, resource allocation, human resources modeling, leadership technique, production methods, and coordination of people and resources. **Chemistry:** The chemical composition, structure, and properties of substances and of the chemical processes and transformations that they undergo. This includes uses of chemicals and their danger signs, production techniques, and disposal methods. **Mechanical Devices:** Machines and tools, including their designs, uses, repair, and maintenance.

WORK ENVIRONMENT—Outdoors; standing; using hands on objects, tools, or controls.

First-Line Supervisors/Managers of Animal Husbandry and Animal Care Workers

This job can be found in the Part I lists under the title Supervisors, Farming, Fishing, and Forestry Workers.

- Education/Training Required: Associate degree
- Annual Earnings: $36,030
- Growth: 3.6%
- Annual Job Openings: 11,000
- Self-Employed: 17.1%
- Part-Time: 9.9%

The job openings listed here are shared with Farm Labor Contractors; First-Line Supervisors/Managers of Agricultural Crop and Horticultural Workers; First-Line Supervisors/Managers of Aquacultural Workers; and First-Line Supervisors/Managers of Logging Workers.

Directly supervise and coordinate activities of animal husbandry or animal care workers. Study feed, weight, health, genetic, or milk production records in order to determine feed formulas and rations and breeding schedules. Assign tasks such as feeding and treatment of animals and cleaning and maintenance of animal quarters. Monitor animal care, maintenance, breeding, or packing and transfer activities to ensure work is done correctly. Train workers in animal care procedures, maintenance duties, and safety precautions. Perform the same animal care duties as subordinates. Observe animals for signs of illness, injury, or unusual behavior, notifying veterinarians or managers as warranted. Plan budgets and arrange for purchase of animals, feed, or supplies. Establish work schedules and procedures. Recruit, hire, and pay workers. Direct and assist workers in maintenance and repair of facilities. Transport or arrange for transport of animals, equipment, food, animal feed, and other supplies to and from worksites. Treat animal illnesses or injuries, following experience or instructions of veterinarians. Inseminate livestock artificially to produce desired offspring. Investigate complaints of animal neglect or cruelty and follow up on complaints appearing to require prosecution. Monitor eggs and adjust incubator thermometers and gauges to facilitate hatching progress and to maintain specified conditions. Operate euthanasia equipment to destroy animals. Prepare reports concerning facility activities, employees' time records, and animal treatment. Inspect buildings, fences, fields or ranges, supplies, and equipment in order to determine work to be performed. Confer with managers to determine production requirements, conditions of equipment and supplies, and work schedules.

LEVEL OF ACTIVITY (out of 100)—General Physical Activity: 42.9. **Sitting:** 41.4. **Outdoors:** 51.4.

SKILLS—Management of Personnel Resources; Management of Financial Resources; Management of Material Resources; Systems Evaluation; Systems Analysis; Instructing; Science; Time Management.

GOE—Interest Area: 01. Agriculture and Natural Resources. **Work Group:** 01.01. Managerial Work in Agriculture and Natural Resources. **Other Jobs in This Work Group:** Aquacultural Managers; Crop and Livestock Managers; Farm Labor Contractors; Farm,

Ranch, and Other Agricultural Managers; Farmers and Ranchers; First-Line Supervisors/ Managers of Agricultural Crop and Horticultural Workers; First-Line Supervisors/Managers of Aquacultural Workers; First-Line Supervisors/Managers of Construction Trades and Extraction Workers; First-Line Supervisors/ Managers of Farming, Fishing, and Forestry Workers; First-Line Supervisors/Managers of Landscaping, Lawn Service, and Groundskeeping Workers; First-Line Supervisors/Managers of Logging Workers; Nursery and Greenhouse Managers; Park Naturalists; Purchasing Agents and Buyers, Farm Products. **PERSONALITY TYPE:** Realistic. Realistic occupations frequently involve work activities that include practical, hands-on problems and solutions. They often deal with plants; animals; and real-world materials like wood, tools, and machinery. Many of the occupations require working outside and do not involve a lot of paperwork or working closely with others.

EDUCATION/TRAINING PROGRAM(S)— Animal/Livestock Husbandry and Production; Dairy Husbandry and Production; Horse Husbandry/Equine Science and Management; Animal Sciences, General; Agricultural Animal Breeding; Animal Nutrition; Dairy Science; Livestock Management; Poultry Science; Agriculture, Agriculture Operations, and Related Sciences, Other. **RELATED KNOWLEDGE/COURSES—Biology:** Plant and animal organisms and their tissues, cells, functions, interdependencies, and interactions with each other and the environment. **Food Production:** Techniques and equipment for planting, growing, and harvesting food products (both plant and animal) for consumption, including storage/handling techniques. **Medicine and Dentistry:** The information and techniques needed to diagnose and treat human injuries, diseases, and deformities. This includes symptoms, treatment alternatives, drug properties and interactions, and preventive health-care measures. **Personnel and Human Resources:** Principles and procedures for personnel recruitment, selection, training, compensation and benefits, labor relations and negotiation, and personnel information systems. **Administration and Management:** Business and management principles involved in strategic planning, resource allocation, human resources modeling, leadership technique, production methods, and coordination of people and resources.

WORK ENVIRONMENT—More often outdoors than indoors; contaminants; standing; walking and running; using hands on objects, tools, or controls.

First-Line Supervisors/Managers of Aquacultural Workers

This job can be found in the Part I lists under the title Supervisors, Farming, Fishing, and Forestry Workers.

- Education/Training Required: Associate degree
- Annual Earnings: $36,030
- Growth: 3.6%
- Annual Job Openings: 11,000
- Self-Employed: 17.1%
- Part-Time: 9.9%

The job openings listed here are shared with Farm Labor Contractors; First-Line Supervisors/Managers of Agricultural Crop and Horticultural Workers; First-Line Supervisors/Managers of Animal Husbandry and Animal Care Workers; and First-Line Supervisors/Managers of Logging Workers.

Directly supervise and coordinate activities of aquacultural workers. Direct and monitor worker activities such as treatment and rearing of fingerlings, maintenance of equipment, and harvesting of fish or shellfish. Confer with managers to determine times and places of seed planting and cultivating, feeding, or harvesting of fish or shellfish. Supervise the artificial spawning of various salmon and trout species. Direct workers to correct problems such as disease, quality of seed distribution, or adequacy of cultivation. Observe fish and beds or ponds to detect diseases, monitor fish growth, determine quality of fish, or determine completeness of harvesting. Plan work schedules according to personnel and equipment availability, tidal levels, feeding schedules, or transfer and harvest needs. Prepare or direct the preparation of fish food and specify medications to be added to food and water to treat fish for diseases. Train workers in spawning, rearing, cultivating, and harvesting methods and in the use of equipment. Interview and select new employees. Maintain workers' time records. Perform both supervisory and management functions, such as accounting, marketing, and personnel work. Record the numbers and types of fish or shellfish reared, harvested, released, sold, and shipped. Requisition supplies. Select and ship eggs to other hatcheries. Assign to workers duties such as fertilizing and incubating spawn; feeding and transferring fish; and planting, cultivating, and harvesting shellfish beds. Engage in the same fishery work as workers supervised.

LEVEL OF ACTIVITY (out of 100)—General Physical Activity: 37.1. **Sitting:** 51.4. **Outdoors:** 54.3.

SKILLS—Management of Personnel Resources; Systems Analysis; Management of Material Resources; Operation and Control; Systems Evaluation; Time Management; Instructing.

GOE—Interest Area: 01. Agriculture and Natural Resources. **Work Group:** 01.01. Managerial Work in Agriculture and Natural Resources. **Other Jobs in This Work Group:** Aquacultural Managers; Crop and Livestock Managers; Farm Labor Contractors; Farm, Ranch, and Other Agricultural Managers; Farmers and Ranchers; First-Line Supervisors/Managers of Agricultural Crop and Horticultural Workers; First-Line Supervisors/Managers of Animal Husbandry and Animal Care Workers; First-Line Supervisors/Managers of Construction Trades and Extraction Workers; First-Line Supervisors/Managers of Farming, Fishing, and Forestry Workers; First-Line Supervisors/Managers of Landscaping, Lawn Service, and Groundskeeping Workers; First-Line Supervisors/Managers of Logging Workers; Nursery and Greenhouse Managers; Park Naturalists; Purchasing Agents and Buyers, Farm Products. **PERSONALITY TYPE:** Realistic. Realistic occupations frequently involve work activities that include practical, hands-on problems and solutions. They often deal with plants; animals; and real-world materials like wood, tools, and machinery. Many of the occupations require working outside and do not involve a lot of paperwork or working closely with others.

EDUCATION/TRAINING PROGRAM(S)—Agricultural Business and Management, Other; Aquaculture; Fishing and Fisheries Sciences and Management. **RELATED KNOWLEDGE/COURSES—Food Production:** Techniques and equipment for planting, growing, and harvesting food products (both plant and animal) for consumption, including storage/handling techniques. **Biology:** Plant and animal organisms and their tissues, cells, functions, interdependencies, and interactions with each other and the environment. **Personnel and Human Resources:** Principles and procedures for personnel recruitment, selection, training, compensation and benefits, labor relations and negotiation, and personnel information systems. **Production and Processing:** Raw materials, production processes, quality control, costs, and other techniques for maximizing the effective manufacture and distribution of goods. **Administration and Management:** Business and management principles involved in strategic planning, resource allocation, human resources modeling, leadership technique, production methods, and coordination of people and resources.

WORK ENVIRONMENT—More often outdoors than indoors; more often sitting than standing; walking and running; using hands on objects, tools, or controls.

First-Line Supervisors/Managers of Construction Trades and Extraction Workers

- Education/Training Required: Work experience in a related occupation
- Annual Earnings: $51,970
- Growth: 10.9%
- Annual Job Openings: 57,000
- Self-Employed: 24.7%
- Part-Time: 3.8%

Directly supervise and coordinate activities of construction or extraction workers. Examine and inspect work progress, equipment, and construction sites to verify safety and to ensure that specifications are met. Train workers in construction methods, operation of equipment, safety procedures, and company policies. Record information such as personnel, production, and operational data on specified forms and reports. Provide assistance to workers engaged in construction or extraction activities, using hand tools and equipment. Order or requisition materials and supplies. Locate, measure, and mark site locations and placement of structures and equipment, using measuring and marking equipment. Arrange for repairs of equipment and machinery. Suggest or initiate personnel actions such as promotions, transfers, and hires.

Analyze worker and production problems and recommend solutions, such as improving production methods or implementing motivational plans. Read specifications such as blueprints to determine construction requirements and to plan procedures. Estimate material and worker requirements to complete jobs. Coordinate work activities with other construction project activities. Confer with managerial and technical personnel, other departments, and contractors in order to resolve problems and to coordinate activities. Assign work to employees based on material and worker requirements of specific jobs. Supervise, coordinate, and schedule the activities of construction or extractive workers.

LEVEL OF ACTIVITY (out of 100)—General Physical Activity: 52.9. **Sitting:** 40.0. **Outdoors:** 54.3.

SKILLS—Management of Personnel Resources; Management of Material Resources; Systems Evaluation; Systems Analysis; Operations Analysis; Management of Financial Resources; Operation Monitoring; Quality Control Analysis.

GOE—Interest Area: 01. Agriculture and Natural Resources. **Work Group:** 01.01. Managerial Work in Agriculture and Natural Resources. **Other Jobs in This Work Group:** Aquacultural Managers; Crop and Livestock Managers; Farm Labor Contractors; Farm, Ranch, and Other Agricultural Managers; Farmers and Ranchers; First-Line Supervisors/Managers of Agricultural Crop and Horticultural Workers; First-Line Supervisors/Managers of Animal Husbandry and Animal Care

Workers; First-Line Supervisors/Managers of Aquacultural Workers; First-Line Supervisors/Managers of Farming, Fishing, and Forestry Workers; First-Line Supervisors/Managers of Landscaping, Lawn Service, and Groundskeeping Workers; First-Line Supervisors/Managers of Logging Workers; Nursery and Greenhouse Managers; Park Naturalists; Purchasing Agents and Buyers, Farm Products. **PERSONALITY TYPE:** Enterprising. Enterprising occupations frequently involve starting up and carrying out projects. These occupations can involve leading people and making many decisions. They sometimes require risk taking and often deal with business.

EDUCATION/TRAINING PROGRAM(S)—Blasting/Blaster; Building/Construction Finishing, Management, and Inspection, Other; Building/Construction Site Management/Manager; Building/Construction Trades, Other; Building/Home/Construction Inspection/Inspector; Building/Property Maintenance and Management; Carpentry/Carpenter; Concrete Finishing/Concrete Finisher; Drywall Installation/Drywaller; others. **RELATED KNOWLEDGE/COURSES—Personnel and Human Resources:** Principles and procedures for personnel recruitment, selection, training, compensation and benefits, labor relations and negotiation, and personnel information systems. **Building and Construction:** The materials, methods, and tools involved in the construction or repair of houses, buildings, or other structures such as highways and roads. **Administration and Management:** Business and management principles involved in strategic planning, resource allocation, human resources modeling, leadership technique, production methods, and coordination of people and resources. **Engineering and Technology:** The practical application of engineering science and technology. This includes applying principles, techniques, procedures, and equipment to the design and production of various goods and services. **Mechanical Devices:** Machines and tools, including their designs, uses, repair, and maintenance. **Physics:** Physical principles and laws and their interrelationships and applications to understanding fluid, material, and atmospheric dynamics and mechanical, electrical, atomic, and subatomic structures and processes.

WORK ENVIRONMENT—Outdoors; contaminants; hazardous equipment; standing; using hands on objects, tools, or controls.

First-Line Supervisors/Managers of Fire Fighting and Prevention Workers

See the descriptions of these jobs:

- **Forest Fire Fighting and Prevention Supervisors**

- **Municipal Fire Fighting and Prevention Supervisors**

First-Line Supervisors/Managers of Food Preparation and Serving Workers

- Education/Training Required: Work experience in a related occupation
- Annual Earnings: $26,050
- Growth: 16.6%
- Annual Job Openings: 187,000
- Self-Employed: 3.7%
- Part-Time: 15.5%

Supervise workers engaged in preparing and serving food. Compile and balance cash receipts at the end of the day or shift. Resolve customer complaints regarding food service. Inspect supplies, equipment, and work areas to ensure efficient service and conformance to standards. Train workers in food preparation and in service, sanitation, and safety procedures. Control inventories of food, equipment, smallware, and liquor; report shortages to designated personnel. Observe and evaluate workers and work procedures in order to ensure quality standards and service. Assign duties, responsibilities, and workstations to employees in accordance with work requirements. Estimate ingredients and supplies required to prepare a recipe. Perform personnel actions such as hiring and firing staff, consulting with other managers as necessary. Analyze operational problems, such as theft and wastage, and establish procedures to alleviate these problems. Specify food portions and courses, production and time sequences, and workstation and equipment arrangements. Recommend measures for improving work procedures and worker performance to increase service quality and enhance job safety. Greet and seat guests and present menus and wine lists. Present bills and accept payments. Forecast staff, equipment, and supply requirements based on a master menu. Record production and operational data on specified forms. Perform serving duties such as carving meat, preparing flambe dishes, or serving wine and liquor. Purchase or requisition supplies and equipment needed to ensure quality and timely delivery of services. Collaborate with other personnel in order to plan menus, serving arrangements, and related details. Supervise and check the assembly of regular and special diet trays and the delivery of food trolleys to hospital patients. Schedule parties and take reservations. Develop departmental objectives, budgets, policies, procedures, and strategies. Develop equipment maintenance schedules and arrange for repairs. Evaluate new products for usefulness and suitability.

LEVEL OF ACTIVITY (out of 100)—General Physical Activity: 44.9. **Sitting:** 24.1. **Outdoors:** 19.9.

SKILLS—Management of Financial Resources; Management of Personnel Resources; Equipment Maintenance; Operation Monitoring; Management of Material Resources; Monitoring; Instructing; Service Orientation.

GOE—Interest Area: 09. Hospitality, Tourism, and Recreation. **Work Group:** 09.01. Managerial Work in Hospitality and Tourism.

Other Jobs in This Work Group: First-Line Supervisors/Managers of Personal Service Workers; Food Service Managers; Gaming Managers; Gaming Supervisors; Lodging Managers. **PERSONALITY TYPE:** Enterprising. Enterprising occupations frequently involve starting up and carrying out projects. These occupations can involve leading people and making many decisions. They sometimes require risk taking and often deal with business.

EDUCATION/TRAINING PROGRAM(S)—Cooking and Related Culinary Arts, General; Restaurant, Culinary, and Catering Management/Manager; Foodservice Systems Administration/Management. **RELATED KNOWLEDGE/COURSES—Food Production:** Techniques and equipment for planting, growing, and harvesting food products (both plant and animal) for consumption, including storage/handling techniques. **Administration and Management:** Business and management principles involved in strategic planning, resource allocation, human resources modeling, leadership technique, production methods, and coordination of people and resources. **Customer and Personal Service:** Principles and processes for providing customer and personal services. This includes customer needs assessment, meeting quality standards for services, and evaluation of customer satisfaction. **Sales and Marketing:** Principles and methods for showing, promoting, and selling products or services. This includes marketing strategy and tactics, product demonstration, sales techniques, and sales control systems. **Economics and Accounting:** Economic and accounting principles and practices, the financial markets, banking, and the analysis and reporting of financial data. **Production and Processing:** Raw materials, production processes, quality control, costs, and other techniques for maximizing the effective manufacture and distribution of goods.

WORK ENVIRONMENT—Indoors; minor burns, cuts, bites, or stings; standing; walking and running; using hands on objects, tools, or controls; repetitive motions.

First-Line Supervisors/Managers of Helpers, Laborers, and Material Movers, Hand

- Education/Training Required: Work experience in a related occupation
- Annual Earnings: $39,000
- Growth: 8.1%
- Annual Job Openings: 15,000
- Self-Employed: 1.3%
- Part-Time: 4.9%

Supervise and coordinate the activities of helpers, laborers, or material movers. Plan work schedules and assign duties to maintain adequate staffing levels, to ensure that activities are performed effectively, and to respond to fluctuating workloads. Collaborate with workers and managers to solve work-related problems. Review work throughout the work process and at completion in order to ensure that it has been performed properly. Transmit and explain work orders to laborers. Check specifications of materials loaded or unloaded against information contained in work orders. Inform designated employees or departments of items loaded and problems encountered. Examine freight to determine loading sequences. Evaluate employee performance and prepare performance appraisals. Perform the same work duties as those whom they supervise and perform more difficult or skilled tasks or assist in their performance. Prepare and maintain work records and reports that include information such as employee time and wages, daily receipts, and inspection results. Counsel employees in work-related activities, personal growth, and career development. Conduct staff meetings to relay general information or to address specific topics such as safety. Inspect equipment for wear and for conformance to specifications. Resolve personnel problems, complaints, and formal grievances when possible or refer them to higher-level supervisors for resolution. Recommend or initiate personnel actions such as promotions, transfers, and disciplinary measures. Assess training needs of staff; then arrange for or provide appropriate instruction. Schedule times of shipment and modes of transportation for materials. Quote prices to customers. Estimate material, time, and staffing requirements for a given project, based on work orders, job specifications, and experience. Provide assistance in balancing books, tracking, monitoring, and projecting a unit's budget needs and in developing unit policies and procedures. Inspect job sites to determine the extent of maintenance or repairs needed. Participate in the hiring process by reviewing credentials, conducting interviews, and making hiring decisions or recommendations.

LEVEL OF ACTIVITY (out of 100)—General Physical Activity: 54.3. **Sitting:** 32.4. **Outdoors:** 32.8.

SKILLS—Management of Personnel Resources; Monitoring; Persuasion; Time Management; Social Perceptiveness; Instructing; Judgment and Decision Making; Systems Evaluation.

GOE—Interest Area: 13. Manufacturing. **Work Group:** 13.01. Managerial Work in Manufacturing. **Other Jobs in This Work Group:** First-Line Supervisors/Managers of Mechanics, Installers, and Repairers; First-Line Supervisors/Managers of Production and Operating Workers; Industrial Production Managers. **PERSONALITY TYPE:** Enterprising. Enterprising occupations frequently involve starting up and carrying out projects. These occupations can involve leading people and making many decisions. They sometimes require risk taking and often deal with business.

EDUCATION/TRAINING PROGRAM(S)—No related CIP programs; this job is learned through work experience in a related occupation. **RELATED KNOWLEDGE/COURSES—Production and Processing:** Raw materials, production processes, quality control, costs, and other techniques for maximizing the effective manufacture and distribution of goods. **Transportation:** Principles and methods for moving people or goods by air, rail, sea, or road, including the relative costs and benefits. **Administration and Management:** Business and management principles involved in strategic planning, resource allocation, human resources modeling, leadership technique, production methods, and coordination of people and resources. **Personnel and Human Resources:** Principles and procedures for personnel recruitment, selection, training, compensation and benefits, labor relations and negotiation, and

personnel information systems. **Customer and Personal Service:** Principles and processes for providing customer and personal services. This includes customer needs assessment, meeting quality standards for services, and evaluation of customer satisfaction. **Public Safety and Security:** Relevant equipment, policies, procedures, and strategies to promote effective local, state, or national security operations for the protection of people, data, property, and institutions.

WORK ENVIRONMENT—Indoors; noisy; very hot or cold; contaminants; standing; walking and running.

First-Line Supervisors/Managers of Housekeeping and Janitorial Workers

- Education/Training Required: Work experience in a related occupation
- Annual Earnings: $30,330
- Growth: 19.0%
- Annual Job Openings: 21,000
- Self-Employed: 8.9%
- Part-Time: 14.9%

Supervise work activities of cleaning personnel in hotels, hospitals, offices, and other establishments. Direct activities for stopping the spread of infections in facilities such as hospitals.

Inspect work performed to ensure that it meets specifications and established standards. Plan and prepare employee work schedules. Perform or assist with cleaning duties as necessary. Investigate complaints about service and equipment and take corrective action. Coordinate activities with other departments to ensure that services are provided in an efficient and timely manner. Check equipment to ensure that it is in working order. Inspect and evaluate the physical condition of facilities in order to determine the type of work required. Select the most suitable cleaning materials for different types of linens, furniture, flooring, and surfaces. Instruct staff in work policies and procedures and the use and maintenance of equipment. Issue supplies and equipment to workers. Forecast necessary levels of staffing and stock at different times in order to facilitate effective scheduling and ordering. Inventory stock to ensure that supplies and equipment are available in adequate amounts. Evaluate employee performance and recommend personnel actions such as promotions, transfers, and dismissals. Confer with staff in order to resolve performance and personnel problems and to discuss company policies. Establish and implement operational standards and procedures for the departments they supervise. Recommend or arrange for additional services such as painting, repair work, renovations, and the replacement of furnishings and equipment. Select and order or purchase new equipment, supplies, and furnishings. Recommend changes that could improve service and increase operational efficiency. Maintain required records of work hours, budgets, payrolls, and other information. Screen job applicants and hire new employees. Supervise in-house services such as laundries, maintenance and repair, dry cleaning, and/or valet services. Advise managers, desk clerks, or admitting personnel of rooms ready for occupancy. Perform financial tasks such as estimating costs and preparing and managing budgets. Prepare activity and personnel reports and reports containing information such as occupancy, hours worked, facility usage, work performed, and departmental expenses.

LEVEL OF ACTIVITY (out of 100)—General Physical Activity: 37.7. **Sitting:** 32.1. **Outdoors:** 21.6.

SKILLS—Management of Personnel Resources; Monitoring; Service Orientation; Equipment Maintenance; Persuasion; Writing; Systems Evaluation; Equipment Selection.

GOE—Interest Area: 04. Business and Administration. **Work Group:** 04.02. Managerial Work in Business Detail. **Other Jobs in This Work Group:** Administrative Services Managers; First-Line Supervisors/Managers of Office and Administrative Support Workers; Meeting and Convention Planners. **PERSONALITY TYPE:** Enterprising. Enterprising occupations frequently involve starting up and carrying out projects. These occupations can involve leading people and making many decisions. They sometimes require risk taking and often deal with business.

EDUCATION/TRAINING PROGRAM(S)—No related CIP programs; this job is learned through work experience in a related occupation. **RELATED KNOWLEDGE/COURSES—Chemistry:** The chemical composition, structure, and properties of substances and of the chemical processes and transformations that they undergo. This includes uses of chemicals and their danger signs, production techniques, and disposal methods. **Building and Construction:** The materials, methods, and tools involved in the construction or repair of houses, buildings, or other structures such as highways and roads. **Administration and Management:** Business and management principles involved in strategic planning, resource allocation, human resources modeling, leadership technique, production methods, and coordination of people and resources. **Public Safety and Security:** Relevant equipment, policies, procedures, and strategies to promote effective local, state, or national security operations for the protection of people, data, property, and institutions. **Mechanical Devices:** Machines and tools, including their designs, uses, repair, and maintenance. **Physics:** Physical principles and laws and their interrelationships and applications to understanding fluid, material, and atmospheric dynamics and mechanical, electrical, atomic, and subatomic structures and processes.

WORK ENVIRONMENT—Indoors; contaminants; disease or infections; standing; walking and running.

First-Line Supervisors/Managers of Landscaping, Lawn Service, and Groundskeeping Workers

- Education/Training Required: Work experience in a related occupation
- Annual Earnings: $36,320
- Growth: 17.8%
- Annual Job Openings: 14,000
- Self-Employed: 42.4%
- Part-Time: 6.3%

Plan, organize, direct, or coordinate activities of workers engaged in landscaping or groundskeeping activities, such as planting and maintaining ornamental trees, shrubs, flowers, and lawns and applying fertilizers, pesticides, and other chemicals, according to contract specifications. May also coordinate activities of workers engaged in terracing hillsides, building retaining walls, constructing pathways, installing patios, and similar activities in following a landscape design plan. Work may involve reviewing contracts to ascertain service, machine, and workforce requirements; answering inquiries from potential customers regarding methods, material, and price ranges; and preparing estimates according to labor, material, and machine costs. Prepare service estimates based on labor, material, and machine costs and maintain budgets for individual projects. Tour grounds such as parks, botanical gardens, cemeteries, or golf courses to inspect conditions of plants and soil. Confer with managers and landscape architects to develop plans and schedules for landscaping maintenance and improvement. Direct and assist workers engaged in the maintenance and repair of equipment such as power tools and motorized equipment. Identify diseases and pests affecting landscaping and order appropriate treatments. Install and maintain landscaped areas, performing tasks such as removing snow, pouring cement curbs, and repairing sidewalks. Maintain required records such as personnel information and project records. Negotiate with customers regarding fees for landscaping, lawn service, or groundskeeping work. Perform administrative duties such as authorizing leaves and processing time sheets. Prepare and maintain required records such as work activity and personnel reports. Recommend changes in working conditions or equipment use in order to increase crew efficiency. Design and supervise the installation of sprinkler systems, calculating water pressure and valve and pipe coverage needs. Review contracts or work assignments to determine service, machine, and workforce requirements for jobs. Plant and maintain vegetation through activities such as mulching, fertilizing, watering, mowing, and pruning. Direct or perform mixing and application of fertilizers, insecticides, herbicides, and fungicides. Answer inquiries from current or prospective customers regarding methods, materials, and price ranges. Direct activities of workers who perform duties such as landscaping, cultivating lawns, or pruning trees and shrubs. Inspect completed work to ensure conformance to specifications, standards, and contract requirements. Train workers in tasks such as

transplanting and pruning trees and shrubs, finishing cement, using equipment, and caring for turf. Confer with other supervisors to coordinate work activities with those of other departments or units.

LEVEL OF ACTIVITY (out of 100)—General Physical Activity: 46.0. **Sitting:** 38.6. **Outdoors:** 60.0.

SKILLS—Management of Personnel Resources; Systems Evaluation; Systems Analysis; Management of Material Resources; Time Management; Coordination.

GOE—Interest Area: 01. Agriculture and Natural Resources. **Work Group:** 01.01. Managerial Work in Agriculture and Natural Resources. **Other Jobs in This Work Group:** Aquacultural Managers; Crop and Livestock Managers; Farm Labor Contractors; Farm, Ranch, and Other Agricultural Managers; Farmers and Ranchers; First-Line Supervisors/Managers of Agricultural Crop and Horticultural Workers; First-Line Supervisors/Managers of Animal Husbandry and Animal Care Workers; First-Line Supervisors/Managers of Aquacultural Workers; First-Line Supervisors/Managers of Construction Trades and Extraction Workers; First-Line Supervisors/Managers of Farming, Fishing, and Forestry Workers; First-Line Supervisors/Managers of Logging Workers; Nursery and Greenhouse Managers; Park Naturalists; Purchasing Agents and Buyers, Farm Products. **PERSONALITY TYPE:** Realistic. Realistic occupations frequently involve work activities that include practical, hands-on problems and solutions. They often deal with plants; animals; and real-world materials like wood, tools, and machinery. Many of the occupations require working outside and do not involve a lot of paperwork or working closely with others.

EDUCATION/TRAINING PROGRAM(S)—
Ornamental Horticulture; Landscaping and
Groundskeeping; Turf and Turfgrass
Management. **RELATED KNOWLEDGE/
COURSES—Personnel and Human
Resources:** Principles and procedures for personnel recruitment, selection, training, compensation and benefits, labor relations and
negotiation, and personnel information systems.
Administration and Management: Business and
management principles involved in strategic
planning, resource allocation, human resources
modeling, leadership technique, production
methods, and coordination of people and
resources. **Chemistry:** The chemical composition, structure, and properties of substances and
of the chemical processes and transformations
that they undergo. This includes uses of chemicals and their danger signs, production techniques, and disposal methods. **Mechanical
Devices:** Machines and tools, including their
designs, uses, repair, and maintenance.

WORK ENVIRONMENT—Outdoors; contaminants; standing; using hands on objects,
tools, or controls.

First-Line Supervisors/Managers of Logging Workers

*This job can be found in the Part I lists under the title
Supervisors, Farming, Fishing, and Forestry Workers.*

- Education/Training Required:
  Bachelor's degree
- Annual Earnings: $36,030
- Growth: 3.6%
- Annual Job Openings: 11,000
- Self-Employed: 17.1%
- Part-Time: 9.9%

*The job openings listed here are shared with Farm
Labor Contractors; First-Line Supervisors/Managers of
Agricultural Crop and Horticultural Workers; First-
Line Supervisors/Managers of Animal Husbandry and
Animal Care Workers; and First-Line Supervisors/
Managers of Aquacultural Workers.*

**Directly supervise and coordinate activities of
logging workers.** Communicate with forestry
personnel regarding forest harvesting and forest
management plans, procedures, and schedules.
Change logging operations or methods to eliminate unsafe conditions. Assign to workers duties
such as trees to be cut; cutting sequences and
specifications; and loading of trucks, railcars, or
rafts. Monitor logging operations to identify and
solve problems; improve work methods; and
ensure compliance with safety, company, and
government regulations. Monitor workers to
ensure that safety regulations are followed, warning or disciplining those who violate safety regulations. Plan and schedule logging operations

such as felling and bucking trees and grading, sorting, yarding, or loading logs. Schedule work crews, equipment, and transportation for several different work locations. Supervise and coordinate the activities of workers engaged in logging operations and silvicultural operations. Train workers in tree felling and bucking, operation of tractors and loading machines, yarding and loading techniques, and safety regulations. Coordinate dismantling equipment, moving it, and setting it up at new work sites. Coordinate the selection and movement of logs from storage areas according to transportation schedules or production requirements. Prepare production and personnel time records for management. Determine logging operation methods, crew sizes, and equipment requirements, conferring with mill, company, and forestry officials as necessary.

LEVEL OF ACTIVITY (out of 100)—General Physical Activity: 65.7. **Sitting:** 34.3. **Outdoors:** 65.7.

SKILLS—Management of Personnel Resources; Management of Material Resources; Systems Analysis; Operation and Control; Systems Evaluation; Time Management; Instructing; Coordination.

GOE—Interest Area: 01. Agriculture and Natural Resources. **Work Group:** 01.01. Managerial Work in Agriculture and Natural Resources. **Other Jobs in This Work Group:** Aquacultural Managers; Crop and Livestock Managers; Farm Labor Contractors; Farm, Ranch, and Other Agricultural Managers; Farmers and Ranchers; First-Line Supervisors/Managers of Agricultural Crop and Horticultural Workers; First-Line Supervisors/Managers of Animal Husbandry and Animal Care Workers; First-Line Supervisors/Managers of Aquacultural Workers; First-Line Supervisors/

Managers of Construction Trades and Extraction Workers; First-Line Supervisors/Managers of Farming, Fishing, and Forestry Workers; First-Line Supervisors/Managers of Landscaping, Lawn Service, and Groundskeeping Workers; Nursery and Greenhouse Managers; Park Naturalists; Purchasing Agents and Buyers, Farm Products. **PERSONALITY TYPE:** Realistic. Realistic occupations frequently involve work activities that include practical, hands-on problems and solutions. They often deal with plants; animals; and real-world materials like wood, tools, and machinery. Many of the occupations require working outside and do not involve a lot of paperwork or working closely with others.

EDUCATION/TRAINING PROGRAM(S)—Farm/Farm and Ranch Management; Agricultural Business and Management, Other. **RELATED KNOWLEDGE/COURSES**—**Administration and Management:** Business and management principles involved in strategic planning, resource allocation, human resources modeling, leadership technique, production methods, and coordination of people and resources. **Production and Processing:** Raw materials, production processes, quality control, costs, and other techniques for maximizing the effective manufacture and distribution of goods. **Personnel and Human Resources:** Principles and procedures for personnel recruitment, selection, training, compensation and benefits, labor relations and negotiation, and personnel information systems. **Mechanical Devices:** Machines and tools, including their designs, uses, repair, and maintenance. **Public Safety and Security:** Relevant equipment, policies, procedures, and strategies to promote effective local, state, or national security operations for the protection of people, data, property, and institutions. **Education and Training:** Principles and methods for curriculum and training design, teaching and instruction for individuals and groups, and the measurement of training effects.

WORK ENVIRONMENT—Outdoors; noisy; hazardous equipment; standing; walking and running; using hands on objects, tools, or controls.

First-Line Supervisors/Managers of Mechanics, Installers, and Repairers

- ◉ Education/Training Required: Work experience in a related occupation
- ◉ Annual Earnings: $51,980
- ◉ Growth: 12.4%
- ◉ Annual Job Openings: 33,000
- ◉ Self-Employed: 0.3%
- ◉ Part-Time: 1.0%

Supervise and coordinate the activities of mechanics, installers, and repairers. Determine schedules, sequences, and assignments for work activities, based on work priority, quantity of equipment, and skill of personnel. Patrol and monitor work areas and examine tools and equipment in order to detect unsafe conditions or violations of procedures or safety rules. Monitor employees' work levels and review work performance. Examine objects, systems, or facilities and analyze information to determine needed installations, services, or repairs. Participate in budget preparation and administration, coordinating purchasing and documentation and monitoring departmental expenditures. Counsel employees about work-related issues and assist employees to correct job-skill deficiencies. Requisition materials and supplies, such as tools, equipment, and replacement parts. Compute estimates and actual costs of factors such as materials, labor, and outside contractors. Conduct or arrange for worker training in safety, repair, and maintenance techniques; operational procedures; or equipment use. Interpret specifications, blueprints, and job orders to construct templates and lay out reference points for workers. Investigate accidents and injuries and prepare reports of findings. Confer with personnel, such as management, engineering, quality control, customer, and union workers' representatives, to coordinate work activities, resolve employee grievances, and identify and review resource needs. Recommend or initiate personnel actions, such as hires, promotions, transfers, discharges, and disciplinary measures. Perform skilled repair and maintenance operations, using equipment such as hand and power tools, hydraulic presses and shears, and welding equipment. Compile operational and personnel records, such as time and production records, inventory data, repair and maintenance statistics, and test results. Develop, implement, and evaluate maintenance policies and procedures. Monitor tool inventories and the condition and maintenance of shops in order to ensure adequate working conditions. Inspect, test, and measure completed work, using devices such as hand tools and gauges to verify conformance to standards and repair requirements.

LEVEL OF ACTIVITY (out of 100)—General Physical Activity: 45.0. **Sitting:** 40.0. **Outdoors:** 44.9.

SKILLS—Installation; Repairing; Management of Personnel Resources; Management of Material Resources; Management of Financial Resources; Equipment Maintenance; Troubleshooting; Negotiation.

GOE—Interest Area: 13. Manufacturing. **Work Group:** 13.01. Managerial Work in Manufacturing. **Other Jobs in This Work Group:** First-Line Supervisors/Managers of Helpers, Laborers, and Material Movers, Hand; First-Line Supervisors/Managers of Production and Operating Workers; Industrial Production Managers. **PERSONALITY TYPE:** Enterprising. Enterprising occupations frequently involve starting up and carrying out projects. These occupations can involve leading people and making many decisions. They sometimes require risk taking and often deal with business.

EDUCATION/TRAINING PROGRAM(S)— Operations Management and Supervision. **RELATED KNOWLEDGE/COURSES**— **Mechanical Devices:** Machines and tools, including their designs, uses, repair, and maintenance. **Building and Construction:** The materials, methods, and tools involved in the construction or repair of houses, buildings, or other structures such as highways and roads. **Design:** Design techniques, tools, and principles involved in production of precision technical plans, blueprints, drawings, and models. **Personnel and Human Resources:** Principles and procedures for personnel recruitment, selection, training, compensation and benefits, labor relations and negotiation, and personnel information systems. **Engineering and Technology:** The practical application of engineering science and technology. This includes applying principles, techniques, procedures, and equipment to the design and production of various goods and services. **Administration and Management:** Business and management principles involved in strategic planning, resource allocation, human resources modeling, leadership technique, production methods, and coordination of people and resources.

WORK ENVIRONMENT—More often indoors than outdoors; noisy; very hot or cold; contaminants; standing.

First-Line Supervisors/Managers of Police and Detectives

- Education/Training Required: Work experience in a related occupation
- Annual Earnings: $65,570
- Growth: 15.5%
- Annual Job Openings: 9,000
- Self-Employed: 0.0%
- Part-Time: 0.9%

Supervise and coordinate activities of members of police force. Explain police operations to subordinates to assist them in performing their job duties. Inform personnel of changes in regulations and policies, implications of new or amended laws, and new techniques of police work. Supervise and coordinate the investigation of criminal cases, offering guidance and expertise to investigators and ensuring that procedures are conducted in accordance with laws and regulations. Investigate and resolve personnel problems within organization and charges of misconduct against staff. Train staff in proper police work procedures. Maintain logs; prepare reports; and direct the preparation, handling, and maintenance of departmental records. Monitor and evaluate the job performance of subordinates and authorize promotions and transfers. Direct collection, preparation, and handling of evidence and personal property of prisoners. Develop, implement, and revise departmental policies and procedures. Conduct raids and order detention of witnesses and suspects for questioning. Prepare work schedules and assign duties to subordinates. Discipline staff for violation of department rules and regulations. Cooperate with court personnel and officials from other law enforcement agencies and testify in court as necessary. Review contents of written orders to ensure adherence to legal requirements. Inspect facilities, supplies, vehicles, and equipment to ensure conformance to standards. Prepare news releases and respond to police correspondence. Requisition and issue equipment and supplies. Meet with civic, educational, and community groups to develop community programs and events and to discuss law enforcement subjects. Direct release or transfer of prisoners. Prepare budgets and manage expenditures of department funds.

LEVEL OF ACTIVITY (out of 100)—General Physical Activity: 68.6. **Sitting:** 52.9. **Outdoors:** 51.1.

SKILLS—Management of Personnel Resources; Persuasion; Negotiation; Social Perceptiveness; Service Orientation; Monitoring; Judgment and Decision Making; Management of Material Resources.

GOE—Interest Area: 12. Law and Public Safety. **Work Group:** 12.01. Managerial Work in Law and Public Safety. **Other Jobs in This Work Group:** Emergency Management Specialists; First-Line Supervisors/Managers of Correctional Officers; First-Line Supervisors/Managers of Fire Fighting and Prevention Workers; Forest Fire Fighting and Prevention Supervisors; Municipal Fire Fighting and Prevention Supervisors. **PERSONALITY TYPE:** Enterprising. Enterprising occupations frequently involve starting up and carrying out projects. These occupations can involve leading people and making many decisions. They sometimes require risk taking and often deal with business.

EDUCATION/TRAINING PROGRAM(S)—Corrections; Criminal Justice/Law Enforcement Administration; Criminal Justice/Safety Studies. **RELATED KNOWLEDGE/COURSES**—**Public Safety and Security:** Relevant equipment, policies, procedures, and strategies to promote effective local, state, or national security operations for the protection of people, data, property, and institutions. **Psychology:** Human behavior and performance; individual differences in ability, personality, and interests; learning and motivation; psychological research methods; and the assessment and treatment of behavioral and affective disorders. **Law and Government:** Laws, legal codes, court procedures, precedents, government regulations, executive orders, agency rules, and the democratic political process. **Personnel and Human Resources:** Principles and procedures for personnel recruitment, selection, training, compensation and benefits, labor relations and negotiation, and personnel information systems. **Education and Training:** Principles and methods for curriculum and training design, teaching and instruction for individuals and groups, and the measurement of training effects. **Customer and Personal Service:** Principles and processes for providing customer and personal services. This includes customer needs assessment, meeting quality standards for services, and evaluation of customer satisfaction.

WORK ENVIRONMENT—More often outdoors than indoors; very hot or cold; very bright or dim lighting; hazardous equipment; sitting.

First-Line Supervisors/Managers of Production and Operating Workers

- Education/Training Required: Work experience in a related occupation
- Annual Earnings: $46,140
- Growth: 2.7%
- Annual Job Openings: 89,000
- Self-Employed: 3.9%
- Part-Time: 2.3%

Supervise and coordinate the activities of production and operating workers, such as inspectors, precision workers, machine setters and operators, assemblers, fabricators, and plant and system operators. Enforce safety and sanitation regulations. Direct and coordinate the activities of employees engaged in the production or processing of goods, such as inspectors, machine setters, and fabricators. Read and analyze charts, work orders, production schedules, and other records and reports in order to determine production requirements and to evaluate current production estimates and outputs. Confer with other supervisors to coordinate operations and activities within or between departments. Plan and establish work schedules, assignments, and production sequences to meet production goals. Inspect materials, products, or equipment to detect defects or malfunctions. Demonstrate equipment operations and work and safety procedures to new employees or assign employees to experienced workers for training. Observe work and monitor gauges, dials, and other indicators to ensure that operators conform to production or processing standards. Interpret specifications, blueprints, job orders, and company policies and procedures for workers. Confer with management or subordinates to resolve worker problems, complaints, or grievances. Maintain operations data such as time, production, and cost records and prepare management reports of production results. Recommend or implement measures to motivate employees and to improve production methods, equipment performance, product quality, or efficiency. Determine standards, budgets, production goals, and rates, based on company policies, equipment and labor availability, and workloads. Requisition materials, supplies, equipment parts, or repair services. Recommend personnel actions such as hirings and promotions. Set up and adjust machines and equipment. Calculate labor and equipment requirements and production specifications, using standard formulas. Plan and develop new products and production processes.

LEVEL OF ACTIVITY (out of 100)—General Physical Activity: 37.6. **Sitting:** 32.1. **Outdoors:** 24.3.

SKILLS—Management of Personnel Resources; Operation Monitoring; Quality Control Analysis; Operation and Control; Systems Analysis; Monitoring; Operations Analysis; Persuasion.

GOE—**Interest Area:** 13. Manufacturing. **Work Group:** 13.01. Managerial Work in Manufacturing. **Other Jobs in This Work Group:** First-Line Supervisors/Managers of Helpers, Laborers, and Material Movers, Hand; First-Line Supervisors/Managers of Mechanics, Installers, and Repairers; Industrial Production Managers. **PERSONALITY TYPE:** Enterprising. Enterprising occupations frequently involve starting up and carrying out projects. These occupations can involve leading people and making many decisions. They sometimes require risk taking and often deal with business.

EDUCATION/TRAINING PROGRAM(S)—Operations Management and Supervision. **RELATED KNOWLEDGE/COURSES**—**Production and Processing:** Raw materials, production processes, quality control, costs, and other techniques for maximizing the effective manufacture and distribution of goods. **Personnel and Human Resources:** Principles and procedures for personnel recruitment, selection, training, compensation and benefits, labor relations and negotiation, and personnel information systems. **Mechanical Devices:** Machines and tools, including their designs, uses, repair, and maintenance. **Administration and Management:** Business and management principles involved in strategic planning, resource allocation, human resources modeling, leadership technique, production methods, and coordina-

tion of people and resources. **Education and Training:** Principles and methods for curriculum and training design, teaching and instruction for individuals and groups, and the measurement of training effects. **Engineering and Technology:** The practical application of engineering science and technology. This includes applying principles, techniques, procedures, and equipment to the design and production of various goods and services.

WORK ENVIRONMENT—Indoors; noisy; contaminants; hazardous equipment; standing; walking and running.

First-Line Supervisors/Managers of Retail Sales Workers

- Education/Training Required: Work experience in a related occupation
- Annual Earnings: $32,840
- Growth: 3.8%
- Annual Job Openings: 229,000
- Self-Employed: 31.9%
- Part-Time: 9.4%

Directly supervise sales workers in a retail establishment or department. Duties may include management functions, such as purchasing, budgeting, accounting, and personnel work, in addition to supervisory duties. Provide customer service by greeting and assisting customers and responding to customer inquiries and complaints. Assign employees to specific duties. Monitor sales activities to ensure that customers receive satisfactory service and quality goods. Direct and supervise employees engaged in sales, inventory-taking, reconciling cash receipts, or performing services for customers. Inventory stock and reorder when inventory drops to a specified level. Keep records of purchases, sales, and requisitions. Enforce safety, health, and security rules. Examine products purchased for resale or received for storage to assess the condition of each product or item. Hire, train, and evaluate personnel in sales or marketing establishments, promoting or firing workers when appropriate. Perform work activities of subordinates, such as cleaning and organizing shelves and displays and selling merchandise. Establish and implement policies, goals, objectives, and procedures for their department. Instruct staff on how to handle difficult and complicated sales. Formulate pricing policies for merchandise according to profitability requirements. Estimate consumer demand and determine the types and amounts of goods to be sold. Examine merchandise to ensure that it is correctly priced and displayed and that it functions as advertised. Plan and prepare work schedules and keep records of employees' work schedules and time cards. Review inventory and sales records to prepare reports for management and budget departments. Plan and coordinate advertising campaigns and sales promotions and prepare merchandise displays and advertising copy. Confer with company officials to develop methods and procedures to increase sales, expand markets, and promote business. Establish credit policies and operating procedures. Plan budgets and authorize payments and merchandise returns.

LEVEL OF ACTIVITY (out of 100)—General Physical Activity: 59.0. **Sitting:** 23.4. **Outdoors:** 18.8.

SKILLS—Management of Personnel Resources; Persuasion; Management of Financial Resources; Instructing; Equipment Maintenance; Repairing; Monitoring; Social Perceptiveness.

GOE—Interest Area: 14. Retail and Wholesale Sales and Service. **Work Group:** 14.01. Managerial Work in Retail/Wholesale Sales and Service. **Other Jobs in This Work Group:** Advertising and Promotions Managers; First-Line Supervisors/Managers of Non-Retail Sales Workers; Funeral Directors; Marketing Managers; Property, Real Estate, and Community Association Managers; Purchasing Managers; Sales Managers. **PERSONALITY TYPE:** Enterprising. Enterprising occupations frequently involve starting up and carrying out projects. These occupations can involve leading people and making many decisions. They sometimes require risk taking and often deal with business.

EDUCATION/TRAINING PROGRAM(S)—Floriculture/Floristry Operations and Management; Consumer Merchandising/Retailing Management; E-Commerce/Electronic Commerce; Retailing and Retail Operations; Selling Skills and Sales Operations; Special Products Marketing Operations; Specialized Merchandising, Sales, and Related Marketing Operations, Other; Business, Management, Marketing, and Related Support Services, Other. **RELATED KNOWLEDGE/COURSES—Sales and Marketing:** Principles and methods for showing, promoting, and selling products or services. This includes marketing strategy and tactics, product demonstration, sales techniques, and sales control systems. **Food Production:** Techniques and equipment for planting, growing, and harvesting food products (both plant and animal) for consumption, including storage/handling techniques. **Administration and Management:** Business and management principles involved in strategic planning, resource allocation, human resources modeling, leadership technique, production methods, and coordination of people and resources. **Customer and Personal Service:** Principles and processes for providing customer and personal services. This includes customer needs assessment, meeting quality standards for services, and evaluation of customer satisfaction. **Economics and Accounting:** Economic and accounting principles and practices, the financial markets, banking, and the analysis and reporting of financial data. **Public Safety and Security:** Relevant equipment, policies, procedures, and strategies to promote effective local, state, or national security operations for the protection of people, data, property, and institutions.

WORK ENVIRONMENT—Indoors; hazardous equipment; standing; walking and running; using hands on objects, tools, or controls.

Fish and Game Wardens

- ☺ Education/Training Required: Long-term on-the-job training
- ☺ Annual Earnings: $42,850
- ☺ Growth: 10.5%
- ☺ Annual Job Openings: 1,000
- ☺ Self-Employed: 0.0%
- ☺ Part-Time: No data available

Patrol assigned area to prevent fish and game law violations. Investigate reports of damage to crops or property by wildlife. Compile biologi-

cal data. Patrol assigned areas by car, boat, airplane, or horse or on foot to enforce game, fish, or boating laws and to manage wildlife programs, lakes, or land. Investigate hunting accidents and reports of fish and game law violations and issue warnings or citations and file reports as necessary. Serve warrants, make arrests, and compile and present evidence for court actions. Protect and preserve native wildlife, plants, and ecosystems. Promote and provide hunter and trapper safety training. Seize equipment used in fish and game law violations and arrange for disposition of fish or game illegally taken or possessed. Provide assistance to other local law enforcement agencies as required. Address schools, civic groups, sporting clubs, and the media to disseminate information concerning wildlife conservation and regulations. Recommend revisions or changes in hunting and trapping regulations or seasons and in animal management programs so that wildlife balances and habitats can be maintained. Inspect commercial operations relating to fish and wildlife, recreation, and protected areas. Collect and report information on populations and conditions of fish and wildlife in their habitats, availability of game food and cover, and suspected pollution. Survey areas and compile figures of bag counts of hunters in order to determine the effectiveness of control measures. Participate in search-and-rescue operations and in firefighting efforts. Investigate crop, property, or habitat damage or destruction or instances of water pollution in order to determine causes and to advise property owners of preventive measures. Design and implement control measures to prevent or counteract damage caused by wildlife or people. Document and detail the extent of crop, property, or habitat damage and make financial loss estimates and compensation recommendations.

Supervise the activities of seasonal workers. Issue licenses, permits, and other documentation. Provide advice and information to park and reserve visitors. Perform facilities maintenance work such as constructing or repairing structures and controlling weeds and pests.

LEVEL OF ACTIVITY (out of 100)—General Physical Activity: 75.9. **Sitting:** 44.1. **Outdoors:** 56.4.

SKILLS—Persuasion; Equipment Maintenance; Social Perceptiveness; Speaking; Negotiation; Writing; Science; Service Orientation.

GOE—Interest Area: 07. Government and Public Administration. **Work Group:** 07.03. Regulations Enforcement. **Other Jobs in This Work Group:** Agricultural Inspectors; Aviation Inspectors; Compliance Officers, Except Agriculture, Construction, Health and Safety, and Transportation; Construction and Building Inspectors; Environmental Compliance Inspectors; Equal Opportunity Representatives and Officers; Financial Examiners; Fire Inspectors; Forest Fire Inspectors and Prevention Specialists; Freight and Cargo Inspectors; Government Property Inspectors and Investigators; Immigration and Customs Inspectors; Licensing Examiners and Inspectors; Nuclear Monitoring Technicians; Occupational Health and Safety Specialists; Occupational Health and Safety Technicians; Tax Examiners, Collectors, and Revenue Agents; Transportation Vehicle, Equipment, and Systems Inspectors, Except Aviation. **PERSONALITY TYPE:** Realistic. Realistic occupations frequently involve work activities that include practical, hands-on problems and solutions. They often deal with plants; animals; and real-world materials like wood, tools, and machinery. Many of the occupations require working outside and do not involve a lot of paperwork or working closely with others.

EDUCATION/TRAINING PROGRAM(S)—Natural Resource Economics; Fishing and Fisheries Sciences and Management; Wildlife and Wildlands Science and Management. **RELATED KNOWLEDGE/COURSES**—**Biology:** Plant and animal organisms and their tissues, cells, functions, interdependencies, and interactions with each other and the environment. **Law and Government:** Laws, legal codes, court procedures, precedents, government regulations, executive orders, agency rules, and the democratic political process. **Public Safety and Security:** Relevant equipment, policies, procedures, and strategies to promote effective local, state, or national security operations for the protection of people, data, property, and institutions. **Geography:** Principles and methods for describing the features of land, sea, and air masses, including their physical characteristics; locations; interrelationships; and distribution of plant, animal, and human life. **Psychology:** Human behavior and performance; individual differences in ability, personality, and interests; learning and motivation; psychological research methods; and the assessment and treatment of behavioral and affective disorders. **Sociology and Anthropology:** Group behavior and dynamics, societal trends and influences, human migrations, ethnicity, and cultures and their history and origins.

WORK ENVIRONMENT—Outdoors; very hot or cold; very bright or dim lighting; contaminants; hazardous equipment; minor burns, cuts, bites, or stings.

Fitness Trainers and Aerobics Instructors

- ◉ Education/Training Required: Postsecondary vocational training
- ◉ Annual Earnings: $25,840
- ◉ Growth: 27.1%
- ◉ Annual Job Openings: 50,000
- ◉ Self-Employed: 6.6%
- ◉ Part-Time: 41.3%

Instruct or coach groups or individuals in exercise activities and the fundamentals of sports. Demonstrate techniques and methods of participation. Observe participants and inform them of corrective measures necessary to improve their skills. Those required to hold teaching degrees should be reported in the appropriate teaching category. Explain and enforce safety rules and regulations governing sports, recreational activities, and the use of exercise equipment. Offer alternatives during classes to accommodate different levels of fitness. Plan routines, choose appropriate music, and choose different movements for each set of muscles, depending on participants' capabilities and limitations. Observe participants and inform them of corrective measures necessary for skill improvement. Teach proper breathing techniques used during physical exertion. Teach and demonstrate use of gymnastic and training equipment such as trampolines and weights. Instruct participants in maintaining exertion levels to maximize benefits from exercise routines. Maintain fitness equipment. Conduct therapeutic, recreational, or athletic activities. Monitor participants' progress and adapt pro-

grams as needed. Evaluate individuals' abilities, needs, and physical conditions and develop suitable training programs to meet any special requirements. Plan physical education programs to promote development of participants' physical attributes and social skills. Provide students with information and resources regarding nutrition, weight control, and lifestyle issues. Administer emergency first aid, wrap injuries, treat minor chronic disabilities, or refer injured persons to physicians. Advise clients about proper clothing and shoes. Wrap ankles, fingers, wrists, or other body parts with synthetic skin, gauze, or adhesive tape to support muscles and ligaments. Teach individual and team sports to participants through instruction and demonstration, utilizing knowledge of sports techniques and of participants' physical capabilities. Promote health clubs through membership sales and record member information. Organize, lead, and referee indoor and outdoor games such as volleyball, baseball, and basketball. Maintain equipment inventories and select, store, or issue equipment as needed. Organize and conduct competitions and tournaments. Advise participants in use of heat or ultraviolet treatments and hot baths. Massage body parts to relieve soreness, strains, and bruises.

LEVEL OF ACTIVITY (out of 100)—General Physical Activity: 75.6. **Sitting:** 24.6. **Outdoors:** 16.6.

SKILLS—Instructing; Equipment Selection; Monitoring; Service Orientation; Coordination; Social Perceptiveness; Time Management; Learning Strategies.

GOE—Interest Area: 05. Education and Training. **Work Group:** 05.06. Counseling, Health, and Fitness Education. **Other Jobs in This Work Group:** Educational, Vocational, and School Counselors; Health Educators. **PERSONALITY TYPE:** Social. Social occupations frequently involve working with, communicating with, and teaching people. These occupations often involve helping or providing service to others.

EDUCATION/TRAINING PROGRAM(S)— Physical Education Teaching and Coaching; Health and Physical Education, General; Sport and Fitness Administration/Management. RELATED KNOWLEDGE/COURSES— **Customer and Personal Service:** Principles and processes for providing customer and personal services. This includes customer needs assessment, meeting quality standards for services, and evaluation of customer satisfaction. **Medicine and Dentistry:** The information and techniques needed to diagnose and treat human injuries, diseases, and deformities. This includes symptoms, treatment alternatives, drug properties and interactions, and preventive health-care measures. **Psychology:** Human behavior and performance; individual differences in ability, personality, and interests; learning and motivation; psychological research methods; and the assessment and treatment of behavioral and affective disorders. **Sociology and Anthropology:** Group behavior and dynamics, societal trends and influences, human migrations, ethnicity, and cultures and their history and origins. **Sales and Marketing:** Principles and methods for showing, promoting, and selling products or services. This includes marketing strategy and tactics, product demonstration, sales techniques, and sales control systems. **Personnel and Human Resources:** Principles and procedures for personnel recruitment, selection, training, compensation and benefits, labor relations and negotiation, and personnel information systems.

WORK ENVIRONMENT—Indoors; standing; walking and running; repetitive motions.

Flight Attendants

- Education/Training Required: Long-term on-the-job training
- Annual Earnings: $46,680
- Growth: 16.3%
- Annual Job Openings: 7,000
- Self-Employed: 0.2%
- Part-Time: 28.8%

Provide personal services to ensure the safety and comfort of airline passengers during flight. Greet passengers, verify tickets, explain use of safety equipment, and serve food or beverages. Direct and assist passengers in the event of an emergency, such as directing passengers to evacuate a plane following an emergency landing. Announce and demonstrate safety and emergency procedures such as the use of oxygen masks, seat belts, and life jackets. Walk aisles of planes to verify that passengers have complied with federal regulations prior to take-offs and landings. Verify that first aid kits and other emergency equipment, including fire extinguishers and oxygen bottles, are in working order. Administer first aid to passengers in distress. Attend preflight briefings concerning weather, altitudes, routes, emergency procedures, crew coordination, lengths of flights, food and beverage services offered, and numbers of passengers. Prepare passengers and aircraft for landing, following procedures. Determine special assistance needs of passengers such as small children, the elderly, or disabled persons. Check to ensure that food, beverages, blankets, reading material, emergency equipment, and other supplies are aboard and are in adequate supply.

Reassure passengers when situations such as turbulence are encountered. Announce flight delays and descent preparations. Inspect passenger tickets to verify information and to obtain destination information. Answer passengers' questions about flights, aircraft, weather, travel routes and services, arrival times, and/or schedules. Assist passengers while entering or disembarking the aircraft. Inspect and clean cabins, checking for any problems and making sure that cabins are in order. Greet passengers boarding aircraft and direct them to assigned seats. Conduct periodic trips through the cabin to ensure passenger comfort and to distribute reading material, headphones, pillows, playing cards, and blankets. Take inventory of headsets, alcoholic beverages, and money collected. Operate audio and video systems. Assist passengers in placing carry-on luggage in overhead, garment, or under-seat storage. Prepare reports showing places of departure and destination, passenger ticket numbers, meal and beverage inventories, the conditions of cabin equipment, and any problems encountered by passengers.

LEVEL OF ACTIVITY (out of 100)—General Physical Activity: 58.7. **Sitting:** 29.3. **Outdoors:** 30.0.

SKILLS—Service Orientation; Social Perceptiveness; Critical Thinking; Reading Comprehension; Coordination; Negotiation; Active Listening; Operation Monitoring.

GOE—**Interest Area:** 09. Hospitality, Tourism, and Recreation. **Work Group:** 09.03. Hospitality and Travel Services. **Other Jobs in This Work Group:** Baggage Porters and Bellhops; Concierges; Hotel, Motel, and Resort Desk Clerks; Janitors and Cleaners, Except Maids and Housekeeping Cleaners; Maids and Housekeeping Cleaners; Reservation and Transportation Ticket Agents and Travel Clerks; Tour Guides and Escorts; Transportation

Attendants, Except Flight Attendants and Baggage Porters; Travel Agents; Travel Guides. **PERSONALITY TYPE:** Enterprising. Enterprising occupations frequently involve starting up and carrying out projects. These occupations can involve leading people and making many decisions. They sometimes require risk taking and often deal with business.

EDUCATION/TRAINING PROGRAM(S)—Airline Flight Attendant. **RELATED KNOWLEDGE/COURSES—Customer and Personal Service:** Principles and processes for providing customer and personal services. This includes customer needs assessment, meeting quality standards for services, and evaluation of customer satisfaction. **Psychology:** Human behavior and performance; individual differences in ability, personality, and interests; learning and motivation; psychological research methods; and the assessment and treatment of behavioral and affective disorders. **Transportation:** Principles and methods for moving people or goods by air, rail, sea, or road, including the relative costs and benefits. **Geography:** Principles and methods for describing the features of land, sea, and air masses, including their physical characteristics; locations; interrelationships; and distribution of plant, animal, and human life. **Public Safety and Security:** Relevant equipment, policies, procedures, and strategies to promote effective local, state, or national security operations for the protection of people, data, property, and institutions. **Philosophy and Theology:** Different philosophical systems and religions. This includes their basic principles, values, ethics, ways of thinking, customs, and practices and their impact on human culture.

WORK ENVIRONMENT—Indoors; noisy; contaminants; disease or infections; high places; standing.

Floor Layers, Except Carpet, Wood, and Hard Tiles

- ⊚ Education/Training Required: Moderate-term on-the-job training
- ⊚ Annual Earnings: $33,010
- ⊚ Growth: 10.2%
- ⊚ Annual Job Openings: 4,000
- ⊚ Self-Employed: 44.7%
- ⊚ Part-Time: 12.3%

Apply blocks, strips, or sheets of shock-absorbing, sound-deadening, or decorative coverings to floors. Sweep, scrape, sand, or chip dirt and irregularities to clean base surfaces, correcting imperfections that may show through the covering. Cut flooring material to fit around obstructions. Inspect surface to be covered to ensure that it is firm and dry. Trim excess covering materials, tack edges, and join sections of covering material to form tight joint. Form a smooth foundation by stapling plywood or Masonite over the floor or by brushing waterproof compound onto surface and filling cracks with plaster, putty, or grout to seal pores. Measure and mark guidelines on surfaces or foundations, using chalk lines and dividers. Cut covering and foundation materials according to blueprints and sketches. Roll and press sheet wall and floor covering into cement base to smooth and finish surface, using hand roller. Apply adhesive cement to floor or wall material to join and adhere foundation material. Determine traffic areas and decide location of seams. Lay out, position, and apply shock-absorbing, sound-deadening, or decorative coverings to floors, walls, and cabinets, following guidelines to keep courses straight and create designs. Remove excess cement to clean finished surface. Disconnect and remove appliances, light fixtures, and worn floor and wall covering from floors, walls, and cabinets. Heat and soften floor covering materials to patch cracks or fit floor coverings around irregular surfaces, using blowtorch.

LEVEL OF ACTIVITY (out of 100)—General Physical Activity: 70.3. **Sitting:** 22.9. **Outdoors:** 24.3.

SKILLS—Installation; Repairing; Equipment Maintenance; Equipment Selection; Mathematics; Operations Analysis; Learning Strategies; Coordination.

GOE—Interest Area: 02. Architecture and Construction. **Work Group:** 02.04. Construction Crafts. **Other Jobs in This Work Group:** Boilermakers; Brickmasons and Blockmasons; Carpet Installers; Cement Masons and Concrete Finishers; Commercial Divers; Construction Carpenters; Crane and Tower Operators; Drywall and Ceiling Tile Installers; Electricians; Fence Erectors; Floor Sanders and Finishers; Glaziers; Hazardous Materials Removal Workers; Insulation Workers, Floor, Ceiling, and Wall; Insulation Workers, Mechanical; Manufactured Building and Mobile Home Installers; Operating Engineers and Other Construction Equipment Operators; Painters, Construction and Maintenance; Paperhangers; Paving, Surfacing, and Tamping Equipment Operators; Pile-Driver Operators; Pipe Fitters and Steamfitters; Pipelayers; Plasterers and Stucco Masons; Plumbers; Plumbers, Pipefitters, and Steamfitters; Rail-Track Laying and Maintenance Equipment Operators; Refractory Materials Repairers, Except Brickmasons;

Reinforcing Iron and Rebar Workers; Riggers; Roofers; Rough Carpenters; Security and Fire Alarm Systems Installers; Segmental Pavers; Sheet Metal Workers; Stone Cutters and Carvers, Manufacturing; Stonemasons; Structural Iron and Steel Workers; Tapers; Terrazzo Workers and Finishers; Tile and Marble Setters. **PERSONALITY TYPE:** Realistic. Realistic occupations frequently involve work activities that include practical, hands-on problems and solutions. They often deal with plants; animals; and real-world materials like wood, tools, and machinery. Many of the occupations require working outside and do not involve a lot of paperwork or working closely with others.

EDUCATION/TRAINING PROGRAM(S)— Construction Trades, Other. **RELATED KNOWLEDGE/COURSES—Building and Construction:** The materials, methods, and tools involved in the construction or repair of houses, buildings, or other structures such as highways and roads. **Design:** Design techniques, tools, and principles involved in production of precision technical plans, blueprints, drawings, and models. **Mechanical Devices:** Machines and tools, including their designs, uses, repair, and maintenance. **Production and Processing:** Raw materials, production processes, quality control, costs, and other techniques for maximizing the effective manufacture and distribution of goods. **Mathematics:** Arithmetic, algebra, geometry, calculus, and statistics and their applications. **Transportation:** Principles and methods for moving people or goods by air, rail, sea, or road, including the relative costs and benefits.

WORK ENVIRONMENT—Indoors; contaminants; cramped work space, awkward positions; kneeling, crouching, stooping, or crawling; using hands on objects, tools, or controls; bending or twisting the body.

Food Service Managers

- Education/Training Required: Work experience in a related occupation
- Annual Earnings: $41,340
- Growth: 11.5%
- Annual Job Openings: 61,000
- Self-Employed: 40.5%
- Part-Time: 9.3%

Plan, direct, or coordinate activities of an organization or department that serves food and beverages. Test cooked food by tasting and smelling it to ensure palatability and flavor conformity. Investigate and resolve complaints regarding food quality, service, or accommodations. Schedule and receive food and beverage deliveries, checking delivery contents to verify product quality and quantity. Monitor food preparation methods, portion sizes, and garnishing and presentation of food to ensure that food is prepared and presented in an acceptable manner. Monitor budgets and payroll records and review financial transactions to ensure that expenditures are authorized and budgeted. Monitor compliance with health and fire regulations regarding food preparation and serving and building maintenance in lodging and dining facilities. Schedule staff hours and assign duties. Coordinate assignments of cooking personnel to ensure economical use of food and timely preparation. Keep records required by government agencies regarding sanitation and food subsidies when appropriate. Establish standards for personnel performance and customer service. Estimate food, liquor, wine, and other beverage consumption to anticipate amounts to be purchased or requisitioned. Review work procedures and operational problems to determine ways to improve service, performance, or safety. Perform some food preparation or service tasks such as cooking, clearing tables, and serving food and drinks when necessary. Maintain food and equipment inventories and keep inventory records. Organize and direct worker training programs, resolve personnel problems, hire new staff, and evaluate employee performance in dining and lodging facilities. Order and purchase equipment and supplies. Review menus and analyze recipes to determine labor and overhead costs and assign prices to menu items. Record the number, type, and cost of items sold to determine which items may be unpopular or less profitable. Assess staffing needs and recruit staff. using methods such as newspaper advertisements or attendance at job fairs. Arrange for equipment maintenance and repairs; coordinate a variety of services such as waste removal and pest control.

LEVEL OF ACTIVITY (out of 100)—General Physical Activity: 50.3. **Sitting:** 28.1. **Outdoors:** 21.9.

SKILLS—Management of Personnel Resources; Management of Financial Resources; Management of Material Resources; Monitoring; Systems Evaluation; Time Management; Speaking; Service Orientation.

GOE—Interest Area: 09. Hospitality, Tourism, and Recreation. **Work Group:** 09.01. Managerial Work in Hospitality and Tourism. **Other Jobs in This Work Group:** First-Line Supervisors/Managers of Food Preparation and Serving Workers; First-Line Supervisors/Managers of Personal Service Workers; Gaming Managers; Gaming Supervisors; Lodging Managers. **PERSONALITY TYPE:** Enterprising. Enterprising occupations frequently involve starting up and carrying out projects. These occupations can involve leading people and making many decisions. They sometimes require risk taking and often deal with business.

EDUCATION/TRAINING PROGRAM(S)—Restaurant, Culinary, and Catering Management/Manager; Hospitality Administration/Management, General; Hotel/Motel Administration/Management; Restaurant/Food Services Management. **RELATED KNOWLEDGE/COURSES—Food Production:** Techniques and equipment for planting, growing, and harvesting food products (both plant and animal) for consumption, including storage/handling techniques. **Sales and Marketing:** Principles and methods for showing, promoting, and selling products or services. This includes marketing strategy and tactics, product demonstration, sales techniques, and sales control systems. **Production and Processing:** Raw materials, production processes, quality control, costs, and other techniques for maximizing the effective manufacture and distribution of goods. **Customer and Personal Service:** Principles and processes for providing customer and personal services. This includes customer needs assessment, meeting quality standards for services, and evaluation of customer satisfaction. **Administration and Management:** Business and management principles involved in strategic planning, resource allocation, human resources modeling, leadership technique, production methods, and coordination of people and resources. **Personnel and Human Resources:** Principles and procedures for personnel recruitment, selection, training, compensation and benefits, labor relations and negotiation, and personnel information systems.

WORK ENVIRONMENT—Indoors; very hot or cold; standing; walking and running; using hands on objects, tools, or controls; repetitive motions.

Forest Fire Fighting and Prevention Supervisors

This job can be found in the Part I lists under the title First-Line Supervisors/Managers of Fire Fighting and Prevention Workers.

◉ Education/Training Required: Work experience in a related occupation

◉ Annual Earnings: $60,840

◉ Growth: 21.1%

◉ Annual Job Openings: 4,000

◉ Self-Employed: 0.0%

◉ Part-Time: 0.4%

The job openings listed here are shared with Municipal Fire Fighting and Prevention Supervisors.

Supervise fire fighters who control and suppress fires in forests or vacant public land. Communicate fire details to superiors, subordinates, and interagency dispatch centers, using two-way radios. Serve as working leader of an engine, hand, helicopter, or prescribed fire crew of three or more firefighters. Maintain fire suppression equipment in good condition, checking equipment periodically in order to ensure that it is ready for use. Evaluate size, location, and condition of forest fires in order to request and dispatch crews and position equipment so fires can be contained safely and effectively. Operate wildland fire engines and hoselays. Direct and supervise prescribed burn projects and prepare post-burn reports analyzing burn conditions and results. Monitor prescribed burns to ensure that they are conducted safely and effectively. Identify staff training and development needs in order to ensure that appropriate training can be arranged. Maintain knowledge of forest fire laws and fire prevention techniques and tactics. Recommend equipment modifications or new equipment purchases. Perform administrative duties such as compiling and maintaining records, completing forms, preparing reports, and composing correspondence. Recruit and hire forest fire-fighting personnel. Train workers in such skills as parachute jumping, fire suppression, aerial observation, and radio communication, both in the classroom and on the job. Review and evaluate employee performance. Observe fires and crews from air to determine fire-fighting force requirements and to note changing conditions that will affect fire-fighting efforts. Inspect all stations, uniforms, equipment, and recreation areas in order to ensure compliance with safety standards, taking corrective action as necessary. Schedule employee work assignments and set work priorities. Regulate open burning by issuing burning permits, inspecting problem sites, issuing citations for violations of laws and ordinances, and educating the public in proper burning practices. Direct investigations of suspected arsons in wildfires, working closely with other investigating agencies. Monitor fire suppression expenditures in order to ensure that they are necessary and reasonable.

LEVEL OF ACTIVITY (out of 100)—General Physical Activity: 82.1. **Sitting:** 30.7. **Outdoors:** 49.2.

SKILLS—Equipment Maintenance; Repairing; Operation Monitoring; Management of Personnel Resources; Operation and Control; Management of Material Resources; Management of Financial Resources; Service Orientation.

GOE—**Interest Area:** 12. Law and Public Safety. **Work Group:** 12.01. Managerial Work in Law and Public Safety. **Other Jobs in This Work Group:** Emergency Management Specialists; First-Line Supervisors/Managers of Correctional Officers; First-Line Supervisors/Managers of Fire Fighting and Prevention Workers; First-Line Supervisors/Managers of Police and Detectives; Municipal Fire Fighting and Prevention Supervisors. **PERSONALITY TYPE:** Realistic. Realistic occupations frequently involve work activities that include practical, hands-on problems and solutions. They often deal with plants; animals; and real-world materials like wood, tools, and machinery. Many of the occupations require working outside and do not involve a lot of paperwork or working closely with others.

EDUCATION/TRAINING PROGRAM(S)—Fire Protection and Safety Technology/Technician; Fire Services Administration. **RELATED KNOWLEDGE/COURSES—Public Safety and Security:** Relevant equipment, policies, procedures, and strategies to promote effective local, state, or national security operations for the protection of people, data, property, and institutions. **Customer and Personal Service:** Principles and processes for providing customer and personal services. This includes customer needs assessment, meeting quality standards for services, and evaluation of customer satisfaction. **Building and Construction:** The materials, methods, and tools involved in the construction or repair of houses, buildings, or other structures such as highways and roads. **Personnel and**

Human Resources: Principles and procedures for personnel recruitment, selection, training, compensation and benefits, labor relations and negotiation, and personnel information systems. **Mechanical Devices:** Machines and tools, including their designs, uses, repair, and maintenance. **Transportation:** Principles and methods for moving people or goods by air, rail, sea, or road, including the relative costs and benefits.

WORK ENVIRONMENT—Outdoors; noisy; very hot or cold; hazardous equipment; minor burns, cuts, bites, or stings; standing.

Foresters

- Education/Training Required: Bachelor's degree
- Annual Earnings: $48,670
- Growth: 6.7%
- Annual Job Openings: 1,000
- Self-Employed: 9.1%
- Part-Time: 6.7%

Manage forested lands for economic, recreational, and conservation purposes. May inventory the type, amount, and location of standing timber; appraise the timber's worth; negotiate the purchase; and draw up contracts for procurement. May determine how to conserve wildlife habitats, creek beds, water quality, and soil stability and how best to comply with environmental regulations. May devise plans for planting and growing new trees, monitor trees for healthy growth, and determine the best time for harvesting. Develop forest manage-

ment plans for public and privately-owned forested lands. Monitor contract compliance and results of forestry activities to assure adherence to government regulations. Establish short- and long-term plans for management of forest lands and forest resources. Supervise activities of other forestry workers. Choose and prepare sites for new trees, using controlled burning, bulldozers, or herbicides to clear weeds, brush, and logging debris. Plan and supervise forestry projects, such as determining the type, number, and placement of trees to be planted; managing tree nurseries; thinning forest; and monitoring growth of new seedlings. Negotiate terms and conditions of agreements and contracts for forest harvesting, forest management, and leasing of forest lands. Direct and participate in forest-fire suppression. Determine methods of cutting and removing timber with minimum waste and environmental damage. Analyze effect of forest conditions on tree growth rates and tree species prevalence and the yield, duration, seed production, growth viability, and germination of different species. Monitor forest-cleared lands to ensure that they are reclaimed to their most suitable end use. Plan and implement projects for conservation of wildlife habitats and soil and water quality. Plan and direct forest surveys and related studies and prepare reports and recommendations. Perform inspections of forests or forest nurseries. Map forest area soils and vegetation to estimate the amount of standing timber and future value and growth. Conduct public educational programs on forest care and conservation. Procure timber from private landowners. Subcontract with loggers or pulpwood cutters for tree removal and to aid in road layout. Plan cutting programs and manage timber sales from harvested areas, assisting compa-

nies to achieve production goals. Monitor wildlife populations and assess the impacts of forest operations on population and habitats. Plan and direct construction and maintenance of recreation facilities, fire towers, trails, roads, and bridges, ensuring that they comply with guidelines and regulations set for forested public lands. Contact local forest owners and gain permission to take inventory of the type, amount, and location of all standing timber on the property.

LEVEL OF ACTIVITY (out of 100)—General Physical Activity: 76.1. **Sitting:** 52.7. **Outdoors:** 37.7.

SKILLS—Management of Financial Resources; Science; Programming; Quality Control Analysis; Coordination; Operations Analysis; Mathematics; Time Management.

GOE—Interest Area: 01. Agriculture and Natural Resources. **Work Group:** 01.02. Resource Science/Engineering for Plants, Animals, and the Environment. **Other Jobs in This Work Group:** Agricultural Engineers; Animal Scientists; Conservation Scientists; Environmental Engineers; Mining and Geological Engineers, Including Mining Safety Engineers; Petroleum Engineers; Range Managers; Soil and Plant Scientists; Soil and Water Conservationists; Zoologists and Wildlife Biologists. **PERSONALITY TYPE:** Realistic. Realistic occupations frequently involve work activities that include practical, hands-on problems and solutions. They often deal with plants; animals; and real-world materials like wood, tools, and machinery. Many of the occupations require working outside and do not involve a lot of paperwork or working closely with others.

EDUCATION/TRAINING PROGRAM(S)—
Natural Resources/Conservation, General; Natural Resources Management and Policy; Natural Resources Management and Policy, Other; Forestry, General; Forest Sciences and Biology; Forest Management/Forest Resources Management; Urban Forestry; Wood Science and Wood Products/Pulp and Paper Technology; Forest Resources Production and Management; Forestry, Other; Natural Resources and Conservation, Other. **RELATED KNOWLEDGE/COURSES—Biology:** Plant and animal organisms and their tissues, cells, functions, interdependencies, and interactions with each other and the environment. **Geography:** Principles and methods for describing the features of land, sea, and air masses, including their physical characteristics; locations; interrelationships; and distribution of plant, animal, and human life. **Mathematics:** Arithmetic, algebra, geometry, calculus, and statistics and their applications. **Law and Government:** Laws, legal codes, court procedures, precedents, government regulations, executive orders, agency rules, and the democratic political process. **Administration and Management:** Business and management principles involved in strategic planning, resource allocation, human resources modeling, leadership technique, production methods, and coordination of people and resources. **Computers and Electronics:** Circuit boards; processors; chips; electronic equipment; and computer hardware and software, including applications and programming.

WORK ENVIRONMENT—More often indoors than outdoors; noisy; sitting.

Freight and Cargo Inspectors

This job can be found in the Part I lists under the title Transportation Inspectors.

- **Education/Training Required: Work experience in a related occupation**
- **Annual Earnings: $49,490**
- **Growth: 11.4%**
- **Annual Job Openings: 2,000**
- **Self-Employed: 1.9%**
- **Part-Time: 2.3%**

The job openings listed here are shared with Aviation Inspectors and with Transportation Vehicle, Equipment, and Systems Inspectors, Except Aviation.

Inspect the handling, storage, and stowing of freight and cargoes. Review commercial vehicle logs, shipping papers, and driver and equipment records to detect any problems and to ensure compliance with regulations. Prepare and submit reports after completion of freight shipments. Recommend remedial procedures to correct any violations found during inspections. Record details about freight conditions, handling of freight, and any problems encountered. Calculate gross and net tonnage, hold capacities, volumes of stored fuel and water, cargo weights, and ship stability factors, using mathematical formulas. Evaluate new methods of packaging, testing, shipping, and transporting hazardous materials to ensure adequate public safety protection. Measure ships' holds and depths of fuel and water in tanks, using sounding lines and tape measures. Write certificates of admeasurement that list details such as designs, lengths, depths, and breadths of vessels and methods of propulsion. Read draft markings to determine depths of vessels in water. Post warning signs on vehicles containing explosives or flammable or radioactive materials. Negotiate with authorities, such as local government officials, to eliminate hazards along transportation routes. Observe loading of freight to ensure that crews comply with procedures. Notify workers of any special treatment required for shipments. Measure heights and widths of loads to ensure that they will pass over bridges or through tunnels on scheduled routes. Issue certificates of compliance for vessels without violations. Inspect shipments to ensure that freight is securely braced and blocked. Inspect loaded cargo, cargo lashed to decks or in storage facilities, and cargo handling devices to determine compliance with health and safety regulations and need for maintenance. Direct crews to reload freight or to insert additional bracing or packing as necessary. Determine types of licenses and safety equipment required and compute applicable fees such as tolls and wharfage fees. Determine cargo transportation capabilities by reading documents that set forth cargo loading and securing procedures, capacities, and stability factors.

LEVEL OF ACTIVITY (out of 100)—General Physical Activity: 28.6. **Sitting:** 38.6. **Outdoors:** 51.4.

SKILLS—Mathematics; Systems Analysis; Systems Evaluation.

GOE—Interest Area: 07. Government and Public Administration. **Work Group:** 07.03. Regulations Enforcement. **Other Jobs in This Work Group:** Agricultural Inspectors; Aviation Inspectors; Compliance Officers, Except Agriculture, Construction, Health and Safety, and Transportation; Construction and Building Inspectors; Environmental Compliance Inspectors; Equal Opportunity Representatives and Officers; Financial Examiners; Fire Inspectors; Fish and Game Wardens; Forest Fire Inspectors and Prevention Specialists; Government Property Inspectors and Investigators; Immigration and Customs Inspectors; Licensing Examiners and Inspectors; Nuclear Monitoring Technicians; Occupational Health and Safety Specialists; Occupational Health and Safety Technicians; Tax Examiners, Collectors, and Revenue Agents; Transportation Vehicle, Equipment, and Systems Inspectors, Except Aviation. **PERSONALITY TYPE:** Conventional. Conventional occupations frequently involve following set procedures and routines. These occupations can include working with data and details more than with ideas. Usually there is a clear line of authority to follow.

EDUCATION/TRAINING PROGRAM(S)—No related CIP programs; this job is learned through work experience in a related occupation. **RELATED KNOWLEDGE/COURSES—Transportation:** Principles and methods for moving people or goods by air, rail, sea, or road, including the relative costs and benefits. **Public Safety and Security:** Relevant equipment, policies, procedures, and strategies to promote effective local, state, or national security operations for the protection of people, data, property, and institutions. **Mathematics:** Arithmetic, algebra, geometry, calculus, and statistics and their applications.

WORK ENVIRONMENT—Outdoors; standing; walking and running; using hands on objects, tools, or controls.

Funeral Directors

- Education/Training Required: Associate degree
- Annual Earnings: $47,630
- Growth: 6.7%
- Annual Job Openings: 3,000
- Self-Employed: 19.7%
- Part-Time: 9.0%

Perform various tasks to arrange and direct funeral services, such as coordinating transportation of body to mortuary for embalming, interviewing family or other authorized person to arrange details, selecting pallbearers, procuring official for religious rites, and providing transportation for mourners. Consult with families or friends of the deceased to arrange funeral details such as obituary notice wording, casket selection, and plans for services. Plan, schedule, and coordinate funerals, burials, and cremations, arranging such details as the time and place of services. Obtain information needed to complete legal documents such as death certificates and burial permits. Oversee the preparation and care of the remains of people who have died. Contact cemeteries to schedule the opening and closing of graves. Provide information on funeral service options, products, and merchandise; maintain a casket display area. Manage funeral home operations, including hiring and supervising embalmers, funeral attendants, and other staff. Offer counsel and comfort to bereaved families and friends. Close caskets and lead funeral corteges to churches or burial sites. Arrange for clergy members to perform needed services. Provide or arrange transportation between sites for the remains, mourners, pallbearers, clergy, and flowers. Perform embalming duties as necessary. Direct preparations and shipment of bodies for out-of-state burial. Discuss and negotiate prearranged funerals with clients. Inform survivors of benefits for which they may be eligible. Maintain financial records, order merchandise, and prepare accounts. Plan placement of caskets at funeral sites and place and adjust lights, fixtures, and floral displays. Arrange for pallbearers and inform pallbearers and honorary groups of their duties. Receive and usher people to their seats for services.

LEVEL OF ACTIVITY (out of 100)—General Physical Activity: 50.7. **Sitting:** 40.6. **Outdoors:** 43.5.

SKILLS—Service Orientation; Management of Financial Resources; Social Perceptiveness; Management of Personnel Resources; Management of Material Resources; Coordination; Negotiation; Time Management.

GOE—Interest Area: 14. Retail and Wholesale Sales and Service. **Work Group:** 14.01. Managerial Work in Retail/Wholesale Sales and Service. **Other Jobs in This Work Group:** Advertising and Promotions Managers; First-Line Supervisors/Managers of Non-Retail Sales Workers; First-Line Supervisors/Managers of Retail Sales Workers; Marketing Managers; Property, Real Estate, and Community Association Managers; Purchasing Managers; Sales Managers. **PERSONALITY TYPE:** Enterprising. Enterprising occupations frequently involve starting up and carrying out projects. These occupations can involve leading people and making many decisions. They sometimes require risk taking and often deal with business.

EDUCATION/TRAINING PROGRAM(S)— Funeral Service and Mortuary Science, General;

Funeral Direction/Service. **RELATED KNOW-LEDGE/COURSES—Customer and Personal Service:** Principles and processes for providing customer and personal services. This includes customer needs assessment, meeting quality standards for services, and evaluation of customer satisfaction. **Therapy and Counseling:** Principles, methods, and procedures for diagnosis, treatment, and rehabilitation of physical and mental dysfunctions and for career counseling and guidance. **Philosophy and Theology:** Different philosophical systems and religions. This includes their basic principles, values, ethics, ways of thinking, customs, and practices and their impact on human culture. **Sales and Marketing:** Principles and methods for showing, promoting, and selling products or services. This includes marketing strategy and tactics, product demonstration, sales techniques, and sales control systems. **Clerical Practices:** Administrative and clerical procedures and systems such as word processing, managing files and records, stenography and transcription, designing forms, and other office procedures and terminology. **Psychology:** Human behavior and performance; individual differences in ability, personality, and interests; learning and motivation; psychological research methods; and the assessment and treatment of behavioral and affective disorders.

WORK ENVIRONMENT—More often indoors than outdoors; contaminants; disease or infections; standing.

Gaming Managers

- ◉ Education/Training Required: Work experience in a related occupation
- ◉ Annual Earnings: $59,940
- ◉ Growth: 22.6%
- ◉ Annual Job Openings: 1,000
- ◉ Self-Employed: 4.0%
- ◉ Part-Time: 5.6%

Plan, organize, direct, control, or coordinate gaming operations in a casino. Formulate gaming policies for their area of responsibility. Resolve customer complaints regarding problems such as payout errors. Remove suspected cheaters, such as card counters and other players who may have systems that shift the odds of winning to their favor. Maintain familiarity with all games used at a facility, as well as strategies and tricks employed in those games. Train new workers and evaluate their performance. Circulate among gaming tables to ensure that operations are conducted properly, that dealers follow house rules, and that players are not cheating. Explain and interpret house rules, such as game rules and betting limits. Monitor staffing levels to ensure that games and tables are adequately staffed for each shift, arranging for staff rotations and breaks and locating substitute employees as necessary. Interview and hire workers. Prepare work schedules and station assignments and keep attendance records. Direct the distribution of complimentary hotel rooms, meals, and other discounts or free items given to players based on their length of play and betting totals. Establish policies on issues such as the type of gambling offered and the odds, the extension of credit, and the serving of food and beverages. Track supplies of money to tables and perform any required paperwork. Set and maintain a bank and table limit for each game. Monitor credit extended to players. Review operational expenses, budget estimates, betting accounts, and collection reports for accuracy. Record, collect, and pay off bets, issuing receipts as necessary. Direct workers compiling summary sheets that show wager amounts and payoffs for races and events. Notify board attendants of table vacancies so that waiting patrons can play.

LEVEL OF ACTIVITY (out of 100)—General Physical Activity: 37.9. **Sitting:** 37.0. **Outdoors:** 18.8.

SKILLS—Management of Personnel Resources; Management of Financial Resources; Service Orientation; Systems Evaluation; Negotiation; Social Perceptiveness; Persuasion; Judgment and Decision Making.

GOE—Interest Area: 09. Hospitality, Tourism, and Recreation. **Work Group:** 09.01. Managerial Work in Hospitality and Tourism. **Other Jobs in This Work Group:** First-Line Supervisors/Managers of Food Preparation and Serving Workers; First-Line Supervisors/ Managers of Personal Service Workers; Food Service Managers; Gaming Supervisors; Lodging Managers. **PERSONALITY TYPE:** Enterprising. Enterprising occupations frequently involve starting up and carrying out projects. These occupations can involve leading people and making many decisions. They sometimes require risk taking and often deal with business.

EDUCATION/TRAINING PROGRAM(S)— Personal and Culinary Services, Other. **RELATED KNOWLEDGE/COURSES—Customer and Personal Service:** Principles and processes for providing customer and personal services. This includes customer needs assessment, meeting quality standards for services, and evaluation of customer satisfaction. **Sales and Marketing:** Principles and methods for showing, promoting, and selling products or services. This includes marketing strategy and tactics, product demonstration, sales techniques, and sales control systems. **Personnel and Human Resources:** Principles and procedures for personnel recruitment, selection, training, compensation and benefits, labor relations and negotiation, and personnel information systems. **Administration and Management:** Business and management principles involved in strategic planning, resource allocation, human resources modeling, leadership technique, production methods, and coordination of people and resources. **Economics and Accounting:** Economic and accounting principles and practices, the financial markets, banking, and the analysis and reporting of financial data. **Mathematics:** Arithmetic, algebra, geometry, calculus, and statistics and their applications.

WORK ENVIRONMENT—Indoors; noisy; contaminants; standing; walking and running.

Gaming Supervisors

⊚ Education/Training Required: Work experience in a related occupation

⊚ Annual Earnings: $40,300

⊚ Growth: 16.3%

⊚ Annual Job Openings: 8,000

⊚ Self-Employed: 29.6%

⊚ Part-Time: 15.0%

Supervise gaming operations and personnel in an assigned area. Circulate among tables and observe operations. Ensure that stations and games are covered for each shift. May explain and interpret operating rules of house to patrons. May plan and organize activities and create friendly atmosphere for guests in hotels/casinos. May adjust service complaints. Monitor game operations to ensure that house rules are followed; that tribal, state, and federal regulations are adhered to; and that employees provide prompt and courteous service. Observe gamblers' behavior for signs of cheating, such as marking, switching, or counting cards; notify security staff of suspected cheating. Maintain familiarity with the games at a facility and with strategies and tricks used by cheaters at such games. Perform paperwork required for monetary transactions. Resolve customer and employee complaints. Greet customers and ask about the quality of service they are receiving. Establish and maintain banks and table limits for each game. Report customer-related incidents occurring in gaming areas to supervisors. Monitor stations and games; move dealers from game to game to ensure adequate staffing. Explain and interpret house rules, such as game rules and betting limits, for patrons. Supervise the distribution of complimentary meals, hotel rooms, discounts, and other items given to players based on length of play and amount bet. Evaluate workers' performance and prepare written performance evaluations. Monitor patrons for signs of compulsive gambling, offering assistance if necessary. Record, issue receipts for, and pay off bets. Monitor and verify the counting, wrapping, weighing, and distribution of currency and coins. Direct workers compiling summary sheets for each race or event to record amounts wagered and amounts to be paid to winners. Determine how many gaming tables to open each day and schedule staff accordingly. Establish policies on types of gambling offered, odds, and extension of credit. Interview, hire, and train workers. Provide fire protection and first-aid assistance when necessary. Review operational expenses, budget estimates, betting accounts, and collection reports for accuracy.

LEVEL OF ACTIVITY (out of 100)—General Physical Activity: 38.7. **Sitting:** 25.7. **Outdoors:** 14.4.

SKILLS—Management of Personnel Resources; Instructing; Service Orientation; Social Perceptiveness; Monitoring; Critical Thinking; Mathematics; Persuasion.

GOE—Interest Area: 09. Hospitality, Tourism, and Recreation. **Work Group:** 09.01. Managerial Work in Hospitality and Tourism. **Other Jobs in This Work Group:** First-Line Supervisors/Managers of Food Preparation and Serving Workers; First-Line Supervisors/Managers of Personal Service Workers; Food Service Managers; Gaming Managers; Lodging Managers. **PERSONALITY TYPE:** Enterprising. Enterprising occupations frequently involve starting up and carrying out projects. These occupations can involve leading people and making many decisions. They sometimes require risk taking and often deal with business.

EDUCATION/TRAINING PROGRAM(S)— Personal and Culinary Services, Other. **RELATED KNOWLEDGE/COURSES—Customer and Personal Service:** Principles and processes for providing customer and personal services. This includes customer needs assessment, meeting quality standards for services, and evaluation of customer satisfaction. **Psychology:** Human behavior and performance; individual differences in ability, personality, and interests; learning and motivation; psychological research methods; and the assessment and treatment of behavioral and affective disorders. **Education and Training:** Principles and methods for curriculum and training design, teaching and instruction for individuals and groups, and the measurement of training effects. **Sales and Marketing:** Principles and methods for showing, promoting, and selling products or services. This includes marketing strategy and tactics, product demonstration, sales techniques, and sales control systems. **Personnel and Human Resources:** Principles and procedures for personnel recruitment, selection, training, compensation and benefits, labor relations and negotiation, and personnel information systems. **Mathematics:** Arithmetic, algebra, geometry, calculus, and statistics and their applications.

WORK ENVIRONMENT—Indoors; noisy; contaminants; standing; walking and running.

Gas Plant Operators

- ◎ Education/Training Required: Long-term on-the-job training
- ◎ Annual Earnings: $51,920
- ◎ Growth: 7.7%
- ◎ Annual Job Openings: 2,000
- ◎ Self-Employed: 0.1%
- ◎ Part-Time: 0.8%

Distribute or process gas for utility companies and others by controlling compressors to maintain specified pressures on main pipelines. Determine causes of abnormal pressure variances and make corrective recommendations, such as installation of pipes to relieve overloading. Distribute or process gas for utility companies or industrial plants, using panel boards, control boards, and semi-automatic equipment. Start and shut down plant equipment. Test gas, chemicals, and air during processing to assess factors such as purity and moisture content and to detect quality problems or gas or chemical leaks. Adjust temperature, pressure, vacuum, level, flow rate, and/or transfer of gas to maintain processes at required levels or to correct problems. Change charts in recording meters. Calculate gas ratios to detect deviations from specifications, using testing apparatus. Clean, maintain, and repair equipment, using hand tools, or request that repair and maintenance work be performed. Collaborate with other operators to solve unit problems. Monitor equipment functioning; observe temperature, level, and flow gauges; and perform regular unit checks in order to ensure that all equipment is operating as it should. Control fractioning columns, compressors, purifying towers, heat exchangers, and related equipment in order to extract nitrogen and oxygen from air. Control equipment to regulate flow and pressure of gas to feedlines of boilers, furnaces, and related steam-generating or heating equipment. Operate construction equipment to install and maintain gas distribution systems. Signal or direct workers who tend auxiliary equipment. Record, review, and compile operations records; test results; and gauge readings such as temperatures, pressures, concentrations, and flows. Read logsheets to determine product demand and disposition or to detect malfunctions. Monitor transportation and storage of flammable and other potentially dangerous products to ensure that safety guidelines are followed. Contact maintenance crews when necessary. Control operation of compressors, scrubbers, evaporators, and refrigeration equipment in order to liquefy, compress, or regasify natural gas.

LEVEL OF ACTIVITY (out of 100)—General Physical Activity: 46.4. **Sitting:** 41.4. **Outdoors:** 32.9.

SKILLS—Operation Monitoring; Operation and Control; Repairing; Equipment Maintenance; Troubleshooting.

GOE—Interest Area: 13. Manufacturing. **Work Group:** 13.16. Utility Operation and Energy Distribution. **Other Jobs in This Work Group:** Chemical Plant and System Operators; Gas Compressor and Gas Pumping Station Operators; Nuclear Power Reactor Operators; Petroleum Pump System Operators, Refinery Operators, and Gaugers; Power Distributors and Dispatchers; Power Plant Operators; Ship Engineers; Stationary Engineers and Boiler Operators; Water and Liquid Waste Treatment

Plant and System Operators. **PERSONALITY TYPE:** Realistic. Realistic occupations frequently involve work activities that include practical, hands-on problems and solutions. They often deal with plants; animals; and real-world materials like wood, tools, and machinery. Many of the occupations require working outside and do not involve a lot of paperwork or working closely with others.

EDUCATION/TRAINING PROGRAM(S)— Mechanic and Repair Technologies/Technicians, Other. **RELATED KNOWLEDGE/COURSES—Mechanical Devices:** Machines and tools, including their designs, uses, repair, and maintenance. **Physics:** Physical principles and laws and their interrelationships and applications to understanding fluid, material, and atmospheric dynamics and mechanical, electrical, atomic, and subatomic structures and processes. **Engineering and Technology:** The practical application of engineering science and technology. This includes applying principles, techniques, procedures, and equipment to the design and production of various goods and services. **Production and Processing:** Raw materials, production processes, quality control, costs, and other techniques for maximizing the effective manufacture and distribution of goods. **Chemistry:** The chemical composition, structure, and properties of substances and of the chemical processes and transformations that they undergo. This includes uses of chemicals and their danger signs, production techniques, and disposal methods.

WORK ENVIRONMENT—Indoors; contaminants; hazardous conditions; standing; using hands on objects, tools, or controls.

Geoscientists, Except Hydrologists and Geographers

- ⊚ Education/Training Required: Master's degree
- ⊚ Annual Earnings: $71,640
- ⊚ Growth: 8.3%
- ⊚ Annual Job Openings: 2,000
- ⊚ Self-Employed: 5.1%
- ⊚ Part-Time: 5.7%

Study the composition, structure, and other physical aspects of the earth. May use geological, physics, and mathematics knowledge in exploration for oil, gas, minerals, or underground water or in waste disposal, land reclamation, or other environmental problems. May study the earth's internal composition, atmospheres, and oceans and its magnetic, electrical, and gravitational forces. Includes mineralogists, crystallographers, paleontologists, stratigraphers, geodesists, and seismologists. Analyze and interpret geological, geochemical, and geophysical information from sources such as survey data, well logs, bore holes, and aerial photos. Plan and conduct geological, geochemical, and geophysical field studies and surveys; sample collection; or drilling and testing programs used to collect data for research or application. Investigate the composition, structure, and history of the Earth's crust through the collection, examination, measurement, and classification of soils, minerals, rocks, or fossil remains. Prepare geological maps, cross-sectional diagrams, charts, and reports concerning mineral extraction, land use, and resource management, using results of field work and laboratory research. Locate and estimate probable natural gas, oil, and mineral ore deposits and underground water resources, using aerial photographs, charts, or research and survey results. Assess ground and surface water movement to provide advice regarding issues such as waste management, route and site selection, and the restoration of contaminated sites. Identify risks for natural disasters such as mud slides, earthquakes, and volcanic eruptions, providing advice on mitigation of potential damage. Conduct geological and geophysical studies to provide information for use in regional development, site selection, and development of public works projects. Inspect construction projects to analyze engineering problems, applying geological knowledge and using test equipment and drilling machinery. Advise construction firms and government agencies on dam and road construction, foundation design, or land use and resource management. Communicate geological findings by writing research papers, participating in conferences, or teaching geological science at universities. Measure characteristics of the Earth, such as gravity and magnetic fields, using equipment such as seismographs, gravimeters, torsion balances, and magnetometers. Test industrial diamonds and abrasives, soil, or rocks to determine their geological characteristics, using optical, X-ray, heat, acid, and precision instruments. Identify deposits of construction materials and assess the materials' characteristics and suitability for use as concrete aggregates, as road fill, or in other applications.

LEVEL OF ACTIVITY (out of 100)—General Physical Activity: 54.4. **Sitting:** 54.6. **Outdoors:** 31.7.

SKILLS—Science; Management of Financial Resources; Active Learning; Time Management; Coordination; Equipment Selection; Operations Analysis; Mathematics.

GOE—**Interest Area:** 15. Scientific Research, Engineering, and Mathematics. **Work Group:** 15.02. Physical Sciences. **Other Jobs in This Work Group:** Astronomers; Atmospheric and Space Scientists; Chemists; Geographers; Hydrologists; Materials Scientists; Physicists. **PERSONALITY TYPE:** Investigative. Investigative occupations frequently involve working with ideas and require an extensive amount of thinking. These occupations can involve searching for facts and figuring out problems mentally.

EDUCATION/TRAINING PROGRAM(S)— Geology/Earth Science, General; Geochemistry; Geophysics and Seismology; Paleontology; Geochemistry and Petrology; Oceanography, Chemical and Physical; Geological and Earth Sciences/Geosciences, Other. **RELATED KNOWLEDGE/COURSES—Geography:** Principles and methods for describing the features of land, sea, and air masses, including their physical characteristics; locations; interrelationships; and distribution of plant, animal, and human life. **Physics:** Physical principles and laws and their interrelationships and applications to understanding fluid, material, and atmospheric dynamics and mechanical, electrical, atomic, and subatomic structures and processes. **Chemistry:** The chemical composition, structure, and properties of substances and of the chemical processes and transformations that they undergo. This includes uses of chemicals and their danger signs, production techniques, and disposal methods. **Biology:** Plant and animal organisms and their tissues, cells, functions, interdependencies, and interactions with each other and the environment. **Engineering and**

Technology: The practical application of engineering science and technology. This includes applying principles, techniques, procedures, and equipment to the design and production of various goods and services. **Mathematics:** Arithmetic, algebra, geometry, calculus, and statistics and their applications.

WORK ENVIRONMENT—More often indoors than outdoors; sitting.

Glaziers

- ◎ Education/Training Required: Long-term on-the-job training
- ◎ Annual Earnings: $33,530
- ◎ Growth: 14.2%
- ◎ Annual Job Openings: 9,000
- ◎ Self-Employed: 11.0%
- ◎ Part-Time: 2.6%

Install glass in windows, skylights, store fronts, and display cases or on surfaces such as building fronts, interior walls, ceilings, and tabletops. Measure mirrors and dimensions of areas to be covered in order to determine work procedures. Cut, assemble, fit, and attach metal-framed glass enclosures for showers, bathtubs, display cases, skylights, solariums, and other structures. Measure, cut, fit, and press anti-glare adhesive film to glass or spray glass with tinting solution to prevent light glare. Pack spaces between moldings and glass with glazing compounds and trim excess material with glazing knives. Prepare glass for cutting by resting it on rack edges or against cutting tables and brushing thin layer of oil along cutting lines or dipping cutting tools in oil. Score glass with cutters' wheels, breaking off excess glass by hand or with notched tools. Read and interpret blueprints and specifications to determine size, shape, color, type, and thickness of glass; location of framing; installation procedures; and staging and scaffolding materials required. Select the type and color of glass or mirror according to specifications. Assemble and cement sections of stained glass together. Assemble, erect, and dismantle scaffolds, rigging, and hoisting equipment. Measure and mark outlines or patterns on glass to indicate cutting lines. Create patterns on glass by etching, sandblasting, or painting designs. Secure mirrors in position, using mastic cement, putty, bolts, or screws. Drive trucks to installation sites and unload mirrors, glass equipment, and tools. Confer with customers to determine project requirements and to provide cost estimates. Move furniture to clear work sites and cover floors and furnishings with drop cloths. Cut, fit, install, repair, and replace glass and glass substitutes, such as plastic and aluminum, in building interiors or exteriors and in furniture or other products. Grind and polish glass and smooth edges when necessary. Fabricate and install metal sashes and moldings for glass installation, using aluminum or steel framing. Load and arrange glass and mirrors onto delivery trucks, using suction cups or cranes to lift glass. Operate cranes or hoists with suction cups to lift large, heavy pieces of glass.

LEVEL OF ACTIVITY (out of 100)—General Physical Activity: 52.3. **Sitting:** 34.3. **Outdoors:** 45.7.

SKILLS—Installation; Technology Design; Repairing.

GOE—Interest Area: 02. Architecture and Construction. **Work Group:** 02.04. Construction Crafts. **Other Jobs in This Work Group:** Boilermakers; Brickmasons and Blockmasons; Carpet Installers; Cement Masons and Concrete Finishers; Commercial Divers; Construction Carpenters; Crane and Tower Operators; Drywall and Ceiling Tile Installers; Electricians; Fence Erectors; Floor Layers, Except Carpet, Wood, and Hard Tiles; Floor Sanders and Finishers; Hazardous Materials Removal Workers; Insulation Workers, Floor, Ceiling, and Wall; Insulation Workers, Mechanical; Manufactured Building and Mobile Home Installers; Operating Engineers and Other Construction Equipment Operators; Painters, Construction and Maintenance; Paperhangers; Paving, Surfacing, and Tamping Equipment Operators; Pile-Driver Operators; Pipe Fitters and Steamfitters; Pipelayers; Plasterers and Stucco Masons; Plumbers; Plumbers, Pipefitters, and Steamfitters; Rail-Track Laying and Maintenance Equipment Operators; Refractory Materials Repairers, Except Brickmasons; Reinforcing Iron and Rebar Workers; Riggers; Roofers; Rough Carpenters; Security and Fire Alarm Systems Installers; Segmental Pavers; Sheet Metal Workers; Stone Cutters and Carvers, Manufacturing; Stonemasons; Structural Iron and Steel Workers; Tapers; Terrazzo Workers and Finishers; Tile and Marble Setters. **PERSONALITY TYPE:** Realistic. Realistic occupations frequently involve work activities that include practical, hands-on problems and solutions. They often deal with plants; animals; and real-world materials like wood, tools, and machinery. Many of the occupations require working outside and do not involve a lot of paperwork or working closely with others.

EDUCATION/TRAINING PROGRAM(S)— Glazier. **RELATED KNOWLEDGE/COURSES—Building and Construction:** The materials, methods, and tools involved in the construction or repair of houses, buildings, or other structures such as highways and roads.

Fine Arts: The theory and techniques required to compose, produce, and perform works of music, dance, visual arts, drama, and sculpture.

WORK ENVIRONMENT—More often indoors than outdoors; minor burns, cuts, bites, or stings; standing; kneeling, crouching, stooping, or crawling; using hands on objects, tools, or controls.

Hairdressers, Hairstylists, and Cosmetologists

- ☺ Education/Training Required: Postsecondary vocational training
- ☺ Annual Earnings: $20,610
- ☺ Growth: 16.1%
- ☺ Annual Job Openings: 59,000
- ☺ Self-Employed: 43.8%
- ☺ Part-Time: 34.8%

Provide beauty services, such as shampooing, cutting, coloring, and styling hair and massaging and treating scalp. May also apply makeup, dress wigs, perform hair removal, and provide nail and skin care services. Keep workstations clean and sanitize tools such as scissors and combs. Cut, trim, and shape hair or hairpieces, based on customers' instructions, hair type and facial features and using clippers, scissors, trimmers, and razors. Analyze patrons' hair and other physical features to determine and recommend beauty treatment or suggest hairstyles. Schedule client appointments. Bleach, dye, or tint hair, using applicator or brush. Update and maintain customer information records, such as beauty services provided. Shampoo, rinse, condition, and dry hair and scalp or hairpieces with water, liquid soap, or other solutions. Operate cash registers to receive payments from patrons. Demonstrate and sell hair care products and cosmetics. Apply water, setting, straightening, or waving solutions to hair and use curlers, rollers, hot combs, and curling irons to press and curl hair. Develop new styles and techniques. Comb, brush, and spray hair or wigs to set style. Shape eyebrows and remove facial hair, using depilatory cream, tweezers, electrolysis, or wax. Administer therapeutic medication and advise patron to seek medical treatment for chronic or contagious scalp conditions. Massage and treat scalp for hygienic and remedial purposes, using hands, fingers, or vibrating equipment. Shave, trim, and shape beards and moustaches. Train or supervise other hairstylists, hairdressers, and assistants. Recommend and explain the use of cosmetics, lotions, and creams to soften and lubricate skin and enhance and restore natural appearance. Give facials to patrons, using special compounds such as lotions and creams. Clean, shape, and polish fingernails and toenails, using files and nail polish. Apply artificial fingernails. Attach wigs or hairpieces to model heads and dress wigs and hairpieces according to instructions, samples, sketches, or photographs.

LEVEL OF ACTIVITY (out of 100)—General Physical Activity: 43.6. **Sitting:** 18.6. **Outdoors:** 14.6.

SKILLS—Science; Management of Financial Resources; Operations Analysis; Learning Strategies; Social Perceptiveness; Equipment Selection; Time Management; Equipment Maintenance.

GOE—**Interest Area:** 09. Hospitality, Tourism, and Recreation. **Work Group:** 09.07. Barber and Beauty Services. **Other Jobs in This Work Group:** Barbers; Manicurists and Pedicurists; Shampooers; Skin Care Specialists. **PERSONALITY TYPE:** Enterprising. Enterprising occupations frequently involve starting up and carrying out projects. These occupations can involve leading people and making many decisions. They sometimes require risk taking and often deal with business.

EDUCATION/TRAINING PROGRAM(S)— Cosmetology/Cosmetologist, General; Electrolysis/Electrology and Electrolysis Technician; Make-Up Artist/Specialist; Hair Styling/Stylist and Hair Design; Permanent Cosmetics/ Makeup and Tattooing; Salon/Beauty Salon Management/Manager; Cosmetology, Barber/ Styling, and Nail Instructor; Cosmetology and Related Personal Grooming Arts, Other. **RELATED KNOWLEDGE/COURSES— Chemistry:** The chemical composition, structure, and properties of substances and of the chemical processes and transformations that they undergo. This includes uses of chemicals and their danger signs, production techniques, and disposal methods. **Sales and Marketing:** Principles and methods for showing, promoting, and selling products or services. This includes marketing strategy and tactics, product demonstration, sales techniques, and sales control systems. **Customer and Personal Service:** Principles and processes for providing customer and personal services. This includes customer needs assessment, meeting quality standards for services, and evaluation of customer satisfaction.

WORK ENVIRONMENT—Indoors; contaminants; minor burns, cuts, bites, or stings; standing; using hands on objects, tools, or controls; repetitive motions.

Hazardous Materials Removal Workers

- ◉ Education/Training Required: Moderate-term on-the-job training
- ◉ Annual Earnings: $33,690
- ◉ Growth: 31.2%
- ◉ Annual Job Openings: 11,000
- ◉ Self-Employed: 0.0%
- ◉ Part-Time: 5.0%

Identify, remove, pack, transport, or dispose of hazardous materials, including asbestos, lead-based paint, waste oil, fuel, transmission fluid, radioactive materials, contaminated soil, etc. Specialized training and certification in hazardous materials handling or a confined entry permit are generally required. May operate earth-moving equipment or trucks. Construct scaffolding or build containment areas prior to beginning abatement or decontamination work. Operate cranes to move and load baskets, casks, and canisters. Unload baskets of irradiated elements onto packaging machines that automatically insert fuel elements into canisters and secure lids. Remove asbestos and/or lead from surfaces, using hand and power tools such as scrapers, vacuums, and high-pressure sprayers. Pull tram cars along underwater tracks and position cars to receive irradiated fuel elements; then pull loaded cars to mechanisms that automatically unload elements onto underwater tables. Package, store, and move irradiated fuel elements in the underwater storage basin of a nuclear reactor plant, using machines and equipment. Manipulate handgrips of mechanical arms to place irradiated fuel elements into baskets. Apply chemical compounds to lead-based paint, allow compounds to dry, and then scrape the hazardous material into containers for removal and/or storage. Record numbers of containers stored at disposal sites and specify amounts and types of equipment and waste disposed. Operate machines and equipment to remove, package, store, or transport loads of waste materials. Mix and pour concrete into forms to encase waste material for disposal. Clean contaminated equipment or areas for re-use, using detergents and solvents, sandblasters, filter pumps, and steam cleaners. Follow prescribed safety procedures and comply with federal laws regulating waste disposal methods. Identify asbestos, lead, or other hazardous materials that need to be removed, using monitoring devices. Load and unload materials into containers and onto trucks, using hoists or forklifts. Drive trucks or other heavy equipment to convey contaminated waste to designated sea or ground locations. Organize and track the locations of hazardous items in landfills.

LEVEL OF ACTIVITY (out of 100)—General Physical Activity: 45.7. **Sitting:** 45.7. **Outdoors:** 60.0.

SKILLS—None met the criteria.

GOE—Interest Area: 02. Architecture and Construction. **Work Group:** 02.04. Construction Crafts. **Other Jobs in This Work Group:** Boilermakers; Brickmasons and Blockmasons; Carpet Installers; Cement Masons and Concrete Finishers; Commercial Divers; Construction Carpenters; Crane and Tower Operators; Drywall and Ceiling Tile Installers; Electricians; Fence Erectors; Floor Layers, Except Carpet, Wood, and Hard Tiles; Floor Sanders and Finishers; Glaziers; Insulation Workers, Floor, Ceiling, and Wall; Insulation Workers,

Mechanical; Manufactured Building and Mobile Home Installers; Operating Engineers and Other Construction Equipment Operators; Painters, Construction and Maintenance; Paperhangers; Paving, Surfacing, and Tamping Equipment Operators; Pile-Driver Operators; Pipe Fitters and Steamfitters; Pipelayers; Plasterers and Stucco Masons; Plumbers; Plumbers, Pipefitters, and Steamfitters; Rail-Track Laying and Maintenance Equipment Operators; Refractory Materials Repairers, Except Brickmasons; Reinforcing Iron and Rebar Workers; Riggers; Roofers; Rough Carpenters; Security and Fire Alarm Systems Installers; Segmental Pavers; Sheet Metal Workers; Stone Cutters and Carvers, Manufacturing; Stonemasons; Structural Iron and Steel Workers; Tapers; Terrazzo Workers and Finishers; Tile and Marble Setters. **PERSONALITY TYPE:** Realistic. Realistic occupations frequently involve work activities that include practical, hands-on problems and solutions. They often deal with plants; animals; and real-world materials like wood, tools, and machinery. Many of the occupations require working outside and do not involve a lot of paperwork or working closely with others.

EDUCATION/TRAINING PROGRAM(S)—Hazardous Materials Management and Waste Technology/Technician; Construction Trades, Other; Mechanic and Repair Technologies/Technicians, Other. **RELATED KNOWLEDGE/COURSES—Transportation:** Principles and methods for moving people or goods by air, rail, sea, or road, including the relative costs and benefits. **Production and Processing:** Raw materials, production processes, quality control, costs, and other techniques for maximizing the effective manufacture and distribution of goods. **Chemistry:** The chemical composition, structure, and properties of substances and of the chemical processes and transformations that they undergo. This includes uses of chemicals and their danger signs, production techniques, and disposal methods. **Public Safety and Security:** Relevant equipment, policies, procedures, and strategies to promote effective local, state, or national security operations for the protection of people, data, property, and institutions. **Law and Government:** Laws, legal codes, court procedures, precedents, government regulations, executive orders, agency rules, and the democratic political process. **Mechanical Devices:** Machines and tools, including their designs, uses, repair, and maintenance.

WORK ENVIRONMENT—Outdoors; contaminants; radiation; more often standing than sitting; using hands on objects, tools, or controls.

Heating and Air Conditioning Mechanics and Installers

This job can be found in the Part I lists under the title Heating, Air Conditioning, and Refrigeration Mechanics and Installers.

- Education/Training Required: Long-term on-the-job training
- Annual Earnings: $37,040
- Growth: 19.0%
- Annual Job Openings: 33,000
- Self-Employed: 13.1%
- Part-Time: 3.6%

The job openings listed here are shared with Refrigeration Mechanics and Installers.

Install, service, and repair heating and air conditioning systems in residences and commercial establishments. Obtain and maintain required certifications. Comply with all applicable standards, policies, and procedures, including safety procedures and the maintenance of a clean work area. Repair or replace defective equipment, components, or wiring. Test electrical circuits and components for continuity, using electrical test equipment. Reassemble and test equipment following repairs. Inspect and test system to verify system compliance with plans and specifications and to detect and locate malfunctions. Discuss heating-cooling system malfunctions with users to isolate problems or to verify that malfunctions have been corrected. Test pipe or tubing joints and connections for leaks, using pressure gauge or soap-and-water solution. Record and report all faults, deficiencies, and other unusual occurrences, as well as the time and materials expended on work orders. Adjust system controls to setting recommended by manufacturer to balance system, using hand tools. Recommend, develop, and perform preventive and general maintenance procedures such as cleaning, power-washing, and vacuuming equipment; oiling parts; and changing filters. Lay out and connect electrical wiring between controls and equipment according to wiring diagram, using electrician's hand tools. Install auxiliary components to heating-cooling equipment, such as expansion and discharge valves, air ducts, pipes, blowers, dampers, flues, and stokers, following blueprints. Assist with other work in coordination with repair and maintenance teams. Install, connect, and adjust thermostats, humidistats, and timers, using hand tools. Generate work orders that address deficiencies in need of correction. Join pipes or tubing to equipment and to fuel, water, or refrigerant source to form complete circuit. Assemble, position, and mount heating or cooling equipment, following blueprints. Study blueprints, design specifications, and manufacturers' recommendations to ascertain the configuration of heating or cooling equipment components and to ensure the proper installation of components. Cut and drill holes in floors, walls, and roof to install equipment, using power saws and drills.

LEVEL OF ACTIVITY (out of 100)—General Physical Activity: 81.6. **Sitting:** 26.6. **Outdoors:** 49.6.

SKILLS—Repairing; Installation; Equipment Maintenance; Troubleshooting; Systems Evaluation; Coordination; Systems Analysis; Operation Monitoring.

GOE—Interest Area: 02. Architecture and Construction. **Work Group:** 02.05. Systems and Equipment Installation, Maintenance, and Repair. **Other Jobs in This Work Group:** Electrical and Electronics Repairers, Powerhouse, Substation, and Relay; Electrical Power-Line Installers and Repairers; Elevator Installers and Repairers; Maintenance and Repair Workers, General; Refrigeration Mechanics and Installers; Telecommunications Equipment Installers and Repairers, Except Line Installers; Telecommunications Line Installers and Repairers. **PERSONALITY TYPE:** Realistic. Realistic occupations frequently involve work activities that include practical, hands-on problems and solutions. They often deal with plants; animals; and real-world materials like wood, tools, and machinery. Many of the occupations require working outside and do not involve a lot of paperwork or working closely with others.

EDUCATION/TRAINING PROGRAM(S)—Heating, Air Conditioning, and Refrigeration Technology/Technician (ACH/ACR/ACHR/HRAC/HVAC); Solar Energy Technology/Technician; Heating, Air Conditioning, Ventilation, and Refrigeration Maintenance Technology/Technician. **RELATED KNOWLEDGE/COURSES—Mechanical Devices:** Machines and tools, including their designs, uses, repair, and maintenance. **Building and Construction:** The materials, methods, and tools involved in the construction or repair of houses, buildings, or other structures such as highways and roads. **Design:** Design techniques, tools, and principles involved in production of precision technical plans, blueprints, drawings, and models. **Physics:** Physical principles and laws and their interrelationships and applications to understanding fluid, material, and atmospheric dynamics and mechanical, electrical, atomic, and subatomic structures and processes. **Engineering and Technology:** The practical application of engineering science and technology. This includes applying principles, techniques, procedures, and equipment to the design and production of various goods and services. **Sales and Marketing:** Principles and methods for showing, promoting, and selling products or services. This includes marketing strategy and tactics, product demonstration, sales techniques, and sales control systems.

WORK ENVIRONMENT—Outdoors; very hot or cold; contaminants; hazardous conditions; minor burns, cuts, bites, or stings; using hands on objects, tools, or controls.

Heating, Air Conditioning, and Refrigeration Mechanics and Installers

See the descriptions of these jobs:

- Heating and Air Conditioning Mechanics and Installers
- Refrigeration Mechanics and Installers

Helpers—Brickmasons, Blockmasons, Stonemasons, and Tile and Marble Setters

- Education/Training Required: Short-term on-the-job training
- Annual Earnings: $24,600
- Growth: 14.9%
- Annual Job Openings: 14,000
- Self-Employed: 0.8%
- Part-Time: 13.1%

Help brickmasons, blockmasons, stonemasons, or tile and marble setters by performing duties of lesser skill. Duties include using, supplying, or holding materials or tools and cleaning work area and equipment. Transport materials, tools, and machines to installation sites manually or using conveyance equipment. Mix mortar, plaster, and grout, manually or using machines, according to standard formulas. Erect scaffolding or other installation structures. Cut materials to specified sizes for installation, using power saws or tile cutters. Clean installation surfaces, equipment, tools, work sites, and storage areas, using water, chemical solutions, oxygen lances, or polishing machines. Arrange and store materials, machines, tools, and equipment. Apply grout between joints of bricks or tiles, using grouting trowels. Apply caulk, sealants, or other agents to installed surfaces. Remove damaged tile, brick, or mortar and clean and prepare surfaces, using pliers, hammers, chisels, drills, wire brushes, and metal wire anchors. Remove excess grout and residue from tile or brick joints, using sponges or trowels. Select or locate and supply materials to masons for installation, following drawings or numbered sequences. Move or position materials such as marble slabs, using cranes, hoists, or dollies. Correct surface imperfections or fill chipped, cracked, or broken bricks or tiles, using fillers, adhesives, and grouting materials. Provide assistance in the preparation, installation, repair, and/or rebuilding of tile, brick, or stone surfaces. Modify material moving, mixing, grouting, grinding, polishing, or cleaning procedures according to installation or material requirements.

LEVEL OF ACTIVITY (out of 100)—General Physical Activity: 68.6. Sitting: 31.4. Outdoors: 57.1.

SKILLS—Installation.

GOE—Interest Area: 02. Architecture and Construction. Work Group: 02.06. Construction Support/Labor. Other Jobs in This Work

Group: Construction Laborers; Helpers—Carpenters; Helpers—Electricians; Helpers—Installation, Maintenance, and Repair Workers; Helpers—Painters, Paperhangers, Plasterers, and Stucco Masons; Helpers—Pipelayers, Plumbers, Pipefitters, and Steamfitters; Helpers—Roofers; Highway Maintenance Workers; Septic Tank Servicers and Sewer Pipe Cleaners. **PERSONALITY TYPE:** Realistic. Realistic occupations frequently involve work activities that include practical, hands-on problems and solutions. They often deal with plants; animals; and real-world materials like wood, tools, and machinery. Many of the occupations require working outside and do not involve a lot of paperwork or working closely with others.

EDUCATION/TRAINING PROGRAM(S)—Mason/Masonry. **RELATED KNOWLEDGE/COURSES—Building and Construction:** The materials, methods, and tools involved in the construction or repair of houses, buildings, or other structures such as highways and roads. **Mechanical Devices:** Machines and tools, including their designs, uses, repair, and maintenance.

WORK ENVIRONMENT—Outdoors; standing; walking and running; kneeling, crouching, stooping, or crawling; using hands on objects, tools, or controls; repetitive motions.

Helpers—Carpenters

- ◎ Education/Training Required: Short-term on-the-job training
- ◎ Annual Earnings: $21,990
- ◎ Growth: 14.5%
- ◎ Annual Job Openings: 24,000
- ◎ Self-Employed: 0.7%
- ◎ Part-Time: 13.1%

Help carpenters by performing duties of lesser skill. Duties include using, supplying, or holding materials or tools and cleaning work area and equipment. Position and hold timbers, lumber, and paneling in place for fastening or cutting. Erect scaffolding, shoring, and braces. Select tools, equipment, and materials from storage and transport items to work site. Fasten timbers and/or lumber with glue, screws, pegs, or nails and install hardware. Clean work areas, machines, and equipment to maintain a clean and safe jobsite. Align, straighten, plumb, and square forms for installation. Hold plumb bobs, sighting rods, and other equipment to aid in establishing reference points and lines. Cut timbers, lumber, and/or paneling to specified dimensions and drill holes in timbers or lumber. Smooth and sand surfaces to remove ridges, tool marks, glue, or caulking. Perform tie spacing layout; then measure, mark, drill, and/or cut. Secure stakes to grids for constructions of footings, nail scabs to footing forms, and vibrate and float concrete. Construct forms; then assist in raising them to the required elevation. Install handrails under the direction of a carpenter. Glue and clamp edges or joints of assembled parts. Cut and install insulating or sound-absorbing material. Cut tile or linoleum to fit; spread adhesives on flooring to install tile or linoleum. Cover surfaces with laminated plastic covering material.

LEVEL OF ACTIVITY (out of 100)—General Physical Activity: 74.0. **Sitting:** 29.6. **Outdoors:** 47.9.

SKILLS—Installation; Repairing; Equipment Maintenance; Management of Material Resources; Troubleshooting; Mathematics; Equipment Selection; Operation and Control.

GOE—**Interest Area:** 02. Architecture and Construction. **Work Group:** 02.06. Construction Support/Labor. **Other Jobs in This Work Group:** Construction Laborers; Helpers—Brickmasons, Blockmasons, Stonemasons, and Tile and Marble Setters; Helpers—Electricians; Helpers—Installation, Maintenance, and Repair Workers; Helpers—Painters, Paperhangers, Plasterers, and Stucco Masons; Helpers—Pipelayers, Plumbers, Pipefitters, and Steamfitters; Helpers—Roofers; Highway Maintenance Workers; Septic Tank Servicers and Sewer Pipe Cleaners. **PERSONALITY TYPE:** Realistic. Realistic occupations frequently involve work activities that include practical, hands-on problems and solutions. They often deal with plants; animals; and real-world materials like wood, tools, and machinery. Many of the occupations require working outside and do not involve a lot of paperwork or working closely with others.

EDUCATION/TRAINING PROGRAM(S)—Carpentry/Carpenter. **RELATED KNOWLEDGE/COURSES**—**Building and Construction:** The materials, methods, and tools involved in the construction or repair of houses, buildings, or other structures such as highways and roads. **Design:** Design techniques, tools, and principles involved in production of precision technical plans, blueprints, drawings, and mod-

els. **Engineering and Technology:** The practical application of engineering science and technology. This includes applying principles, techniques, procedures, and equipment to the design and production of various goods and services. **Public Safety and Security:** Relevant equipment, policies, procedures, and strategies to promote effective local, state, or national security operations for the protection of people, data, property, and institutions. **Mechanical Devices:** Machines and tools, including their designs, uses, repair, and maintenance.

WORK ENVIRONMENT—Noisy; very hot or cold; hazardous equipment; standing; walking and running; using hands on objects, tools, or controls.

Helpers—Installation, Maintenance, and Repair Workers

- ☉ Education/Training Required: Short-term on-the-job training
- ☉ Annual Earnings: $21,230
- ☉ Growth: 16.4%
- ☉ Annual Job Openings: 41,000
- ☉ Self-Employed: 0.9%
- ☉ Part-Time: 32.9%

Help installation, maintenance, and repair workers in maintenance, parts replacement, and repair of vehicles, industrial machinery, and electrical and electronic equipment.

Perform duties such as furnishing tools, materials, and supplies to other workers; cleaning work area, machines, and tools; and holding materials or tools for other workers. Tend and observe equipment and machinery in order to verify efficient and safe operation. Examine and test machinery, equipment, components, and parts for defects and to ensure proper functioning. Adjust, connect, or disconnect wiring, piping, tubing, and other parts, using hand tools or power tools. Install or replace machinery, equipment, and new or replacement parts and instruments, using hand tools or power tools. Clean or lubricate vehicles, machinery, equipment, instruments, tools, work areas, and other objects, using hand tools, power tools, and cleaning equipment. Apply protective materials to equipment, components, and parts in order to prevent defects and corrosion. Transfer tools, parts, equipment, and supplies to and from workstations and other areas. Disassemble broken or defective equipment in order to facilitate repair; reassemble equipment when repairs are complete. Assemble and maintain physical structures, using hand tools or power tools. Provide assistance to more-skilled workers involved in the adjustment, maintenance, part replacement, and repair of tools, equipment, and machines. Position vehicles, machinery, equipment, physical structures, and other objects for assembly or installation, using hand tools, power tools, and moving equipment. Hold or supply tools, parts, equipment, and supplies for other workers. Prepare workstations so mechanics and repairers can conduct work.

LEVEL OF ACTIVITY (out of 100)—General Physical Activity: 61.7. **Sitting:** 31.1. **Outdoors:** 37.8.

SKILLS—Installation; Operation Monitoring; Repairing; Equipment Maintenance; Troubleshooting; Operations Analysis; Operation and Control; Science.

GOE—Interest Area: 02. Architecture and Construction. **Work Group:** 02.06. Construction Support/Labor. **Other Jobs in This Work Group:** Construction Laborers; Helpers—Brickmasons, Blockmasons, Stonemasons, and Tile and Marble Setters; Helpers—Carpenters; Helpers—Electricians; Helpers—Painters, Paperhangers, Plasterers, and Stucco Masons; Helpers—Pipelayers, Plumbers, Pipefitters, and Steamfitters; Helpers—Roofers; Highway Maintenance Workers; Septic Tank Servicers and Sewer Pipe Cleaners. **PERSONALITY TYPE:** Realistic. Realistic occupations frequently involve work activities that include practical, hands-on problems and solutions. They often deal with plants; animals; and real-world materials like wood, tools, and machinery. Many of the occupations require working outside and do not involve a lot of paperwork or working closely with others.

EDUCATION/TRAINING PROGRAM(S)—Industrial Mechanics and Maintenance Technology. **RELATED KNOWLEDGE/COURSES—Mechanical Devices:** Machines and tools, including their designs, uses, repair, and maintenance. **Engineering and Technology:** The practical application of engineering science and technology. This includes applying principles, techniques, procedures, and equipment to the design and production of various goods and services. **Design:** Design techniques, tools, and principles involved in production of precision technical plans, blueprints, drawings, and models. **Chemistry:** The chemical composition, structure, and properties of substances and of the chemical processes and transformations that they undergo. This includes uses of chemicals and their danger signs, production techniques, and disposal methods. **Building and Construction:** The materials, methods, and tools involved in the construction or repair of houses, buildings, or other structures such as highways and roads. **Public Safety and Security:** Relevant equipment, policies, procedures, and strategies to promote effective local, state, or national security operations for the protection of people, data, property, and institutions.

WORK ENVIRONMENT—Noisy; hazardous conditions; hazardous equipment; standing; using hands on objects, tools, or controls; bending or twisting the body.

Helpers—Pipelayers, Plumbers, Pipefitters, and Steamfitters

- ◉ Education/Training Required: Short-term on-the-job training
- ◉ Annual Earnings: $22,820
- ◉ Growth: 16.6%
- ◉ Annual Job Openings: 17,000
- ◉ Self-Employed: 0.8%
- ◉ Part-Time: 13.1%

Help plumbers, pipefitters, steamfitters, or pipelayers by performing duties of lesser skill. Duties include using, supplying, or holding materials or tools and cleaning work area and equipment. Assist plumbers by performing rough-ins, repairing and replacing fixtures, and locating and repairing leaking or broken pipes. Cut or drill holes in walls or floors to accommodate the passage of pipes. Measure, cut, thread, and assemble new pipe, placing the assembled pipe in hangers or other supports. Mount brackets and hangers on walls and ceilings to hold pipes and set sleeves or inserts to provide support for pipes. Requisition tools and equipment, select type and size of pipe, and collect and transport materials and equipment to worksite. Fit or assist in fitting valves, couplings, or assemblies to tanks, pumps, or systems, using hand tools. Assist pipe fitters in the layout, assembly, and installation of piping for air, ammonia, gas, and water systems. Excavate and grade ditches and lay and join pipe for water and sewer service. Cut pipe and lift up to fitters. Disassemble and remove damaged or worn pipe. Clean shop, work area, and machines, using solvent and rags. Install gas burners to convert furnaces from wood, coal, or oil. Immerse pipe in chemical solution to remove dirt, oil, and scale. Clean and renew steam traps. Fill pipes with sand or resin to prevent distortion and hold pipes during bending and installation.

LEVEL OF ACTIVITY (out of 100)—General Physical Activity: 64.9. **Sitting:** 26.6. **Outdoors:** 48.2.

SKILLS—Installation; Repairing; Equipment Maintenance; Troubleshooting; Mathematics; Quality Control Analysis; Equipment Selection; Negotiation.

GOE—**Interest Area:** 02. Architecture and Construction. **Work Group:** 02.06. Construction Support/Labor. **Other Jobs in This Work Group:** Construction Laborers; Helpers—Brickmasons, Blockmasons, Stonemasons, and Tile and Marble Setters; Helpers—Carpenters; Helpers—Electricians; Helpers—Installation, Maintenance, and Repair Workers; Helpers—Painters, Paperhangers, Plasterers, and Stucco Masons; Helpers—Roofers; Highway Maintenance Workers; Septic Tank Servicers and Sewer Pipe Cleaners. **PERSONALITY TYPE:** Realistic. Realistic occupations frequently involve work activities that include practical, hands-on problems and solutions. They often deal with plants; animals; and real-world materials like wood, tools, and machinery. Many of the occupations require working outside and do not involve a lot of paperwork or working closely with others.

EDUCATION/TRAINING PROGRAM(S)—Plumbing Technology/Plumber. **RELATED KNOWLEDGE/COURSES—Building and Construction:** The materials, methods, and tools involved in the construction or repair of houses, buildings, or other structures such as highways and roads. **Mechanical Devices:** Machines and tools, including their designs, uses, repair, and maintenance. **Design:** Design techniques, tools, and principles involved in production of precision technical plans, blueprints, drawings, and models. **Public Safety and Security:** Relevant equipment, policies, procedures, and strategies to promote effective local, state, or national security operations for the protection of people, data, property, and institutions. **Engineering and Technology:** The practical application of engineering science and technology. This includes applying principles, techniques, procedures, and equipment to the design and production of various goods and

services. **Law and Government:** Laws, legal codes, court procedures, precedents, government regulations, executive orders, agency rules, and the democratic political process.

WORK ENVIRONMENT—Outdoors; noisy; contaminants; hazardous equipment; standing; using hands on objects, tools, or controls.

Helpers—Production Workers

- Education/Training Required: Short-term on-the-job training
- Annual Earnings: $20,390
- Growth: 7.9%
- Annual Job Openings: 107,000
- Self-Employed: 0.1%
- Part-Time: 23.3%

Help production workers by performing duties of lesser skill. Duties include supplying or holding materials or tools and cleaning work area and equipment. Observe equipment operations so that malfunctions can be detected and notify operators of any malfunctions. Operate machinery used in the production process or assist machine operators. Pack and store materials and products. Start machines or equipment in order to begin production processes. Break up defective products for reprocessing. Unclamp and hoist full reels from braiding, winding, and other fabricating machines, using power hoists. Signal co-workers to direct them to move products during the production process. Separate products according to weight, grade, size, and composition of materials used to produce them. Record information such as the number of products tested, meter readings, and dates and times of product production. Perform minor repairs to machines, such as replacing damaged or worn parts. Pack food products in paper bags and boxes and stack them in warehouses and coolers. Measure amounts of products, lengths of extruded articles, or weights of filled containers to ensure conformance to specifications. Fold products and product parts during processing. Examine products to verify conformance to quality standards. Read gauges and charts and record data obtained. Change machine gears, using wrenches. Thread ends of items such as thread, cloth, and lace through needles and rollers and around take-up tubes. Wash work areas, machines, equipment, vehicles, and products. Turn valves to regulate flow of liquids or air, to reverse machines, to start pumps, or to regulate equipment. Transfer finished products, raw materials, tools, or equipment between storage and work areas of plants and warehouses by hand or using hand trucks or powered lift trucks. Tie products in bundles for further processing or shipment, following prescribed procedures. Remove products, machine attachments, and waste material from machines. Prepare raw materials for processing. Position spouts or chutes of storage bins so that containers can be filled. Place products in equipment or on work surfaces for further processing, inspecting, or wrapping. Mix ingredients according to specified procedures and formulas.

LEVEL OF ACTIVITY (out of 100)—General Physical Activity: 61.4. **Sitting:** 32.9. **Outdoors:** 34.3.

SKILLS—Repairing; Equipment Maintenance; Installation; Operation Monitoring.

GOE—Interest Area: 13. Manufacturing. **Work Group:** 13.03. Production Work, Assorted Materials Processing. **Other Jobs in This Work Group:** Bakers; Cementing and Gluing Machine Operators and Tenders; Chemical Equipment Operators and Tenders; Cleaning, Washing, and Metal Pickling Equipment Operators and Tenders; Coating, Painting, and Spraying Machine Setters, Operators, and Tenders; Cooling and Freezing Equipment Operators and Tenders; Cutting and Slicing Machine Setters, Operators, and Tenders; Extruding and Forming Machine Setters, Operators, and Tenders, Synthetic and Glass Fibers; Extruding, Forming, Pressing, and Compacting Machine Setters, Operators, and Tenders; Food and Tobacco Roasting, Baking, and Drying Machine Operators and Tenders; Food Batchmakers; Food Cooking Machine Operators and Tenders; Furnace, Kiln, Oven, Drier, and Kettle Operators and Tenders; Heat Treating Equipment Setters, Operators, and Tenders, Metal and Plastic; Meat, Poultry, and Fish Cutters and Trimmers; Metal-Refining Furnace Operators and Tenders; Mixing and Blending Machine Setters, Operators, and Tenders; Packaging and Filling Machine Operators and Tenders; Plating and Coating Machine Setters, Operators, and Tenders, Metal and Plastic; Pourers and Casters, Metal; Sawing Machine Setters, Operators, and Tenders, Wood; Separating, Filtering, Clarifying, Precipitating, and Still Machine Setters, Operators, and Tenders; Sewing Machine Operators; Shoe Machine Operators and Tenders; Slaughterers and Meat Packers; Team Assemblers; Textile Bleaching and Dyeing Machine Operators and Tenders; Tire Builders; Woodworking Machine Setters, Operators, and Tenders, Except Sawing. **PERSONALITY TYPE:** Realistic. Realistic occupations frequently involve work activities that include practical, hands-on problems and solutions. They often deal with plants; animals; and real-world materials like wood, tools, and machinery. Many of the occupations require working outside and do not involve a lot of paperwork or working closely with others.

EDUCATION/TRAINING PROGRAM(S)— No related CIP programs; this job is learned through informal short-term on-the-job training. RELATED KNOWLEDGE/COURSES— Production and Processing: Raw materials, production processes, quality control, costs, and other techniques for maximizing the effective manufacture and distribution of goods. Mechanical Devices: Machines and tools, including their designs, uses, repair, and maintenance.

WORK ENVIRONMENT—Indoors; hazardous equipment; standing; using hands on objects, tools, or controls; bending or twisting the body; repetitive motions.

Highway Maintenance Workers

- Education/Training Required: Moderate-term on-the-job training
- Annual Earnings: $30,250
- Growth: 23.3%
- Annual Job Openings: 27,000
- Self-Employed: 1.2%
- Part-Time: 6.3%

Maintain highways, municipal and rural roads, airport runways, and rights-of-way. Duties include patching broken or eroded pavement and repairing guardrails, highway markers, and snow fences. May also mow or clear brush from along road or plow snow from roadway. Flag motorists to warn them of obstacles or repair work ahead. Set out signs and cones around work areas to divert traffic. Drive trucks or tractors with adjustable attachments to sweep debris from paved surfaces, mow grass and weeds, and remove snow and ice. Dump, spread, and tamp asphalt, using pneumatic tampers, to repair joints and patch broken pavement. Drive trucks to transport crews and equipment to worksites. Inspect, clean, and repair drainage systems, bridges, tunnels, and other structures. Haul and spread sand, gravel, and clay to fill washouts and repair road shoulders. Erect, install, or repair guardrails, road shoulders, berms, highway markers, warning signals, and highway lighting, using hand tools and power tools. Remove litter and debris from roadways, including debris from rock and mud slides. Clean and clear debris from culverts, catch basins, drop inlets, ditches, and other drain structures. Perform roadside landscaping work, such as clearing weeds and brush and planting and trimming trees. Paint traffic control lines and place pavement traffic messages by hand or using machines. Inspect markers to verify accurate installation. Apply poisons along roadsides and in animal burrows to eliminate unwanted roadside vegetation and rodents. Measure and mark locations for installation of markers, using tape, string, or chalk. Apply oil to road surfaces, using sprayers. Blend compounds to form adhesive mixtures used for marker installation. Place and remove snow fences used to prevent the accumulation of drifting snow on highways.

LEVEL OF ACTIVITY (out of 100)—General Physical Activity: 60.6. Sitting: 37.6. Outdoors: 53.9.

SKILLS—Equipment Maintenance; Repairing; Installation; Management of Material Resources; Operation and Control; Troubleshooting; Equipment Selection; Operation Monitoring.

GOE—**Interest Area:** 02. Architecture and Construction. **Work Group:** 02.06. Construction Support/Labor. **Other Jobs in This Work Group:** Construction Laborers; Helpers— Brickmasons, Blockmasons, Stone-masons, and Tile and Marble Setters; Helpers—Carpenters; Helpers—Electricians; Helpers—Installation, Maintenance, and Repair Workers; Helpers— Painters, Paperhangers, Plasterers, and Stucco Masons; Helpers—Pipelayers, Plumbers, Pipefitters, and Steamfitters; Helpers—Roofers; Septic Tank Servicers and Sewer Pipe Cleaners. **PERSONALITY TYPE:** Realistic. Realistic occupations frequently involve work activities that include practical, hands-on problems and solutions. They often deal with plants; animals; and real-world materials like wood, tools, and machinery. Many of the occupations require working outside and do not involve a lot of paperwork or working closely with others.

EDUCATION/TRAINING PROGRAM(S)— Construction/Heavy Equipment/Earthmoving Equipment Operation. **RELATED KNOWLEDGE/COURSES**—**Building and Construction:** The materials, methods, and tools involved in the construction or repair of houses, buildings, or other structures such as highways and roads. **Transportation:** Principles and methods for moving people or goods by air, rail, sea, or road, including the relative costs and benefits. **Mechanical Devices:** Machines and tools, including their designs, uses, repair, and maintenance. **Public Safety and Security:** Relevant equipment, policies, procedures, and strategies to promote effective local, state, or national security operations for the protection of people, data, property, and institutions. **Customer and Personal Service:** Principles and processes for providing customer and personal services. This includes customer needs assessment, meeting quality standards for services, and evaluation of customer satisfaction. **Geography:** Principles and methods for describing the features of land, sea, and air masses, including their physical characteristics; locations; interrelationships; and distribution of plant, animal, and human life.

WORK ENVIRONMENT—Outdoors; noisy; very hot or cold; contaminants; hazardous equipment; using hands on objects, tools, or controls.

Immigration and Customs Inspectors

This job can be found in the Part I lists under the title Detectives and Criminal Investigators.

- Education/Training Required: Work experience in a related occupation
- Annual Earnings: $55,790
- Growth: 16.3%
- Annual Job Openings: 9,000
- Self-Employed: 0.0%
- Part-Time: 2.5%

The job openings listed here are shared with Criminal Investigators and Special Agents; Police Detectives; and Police Identification and Records Officers.

Investigate and inspect persons, common carriers, goods, and merchandise arriving in or departing from the United States or moving between states to detect violations of immigration and customs laws and regulations. Examine immigration applications, visas, and passports; interview persons in order to determine eligibility for admission, residence, and travel in the United States. Detain persons found to be in violation of customs or immigration laws and arrange for legal action such as deportation. Locate and seize contraband; undeclared merchandise; and vehicles, aircraft, or boats that contain such merchandise. Interpret and explain laws and regulations to travelers, prospective immigrants, shippers, and manufacturers. Inspect cargo, baggage, and personal articles entering or leaving the United States. for compliance with revenue laws and U.S. Customs Service regulations. Record and report job-related activities, findings, transactions, violations, discrepancies, and decisions. Institute civil and criminal prosecutions and cooperate with other law enforcement agencies in the investigation and prosecution of those in violation of immigration or customs laws. Testify regarding decisions at immigration appeals or in federal court. Determine duty and taxes to be paid on goods. Collect samples of merchandise for examination, appraisal, or testing. Investigate applications for duty refunds and petition for remission or mitigation of penalties when warranted.

LEVEL OF ACTIVITY (out of 100)—General Physical Activity: 74.6. **Sitting:** 46.7. **Outdoors:** 50.0.

SKILLS—Persuasion; Negotiation; Social Perceptiveness; Speaking; Operations Analysis; Instructing; Equipment Selection; Learning Strategies.

GOE—Interest Area: 07. Government and Public Administration. **Work Group:** 07.03. Regulations Enforcement. **Other Jobs in This Work Group:** Agricultural Inspectors; Aviation Inspectors; Compliance Officers, Except Agriculture, Construction, Health and Safety, and Transportation; Construction and Building Inspectors; Environmental Compliance Inspectors; Equal Opportunity Representatives and Officers; Financial Examiners; Fire Inspectors; Fish and Game Wardens; Forest Fire Inspectors and Prevention Specialists; Freight and Cargo Inspectors; Government Property Inspectors and Investigators; Licensing Examiners and Inspectors; Nuclear Monitoring Technicians; Occupational Health and Safety Specialists; Occupational Health and Safety Technicians; Tax Examiners, Collectors, and Revenue Agents; Transportation Vehicle, Equipment, and Systems Inspectors, Except Aviation. **PERSONALITY TYPE:** Conventional. Conventional occupations frequently involve following set procedures and routines. These occupations can include working with data and details more than with ideas. Usually there is a clear line of authority to follow.

EDUCATION/TRAINING PROGRAM(S)—Criminal Justice/Police Science; Criminalistics and Criminal Science. **RELATED KNOWLEDGE/COURSES—Public Safety and Security:** Relevant equipment, policies, procedures, and strategies to promote effective local, state, or national security operations for the protection of people, data, property, and institutions. **Law and Government:** Laws, legal codes, court procedures, precedents, government regulations, executive orders, agency rules, and the democratic political process. **Foreign Language:** The structure and content of a foreign (non-English) language, including the meaning and spelling of words, rules of composition and grammar, and pronunciation. **Customer and Personal Service:** Principles and processes for providing customer and personal services. This includes customer needs assessment, meeting quality standards for services, and evaluation of customer satisfaction. **Geography:** Principles and methods for describing the features of land, sea, and air masses, including their physical characteristics; locations; interrelationships; and distribution of plant, animal, and human life. **Philosophy and Theology:** Different philosophical systems and religions. This includes their basic principles, values, ethics, ways of thinking, customs, and practices and their impact on human culture.

WORK ENVIRONMENT—More often outdoors than indoors; noisy; contaminants; radiation; hazardous equipment.

Industrial Machinery Mechanics

- ◎ Education/Training Required: Long-term on-the-job training
- ◎ Annual Earnings: $39,740
- ◎ Growth: –0.2%
- ◎ Annual Job Openings: 13,000
- ◎ Self-Employed: 2.3%
- ◎ Part-Time: 1.5%

Repair, install, adjust, or maintain industrial production and processing machinery or refinery and pipeline distribution systems. Clean, lubricate, and adjust parts, equipment, and machinery. Repair and replace broken or malfunctioning components of machinery and equipment. Record repairs and maintenance performed. Record parts and materials used and order or requisition new parts and materials as necessary. Enter codes and instructions to program computer-controlled machinery. Demonstrate equipment functions and features to machine operators. Cut and weld metal to repair broken metal parts, fabricate new parts, and assemble new equipment. Study blueprints and manufacturers' manuals to determine correct installation and operation of machinery. Repair and maintain the operating condition of industrial production and processing machinery and equipment. Reassemble equipment after completion of inspections, testing, or repairs. Operate newly repaired machinery and equipment to verify the adequacy of repairs. Observe and test the operation of machinery and equipment in order to diagnose malfunctions, using voltmeters and other testing devices. Disassemble machinery and equipment to remove parts and make repairs. Examine parts for defects such as breakage and excessive wear. Analyze test results, machine error messages, and information obtained from operators in order to diagnose equipment problems.

LEVEL OF ACTIVITY (out of 100)—**General Physical Activity:** 61.9. **Sitting:** 42.9. **Outdoors:** 28.6.

SKILLS—Repairing; Equipment Maintenance; Troubleshooting; Operation Monitoring; Quality Control Analysis; Installation; Operation and Control.

GOE—**Interest Area:** 13. Manufacturing. **Work Group:** 13.13. Machinery Repair. **Other Jobs in This Work Group:** Bicycle Repairers; Control and Valve Installers and Repairers, Except Mechanical Door; Home Appliance Repairers;

Locksmiths and Safe Repairers; Maintenance Workers, Machinery; Mechanical Door Repairers; Millwrights; Signal and Track Switch Repairers. **PERSONALITY TYPE:** Realistic. Realistic occupations frequently involve work activities that include practical, hands-on problems and solutions. They often deal with plants; animals; and real-world materials like wood, tools, and machinery. Many of the occupations require working outside and do not involve a lot of paperwork or working closely with others.

EDUCATION/TRAINING PROGRAM(S)— Industrial Mechanics and Maintenance Technology; Heavy/Industrial Equipment Maintenance Technologies, Other. **RELATED KNOWLEDGE/COURSES—Mechanical Devices:** Machines and tools, including their designs, uses, repair, and maintenance. **Engineering and Technology:** The practical application of engineering science and technology. This includes applying principles, techniques, procedures, and equipment to the design and production of various goods and services. **Physics:** Physical principles and laws and their interrelationships and applications to understanding fluid, material, and atmospheric dynamics and mechanical, electrical, atomic, and subatomic structures and processes. **Computers and Electronics:** Circuit boards; processors; chips; electronic equipment; and computer hardware and software, including applications and programming. **Public Safety and Security:** Relevant equipment, policies, procedures, and strategies to promote effective local, state, or national security operations for the protection of people, data, property, and institutions.

WORK ENVIRONMENT—Indoors; noisy; hazardous equipment; standing; kneeling, crouching, stooping, or crawling; using hands on objects, tools, or controls.

Industrial Production Managers

- Education/Training Required: Work experience in a related occupation
- Annual Earnings: $75,580
- Growth: 0.8%
- Annual Job Openings: 13,000
- Self-Employed: 1.7%
- Part-Time: 2.3%

Plan, direct, or coordinate the work activities and resources necessary for manufacturing products in accordance with cost, quality, and quantity specifications. Direct and coordinate production, processing, distribution, and marketing activities of industrial organization. Develop budgets and approve expenditures for supplies, materials, and human resources, ensuring that materials, labor, and equipment are used efficiently to meet production targets. Review processing schedules and production orders to make decisions concerning inventory requirements, staffing requirements, work procedures, and duty assignments, considering budgetary limitations and time constraints.

Review operations and confer with technical or administrative staff to resolve production or processing problems. Hire, train, evaluate, and discharge staff and resolve personnel grievances. Initiate and coordinate inventory and cost control programs. Prepare and maintain production reports and personnel records. Set and monitor product standards, examining samples of raw products or directing testing during processing to ensure that finished products are of prescribed quality. Develop and implement production tracking and quality control systems, analyzing production, quality control, maintenance, and other operational reports to detect production problems. Review plans and confer with research and support staff to develop new products and processes. Institute employee suggestion or involvement programs. Coordinate and recommend procedures for facility and equipment maintenance or modification, including the replacement of machines. Maintain current knowledge of the quality control field, relying on current literature pertaining to materials use, technological advances, and statistical studies. Negotiate materials prices with suppliers.

LEVEL OF ACTIVITY (out of 100)—General Physical Activity: 49.3. **Sitting:** 49.3. **Outdoors:** 28.6.

SKILLS—Management of Material Resources; Systems Evaluation; Management of Personnel Resources; Persuasion; Operations Analysis; Systems Analysis; Quality Control Analysis; Monitoring.

GOE—Interest Area: 13. Manufacturing. **Work Group:** 13.01. Managerial Work in Manufacturing. **Other Jobs in This Work Group:** First-Line Supervisors/Managers of Helpers, Laborers, and Material Movers, Hand; First-Line Supervisors/Managers of Mechanics, Installers, and Repairers; First-Line Supervisors/ Managers of Production and Operating Workers. **PERSONALITY TYPE:** Enterprising. Enterprising occupations frequently involve starting up and carrying out projects. These occupations can involve leading people and making many decisions. They sometimes require risk taking and often deal with business.

EDUCATION/TRAINING PROGRAM(S)—Business/Commerce, General; Business Administration and Management, General; Operations Management and Supervision. **RELATED KNOWLEDGE/COURSES—Production and Processing:** Raw materials, production processes, quality control, costs, and other techniques for maximizing the effective manufacture and distribution of goods. **Personnel and Human Resources:** Principles and procedures for personnel recruitment, selection, training, compensation and benefits, labor relations and negotiation, and personnel information systems. **Education and Training:** Principles and methods for curriculum and training design, teaching and instruction for individuals and groups, and the measurement of training effects. **Mechanical Devices:** Machines and tools, including their designs, uses, repair, and maintenance. **Design:** Design techniques, tools, and principles involved in production of precision technical plans, blueprints, drawings, and models. **Engineering and Technology:** The practical application of engineering science and technology. This includes applying principles, techniques, procedures, and equipment to the design and production of various goods and services.

WORK ENVIRONMENT—Indoors; sitting.

Industrial Truck and Tractor Operators

- Education/Training Required: Short-term on-the-job training
- Annual Earnings: $27,080
- Growth: 7.9%
- Annual Job Openings: 114,000
- Self-Employed: 0.2%
- Part-Time: 3.3%

Operate industrial trucks or tractors equipped to move materials around a warehouse, storage yard, factory, construction site, or similar location. Move controls to drive gasoline- or electric-powered trucks, cars, or tractors and transport materials between loading, processing, and storage areas. Move levers and controls that operate lifting devices, such as forklifts, lift beams and swivel-hooks, hoists, and elevating platforms, to load, unload, transport, and stack material. Position lifting devices under, over, or around loaded pallets, skids, and boxes and secure material or products for transport to designated areas. Manually load or unload materials onto or off pallets, skids, platforms, cars, or lifting devices. Perform routine maintenance on vehicles and auxiliary equipment, such as cleaning, lubricating, recharging batteries, fueling, or replacing liquefied-gas tank. Weigh materials or products and record weight and other production data on tags or labels. Operate or tend automatic stacking, loading, packaging, or cutting machines. Signal workers to discharge, dump, or level materials. Hook tow trucks to trailer hitches and fasten attachments such as graders, plows, rollers, and winch cables to tractors, using hitchpins. Turn valves and open chutes to dump, spray, or release materials from dump cars or storage bins into hoppers.

LEVEL OF ACTIVITY (out of 100)—General Physical Activity: 62.7. **Sitting:** 40.0. **Outdoors:** 35.3.

SKILLS—Operation Monitoring; Equipment Maintenance; Repairing; Operation and Control; Systems Analysis; Troubleshooting; Instructing; Equipment Selection.

GOE—Interest Area: 13. Manufacturing. **Work Group:** 13.17. Loading, Moving, Hoisting, and Conveying. **Other Jobs in This Work Group:** Conveyor Operators and Tenders; Hoist and Winch Operators; Machine Feeders and Offbearers; Packers and Packagers, Hand; Pump Operators, Except Wellhead Pumpers; Refuse and Recyclable Material Collectors; Tank Car, Truck, and Ship Loaders. **PERSONALITY TYPE:** Realistic. Realistic occupations frequently involve work activities that include practical, hands-on problems and solutions. They often deal with plants; animals; and real-world materials like wood, tools, and machinery. Many of the occupations require working outside and do not involve a lot of paperwork or working closely with others.

EDUCATION/TRAINING PROGRAM(S)—Ground Transportation, Other. **RELATED KNOWLEDGE/COURSES—Transportation:** Principles and methods for moving people or goods by air, rail, sea, or road, including the relative costs and benefits. **Mechanical Devices:** Machines and tools, including their designs, uses, repair, and maintenance. **Production and Processing:** Raw materials, production processes, quality control, costs, and other techniques for maximizing the effective manufacture and distribution of goods. **Mathematics:** Arithmetic, algebra, geometry, calculus, and statistics and their applications.

WORK ENVIRONMENT—Noisy; very hot or cold; contaminants; standing; using hands on objects, tools, or controls; bending or twisting the body.

Kindergarten Teachers, Except Special Education

◉ Education/Training Required: Bachelor's degree

◉ Annual Earnings: $42,230

◉ Growth: 22.4%

◉ Annual Job Openings: 28,000

◉ Self-Employed: 1.5%

◉ Part-Time: 25.1%

Teach elemental, natural, and social science; personal hygiene; music; art; and literature to children from 4 to 6 years old. Promote physical, mental, and social development. May be required to hold state certification. Teach basic skills such as color, shape, number, and letter recognition; personal hygiene; and social skills. Establish and enforce rules for behavior and policies and procedures to maintain order among students. Observe and evaluate children's performance, behavior, social development, and physical health. Instruct students individually and in groups, adapting teaching methods to meet students' varying needs and interests. Read books to entire classes or to small groups. Demonstrate activities to children. Provide a variety of materials and resources for children to explore, manipulate, and use, both in learning activities and in imaginative play. Plan and conduct activities for a balanced program of instruction, demonstration, and work time that provides students with opportunities to observe, question, and investigate. Confer with parents or guardians, other teachers, counselors, and administrators to resolve students' behavioral and academic problems. Prepare children for later grades by encouraging them to explore learning opportunities and to persevere with challenging tasks. Establish clear objectives for all lessons, units, and projects and communicate those objectives to children. Prepare and implement remedial programs for students requiring extra help. Meet with parents and guardians to discuss their children's progress and to determine their priorities for their children and their resource needs. Prepare objectives and outlines for courses of study, following curriculum guidelines or requirements of states and schools. Organize and lead activities designed to promote physical, mental, and social development such as games, arts and crafts, music, and storytelling. Guide and counsel students with adjustment or academic problems or special academic interests. Identify children showing signs of emotional, developmental, or health-related problems and discuss them with supervisors, parents or guardians, and child development specialists. Instruct and monitor students in the use and care of equipment and materials to prevent injuries and damage. Assimilate arriving children to the school environment by greeting them, helping them remove outerwear, and selecting activities of interest to them.

LEVEL OF ACTIVITY (out of 100)—General Physical Activity: 38.7. Sitting: 33.1. Outdoors: 19.8.

SKILLS—Instructing; Learning Strategies; Social Perceptiveness; Monitoring; Time Management; Coordination; Writing; Persuasion.

GOE—Interest Area: 05. Education and Training. **Work Group:** 05.02. Preschool, Elementary, and Secondary Teaching and Instructing. **Other Jobs in This Work Group:** Elementary School Teachers, Except Special Education; Middle School Teachers, Except Special and Vocational Education; Preschool Teachers, Except Special Education; Secondary School Teachers, Except Special and Vocational Education; Special Education Teachers, Middle School; Special Education Teachers, Preschool, Kindergarten, and Elementary School; Special Education Teachers, Secondary School; Teacher Assistants; Vocational Education Teachers, Middle School; Vocational Education Teachers, Secondary School. **PERSONALITY TYPE:** Social. Social occupations frequently involve working with, communicating with, and teaching people. These occupations often involve helping or providing service to others.

EDUCATION/TRAINING PROGRAM(S)—Montessori Teacher Education; Waldorf/Steiner Teacher Education; Kindergarten/Preschool Education and Teaching; Early Childhood Education and Teaching. **RELATED KNOWLEDGE/COURSES—History and Archeology:** Historical events and their causes, indicators, and effects on civilizations and cultures. **Education and Training:** Principles and methods for curriculum and training design, teaching and instruction for individuals and groups, and the measurement of training effects. **Geography:** Principles and methods for describing the features of land, sea, and air masses, including their physical characteristics; locations; interrelationships; and distribution of plant, animal, and human life. **Sociology and Anthropology:** Group behavior and dynamics, societal trends and influences, human migrations, ethnicity, and cultures and their history and origins. **Philosophy and Theology:** Different philosophical systems and religions. This includes their basic principles, values, ethics, ways of thinking, customs, and practices and their impact on human culture. **Psychology:** Human behavior and performance; individual differences in ability, personality, and interests; learning and motivation; psychological research methods; and the assessment and treatment of behavioral and affective disorders.

WORK ENVIRONMENT—Indoors; disease or infections; standing.

Laborers and Freight, Stock, and Material Movers, Hand

- ◉ Education/Training Required: Short-term on-the-job training
- ◉ Annual Earnings: $20,610
- ◉ Growth: 10.2%
- ◉ Annual Job Openings: 671,000
- ◉ Self-Employed: 0.6%
- ◉ Part-Time: 25.1%

Manually move freight, stock, or other materials or perform other unskilled general labor. Includes all unskilled manual laborers not elsewhere classified. Attach identifying tags to containers or mark them with identifying information. Read work orders or receive oral instructions to determine work assignments and material and equipment needs. Record numbers of units handled and moved, using daily production sheets or work tickets. Move freight, stock, and other materials to and from storage and production areas, loading docks, delivery vehicles, ships, and containers by hand or using trucks, tractors, and other equipment. Sort cargo before loading and unloading. Assemble product containers and crates, using hand tools and precut lumber. Load and unload ship cargo, using winches and other hoisting devices. Connect hoses and operate equipment to move liquid materials into and out of storage tanks on vessels. Pack containers and re-pack damaged containers. Carry needed tools and supplies from storage or trucks and return them after use. Install protective devices, such as bracing, padding, or strapping, to prevent shifting or damage to items being transported. Maintain equipment storage areas to ensure that inventory is protected. Attach slings, hooks, and other devices to lift cargo and guide loads. Carry out general yard duties such as performing shunting on railway lines. Adjust controls to guide, position, and move equipment such as cranes, booms, and cameras. Guide loads being lifted in order to prevent swinging. Adjust or replace equipment parts, such as rollers, belts, plugs, and caps, using hand tools. Stack cargo in locations such as transit sheds or in holds of ships as directed, using pallets or cargo boards. Connect electrical equipment to power sources so that it can be tested before use. Set up the equipment needed to produce special lighting and sound effects during performances. Bundle and band material such as fodder and tobacco leaves, using banding machines. Rig and dismantle props and equipment such as frames, scaffolding, platforms, or backdrops, using hand tools. Check out, rent, or requisition all equipment needed for productions or for set construction. Direct spouts and position receptacles such as bins, carts, and containers so they can be loaded.

LEVEL OF ACTIVITY (out of 100)—General Physical Activity: 72.0. **Sitting:** 27.7. **Outdoors:** 41.8.

SKILLS—None met the criteria.

GOE—Interest Area: 16. Transportation, Distribution, and Logistics. **Work Group:** 16.07. Transportation Support Work. **Other Jobs in This Work Group:** Bridge and Lock Tenders; Cargo and Freight Agents; Cleaners of Vehicles and Equipment; Railroad Brake, Signal, and

Switch Operators; Traffic Technicians. **PER-SONALITY TYPE:** Realistic. Realistic occupations frequently involve work activities that include practical, hands-on problems and solutions. They often deal with plants; animals; and real-world materials like wood, tools, and machinery. Many of the occupations require working outside and do not involve a lot of paperwork or working closely with others.

EDUCATION/TRAINING PROGRAM(S)— No related CIP programs; this job is learned through informal short-term on-the-job training. **RELATED KNOWLEDGE/COURSES— Transportation:** Principles and methods for moving people or goods by air, rail, sea, or road, including the relative costs and benefits. **Public Safety and Security:** Relevant equipment, policies, procedures, and strategies to promote effective local, state, or national security operations for the protection of people, data, property, and institutions. **Production and Processing:** Raw materials, production processes, quality control, costs, and other techniques for maximizing the effective manufacture and distribution of goods.

WORK ENVIRONMENT—Outdoors; noisy; very hot or cold; contaminants; standing; using hands on objects, tools, or controls.

Landscaping and Groundskeeping Workers

- Education/Training Required: Short-term on-the-job training
- Annual Earnings: $20,670
- Growth: 19.5%
- Annual Job Openings: 243,000
- Self-Employed: 20.5%
- Part-Time: 24.4%

Landscape or maintain grounds of property, using hand or power tools or equipment. Workers typically perform a variety of tasks, which may include any combination of the following: sod laying, mowing, trimming, planting, watering, fertilizing, digging, raking, sprinkler installation, and installation of mortarless segmental concrete masonry wall units. Operate powered equipment such as mowers, tractors, twin-axle vehicles, snowblowers, chainsaws, electric clippers, sod cutters, and pruning saws. Mow and edge lawns, using power mowers and edgers. Shovel snow from walks, driveways, and parking lots and spread salt in those areas. Care for established lawns by mulching; aerating; weeding; grubbing and removing thatch; and trimming and edging around flowerbeds, walks, and walls. Use hand tools such as shovels, rakes, pruning saws, saws, hedge and brush trimmers, and axes. Prune and trim trees, shrubs, and hedges, using shears, pruners, or chain saws. Maintain and repair tools; equipment; and structures such as buildings, greenhouses, fences, and benches, using hand and power tools. Gather and remove litter. Mix and spray or spread fertilizers, herbicides, or insecticides onto grass, shrubs, and trees, using hand or automatic sprayers or spreaders. Provide proper upkeep of sidewalks, driveways, parking lots, fountains, planters, burial sites, and other grounds features. Water lawns, trees, and plants, using portable sprinkler systems, hoses, or watering cans. Trim and pick flowers and clean flowerbeds. Rake, mulch, and compost leaves. Plant seeds, bulbs, foliage, flowering plants, grass, ground covers, trees, and shrubs, and apply mulch for protection, using gardening tools. Follow planned landscaping designs to determine where to lay sod, sow grass, or plant flowers and foliage. Decorate gardens with stones and plants. Maintain irrigation systems, including winterizing the systems and starting them up in spring. Care for natural turf fields, making sure the underlying soil has the required composition to allow proper drainage and to support the grasses used on the fields. Use irrigation methods to adjust the amount of water consumption and to prevent waste. Haul or spread topsoil and spread straw over seeded soil to hold soil in place. Advise customers on plant selection and care. Care for artificial turf fields, removing the turf and replacing cushioning pads periodically and vacuuming and disinfecting the turf after use to prevent the growth of harmful bacteria.

LEVEL OF ACTIVITY (out of 100)—General Physical Activity: 64.4. **Sitting:** 32.0. **Outdoors:** 52.9.

SKILLS—Equipment Maintenance; Repairing; Operation Monitoring; Installation; Troubleshooting; Active Listening; Equipment Selection.

GOE—Interest Area: 01. Agriculture and Natural Resources. **Work Group:** 01.05. Nursery, Groundskeeping, and Pest Control. **Other Jobs in This Work Group:** Nursery Workers; Pest Control Workers; Pesticide Handlers, Sprayers, and Applicators, Vegetation; Tree Trimmers and Pruners. **PERSONALITY TYPE:** Realistic. Realistic occupations frequently involve work activities that include practical, hands-on problems and solutions. They often deal with plants; animals; and real-world materials like wood, tools, and machinery. Many of the occupations require working outside and do not involve a lot of paperwork or working closely with others.

EDUCATION/TRAINING PROGRAM(S)—Landscaping and Groundskeeping; Turf and Turfgrass Management. **RELATED KNOWLEDGE/COURSES—Mechanical Devices:** Machines and tools, including their designs, uses, repair, and maintenance. **Building and Construction:** The materials, methods, and tools involved in the construction or repair of houses, buildings, or other structures such as highways and roads.

WORK ENVIRONMENT—Outdoors; noisy; very hot or cold; contaminants; standing; using hands on objects, tools, or controls.

Licensed Practical and Licensed Vocational Nurses

◉ Education/Training Required: Postsecondary vocational training

◉ Annual Earnings: $35,230

◉ Growth: 17.1%

◉ Annual Job Openings: 84,000

◉ Self-Employed: 0.6%

◉ Part-Time: 21.9%

Care for ill, injured, convalescent, or disabled persons in hospitals, nursing homes, clinics, private homes, group homes, and similar institutions. May work under the supervision of a registered nurse. Licensing required. Observe patients, charting and reporting changes in patients' conditions (such as adverse reactions to medication or treatment) and taking any necessary action. Administer prescribed medications or start intravenous fluids and note times and amounts on patients' charts. Answer patients' calls and determine how to assist them. Measure and record patients' vital signs, such as height, weight, temperature, blood pressure, pulse, and respiration. Provide basic patient care and treatments, such as taking temperatures or blood pressures, dressing wounds, treating bedsores, giving enemas or douches, rubbing with alcohol, massaging, or performing catheterizations. Help patients with bathing, dressing, maintaining personal hygiene, moving in bed, or standing and walking. Supervise nurses' aides and assistants. Work as part of a health care team to assess patient needs, plan and modify care, and implement interventions. Record food and fluid intake and output. Evaluate nursing intervention outcomes, conferring with other health care team members as necessary. Assemble and use equipment such as catheters, tracheotomy tubes, and oxygen suppliers. Collect samples such as blood, urine, and sputum from patients and perform routine laboratory tests on samples. Prepare patients for examinations, tests, or treatments and explain procedures. Prepare food trays and examine them for conformance to prescribed diet. Apply compresses, ice bags, and hot water bottles. Clean rooms and make beds. Inventory and requisition supplies and instruments. Provide medical treatment and personal care to patients in private home settings, such as cooking, keeping rooms orderly, seeing that patients are comfortable and in good spirits, and instructing family members in simple nursing tasks. Sterilize equipment and supplies, using germicides, sterilizer, or autoclave. Assist in delivery, care, and feeding of infants. Wash and dress bodies of deceased persons. Make appointments, keep records, and perform other clerical duties in doctors' offices and clinics. Set up equipment and prepare medical treatment rooms.

LEVEL OF ACTIVITY (out of 100)—General Physical Activity: 51.1. **Sitting:** 39.1. **Outdoors:** 18.8.

SKILLS—Science; Service Orientation; Operation Monitoring; Judgment and Decision Making; Active Listening; Management of Personnel Resources; Writing; Time Management.

GOE—Interest Area: 08. Health Science. **Work Group:** 08.08. Patient Care and Assistance. **Other Jobs in This Work Group:** Home Health Aides; Nursing Aides, Orderlies, and

Attendants; Psychiatric Aides; Psychiatric Technicians. **PERSONALITY TYPE:** Social. Social occupations frequently involve working with, communicating with, and teaching people. These occupations often involve helping or providing service to others.

EDUCATION/TRAINING PROGRAM(S)— Licensed Practical /Vocational Nurse Training (LPN, LVN, Cert, Dipl, AAS). **RELATED KNOWLEDGE/COURSES—Psychology:** Human behavior and performance; individual differences in ability, personality, and interests; learning and motivation; psychological research methods; and the assessment and treatment of behavioral and affective disorders. **Therapy and Counseling:** Principles, methods, and procedures for diagnosis, treatment, and rehabilitation of physical and mental dysfunctions and for career counseling and guidance. **Medicine and Dentistry:** The information and techniques needed to diagnose and treat human injuries, diseases, and deformities. This includes symptoms, treatment alternatives, drug properties and interactions, and preventive health-care measures. **Customer and Personal Service:** Principles and processes for providing customer and personal services. This includes customer needs assessment, meeting quality standards for services, and evaluation of customer satisfaction. **Philosophy and Theology:** Different philosophical systems and religions. This includes their basic principles, values, ethics, ways of thinking, customs, and practices and their impact on human culture. **Sociology and Anthropology:** Group behavior and dynamics, societal trends and influences, human migrations, ethnicity, and cultures and their history and origins.

WORK ENVIRONMENT—Indoors; disease or infections; standing; walking and running.

Locksmiths and Safe Repairers

- Education/Training Required: Moderate-term on-the-job training
- Annual Earnings: $30,880
- Growth: 16.1%
- Annual Job Openings: 5,000
- Self-Employed: 37.6%
- Part-Time: 18.2%

Repair and open locks, make keys, change locks and safe combinations, and install and repair safes. Cut new or duplicate keys, using keycutting machines. Keep records of company locks and keys. Insert new or repaired tumblers into locks to change combinations. Move picklocks in cylinders to open door locks without keys. Disassemble mechanical or electrical locking devices and repair or replace worn tumblers, springs, and other parts, using hand tools. Repair and adjust safes, vault doors, and vault components, using hand tools, lathes, drill presses, and welding and acetylene cutting apparatus. Install safes, vault doors, and deposit boxes according to blueprints, using equipment such as powered drills, taps, dies, truck cranes, and dollies. Open safe locks by drilling. Remove interior and exterior finishes on safes and vaults and spray on new finishes.

LEVEL OF ACTIVITY (out of 100)—General Physical Activity: 60.3. **Sitting:** 33.9. **Outdoors:** 46.9.

SKILLS—Installation; Repairing; Equipment Maintenance; Troubleshooting; Service

Orientation; Equipment Selection; Management of Material Resources; Technology Design.

GOE—Interest Area: 13. Manufacturing. **Work Group:** 13.13. Machinery Repair. **Other Jobs in This Work Group:** Bicycle Repairers; Control and Valve Installers and Repairers, Except Mechanical Door; Home Appliance Repairers; Industrial Machinery Mechanics; Maintenance Workers, Machinery; Mechanical Door Repairers; Millwrights; Signal and Track Switch Repairers. **PERSONALITY TYPE:** Realistic. Realistic occupations frequently involve work activities that include practical, hands-on problems and solutions. They often deal with plants; animals; and real-world materials like wood, tools, and machinery. Many of the occupations require working outside and do not involve a lot of paperwork or working closely with others.

EDUCATION/TRAINING PROGRAM(S)— Locksmithing and Safe Repair. **RELATED KNOWLEDGE/COURSES—Customer and Personal Service:** Principles and processes for providing customer and personal services. This includes customer needs assessment, meeting quality standards for services, and evaluation of customer satisfaction. **Sales and Marketing:** Principles and methods for showing, promoting, and selling products or services. This includes marketing strategy and tactics, product demonstration, sales techniques, and sales control systems. **Administration and Management:** Business and management principles involved in strategic planning, resource allocation, human resources modeling, leadership technique, production methods, and coordination of people and resources. **Clerical Practices:** Administrative and clerical procedures and systems such as word processing, managing files and records, stenography and transcription, designing forms, and other office procedures and terminology. **Mechanical Devices:** Machines and tools, including their designs, uses, repair, and maintenance. **Public Safety and Security:** Relevant equipment, policies, procedures, and strategies to promote effective local, state, or national security operations for the protection of people, data, property, and institutions.

WORK ENVIRONMENT—More often outdoors than indoors; noisy; very bright or dim lighting; standing; using hands on objects, tools, or controls.

Machinists

- Education/Training Required: Long-term on-the-job training
- Annual Earnings: $34,350
- Growth: 4.3%
- Annual Job Openings: 33,000
- Self-Employed: 1.0%
- Part-Time: 1.8%

Set up and operate a variety of machine tools to produce precision parts and instruments. Includes precision instrument makers who fabricate, modify, or repair mechanical instruments. May also fabricate and modify parts to make or repair machine tools or maintain industrial machines, applying knowledge of mechanics, shop mathematics, metal properties, layout, and machining procedures. Calculate dimensions and tolerances, using knowledge of mathematics and instruments such as micrometers and vernier calipers. Machine parts to specifications, using machine tools such as lathes, milling machines, shapers,

or grinders. Measure, examine, and test completed units to detect defects and ensure conformance to specifications, using precision instruments such as micrometers. Set up, adjust, and operate all of the basic machine tools and many specialized or advanced variation tools to perform precision machining operations. Align and secure holding fixtures, cutting tools, attachments, accessories, and materials onto machines. Monitor the feed and speed of machines during the machining process. Study sample parts, blueprints, drawings, and engineering information to determine methods and sequences of operations needed to fabricate products and determine product dimensions and tolerances. Select the appropriate tools, machines, and materials to be used in preparation of machinery work. Lay out, measure, and mark metal stock to display placement of cuts. Observe and listen to operating machines or equipment to diagnose machine malfunctions and to determine need for adjustments or repairs. Check workpieces to ensure that they are properly lubricated and cooled. Maintain industrial machines, applying knowledge of mechanics, shop mathematics, metal properties, layout, and machining procedures. Position and fasten workpieces. Operate equipment to verify operational efficiency. Install repaired parts into equipment or install new equipment. Clean and lubricate machines, tools, and equipment to remove grease, rust, stains, and foreign matter. Advise clients about the materials being used for finished products. Program computers and electronic instruments such as numerically controlled machine tools. Set controls to regulate machining or enter commands to retrieve, input, or edit computerized machine control media. Confer with engineering, supervisory, and manufacturing personnel to exchange technical information. Dismantle machines or equipment, using hand tools and power tools, to examine parts for defects and replace defective parts where needed.

LEVEL OF ACTIVITY (out of 100)—General Physical Activity: 58.3. **Sitting:** 24.7. **Outdoors:** 21.1.

SKILLS—Operation Monitoring; Operation and Control; Equipment Maintenance; Quality Control Analysis; Installation; Equipment Selection; Repairing; Troubleshooting.

GOE—Interest Area: 13. Manufacturing. **Work Group:** 13.05. Production Machining Technology. **Other Jobs in This Work Group:** Computer-Controlled Machine Tool Operators, Metal and Plastic; Foundry Mold and Coremakers; Lay-Out Workers, Metal and Plastic; Model Makers, Metal and Plastic; Numerical Tool and Process Control Programmers; Patternmakers, Metal and Plastic; Tool and Die Makers; Tool Grinders, Filers, and Sharpeners. **PERSONALITY TYPE:** Realistic. Realistic occupations frequently involve work activities that include practical, hands-on problems and solutions. They often deal with plants; animals; and real-world materials like wood, tools, and machinery. Many of the occupations require working outside and do not involve a lot of paperwork or working closely with others.

EDUCATION/TRAINING PROGRAM(S)—Machine Tool Technology/Machinist; Machine Shop Technology/Assistant. **RELATED KNOWLEDGE/COURSES—Mechanical Devices:** Machines and tools, including their designs, uses, repair, and maintenance. **Mathematics:** Arithmetic, algebra, geometry, calculus, and statistics and their applications. **Engineering and Technology:** The practical application of engineering science and technology. This includes applying principles, techniques, procedures, and equipment to the design and production of various goods and services.

Design: Design techniques, tools, and principles involved in production of precision technical plans, blueprints, drawings, and models. **Production and Processing:** Raw materials, production processes, quality control, costs, and other techniques for maximizing the effective manufacture and distribution of goods. **Computers and Electronics:** Circuit boards; processors; chips; electronic equipment; and computer hardware and software, including applications and programming.

WORK ENVIRONMENT—Indoors; noisy; hazardous equipment; standing; using hands on objects, tools, or controls; repetitive motions.

Maintenance and Repair Workers, General

- ◎ Education/Training Required: Moderate-term on-the-job training
- ◎ Annual Earnings: $31,210
- ◎ Growth: 15.2%
- ◎ Annual Job Openings: 154,000
- ◎ Self-Employed: 0.6%
- ◎ Part-Time: 6.0%

Perform work involving the skills of two or more maintenance or craft occupations to keep machines, mechanical equipment, or the structure of an establishment in repair. Duties may involve pipefitting; boilermaking; insulating; welding; machining; carpentry; repairing electrical or mechanical equipment; installing, aligning, and balancing new equipment; and repairing buildings, floors, or stairs. Repair or replace defective equipment parts, using hand tools and power tools, and reassemble equipment. Perform routine preventive maintenance to ensure that machines continue to run smoothly, building systems operate efficiently, and the physical condition of buildings does not deteriorate. Inspect drives, motors, and belts; check fluid levels; replace filters; and perform other maintenance actions, following checklists. Use tools ranging from common hand and power tools, such as hammers, hoists, saws, drills, and wrenches, to precision measuring instruments and electrical and electronic testing devices. Assemble, install, and/or repair wiring, electrical and electronic components, pipe systems and plumbing, machinery, and equipment. Diagnose mechanical problems and determine how to correct them, checking blueprints, repair manuals, and parts catalogs as necessary. Inspect, operate, and test machinery and equipment in order to diagnose machine malfunctions. Record maintenance and repair work performed and the costs of the work. Clean and lubricate shafts, bearings, gears, and other parts of machinery. Dismantle devices to gain access to and remove defective parts, using hoists, cranes, hand tools, and power tools. Plan and lay out repair work, using diagrams, drawings, blueprints, maintenance manuals, and schematic diagrams. Adjust functional parts of devices and control instruments, using hand tools, levels, plumb bobs, and straightedges. Order parts, supplies, and equipment from catalogs and suppliers or obtain them from storerooms. Paint and repair roofs, windows, doors, floors, woodwork, plaster, drywall, and other parts of building structures. Operate cutting torches or welding equipment to cut or join metal parts. Align and balance new equipment after installation. Inspect used parts to determine changes in dimensional requirements, using rules, calipers, micrometers, and other measuring instruments. Set up and operate machine tools to repair or fabricate machine parts, jigs and fixtures, and tools. Maintain and repair specialized equipment and machinery found in cafeterias, laundries, hospitals, stores, offices, and factories.

LEVEL OF ACTIVITY (out of 100)—General Physical Activity: 69.7. **Sitting:** 24.7. **Outdoors:** 40.5.

SKILLS—Equipment Maintenance; Installation; Repairing; Troubleshooting; Operation Monitoring; Operation and Control; Equipment Selection; Technology Design.

GOE—Interest Area: 02. Architecture and Construction. **Work Group:** 02.05. Systems and Equipment Installation, Maintenance, and Repair. **Other Jobs in This Work Group:** Electrical and Electronics Repairers, Powerhouse, Substation, and Relay; Electrical Power-Line Installers and Repairers; Elevator Installers and Repairers; Heating and Air Conditioning Mechanics and Installers; Refrigeration Mechanics and Installers; Telecommunications Equipment Installers and Repairers, Except Line Installers; Telecommunications Line Installers and Repairers. **PERSONALITY TYPE:** Realistic. Realistic occupations frequently involve work activities that include practical, hands-on

problems and solutions. They often deal with plants; animals; and real-world materials like wood, tools, and machinery. Many of the occupations require working outside and do not involve a lot of paperwork or working closely with others.

EDUCATION/TRAINING PROGRAM(S)—Building/Construction Site Management/ Manager. **RELATED KNOWLEDGE/ COURSES—Building and Construction:** The materials, methods, and tools involved in the construction or repair of houses, buildings, or other structures such as highways and roads. **Mechanical Devices:** Machines and tools, including their designs, uses, repair, and maintenance. **Design:** Design techniques, tools, and principles involved in production of precision technical plans, blueprints, drawings, and models. **Physics:** Physical principles and laws and their interrelationships and applications to understanding fluid, material, and atmospheric dynamics and mechanical, electrical, atomic, and subatomic structures and processes. **Engineering and Technology:** The practical application of engineering science and technology. This includes applying principles, techniques, procedures, and equipment to the design and production of various goods and services. **Public Safety and Security:** Relevant equipment, policies, procedures, and strategies to promote effective local, state, or national security operations for the protection of people, data, property, and institutions.

WORK ENVIRONMENT—Indoors; noisy; minor burns, cuts, bites, or stings; standing; walking and running; using hands on objects, tools, or controls.

M

Mechanical Engineering Technicians

- ⊚ Education/Training Required: Associate degree
- ⊚ Annual Earnings: $44,830
- ⊚ Growth: 12.3%
- ⊚ Annual Job Openings: 5,000
- ⊚ Self-Employed: 0.4%
- ⊚ Part-Time: 6.7%

Apply theory and principles of mechanical engineering to modify, develop, and test machinery and equipment under direction of engineering staff or physical scientists. Prepare parts sketches and write work orders and purchase requests to be furnished by outside contractors. Draft detail drawing or sketch for drafting room completion or to request parts fabrication by machine, sheet, or wood shops. Review project instructions and blueprints to ascertain test specifications, procedures, and objectives and testing requirements created by technical problems such as redesign. Review project instructions and specifications to identify, modify, and plan requirements for fabrication, assembly, and testing. Devise, fabricate, and assemble new or modified mechanical components for products such as industrial machinery or equipment and measuring instruments. Discuss changes in design, method of manufacture and assembly, and drafting techniques and procedures with staff and coordinate corrections. Set up and conduct tests of complete units and components under operational conditions to investigate proposals for improving equipment performance. Inspect lines and figures for clarity and return erroneous drawings to designer for correction. Analyze test results in relation to design or rated specifications and test objectives and modify or adjust equipment to meet specifications. Evaluate tool drawing designs by measuring drawing dimensions and comparing with original specifications for form and function, using engineering skills. Confer with technicians and submit reports of test results to engineering department and recommend design or material changes. Calculate required capacities for equipment of proposed system to obtain specified performance and submit data to engineering personnel for approval. Record test procedures and results, numerical and graphical data, and recommendations for changes in product or test methods. Read dials and meters to determine amperage, voltage, and electrical output and input at specific operating temperature to analyze parts performance. Estimate cost factors, including labor and material for purchased and fabricated parts and costs for assembly, testing, or installing. Set up prototype and test apparatus and operate test-controlling equipment to observe and record prototype test results.

LEVEL OF ACTIVITY (out of 100)—General Physical Activity: 52.4. **Sitting:** 44.3. **Outdoors:** 28.5.

SKILLS—Installation; Troubleshooting; Technology Design; Operations Analysis; Coordination; Equipment Selection; Operation Monitoring; Systems Evaluation.

GOE—**Interest Area:** 15. Scientific Research, Engineering, and Mathematics. **Work Group:** 15.09. Engineering Technology. **Other Jobs in This Work Group:** Aerospace Engineering and Operations Technicians; Cartographers and Photogrammetrists; Civil Engineering Technicians; Electrical and Electronic Engineering Technicians; Electrical and Electronics Drafters;

Electrical Drafters; Electrical Engineering Technicians; Electro-Mechanical Technicians; Electronic Drafters; Electronics Engineering Technicians; Environmental Engineering Technicians; Mapping Technicians; Mechanical Drafters; Surveying and Mapping Technicians; Surveying Technicians. **PERSONALITY TYPE:** Realistic. Realistic occupations frequently involve work activities that include practical, hands-on problems and solutions. They often deal with plants; animals; and real-world materials like wood, tools, and machinery. Many of the occupations require working outside and do not involve a lot of paperwork or working closely with others.

EDUCATION/TRAINING PROGRAM(S)— Mechanical Engineering/Mechanical Technology/Technician; Mechanical Engineering Related Technologies/Technicians, Other. **RELATED KNOWLEDGE/COURSES— Engineering and Technology:** The practical application of engineering science and technology. This includes applying principles, techniques, procedures, and equipment to the design and production of various goods and services. **Design:** Design techniques, tools, and principles involved in production of precision technical plans, blueprints, drawings, and models. **Mechanical Devices:** Machines and tools, including their designs, uses, repair, and maintenance. **Physics:** Physical principles and laws and their interrelationships and applications to understanding fluid, material, and atmospheric dynamics and mechanical, electrical, atomic, and subatomic structures and processes. **Production and Processing:** Raw materials, production processes, quality control, costs, and other techniques for maximizing the effective manufacture and distribution of goods. **Chemistry:** The chemical composition, struc-ture, and properties of substances and of the chemical processes and transformations that they undergo. This includes uses of chemicals and their danger signs, production techniques, and disposal methods.

WORK ENVIRONMENT—Indoors; noisy; contaminants; hazardous equipment; sitting.

Medical Assistants

- Education/Training Required: Moderate-term on-the-job training
- Annual Earnings: $25,350
- Growth: 52.1%
- Annual Job Openings: 93,000
- Self-Employed: 0.0%
- Part-Time: 27.5%

Perform administrative and certain clinical duties under the direction of physician. Administrative duties may include scheduling appointments, maintaining medical records, billing, and coding for insurance purposes. Clinical duties may include taking and recording vital signs and medical histories, preparing patients for examination, drawing blood, and administering medications as directed by physician. Interview patients to obtain medical information and measure their vital signs, weight, and height. Show patients to examination rooms and prepare them for the physician. Record patients' medical history, vital statistics, and information such as test results in medical records. Prepare and administer medications as directed by a physician. Collect blood, tissue, or other laboratory specimens; log the specimens; and prepare them for testing. Explain treatment procedures, medications, diets, and physicians' instructions to patients. Help physicians examine and treat patients, handing them instruments and materials or performing such tasks as giving injections or removing sutures. Authorize drug refills and provide prescription information to pharmacies. Prepare treatment rooms for patient examinations, keeping the rooms neat and clean. Clean and sterilize instruments and dispose of contaminated supplies. Schedule appointments for patients. Change dressings on wounds. Greet and log in patients arriving at office or clinic. Contact medical facilities or departments to schedule patients for tests or admission. Perform general office duties such as answering telephones, taking dictation, or completing insurance forms. Inventory and order medical, lab, or office supplies and equipment. Perform routine laboratory tests and sample analyses. Set up medical laboratory equipment. Keep financial records and perform other bookkeeping duties, such as handling credit and collections and mailing monthly statements to patients. Operate X-ray, electrocardiogram (EKG), and other equipment to administer routine diagnostic tests. Give physiotherapy treatments such as diathermy, galvanics, and hydrotherapy.

LEVEL OF ACTIVITY (out of 100)—General Physical Activity: 40.1. **Sitting:** 33.6. **Outdoors:** 14.7.

SKILLS—Social Perceptiveness; Service Orientation; Instructing; Active Listening; Operation Monitoring; Operation and Control; Learning Strategies; Troubleshooting.

GOE—Interest Area: 08. Health Science. **Work Group:** 08.02. Medicine and Surgery. **Other Jobs in This Work Group:** Anesthesiologists; Family and General Practitioners; Internists, General; Medical Transcriptionists; Obstetricians and Gynecologists; Pediatricians, General; Pharmacists; Pharmacy Aides; Pharmacy Technicians; Physician Assistants; Psychiatrists; Registered Nurses; Surgeons; Surgical Technologists. **PERSONALITY TYPE:** Social. Social occupations frequently involve working with, communicating with, and teaching people. These occupations often involve helping or providing service to others.

EDUCATION/TRAINING PROGRAM(S)—Medical Office Management/Administration; Medical Office Assistant/Specialist; Medical Reception/Receptionist; Medical Insurance Coding Specialist/Coder; Medical Administrative/Executive Assistant and Medical Secretary; Medical/Clinical Assistant; Anesthesiologist Assistant; Chiropractic Assistant/Technician; Allied Health and Medical Assisting Services, Other; Optomeric Technician/Assistant; others. **RELATED KNOWLEDGE/COURSES**—**Medicine and Dentistry:** The information and techniques needed to diagnose and treat human injuries, diseases, and deformities. This includes symptoms, treatment alternatives, drug properties and interactions, and preventive health-care measures. **Therapy and Counseling:** Principles, methods, and procedures for diagnosis, treatment, and rehabilitation of physical and mental dysfunctions and for career counseling and guidance. **Customer and Personal Service:** Principles and processes for providing customer and personal services. This includes customer needs assessment, meeting quality standards for services, and evaluation of customer satisfaction. **Clerical Practices:** Administrative and clerical procedures and systems such as word processing, managing files and records, stenography and transcription, designing forms, and other office procedures and terminology. **Psychology:**

Human behavior and performance; individual differences in ability, personality, and interests; learning and motivation; psychological research methods; and the assessment and treatment of behavioral and affective disorders. **English Language:** The structure and content of the English language, including the meaning and spelling of words, rules of composition, and grammar.

WORK ENVIRONMENT—Indoors; disease or infections; standing; walking and running; using hands on objects, tools, or controls.

Medical Equipment Preparers

- Education/Training Required: Short-term on-the-job training
- Annual Earnings: $24,880
- Growth: 20.0%
- Annual Job Openings: 8,000
- Self-Employed: 2.7%
- Part-Time: 27.5%

Prepare, sterilize, install, or clean laboratory or healthcare equipment. May perform routine laboratory tasks and operate or inspect equipment. Organize and assemble routine and specialty surgical instrument trays and other sterilized supplies, filling special requests as needed. Clean instruments to prepare them for sterilization. Operate and maintain steam autoclaves, keeping records of loads completed, items in loads, and maintenance procedures per-

formed. Record sterilizer test results. Disinfect and sterilize equipment such as respirators, hospital beds, and oxygen and dialysis equipment, using sterilizers, aerators, and washers. Start equipment and observe gauges and equipment operation to detect malfunctions and to ensure equipment is operating to prescribed standards. Examine equipment to detect leaks, worn or loose parts, or other indications of disrepair. Report defective equipment to appropriate supervisors or staff. Check sterile supplies to ensure that they are not outdated. Maintain records of inventory and equipment usage. Attend hospital in-service programs related to areas of work specialization. Purge wastes from equipment by connecting equipment to water sources and flushing water through systems. Deliver equipment to specified hospital locations or to patients' residences. Assist hospital staff with patient care duties such as providing transportation or setting up traction. Install and set up medical equipment, using hand tools.

LEVEL OF ACTIVITY (out of 100)—General Physical Activity: 50.6. **Sitting:** 25.3. **Outdoors:** 15.0.

SKILLS—Operation Monitoring; Management of Material Resources; Equipment Maintenance; Quality Control Analysis; Service Orientation; Management of Personnel Resources; Learning Strategies; Monitoring.

GOE—Interest Area: 08. Health Science. **Work Group:** 08.06. Medical Technology. **Other Jobs in This Work Group:** Biological Technicians; Cardiovascular Technologists and Technicians; Diagnostic Medical Sonographers; Medical and Clinical Laboratory Technicians; Medical and Clinical Laboratory Technologists; Medical Records and Health Information Technicians; Nuclear Medicine Technologists; Opticians, Dispensing; Orthotists and Prosthetists;

Radiologic Technicians; Radiologic Technologists; Radiologic Technologists and Technicians. **PERSONALITY TYPE:** Realistic. Realistic occupations frequently involve work activities that include practical, hands-on problems and solutions. They often deal with plants; animals; and real-world materials like wood, tools, and machinery. Many of the occupations require working outside and do not involve a lot of paperwork or working closely with others.

EDUCATION/TRAINING PROGRAM(S)— Medical/Clinical Assistant; Allied Health and Medical Assisting Services, Other. **RELATED KNOWLEDGE/COURSES—Chemistry:** The chemical composition, structure, and properties of substances and of the chemical processes and transformations that they undergo. This includes uses of chemicals and their danger signs, production techniques, and disposal methods. **Biology:** Plant and animal organisms and their tissues, cells, functions, interdependencies, and interactions with each other and the environment. **Medicine and Dentistry:** The information and techniques needed to diagnose and treat human injuries, diseases, and deformities. This includes symptoms, treatment alternatives, drug properties and interactions, and preventive health-care measures. **Production and Processing:** Raw materials, production processes, quality control, costs, and other techniques for maximizing the effective manufacture and distribution of goods. **Education and Training:** Principles and methods for curriculum and training design, teaching and instruction for individuals and groups, and the measurement of training effects. **Customer and Personal Service:** Principles and processes for providing customer and personal services. This includes customer needs assessment, meeting quality standards for services, and evaluation of customer satisfaction.

WORK ENVIRONMENT—Indoors; contaminants; disease or infections; standing; using hands on objects, tools, or controls; repetitive motions.

Medical Equipment Repairers

- Education/Training Required: Associate degree
- Annual Earnings: $39,570
- Growth: 14.8%
- Annual Job Openings: 4,000
- Self-Employed: 16.2%
- Part-Time: 12.1%

Test, adjust, or repair biomedical or electromedical equipment. Inspect and test malfunctioning medical and related equipment following manufacturers' specifications, using test and analysis instruments. Examine medical equipment and facility's structural environment and check for proper use of equipment to protect patients and staff from electrical or mechanical hazards and to ensure compliance with safety regulations. Disassemble malfunctioning equipment and remove, repair, and replace defective parts such as motors, clutches, or transformers. Keep records of maintenance, repair, and required updates of equipment. Perform preventive maintenance or service such as cleaning, lubricating, and adjusting equipment. Test and calibrate components and equipment, following manufacturers' manuals and troubleshooting techniques and using hand tools, power tools, and measuring devices. Explain and demonstrate correct operation and preventive maintenance of medical equipment to personnel. Study technical manuals and attend training sessions provided by equipment manufacturers to maintain current knowledge. Plan and carry out work assignments, using blueprints, schematic drawings, technical manuals, wiring diagrams, and liquid and air flow sheets, following prescribed regulations, directives, and other instructions as required. Solder loose connections, using soldering iron. Test, evaluate, and classify excess or in-use medical equipment and determine serviceability, condition, and disposition in accordance with regulations. Research catalogs and repair part lists to locate sources for repair parts, requisitioning parts and recording their receipt. Evaluate technical specifications to identify equipment and systems best suited for intended use and possible purchase based on specifications, user needs, and technical requirements. Contribute expertise to develop medical maintenance standard operating procedures. Compute power and space requirements for installing medical, dental, or related equipment and install units to manufacturers' specifications. Supervise and advise subordinate personnel. Repair shop equipment; metal furniture; and hospital equipment, including welding broken parts and replacing missing parts, or bring item into local shop for major repairs.

LEVEL OF ACTIVITY (out of 100)—General Physical Activity: 51.0. **Sitting:** 33.7. **Outdoors:** 25.9.

SKILLS—Repairing; Installation; Equipment Maintenance; Troubleshooting; Systems Analysis; Operation Monitoring; Quality Control Analysis; Science.

GOE—Interest Area: 13. Manufacturing. **Work Group:** 13.15. Medical and Technical Equipment Repair. **Other Jobs in This Work Group:**

Camera and Photographic Equipment Repairers; Watch Repairers. **PERSONALITY TYPE:** Realistic. Realistic occupations frequently involve work activities that include practical, hands-on problems and solutions. They often deal with plants; animals; and real-world materials like wood, tools, and machinery. Many of the occupations require working outside and do not involve a lot of paperwork or working closely with others.

EDUCATION/TRAINING PROGRAM(S)—Biomedical Technology/Technician. **RELATED KNOWLEDGE/COURSES—Mechanical Devices:** Machines and tools, including their designs, uses, repair, and maintenance. **Computers and Electronics:** Circuit boards; processors; chips; electronic equipment; and computer hardware and software, including applications and programming. **Engineering and Technology:** The practical application of engineering science and technology. This includes applying principles, techniques, procedures, and equipment to the design and production of various goods and services. **Physics:** Physical principles and laws and their interrelationships and applications to understanding fluid, material, and atmospheric dynamics and mechanical, electrical, atomic, and subatomic structures and processes. **Customer and Personal Service:** Principles and processes for providing customer and personal services. This includes customer needs assessment, meeting quality standards for services, and evaluation of customer satisfaction. **Telecommunications:** Transmission, broadcasting, switching, control, and operation of telecommunications systems.

WORK ENVIRONMENT—Indoors; contaminants; disease or infections; standing; using hands on objects, tools, or controls.

Middle School Teachers, Except Special and Vocational Education

- Education/Training Required: Bachelor's degree
- Annual Earnings: $44,640
- Growth: 13.7%
- Annual Job Openings: 83,000
- Self-Employed: 0.0%
- Part-Time: 12.6%

Teach students in public or private schools in one or more subjects at the middle, intermediate, or junior high level, which falls between elementary and senior high school, as defined by applicable state laws and regulations. Establish and enforce rules for behavior and procedures for maintaining order among the students for whom they are responsible. Adapt teaching methods and instructional materials to meet students' varying needs and interests. Instruct through lectures, discussions, and demonstrations in one or more subjects, such as English, mathematics, or social studies. Prepare, administer, and grade tests and assignments in order to evaluate students' progress. Establish clear objectives for all lessons, units, and projects and communicate these objectives to students. Plan and conduct activities for a balanced program of instruction, demonstration, and work time that provides students with opportunities to observe, question, and investigate. Maintain accurate, complete, and correct student records as required by laws, district policies, and admin-

istrative regulations. Observe and evaluate students' performance, behavior, social development, and physical health. Assign lessons and correct homework. Prepare materials and classrooms for class activities. Enforce all administration policies and rules governing students. Confer with parents or guardians, other teachers, counselors, and administrators in order to resolve students' behavioral and academic problems. Prepare students for later grades by encouraging them to explore learning opportunities and to persevere with challenging tasks. Prepare objectives and outlines for courses of study, following curriculum guidelines or requirements of states and schools. Guide and counsel students with adjustment and/or academic problems or special academic interests. Meet with parents and guardians to discuss their children's progress and to determine their priorities for their children and their resource needs. Meet with other professionals to discuss individual students' needs and progress. Prepare and implement remedial programs for students requiring extra help. Prepare for assigned classes and show written evidence of preparation upon request of immediate supervisors. Instruct and monitor students in the use and care of equipment and materials in order to prevent injury and damage.

LEVEL OF ACTIVITY (out of 100)—General Physical Activity: 36.6. **Sitting:** 30.6. **Outdoors:** 19.0.

SKILLS—Learning Strategies; Instructing; Social Perceptiveness; Monitoring; Time Management; Persuasion; Negotiation; Service Orientation.

GOE—Interest Area: 05. Education and Training. **Work Group:** 05.02. Preschool, Elementary, and Secondary Teaching and Instructing. **Other Jobs in This Work Group:**

Elementary School Teachers, Except Special Education; Kindergarten Teachers, Except Special Education; Preschool Teachers, Except Special Education; Secondary School Teachers, Except Special and Vocational Education; Special Education Teachers, Middle School; Special Education Teachers, Preschool, Kindergarten, and Elementary School; Special Education Teachers, Secondary School; Teacher Assistants; Vocational Education Teachers, Middle School; Vocational Education Teachers, Secondary School. **PERSONALITY TYPE:** Social. Social occupations frequently involve working with, communicating with, and teaching people. These occupations often involve helping or providing service to others.

EDUCATION/TRAINING PROGRAM(S)— Junior High/Intermediate/Middle School Education and Teaching; Montessori Teacher Education; Waldorf/Steiner Teacher Education; Art Teacher Education; English/Language Arts Teacher Education; Foreign Language Teacher Education; Health Teacher Education; Family and Consumer Sciences/Home Economics Teacher Education; Technology Teacher Education/Industrial Arts Teacher Education; Mathematics Teacher Education; others. **RELATED KNOWLEDGE/COURSES— Education and Training:** Principles and methods for curriculum and training design, teaching and instruction for individuals and groups, and the measurement of training effects. **Sociology and Anthropology:** Group behavior and dynamics, societal trends and influences, human migrations, ethnicity, and cultures and their history and origins. **History and Archeology:** Historical events and their causes, indicators, and effects on civilizations and cultures. **Philosophy and Theology:** Different philosophical systems and religions. This includes their basic principles, values, ethics, ways of thinking,

customs, and practices and their impact on human culture. **Geography:** Principles and methods for describing the features of land, sea, and air masses, including their physical characteristics; locations; interrelationships; and distribution of plant, animal, and human life. **Therapy and Counseling:** Principles, methods, and procedures for diagnosis, treatment, and rehabilitation of physical and mental dysfunctions and for career counseling and guidance.

WORK ENVIRONMENT—Indoors; noisy; standing.

Millwrights

- Education/Training Required: Long-term on-the-job training
- Annual Earnings: $44,780
- Growth: 5.9%
- Annual Job Openings: 5,000
- Self-Employed: 1.1%
- Part-Time: 1.1%

Install, dismantle, or move machinery and heavy equipment according to layout plans, blueprints, or other drawings. Replace defective parts of machine or adjust clearances and alignment of moving parts. Align machines and equipment, using hoists, jacks, hand tools, squares, rules, micrometers, and plumb bobs. Connect power unit to machines or steam piping to equipment and test unit to evaluate its mechanical operation. Repair and lubricate machines and equipment. Assemble and install equipment, using hand tools and power tools.

Position steel beams to support bedplates of machines and equipment, using blueprints and schematic drawings to determine work procedures. Signal crane operator to lower basic assembly units to bedplate and align unit to centerline. Insert shims, adjust tension on nuts and bolts, or position parts, using hand tools and measuring instruments to set specified clearances between moving and stationary parts. Move machinery and equipment, using hoists, dollies, rollers, and trucks. Attach moving parts and subassemblies to basic assembly unit, using hand tools and power tools. Assemble machines and bolt, weld, rivet, or otherwise fasten them to foundation or other structures, using hand tools and power tools. Lay out mounting holes, using measuring instruments, and drill holes with power drill. Bolt parts, such as side and deck plates, jaw plates, and journals, to basic assembly unit. Dismantle machines, using hammers, wrenches, crowbars, and other hand tools. Level bedplate and establish centerline, using straightedge, levels, and transit. Shrink-fit bushings, sleeves, rings, liners, gears, and wheels to specified items, using portable gas heating equipment. Dismantle machinery and equipment for shipment to installation site, usually performing installation and maintenance work as part of team. Construct foundation for machines, using hand tools and building materials such as wood, cement, and steel. Install robot and modify its program, using teach pendant. Operate engine lathe to grind, file, and turn machine parts to dimensional specifications.

LEVEL OF ACTIVITY (out of 100)—General Physical Activity: 73.7. **Sitting:** 23.1. **Outdoors:** 40.5.

SKILLS—Installation; Repairing; Troubleshooting; Equipment Maintenance; Mathematics; Equipment Selection; Technology Design; Operation Monitoring.

GOE—Interest Area: 13. Manufacturing. **Work Group:** 13.13. Machinery Repair. **Other Jobs in This Work Group:** Bicycle Repairers; Control and Valve Installers and Repairers, Except Mechanical Door; Home Appliance Repairers; Industrial Machinery Mechanics; Locksmiths and Safe Repairers; Maintenance Workers, Machinery; Mechanical Door Repairers; Signal and Track Switch Repairers. **PERSONALITY TYPE:** Realistic. Realistic occupations frequently involve work activities that include practical, hands-on problems and solutions. They often deal with plants; animals; and real-world materials like wood, tools, and machinery. Many of the occupations require working outside and do not involve a lot of paperwork or working closely with others.

EDUCATION/TRAINING PROGRAM(S)—Industrial Mechanics and Maintenance Technology; Heavy/Industrial Equipment Maintenance Technologies, Other. **RELATED KNOWLEDGE/COURSES—Mechanical Devices:** Machines and tools, including their designs, uses, repair, and maintenance. **Building and Construction:** The materials, methods, and tools involved in the construction or repair of houses, buildings, or other structures such as highways and roads. **Design:** Design techniques, tools, and principles involved in production of precision technical plans, blueprints, drawings, and models. **Engineering and Technology:** The practical application of engineering science and technology. This includes applying principles, techniques, procedures, and equipment to the design and production of various goods and services. **Physics:** Physical principles and laws and their interrelationships and applications to understanding fluid, material, and atmospheric dynamics and mechanical, electrical, atomic, and subatomic structures and processes. **Public Safety and Security:** Relevant equipment, policies, procedures, and strategies to promote effective local, state, or national security operations for the protection of people, data, property, and institutions.

WORK ENVIRONMENT—Noisy; very hot or cold; very bright or dim lighting; contaminants; hazardous equipment; using hands on objects, tools, or controls.

Mobile Heavy Equipment Mechanics, Except Engines

- ◎ Education/Training Required: Postsecondary vocational training
- ◎ Annual Earnings: $39,410
- ◎ Growth: 8.8%
- ◎ Annual Job Openings: 14,000
- ◎ Self-Employed: 2.9%
- ◎ Part-Time: 3.0%

Diagnose, adjust, repair, or overhaul mobile mechanical, hydraulic, and pneumatic equipment, such as cranes, bulldozers, graders, and conveyors, used in construction, logging, and surface mining. Test mechanical products and equipment after repair or assembly to ensure proper performance and compliance with manufacturers' specifications. Repair and replace damaged or worn parts. Diagnose faults or malfunctions to determine required repairs, using engine diagnostic equipment such as computerized test equipment and calibration devices. Operate and inspect machines or heavy equip-

ment to diagnose defects. Dismantle and reassemble heavy equipment, using hoists and hand tools. Clean, lubricate, and perform other routine maintenance work on equipment and vehicles. Examine parts for damage or excessive wear, using micrometers and gauges. Read and understand operating manuals, blueprints, and technical drawings. Schedule maintenance for industrial machines and equipment and keep equipment service records. Overhaul and test machines or equipment to ensure operating efficiency. Assemble gear systems and align frames and gears. Fit bearings to adjust, repair, or overhaul mobile mechanical, hydraulic, and pneumatic equipment. Weld or solder broken parts and structural members, using electric or gas welders and soldering tools. Clean parts by spraying them with grease solvent or immersing them in tanks of solvent. Adjust, maintain, and repair or replace subassemblies, such as transmissions and crawler heads, using hand tools, jacks, and cranes. Adjust and maintain industrial machinery, using control and regulating devices. Fabricate needed parts or items from sheet metal. Direct workers who are assembling or disassembling equipment or cleaning parts.

LEVEL OF ACTIVITY (out of 100)—General Physical Activity: 61.6. Sitting: 27.6. Outdoors: 50.2.

SKILLS—Installation; Repairing; Equipment Maintenance; Operation Monitoring; Troubleshooting; Operation and Control; Equipment Selection; Technology Design.

GOE—Interest Area: 13. Manufacturing. Work Group: 13.14. Vehicle and Facility Mechanical Work. Other Jobs in This Work Group: Aircraft Mechanics and Service Technicians; Aircraft Structure, Surfaces, Rigging, and Systems Assemblers; Automotive Body and Related Repairers; Automotive Glass Installers and

M

Repairers; Automotive Master Mechanics; Automotive Service Technicians and Mechanics; Automotive Specialty Technicians; Bus and Truck Mechanics and Diesel Engine Specialists; Farm Equipment Mechanics; Fiberglass Laminators and Fabricators; Motorboat Mechanics; Motorcycle Mechanics; Outdoor Power Equipment and Other Small Engine Mechanics; Rail Car Repairers; Recreational Vehicle Service Technicians; Tire Repairers and Changers. **PERSONALITY TYPE:** Realistic. Realistic occupations frequently involve work activities that include practical, hands-on problems and solutions. They often deal with plants; animals; and real-world materials like wood, tools, and machinery. Many of the occupations require working outside and do not involve a lot of paperwork or working closely with others.

EDUCATION/TRAINING PROGRAM(S)— Agricultural Mechanics and Equipment/ Machine Technology; Heavy Equipment Maintenance Technology/Technician. **RELATED KNOWLEDGE/COURSES—Mechanical Devices:** Machines and tools, including their designs, uses, repair, and maintenance. **Engineering and Technology:** The practical application of engineering science and technology. This includes applying principles, techniques, procedures, and equipment to the design and production of various goods and services. **Physics:** Physical principles and laws and their interrelationships and applications to understanding fluid, material, and atmospheric dynamics and mechanical, electrical, atomic, and subatomic structures and processes. **Customer and Personal Service:** Principles and processes for providing customer and personal services. This includes customer needs assessment, meeting quality standards for services, and evaluation of customer satisfaction. **Production and Processing:** Raw materials, production processes, quali-

ty control, costs, and other techniques for maximizing the effective manufacture and distribution of goods.

WORK ENVIRONMENT—Noisy; contaminants; hazardous equipment; minor burns, cuts, bites, or stings; standing; using hands on objects, tools, or controls.

Motorboat Mechanics

- Education/Training Required: Long-term on-the-job training
- Annual Earnings: $32,780
- Growth: 15.1%
- Annual Job Openings: 7,000
- Self-Employed: 18.9%
- Part-Time: 13.2%

Repairs and adjusts electrical and mechanical equipment of gasoline- or diesel-powered inboard or inboard-outboard boat engines. Replace parts such as gears, magneto points, piston rings, and spark plugs and reassemble engines. Adjust generators and replace faulty wiring, using hand tools and soldering irons. Mount motors to boats and operate boats at various speeds on waterways to conduct operational tests. Document inspection and test results and work performed or to be performed. Start motors and monitor performance for signs of malfunctioning, such as smoke, excessive vibration, and misfiring. Set starter locks and align and repair steering or throttle controls, using gauges, screwdrivers, and wrenches. Repair engine mechanical equipment, such as power-tilts, bilge pumps, or power take-offs. Inspect and repair or adjust propellers and propeller shafts. Disassemble and inspect motors to locate defective parts, using mechanic's hand tools and gauges. Adjust carburetor mixtures, electrical point settings, and timing while motors are running in water-filled test tanks. Repair or rework parts, using machine tools such as lathes, mills, drills, and grinders. Idle motors and observe thermometers to determine the effectiveness of cooling systems.

LEVEL OF ACTIVITY (out of 100)—General Physical Activity: 47.6. **Sitting:** 34.3. **Outdoors:** 45.7.

SKILLS—Repairing; Quality Control Analysis; Installation; Troubleshooting; Equipment Maintenance; Operation Monitoring; Operation and Control.

GOE—Interest Area: 13. Manufacturing. **Work Group:** 13.14. Vehicle and Facility Mechanical Work. **Other Jobs in This Work Group:** Aircraft Mechanics and Service Technicians; Aircraft Structure, Surfaces, Rigging, and Systems Assemblers; Automotive Body and Related Repairers; Automotive Glass Installers and Repairers; Automotive Master Mechanics; Automotive Service Technicians and Mechanics; Automotive Specialty Technicians; Bus and Truck Mechanics and Diesel Engine Specialists; Farm Equipment Mechanics; Fiberglass Laminators and Fabricators; Mobile Heavy Equipment Mechanics, Except Engines; Motorcycle Mechanics; Outdoor Power Equipment and Other Small Engine Mechanics; Rail Car Repairers; Recreational Vehicle Service Technicians; Tire Repairers and Changers. **PERSONALITY TYPE:** Realistic. Realistic occupations frequently involve work activities that include practical, hands-on problems and solutions. They often deal with plants; animals; and

real-world materials like wood, tools, and machinery. Many of the occupations require working outside and do not involve a lot of paperwork or working closely with others.

EDUCATION/TRAINING PROGRAM(S)—Small Engine Mechanics and Repair Technology/Technician; Marine Maintenance/Fitter and Ship Repair Technology/Technician. **RELATED KNOWLEDGE/COURSES**—**Mechanical Devices:** Machines and tools, including their designs, uses, repair, and maintenance. **Engineering and Technology:** The practical application of engineering science and technology. This includes applying principles, techniques, procedures, and equipment to the design and production of various goods and services.

WORK ENVIRONMENT—More often indoors than outdoors; standing; using hands on objects, tools, or controls.

Motorcycle Mechanics

- Education/Training Required: Long-term on-the-job training
- Annual Earnings: $29,450
- Growth: 13.7%
- Annual Job Openings: 6,000
- Self-Employed: 15.7%
- Part-Time: 13.2%

Diagnose, adjust, repair, or overhaul motorcycles, scooters, mopeds, dirt bikes, or similar motorized vehicles. Repair and adjust motorcycle subassemblies such as forks, transmissions, brakes, and drive chains according to specifications. Replace defective parts, using hand tools, arbor presses, flexible power presses, or power tools. Connect test panels to engines and measure generator output, ignition timing, and other engine performance indicators. Listen to engines, examine vehicle frames, and confer with customers in order to determine nature and extent of malfunction or damage. Reassemble and test subassembly units. Dismantle engines and repair or replace defective parts, such as magnetos, carburetors, and generators. Remove cylinder heads, grind valves, and scrape off carbon and replace defective valves, pistons, cylinders, and rings, using hand tools and power tools. Repair or replace other parts, such as headlights, horns, handlebar controls, gasoline and oil tanks, starters, and mufflers. Disassemble subassembly units and examine condition, movement, or alignment of parts visually or using gauges. Hammer out dents and bends in frames, weld tears and breaks, and then reassemble frames and reinstall engines.

LEVEL OF ACTIVITY (out of 100)—General Physical Activity: 67.1. **Sitting:** 27.1. **Outdoors:** 37.9.

SKILLS—Repairing; Installation; Troubleshooting; Equipment Maintenance; Technology Design; Science; Mathematics; Learning Strategies.

GOE—Interest Area: 13. Manufacturing. **Work Group:** 13.14. Vehicle and Facility Mechanical Work. **Other Jobs in This Work Group:** Aircraft Mechanics and Service Technicians; Aircraft Structure, Surfaces, Rigging, and Systems Assemblers; Automotive Body and Related Repairers; Automotive Glass Installers and Repairers; Automotive Master Mechanics; Automotive Service Technicians and Mechanics; Automotive Specialty Technicians; Bus and Truck Mechanics and Diesel Engine Specialists;

Farm Equipment Mechanics; Fiberglass Laminators and Fabricators; Mobile Heavy Equipment Mechanics, Except Engines; Motorboat Mechanics; Outdoor Power Equipment and Other Small Engine Mechanics; Rail Car Repairers; Recreational Vehicle Service Technicians; Tire Repairers and Changers. **PERSONALITY TYPE:** Realistic. Realistic occupations frequently involve work activities that include practical, hands-on problems and solutions. They often deal with plants; animals; and real-world materials like wood, tools, and machinery. Many of the occupations require working outside and do not involve a lot of paperwork or working closely with others.

EDUCATION/TRAINING PROGRAM(S)—Motorcycle Maintenance and Repair Technology/Technician. **RELATED KNOWLEDGE/COURSES—Mechanical Devices:** Machines and tools, including their designs, uses, repair, and maintenance. **Design:** Design techniques, tools, and principles involved in production of precision technical plans, blueprints, drawings, and models. **Engineering and Technology:** The practical application of engineering science and technology. This includes applying principles, techniques, procedures, and equipment to the design and production of various goods and services. **Physics:** Physical principles and laws and their interrelationships and applications to understanding fluid, material, and atmospheric dynamics and mechanical, electrical, atomic, and subatomic structures and processes. **Transportation:** Principles and methods for moving people or goods by air, rail, sea, or road, including the relative costs and benefits. **Sales and Marketing:** Principles and methods for showing, promoting, and selling products or services. This includes marketing strategy and tactics, product demonstration, sales techniques, and sales control systems.

WORK ENVIRONMENT—Indoors; noisy; contaminants; standing; using hands on objects, tools, or controls; bending or twisting the body.

Municipal Fire Fighting and Prevention Supervisors

This job can be found in the Part I lists under the title First-Line Supervisors/Managers of Fire Fighting and Prevention Workers.

- ◉ Education/Training Required: Work experience in a related occupation
- ◉ Annual Earnings: $60,840
- ◉ Growth: 21.1%
- ◉ Annual Job Openings: 4,000
- ◉ Self-Employed: 0.0%
- ◉ Part-Time: 0.4%

The job openings listed here are shared with Forest Fire Fighting and Prevention Supervisors.

Supervise fire fighters who control and extinguish municipal fires, protect life and property, and conduct rescue efforts. Assign firefighters to jobs at strategic locations to facilitate rescue of persons and maximize application of extinguishing agents. Provide emergency medical services as required and perform light to heavy rescue functions at emergencies. Assess nature and extent of fire, condition of building, danger to adjacent buildings, and water supply status to determine crew or company requirements. Instruct and drill fire department personnel in assigned duties, including firefighting, medical care, hazardous materials response, fire prevention, and related subjects. Evaluate the performance of assigned firefighting personnel. Direct the training of firefighters, assigning of instructors to training classes, and providing of supervisors with reports on training progress and status. Prepare activity reports listing fire call locations, actions taken, fire types and probable causes, damage estimates, and situation dispositions. Maintain required maps and records. Attend in-service training classes to remain current in knowledge of codes, laws, ordinances, and regulations. Evaluate fire station procedures to ensure efficiency and enforcement of departmental regulations. Direct firefighters in station maintenance duties and participate in these duties. Compile and maintain equipment and personnel records, including accident reports. Direct investigation of cases of suspected arson, hazards, and false alarms and submit reports outlining findings. Recommend personnel actions related to disciplinary procedures, performance, leaves of absence, and grievances. Supervise and participate in the inspection of properties to ensure that they are in compliance with applicable fire codes, ordinances, laws, regulations, and standards. Write and submit proposals for repair, modification, or replacement of firefighting equipment. Coordinate the distribution of fire-prevention promotional materials. Identify corrective actions needed to bring properties into compliance with applicable fire codes and ordinances and conduct follow-up inspections to see if corrective actions have been taken. Participate in creating fire safety guidelines and evacuation schemes for non-residential buildings.

LEVEL OF ACTIVITY (out of 100)—General Physical Activity: 80.4. **Sitting:** 35.1. **Outdoors:** 49.8.

SKILLS—Management of Personnel Resources; Equipment Maintenance; Service Orientation; Operation Monitoring; Coordination; Management of Material Resources; Judgment and Decision Making; Operation and Control.

GOE—**Interest Area:** 12. Law and Public Safety. **Work Group:** 12.01. Managerial Work in Law and Public Safety. **Other Jobs in This Work Group:** Emergency Management Specialists; First-Line Supervisors/Managers of Correctional Officers; First-Line Supervisors/Managers of Fire Fighting and Prevention Workers; First-Line Supervisors/Managers of Police and Detectives; Forest Fire Fighting and Prevention Supervisors. **PERSONALITY TYPE:** Realistic. Realistic occupations frequently involve work activities that include practical, hands-on problems and solutions. They often deal with plants; animals; and real-world materials like wood, tools, and machinery. Many of the occupations require working outside and do not involve a lot of paperwork or working closely with others.

EDUCATION/TRAINING PROGRAM(S)—Fire Protection and Safety Technology/Technician; Fire Services Administration. **RELATED KNOWLEDGE/COURSES**—**Public Safety and Security:** Relevant equipment, policies, procedures, and strategies to promote effective local, state, or national security operations for the protection of people, data, property, and institutions. **Building and Construction:** The materials, methods, and tools involved in the construction or repair of houses, buildings, or other structures such as highways and roads. **Medicine and Dentistry:** The information and techniques needed to diagnose and treat human injuries, diseases, and deformities. This includes symptoms, treatment alternatives, drug properties and interactions, and preventive health-care measures. **Education and Training:** Principles and methods for curriculum and training design, teaching and instruction for individuals and groups, and the measurement of training effects. **Customer and Personal Service:** Principles and processes for providing customer and personal services. This includes customer needs assessment, meeting quality standards for services, and evaluation of customer satisfaction. **Mechanical Devices:** Machines and tools, including their designs, uses, repair, and maintenance.

WORK ENVIRONMENT—More often outdoors than indoors; noisy; contaminants; disease or infections; hazardous equipment.

Museum Technicians and Conservators

- Education/Training Required: Bachelor's degree
- Annual Earnings: $34,090
- Growth: 14.1%
- Annual Job Openings: 2,000
- Self-Employed: 9.4%
- Part-Time: 23.4%

Prepare specimens, such as fossils, skeletal parts, lace, and textiles, for museum collection and exhibits. May restore documents or install, arrange, and exhibit materials. Install, arrange, assemble, and prepare artifacts for exhibition, ensuring the artifacts' safety, reporting their status and condition, and identifying and correcting any problems with the setup. Coordinate exhibit installations, assisting with design; constructing displays, dioramas, display cases, and models; and ensuring the availability of necessary materials. Determine whether objects need repair and choose the safest and most effective method of repair. Clean objects, such as paper, textiles, wood, metal, glass, rock, pottery, and furniture, using cleansers, solvents, soap solutions, and polishes. Prepare artifacts for storage and shipping. Supervise and work with volunteers. Present public programs and tours. Specialize in particular materials or types of object, such as documents and books, paintings, decorative arts, textiles, metals, or architectural materials. Recommend preservation procedures, such as control of temperature and humidity, to curatorial and building staff. Classify and assign registration numbers to artifacts and supervise inventory control. Direct and supervise curatorial and technical staff in the handling, mounting, care, and storage of art objects. Perform on-site field work, which may involve interviewing people, inspecting and identifying artifacts, note-taking, viewing sites and collections, and repainting exhibition spaces. Repair, restore, and reassemble artifacts, designing and fabricating missing or broken parts, to restore them to their original appearance and prevent deterioration. Prepare reports on the operation of conservation laboratories, documenting the condition of artifacts, treatment options, and the methods of preservation and repair used. Study object documentation or conduct standard chemical and physical tests to ascertain the object's age, composition, original appearance, need for treatment or restoration, and appropriate preservation method. Cut and weld metal sections in reconstruction or renovation of exterior structural sections and accessories of exhibits.

Perform tests and examinations to establish storage and conservation requirements, policies, and procedures.

LEVEL OF ACTIVITY (out of 100)—General Physical Activity: 55.7. **Sitting:** 38.9. **Outdoors:** 27.1.

SKILLS—Management of Material Resources; Repairing; Installation; Technology Design; Equipment Maintenance; Time Management; Operations Analysis; Equipment Selection.

GOE—Interest Area: 05. Education and Training. **Work Group:** 05.05. Archival and Museum Services. **Other Jobs in This Work Group:** Archivists; Audio-Visual Collections Specialists; Curators. **PERSONALITY TYPE:** Artistic. Artistic occupations frequently involve working with forms, designs, and patterns. They often require self-expression, and the work can be done without following a clear set of rules.

EDUCATION/TRAINING PROGRAM(S)—Museology/Museum Studies; Art History, Criticism, and Conservation; Public/Applied History and Archival Administration. **RELATED KNOWLEDGE/COURSES—History and Archeology:** Historical events and their causes, indicators, and effects on civilizations and cultures. **Fine Arts:** The theory and techniques required to compose, produce, and perform works of music, dance, visual arts, drama, and sculpture. **Sociology and Anthropology:** Group behavior and dynamics, societal trends and influences, human migrations, ethnicity, and cultures and their history and origins. **Design:** Design techniques, tools, and principles involved in production of precision technical plans, blueprints, drawings, and models. **Education and Training:** Principles and methods for curriculum and training design, teaching and instruction for individuals and groups, and the measurement of training effects. **Clerical**

Practices: Administrative and clerical procedures and systems such as word processing, managing files and records, stenography and transcription, designing forms, and other office procedures and terminology.

WORK ENVIRONMENT—Indoors; standing; using hands on objects, tools, or controls.

Nuclear Equipment Operation Technicians

This job can be found in the Part I lists under the title Nuclear Technicians.

- Education/Training Required: Associate degree
- Annual Earnings: $61,120
- Growth: 13.7%
- Annual Job Openings: 1,000
- Self-Employed: 0.0%
- Part-Time: No data available

The job openings listed here are shared with Nuclear Monitoring Technicians.

Operate equipment used for the release, control, and utilization of nuclear energy to assist scientists in laboratory and production activities. Follow policies and procedures for radiation workers in order to ensure personnel safety. Modify, devise, and maintain equipment used in operations. Set control panel switches, according to standard procedures, in order to route electric power from sources and direct particle beams through injector units. Submit computations to supervisors for review. Calculate equipment operating factors, such as radiation times, dosages, temperatures, gamma intensities, and pressures, using standard formulas and conversion tables. Perform testing, maintenance, repair, and upgrading of accelerator systems. Warn maintenance workers of radiation hazards and direct workers to vacate hazardous areas. Monitor instruments, gauges, and recording devices in control rooms during operation of equipment under direction of nuclear experimenters. Write summaries of activities and record experimental data, such as accelerator performance, systems status, particle beam specification, and beam conditions obtained.

LEVEL OF ACTIVITY (out of 100)—General Physical Activity: 69.9. **Sitting:** 37.9. **Outdoors:** 35.9.

SKILLS—Operation Monitoring; Operation and Control; Science; Equipment Maintenance; Mathematics; Quality Control Analysis; Troubleshooting; Active Listening.

GOE—Interest Area: 15. Scientific Research, Engineering, and Mathematics. **Work Group:** 15.05. Physical Science Laboratory Technology. **Other Jobs in This Work Group:** Chemical Technicians; Nuclear Technicians. **PERSONALITY TYPE:** Realistic. Realistic occupations frequently involve work activities that include practical, hands-on problems and solutions. They often deal with plants; animals; and real-world materials like wood, tools, and machinery. Many of the occupations require working outside and do not involve a lot of paperwork or working closely with others.

EDUCATION/TRAINING PROGRAM(S)— Nuclear Engineering Technology/Technician; Industrial Radiologic Technology/Technician; Nuclear/Nuclear Power Technology/Technician; Nuclear and Industrial Radiologic Technologies/ Technicians, Other; Radiation Protection/ Health Physics Technician. **RELATED KNOWLEDGE/COURSES—Physics:** Physical principles and laws and their interrelationships and applications to understanding fluid, material, and atmospheric dynamics and mechanical, electrical, atomic, and subatomic structures and processes. **Chemistry:** The chemical composition, structure, and properties of substances and of the chemical processes and transformations that they undergo. This includes uses of chemicals and their danger signs, production techniques, and disposal methods. **Engineering and Technology:** The practical application of engineering science and technology. This includes applying principles, techniques, procedures, and equipment to the design and production of various goods and services. **Public Safety and Security:** Relevant equipment, policies, procedures, and strategies to promote effective local, state, or national security operations for the protection of people, data, property, and institutions. **Mechanical Devices:** Machines and tools, including their designs, uses, repair, and maintenance. **Computers and Electronics:** Circuit boards; processors; chips; electronic equipment; and computer hardware and software, including applications and programming.

WORK ENVIRONMENT—Indoors; noisy; very hot or cold; radiation; hazardous conditions; hazardous equipment.

Nuclear Medicine Technologists

- Education/Training Required: Associate degree
- Annual Earnings: $59,670
- Growth: 21.5%
- Annual Job Openings: 2,000
- Self-Employed: 0.5%
- Part-Time: 17.2%

Prepare, administer, and measure radioactive isotopes in therapeutic, diagnostic, and tracer studies, utilizing a variety of radioisotope equipment. Prepare stock solutions of radioactive materials and calculate doses to be administered by radiologists. Subject patients to radiation. Execute blood volume, red cell survival, and fat absorption studies following standard laboratory techniques. Calculate, measure, and record radiation dosage or radiopharmaceuticals received, used, and disposed, using computer and following physician's prescription. Detect and map radiopharmaceuticals in patients' bodies, using a camera to produce photographic or computer images. Explain test procedures and safety precautions to patients and provide them with assistance during test procedures. Administer radiopharmaceuticals or radiation to patients to detect or treat diseases under direction of physician, using radioisotope equipment. Produce a computer-generated or film image for interpretation by a physician. Process cardiac function studies, using computer.

N

Dispose of radioactive materials and store radio-pharmaceuticals, following radiation safety procedures. Record and process results of procedures. Prepare stock radiopharmaceuticals, adhering to safety standards that minimize radiation exposure to workers and patients. Maintain and calibrate radioisotope and laboratory equipment. Gather information on patients' illnesses and medical history to guide the choice of diagnostic procedures for therapy. Measure glandular activity, blood volume, red cell survival, and radioactivity of patient, using scanners, Geiger counters, scintillometers, and other laboratory equipment. Train and supervise student or subordinate nuclear medicine technologists. Position radiation fields, radiation beams, and patient to allow for most effective treatment of patient's disease, using computer. Add radioactive substances to biological specimens, such as blood, urine, and feces, to determine therapeutic drug or hormone levels. Develop treatment procedures for nuclear medicine treatment programs.

LEVEL OF ACTIVITY (out of 100)—General Physical Activity: 53.1. **Sitting:** 36.9. **Outdoors:** 14.6.

SKILLS—Science; Operation Monitoring; Operation and Control; Social Perceptiveness; Service Orientation; Quality Control Analysis; Troubleshooting; Instructing.

GOE—Interest Area: 08. Health Science. **Work Group:** 08.06. Medical Technology. **Other Jobs in This Work Group:** Biological Technicians; Cardiovascular Technologists and Technicians; Diagnostic Medical Sonographers; Medical and Clinical Laboratory Technicians; Medical and Clinical Laboratory Technologists; Medical Equipment Preparers; Medical Records and Health Information Technicians; Opticians, Dispensing; Orthotists and Prosthetists;

Radiologic Technicians; Radiologic Technologists; Radiologic Technologists and Technicians. **PERSONALITY TYPE:** Investigative. Investigative occupations frequently involve working with ideas and require an extensive amount of thinking. These occupations can involve searching for facts and figuring out problems mentally.

EDUCATION/TRAINING PROGRAM(S)—Nuclear Medical Technology/Technologist; Radiation Protection/Health Physics Technician. **RELATED KNOWLEDGE/COURSES**—**Medicine and Dentistry:** The information and techniques needed to diagnose and treat human injuries, diseases, and deformities. This includes symptoms, treatment alternatives, drug properties and interactions, and preventive health-care measures. **Biology:** Plant and animal organisms and their tissues, cells, functions, interdependencies, and interactions with each other and the environment. **Physics:** Physical principles and laws and their interrelationships and applications to understanding fluid, material, and atmospheric dynamics and mechanical, electrical, atomic, and subatomic structures and processes. **Chemistry:** The chemical composition, structure, and properties of substances and of the chemical processes and transformations that they undergo. This includes uses of chemicals and their danger signs, production techniques, and disposal methods. **Customer and Personal Service:** Principles and processes for providing customer and personal services. This includes customer needs assessment, meeting quality standards for services, and evaluation of customer satisfaction. **Computers and Electronics:** Circuit boards; processors; chips; electronic equipment; and computer hardware and software, including applications and programming.

WORK ENVIRONMENT—Indoors; contaminants; radiation; disease or infections; standing; using hands on objects, tools, or controls.

Nuclear Monitoring Technicians

This job can be found in the Part I lists under the title Nuclear Technicians.

- Education/Training Required: Associate degree
- Annual Earnings: $61,120
- Growth: 13.7%
- Annual Job Openings: 1,000
- Self-Employed: 0.0%
- Part-Time: No data available

The job openings listed here are shared with Nuclear Equipment Operation Technicians.

Collect and test samples to monitor results of nuclear experiments and contamination of humans, facilities, and environment. Calculate safe radiation exposure times for personnel, using plant contamination readings and prescribed safe levels of radiation. Provide initial response to abnormal events and to alarms from radiation monitoring equipment. Monitor personnel in order to determine the amounts and intensities of radiation exposure. Inform supervisors when individual exposures or area radiation levels approach maximum permissible limits. Instruct personnel in radiation safety procedures and demonstrate use of protective clothing and equipment. Determine intensities and types of radiation in work areas, equipment, and materials, using radiation detectors and other instruments. Collect samples of air, water, gases, and solids in order to determine radioactivity levels of contamination. Set up equipment that automatically detects area radiation deviations and test detection equipment in order to ensure its accuracy. Determine or recommend radioactive decontamination procedures according to the size and nature of equipment and the degree of contamination. Decontaminate objects by cleaning with soap or solvents or by abrading with wire brushes, buffing wheels, or sandblasting machines. Place radioactive waste, such as sweepings and broken sample bottles, into containers for disposal. Calibrate and maintain chemical instrumentation sensing elements and sampling system equipment, using calibration instruments and hand tools. Place irradiated nuclear fuel materials in environmental chambers for testing and observe reactions through cell windows. Enter data into computers in order to record characteristics of nuclear events and locating coordinates of particles. Operate manipulators from outside cells to move specimens into and out of shielded containers, to remove specimens from cells, or to place specimens on benches or equipment workstations. Prepare reports describing contamination tests, material and equipment decontaminated, and methods used in decontamination processes. Confer with scientists directing projects in order to determine significant events to monitor during tests. Immerse samples in chemical compounds in order to prepare them for testing.

LEVEL OF ACTIVITY (out of 100)—General Physical Activity: 37.1. **Sitting:** 38.4. **Outdoors:** 31.8.

SKILLS—Science; Operation Monitoring; Equipment Maintenance; Mathematics;

Systems Analysis; Coordination; Technology Design; Operation and Control.

GOE—Interest Area: 07. Government and Public Administration. **Work Group:** 07.03. Regulations Enforcement. **Other Jobs in This Work Group:** Agricultural Inspectors; Aviation Inspectors; Compliance Officers, Except Agriculture, Construction, Health and Safety, and Transportation; Construction and Building Inspectors; Environmental Compliance Inspectors; Equal Opportunity Representatives and Officers; Financial Examiners; Fire Inspectors; Fish and Game Wardens; Forest Fire Inspectors and Prevention Specialists; Freight and Cargo Inspectors; Government Property Inspectors and Investigators; Immigration and Customs Inspectors; Licensing Examiners and Inspectors; Occupational Health and Safety Specialists; Occupational Health and Safety Technicians; Tax Examiners, Collectors, and Revenue Agents; Transportation Vehicle, Equipment, and Systems Inspectors, Except Aviation. **PERSONALITY TYPE:** Realistic. Realistic occupations frequently involve work activities that include practical, hands-on problems and solutions. They often deal with plants; animals; and real-world materials like wood, tools, and machinery. Many of the occupations require working outside and do not involve a lot of paperwork or working closely with others.

EDUCATION/TRAINING PROGRAM(S)— Nuclear Engineering Technology/Technician; Industrial Radiologic Technology/Technician; Nuclear/Nuclear Power Technology/Technician; Nuclear and Industrial Radiologic Technologies/Technicians, Other; Radiation Protection/Health Physics Technician. **RELATED KNOWLEDGE/COURSES—Physics:** Physical principles and laws and their interrelationships and applications to understanding fluid, material,

and atmospheric dynamics and mechanical, electrical, atomic, and subatomic structures and processes. **Chemistry:** The chemical composition, structure, and properties of substances and of the chemical processes and transformations that they undergo. This includes uses of chemicals and their danger signs, production techniques, and disposal methods. **Public Safety and Security:** Relevant equipment, policies, procedures, and strategies to promote effective local, state, or national security operations for the protection of people, data, property, and institutions. **Engineering and Technology:** The practical application of engineering science and technology. This includes applying principles, techniques, procedures, and equipment to the design and production of various goods and services. **Design:** Design techniques, tools, and principles involved in production of precision technical plans, blueprints, drawings, and models. **Biology:** Plant and animal organisms and their tissues, cells, functions, interdependencies, and interactions with each other and the environment.

WORK ENVIRONMENT—Indoors; noisy; very hot or cold; contaminants; radiation; hazardous conditions.

Nuclear Technicians

See the descriptions of these jobs:

- **Nuclear Equipment Operation Technicians**
- **Nuclear Monitoring Technicians**

Nursing Aides, Orderlies, and Attendants

◎ Education/Training Required:
Short-term on-the-job training

◎ Annual Earnings: $21,440

◎ Growth: 22.3%

◎ Annual Job Openings: 307,000

◎ Self-Employed: 1.9%

◎ Part-Time: 28.0%

Provide basic patient care under direction of nursing staff. Perform duties such as feeding, bathing, dressing, grooming, or moving patients or changing linens. Turn and reposition bedridden patients, alone or with assistance, to prevent bedsores. Answer patients' call signals. Feed patients who are unable to feed themselves. Observe patients' conditions, measuring and recording food and liquid intake and output and vital signs, and report changes to professional staff. Provide patient care by supplying and emptying bedpans, applying dressings, and supervising exercise routines. Provide patients with help walking, exercising, and moving in and out of bed. Bathe, groom, shave, dress, or drape patients to prepare them for surgery, treatment, or examination. Collect specimens such as urine, feces, or sputum. Prepare, serve, and collect food trays. Clean rooms and change linens. Transport patients to treatment units, using a wheelchair or stretcher. Deliver messages, docu-ments, and specimens. Answer phones and direct visitors. Administer medications and treatments, such as catheterizations, suppositories, irrigations, enemas, massages, and douches, as directed by a physician or nurse. Restrain patients if necessary. Maintain inventory by storing, preparing, sterilizing, and issuing supplies such as dressing packs and treatment trays. Explain medical instructions to patients and family members. Perform clerical duties such as processing documents and scheduling appointments. Work as part of a medical team that examines and treats clinic outpatients. Set up equipment such as oxygen tents, portable X-ray machines, and overhead irrigation bottles.

LEVEL OF ACTIVITY (out of 100)—General Physical Activity: 48.6. **Sitting:** 34.1. **Outdoors:** 16.9.

SKILLS—Social Perceptiveness; Operation Monitoring; Time Management; Service Orientation; Instructing; Monitoring; Technology Design; Speaking.

GOE—Interest Area: 08. Health Science. **Work Group:** 08.08. Patient Care and Assistance. **Other Jobs in This Work Group:** Home Health Aides; Licensed Practical and Licensed Vocational Nurses; Psychiatric Aides; Psychiatric Technicians. **PERSONALITY TYPE:** Social. Social occupations frequently involve working with, communicating with, and teaching people. These occupations often involve helping or providing service to others.

EDUCATION/TRAINING PROGRAM(S)—Nurse/Nursing Assistant/Aide and Patient Care Assistant; Health Aide. **RELATED KNOWLEDGE/COURSES—Psychology:** Human behavior and performance; individual differences in ability, personality, and interests; learning and motivation; psychological research methods; and the assessment and treatment of behavioral and affective disorders. **Medicine and Dentistry:** The information and techniques needed to diagnose and treat human injuries, diseases, and deformities. This includes symptoms, treatment alternatives, drug properties and interactions, and preventive health-care measures. **Customer and Personal Service:** Principles and processes for providing customer and personal services. This includes customer needs assessment, meeting quality standards for services, and evaluation of customer satisfaction. **Chemistry:** The chemical composition, structure, and properties of substances and of the chemical processes and transformations that they undergo. This includes uses of chemicals and their danger signs, production techniques, and disposal methods. **Education and Training:** Principles and methods for curriculum and training design, teaching and instruction for individuals and groups, and the measurement of training effects. **English Language:** The structure and content of the English language, including the meaning and spelling of words, rules of composition, and grammar.

WORK ENVIRONMENT—Indoors; disease or infections; standing; walking and running; using hands on objects, tools, or controls; bending or twisting the body.

Occupational Therapist Assistants

- Education/Training Required: Associate degree
- Annual Earnings: $39,750
- Growth: 34.1%
- Annual Job Openings: 2,000
- Self-Employed: 0.0%
- Part-Time: 18.6%

Assist occupational therapists in providing occupational therapy treatments and procedures. May, in accordance with state laws, assist in development of treatment plans, carry out routine functions, direct activity programs, and document the progress of treatments. Generally requires formal training. Observe and record patients' progress, attitudes, and behavior and maintain this information in client records. Maintain and promote a positive attitude toward clients and their treatment programs. Monitor patients' performance in therapy activities, providing encouragement. Select therapy activities to fit patients' needs and capabilities. Instruct, or assist in instructing, patients and families in home programs, basic living skills, and the care and use of adaptive equipment. Evaluate the daily living skills and capacities of physically, developmentally, or emotionally disabled clients. Aid patients in dressing and grooming themselves. Implement, or assist occupational therapists with implementing, treatment plans designed to help clients function independently. Report to supervisors, verbally or in writing, on patients' progress, attitudes, and behavior. Alter treatment programs to obtain better results if treatment is not having the intended effect. Work under the direction of occupational therapists to plan, implement, and administer educational, vocational, and recreational programs that restore and enhance performance in individuals with functional impairments. Design, fabricate, and repair assistive devices and make adaptive changes to equipment and environments. Assemble, clean, and maintain equipment and materials for patient use. Teach patients how to deal constructively with their emotions. Perform clerical duties such as scheduling appointments, collecting data, and documenting health insurance billings. Transport patients to and from the occupational therapy work area. Demonstrate therapy techniques such as manual and creative arts or games. Order any needed educational or treatment supplies. Assist educational specialists or clinical psychologists in administering situational or diagnostic tests to measure client's abilities or progress.

LEVEL OF ACTIVITY (out of 100)—General Physical Activity: 47.7. **Sitting:** 29.9. **Outdoors:** 21.4.

SKILLS—Social Perceptiveness; Service Orientation; Persuasion; Time Management; Operations Analysis; Instructing; Learning Strategies; Monitoring.

GOE—Interest Area: 08. Health Science. **Work Group:** 08.07. Medical Therapy. **Other Jobs in This Work Group:** Audiologists; Massage Therapists; Occupational Therapist Aides; Occupational Therapists; Physical Therapist Aides; Physical Therapist Assistants; Physical Therapists; Radiation Therapists; Recreational Therapists; Respiratory Therapists; Respiratory Therapy Technicians; Speech-Language Pathologists. **PERSONALITY TYPE:** Social. Social occupations frequently involve working with, communicating with, and teaching people. These occupations often involve helping or providing service to others.

EDUCATION/TRAINING PROGRAM(S)— Occupational Therapist Assistant. **RELATED KNOWLEDGE/COURSES—Therapy and Counseling:** Principles, methods, and procedures for diagnosis, treatment, and rehabilitation of physical and mental dysfunctions and for career counseling and guidance. **Psychology:** Human behavior and performance; individual differences in ability, personality, and interests; learning and motivation; psychological research methods; and the assessment and treatment of behavioral and affective disorders. **Sociology and Anthropology:** Group behavior and dynamics, societal trends and influences, human migrations, ethnicity, and cultures and their history and origins. **Philosophy and Theology:** Different philosophical systems and religions. This includes their basic principles, values, ethics, ways of thinking, customs, and practices and their impact on human culture. **Medicine and Dentistry:** The information and techniques needed to diagnose and treat human injuries, diseases, and deformities. This includes symptoms, treatment alternatives, drug properties and interactions, and preventive health-care measures. **Biology:** Plant and animal organisms and their tissues, cells, functions, interdependencies, and interactions with each other and the environment.

WORK ENVIRONMENT—Indoors; disease or infections; standing; walking and running; using hands on objects, tools, or controls; bending or twisting the body.

Occupational Therapists

◉ Education/Training Required:
Bachelor's degree

◉ Annual Earnings: $56,860

◉ Growth: 33.6%

◉ Annual Job Openings: 7,000

◉ Self-Employed: 6.0%

◉ Part-Time: 29.4%

**Assess, plan, organize, and participate in reha-
bilitative programs that help restore vocational,
homemaking, and daily living skills, as well as
general independence, to disabled persons.**
Complete and maintain necessary records.
Evaluate patients' progress and prepare reports
that detail progress. Test and evaluate patients'
physical and mental abilities and analyze medical data to determine realistic rehabilitation
goals for patients. Select activities that will help
individuals learn work and life-management
skills within limits of their mental and physical
capabilities. Plan, organize, and conduct occupational therapy programs in hospital, institutional, or community settings to help
rehabilitate those impaired because of illness,
injury, or psychological or developmental problems. Recommend changes in patients' work or
living environments consistent with their needs
and capabilities. Consult with rehabilitation
team to select activity programs and coordinate
occupational therapy with other therapeutic
activities. Help clients improve decisionmaking,
abstract reasoning, memory, sequencing, coordination, and perceptual skills, using computer

programs. Develop and participate in health
promotion programs, group activities, or discussions to promote client health, facilitate social
adjustment, alleviate stress, and prevent physical
or mental disability. Provide training and supervision in therapy techniques and objectives for
students and nurses and other medical staff.
Design and create, or requisition, special supplies and equipment, such as splints, braces, and
computer-aided adaptive equipment. Plan and
implement programs and social activities to help
patients learn work and school skills and adjust
to handicaps. Lay out materials such as puzzles,
scissors, and eating utensils for use in therapy
and clean and repair these tools after therapy sessions. Advise on health risks in the workplace
and on health-related transition to retirement.
Conduct research in occupational therapy.
Provide patients with assistance in locating and
holding jobs.

**LEVEL OF ACTIVITY (out of 100)—General
Physical Activity: 65.7. Sitting: 38.6.
Outdoors: 21.0.**

SKILLS—Social Perceptiveness; Service Orientation; Science; Technology Design; Reading
Comprehension; Coordination; Active Learning; Writing.

GOE—Interest Area: 08. Health Science. **Work
Group:** 08.07. Medical Therapy. **Other Jobs in
This Work Group:** Audiologists; Massage
Therapists; Occupational Therapist Aides;
Occupational Therapist Assistants; Physical
Therapist Aides; Physical Therapist Assistants;
Physical Therapists; Radiation Therapists;
Recreational Therapists; Respiratory Therapists;
Respiratory Therapy Technicians; Speech-
Language Pathologists. **PERSONALITY
TYPE:** Social. Social occupations frequently

involve working with, communicating with, and teaching people. These occupations often involve helping or providing service to others.

EDUCATION/TRAINING PROGRAM(S)— Occupational Therapy/Therapist. **RELATED KNOWLEDGE/COURSES—Therapy and Counseling:** Principles, methods, and procedures for diagnosis, treatment, and rehabilitation of physical and mental dysfunctions and for career counseling and guidance. **Psychology:** Human behavior and performance; individual differences in ability, personality, and interests; learning and motivation; psychological research methods; and the assessment and treatment of behavioral and affective disorders. **Medicine and Dentistry:** The information and techniques needed to diagnose and treat human injuries, diseases, and deformities. This includes symptoms, treatment alternatives, drug properties and interactions, and preventive health-care measures. **Customer and Personal Service:** Principles and processes for providing customer and personal services. This includes customer needs assessment, meeting quality standards for services, and evaluation of customer satisfaction. **Biology:** Plant and animal organisms and their tissues, cells, functions, interdependencies, and interactions with each other and the environment. **Sociology and Anthropology:** Group behavior and dynamics, societal trends and influences, human migrations, ethnicity, and cultures and their history and origins.

WORK ENVIRONMENT—Indoors; disease or infections; standing.

Operating Engineers and Other Construction Equipment Operators

- Education/Training Required: Moderate-term on-the-job training
- Annual Earnings: $35,830
- Growth: 11.6%
- Annual Job Openings: 37,000
- Self-Employed: 5.4%
- Part-Time: 2.9%

Operate one or several types of power construction equipment, such as motor graders, bulldozers, scrapers, compressors, pumps, derricks, shovels, tractors, or front-end loaders, to excavate, move, and grade earth; erect structures; or pour concrete or other hard-surface pavement. May repair and maintain equipment in addition to other duties. Learn and follow safety regulations. Take actions to avoid potential hazards and obstructions such as utility lines, other equipment, other workers, and falling objects. Adjust handwheels and depress pedals to control attachments such as blades, buckets, scrapers, and swing booms. Start engines, move throttles, switches, and levers; and depress pedals to operate machines such as bulldozers, trench excavators, road graders, and backhoes. Locate underground services, such as pipes and wires, prior to beginning work. Monitor operations to ensure that health and safety standards are met. Align machines, cutterheads, or depth gauge makers with reference stakes and guidelines or with ground or position equipment, following hand signals of other workers. Load and move dirt, rocks, equipment, and materials, using trucks, crawler tractors, power cranes, shovels, graders, and related equipment. Drive and maneuver equipment equipped with blades in successive passes over working areas to remove topsoil, vegetation, and rocks and to distribute and level earth or terrain. Coordinate machine actions with other activities, positioning or moving loads in response to hand or audio signals from crew members. Operate tractors and bulldozers to perform such tasks as clearing land, mixing sludge, trimming backfills, and building roadways and parking lots. Repair and maintain equipment, making emergency adjustments or assisting with major repairs as necessary. Check fuel supplies at sites to ensure adequate availability. Connect hydraulic hoses, belts, mechanical linkages, or power takeoff shafts to tractors. Operate loaders to pull out stumps, rip asphalt or concrete, rough-grade properties, bury refuse, or perform general cleanup. Select and fasten bulldozer blades or other attachments to tractors, using hitches. Test atmosphere for adequate oxygen and explosive conditions when working in confined spaces. Operate compactors, scrapers, and rollers to level, compact, and cover refuse at disposal grounds. Talk to clients and study instructions, plans, and diagrams in order to establish work requirements.

LEVEL OF ACTIVITY (out of 100)—General Physical Activity: 57.6. **Sitting:** 53.7. **Outdoors:** 54.1.

SKILLS—Equipment Maintenance; Installation; Operation Monitoring; Operation and Control; Repairing; Management of Financial Resources; Management of Material Resources; Equipment Selection.

GOE—Interest Area: 02. Architecture and Construction. **Work Group:** 02.04. Construction Crafts. **Other Jobs in This Work Group:** Boilermakers; Brickmasons and Blockmasons; Carpet Installers; Cement Masons and Concrete Finishers; Commercial Divers; Construction Carpenters; Crane and Tower Operators; Drywall and Ceiling Tile Installers; Electricians; Fence Erectors; Floor Layers, Except Carpet, Wood, and Hard Tiles; Floor Sanders and Finishers; Glaziers; Hazardous Materials Removal Workers; Insulation Workers, Floor, Ceiling, and Wall; Insulation Workers, Mechanical; Manufactured Building and Mobile Home Installers; Painters, Construction and Maintenance; Paperhangers; Paving, Surfacing, and Tamping Equipment Operators; Pile-Driver Operators; Pipe Fitters and Steamfitters; Pipelayers; Plasterers and Stucco Masons; Plumbers; Plumbers, Pipefitters, and Steamfitters; Rail-Track Laying and Maintenance Equipment Operators; Refractory Materials Repairers, Except Brickmasons; Reinforcing Iron and Rebar Workers; Riggers; Roofers; Rough Carpenters; Security and Fire Alarm Systems Installers; Segmental Pavers; Sheet Metal Workers; Stone Cutters and Carvers, Manufacturing; Stonemasons; Structural Iron and Steel Workers; Tapers; Terrazzo Workers and Finishers; Tile and Marble Setters. **PERSONALITY TYPE:** Realistic. Realistic occupations frequently involve work activities that include practical, hands-on problems and solutions. They often deal with plants; animals; and real-world materials like wood, tools, and machinery. Many of the occupations require working outside and do not involve a lot of paperwork or working closely with others.

EDUCATION/TRAINING PROGRAM(S)—Construction/Heavy Equipment/Earthmoving Equipment Operation; Mobile Crane Operation/Operator. **RELATED KNOWLEDGE/COURSES—Building and Construction:** The materials, methods, and tools involved in the construction or repair of houses, buildings, or other structures such as highways and roads. **Mechanical Devices:** Machines and tools, including their designs, uses, repair, and maintenance. **Engineering and Technology:** The practical application of engineering science and technology. This includes applying principles, techniques, procedures, and equipment to the design and production of various goods and services. **Design:** Design techniques, tools, and principles involved in production of precision technical plans, blueprints, drawings, and models. **Production and Processing:** Raw materials, production processes, quality control, costs, and other techniques for maximizing the effective manufacture and distribution of goods. **Public Safety and Security:** Relevant equipment, policies, procedures, and strategies to promote effective local, state, or national security operations for the protection of people, data, property, and institutions.

WORK ENVIRONMENT—Outdoors; noisy; very hot or cold; contaminants; whole-body vibration; using hands on objects, tools, or controls.

Oral and Maxillofacial Surgeons

- ◎ Education/Training Required: First professional degree
- ◎ Annual Earnings: More than $145,600
- ◎ Growth: 16.2%
- ◎ Annual Job Openings: Fewer than 500
- ◎ Self-Employed: 15.7%
- ◎ Part-Time: 22.4%

Perform surgery on mouth, jaws, and related head and neck structure to execute difficult and multiple extractions of teeth, to remove tumors and other abnormal growths, to correct abnormal jaw relations by mandibular or maxillary revision, to prepare mouth for insertion of dental prosthesis, or to treat fractured jaws. Administer general and local anesthetics. Remove impacted, damaged, and non-restorable teeth. Evaluate the position of the wisdom teeth in order to determine whether problems exist currently or might occur in the future. Collaborate with other professionals such as restorative dentists and orthodontists in order to plan treatment. Perform surgery to prepare the mouth for dental implants and to aid in the regeneration of deficient bone and gum tissues. Remove tumors and other abnormal growths of the oral and facial regions, using surgical instruments. Treat infections of the oral cavity, salivary glands, jaws, and neck. Treat problems affecting the oral mucosa such as mouth ulcers and infections. Provide emergency treatment of facial injuries, including facial lacerations, intra-oral lacerations, and fractured facial bones. Perform surgery on the mouth and jaws in order to treat conditions such as cleft lip and palate and jaw growth problems. Restore form and function by moving skin, bone, nerves, and other tissues from other parts of the body in order to reconstruct the jaws and face. Perform minor cosmetic procedures, such as chin and cheek-bone enhancements, and minor facial rejuvenation procedures, including the use of Botox and laser technology. Treat snoring problems, using laser surgery.

LEVEL OF ACTIVITY (out of 100)—General Physical Activity: 55.0. **Sitting:** 43.7. **Outdoors:** 14.7.

SKILLS—Science; Management of Financial Resources; Service Orientation; Equipment Selection; Management of Personnel Resources; Active Learning; Complex Problem Solving; Coordination.

GOE—Interest Area: 08. Health Science. **Work Group:** 08.03. Dentistry. **Other Jobs in This Work Group:** Dental Assistants; Dental Hygienists; Dentists, General; Orthodontists; Prosthodontists. **PERSONALITY TYPE:** Investigative. Investigative occupations frequently involve working with ideas and require an extensive amount of thinking. These occupations can involve searching for facts and figuring out problems mentally.

EDUCATION/TRAINING PROGRAM(S)— Oral/Maxillofacial Surgery (Cert, MS, PhD);

Dental/Oral Surgery Specialty. **RELATED KNOWLEDGE/COURSES—Medicine and Dentistry:** The information and techniques needed to diagnose and treat human injuries, diseases, and deformities. This includes symptoms, treatment alternatives, drug properties and interactions, and preventive health-care measures. **Biology:** Plant and animal organisms and their tissues, cells, functions, interdependencies, and interactions with each other and the environment. **Therapy and Counseling:** Principles, methods, and procedures for diagnosis, treatment, and rehabilitation of physical and mental dysfunctions and for career counseling and guidance. **Chemistry:** The chemical composition, structure, and properties of substances and of the chemical processes and transformations that they undergo. This includes uses of chemicals and their danger signs, production techniques, and disposal methods. **Customer and Personal Service:** Principles and processes for providing customer and personal services. This includes customer needs assessment, meeting quality standards for services, and evaluation of customer satisfaction. **Psychology:** Human behavior and performance; individual differences in ability, personality, and interests; learning and motivation; psychological research methods; and the assessment and treatment of behavioral and affective disorders.

WORK ENVIRONMENT—Indoors; disease or infections; standing; using hands on objects, tools, or controls; bending or twisting the body; repetitive motions.

Orthotists and Prosthetists

- ◉ Education/Training Required: Bachelor's degree
- ◉ Annual Earnings: $53,760
- ◉ Growth: 18.0%
- ◉ Annual Job Openings: Fewer than 500
- ◉ Self-Employed: 14.4%
- ◉ Part-Time: 18.2%

Assist patients with disabling conditions of limbs and spine or with partial or total absence of limb by fitting and preparing orthopedic braces or prostheses. Examine, interview, and measure patients in order to determine their appliance needs and to identify factors that could affect appliance fit. Fit, test, and evaluate devices on patients and make adjustments for proper fit, function, and comfort. Instruct patients in the use and care of orthoses and prostheses. Design orthopedic and prosthetic devices based on physicians' prescriptions and examination and measurement of patients. Maintain patients' records. Make and modify plaster casts of areas that will be fitted with prostheses or orthoses for use in the device construction process. Select materials and components to be used based on device design. Confer with physicians in order to formulate specifications and prescriptions for orthopedic and/or prosthetic devices. Repair, rebuild, and modify prosthetic and orthopedic appliances. Construct and fabricate appliances or supervise others who are constructing the appliances. Train and supervise orthopedic and prosthetic assistants and technicians and other support staff. Update skills and knowledge by attending conferences and seminars. Show and explain orthopedic and prosthetic appliances to healthcare workers. Research new ways to construct and use orthopedic and prosthetic devices. Publish research findings and present them at conferences and seminars.

LEVEL OF ACTIVITY (out of 100)—General Physical Activity: 46.7. **Sitting:** 39.0. **Outdoors:** 20.3.

SKILLS—Technology Design; Management of Financial Resources; Management of Material Resources; Service Orientation; Management of Personnel Resources; Operations Analysis; Social Perceptiveness; Equipment Selection.

GOE—Interest Area: 08. Health Science. **Work Group:** 08.06. Medical Technology. **Other Jobs in This Work Group:** Biological Technicians; Cardiovascular Technologists and Technicians; Diagnostic Medical Sonographers; Medical and Clinical Laboratory Technicians; Medical and Clinical Laboratory Technologists; Medical Equipment Preparers; Medical Records and Health Information Technicians; Nuclear Medicine Technologists; Opticians, Dispensing; Radiologic Technicians; Radiologic Technologists; Radiologic Technologists and Technicians. **PERSONALITY TYPE:** Social. Social occupations frequently involve working with, communicating with, and teaching people. These occupations often involve helping or providing service to others.

EDUCATION/TRAINING PROGRAM(S)—Orthotist/Prosthetist; Assistive/Augmentative Technology and Rehabiliation Engineering. **RELATED KNOWLEDGE/COURSES— Engineering and Technology:** The practical application of engineering science and technology. This includes applying principles, techniques, procedures, and equipment to the design and production of various goods and services. **Medicine and Dentistry:** The information and techniques needed to diagnose and treat human injuries, diseases, and deformities. This includes symptoms, treatment alternatives, drug properties and interactions, and preventive health-care measures. **Design:** Design techniques, tools, and principles involved in production of precision technical plans, blueprints, drawings, and models. **Therapy and Counseling:** Principles, methods, and procedures for diagnosis, treatment, and rehabilitation of physical and mental dysfunctions and for career counseling and guidance. **Psychology:** Human behavior and performance; individual differences in ability, personality, and interests; learning and motivation; psychological research methods; and the assessment and treatment of behavioral and affective disorders. **Production and Processing:** Raw materials, production processes, quality control, costs, and other techniques for maximizing the effective manufacture and distribution of goods.

WORK ENVIRONMENT—Indoors; noisy; contaminants; disease or infections; hazardous equipment; using hands on objects, tools, or controls.

Outdoor Power Equipment and Other Small Engine Mechanics

- Education/Training Required: Moderate-term on-the-job training
- Annual Earnings: $25,810
- Growth: 14.0%
- Annual Job Openings: 10,000
- Self-Employed: 19.2%
- Part-Time: 13.2%

Diagnose, adjust, repair, or overhaul small engines used to power lawn mowers, chain saws, and related equipment. Reassemble engines after repair or maintenance work is complete. Sell parts and equipment. Show customers how to maintain equipment. Record repairs made, time spent, and parts used. Grind, ream, rebore, and retap parts to obtain specified clearances, using grinders, lathes, taps, reamers, boring machines, and micrometers. Test and inspect engines to determine malfunctions, to locate missing and broken parts, and to verify repairs, using diagnostic instruments. Replace motors. Repair or replace defective parts such as magnetos, water pumps, gears, pistons, and carburetors, using hand tools. Remove engines from equipment and position and bolt engines to repair stands. Perform routine maintenance such as cleaning and oiling parts, honing cylinders, and tuning ignition systems. Obtain problem descriptions from customers and prepare cost estimates for repairs. Dismantle engines, using hand tools, and examine parts for defects. Adjust points, valves, carburetors, distributors, and spark plug gaps, using feeler gauges. Repair and maintain gasoline engines used to power equipment such as portable saws, lawn mowers, generators, and compressors.

LEVEL OF ACTIVITY (out of 100)—General Physical Activity: 45.1. **Sitting:** 31.4. **Outdoors:** 34.3.

SKILLS—Repairing; Equipment Maintenance; Troubleshooting; Installation; Quality Control Analysis; Operation Monitoring; Operation and Control.

GOE—Interest Area: 13. Manufacturing. **Work Group:** 13.14. Vehicle and Facility Mechanical Work. **Other Jobs in This Work Group:** Aircraft Mechanics and Service Technicians; Aircraft Structure, Surfaces, Rigging, and Systems Assemblers; Automotive Body and Related Repairers; Automotive Glass Installers and Repairers; Automotive Master Mechanics; Automotive Service Technicians and Mechanics; Automotive Specialty Technicians; Bus and Truck Mechanics and Diesel Engine Specialists; Farm Equipment Mechanics; Fiberglass Laminators and Fabricators; Mobile Heavy Equipment Mechanics, Except Engines; Motorboat Mechanics; Motorcycle Mechanics; Rail Car Repairers; Recreational Vehicle Service Technicians; Tire Repairers and Changers. **PERSONALITY TYPE:** Realistic. Realistic occupations frequently involve work activities that include practical, hands-on problems and solutions. They often deal with plants; animals; and

real-world materials like wood, tools, and machinery. Many of the occupations require working outside and do not involve a lot of paperwork or working closely with others.

EDUCATION/TRAINING PROGRAM(S)— Small Engine Mechanics and Repair Technology/Technician. **RELATED KNOWLEDGE/COURSES—Mechanical Devices:** Machines and tools, including their designs, uses, repair, and maintenance. **Engineering and Technology:** The practical application of engineering science and technology. This includes applying principles, techniques, procedures, and equipment to the design and production of various goods and services.

WORK ENVIRONMENT—Indoors; contaminants; hazardous equipment; standing; kneeling, crouching, stooping, or crawling; using hands on objects, tools, or controls.

Painters, Construction and Maintenance

- ◉ Education/Training Required: Moderate-term on-the-job training
- ◉ Annual Earnings: $30,800
- ◉ Growth: 12.6%
- ◉ Annual Job Openings: 102,000
- ◉ Self-Employed: 44.6%
- ◉ Part-Time: 15.0%

Paint walls, equipment, buildings, bridges, and other structural surfaces, using brushes, rollers, and spray guns. May remove old paint to pre-

pare surface prior to painting. **May mix colors or oils to obtain desired color or consistency.** Bake finishes on painted and enameled articles, using baking ovens. Cut stencils and brush and spray lettering and decorations on surfaces. Erect scaffolding and swing gates or set up ladders to work above ground level. Select and purchase tools and finishes for surfaces to be covered, considering durability, ease of handling, methods of application, and customers' wishes. Spray or brush hot plastics or pitch onto surfaces. Smooth surfaces, using sandpaper, scrapers, brushes, steel wool, and/or sanding machines. Waterproof buildings, using waterproofers and caulking. Remove old finishes by stripping, sanding, wire brushing, burning, or using water and/or abrasive blasting. Use special finishing techniques such as sponging, ragging, layering, or faux finishing. Calculate amounts of required materials and estimate costs based on surface measurements and/or work orders. Wash and treat surfaces with oil, turpentine, mildew remover, or other preparations and sand rough spots to ensure that finishes will adhere properly. Apply primers or sealers to prepare new surfaces, such as bare wood or metal, for finish coats. Cover surfaces with drop cloths or masking tape and paper to protect surfaces during painting. Fill cracks, holes, and joints with caulk, putty, plaster, or other fillers, using caulking guns or putty knives. Mix and match colors of paint, stain, or varnish with oil and thinning and drying additives in order to obtain desired colors and consistencies. Polish final coats to specified finishes. Read work orders or receive instructions from supervisors or homeowners in order to determine work requirements. Remove fixtures such as pictures, door knobs, lamps, and electric switch covers prior to painting. Apply paint, stain, varnish, enamel, and other finishes to equipment, buildings, bridges, and/or other structures, using brushes, spray guns, or rollers.

LEVEL OF ACTIVITY (out of 100)—General Physical Activity: 59.4. **Sitting:** 25.7. **Outdoors:** 45.7.

SKILLS—None met the criteria.

GOE—Interest Area: 02. Architecture and Construction. **Work Group:** 02.04. Construction Crafts. **Other Jobs in This Work Group:** Boilermakers; Brickmasons and Blockmasons; Carpet Installers; Cement Masons and Concrete Finishers; Commercial Divers; Construction Carpenters; Crane and Tower Operators; Drywall and Ceiling Tile Installers; Electricians; Fence Erectors; Floor Layers, Except Carpet, Wood, and Hard Tiles; Floor Sanders and Finishers; Glaziers; Hazardous Materials Removal Workers; Insulation Workers, Floor, Ceiling, and Wall; Insulation Workers, Mechanical; Manufactured Building and Mobile Home Installers; Operating Engineers and Other Construction Equipment Operators; Paperhangers; Paving, Surfacing, and Tamping Equipment Operators; Pile-Driver Operators; Pipe Fitters and Steamfitters; Pipelayers; Plasterers and Stucco Masons; Plumbers; Plumbers, Pipefitters, and Steamfitters; Rail-Track Laying and Maintenance Equipment Operators; Refractory Materials Repairers, Except Brickmasons; Reinforcing Iron and Rebar Workers; Riggers; Roofers; Rough Carpenters; Security and Fire Alarm Systems Installers; Segmental Pavers; Sheet Metal Workers; Stone Cutters and Carvers, Manufacturing; Stonemasons; Structural Iron and Steel Workers; Tapers; Terrazzo Workers and Finishers; Tile and Marble Setters. **PERSONALITY TYPE:** Realistic. Realistic occupations frequently involve work activities that include practical, hands-on problems and solutions. They often deal with plants; animals; and real-world materials like wood, tools, and machinery. Many of the occupations require working outside and do not involve a lot of paperwork or working closely with others.

EDUCATION/TRAINING PROGRAM(S)—Painting/Painter and Wall Coverer. **RELATED KNOWLEDGE/COURSES—Building and Construction:** The materials, methods, and tools involved in the construction or repair of houses, buildings, or other structures such as highways and roads. **Fine Arts:** The theory and techniques required to compose, produce, and perform works of music, dance, visual arts, drama, and sculpture.

WORK ENVIRONMENT—Indoors; contaminants; high places; standing; using hands on objects, tools, or controls; repetitive motions.

Painters, Transportation Equipment

- Education/Training Required: Moderate-term on-the-job training
- Annual Earnings: $34,840
- Growth: 14.1%
- Annual Job Openings: 10,000
- Self-Employed: 5.4%
- Part-Time: 5.7%

Operate or tend painting machines to paint surfaces of transportation equipment, such as automobiles, buses, trucks, trains, boats, and airplanes. Dispose of hazardous waste in an appropriate manner. Select paint according to company requirements and match colors of paint following specified color charts. Mix paints to match color specifications or vehicles' original colors and then stir and thin the paints, using spatulas or power mixing equipment. Remove grease, dirt, paint, and rust from vehicle surfaces in preparation for paint application, using abrasives, solvents, brushes, blowtorches, washing tanks, or sandblasters. Pour paint into spray guns and adjust nozzles and paint mixes in order to get the proper paint flow and coating thickness. Monitor painting operations in order to identify flaws such as blisters and streaks so that their causes can be corrected. Sand vehicle surfaces between coats of paint and/or primer in order to remove flaws and enhance adhesion for subsequent coats. Disassemble, clean, and reassemble sprayers and power equipment, using solvents, wire brushes, and cloths for cleaning duties. Remove accessories from vehicles, such as chrome or mirrors, and mask other surfaces with tape or paper in order to protect them from paint. Spray prepared surfaces with specified amounts of primers and decorative or finish coatings. Allow the sprayed product to dry and then touch up any spots that may have been missed. Apply rust-resistant undercoats and caulk and seal seams. Select the correct spray gun system for the material being applied. Apply primer over any repairs made to vehicle surfaces. Adjust controls on infrared ovens, heat lamps, portable ventilators, and exhaust units in order to speed the drying of vehicles between coats. Fill small dents and scratches with body fillers and smooth surfaces in order to prepare vehicles for painting. Apply designs, lettering, or other identifying or decorative items to finished products, using paint brushes or paint sprayers. Paint by hand areas that cannot be reached with a spray gun or those that need retouching, using brushes. Sand the final finish and apply sealer once a vehicle has dried properly. Buff and wax the finished paintwork. Lay out logos, symbols, or designs on painted surfaces according to blueprint specifications, using measuring instruments, stencils, and patterns.

LEVEL OF ACTIVITY (out of 100)—General Physical Activity: 63.3. **Sitting:** 21.1. **Outdoors:** 29.7.

SKILLS—Equipment Maintenance; Repairing; Monitoring; Technology Design; Operation and Control; Coordination; Equipment Selection; Active Learning.

GOE—**Interest Area:** 13. Manufacturing. **Work Group:** 13.09. Hands-On Work, Assorted Materials. **Other Jobs in This Work Group:** Coil Winders, Tapers, and Finishers; Cutters and Trimmers, Hand; Fabric and Apparel Patternmakers; Glass Blowers, Molders, Benders, and Finishers; Grinding and Polishing Workers, Hand; Molding and Casting Workers; Painting, Coating, and Decorating Workers; Sewers, Hand. **PERSONALITY TYPE:** Realistic. Realistic occupations frequently involve work activities that include practical, hands-on problems and solutions. They often deal with plants; animals; and real-world materials like wood, tools, and machinery. Many of the occupations require working outside and do not involve a lot of paperwork or working closely with others.

EDUCATION/TRAINING PROGRAM(S)—Auto Body/Collision and Repair Technology/Technician. **RELATED KNOWLEDGE/COURSES**—**Chemistry:** The chemical composition, structure, and properties of substances and of the chemical processes and transformations that they undergo. This includes uses of chemicals and their danger signs, production techniques, and disposal methods. **Production and Processing:** Raw materials, production processes, quality control, costs, and other techniques for maximizing the effective manufacture and distribution of goods. **Mechanical Devices:**

Machines and tools, including their designs, uses, repair, and maintenance.

WORK ENVIRONMENT—Noisy; contaminants; hazardous conditions; standing; using hands on objects, tools, or controls; repetitive motions.

Paper Goods Machine Setters, Operators, and Tenders

- Education/Training Required: Moderate-term on-the-job training
- Annual Earnings: $31,160
- Growth: 2.4%
- Annual Job Openings: 15,000
- Self-Employed: 0.7%
- Part-Time: 4.1%

Set up, operate, or tend paper goods machines that perform a variety of functions, such as converting, sawing, corrugating, banding, wrapping, boxing, stitching, forming, or sealing paper or paperboard sheets into products. Cut products to specified dimensions, using hand or power cutters. Stamp products with information such as dates, using hand stamps or automatic stamping devices. Lift tote boxes of finished cartons and dump cartons into feed hoppers. Disassemble machines to maintain, repair, or replace broken or worn parts, using hand or power tools. Start machines and move controls to regulate tension on pressure rolls, to synchronize speed of machine components, and to adjust temperatures of glue or paraffin. Observe operation of various machines to detect and correct machine malfunctions such as improper forming, glue flow, or pasteboard tension. Remove finished cores and stack or place them on conveyors for transfer to other work areas. Adjust guide assemblies, forming bars, and folding mechanisms according to specifications, using hand tools. Examine completed work to detect defects and verify conformance to work orders and adjust machinery as necessary to correct production problems. Fill glue and paraffin reservoirs and position rollers to dispense glue onto paperboard. Install attachments to machines for gluing, folding, printing, or cutting. Load automatic stapling mechanisms. Measure, space, and set saw blades, cutters, and perforators according to product specifications. Monitor finished cartons as they drop from forming machines into rotating hoppers and then into gravity feed chutes in order to prevent jamming. Place rolls of paper or cardboard on machine feedtracks and thread paper through gluing, coating, and slitting rollers.

LEVEL OF ACTIVITY (out of 100)—General Physical Activity: 47.6. **Sitting:** 40.0. **Outdoors:** 14.3.

SKILLS—Operation Monitoring; Operation and Control; Installation; Equipment Maintenance; Repairing; Quality Control Analysis; Troubleshooting.

GOE—Interest Area: 13. Manufacturing. **Work Group:** 13.02. Machine Setup and Operation. **Other Jobs in This Work Group:** Crushing, Grinding, and Polishing Machine Setters, Operators, and Tenders; Cutting, Punching, and Press Machine Setters, Operators, and Tenders, Metal and Plastic; Drilling and Boring Machine Tool Setters, Operators, and Tenders, Metal and Plastic; Extruding and Drawing Machine Setters, Operators, and Tenders, Metal and Plastic; Forging Machine Setters, Operators, and Tenders, Metal and Plastic; Grinding, Lapping, Polishing, and Buffing Machine Tool Setters, Operators, and Tenders, Metal and Plastic; Lathe and Turning Machine Tool Setters, Operators, and Tenders, Metal and Plastic; Milling and Planing Machine Setters, Operators, and Tenders, Metal and Plastic; Multiple Machine Tool Setters, Operators, and Tenders, Metal and Plastic; Rolling Machine Setters, Operators, and Tenders, Metal and Plastic; Textile Cutting Machine Setters, Operators, and Tenders; Textile Knitting and Weaving Machine Setters, Operators, and Tenders; Textile Winding, Twisting, and Drawing Out Machine Setters, Operators, and Tenders. **PERSONALITY TYPE:** Realistic. Realistic occupations frequently involve work activities that include practical, hands-on problems and solutions. They often deal with plants; animals; and real-world materials like wood, tools, and machinery. Many of the occupations require working outside and do not involve a lot of paperwork or working closely with others.

EDUCATION/TRAINING PROGRAM(S)—No related CIP programs; this job is learned through informal moderate-term on-the-job training. **RELATED KNOWLEDGE/ COURSES—Mechanical Devices:** Machines and tools, including their designs, uses, repair, and maintenance. **Production and Processing:** Raw materials, production processes, quality control, costs, and other techniques for maximizing the effective manufacture and distribution of goods.

WORK ENVIRONMENT—Indoors; noisy; hazardous equipment; standing; using hands on objects, tools, or controls.

Park Naturalists

This job can be found in the Part I lists under the title Conservation Scientists.

- ◎ Education/Training Required: Bachelor's degree
- ◎ Annual Earnings: $53,350
- ◎ Growth: 6.3%
- ◎ Annual Job Openings: 2,000
- ◎ Self-Employed: 9.0%
- ◎ Part-Time: 6.7%

The job openings listed here are shared with Range Managers and with Soil and Water Conservationists.

Plan, develop, and conduct programs to inform public of historical, natural, and scientific features of national, state, or local park. Provide visitor services by explaining regulations; answering visitor requests, needs, and complaints; and providing information about the park and surrounding areas. Conduct field trips to point out scientific, historic, and natural features of parks, forests, historic sites, or other attractions. Prepare and present illustrated lectures and interpretive talks about park features. Perform emergency duties to protect human life, government property, and natural features of park. Confer with park staff to determine subjects and schedules for park programs. Assist with operations of general facilities, such as visitor centers. Plan, organize, and direct activities of seasonal staff members. Perform routine maintenance on park structures. Prepare brochures and write newspaper articles. Construct historical, scientific, and nature visi-tor-center displays. Research stories regarding the area's natural history or environment. Interview specialists in desired fields to obtain and develop data for park information programs. Compile and maintain official park photographic and information files. Take photographs and motion pictures for use in lectures and publications and to develop displays. Survey park to determine forest conditions and distribution and abundance of fauna and flora. Plan and develop audiovisual devices for public programs.

LEVEL OF ACTIVITY (out of 100)—General Physical Activity: 71.1. **Sitting:** 44.0. **Outdoors:** 45.8.

SKILLS—Management of Personnel Resources; Management of Financial Resources; Service Orientation; Writing; Persuasion; Management of Material Resources; Instructing; Science.

GOE—Interest Area: 01. Agriculture and Natural Resources. **Work Group:** 01.01. Managerial Work in Agriculture and Natural Resources. **Other Jobs in This Work Group:** Aquacultural Managers; Crop and Livestock Managers; Farm Labor Contractors; Farm, Ranch, and Other Agricultural Managers; Farmers and Ranchers; First-Line Supervisors/ Managers of Agricultural Crop and Horticultural Workers; First-Line Supervisors/ Managers of Animal Husbandry and Animal Care Workers; First-Line Supervisors/Managers of Aquacultural Workers; First-Line Supervisors/ Managers of Construction Trades and Extraction Workers; First-Line Supervisors/ Managers of Farming, Fishing, and Forestry Workers; First-Line Supervisors/Managers of Landscaping, Lawn Service, and Groundskeeping Workers; First-Line Supervisors/Managers of Logging Workers; Nursery and Greenhouse

Managers; Purchasing Agents and Buyers, Farm Products. **PERSONALITY TYPE:** Social. Social occupations frequently involve working with, communicating with, and teaching people. These occupations often involve helping or providing service to others.

EDUCATION/TRAINING PROGRAM(S)— Natural Resources/Conservation, General; Water, Wetlands, and Marine Resources Management; Land Use Planning and Management/Development; Natural Resources Management and Policy, Other; Forestry, General; Forest Sciences and Biology; Forest Management/Forest Resources Management; Forestry, Other; Wildlife and Wildlands Science and Management; Natural Resources and Conservation, Other. **RELATED KNOWL-EDGE/COURSES—Biology:** Plant and animal organisms and their tissues, cells, functions, interdependencies, and interactions with each other and the environment. **History and Archeology:** Historical events and their causes, indicators, and effects on civilizations and cultures. **Geography:** Principles and methods for describing the features of land, sea, and air masses, including their physical characteristics; locations; interrelationships; and distribution of plant, animal, and human life. **Customer and Personal Service:** Principles and processes for providing customer and personal services. This includes customer needs assessment, meeting quality standards for services, and evaluation of customer satisfaction. **Sociology and Anthropology:** Group behavior and dynamics, societal trends and influences, human migrations, ethnicity, and cultures and their history and origins. **Communications and Media:** Media production, communication, and dissemination techniques and methods. This includes alternative ways to inform and entertain via written, oral, and visual media.

WORK ENVIRONMENT—More often indoors than outdoors; very hot or cold; minor burns, cuts, bites, or stings; sitting; using hands on objects, tools, or controls.

Paving, Surfacing, and Tamping Equipment Operators

- Education/Training Required: Moderate-term on-the-job training
- Annual Earnings: $30,320
- Growth: 15.6%
- Annual Job Openings: 7,000
- Self-Employed: 1.2%
- Part-Time: 6.3%

Operate equipment used for applying concrete, asphalt, or other materials to roadbeds, parking lots, or airport runways and taxiways or equipment used for tamping gravel, dirt, or other materials. Includes concrete and asphalt paving machine operators, form tampers, tamping machine operators, and stone spreader operators. Start machine, engage clutch, and push and move levers to guide machine along forms or guidelines and to control the operation of machine attachments. Operate machines to spread, smooth, level, or steel-reinforce stone, concrete, or asphalt on roadbeds. Inspect, clean, maintain, and repair equipment, using mechanics' hand tools, or report malfunctions to supervisors. Operate oil distributors, loaders, chip spreaders, dump trucks, and snowplows.

Coordinate truck dumping. Set up and tear down equipment. Operate tamping machines or manually roll surfaces to compact earth fills, foundation forms, and finished road materials according to grade specifications. Shovel blacktop. Drive machines onto truck trailers and drive trucks to transport machines and material to and from job sites. Observe distribution of paving material to adjust machine settings or material flow and indicate low spots for workers to add material. Light burners or start heating units of machines and regulate screed temperatures and asphalt flow rates. Control paving machines to push dump trucks and to maintain a constant flow of asphalt or other material into hoppers or screeds. Set up forms and lay out guidelines for curbs according to written specifications, using string, spray paint, and concrete/water mixes. Fill tanks, hoppers, or machines with paving materials. Drive and operate curbing machines to extrude concrete or asphalt curbing. Cut or break up pavement and drive guardrail posts, using machines equipped with interchangeable hammers. Install dies, cutters, and extensions to screeds onto machines, using hand tools. Operate machines that clean or cut expansion joints in concrete or asphalt and that rout out cracks in pavement. Place strips of material such as cork, asphalt, or steel into joints or place rolls of expansion-joint material on machines that automatically insert material.

LEVEL OF ACTIVITY (out of 100)—General Physical Activity: 70.7. **Sitting:** 38.9. **Outdoors:** 53.6.

SKILLS—Operation Monitoring; Equipment Maintenance; Operation and Control; Repairing; Installation; Equipment Selection; Troubleshooting; Technology Design.

GOE—Interest Area: 02. Architecture and Construction. **Work Group:** 02.04. Construction Crafts. **Other Jobs in This Work Group:** Boilermakers; Brickmasons and Blockmasons; Carpet Installers; Cement Masons and Concrete Finishers; Commercial Divers; Construction Carpenters; Crane and Tower Operators; Drywall and Ceiling Tile Installers; Electricians; Fence Erectors; Floor Layers, Except Carpet, Wood, and Hard Tiles; Floor Sanders and Finishers; Glaziers; Hazardous Materials Removal Workers; Insulation Workers, Floor, Ceiling, and Wall; Insulation Workers, Mechanical; Manufactured Building and Mobile Home Installers; Operating Engineers and Other Construction Equipment Operators; Painters, Construction and Maintenance; Paperhangers; Pile-Driver Operators; Pipe Fitters and Steamfitters; Pipelayers; Plasterers and Stucco Masons; Plumbers; Plumbers, Pipefitters, and Steamfitters; Rail-Track Laying and Maintenance Equipment Operators; Refractory Materials Repairers, Except Brickmasons; Reinforcing Iron and Rebar Workers; Riggers; Roofers; Rough Carpenters; Security and Fire Alarm Systems Installers; Segmental Pavers; Sheet Metal Workers; Stone Cutters and Carvers, Manufacturing; Stonemasons; Structural Iron and Steel Workers; Tapers; Terrazzo Workers and Finishers; Tile and Marble Setters. **PERSONALITY TYPE:** Realistic. Realistic occupations frequently involve work activities that include practical, hands-on problems and solutions. They often deal with plants; animals; and real-world materials like wood, tools, and machinery. Many of the occupations require working outside and do not involve a lot of paperwork or working closely with others.

EDUCATION/TRAINING PROGRAM(S)—Construction/Heavy Equipment/Earthmoving Equipment Operation. **RELATED KNOWLEDGE/COURSES—Building and Construction:** The materials, methods, and tools involved in the construction or repair of houses, buildings, or other structures such as highways and roads. **Mechanical Devices:** Machines and tools, including their designs, uses, repair, and maintenance. **Transportation:** Principles and methods for moving people or goods by air, rail, sea, or road, including the relative costs and benefits. **Public Safety and Security:** Relevant equipment, policies, procedures, and strategies to promote effective local, state, or national security operations for the protection of people, data, property, and institutions. **Engineering and Technology:** The practical application of engineering science and technology. This includes applying principles, techniques, procedures, and equipment to the design and production of various goods and services. **Administration and Management:** Business and management principles involved in strategic planning, resource allocation, human resources modeling, leadership technique, production methods, and coordination of people and resources.

WORK ENVIRONMENT—Outdoors; noisy; very hot or cold; contaminants; hazardous equipment; using hands on objects, tools, or controls.

Pest Control Workers

- Education/Training Required: Moderate-term on-the-job training
- Annual Earnings: $27,170
- Growth: 18.4%
- Annual Job Openings: 4,000
- Self-Employed: 9.7%
- Part-Time: 6.0%

Spray or release chemical solutions or toxic gases and set traps to kill pests and vermin, such as mice, termites, and roaches, that infest buildings and surrounding areas. Record work activities performed. Inspect premises to identify infestation source and extent of damage to property, wall and roof porosity, and access to infested locations. Spray or dust chemical solutions, powders, or gases into rooms; onto clothing, furnishings, or wood; and over marshlands, ditches, and catch-basins. Clean worksite after completion of job. Direct and/or assist other workers in treatment and extermination processes to eliminate and control rodents, insects, and weeds. Drive truck equipped with power spraying equipment. Measure area dimensions requiring treatment, using rule; calculate fumigant requirements; and estimate cost for service. Post warning signs and lock building doors to secure

P

area to be fumigated. Cut or bore openings in building or surrounding concrete, access infested areas, insert nozzle, and inject pesticide to impregnate ground. Study preliminary reports and diagrams of infested area and determine treatment type required to eliminate and prevent recurrence of infestation. Dig up and burn weeds or spray them with herbicides. Set mechanical traps and place poisonous paste or bait in sewers, burrows, and ditches. Clean and remove blockages from infested areas to facilitate spraying procedure and provide drainage, using broom, mop, shovel, and rake. Position and fasten edges of tarpaulins over building and tape vents to ensure airtight environment and check for leaks.

LEVEL OF ACTIVITY (out of 100)—General Physical Activity: 67.4. **Sitting:** 36.6. **Outdoors:** 51.0.

SKILLS—Persuasion; Service Orientation; Social Perceptiveness; Active Learning; Equipment Selection; Management of Material Resources; Time Management; Coordination.

GOE—**Interest Area:** 01. Agriculture and Natural Resources. **Work Group:** 01.05. Nursery, Groundskeeping, and Pest Control. **Other Jobs in This Work Group:** Landscaping and Groundskeeping Workers; Nursery Workers; Pesticide Handlers, Sprayers, and Applicators, Vegetation; Tree Trimmers and Pruners. **PERSONALITY TYPE:** Realistic. Realistic occupations frequently involve work activities that include practical, hands-on problems and solutions. They often deal with plants; animals; and real-world materials like wood, tools, and machinery. Many of the occupations require working outside and do not involve a lot of paperwork or working closely with others.

EDUCATION/TRAINING PROGRAM(S)—Agricultural/Farm Supplies Retailing and Wholesaling. **RELATED KNOWLEDGE/COURSES**—**Sales and Marketing:** Principles and methods for showing, promoting, and selling products or services. This includes marketing strategy and tactics, product demonstration, sales techniques, and sales control systems. **Chemistry:** The chemical composition, structure, and properties of substances and of the chemical processes and transformations that they undergo. This includes uses of chemicals and their danger signs, production techniques, and disposal methods. **Biology:** Plant and animal organisms and their tissues, cells, functions, interdependencies, and interactions with each other and the environment. **Customer and Personal Service:** Principles and processes for providing customer and personal services. This includes customer needs assessment, meeting quality standards for services, and evaluation of customer satisfaction. **Education and Training:** Principles and methods for curriculum and training design, teaching and instruction for individuals and groups, and the measurement of training effects. **Building and Construction:** The materials, methods, and tools involved in the construction or repair of houses, buildings, or other structures such as highways and roads.

WORK ENVIRONMENT—More often outdoors than indoors; very hot or cold; contaminants; hazardous conditions; using hands on objects, tools, or controls.

Pesticide Handlers, Sprayers, and Applicators, Vegetation

- ◎ Education/Training Required:
  Moderate-term on-the-job training
- ◎ Annual Earnings: $26,120
- ◎ Growth: 16.6%
- ◎ Annual Job Openings: 6,000
- ◎ Self-Employed: 19.6%
- ◎ Part-Time: 6.0%

Mix or apply pesticides, herbicides, fungicides, or insecticides through sprays; dusts; vapors; soil incorporation; or chemical application on trees, shrubs, lawns, or botanical crops. Usually requires specific training and state or federal certification. Fill sprayer tanks with water and chemicals according to formulas. Provide driving instructions to truck drivers to ensure complete coverage of designated areas, using hand and horn signals. Plant grass with seed spreaders and operate straw blowers to cover seeded areas with mixtures of asphalt and straw. Start motors and engage machinery, such as sprayer agitators and pumps or portable spray equipment. Cover areas to specified depths with pesticides, applying knowledge of weather conditions, droplet sizes, elevation-to-distance ratios, and obstructions. Connect hoses and nozzles selected according to terrain, distribution pattern requirements, types of infestations, and velocities. Clean and service machinery to ensure operating efficiency, using water, gasoline, lubricants, and/or hand tools. Lift, push, and swing nozzles, hoses, and tubes in order to direct spray over designated areas. Mix pesticides, herbicides, and fungicides for application to trees, shrubs, lawns, or botanical crops.

LEVEL OF ACTIVITY (out of 100)—General Physical Activity: 57.1. **Sitting:** 28.6. **Outdoors:** 65.7.

SKILLS—Operation and Control; Equipment Maintenance.

GOE—Interest Area: 01. Agriculture and Natural Resources. **Work Group:** 01.05. Nursery, Groundskeeping, and Pest Control. **Other Jobs in This Work Group:** Landscaping and Groundskeeping Workers; Nursery Workers; Pest Control Workers; Tree Trimmers and Pruners. **PERSONALITY TYPE:** Realistic. Realistic occupations frequently involve work activities that include practical, hands-on problems and solutions. They often deal with plants; animals; and real-world materials like wood, tools, and machinery. Many of the occupations require working outside and do not involve a lot of paperwork or working closely with others.

EDUCATION/TRAINING PROGRAM(S)—Landscaping and Groundskeeping; Plant Nursery Operations and Management; Turf and Turfgrass Management. **RELATED KNOWLEDGE/COURSES—Chemistry:** The chemical composition, structure, and properties of substances and of the chemical processes and transformations that they undergo. This includes uses of chemicals and their danger signs, production techniques, and disposal methods. **Mechanical Devices:** Machines and tools, including their designs, uses, repair, and maintenance. **Engineering and Technology:** The practical application of engineering science and technology. This includes applying principles, techniques, procedures, and equipment to the design and production of various goods and services.

P

WORK ENVIRONMENT—Outdoors; contaminants; hazardous conditions; standing; using hands on objects, tools, or controls.

Petroleum Pump System Operators, Refinery Operators, and Gaugers

- ◉ Education/Training Required: Long-term on-the-job training
- ◉ Annual Earnings: $51,060
- ◉ Growth: –8.6%
- ◉ Annual Job Openings: 6,000
- ◉ Self-Employed: 0.1%
- ◉ Part-Time: 0.8%

Control the operation of petroleum-refining or -processing units. May specialize in controlling manifold and pumping systems, gauging or testing oil in storage tanks, or regulating the flow of oil into pipelines. Calculate test result values, using standard formulas. Clamp seals around valves to secure tanks. Signal other workers by telephone or radio to operate pumps, open and close valves, and check temperatures. Start pumps and open valves or use automated equipment to regulate the flow of oil in pipelines and into and out of tanks. Synchronize activities with other pumphouses to ensure a continuous flow of products and a minimum of contamination between products. Verify that incoming and outgoing products are moving through the correct meters and that meters are working properly. Prepare calculations for receipts and deliveries of oil and oil products. Read automatic gauges at specified intervals to determine the flow rate of oil into or from tanks and the amount of oil in tanks. Record and compile operating data, instrument readings, documentation, and results of laboratory analyses. Control or operate manifold and pumping systems to circulate liquids through a petroleum refinery. Monitor process indicators, instruments, gauges, and meters in order to detect and report any possible problems. Clean interiors of processing units by circulating chemicals and solvents within units. Operate control panels to coordinate and regulate process variables such as temperature and pressure and to direct product flow rate according to process schedules. Read and analyze specifications, schedules, logs, test results, and laboratory recommendations to determine how to set equipment controls to produce the required qualities and quantities of products. Perform tests to check the qualities and grades of products, such as assessing levels of bottom sediment, water, and foreign materials in oil samples, using centrifugal testers. Collect product samples by turning bleeder valves or by lowering containers into tanks to obtain oil samples. Patrol units to monitor the amount of oil in storage tanks and to verify that activities and operations are safe, efficient, and in compliance with regulations. Operate auxiliary equipment and control multiple processing units during distilling or treating operations, moving controls that regulate valves, pumps, compressors, and auxiliary equipment.

LEVEL OF ACTIVITY (out of 100)—General Physical Activity: 42.1. **Sitting:** 36.9. **Outdoors:** 37.6.

SKILLS—Operation Monitoring; Operation and Control; Repairing; Equipment Maintenance; Troubleshooting; Science; Quality Control Analysis; Mathematics.

GOE—**Interest Area:** 13. Manufacturing. **Work Group:** 13.16. Utility Operation and Energy Distribution. **Other Jobs in This Work Group:** Chemical Plant and System Operators; Gas Compressor and Gas Pumping Station Operators; Gas Plant Operators; Nuclear Power Reactor Operators; Power Distributors and Dispatchers; Power Plant Operators; Ship Engineers; Stationary Engineers and Boiler Operators; Water and Liquid Waste Treatment Plant and System Operators. **PERSONALITY TYPE:** Realistic. Realistic occupations frequently involve work activities that include practical, hands-on problems and solutions. They often deal with plants; animals; and real-world materials like wood, tools, and machinery. Many of the occupations require working outside and do not involve a lot of paperwork or working closely with others.

EDUCATION/TRAINING PROGRAM(S)— Mechanic and Repair Technologies/Technicians, Other. **RELATED KNOWLEDGE/COURS-ES—Mechanical Devices:** Machines and tools, including their designs, uses, repair, and maintenance. **Chemistry:** The chemical composition, structure, and properties of substances and of the chemical processes and transformations that they undergo. This includes uses of chemicals and their danger signs, production techniques, and disposal methods. **Physics:** Physical principles and laws and their interrelationships and applications to understanding fluid, material, and atmospheric dynamics and mechanical, electrical, atomic, and subatomic structures and processes. **Production and Processing:** Raw materials, production processes, quality control, costs, and other techniques for maximizing the effective manufacture and distribution of goods. **Engineering and Technology:** The practical application of engineering science and technology. This includes applying principles, tech-niques, procedures, and equipment to the design and production of various goods and services.

WORK ENVIRONMENT—Indoors; contaminants; hazardous conditions; standing; using hands on objects, tools, or controls.

Photographers

- Education/Training Required: Long-term on-the-job training
- Annual Earnings: $26,100
- Growth: 12.3%
- Annual Job Openings: 23,000
- Self-Employed: 58.8%
- Part-Time: 28.9%

Photograph persons, subjects, merchandise, or other commercial products. May develop negatives and produce finished prints. Take pictures of individuals, families, and small groups, either in studio or on location. Adjust apertures, shutter speeds, and camera focus based on a combination of factors such as lighting, field depth, subject motion, film type, and film speed. Use traditional or digital cameras along with a variety of equipment such as tripods, filters, and flash attachments. Create artificial light, using flashes and reflectors. Determine desired images and picture composition and select and adjust subjects, equipment, and lighting to achieve desired effects. Scan photographs into computers for editing, storage, and electronic transmission. Test equipment prior to use to ensure that it is in good working order. Review sets of photographs to select the best work. Estimate or

P

measure light levels, distances, and numbers of exposures needed, using measuring devices and formulas. Manipulate and enhance scanned or digital images to create desired effects, using computers and specialized software. Perform maintenance tasks necessary to keep equipment working properly. Perform general office duties such as scheduling appointments, keeping books, and ordering supplies. Consult with clients or advertising staff and study assignments to determine project goals, locations, and equipment needs. Select and assemble equipment and required background properties according to subjects, materials, and conditions. Enhance, retouch, and resize photographs and negatives, using airbrushing and other techniques. Set up, mount, or install photographic equipment and cameras. Produce computer-readable digital images from film, using flatbed scanners and photofinishing laboratories. Develop and print exposed film, using chemicals, touchup tools, and developing and printing equipment, or send film to photofinishing laboratories for processing. Direct activities of workers who are setting up photographic equipment. Employ a variety of specialized photographic materials and techniques, including infrared and ultraviolet films, macrophotography, photogrammetry, and sensitometry. Engage in research to develop new photographic procedures and materials.

LEVEL OF ACTIVITY (out of 100)—General Physical Activity: 51.1. **Sitting:** 49.4. **Outdoors:** 32.3.

SKILLS—Persuasion; Equipment Maintenance; Management of Financial Resources; Operation Monitoring; Service Orientation; Active Learning; Monitoring; Technology Design.

GOE—Interest Area: 03. Arts and Communication. **Work Group:** 03.09. Media Technology. **Other Jobs in This Work Group:**

Audio and Video Equipment Technicians; Broadcast Technicians; Camera Operators, Television, Video, and Motion Picture; Film and Video Editors; Multi-Media Artists and Animators; Radio Operators; Sound Engineering Technicians. **PERSONALITY TYPE:** Artistic. Artistic occupations frequently involve working with forms, designs, and patterns. They often require self-expression, and the work can be done without following a clear set of rules.

EDUCATION/TRAINING PROGRAM(S)— Photojournalism; Visual and Performing Arts, General; Commercial Photography; Photography; Film/Video and Photographic Arts, Other; Art/Art Studies, General. **RELATED KNOWLEDGE/COURSES—Sales and Marketing:** Principles and methods for showing, promoting, and selling products or services. This includes marketing strategy and tactics, product demonstration, sales techniques, and sales control systems. **Fine Arts:** The theory and techniques required to compose, produce, and perform works of music, dance, visual arts, drama, and sculpture. **Clerical Practices:** Administrative and clerical procedures and systems such as word processing, managing files and records, stenography and transcription, designing forms, and other office procedures and terminology. **Customer and Personal Service:** Principles and processes for providing customer and personal services. This includes customer needs assessment, meeting quality standards for services, and evaluation of customer satisfaction. **Production and Processing:** Raw materials, production processes, quality control, costs, and other techniques for maximizing the effective manufacture and distribution of goods. **Communications and Media:** Media production, communication, and dissemination techniques and methods. This includes alternative ways to inform and entertain via written, oral, and visual media.

WORK ENVIRONMENT—More often indoors than outdoors; sitting; using hands on objects, tools, or controls.

Physical Therapist Aides

- Education/Training Required: Short-term on-the-job training
- Annual Earnings: $21,510
- Growth: 34.4%
- Annual Job Openings: 5,000
- Self-Employed: 0.2%
- Part-Time: 28.6%

Under close supervision of a physical therapist or physical therapy assistant, perform only delegated, selected, or routine tasks in specific situations. These duties include preparing the patient and the treatment area. Clean and organize work area and disinfect equipment after treatment. Observe patients during treatment to compile and evaluate data on patients' responses and progress and report to physical therapist. Instruct, motivate, safeguard, and assist patients practicing exercises and functional activities under direction of medical staff. Secure patients into or onto therapy equipment. Transport patients to and from treatment areas, using wheelchairs or providing standing support. Confer with physical therapy staff or others to discuss and evaluate patient information for planning, modifying, and coordinating treat-

ment. Record treatment given and equipment used. Perform clerical duties, such as taking inventory, ordering supplies, answering telephone, taking messages, and filling out forms. Maintain equipment and furniture to keep it in good working condition, including performing the assembly and disassembly of equipment and accessories. Administer active and passive manual therapeutic exercises; therapeutic massage; and heat, light, sound, water, or electrical modality treatments, such as ultrasound. Change linens, such as bed sheets and pillowcases. Arrange treatment supplies to keep them in order. Assist patients to dress; undress; and put on and remove supportive devices, such as braces, splints, and slings. Measure patient's range of joint motion, body parts, and vital signs to determine effects of treatments or for patient evaluations. Train patients to use orthopedic braces, prostheses, or supportive devices. Fit patients for orthopedic braces, prostheses, or supportive devices, adjusting fit as needed. Participate in patient care tasks, such as assisting with passing food trays, feeding residents, or bathing residents on bed rest. Administer traction to relieve neck and back pain, using intermittent and static traction equipment.

LEVEL OF ACTIVITY (out of 100)—General Physical Activity: 56.0. **Sitting:** 32.1. **Outdoors:** 19.2.

SKILLS—Social Perceptiveness; Service Orientation; Operation Monitoring; Equipment Maintenance; Time Management; Learning Strategies; Negotiation; Persuasion.

GOE—Interest Area: 08. Health Science. **Work Group:** 08.07. Medical Therapy. **Other Jobs in This Work Group:** Audiologists; Massage Therapists; Occupational Therapist Aides; Occupational Therapist Assistants; Occupational Therapists; Physical Therapist Assistants;

Physical Therapists; Radiation Therapists; Recreational Therapists; Respiratory Therapists; Respiratory Therapy Technicians; Speech-Language Pathologists. **PERSONALITY TYPE:** Social. Social occupations frequently involve working with, communicating with, and teaching people. These occupations often involve helping or providing service to others.

EDUCATION/TRAINING PROGRAM(S)— Physical Therapist Assistant. **RELATED KNOWLEDGE/COURSES—Psychology:** Human behavior and performance; individual differences in ability, personality, and interests; learning and motivation; psychological research methods; and the assessment and treatment of behavioral and affective disorders. **Medicine and Dentistry:** The information and techniques needed to diagnose and treat human injuries, diseases, and deformities. This includes symptoms, treatment alternatives, drug properties and interactions, and preventive health-care measures. **Therapy and Counseling:** Principles, methods, and procedures for diagnosis, treatment, and rehabilitation of physical and mental dysfunctions and for career counseling and guidance. **Customer and Personal Service:** Principles and processes for providing customer and personal services. This includes customer needs assessment, meeting quality standards for services, and evaluation of customer satisfaction. **Clerical Practices:** Administrative and clerical procedures and systems such as word processing, managing files and records, stenography and transcription, designing forms, and other office procedures and terminology. **Education and Training:** Principles and methods for curriculum and training design, teaching and instruction for individuals and groups, and the measurement of training effects.

WORK ENVIRONMENT—Indoors; disease or infections; standing; walking and running; using hands on objects, tools, or controls; repetitive motions.

Physical Therapist Assistants

- Education/Training Required: Associate degree
- Annual Earnings: $39,490
- Growth: 44.2%
- Annual Job Openings: 7,000
- Self-Employed: 0.2%
- Part-Time: 28.6%

Assist physical therapists in providing physical therapy treatments and procedures. May, in accordance with state laws, assist in the development of treatment plans, carry out routine functions, document the progress of treatment, and modify specific treatments in accordance with patient status and within the scope of treatment plans established by a physical therapist. Generally requires formal training. Instruct, motivate, safeguard, and assist patients as they practice exercises and functional activities. Confer with physical therapy staff or others to discuss and evaluate patient information for planning, modifying, and coordinating treatment. Administer active and passive manual therapeutic exercises; therapeutic massage; and heat, light, sound, water, and electrical modality treatments, such as ultrasound. Observe patients during treatments to compile and evaluate data on patients' responses and progress; report to physical therapist. Measure patients' range of joint motion, body parts, and vital signs to determine effects of treatments or for patient evaluations. Secure patients into or onto therapy equipment. Fit patients for orthopedic braces, prostheses, and supportive devices such as crutches. Train patients in the use of orthopedic braces, prostheses, or supportive devices. Transport patients to and from treatment areas, lifting and transferring them according to positioning requirements. Monitor operation of equipment and record use of equipment and administration of treatment. Clean work area and check and store equipment after treatment. Assist patients to dress; undress; or put on and remove supportive devices, such as braces, splints, and slings. Administer traction to relieve neck and back pain, using intermittent and static traction equipment. Perform clerical duties, such as taking inventory, ordering supplies, answering telephone, taking messages, and filling out forms. Prepare treatment areas and electrotherapy equipment for use by physiotherapists. Perform postural drainage, percussions, and vibrations and teach deep breathing exercises to treat respiratory conditions.

LEVEL OF ACTIVITY (out of 100)—General Physical Activity: 73.3. **Sitting:** 31.6. **Outdoors:** 17.5.

SKILLS—Social Perceptiveness; Science; Service Orientation; Instructing; Time Management; Writing; Speaking; Active Learning.

GOE—Interest Area: 08. Health Science. **Work Group:** 08.07. Medical Therapy. **Other Jobs in This Work Group:** Audiologists; Massage Therapists; Occupational Therapist Aides; Occupational Therapist Assistants; Occupational Therapists; Physical Therapist Aides; Physical Therapists; Radiation Therapists; Recreational Therapists; Respiratory Therapists; Respiratory Therapy Technicians; Speech-Language Pathologists. **PERSONALITY TYPE:** Social. Social occupations frequently involve working with, communicating with, and teaching people. These occupations often involve helping or providing service to others.

EDUCATION/TRAINING PROGRAM(S)— Physical Therapist Assistant. **RELATED KNOWLEDGE/COURSES—Psychology:** Human behavior and performance; individual differences in ability, personality, and interests; learning and motivation; psychological research methods; and the assessment and treatment of behavioral and affective disorders. **Therapy and Counseling:** Principles, methods, and procedures for diagnosis, treatment, and rehabilitation of physical and mental dysfunctions and for career counseling and guidance. **Medicine and Dentistry:** The information and techniques needed to diagnose and treat human injuries, diseases, and deformities. This includes symptoms, treatment alternatives, drug properties and interactions, and preventive health-care measures. **Education and Training:** Principles and methods for curriculum and training design, teaching and instruction for individuals and groups, and the measurement of training effects. **Sociology and Anthropology:** Group behavior and dynamics, societal trends and influences, human migrations, ethnicity, and cultures and their history and origins. **Biology:** Plant and animal organisms and their tissues, cells, functions, interdependencies, and interactions with each other and the environment.

WORK ENVIRONMENT—Indoors; disease or infections; standing; walking and running; using hands on objects, tools, or controls; bending or twisting the body.

Physical Therapists

◎ Education/Training Required: Master's degree

◎ Annual Earnings: $63,080

◎ Growth: 36.7%

◎ Annual Job Openings: 13,000

◎ Self-Employed: 4.5%

◎ Part-Time: 24.7%

Assess, plan, organize, and participate in rehabilitative programs that improve mobility, relieve pain, increase strength, and decrease or prevent deformity of patients suffering from disease or injury. Plan, prepare, and carry out individually designed programs of physical treatment to maintain, improve, or restore physical functioning; alleviate pain; and prevent physical dysfunction in patients. Perform and document an initial exam, evaluating data to identify problems and determine a diagnosis prior to intervention. Evaluate effects of treatment at various stages and adjust treatments to achieve maximum benefit. Administer manual exercises, massage, or traction to help relieve pain, increase patient strength, or decrease or prevent deformity or crippling. Instruct patient and family in treatment procedures to be continued at home. Confer with the patient, medical practitioners, and appropriate others to plan, implement, and assess the intervention program. Review physician's referral and patient's medical records to help determine diagnosis and physical therapy treatment required. Obtain patients' informed consent to proposed interventions. Record prognosis, treatment, response, and progress in patient's chart or enter information into com-

puter. Discharge patient from physical therapy when goals or projected outcomes have been attained and provide for appropriate follow-up care or referrals. Test and measure patient's strength, motor development and function, sensory perception, functional capacity, and respiratory and circulatory efficiency and record data. Identify and document goals, anticipated progress, and plans for reevaluation. Provide information to the patient about the proposed intervention, its material risks and expected benefits, and any reasonable alternatives. Inform patients when diagnosis reveals findings outside physical therapy and refer to appropriate practitioners. Direct, supervise, assess, and communicate with supportive personnel. Administer treatment involving application of physical agents, using equipment, moist packs, ultraviolet and infrared lamps, and ultrasound machines. Teach physical therapy students as well as those in other health professions. Evaluate, fit, and adjust prosthetic and orthotic devices and recommend modification to orthotist. Provide educational information about physical therapy and physical therapists, injury prevention, ergonomics, and ways to promote health.

LEVEL OF ACTIVITY (out of 100)—General Physical Activity: 63.9. **Sitting:** 29.9. **Outdoors:** 19.8.

SKILLS—Science; Reading Comprehension; Social Perceptiveness; Instructing; Learning Strategies; Service Orientation; Monitoring; Time Management.

GOE—Interest Area: 08. Health Science. **Work Group:** 08.07. Medical Therapy. **Other Jobs in This Work Group:** Audiologists; Massage Therapists; Occupational Therapist Aides; Occupational Therapist Assistants; Occupational Therapists; Physical Therapist Aides;

Physical Therapist Assistants; Radiation Therapists; Recreational Therapists; Respiratory Therapists; Respiratory Therapy Technicians; Speech-Language Pathologists. **PERSONALITY TYPE:** Social. Social occupations frequently involve working with, communicating with, and teaching people. These occupations often involve helping or providing service to others.

EDUCATION/TRAINING PROGRAM(S)— Physical Therapy/Therapist; Kinesiotherapy/ Kinesiotherapist. **RELATED KNOWLEDGE/ COURSES—Therapy and Counseling:** Principles, methods, and procedures for diagnosis, treatment, and rehabilitation of physical and mental dysfunctions and for career counseling and guidance. **Psychology:** Human behavior and performance; individual differences in ability, personality, and interests; learning and motivation; psychological research methods; and the assessment and treatment of behavioral and affective disorders. **Medicine and Dentistry:** The information and techniques needed to diagnose and treat human injuries, diseases, and deformities. This includes symptoms, treatment alternatives, drug properties and interactions, and preventive health-care measures. **Biology:** Plant and animal organisms and their tissues, cells, functions, interdependencies, and interactions with each other and the environment. **Customer and Personal Service:** Principles and processes for providing customer and personal services. This includes customer needs assessment, meeting quality standards for services, and evaluation of customer satisfaction. **Sociology and Anthropology:** Group behavior and dynamics, societal trends and influences, human migrations, ethnicity, and cultures and their history and origins.

WORK ENVIRONMENT—Indoors; contaminants; disease or infections; standing; walking and running; bending or twisting the body.

Physician Assistants

- Education/Training Required: Bachelor's degree
- Annual Earnings: $72,030
- Growth: 49.6%
- Annual Job Openings: 10,000
- Self-Employed: 1.3%
- Part-Time: 16.7%

Under the supervision of a physician, provide healthcare services typically performed by a physician. Conduct complete physicals, provide treatment, and counsel patients. May, in some cases, prescribe medication. Must graduate from an accredited educational program for physician assistants. Examine patients to obtain information about their physical condition. Make tentative diagnoses and decisions about management and treatment of patients. Interpret diagnostic test results for deviations from normal. Obtain, compile, and record patient medical data, including health history, progress notes, and results of physical examination. Administer or order diagnostic tests, such as X-ray, electrocardiogram, and laboratory tests. Prescribe therapy or medication with physician approval. Perform therapeutic procedures, such as injections, immunizations, suturing and wound care, and infection management.

Instruct and counsel patients about prescribed therapeutic regimens, normal growth and development, family planning, emotional problems of daily living, and health maintenance. Provide physicians with assistance during surgery or complicated medical procedures. Supervise and coordinate activities of technicians and technical assistants. Visit and observe patients on hospital rounds or house calls, updating charts, ordering therapy, and reporting back to physician. Order medical and laboratory supplies and equipment.

LEVEL OF ACTIVITY (out of 100)—General Physical Activity: 43.4. **Sitting:** 35.4. **Outdoors:** 16.2.

SKILLS—Science; Social Perceptiveness; Reading Comprehension; Critical Thinking; Instructing; Active Listening; Time Management; Active Learning.

GOE—Interest Area: 08. Health Science. **Work Group:** 08.02. Medicine and Surgery. **Other Jobs in This Work Group:** Anesthesiologists; Family and General Practitioners; Internists, General; Medical Assistants; Medical Transcriptionists; Obstetricians and Gynecologists; Pediatricians, General; Pharmacists; Pharmacy Aides; Pharmacy Technicians; Psychiatrists; Registered Nurses; Surgeons; Surgical Technologists. **PERSONALITY TYPE:** Investigative. Investigative occupations frequently involve working with ideas and require an extensive amount of thinking. These occupations can involve searching for facts and figuring out problems mentally.

EDUCATION/TRAINING PROGRAM(S)—Physician Assistant. **RELATED KNOWLEDGE/COURSES—Medicine and Dentistry:** The information and techniques needed to diagnose and treat human injuries, diseases, and deformities. This includes symptoms, treatment alternatives, drug properties and interactions, and preventive health-care measures. **Biology:** Plant and animal organisms and their tissues, cells, functions, interdependencies, and interactions with each other and the environment. **Therapy and Counseling:** Principles, methods, and procedures for diagnosis, treatment, and rehabilitation of physical and mental dysfunctions and for career counseling and guidance. **Psychology:** Human behavior and performance; individual differences in ability, personality, and interests; learning and motivation; psychological research methods; and the assessment and treatment of behavioral and affective disorders. **Chemistry:** The chemical composition, structure, and properties of substances and of the chemical processes and transformations that they undergo. This includes uses of chemicals and their danger signs, production techniques, and disposal methods. **Customer and Personal Service:** Principles and processes for providing customer and personal services. This includes customer needs assessment, meeting quality standards for services, and evaluation of customer satisfaction.

WORK ENVIRONMENT—Indoors; disease or infections; standing.

Pipe Fitters and Steamfitters

This job can be found in the Part I lists under the title Plumbers, Pipefitters, and Steamfitters.

- ◉ Education/Training Required: Long-term on-the-job training
- ◉ Annual Earnings: $42,160
- ◉ Growth: 15.7%
- ◉ Annual Job Openings: 61,000
- ◉ Self-Employed: 13.3%
- ◉ Part-Time: 3.6%

The job openings listed here are shared with Plumbers.

Lay out, assemble, install, and maintain pipe systems, pipe supports, and related hydraulic and pneumatic equipment for steam, hot water, heating, cooling, lubricating, sprinkling, and industrial production and processing systems. Cut, thread, and hammer pipe to specifications, using tools such as saws, cutting torches, and pipe threaders and benders. Assemble and secure pipes, tubes, fittings, and related equipment, according to specifications, by welding, brazing, cementing, soldering, and threading joints. Attach pipes to walls, structures, and fixtures such as radiators or tanks, using brackets, clamps, tools, or welding equipment. Inspect, examine, and test installed systems and pipelines, using pressure gauge, hydrostatic test-

ing, observation, or other methods. Measure and mark pipes for cutting and threading. Lay out full-scale drawings of pipe systems, supports, and related equipment, following blueprints. Plan pipe system layout, installation, or repair according to specifications. Select pipe sizes and types and related materials, such as supports, hangers, and hydraulic cylinders, according to specifications. Cut and bore holes in structures such as bulkheads, decks, walls, and mains prior to pipe installation, using hand and power tools. Modify, clean, and maintain pipe systems, units, fittings, and related machines and equipment, following specifications and using hand and power tools. Install automatic controls used to regulate pipe systems. Turn valves to shut off steam, water, or other gases or liquids from pipe sections, using valve keys or wrenches. Remove and replace worn components. Prepare cost estimates for clients. Inspect worksites for obstructions and to ensure that holes will not cause structural weakness. Operate motorized pumps to remove water from flooded manholes, basements, or facility floors. Dip nonferrous piping materials in a mixture of molten tin and lead to obtain a coating that prevents erosion or galvanic and electrolytic action.

LEVEL OF ACTIVITY (out of 100)—General Physical Activity: 38.6. **Sitting:** 40.6. **Outdoors:** 42.0.

SKILLS—Installation; Repairing; Management of Personnel Resources; Systems Analysis; Equipment Maintenance; Coordination; Operation Monitoring; Technology Design.

GOE—Interest Area: 02. Architecture and Construction. **Work Group:** 02.04.

Construction Crafts. **Other Jobs in This Work Group:** Boilermakers; Brickmasons and Blockmasons; Carpet Installers; Cement Masons and Concrete Finishers; Commercial Divers; Construction Carpenters; Crane and Tower Operators; Drywall and Ceiling Tile Installers; Electricians; Fence Erectors; Floor Layers, Except Carpet, Wood, and Hard Tiles; Floor Sanders and Finishers; Glaziers; Hazardous Materials Removal Workers; Insulation Workers, Floor, Ceiling, and Wall; Insulation Workers, Mechanical; Manufactured Building and Mobile Home Installers; Operating Engineers and Other Construction Equipment Operators; Painters, Construction and Maintenance; Paperhangers; Paving, Surfacing, and Tamping Equipment Operators; Pile-Driver Operators; Pipelayers; Plasterers and Stucco Masons; Plumbers; Plumbers, Pipefitters, and Steamfitters; Rail-Track Laying and Maintenance Equipment Operators; Refractory Materials Repairers, Except Brickmasons; Reinforcing Iron and Rebar Workers; Riggers; Roofers; Rough Carpenters; Security and Fire Alarm Systems Installers; Segmental Pavers; Sheet Metal Workers; Stone Cutters and Carvers, Manufacturing; Stonemasons; Structural Iron and Steel Workers; Tapers; Terrazzo Workers and Finishers; Tile and Marble Setters. **PERSONALITY TYPE:** Realistic. Realistic occupations frequently involve work activities that include practical, hands-on problems and solutions. They often deal with plants; animals; and real-world materials like wood, tools, and machinery. Many of the occupations require working outside and do not involve a lot of paperwork or working closely with others.

EDUCATION/TRAINING PROGRAM(S)— Pipefitting/Pipefitter and Sprinkler Fitter. **RELATED KNOWLEDGE/COURSES— Building and Construction:** The materials, methods, and tools involved in the construction or repair of houses, buildings, or other structures such as highways and roads. **Design:** Design techniques, tools, and principles involved in production of precision technical plans, blueprints, drawings, and models. **Mechanical Devices:** Machines and tools, including their designs, uses, repair, and maintenance. **Engineering and Technology:** The practical application of engineering science and technology. This includes applying principles, techniques, procedures, and equipment to the design and production of various goods and services. **Economics and Accounting:** Economic and accounting principles and practices, the financial markets, banking, and the analysis and reporting of financial data. **Transportation:** Principles and methods for moving people or goods by air, rail, sea, or road, including the relative costs and benefits.

WORK ENVIRONMENT—Outdoors; hazardous equipment; minor burns, cuts, bites, or stings; standing; using hands on objects, tools, or controls; repetitive motions.

Pipelayers

- Education/Training Required: Moderate-term on-the-job training
- Annual Earnings: $28,760
- Growth: 9.9%
- Annual Job Openings: 7,000
- Self-Employed: 11.9%
- Part-Time: 3.6%

Lay pipe for storm or sanitation sewers, drains, and water mains. Perform any combination of the following tasks: grade trenches or culverts, position pipe, or seal joints. Operate mechanized equipment such as pickup trucks, rollers, tandem dump trucks, front-end loaders, and backhoes. Install and repair sanitary and stormwater sewer structures and pipe systems. Train others in pipelaying and provide supervision. Install and use instruments such as lasers, grade rods, and transit levels. Tap and drill holes into pipes to introduce auxiliary lines or devices. Locate existing pipes needing repair or replacement, using magnetic or radio indicators. Lay out pipe routes, following written instructions or blueprints and coordinating layouts with supervisors. Dig trenches to desired or required depths by hand or using trenching tools. Cut pipes to required lengths. Cover pipes with earth or other materials. Connect pipe pieces and seal joints, using welding equipment, cement, or glue. Check slopes for conformance to requirements, using levels or lasers. Align and position pipes to prepare them for welding or sealing. Grade and level trench bases, using tamping machines and hand tools.

LEVEL OF ACTIVITY (out of 100)—General Physical Activity: 74.3. **Sitting:** 31.4. **Outdoors:** 68.6.

SKILLS—Installation.

GOE—Interest Area: 02. Architecture and Construction. **Work Group:** 02.04. Construction Crafts. **Other Jobs in This Work Group:** Boilermakers; Brickmasons and Blockmasons; Carpet Installers; Cement Masons and Concrete Finishers; Commercial Divers; Construction Carpenters; Crane and Tower Operators; Drywall and Ceiling Tile Installers; Electricians; Fence Erectors; Floor Layers, Except Carpet, Wood, and Hard Tiles; Floor Sanders and Finishers; Glaziers; Hazardous Materials Removal Workers; Insulation Workers, Floor, Ceiling, and Wall; Insulation Workers, Mechanical; Manufactured Building and Mobile Home Installers; Operating Engineers and Other Construction Equipment Operators; Painters, Construction and Maintenance; Paperhangers; Paving, Surfacing, and Tamping Equipment Operators; Pile-Driver Operators; Pipe Fitters and Steamfitters; Plasterers and Stucco Masons; Plumbers; Plumbers, Pipefitters, and Steamfitters; Rail-Track Laying and Maintenance Equipment Operators; Refractory Materials Repairers, Except Brickmasons; Reinforcing Iron and Rebar Workers; Riggers; Roofers; Rough Carpenters; Security and Fire Alarm Systems Installers; Segmental Pavers; Sheet Metal Workers; Stone Cutters and Carvers, Manufacturing; Stonemasons; Structural Iron and Steel Workers; Tapers; Terrazzo Workers and Finishers; Tile and Marble Setters.
PERSONALITY TYPE: Realistic. Realistic occupations frequently involve work activities that include practical, hands-on problems and solutions. They often deal with plants; animals; and real-world materials like wood, tools, and machinery. Many of the occupations require working outside and do not involve a lot of paperwork or working closely with others.

EDUCATION/TRAINING PROGRAM(S)— Plumbing Technology/Plumber. **RELATED KNOWLEDGE/COURSES—Building and Construction:** The materials, methods, and tools involved in the construction or repair of houses, buildings, or other structures such as highways and roads. **Mechanical Devices:** Machines and tools, including their designs, uses, repair, and maintenance. **Design:** Design techniques, tools, and principles involved in production of precision technical plans, blueprints, drawings, and models. **Physics:** Physical

P

principles and laws and their interrelationships and applications to understanding fluid, material, and atmospheric dynamics and mechanical, electrical, atomic, and subatomic structures and processes.

WORK ENVIRONMENT—Outdoors; hazardous equipment; standing; kneeling, crouching, stooping, or crawling; using hands on objects, tools, or controls; repetitive motions.

Plasterers and Stucco Masons

- Education/Training Required: Long-term on-the-job training
- Annual Earnings: $33,440
- Growth: 8.2%
- Annual Job Openings: 6,000
- Self-Employed: 5.0%
- Part-Time: 8.6%

Apply interior or exterior plaster, cement, stucco, or similar materials. May also set ornamental plaster. Apply coats of plaster or stucco to walls, ceilings, or partitions of buildings, using trowels, brushes, or spray guns. Mix mortar and plaster to desired consistency or direct workers who perform mixing. Create decorative textures in finish coat, using brushes or trowels, sand, pebbles, or stones. Apply insulation to building exteriors by installing prefabricated insulation systems over existing walls or by covering the outer wall with insulation board, reinforcing mesh, and a base coat. Cure freshly plastered surfaces. Clean and prepare surfaces for applications of plaster, cement, stucco, or similar materials, such as by drywall taping. Rough the undercoat surface with a scratcher so the finish coat will adhere. Apply weatherproof decorative coverings to exterior surfaces of buildings, such as troweling or spraying on coats of stucco. Install guidewires on exterior surfaces of buildings to indicate thickness of plaster or stucco and nail wire mesh, lath, or similar materials to the outside surface to hold stucco in place. Spray acoustic materials or texture finish over walls and ceilings. Mold and install ornamental plaster pieces, panels, and trim.

LEVEL OF ACTIVITY (out of 100)—General Physical Activity: 79.1. Sitting: 22.6. Outdoors: 34.8.

SKILLS—Management of Material Resources; Repairing; Technology Design; Installation; Management of Financial Resources; Management of Personnel Resources; Equipment Maintenance; Equipment Selection.

GOE—Interest Area: 02. Architecture and Construction. Work Group: 02.04. Construction Crafts. Other Jobs in This Work Group: Boilermakers; Brickmasons and Blockmasons; Carpet Installers; Cement Masons and Concrete Finishers; Commercial Divers; Construction Carpenters; Crane and Tower Operators; Drywall and Ceiling Tile Installers; Electricians; Fence Erectors; Floor Layers, Except Carpet, Wood, and Hard Tiles; Floor Sanders and Finishers; Glaziers; Hazardous Materials Removal Workers; Insulation Workers, Floor, Ceiling, and Wall; Insulation Workers, Mechanical; Manufactured Building and Mobile Home Installers; Operating Engineers and Other Construction Equipment Operators; Painters, Construction and Maintenance; Paperhangers; Paving, Surfacing, and Tamping

Equipment Operators; Pile-Driver Operators; Pipe Fitters and Steamfitters; Pipelayers; Plumbers; Plumbers, Pipefitters, and Steamfitters; Rail-Track Laying and Maintenance Equipment Operators; Refractory Materials Repairers, Except Brickmasons; Reinforcing Iron and Rebar Workers; Riggers; Roofers; Rough Carpenters; Security and Fire Alarm Systems Installers; Segmental Pavers; Sheet Metal Workers; Stone Cutters and Carvers, Manufacturing; Stonemasons; Structural Iron and Steel Workers; Tapers; Terrazzo Workers and Finishers; Tile and Marble Setters. **PERSONALITY TYPE:** Realistic. Realistic occupations frequently involve work activities that include practical, hands-on problems and solutions. They often deal with plants; animals; and real-world materials like wood, tools, and machinery. Many of the occupations require working outside and do not involve a lot of paperwork or working closely with others.

EDUCATION/TRAINING PROGRAM(S)—Construction Trades, Other. **RELATED KNOWLEDGE/COURSES—Building and Construction:** The materials, methods, and tools involved in the construction or repair of houses, buildings, or other structures such as highways and roads. **Public Safety and Security:** Relevant equipment, policies, procedures, and strategies to promote effective local, state, or national security operations for the protection of people, data, property, and institutions.

WORK ENVIRONMENT—High places; standing; walking and running; using hands on objects, tools, or controls; bending or twisting the body; repetitive motions.

Plumbers

This job can be found in the Part I lists under the title Plumbers, Pipefitters, and Steamfitters.

- Education/Training Required: Long-term on-the-job training
- Annual Earnings: $42,160
- Growth: 15.7%
- Annual Job Openings: 61,000
- Self-Employed: 13.3%
- Part-Time: 3.6%

The job openings listed here are shared with Pipe Fitters and Steamfitters.

Assemble, install, and repair pipes, fittings, and fixtures of heating, water, and drainage systems according to specifications and plumbing codes. Assemble pipe sections, tubing, and fittings, using couplings; clamps; screws; bolts; cement; plastic solvent; caulking; or soldering, brazing, and welding equipment. Fill pipes or plumbing fixtures with water or air and observe pressure gauges to detect and locate leaks. Review blueprints and building codes and specifications to determine work details and procedures. Prepare written work cost estimates and negotiate contracts. Study building plans and inspect structures to assess material and equipment needs, to establish the sequence of pipe installations, and to plan installation around obstructions such as electrical wiring. Keep records of assignments and produce detailed work reports. Perform complex calculations and planning for special or very large jobs. Locate and mark the position of pipe installations, connections, passage holes, and fixtures in structures, using measuring instruments such as rulers and levels. Measure, cut, thread, and bend pipe to required angle, using hand and power tools or machines such as pipe cutters, pipe-threading machines, and pipe-bending machines. Cut openings in structures to accommodate pipes and pipe fittings, using hand and power tools. Install pipe assemblies, fittings, valves, appliances such as dishwashers and water heaters, and fixtures such as sinks and toilets, using hand and power tools. Hang steel supports from ceiling joists to hold pipes in place. Repair and maintain plumbing, replacing defective washers, replacing or mending broken pipes, and opening clogged drains. Direct workers engaged in pipe cutting and preassembly and installation of plumbing systems and components. Install underground storm, sanitary, and water piping systems and extend piping to connect fixtures and plumbing to these systems. Clear away debris in a renovation. Install oxygen and medical gas in hospitals. Use specialized techniques, equipment, or materials, such as performing computer-assisted welding of small pipes or working with the special piping used in microchip fabrication.

LEVEL OF ACTIVITY (out of 100)—General Physical Activity: 76.1. **Sitting:** 33.1. **Outdoors:** 50.2.

SKILLS—Installation; Repairing; Systems Evaluation; Management of Material Resources; Management of Financial Resources; Science; Equipment Maintenance; Equipment Selection.

GOE—**Interest Area:** 02. Architecture and Construction. **Work Group:** 02.04. Construction Crafts. **Other Jobs in This Work Group:** Boilermakers; Brickmasons and Blockmasons; Carpet Installers; Cement Masons and Concrete Finishers; Commercial Divers; Construction Carpenters; Crane and Tower Operators; Drywall and Ceiling Tile Installers; Electricians; Fence Erectors; Floor Layers, Except Carpet, Wood, and Hard Tiles; Floor Sanders and Finishers; Glaziers; Hazardous Materials Removal Workers; Insulation Workers, Floor, Ceiling, and Wall; Insulation Workers, Mechanical; Manufactured Building and Mobile Home Installers; Operating Engineers and Other Construction Equipment Operators; Painters, Construction and Maintenance; Paperhangers; Paving, Surfacing, and Tamping Equipment Operators; Pile-Driver Operators; Pipe Fitters and Steamfitters; Pipelayers; Plasterers and Stucco Masons; Plumbers, Pipefitters, and Steamfitters; Rail-Track Laying and Maintenance Equipment Operators; Refractory Materials Repairers, Except Brickmasons; Reinforcing Iron and Rebar Workers; Riggers; Roofers; Rough Carpenters; Security and Fire Alarm Systems Installers; Segmental Pavers; Sheet Metal Workers; Stone Cutters and Carvers, Manufacturing; Stonemasons; Structural Iron and Steel Workers; Tapers; Terrazzo Workers and Finishers; Tile and Marble Setters. **PERSONALITY TYPE:** Realistic. Realistic occupations frequently involve work activities that include practical, hands-on problems and solutions. They often deal with plants; animals; and real-world materials like wood, tools, and machinery. Many of the occupations require working outside and do not involve a lot of paperwork or working closely with others.

EDUCATION/TRAINING PROGRAM(S)—Pipefitting/Pipefitter and Sprinkler Fitter; Plumbing Technology/Plumber; Plumbing and Related Water Supply Services, Other. **RELATED KNOWLEDGE/COURSES**—**Building and Construction:** The materials, methods, and tools involved in the construction or repair of houses, buildings, or other structures such as highways and roads. **Physics:** Physical principles and laws and their interrelationships and applications to understanding fluid, material, and atmospheric dynamics and mechanical, electrical, atomic, and subatomic structures and processes. **Mechanical Devices:** Machines and tools, including their designs, uses, repair, and maintenance. **Chemistry:** The chemical composition, structure, and properties of substances and of the chemical processes and transformations that they undergo. This includes uses of chemicals and their danger signs, production techniques, and disposal methods. **Design:** Design techniques, tools, and principles involved in production of precision technical plans, blueprints, drawings, and models. **Sales and Marketing:** Principles and methods for showing, promoting, and selling products or services. This includes marketing strategy and tactics, product demonstration, sales techniques, and sales control systems.

WORK ENVIRONMENT—Outdoors; contaminants; cramped work space, awkward positions; hazardous equipment; minor burns, cuts, bites, or stings; using hands on objects, tools, or controls.

Plumbers, Pipefitters, and Steamfitters

See the descriptions of these jobs:

- Pipe Fitters and Steamfitters
- Plumbers

Police and Sheriff's Patrol Officers

See the descriptions of these jobs:

- Police Patrol Officers
- Sheriffs and Deputy Sheriffs

Police Detectives

This job can be found in the Part I lists under the title Detectives and Criminal Investigators.

- Education/Training Required: Work experience in a related occupation
- Annual Earnings: $55,790
- Growth: 16.3%
- Annual Job Openings: 9,000
- Self-Employed: 0.0%
- Part-Time: 2.5%

The job openings listed here are shared with Criminal Investigators and Special Agents; Immigration and Customs Inspectors; and Police Identification and Records Officers.

Conduct investigations to prevent crimes or solve criminal cases. Examine crime scenes to obtain clues and evidence, such as loose hairs, fibers, clothing, or weapons. Secure deceased body and obtain evidence from it, preventing bystanders from tampering with it prior to medical examiner's arrival. Obtain evidence from suspects. Provide testimony as a witness in court. Analyze completed police reports to determine what additional information and investigative work is needed. Prepare charges, responses to charges, or information for court cases according to formalized procedures. Note, mark, and photograph location of objects found, such as footprints, tire tracks, bullets, and bloodstains, and take measurements of the scene. Obtain facts or statements from complainants, witnesses, and accused persons and record interviews, using recording device. Obtain summary of incident from officer in charge at crime scene, taking care to avoid disturbing evidence. Examine records and governmental agency files to find identifying data about suspects. Prepare and serve search and arrest warrants. Block or rope off scene and check perimeter to ensure that entire scene is secured. Summon medical help for injured individuals and alert medical personnel to take statements from them. Provide information to lab personnel concerning the source of an item of evidence and tests to be performed. Monitor conditions of victims who are unconscious so that arrangements can be made to take statements if consciousness is regained. Secure persons at scene, keeping witnesses from conversing or leaving the scene before investigators arrive. Preserve, process, and analyze items of evidence obtained from crime scenes and suspects, placing them in proper containers and destroying evidence no longer needed. Record progress of investigation, maintain informational files on suspects, and submit reports to commanding officer or magistrate to authorize warrants. Organize scene search, assigning specific tasks and areas of search to individual officers and obtaining adequate lighting as necessary. Take photographs from all angles of relevant parts of a crime scene, including entrance and exit routes and streets and intersections.

LEVEL OF ACTIVITY (out of 100)—General Physical Activity: 67.6. **Sitting:** 45.0. **Outdoors:** 45.6.

SKILLS—Persuasion; Negotiation; Social Perceptiveness; Coordination; Service Orientation; Speaking; Active Listening; Writing.

GOE—Interest Area: 12. Law and Public Safety. **Work Group:** 12.04. Law Enforcement and Public Safety. **Other Jobs in This Work Group:** Bailiffs; Correctional Officers and Jailers; Criminal Investigators and Special Agents; Detectives and Criminal Investigators; Fire Investigators; Forensic Science Technicians; Parking Enforcement Workers; Police and Sheriff's Patrol Officers; Police Identification and Records Officers; Police Patrol Officers; Sheriffs and Deputy Sheriffs; Transit and Railroad Police. **PERSONALITY TYPE:** Enterprising. Enterprising occupations frequently involve starting up and carrying out projects. These occupations can involve leading people and making many decisions. They sometimes require risk taking and often deal with business.

EDUCATION/TRAINING PROGRAM(S)—Criminal Justice/Police Science; Criminalistics and Criminal Science. **RELATED KNOWLEDGE/COURSES—Public Safety and Security:** Relevant equipment, policies, procedures, and strategies to promote effective local, state, or national security operations for the protection of people, data, property, and institutions. **Law and Government:** Laws, legal codes, court procedures, precedents, government regulations, executive orders, agency rules, and the democratic political process. **Psychology:** Human behavior and performance; individual differences in ability, personality, and interests;

learning and motivation; psychological research methods; and the assessment and treatment of behavioral and affective disorders. **Therapy and Counseling:** Principles, methods, and procedures for diagnosis, treatment, and rehabilitation of physical and mental dysfunctions and for career counseling and guidance. **Philosophy and Theology:** Different philosophical systems and religions. This includes their basic principles, values, ethics, ways of thinking, customs, and practices and their impact on human culture. **Education and Training:** Principles and methods for curriculum and training design, teaching and instruction for individuals and groups, and the measurement of training effects.

WORK ENVIRONMENT—More often indoors than outdoors; very hot or cold; sitting.

Police Identification and Records Officers

This job can be found in the Part I lists under the title Detectives and Criminal Investigators.

- Education/Training Required: Work experience in a related occupation
- Annual Earnings: $55,790
- Growth: 16.3%
- Annual Job Openings: 9,000
- Self-Employed: 0.0%
- Part-Time: 2.5%

The job openings listed here are shared with Criminal Investigators and Special Agents; Immigration and Customs Inspectors; and Police Detectives.

Collect evidence at crime scene, classify and identify fingerprints, and photograph evidence for use in criminal and civil cases. Photograph crime or accident scenes for evidence records. Analyze and process evidence at crime scenes and in the laboratory, wearing protective equipment and using powders and chemicals. Look for trace evidence, such as fingerprints, hairs, fibers, or shoe impressions, using alternative light sources when necessary. Dust selected areas of crime scene and lift latent fingerprints, adhering to proper preservation procedures. Testify in court and present evidence. Package, store, and retrieve evidence. Serve as technical advisor and coordinate with other law enforcement workers to exchange information on crime scene collection activities. Perform emergency work during off-hours. Submit evidence to supervisors. Process film and prints from crime or accident scenes. Identify, classify, and file fingerprints, using systems such as the Henry Classification system.

LEVEL OF ACTIVITY (out of 100)—General Physical Activity: 55.0. **Sitting:** 52.4. **Outdoors:** 46.3.

SKILLS—Persuasion; Negotiation; Judgment and Decision Making; Service Orientation; Social Perceptiveness; Critical Thinking; Time Management; Speaking.

GOE—Interest Area: 12. Law and Public Safety. **Work Group:** 12.04. Law Enforcement and Public Safety. **Other Jobs in This Work Group:** Bailiffs; Correctional Officers and Jailers; Criminal Investigators and Special Agents; Detectives and Criminal Investigators; Fire Investigators; Forensic Science Technicians; Parking Enforcement Workers; Police and

P.

Sheriff's Patrol Officers; Police Detectives; Police Patrol Officers; Sheriffs and Deputy Sheriffs; Transit and Railroad Police. **PERSONALITY TYPE:** Conventional. Conventional occupations frequently involve following set procedures and routines. These occupations can include working with data and details more than with ideas. Usually there is a clear line of authority to follow.

EDUCATION/TRAINING PROGRAM(S)— Criminal Justice/Police Science; Criminalistics and Criminal Science. **RELATED KNOWLEDGE/COURSES—Law and Government:** Laws, legal codes, court procedures, precedents, government regulations, executive orders, agency rules, and the democratic political process. **Public Safety and Security:** Relevant equipment, policies, procedures, and strategies to promote effective local, state, or national security operations for the protection of people, data, property, and institutions. **Customer and Personal Service:** Principles and processes for providing customer and personal services. This includes customer needs assessment, meeting quality standards for services, and evaluation of customer satisfaction. **Telecommunications:** Transmission, broadcasting, switching, control, and operation of telecommunications systems. **Psychology:** Human behavior and performance; individual differences in ability, personality, and interests; learning and motivation; psychological research methods; and the assessment and treatment of behavioral and affective disorders. **Computers and Electronics:** Circuit boards; processors; chips; electronic equipment; and computer hardware and software, including applications and programming.

WORK ENVIRONMENT—More often outdoors than indoors; noisy; very hot or cold; contaminants; using hands on objects, tools, or controls.

Police Patrol Officers

This job can be found in the Part I lists under the title Police and Sheriff's Patrol Officers.

- Education/Training Required: Long-term on-the-job training
- Annual Earnings: $46,290
- Growth: 15.5%
- Annual Job Openings: 47,000
- Self-Employed: 0.0%
- Part-Time: 1.4%

The job openings listed here are shared with Sheriffs and Deputy Sheriffs.

Patrol assigned area to enforce laws and ordinances, regulate traffic, control crowds, prevent crime, and arrest violators. Provide for public safety by maintaining order, responding to emergencies, protecting people and property, enforcing motor vehicle and criminal laws, and promoting good community relations. Identify, pursue, and arrest suspects and perpetrators of criminal acts. Record facts to prepare reports that document incidents and activities. Review facts of incidents to determine if criminal act or statute violations were involved. Render aid to accident victims and other persons requiring first aid for physical injuries. Testify in court to present evidence or act as witness in traffic and criminal cases. Evaluate complaint and emergency-request information to determine response requirements. Patrol specific area on foot, horseback, or motorized conveyance, responding promptly to calls for assistance. Monitor, note, report, and investigate suspicious persons and situations, safety hazards, and unusual or illegal activity in patrol area. Investigate traffic accidents and other accidents to determine causes and to determine if a crime has been committed. Photograph or draw diagrams of crime or accident scenes and interview principals and eyewitnesses. Monitor traffic to ensure that motorists observe traffic regulations and exhibit safe driving procedures. Relay complaint and emergency-request information to appropriate agency dispatchers. Issue citations or warnings to violators of motor vehicle ordinances. Direct traffic flow and reroute traffic in case of emergencies. Inform citizens of community services and recommend options to facilitate longer-term problem resolution. Provide road information to assist motorists. Process prisoners and prepare and maintain records of prisoner bookings and prisoner status during booking and pre-trial process. Inspect public establishments to ensure compliance with rules and regulations. Act as official escorts, such as when leading funeral processions or firefighters.

LEVEL OF ACTIVITY (out of 100)—General Physical Activity: 72.0. **Sitting:** 48.4. **Outdoors:** 46.6.

SKILLS—Persuasion; Negotiation; Social Perceptiveness; Judgment and Decision Making; Service Orientation; Active Listening; Complex Problem Solving; Coordination.

GOE—Interest Area: 12. Law and Public Safety. **Work Group:** 12.04. Law Enforcement and Public Safety. **Other Jobs in This Work Group:** Bailiffs; Correctional Officers and Jailers; Criminal Investigators and Special Agents; Detectives and Criminal Investigators; Fire Investigators; Forensic Science Technicians; Parking Enforcement Workers; Police and Sheriff's Patrol Officers; Police Detectives; Police Identification and Records Officers;

Sheriffs and Deputy Sheriffs; Transit and Railroad Police. **PERSONALITY TYPE:** Social. Social occupations frequently involve working with, communicating with, and teaching people. These occupations often involve helping or providing service to others.

EDUCATION/TRAINING PROGRAM(S)— Criminal Justice/Police Science; Criminalistics and Criminal Science. **RELATED KNOWLEDGE/COURSES—Public Safety and Security:** Relevant equipment, policies, procedures, and strategies to promote effective local, state, or national security operations for the protection of people, data, property, and institutions. **Law and Government:** Laws, legal codes, court procedures, precedents, government regulations, executive orders, agency rules, and the democratic political process. **Psychology:** Human behavior and performance; individual differences in ability, personality, and interests; learning and motivation; psychological research methods; and the assessment and treatment of behavioral and affective disorders. **Customer and Personal Service:** Principles and processes for providing customer and personal services. This includes customer needs assessment, meeting quality standards for services, and evaluation of customer satisfaction. **Therapy and Counseling:** Principles, methods, and procedures for diagnosis, treatment, and rehabilitation of physical and mental dysfunctions and for career counseling and guidance. **Telecommunications:** Transmission, broadcasting, switching, control, and operation of telecommunications systems.

WORK ENVIRONMENT—Outdoors; noisy; very hot or cold; contaminants; hazardous equipment; using hands on objects, tools, or controls.

Postal Service Clerks

- ☺ Education/Training Required: Short-term on-the-job training
- ☺ Annual Earnings: $48,310
- ☺ Growth: 0.0%
- ☺ Annual Job Openings: 4,000
- ☺ Self-Employed: 0.0%
- ☺ Part-Time: 6.7%

Perform any combination of tasks in a post office, such as receiving letters and parcels; selling postage and revenue stamps, postal cards, and stamped envelopes; filling out and selling money orders; placing mail in pigeonholes of mail rack or in bags according to state, address, or other scheme; and examining mail for correct postage. Provide customers with assistance in filing claims for mail theft or lost or damaged mail. Receive letters and parcels and place mail into bags. Put undelivered parcels away, retrieve them when customers come to claim them, and complete any related documentation. Obtain signatures from recipients of registered or special delivery mail. Complete forms regarding changes of address or theft or loss of mail or for special services such as registered or priority mail. Rent post office boxes to customers. Respond to complaints regarding mail theft, delivery problems, and lost or damaged mail, filling out forms and making appropriate referrals for investigation. Sell and collect payment for products such as stamps, prepaid mail envelopes, and money orders. Set postage meters and calibrate them to ensure correct operation. Sort incoming and outgoing mail according to type and destination by hand or by operating electronic mail-sorting and scanning devices. Transport mail from one workstation to another. Register, certify, and insure letters and parcels. Provide assistance to the public in complying with federal regulations of Postal Service and other federal agencies. Weigh letters and parcels; compute mailing costs based on type, weight, and destination; and affix correct postage. Cash money orders. Post announcements or government information on public bulletin boards. Answer questions regarding mail regulations and procedures, postage rates, and post office boxes. Check mail in order to ensure correct postage and that packages and letters are in proper condition for mailing. Keep money drawers in order and record and balance daily transactions. Feed mail into postage-canceling devices or hand-stamp mail to cancel postage.

LEVEL OF ACTIVITY (out of 100)—General Physical Activity: 40.0. **Sitting:** 40.0. **Outdoors:** 22.9.

SKILLS—None met the criteria.

GOE—Interest Area: 04. Business and Administration. **Work Group:** 04.07. Records and Materials Processing. **Other Jobs in This Work Group:** Correspondence Clerks; File Clerks; Human Resources Assistants, Except Payroll and Timekeeping; Marking Clerks; Meter Readers, Utilities; Office Clerks, General; Order Fillers, Wholesale and Retail Sales; Postal Service Mail Sorters, Processors, and Processing Machine Operators; Procurement Clerks; Production, Planning, and Expediting Clerks; Shipping, Receiving, and Traffic Clerks; Stock Clerks and Order Fillers; Stock Clerks, Sales Floor; Stock Clerks—Stockroom, Warehouse, or Storage Yard; Weighers, Measurers, Checkers, and Samplers, Recordkeeping. **PERSONALITY TYPE:** Conventional. Conventional occupations frequently involve following set procedures and routines. These occupations can include working with data and details more than with ideas. Usually there is a clear line of authority to follow.

EDUCATION/TRAINING PROGRAM(S)— General Office Occupations and Clerical Services. **RELATED KNOWLEDGE/COURSES—Clerical Practices:** Administrative and clerical procedures and systems such as word processing, managing files and records, stenography and transcription, designing forms, and other office procedures and terminology. **Geography:** Principles and methods for describing the features of land, sea, and air masses, including their physical characteristics; locations; interrelationships; and distribution of plant, animal, and human life.

WORK ENVIRONMENT—Indoors; standing; repetitive motions.

Postal Service Mail Carriers

- ☙ Education/Training Required: Short-term on-the-job training
- ☙ Annual Earnings: $46,330
- ☙ Growth: 0.0%
- ☙ Annual Job Openings: 19,000
- ☙ Self-Employed: 0.0%
- ☙ Part-Time: 9.8%

Sort mail for delivery. Deliver mail on established route by vehicle or on foot. Sell stamps and money orders. Report any unusual circumstances concerning mail delivery, including the condition of street letter boxes. Register, certify, and insure parcels and letters. Record address changes and redirect mail for those addresses. Sort mail for delivery, arranging it in delivery sequence. Travel to post offices to pick up the mail for routes and/or pick up mail from postal relay boxes. Obtain signed receipts for registered, certified, and insured mail; collect associated charges; and complete any necessary paperwork. Complete forms that notify publishers of address changes. Answer customers' questions about postal services and regulations. Provide customers with change-of-address cards and other forms. Sign for cash-on-delivery and registered mail before leaving the post office. Return incorrectly addressed mail to senders. Meet schedules for the collection and return of mail. Maintain accurate records of deliveries. Leave notices telling patrons where to collect mail that could not be delivered. Bundle mail in preparation for delivery or transportation to relay boxes. Deliver mail to residences and business establishments along specified routes by walking and/or driving, using a combination of satchels, carts, cars, and small trucks. Enter change-of-address orders into computers that process forwarding address stickers. Hold mail for customers who are away from delivery locations. Turn in money and receipts collected along mail routes. Return to the post office with mail collected from homes, businesses, and public mailboxes.

LEVEL OF ACTIVITY (out of 100)—**General Physical Activity:** 83.3. **Sitting:** 42.9. **Outdoors:** 62.9.

SKILLS—None met the criteria.

GOE—Interest Area: 16. Transportation, Distribution, and Logistics. Work Group: 16.06. Other Services Requiring Driving. Other Jobs in This Work Group: Ambulance Drivers and Attendants, Except Emergency Medical Technicians; Bus Drivers, School; Bus Drivers, Transit and Intercity; Couriers and Messengers; Driver/Sales Workers; Parking Lot Attendants; Taxi Drivers and Chauffeurs. PERSONALITY TYPE: Conventional. Conventional occupations frequently involve following set procedures and routines. These occupations can include working with data and details more than with ideas. Usually there is a clear line of authority to follow.

EDUCATION/TRAINING PROGRAM(S)— General Office Occupations and Clerical Services. RELATED KNOWLEDGE/COURS-ES—Transportation: Principles and methods for moving people or goods by air, rail, sea, or road, including the relative costs and benefits. Geography: Principles and methods for describing the features of land, sea, and air masses, including their physical characteristics; locations; interrelationships; and distribution of plant, animal, and human life.

WORK ENVIRONMENT—Outdoors; very hot or cold; standing; walking and running; using hands on objects, tools, or controls.

Preschool Teachers, Except Special Education

- Education/Training Required: Postsecondary vocational training
- Annual Earnings: $21,990
- Growth: 33.1%
- Annual Job Openings: 77,000
- Self-Employed: 1.4%
- Part-Time: 25.1%

Instruct children (normally up to 5 years of age) in activities designed to promote social, physical, and intellectual growth needed for primary school in preschool, day care center, or other child development facility. May be required to hold state certification. Provide a variety of materials and resources for children to explore, manipulate, and use, both in learning activities and in imaginative play. Attend to children's basic needs by feeding them, dressing them, and changing their diapers. Establish and enforce rules for behavior and procedures for maintaining order. Read books to entire classes or to small groups. Teach basic skills such as color, shape, number, and letter recognition; personal hygiene; and social skills. Organize and lead activities designed to promote physical, mental, and social development, such as games, arts and crafts, music, storytelling, and field trips. Observe and evaluate children's performance, behavior, social development, and physical health. Meet with parents and guardians to discuss their children's progress and needs, determine their priorities for their children, and suggest ways that they can promote learning and development. Identify children showing signs of emotional, developmental, or health-related problems and discuss them with supervisors, parents or guardians, and child development specialists. Enforce all administration policies and rules governing students. Prepare materials and classrooms for class activities. Serve meals and snacks in accordance with nutritional guidelines. Teach proper eating habits and personal hygiene. Assimilate arriving children to the school environment by greeting them, helping them remove outerwear, and selecting activities of interest to them. Adapt teaching methods and instructional materials to meet students' varying needs and interests. Establish clear objectives for all lessons, units, and projects and communicate those objectives to children. Demonstrate activities to children. Arrange indoor and outdoor space to facilitate creative play, motor-skill activities, and safety. Plan and conduct activities for a balanced program of instruction, demonstration, and work time that provides students with opportunities to observe, question, and investigate. Maintain accurate and complete student records as required by laws, district policies, and administrative regulations.

LEVEL OF ACTIVITY (out of 100)—General Physical Activity: 49.9. **Sitting:** 33.0. **Outdoors:** 25.4.

SKILLS—Learning Strategies; Social Perceptiveness; Instructing; Writing; Negotiation; Monitoring; Service Orientation; Speaking.

GOE—Interest Area: 05. Education and Training. **Work Group:** 05.02. Preschool, Elementary, and Secondary Teaching and Instructing. **Other Jobs in This Work Group:** Elementary School Teachers, Except Special Education; Kindergarten Teachers, Except Special Education; Middle School Teachers, Except Special and Vocational Education; Secondary School Teachers, Except Special and Vocational Education; Special Education Teachers, Middle School; Special Education Teachers, Preschool, Kindergarten, and Elementary School; Special Education Teachers, Secondary School; Teacher Assistants; Vocational Education Teachers, Middle School; Vocational Education Teachers, Secondary School. **PERSONALITY TYPE:** Social. Social occupations frequently involve working with, communicating with, and teaching people. These occupations often involve helping or providing service to others.

EDUCATION/TRAINING PROGRAM(S)— Montessori Teacher Education; Early Childhood Education and Teaching; Child Care and Support Services Management. **RELATED KNOWLEDGE/COURSES—Philosophy and Theology:** Different philosophical systems and religions. This includes their basic principles, values, ethics, ways of thinking, customs, and practices and their impact on human culture. **Customer and Personal Service:** Principles and processes for providing customer and personal services. This includes customer needs assessment, meeting quality standards for services, and evaluation of customer satisfaction. **Sociology and Anthropology:** Group behavior and dynamics, societal trends and influences, human migrations, ethnicity, and cultures and their history and origins. **Psychology:** Human behavior and performance; individual differences in ability, personality, and interests; learning and motivation; psychological research methods; and the assessment and treatment of behavioral and affective disorders. **Education and Training:** Principles and methods for curriculum and training design, teaching and instruction for individuals and groups, and the measurement of training effects. **Public Safety and Security:** Relevant equipment, policies, procedures, and strategies to promote effective local, state, or national security operations for the protection of people, data, property, and institutions.

WORK ENVIRONMENT—Indoors; standing; walking and running; bending or twisting the body.

Printing Machine Operators

- Education/Training Required: Moderate-term on-the-job training
- Annual Earnings: $30,730
- Growth: 2.9%
- Annual Job Openings: 26,000
- Self-Employed: 3.2%
- Part-Time: 8.1%

Set up or operate various types of printing machines, such as offset, letterset, intaglio, or gravure presses or screen printers, to produce print on paper or other materials. Inspect and examine printed products for print clarity, color accuracy, conformance to specifications, and external defects. Push buttons, turn handles, or move controls and levers to start and control printing machines. Reposition printing plates, adjust pressure rolls, or otherwise adjust machines to improve print quality, using knobs, handwheels, or hand tools. Set and adjust speed, temperature, ink flow, and positions and pressure tolerances of equipment. Examine job orders to determine details such as quantities to be printed, production times, stock specifications, colors, and color sequences. Select and install printing plates, rollers, feed guides, gauges, screens, stencils, type, dies, and cylinders in machines according to specifications, using hand tools. Monitor feeding, printing, and racking processes of presses in order to maintain specified operating levels and to detect malfunctions; make any necessary adjustments. Operate equipment at slow speed to ensure proper ink coverage, alignment, and registration. Load, position, and adjust unprinted materials on holding fixtures or in equipment-loading and -feeding mechanisms. Pour or spread paint, ink, color compounds, and other materials into reservoirs, troughs, hoppers, or color holders of printing units, making measurements and adjustments to control color and viscosity. Repair, maintain, or adjust equipment. Blend and test paint, inks, stains, and solvents according to types of material being printed and work order specifications. Clean and lubricate printing machines and components, using oil, solvents, brushes, rags, and hoses. Remove printed materials from presses, using handtrucks, electric lifts, or hoists, and transport them to drying, storage, or finishing areas. Input instructions in order to program automated machinery, using a computer keyboard. Place printed items in ovens to dry or set ink. Squeeze or spread ink on plates, pads, or rollers, using putty knives, brushes, or sponges. Measure screens and use measurements to center and align screens in proper positions and sequences on machines, using gauges and hand tools.

LEVEL OF ACTIVITY (out of 100)—General Physical Activity: 62.0. **Sitting:** 21.3. **Outdoors:** 17.6.

SKILLS—Operation Monitoring; Equipment Maintenance; Operation and Control; Repairing; Quality Control Analysis; Troubleshooting; Technology Design; Equipment Selection.

GOE—**Interest Area:** 13. Manufacturing. **Work Group:** 13.08. Graphic Arts Production. **Other Jobs in This Work Group:** Bindery Workers; Desktop Publishers; Etchers and Engravers; Job Printers; Photographic Process Workers; Photographic Processing Machine Operators; Prepress Technicians and Workers. **PERSONALITY TYPE:** Realistic. Realistic occupations frequently involve work activities that include practical, hands-on problems and solutions. They often deal with plants; animals; and real-world materials like wood, tools, and machinery. Many of the occupations require working outside and do not involve a lot of paperwork or working closely with others.

EDUCATION/TRAINING PROGRAM(S)— Printing Management; Graphic and Printing Equipment Operator, General Production; Printing Press Operator; Graphic Communications, Other. **RELATED KNOWLEDGE/ COURSES—Mechanical Devices:** Machines and tools, including their designs, uses, repair, and maintenance. **Production and Processing:** Raw materials, production processes, quality control, costs, and other techniques for maximizing the effective manufacture and distribution of goods. **Chemistry:** The chemical composition, structure, and properties of substances and of the chemical processes and transformations that they undergo. This includes uses of chemicals and their danger signs, production techniques, and disposal methods. **Administration and Management:** Business and management principles involved in strategic planning, resource allocation, human resources modeling, leadership technique, production methods, and coordination of people and resources.

WORK ENVIRONMENT—Noisy; contaminants; hazardous conditions; hazardous equipment; standing; using hands on objects, tools, or controls.

Radiation Therapists

- Education/Training Required: Associate degree
- Annual Earnings: $62,340
- Growth: 26.3%
- Annual Job Openings: 1,000
- Self-Employed: 0.0%
- Part-Time: 6.0%

Provide radiation therapy to patients as prescribed by a radiologist according to established practices and standards. Duties may include reviewing prescription and diagnosis; acting as liaison with physician and supportive care personnel; preparing equipment, such as immobilization, treatment, and protection devices; and maintaining records, reports, and files. May assist in dosimetry procedures and tumor localization. Administer prescribed doses of radiation to specific body parts, using radiation therapy equipment according to established practices and standards. Position patients for treatment with accuracy according to prescription. Enter data into computer and set controls to operate and adjust equipment and regulate dosage. Follow principles of radiation protection for patient, self, and others. Maintain records, reports, and files as required, including such information as radiation dosages, equipment settings, and patients' reactions. Review prescription, diagnosis, patient chart, and identification. Conduct most treatment sessions independently in accordance with the long-term treatment plan and under the general direction of the patient's physician. Check radiation therapy equipment to ensure proper operation. Observe and reassure patients during treatment and report unusual reactions to physician or turn equipment off if unexpected adverse reactions occur. Check for side effects such as skin irritation, nausea, and hair loss to assess patients' reaction to treatment. Educate, prepare, and reassure patients and their families by answering questions, providing physical assistance, and reinforcing physicians' advice regarding treatment reactions and post-treatment care. Calculate actual treatment dosages delivered during each session. Prepare and construct equipment such as immobilization, treatment, and protection devices. Photograph treated area of patient and process film. Help physicians, radiation oncologists, and clinical physicists to prepare physical and technical aspects of radiation treatment plans, using information about patient condition and anatomy. Train and supervise student or subordinate radiotherapy technologists. Provide assistance to other health care personnel during dosimetry procedures and tumor localization. Implement appropriate follow-up care plans. Act as liaison with physicist and supportive care personnel. Store, sterilize, or prepare the special applicators containing the radioactive substance implanted by the physician. Assist in the preparation of sealed radioactive materials, such as cobalt, radium, cesium, and isotopes, for use in radiation treatments.

LEVEL OF ACTIVITY (out of 100)—General Physical Activity: 46.7. **Sitting:** 27.1. **Outdoors:** 14.3.

SKILLS—Operation Monitoring; Operation and Control; Technology Design; Time Management; Science; Management of Personnel Resources; Service Orientation; Instructing.

GOE—Interest Area: 08. Health Science. **Work Group:** 08.07. Medical Therapy. **Other Jobs in This Work Group:** Audiologists; Massage Therapists; Occupational Therapist Aides; Occupational Therapist Assistants; Occupational Therapists; Physical Therapist Aides; Physical Therapist Assistants; Physical Therapists; Recreational Therapists; Respiratory Therapists; Respiratory Therapy Technicians; Speech-Language Pathologists. **PERSONALITY TYPE:** Social. Social occupations frequently involve working with, communicating with, and teaching people. These occupations often involve helping or providing service to others.

EDUCATION/TRAINING PROGRAM(S)—Medical Radiologic Technology/Science—Radiation Therapist. **RELATED KNOWLEDGE/COURSES—Medicine and Dentistry:** The information and techniques needed to diagnose and treat human injuries, diseases, and deformities. This includes symptoms, treatment alternatives, drug properties and interactions, and preventive health-care measures. **Biology:** Plant and animal organisms and their tissues, cells, functions, interdependencies, and interactions with each other and the environment. **Psychology:** Human behavior and performance; individual differences in ability, personality, and interests; learning and motivation; psychological research methods; and the assessment and treatment of behavioral and affective disorders. **Physics:** Physical principles and laws and their interrelationships and applications to understanding fluid, material, and atmospheric dynamics and mechanical, electrical, atomic, and subatomic structures and processes. **Customer and Personal Service:** Principles and processes for providing customer and personal services. This includes customer needs assessment, meeting quality standards for services, and evaluation of customer satisfaction. **Therapy and Counseling:** Principles, methods, and procedures for diagnosis, treatment, and rehabilitation of physical and mental dysfunctions and for career counseling and guidance.

WORK ENVIRONMENT—Indoors; disease or infections; standing; walking and running; using hands on objects, tools, or controls; repetitive motions.

Radiologic Technicians

This job can be found in the Part I lists under the title Radiologic Technologists and Technicians.

- ◎ Education/Training Required: Associate degree
- ◎ Annual Earnings: $45,950
- ◎ Growth: 23.2%
- ◎ Annual Job Openings: 17,000
- ◎ Self-Employed: 0.4%
- ◎ Part-Time: 17.2%

The job openings listed here are shared with Radiologic Technologists.

Maintain and use equipment and supplies necessary to demonstrate portions of the human body on X-ray film or fluoroscopic screen for diagnostic purposes. Use beam-restrictive devices and patient-shielding techniques to minimize radiation exposure to patient and staff. Position X-ray equipment and adjust controls to set exposure factors, such as time and distance. Position patient on examining table and set up and adjust equipment to obtain optimum view of specific body area as requested by physician. Determine patients' X-ray needs by reading requests or instructions from physicians. Make exposures necessary for the requested procedures, rejecting and repeating work that does not meet established standards. Process exposed radiographs, using film processors or computer-generated methods. Explain procedures to patients to reduce anxieties and obtain cooperation. Perform procedures such as linear tomography; mammography; sonograms; joint and cyst aspirations; routine contrast studies; routine fluoroscopy; and examinations of the head, trunk, and extremities under supervision of physician. Prepare and set up X-ray room for patient. Assure that sterile supplies, contrast materials, catheters, and other required equipment are present and in working order, requisitioning materials as necessary. Maintain records of patients examined, examinations performed, views taken, and technical factors used. Provide assistance to physicians or other technologists in the performance of more complex procedures. Monitor equipment operation and report malfunctioning equipment to supervisor. Provide students and other technologists with suggestions of additional views, alternate positioning, or improved techniques to ensure that the images produced are of the highest quality. Coordinate work of other technicians or technologists when procedures require more than one person. Assist with on-the-job training of new employees and students and provide input to supervisors regarding training performance. Maintain a current file of examination protocols. Operate mobile X-ray equipment in operating room, in emergency room, or at patient's bedside. Provide assistance in radiopharmaceutical administration, monitoring patients' vital signs and notifying the radiologist of any relevant changes.

LEVEL OF ACTIVITY (out of 100)—General Physical Activity: 55.6. **Sitting:** 28.0. **Outdoors:** 16.2.

SKILLS—Science; Operation Monitoring; Service Orientation; Equipment Selection; Operation and Control; Negotiation; Active Listening; Speaking.

GOE—**Interest Area:** 08. Health Science. **Work Group:** 08.06. Medical Technology. **Other Jobs in This Work Group:** Biological Technicians; Cardiovascular Technologists and Technicians; Diagnostic Medical Sonographers; Medical and Clinical Laboratory Technicians; Medical and Clinical Laboratory Technologists; Medical Equipment Preparers; Medical Records and Health Information Technicians; Nuclear Medicine Technologists; Opticians, Dispensing; Orthotists and Prosthetists; Radiologic Technologists; Radiologic Technologists and Technicians. **PERSONALITY TYPE:** Realistic. Realistic occupations frequently involve work activities that include practical, hands-on problems and solutions. They often deal with plants; animals; and real-world materials like wood, tools, and machinery. Many of the occupations require working outside and do not involve a lot of paperwork or working closely with others.

EDUCATION/TRAINING PROGRAM(S)—Medical Radiologic Technology/Science—

Radiation Therapist; Radiologic Technology/Science—Radiographer; Allied Health Diagnostic, Intervention, and Treatment Professions, Other. **RELATED KNOWLEDGE/COURSES**—**Clerical Practices:** Administrative and clerical procedures and systems such as word processing, managing files and records, stenography and transcription, designing forms, and other office procedures and terminology. **Medicine and Dentistry:** The information and techniques needed to diagnose and treat human injuries, diseases, and deformities. This includes symptoms, treatment alternatives, drug properties and interactions, and preventive health-care measures. **Psychology:** Human behavior and performance; individual differences in ability, personality, and interests; learning and motivation; psychological research methods; and the assessment and treatment of behavioral and affective disorders. **Physics:** Physical principles and laws and their interrelationships and applications to understanding fluid, material, and atmospheric dynamics and mechanical, electrical, atomic, and subatomic structures and processes. **Biology:** Plant and animal organisms and their tissues, cells, functions, interdependencies, and interactions with each other and the environment. **Customer and Personal Service:** Principles and processes for providing customer and personal services. This includes customer needs assessment, meeting quality standards for services, and evaluation of customer satisfaction.

WORK ENVIRONMENT—Indoors; radiation; disease or infections; standing; walking and running; using hands on objects, tools, or controls.

Radiologic Technologists

This job can be found in the Part I lists under the title Radiologic Technologists and Technicians.

- ◉ Education/Training Required: Associate degree
- ◉ Annual Earnings: $45,950
- ◉ Growth: 23.2%
- ◉ Annual Job Openings: 17,000
- ◉ Self-Employed: 0.4%
- ◉ Part-Time: 17.2%

The job openings listed here are shared with Radiologic Technicians.

Take X rays and Computerized Axial Tomography (CAT or CT) scans or administer nonradioactive materials into patient's bloodstream for diagnostic purposes. Includes technologists who specialize in other modalities, such as computed tomography, ultrasound, and magnetic resonance. Review and evaluate developed X rays, videotape, or computer-generated information to determine if images are satisfactory for diagnostic purposes. Use radiation safety measures and protection devices to comply with government regulations and to ensure safety of patients and staff. Explain procedures and observe patients to ensure safety and comfort during scan. Operate or oversee operation of radiologic and magnetic imaging equipment to produce images of the body for diagnostic purposes. Position and immobilize patient on examining table. Position imaging equipment and adjust controls to set exposure time and distance, according to specification of examination.

Key commands and data into computer to document and specify scan sequences, adjust transmitters and receivers, or photograph certain images. Monitor video display of area being scanned and adjust density or contrast to improve picture quality. Monitor patients' conditions and reactions, reporting abnormal signs to physician. Prepare and administer oral or injected contrast media to patients. Set up examination rooms, ensuring that all necessary equipment is ready. Take thorough and accurate patient medical histories. Remove and process film. Record, process, and maintain patient data and treatment records and prepare reports. Coordinate work with clerical personnel or other technologists. Demonstrate new equipment, procedures, and techniques to staff and provide technical assistance. Provide assistance in dressing or changing seriously ill, injured, or disabled patients. Move ultrasound scanner over patient's body and watch pattern produced on video screen. Measure thickness of section to be radiographed, using instruments similar to measuring tapes. Operate fluoroscope to aid physician to view and guide wire or catheter through blood vessels to area of interest. Assign duties to radiologic staff to maintain patient flows and achieve production goals. Collaborate with other medical team members, such as physicians and nurses, to conduct angiography or special vascular procedures. Perform administrative duties such as developing departmental operating budget, coordinating purchases of supplies and equipment, and preparing work schedules.

LEVEL OF ACTIVITY (out of 100)—General Physical Activity: 62.9. **Sitting:** 39.7. **Outdoors:** 21.1.

SKILLS—Operation Monitoring; Social Perceptiveness; Instructing; Reading Comprehension; Service Orientation; Active Listening; Speaking; Science.

GOE—**Interest Area:** 08. Health Science. **Work Group:** 08.06. Medical Technology. **Other Jobs in This Work Group:** Biological Technicians; Cardiovascular Technologists and Technicians; Diagnostic Medical Sonographers; Medical and Clinical Laboratory Technicians; Medical and Clinical Laboratory Technologists; Medical Equipment Preparers; Medical Records and Health Information Technicians; Nuclear Medicine Technologists; Opticians, Dispensing; Orthotists and Prosthetists; Radiologic Technicians; Radiologic Technologists and Technicians. **PERSONALITY TYPE:** Realistic. Realistic occupations frequently involve work activities that include practical, hands-on problems and solutions. They often deal with plants; animals; and real-world materials like wood, tools, and machinery. Many of the occupations require working outside and do not involve a lot of paperwork or working closely with others.

EDUCATION/TRAINING PROGRAM(S)— Medical Radiologic Technology/Science— Radiation Therapist; Radiologic Technology/ Science—Radiographer; Allied Health Diagnostic, Intervention, and Treatment Professions, Other. **RELATED KNOWLEDGE/COURSES—Medicine and Dentistry:** The information and techniques needed to diagnose and treat human injuries, diseases, and deformities. This includes symptoms, treatment alternatives, drug properties and interactions, and preventive health-care measures. **Biology:** Plant and animal organisms and their tissues, cells, functions, interdependencies, and interactions with each other and the environment. **Physics:** Physical principles and laws and their interrelationships and applications to understanding fluid, material, and atmospheric dynamics and mechanical, electrical, atomic, and subatomic structures and processes. **Psychology:** Human behavior and performance; individual differences in ability, personality, and interests; learning and motivation; psychological research methods; and the assessment and treatment of behavioral and affective disorders. **Chemistry:** The chemical composition, structure, and properties of substances and of the chemical processes and transformations that they undergo. This includes uses of chemicals and their danger signs, production techniques, and disposal methods. **Customer and Personal Service:** Principles and processes for providing customer and personal services. This includes customer needs assessment, meeting quality standards for services, and evaluation of customer satisfaction.

WORK ENVIRONMENT—Indoors; disease or infections; standing; walking and running; using hands on objects, tools, or controls; repetitive motions.

Radiologic Technologists and Technicians

See the descriptions of these jobs:

- **Radiologic Technicians**
- **Radiologic Technologists**

Railroad Conductors and Yardmasters

◉ Education/Training Required: Work experience in a related occupation

◉ Annual Earnings: $54,040

◉ Growth: 20.3%

◉ Annual Job Openings: 3,000

◉ Self-Employed: 0.0%

◉ Part-Time: 0.6%

Conductors coordinate activities of train crew on passenger or freight train. Coordinate activities of switch-engine crew within yard of railroad, industrial plant, or similar location. Yardmasters coordinate activities of workers engaged in railroad traffic operations, such as the makeup or breakup of trains and yard switching, and review train schedules and switching orders. Signal engineers to begin train runs, stop trains, or change speed, using telecommunications equipment or hand signals. Receive information regarding train or rail problems from dispatchers or from electronic monitoring devices. Direct and instruct workers engaged in yard activities, such as switching tracks, coupling and uncoupling cars, and routing inbound and outbound traffic. Keep records of the contents and destination of each train car and make sure that cars are added or removed at proper points on routes. Operate controls to activate track switches and traffic signals. Instruct workers to set warning signals in front and at rear of trains during emergency stops.

Direct engineers to move cars to fit planned train configurations, combining or separating cars to make up or break up trains. Receive instructions from dispatchers regarding trains' routes, timetables, and cargoes. Review schedules, switching orders, way bills, and shipping records to obtain cargo loading and unloading information and to plan work. Confer with engineers regarding train routes, timetables, and cargoes and to discuss alternative routes when there are rail defects or obstructions. Arrange for the removal of defective cars from trains at stations or stops. Inspect each car periodically during runs. Observe yard traffic to determine tracks available to accommodate inbound and outbound traffic. Document and prepare reports of accidents, unscheduled stops, or delays. Confirm routes and destination information for freight cars. Supervise and coordinate crew activities to transport freight and passengers and to provide boarding, porter, maid, and meal services to passengers. Supervise workers in the inspection and maintenance of mechanical equipment in order to ensure efficient and safe train operation. Record departure and arrival times, messages, tickets and revenue collected, and passenger accommodations and destinations. Inspect freight cars for compliance with sealing procedures and record car numbers and seal numbers. Collect tickets, fares, or passes from passengers. Verify accuracy of timekeeping instruments with engineers to ensure that trains depart on time.

LEVEL OF ACTIVITY (out of 100)—General Physical Activity: 56.6. **Sitting:** 47.0. **Outdoors:** 43.0.

SKILLS—Operation and Control; Operation Monitoring; Coordination; Equipment Maintenance; Instructing; Troubleshooting; Active Listening; Reading Comprehension.

GOE—Interest Area: 16. Transportation, Distribution, and Logistics. Work Group: 16.01. Managerial Work in Transportation. Other Jobs in This Work Group: Aircraft Cargo Handling Supervisors; First-Line Supervisors/Managers of Transportation and Material-Moving Machine and Vehicle Operators; Postmasters and Mail Superintendents; Storage and Distribution Managers; Transportation Managers; Transportation, Storage, and Distribution Managers. PERSONALITY TYPE: Realistic. Realistic occupations frequently involve work activities that include practical, hands-on problems and solutions. They often deal with plants; animals; and real-world materials like wood, tools, and machinery. Many of the occupations require working outside and do not involve a lot of paperwork or working closely with others.

EDUCATION/TRAINING PROGRAM(S)—Truck and Bus Driver/Commercial Vehicle Operation. RELATED KNOWLEDGE/COURSES—Transportation: Principles and methods for moving people or goods by air, rail, sea, or road, including the relative costs and benefits. Public Safety and Security: Relevant equipment, policies, procedures, and strategies to promote effective local, state, or national security operations for the protection of people, data, property, and institutions. Mechanical Devices: Machines and tools, including their designs, uses, repair, and maintenance. Clerical Practices: Administrative and clerical procedures and systems such as word processing, managing files and records, stenography and transcription, designing forms, and other office procedures and terminology. Law and Government: Laws, legal codes, court procedures, precedents, government regulations, executive orders, agency rules, and the democratic political process.

WORK ENVIRONMENT—Outdoors; noisy; very hot or cold; very bright or dim lighting; contaminants; hazardous equipment.

Range Managers

This job can be found in the Part I lists under the title Conservation Scientists.

- Education/Training Required: Bachelor's degree
- Annual Earnings: $53,350
- Growth: 6.3%
- Annual Job Openings: 2,000
- Self-Employed: 9.0%
- Part-Time: 6.7%

The job openings listed here are shared with Park Naturalists and with Soil and Water Conservationists.

Research or study range land management practices to provide sustained production of forage, livestock, and wildlife. Regulate grazing and help ranchers plan and organize grazing systems in order to manage, improve, and protect rangelands and maximize their use. Measure and assess vegetation resources for biological assessment companies, environmental impact statements, and rangeland monitoring programs. Maintain soil stability and vegetation for non-grazing uses, such as wildlife habitats and outdoor recreation. Mediate agreements among rangeland users and preservationists as to appropriate land use and management. Study rangeland management practices and research range problems to provide sustained production of forage, livestock, and wildlife. Manage forage resources through fire, herbicide use, or revegetation to maintain a sustainable yield from the land. Offer advice to rangeland users on water management, forage production methods, and control of brush. Develop technical standards and specifications used to manage, protect, and improve the natural resources of range lands and related grazing lands. Tailor conservation plans to landowners' goals, such as livestock support, wildlife, or recreation. Plan and direct construction and maintenance of range improvements such as fencing, corrals, stock-watering reservoirs, and soil-erosion control structures. Study grazing patterns to determine number and kind of livestock that can be most profitably grazed and to determine the best grazing seasons. Plan and implement revegetation of disturbed sites. Study forage plants and their growth requirements to determine varieties best suited to particular range. Develop methods for protecting range from fire and rodent damage and for controlling poisonous plants. Manage private livestock operations. Develop new and improved instruments and techniques for activities such as range reseeding.

LEVEL OF ACTIVITY (out of 100)—General Physical Activity: 72.6. **Sitting:** 46.4. **Outdoors:** 42.8.

SKILLS—Negotiation; Management of Financial Resources; Science; Persuasion; Coordination; Complex Problem Solving; Judgment and Decision Making; Systems Evaluation.

GOE—Interest Area: 01. Agriculture and Natural Resources. **Work Group:** 01.02. Resource Science/Engineering for Plants, Animals, and the Environment. **Other Jobs in This Work Group:** Agricultural Engineers; Animal Scientists; Conservation Scientists; Environmental Engineers; Foresters; Mining and Geological Engineers, Including Mining Safety Engineers; Petroleum Engineers; Soil and Plant Scientists; Soil and Water Conservationists; Zoologists and Wildlife Biologists. **PERSONALITY TYPE:** Investigative. Investigative occupations frequently involve working with ideas and require an extensive amount of thinking. These occupations can involve searching for facts and figuring out problems mentally.

EDUCATION/TRAINING PROGRAM(S)—Natural Resources/Conservation, General; Natural Resources Management and Policy; Water, Wetlands, and Marine Resources Management; Land Use Planning and Management/Development; Natural Resources Management and Policy, Other; Forestry, General; Forest Sciences and Biology; Forest Management/Forest Resources Management; Forestry, Other; Wildlife and Wildlands Science and Management; others. **RELATED KNOWLEDGE/COURSES—Biology:** Plant and animal organisms and their tissues, cells, functions, interdependencies, and interactions with each other and the environment. **Geography:** Principles and methods for describing the features of land, sea, and air masses, including their physical characteristics; locations; interrelationships; and distribution of plant, animal, and human life. **Food Production:** Techniques and equipment for planting, growing, and harvesting food products (both plant and animal) for consumption, including storage/handling techniques. **History and Archeology:** Historical events and their causes, indicators, and effects on civilizations and cultures. **Law and Government:** Laws, legal codes, court procedures, precedents, government regulations, executive orders, agency rules, and the democratic political process. **Engineering and Technology:** The practical application of engineering science and technology. This includes applying principles, techniques, procedures, and equipment to the design and production of various goods and services.

WORK ENVIRONMENT—More often outdoors than indoors; noisy; very hot or cold; minor burns, cuts, bites, or stings; sitting.

Recreation Workers

- Education/Training Required: Bachelor's degree
- Annual Earnings: $20,110
- Growth: 17.3%
- Annual Job Openings: 69,000
- Self-Employed: 6.7%
- Part-Time: 41.3%

Conduct recreation activities with groups in public, private, or volunteer agencies or recreation facilities. Organize and promote activities such as arts and crafts, sports, games, music, dramatics, social recreation, camping, and hobbies, taking into account the needs and interests of individual members. Enforce rules and regulations of recreational facilities to maintain discipline and ensure safety. Organize, lead, and promote interest in recreational activities such as arts, crafts, sports, games, camping, and hobbies. Manage the daily operations of recreational facilities. Administer first aid according to prescribed procedures and notify emergency medical personnel when necessary. Ascertain and interpret group interests, evaluate equipment and facilities, and adapt activities to meet partic-

ipant needs. Greet new arrivals to activities, introducing them to other participants, explaining facility rules, and encouraging participation. Complete and maintain time and attendance forms and inventory lists. Explain principles, techniques, and safety procedures to participants in recreational activities and demonstrate use of materials and equipment. Evaluate recreation areas, facilities, and services to determine if they are producing desired results. Confer with management to discuss and resolve participant complaints. Supervise and coordinate the work activities of personnel, such as training staff members and assigning work duties. Meet and collaborate with agency personnel, community organizations, and other professional personnel to plan balanced recreational programs for participants. Schedule maintenance and use of facilities. Direct special activities or events such as aquatics, gymnastics, or performing arts. Meet with staff to discuss rules, regulations, and work-related problems. Provide for entertainment and set up related decorations and equipment. Encourage participants to develop their own activities and leadership skills through group discussions. Serve as liaison between park or recreation administrators and activity instructors. Evaluate staff performance, recording evaluations on appropriate forms. Oversee the purchase, planning, design, construction, and upkeep of recreation facilities and areas.

LEVEL OF ACTIVITY (out of 100)—General Physical Activity: 52.9. **Sitting:** 43.9. **Outdoors:** 29.3.

SKILLS—Management of Financial Resources; Management of Personnel Resources; Service Orientation; Management of Material Resources; Social Perceptiveness; Time Management; Coordination; Writing.

GOE—**Interest Area:** 09. Hospitality, Tourism, and Recreation. **Work Group:** 09.02. Recreational Services. **Other Jobs in This Work Group:** Amusement and Recreation Attendants; Gaming and Sports Book Writers and Runners; Gaming Dealers; Locker Room, Coatroom, and Dressing Room Attendants; Motion Picture Projectionists; Slot Key Persons; Ushers, Lobby Attendants, and Ticket Takers. **PERSONALITY TYPE:** Social. Social occupations frequently involve working with, communicating with, and teaching people. These occupations often involve helping or providing service to others.

EDUCATION/TRAINING PROGRAM(S)— Parks, Recreation, and Leisure Studies; Parks, Recreation and Leisure Facilities Management; Sport and Fitness Administration/Management; Health and Physical Education/Fitness, Other; Parks, Recreation, Leisure, and Fitness Studies, Other. **RELATED KNOWLEDGE/COURS-ES—Psychology:** Human behavior and performance; individual differences in ability, personality, and interests; learning and motivation; psychological research methods; and the assessment and treatment of behavioral and affective disorders. **Customer and Personal Service:** Principles and processes for providing customer and personal services. This includes customer needs assessment, meeting quality standards for services, and evaluation of customer satisfaction. **Therapy and Counseling:** Principles, methods, and procedures for diagnosis, treatment, and rehabilitation of physical and mental dysfunctions and for career counseling and guidance. **Education and Training:** Principles and methods for curriculum and training design, teaching and instruction for individuals and groups, and the measurement of training effects. **Sales and Marketing:** Principles and methods for showing, promoting, and selling products or services. This includes marketing strategy and tactics, product demonstration,

sales techniques, and sales control systems. **Sociology and Anthropology:** Group behavior and dynamics, societal trends and influences, human migrations, ethnicity, and cultures and their history and origins.

WORK ENVIRONMENT—Indoors; noisy; more often standing than sitting; using hands on objects, tools, or controls.

Recreational Vehicle Service Technicians

- Education/Training Required: Long-term on-the-job training
- Annual Earnings: $30,480
- Growth: 19.5%
- Annual Job Openings: 3,000
- Self-Employed: 3.6%
- Part-Time: 19.6%

Diagnose, inspect, adjust, repair, or overhaul recreational vehicles, including travel trailers. May specialize in maintaining gas, electrical, hydraulic, plumbing, or chassis/towing systems as well as repairing generators, appliances, and interior components. Examine or test operation of parts or systems that have been repaired to ensure completeness of repairs. Repair plumbing and propane gas lines, using caulking compounds and plastic or copper pipe. Inspect recreational vehicles to diagnose problems; then perform necessary adjustment, repair, or overhaul. Locate and repair frayed wiring, broken connections, or incorrect wiring, using ohmmeters, soldering irons, tape, and hand tools.

Confer with customers, read work orders, and examine vehicles needing repair in order to determine the nature and extent of damage. List parts needed, estimate costs, and plan work procedures, using parts lists, technical manuals, and diagrams. Connect electrical systems to outside power sources and activate switches to test the operation of appliances and light fixtures. Connect water hoses to inlet pipes of plumbing systems and test operation of toilets and sinks. Remove damaged exterior panels and repair and replace structural frame members. Open and close doors, windows, and drawers to test their operation, trimming edges to fit as necessary. Repair leaks with caulking compound or replace pipes, using pipe wrenches. Refinish wood surfaces on cabinets, doors, moldings, and floors, using power sanders, putty, spray equipment, brushes, paints, or varnishes. Reset hardware, using chisels, mallets, and screwdrivers. Seal open sides of modular units to prepare them for shipment, using polyethylene sheets, nails, and hammers.

LEVEL OF ACTIVITY (out of 100)—General Physical Activity: 73.3. **Sitting:** 26.1. **Outdoors:** 57.0.

SKILLS—Repairing; Installation; Troubleshooting; Equipment Maintenance; Operation Monitoring; Technology Design; Equipment Selection; Systems Evaluation.

GOE—Interest Area: 13. Manufacturing. **Work Group:** 13.14. Vehicle and Facility Mechanical Work. **Other Jobs in This Work Group:** Aircraft Mechanics and Service Technicians; Aircraft Structure, Surfaces, Rigging, and Systems Assemblers; Automotive Body and Related Repairers; Automotive Glass Installers and Repairers; Automotive Master Mechanics; Automotive Service Technicians and Mechanics; Automotive Specialty Technicians; Bus and Truck Mechanics and Diesel Engine Specialists; Farm Equipment Mechanics; Fiberglass Laminators and Fabricators; Mobile Heavy Equipment Mechanics, Except Engines; Motorboat Mechanics; Motorcycle Mechanics; Outdoor Power Equipment and Other Small Engine Mechanics; Rail Car Repairers; Tire Repairers and Changers. **PERSONALITY TYPE:** Realistic. Realistic occupations frequently involve work activities that include practical, hands-on problems and solutions. They often deal with plants; animals; and real-world materials like wood, tools, and machinery. Many of the occupations require working outside and do not involve a lot of paperwork or working closely with others.

EDUCATION/TRAINING PROGRAM(S)—Vehicle Maintenance and Repair Technologies, Other. **RELATED KNOWLEDGE/COURSES—Mechanical Devices:** Machines and tools, including their designs, uses, repair, and maintenance. **Building and Construction:** The materials, methods, and tools involved in the construction or repair of houses, buildings, or other structures such as highways and roads. **Chemistry:** The chemical composition, structure, and properties of substances and of the chemical processes and transformations that they undergo. This includes uses of chemicals and their danger signs, production techniques, and disposal methods. **Physics:** Physical principles and laws and their interrelationships and applications to understanding fluid, material, and atmospheric dynamics and mechanical, electrical, atomic, and subatomic structures and processes. **Design:** Design techniques, tools, and principles involved in production of precision technical plans, blueprints, drawings, and models. **Engineering and Technology:** The practical application of engineering science and technology. This includes applying principles, techniques, procedures, and equipment to the design and production of various goods and services.

WORK ENVIRONMENT—Noisy; contaminants; cramped work space, awkward positions; hazardous equipment; standing; using hands on objects, tools, or controls.

Refrigeration Mechanics and Installers

This job can be found in the Part I lists under the title Heating, Air Conditioning, and Refrigeration Mechanics and Installers.

- Education/Training Required: Long-term on-the-job training
- Annual Earnings: $37,040
- Growth: 19.0%
- Annual Job Openings: 33,000
- Self-Employed: 13.1%
- Part-Time: 3.6%

The job openings listed here are shared with Heating and Air Conditioning Mechanics and Installers.

Install and repair industrial and commercial refrigerating systems. Braze or solder parts to repair defective joints and leaks. Observe and test system operation, using gauges and instruments. Test lines, components, and connections for leaks. Dismantle malfunctioning systems and test components, using electrical, mechanical, and pneumatic testing equipment. Adjust or replace worn or defective mechanisms and parts; reassemble repaired systems. Read blueprints to determine location, size, capacity, and type of components needed to build refrigeration system. Supervise and instruct assistants. Perform mechanical overhauls and refrigerant reclaiming. Install wiring to connect components to an electric power source. Cut, bend, thread, and connect pipe to functional components and water, power, or refrigeration system. Adjust valves according to specifications and charge system with proper type of refrigerant by pumping the specified gas or fluid into the system. Estimate, order, pick up, deliver, and install materials and supplies needed to maintain equipment in good working condition. Install expansion and control valves, using acetylene torches and wrenches. Mount compressor, condenser, and other components in specified locations on frames, using hand tools and acetylene welding equipment. Keep records of repairs and replacements made and causes of malfunctions. Schedule work with customers and initiate work orders, house requisitions, and orders from stock. Lay out reference points for installation of structural and functional components, using measuring instruments. Fabricate and assemble structural and functional components of refrigeration system, using hand tools, power tools, and welding equipment. Lift and align components into position, using hoist or block and tackle. Drill holes and install mounting brackets and hangers into floor and walls of building. Insulate shells and cabinets of systems.

LEVEL OF ACTIVITY (out of 100)—General Physical Activity: 73.4. **Sitting:** 26.6. **Outdoors:** 44.4.

SKILLS—Installation; Repairing; Equipment Maintenance; Operation Monitoring; Systems Evaluation; Systems Analysis; Science; Troubleshooting.

GOE—Interest Area: 02. Architecture and Construction. Work Group: 02.05. Systems and Equipment Installation, Maintenance, and Repair. Other Jobs in This Work Group: Electrical and Electronics Repairers, Power-house, Substation, and Relay; Electrical Power-Line Installers and Repairers; Elevator Installers and Repairers; Heating and Air Conditioning Mechanics and Installers; Maintenance and Repair Workers, General; Telecommunications Equipment Installers and Repairers, Except Line Installers; Telecommunications Line Installers and Repairers. PERSONALITY TYPE: Real-istic. Realistic occupations frequently involve work activities that include practical, hands-on problems and solutions. They often deal with plants; animals; and real-world materials like wood, tools, and machinery. Many of the occu-pations require working outside and do not involve a lot of paperwork or working closely with others.

EDUCATION/TRAINING PROGRAM(S)—Heating, Air Conditioning, and Refrigeration Technology/Technician (ACH/ACR/ACHR/HRAC/HVAC); Solar Energy Technology/Technician; Heating, Air Conditioning, Ventilation, and Refrigeration Maintenance Technology/Technician. RELATED KNOWL-EDGE/COURSES—Building and Construc-tion: The materials, methods, and tools involved in the construction or repair of houses, build-ings, or other structures such as highways and roads. Mechanical Devices: Machines and tools, including their designs, uses, repair, and mainte-nance. Engineering and Technology: The prac-tical application of engineering science and technology. This includes applying principles, techniques, procedures, and equipment to the design and production of various goods and services. Physics: Physical principles and laws and their interrelationships and applications to understanding fluid, material, and atmospheric dynamics and mechanical, electrical, atomic, and subatomic structures and processes. Design: Design techniques, tools, and principles involved in production of precision technical plans, blueprints, drawings, and models. Chemistry: The chemical composition, struc-ture, and properties of substances and of the chemical processes and transformations that they undergo. This includes uses of chemicals and their danger signs, production techniques, and disposal methods.

WORK ENVIRONMENT—Outdoors; very hot or cold; cramped work space, awkward posi-tions; minor burns, cuts, bites, or stings; stand-ing; using hands on objects, tools, or controls.

Refuse and Recyclable Material Collectors

- Education/Training Required: Short-term on-the-job training
- Annual Earnings: $28,460
- Growth: 8.9%
- Annual Job Openings: 31,000
- Self-Employed: 4.2%
- Part-Time: 18.2%

Collect and dump refuse or recyclable materials from containers into truck. May drive truck. Inspect trucks prior to beginning routes to ensure safe operating condition. Refuel trucks and add other necessary fluids, such as oil. Fill out any needed reports for defective equipment.

Drive to disposal sites to empty trucks that have been filled. Drive trucks along established routes through residential streets and alleys or through business and industrial areas. Operate equipment that compresses the collected refuse. Operate automated or semi-automated hoisting devices that raise refuse bins and dump contents into openings in truck bodies. Dismount garbage trucks to collect garbage and remount trucks to ride to the next collection point. Communicate with dispatchers concerning delays, unsafe sites, accidents, equipment breakdowns, and other maintenance problems. Keep informed of road and weather conditions to determine how routes will be affected. Tag garbage or recycling containers to inform customers of problems such as excess garbage or inclusion of items that are not permitted. Clean trucks and compactor bodies after routes have been completed. Sort items set out for recycling and throw materials into designated truck compartments. Organize schedules for refuse collection. Provide quotes for refuse collection contracts.

LEVEL OF ACTIVITY (out of 100)—General Physical Activity: 60.4. **Sitting:** 47.1. **Outdoors:** 50.9.

SKILLS—Equipment Maintenance; Operation Monitoring; Operation and Control; Repairing.

GOE—Interest Area: 13. Manufacturing. **Work Group:** 13.17. Loading, Moving, Hoisting, and Conveying. **Other Jobs in This Work Group:** Conveyor Operators and Tenders; Hoist and Winch Operators; Industrial Truck and Tractor Operators; Machine Feeders and Offbearers; Packers and Packagers, Hand; Pump Operators, Except Wellhead Pumpers; Tank Car, Truck, and Ship Loaders. **PERSONALITY TYPE:** Realistic. Realistic occupations frequently involve work activities that include practical, hands-on problems and solutions. They often deal with plants; animals; and real-world materials like wood, tools, and machinery. Many of the occupations require working outside and do not involve a lot of paperwork or working closely with others.

EDUCATION/TRAINING PROGRAM(S)— No related CIP programs; this job is learned through informal short-term on-the-job training. **RELATED KNOWLEDGE/COURSES— Transportation:** Principles and methods for moving people or goods by air, rail, sea, or road, including the relative costs and benefits. **Customer and Personal Service:** Principles and processes for providing customer and personal services. This includes customer needs assessment, meeting quality standards for services, and evaluation of customer satisfaction. **Public Safety and Security:** Relevant equipment, policies, procedures, and strategies to promote effective local, state, or national security operations for the protection of people, data, property, and institutions. **Education and Training:** Principles and methods for curriculum and training design, teaching and instruction for individuals and groups, and the measurement of training effects. **Mechanical Devices:** Machines and tools, including their designs, uses, repair, and maintenance.

WORK ENVIRONMENT—Outdoors; noisy; contaminants; using hands on objects, tools, or controls; bending or twisting the body; repetitive motions.

Registered Nurses

- Education/Training Required: Associate degree
- Annual Earnings: $54,670
- Growth: 29.4%
- Annual Job Openings: 229,000
- Self-Employed: 0.7%
- Part-Time: 24.1%

Assess patient health problems and needs, develop and implement nursing care plans, and maintain medical records. Administer nursing care to ill, injured, convalescent, or disabled patients. May advise patients on health maintenance and disease prevention or provide case management. Licensing or registration required. Includes advance practice nurses such as nurse practitioners, clinical nurse specialists, certified nurse midwives, and certified registered nurse anesthetists. Advanced practice nursing is practiced by RNs who have specialized formal, post-basic education and who function in highly autonomous and specialized roles. Maintain accurate, detailed reports and records. Monitor, record, and report symptoms and changes in patients' conditions. Record patients' medical information and vital signs. Modify patient treatment plans as indicated by patients' responses and conditions. Consult and coordinate with health care team members to assess, plan, implement, and evaluate patient care plans. Order, interpret, and evaluate diagnostic tests to identify and assess patient's condition. Monitor all aspects of patient care, including diet and physical activity. Direct and supervise less-skilled nursing or health care personnel or supervise a particular unit. Prepare patients for, and assist with, examinations and treatments. Observe nurses and visit patients to ensure proper nursing care. Assess the needs of individuals, families, or communities, including assessment of individuals' home or work environments to identify potential health or safety problems. Instruct individuals, families, and other groups on topics such as health education, disease prevention, and childbirth, and develop health improvement programs. Prepare rooms, sterile instruments, equipment, and supplies and ensure that stock of supplies is maintained. Inform physician of patient's condition during anesthesia. Deliver infants and provide prenatal and postpartum care and treatment under obstetrician's supervision. Administer local, inhalation, intravenous, and other anesthetics. Provide health care, first aid, immunizations, and assistance in convalescence and rehabilitation in locations such as schools, hospitals, and industry. Conduct specified laboratory tests. Perform physical examinations, make tentative diagnoses, and treat patients en route to hospitals or at disaster site triage centers. Hand items to surgeons during operations. Prescribe or recommend drugs, medical devices, or other forms of treatment, such as physical therapy, inhalation therapy, or related therapeutic procedures. Direct and coordinate infection control programs, advising and consulting with specified personnel about necessary precautions. Perform administrative and managerial functions, such as taking responsibility for a unit's staff, budget, planning, and long-range goals.

LEVEL OF ACTIVITY (out of 100)—General Physical Activity: 48.1. **Sitting:** 34.4. **Outdoors:** 18.3.

SKILLS—Social Perceptiveness; Service Orientation; Science; Time Management;

Instructing; Monitoring; Critical Thinking; Learning Strategies.

GOE—Interest Area: 08. Health Science. **Work Group:** 08.02. Medicine and Surgery. **Other Jobs in This Work Group:** Anesthesiologists; Family and General Practitioners; Internists, General; Medical Assistants; Medical Transcriptionists; Obstetricians and Gynecologists; Pediatricians, General; Pharmacists; Pharmacy Aides; Pharmacy Technicians; Physician Assistants; Psychiatrists; Surgeons; Surgical Technologists. **PERSONALITY TYPE:** Social. Social occupations frequently involve working with, communicating with, and teaching people. These occupations often involve helping or providing service to others.

EDUCATION/TRAINING PROGRAM(S)— Nursing—Registered Nurse Training (RN, ASN, BSN, MSN); Adult Health Nurse/Nursing; Nurse Anesthetist; Family Practice Nurse/Nurse Practitioner; Maternal/Child Health and Neonatal Nurse/Nursing; Nurse Midwife/Nursing Midwifery; Nursing Science (MS, PhD); Pediatric Nurse/Nursing; Psychiatric/Mental Health Nurse/Nursing; Public Health/Community Nurse/Nursing; others. **RELATED KNOWLEDGE/COURSES— Medicine and Dentistry:** The information and techniques needed to diagnose and treat human injuries, diseases, and deformities. This includes symptoms, treatment alternatives, drug properties and interactions, and preventive health-care measures. **Psychology:** Human behavior and performance; individual differences in ability, personality, and interests; learning and motivation; psychological research methods; and the assessment and treatment of behavioral and affective disorders. **Therapy and Counseling:** Principles, methods, and procedures for diagnosis, treatment, and rehabilitation of physical and mental dysfunctions and for career counseling

and guidance. **Biology:** Plant and animal organisms and their tissues, cells, functions, interdependencies, and interactions with each other and the environment. **Customer and Personal Service:** Principles and processes for providing customer and personal services. This includes customer needs assessment, meeting quality standards for services, and evaluation of customer satisfaction. **Sociology and Anthropology:** Group behavior and dynamics, societal trends and influences, human migrations, ethnicity, and cultures and their history and origins.

WORK ENVIRONMENT—Indoors; noisy; contaminants; disease or infections; standing; using hands on objects, tools, or controls.

Reinforcing Iron and Rebar Workers

- Education/Training Required: Long-term on-the-job training
- Annual Earnings: $34,910
- Growth: 14.1%
- Annual Job Openings: 6,000
- Self-Employed: 2.3%
- Part-Time: 3.9%

Position and secure steel bars or mesh in concrete forms in order to reinforce concrete. Use a variety of fasteners, rod-bending machines, blowtorches, and hand tools. Space and fasten together rods in forms according to blueprints, using wire and pliers. Cut and fit wire mesh or fabric, using hooked rods, and position fabric or mesh in concrete to reinforce concrete. Cut rods to required lengths, using metal shears, hacksaws, bar cutters, or acetylene torches. Bend steel rods with hand tools and rodbending machines and weld them with arc-welding equipment. Position and secure steel bars, rods, cables, or mesh in concrete forms, using fasteners, rod-bending machines, blowtorches, and hand tools. Place blocks under rebar to hold the bars off the deck when reinforcing floors. Determine quantities, sizes, shapes, and locations of reinforcing rods from blueprints, sketches, or oral instructions.

LEVEL OF ACTIVITY (out of 100)—General Physical Activity: 61.9. **Sitting:** 35.7. **Outdoors:** 53.6.

SKILLS—None met the criteria.

GOE—Interest Area: 02. Architecture and Construction. **Work Group:** 02.04. Construction Crafts. **Other Jobs in This Work Group:** Boilermakers; Brickmasons and Blockmasons; Carpet Installers; Cement Masons and Concrete Finishers; Commercial Divers; Construction Carpenters; Crane and Tower Operators; Drywall and Ceiling Tile Installers; Electricians; Fence Erectors; Floor Layers, Except Carpet, Wood, and Hard Tiles; Floor Sanders and Finishers; Glaziers; Hazardous Materials Removal Workers; Insulation Workers, Floor, Ceiling, and Wall; Insulation Workers, Mechanical; Manufactured Building and Mobile Home Installers; Operating Engineers and Other Construction Equipment Operators; Painters, Construction and Maintenance; Paperhangers; Paving, Surfacing, and Tamping Equipment Operators; Pile-Driver Operators; Pipe Fitters and Steamfitters; Pipelayers; Plasterers and Stucco Masons; Plumbers; Plumbers, Pipefitters, and Steamfitters; Rail-Track Laying and Maintenance Equipment Operators; Refractory Materials Repairers, Except Brickmasons; Riggers; Roofers; Rough Carpenters; Security and Fire Alarm Systems Installers; Segmental Pavers; Sheet Metal Workers; Stone Cutters and Carvers, Manufacturing; Stonemasons; Structural Iron and Steel Workers; Tapers; Terrazzo Workers and Finishers; Tile and Marble Setters. **PERSONALITY TYPE:** Realistic. Realistic occupations frequently involve work activities that include practical, hands-on problems and solutions. They often deal with plants; animals; and real-world materials like wood, tools, and machinery. Many of the occupations require working outside and do not involve a lot of paperwork or working closely with others.

EDUCATION/TRAINING PROGRAM(S)—Construction Trades, Other. **RELATED KNOWLEDGE/COURSES—Building and Construction:** The materials, methods, and tools involved in the construction or repair of houses, buildings, or other structures such as highways and roads. **Physics:** Physical principles and laws and their interrelationships and applications to understanding fluid, material, and atmospheric dynamics and mechanical, electrical, atomic, and subatomic structures and processes. **Design:** Design techniques, tools, and principles involved in production of precision technical plans, blueprints, drawings, and models. **Engineering and Technology:** The practical application of engineering science and technology. This includes applying principles, techniques, procedures, and equipment to the design and production of various goods and services.

WORK ENVIRONMENT—Outdoors; noisy; contaminants; minor burns, cuts, bites, or stings; standing; using hands on objects, tools, or controls.

Respiratory Therapists

- ◉ Education/Training Required: Associate degree
- ◉ Annual Earnings: $45,140
- ◉ Growth: 28.4%
- ◉ Annual Job Openings: 7,000
- ◉ Self-Employed: 0.4%
- ◉ Part-Time: 15.9%

Assess, treat, and care for patients with breathing disorders. Assume primary responsibility for all respiratory care modalities, including the supervision of respiratory therapy technicians. Initiate and conduct therapeutic procedures; maintain patient records; and select, assemble, check, and operate equipment. Set up and operate devices such as mechanical ventilators, therapeutic gas administration apparatus, environmental control systems, and aerosol generators, following specified parameters of treatment. Provide emergency care, including artificial respiration, external cardiac massage, and assistance with cardiopulmonary resuscitation. Determine requirements for treatment, such as type, method, and duration of therapy; precautions to be taken; and medication and dosages, compatible with physicians' orders. Monitor patient's physiological responses to therapy, such as vital signs, arterial blood gases, and blood chemistry changes, and consult with physician if adverse reactions occur. Read prescription, measure arterial blood gases, and review patient information to assess patient condition. Work as part of a team of physicians, nurses, and other health care professionals to manage patient care. Enforce safety rules and ensure careful adherence to physicians' orders. Maintain charts that contain patients' pertinent identification and therapy information. Inspect, clean, test, and maintain respiratory therapy equipment to ensure equipment is functioning safely and efficiently, ordering repairs when necessary. Educate patients and their families about their conditions and teach appropriate disease management techniques, such as breathing exercises and the use of medications and respiratory equipment. Explain treatment procedures to patients to gain cooperation and allay fears. Relay blood analysis results to a physician. Perform pulmonary function and adjust equipment to obtain optimum results in therapy. Perform bronchopulmonary drainage and assist or instruct patients in performance of breathing exercises. Demonstrate respiratory care procedures to trainees and other health care personnel. Teach, train, supervise, and utilize the assistance of students, respiratory therapy technicians, and assistants. Make emergency visits to resolve equipment problems. Use a variety of testing techniques to assist doctors in cardiac and pulmonary research and to diagnose disorders. Conduct tests, such as electrocardiograms (EKGs), stress testing, and lung capacity tests, to evaluate patients' cardiopulmonary functions.

LEVEL OF ACTIVITY (out of 100)—General Physical Activity: 49.1. **Sitting:** 34.6. **Outdoors:** 15.1.

SKILLS—Science; Instructing; Operation Monitoring; Active Learning; Mathematics; Service Orientation; Reading Comprehension; Troubleshooting.

GOE—Interest Area: 08. Health Science. **Work Group:** 08.07. Medical Therapy. **Other Jobs in This Work Group:** Audiologists; Massage Therapists; Occupational Therapist Aides; Occupational Therapist Assistants; Occupational Therapists; Physical Therapist Aides; Physical Therapist Assistants; Physical Therapists; Radiation Therapists; Recreational Therapists; Respiratory Therapy Technicians; Speech-Language Pathologists. **PERSONALITY TYPE:** Investigative. Investigative occupations frequently involve working with ideas and require an extensive amount of thinking. These occupations can involve searching for facts and figuring out problems mentally.

EDUCATION/TRAINING PROGRAM(S)— Respiratory Care Therapy/Therapist. **RELATED KNOWLEDGE/COURSES—Medicine and Dentistry:** The information and techniques needed to diagnose and treat human injuries, diseases, and deformities. This includes symptoms, treatment alternatives, drug properties and interactions, and preventive health-care measures. **Psychology:** Human behavior and performance; individual differences in ability, personality, and interests; learning and motivation; psychological research methods; and the assessment and treatment of behavioral and affective disorders. **Biology:** Plant and animal organisms and their tissues, cells, functions, interdependencies, and interactions with each other and the environment. **Customer and Personal Service:** Principles and processes for providing customer and personal services. This includes customer needs assessment, meeting quality standards for services, and evaluation of customer satisfaction. **Therapy and Counseling:** Principles, methods, and procedures for diagnosis, treatment, and rehabilitation of physical and mental dysfunctions and for career counseling and guidance. **Chemistry:** The chemical composition, structure, and properties of substances and of the chemical processes and transformations that they undergo. This includes uses of chemicals and their danger signs, production techniques, and disposal methods.

WORK ENVIRONMENT—Indoors; disease or infections; standing.

Riggers

- ◎ Education/Training Required: Short-term on-the-job training
- ◎ Annual Earnings: $37,010
- ◎ Growth: 13.9%
- ◎ Annual Job Openings: 2,000
- ◎ Self-Employed: 0.0%
- ◎ Part-Time: 1.9%

Set up or repair rigging for construction projects, manufacturing plants, logging yards, ships and shipyards, or the entertainment industry. Manipulate rigging lines, hoists, and pulling gear to move or support materials such as heavy equipment, ships, or theatrical sets. Signal or verbally direct workers engaged in hoisting and moving loads in order to ensure safety of workers and materials. Dismantle and store rigging equipment after use. Control movement of heavy equipment through narrow openings or confined spaces, using chainfalls, gin poles, gallows frames, and other equipment. Attach pulleys and blocks to fixed overhead structures such as beams, ceilings, and gin pole booms, using bolts and clamps. Attach loads to rigging to provide support or prepare them for moving, using hand and power tools. Align, level, and anchor machinery. Select gear such as cables, pulleys, and winches according to load weights and sizes, facilities, and work schedules. Tilt, dip, and turn suspended loads to maneuver over, under, and/or around obstacles, using multi-point suspension techniques. Test rigging to ensure safety and reliability. Fabricate, set up, and repair rigging, supporting structures, hoists, and pulling gear, using hand and power tools. Install ground rigging for yarding lines, attaching chokers to logs and then to the lines. Clean and dress machine surfaces and component parts.

LEVEL OF ACTIVITY (out of 100)—General Physical Activity: 57.1. **Sitting:** 31.4. **Outdoors:** 54.3.

SKILLS—Repairing; Technology Design; Science; Operation Monitoring; Operation and Control; Installation; Management of Material Resources; Equipment Maintenance.

GOE—Interest Area: 02. Architecture and Construction. **Work Group:** 02.04. Construction Crafts. **Other Jobs in This Work Group:** Boilermakers; Brickmasons and Blockmasons; Carpet Installers; Cement Masons and Concrete Finishers; Commercial Divers; Construction Carpenters; Crane and Tower Operators; Drywall and Ceiling Tile Installers; Electricians; Fence Erectors; Floor Layers, Except Carpet, Wood, and Hard Tiles; Floor Sanders and Finishers; Glaziers; Hazardous Materials Removal Workers; Insulation Workers, Floor, Ceiling, and Wall; Insulation Workers, Mechanical; Manufactured Building and Mobile Home Installers; Operating Engineers and Other Construction Equipment Operators; Painters, Construction and Maintenance; Paperhangers; Paving, Surfacing, and Tamping Equipment Operators; Pile-Driver Operators; Pipe Fitters and Steamfitters; Pipelayers; Plasterers and Stucco Masons; Plumbers; Plumbers, Pipefitters, and Steamfitters; Rail-Track Laying and Maintenance Equipment Operators; Refractory Materials Repairers, Except Brickmasons; Reinforcing Iron and Rebar Workers; Roofers; Rough Carpenters; Security and Fire Alarm Systems Installers; Segmental Pavers; Sheet Metal Workers; Stone Cutters and Carvers, Manufacturing; Stonemasons; Structural Iron and Steel Workers; Tapers; Terrazzo Workers and Finishers; Tile and Marble Setters. **PERSONALITY TYPE:** Realistic. Realistic occupations frequently involve work activities that include practical, hands-on problems and solutions. They often deal with plants; animals; and real-world materials like wood, tools, and machinery. Many of the occupations require working outside and do not involve a lot of paperwork or working closely with others.

EDUCATION/TRAINING PROGRAM(S)— Construction/Heavy Equipment/Earthmoving Equipment Operation. **RELATED KNOWLEDGE/COURSES—Mechanical Devices:** Machines and tools, including their designs, uses, repair, and maintenance. **Public Safety and Security:** Relevant equipment, policies, procedures, and strategies to promote effective local, state, or national security operations for the protection of people, data, property, and institutions. **Engineering and Technology:** The practical application of engineering science and technology. This includes applying principles, techniques, procedures, and equipment to the design and production of various goods and services. **Building and Construction:** The materials, methods, and tools involved in the construction or repair of houses, buildings, or other structures such as highways and roads.

WORK ENVIRONMENT—Outdoors; high places; standing; climbing ladders, scaffolds, or poles; using hands on objects, tools, or controls; bending or twisting the body.

Roofers

⊚ Education/Training Required: Moderate-term on-the-job training

⊚ Annual Earnings: $31,230

⊚ Growth: 16.8%

⊚ Annual Job Openings: 38,000

⊚ Self-Employed: 23.8%

⊚ Part-Time: 10.3%

Cover roofs of structures with shingles, slate, asphalt, aluminum, wood, and related materials. May spray roofs, sidings, and walls with material to bind, seal, insulate, or soundproof sections of structures. Cement or nail flashing-strips of metal or shingle over joints to make them watertight. Cut roofing paper to size, using knives, and nail or staple roofing paper to roofs in overlapping strips to form bases for other materials. Apply gravel or pebbles over top layers of roofs, using rakes or stiff-bristled brooms. Apply plastic coatings and membranes, fiberglass, or felt over sloped roofs before applying shingles. Hammer and chisel away rough spots or remove them with rubbing bricks to prepare surfaces for waterproofing. Spray roofs, sidings, and walls with material to bind, seal, insulate, or soundproof sections of structures, using spray guns, air compressors, and heaters. Cover exposed nailheads with roofing cement or caulking to prevent water leakage and rust. Clean and maintain equipment. Cut felt, shingles, and strips of flashing and fit them into angles formed by walls, vents, and intersecting roof surfaces. Glaze top layers to make a smooth finish or embed gravel in the bitumen for rough surfaces. Inspect problem roofs to determine the best procedures for repairing them. Install par-tially overlapping layers of material over roof insulation surfaces, determining distance of roofing material overlap by using chalk lines, gauges on shingling hatchets, or lines on shingles. Install vapor barriers and/or layers of insulation on the roof decks of flat roofs and seal the seams. Install, repair, or replace single-ply roofing systems, using waterproof sheet materials such as modified plastics, elastomeric, or other asphaltic compositions. Mop or pour hot asphalt or tar onto roof bases. Apply alternate layers of hot asphalt or tar and roofing paper to roofs according to specification. Cover roofs and exterior walls of structures with slate, asphalt, aluminum, wood, gravel, gypsum, and/or related materials, using brushes, knives, punches, hammers, and other tools. Waterproof and damp-proof walls, floors, roofs, foundations, and basements by painting or spraying surfaces with waterproof coatings or by attaching waterproofing membranes to surfaces. Estimate roofing materials and labor required to complete jobs and provide price quotes.

LEVEL OF ACTIVITY (out of 100)—General Physical Activity: 71.4. **Sitting:** 31.4. **Outdoors:** 71.4.

SKILLS—Repairing; Installation; Operation and Control.

GOE—Interest Area: 02. Architecture and Construction. **Work Group:** 02.04. Construction Crafts. **Other Jobs in This Work Group:** Boilermakers; Brickmasons and Blockmasons; Carpet Installers; Cement Masons and Concrete Finishers; Commercial Divers; Construction Carpenters; Crane and Tower Operators; Drywall and Ceiling Tile Installers; Electricians; Fence Erectors; Floor Layers, Except Carpet, Wood, and Hard Tiles; Floor Sanders and Finishers; Glaziers; Hazardous Materials Removal Workers; Insulation Workers, Floor, Ceiling, and Wall; Insulation Workers,

Mechanical; Manufactured Building and Mobile Home Installers; Operating Engineers and Other Construction Equipment Operators; Painters, Construction and Maintenance; Paperhangers; Paving, Surfacing, and Tamping Equipment Operators; Pile-Driver Operators; Pipe Fitters and Steamfitters; Pipelayers; Plasterers and Stucco Masons; Plumbers; Plumbers, Pipefitters, and Steamfitters; Rail-Track Laying and Maintenance Equipment Operators; Refractory Materials Repairers, Except Brickmasons; Reinforcing Iron and Rebar Workers; Riggers; Rough Carpenters; Security and Fire Alarm Systems Installers; Segmental Pavers; Sheet Metal Workers; Stone Cutters and Carvers, Manufacturing; Stonemasons; Structural Iron and Steel Workers; Tapers; Terrazzo Workers and Finishers; Tile and Marble Setters. **PERSONALITY TYPE:** Realistic. Realistic occupations frequently involve work activities that include practical, hands-on problems and solutions. They often deal with plants; animals; and real-world materials like wood, tools, and machinery. Many of the occupations require working outside and do not involve a lot of paperwork or working closely with others.

EDUCATION/TRAINING PROGRAM(S)— Roofer. **RELATED KNOWLEDGE/COURSES—Building and Construction:** The materials, methods, and tools involved in the construction or repair of houses, buildings, or other structures such as highways and roads. **Mechanical Devices:** Machines and tools, including their designs, uses, repair, and maintenance.

WORK ENVIRONMENT—Outdoors; high places; kneeling, crouching, stooping, or crawling; keeping or regaining balance; using hands on objects, tools, or controls; bending or twisting the body.

Rough Carpenters

This job can be found in the Part I lists under the title Carpenters.

- Education/Training Required: Long-term on-the-job training
- Annual Earnings: $35,580
- Growth: 13.8%
- Annual Job Openings: 210,000
- Self-Employed: 32.4%
- Part-Time: 8.2%

The job openings listed here are shared with Construction Carpenters.

Build rough wooden structures, such as concrete forms; scaffolds; tunnel, bridge, or sewer supports; billboard signs; and temporary frame shelters, according to sketches, blueprints, or oral instructions. Study blueprints and diagrams to determine dimensions of structure or form to be constructed. Measure materials or distances, using square, measuring tape, or rule to lay out work. Cut or saw boards, timbers, or plywood to required size, using handsaw, power saw, or woodworking machine. Assemble and fasten material together to construct wood or metal framework of structure, using bolts, nails, or screws. Anchor and brace forms and other structures in place, using nails, bolts, anchor rods, steel cables, planks, wedges, and timbers. Mark cutting lines on materials, using pencil and scriber. Erect forms, framework, scaffolds, hoists, roof supports, or chutes, using hand tools, plumb rule, and level. Install rough door and window frames, subflooring, fixtures, or temporary supports in structures undergoing construction or repair. Examine structural timbers and supports to detect decay and replace timbers as required, using hand tools, nuts, and bolts. Bore bolt holes in timber, masonry, or concrete walls, using power drill. Fabricate parts, using woodworking and metalworking machines. Dig or direct digging of post holes and set poles to support structures. Build sleds from logs and timbers for use in hauling camp buildings and machinery through wooded areas. Build chutes for pouring concrete.

LEVEL OF ACTIVITY (out of 100)—General Physical Activity: 72.9. **Sitting:** 25.3. **Outdoors:** 44.8.

SKILLS—Repairing; Installation; Management of Personnel Resources; Equipment Selection; Mathematics; Technology Design; Coordination; Equipment Maintenance.

GOE—Interest Area: 02. Architecture and Construction. **Work Group:** 02.04. Construction Crafts. **Other Jobs in This Work Group:** Boilermakers; Brickmasons and Blockmasons; Carpet Installers; Cement Masons and Concrete Finishers; Commercial Divers; Construction Carpenters; Crane and Tower Operators; Drywall and Ceiling Tile Installers; Electricians; Fence Erectors; Floor Layers, Except Carpet, Wood, and Hard Tiles; Floor Sanders and Finishers; Glaziers; Hazardous Materials Removal Workers; Insulation Workers, Floor, Ceiling, and Wall; Insulation Workers, Mechanical; Manufactured Building and Mobile Home Installers; Operating Engineers and Other Construction Equipment Operators; Painters, Construction and Maintenance; Paperhangers; Paving, Surfacing, and Tamping Equipment Operators; Pile-Driver Operators; Pipe Fitters and Steamfitters; Pipelayers; Plasterers and Stucco Masons; Plumbers; Plumbers, Pipefitters, and Steamfitters; Rail-Track Laying and Maintenance Equipment Operators; Refractory Materials Repairers, Except Brickmasons; Reinforcing Iron and Rebar Workers; Riggers; Roofers; Security and Fire Alarm Systems Installers; Segmental Pavers; Sheet Metal Workers; Stone Cutters and Carvers, Manufacturing; Stonemasons; Structural Iron and Steel Workers; Tapers; Terrazzo Workers and Finishers; Tile and Marble Setters. **PERSONALITY TYPE:** Realistic. Realistic occupations frequently involve work activities that include practical, hands-on problems and solutions. They often deal with plants; animals; and real-world materials like wood, tools, and machinery. Many of the occupations require working outside and do not involve a lot of paperwork or working closely with others.

EDUCATION/TRAINING PROGRAM(S)— Carpentry/Carpenter. **RELATED KNOWLEDGE/COURSES—Building and Construction:** The materials, methods, and tools involved in the construction or repair of houses, buildings, or other structures such as highways and roads. **Design:** Design techniques, tools, and principles involved in production of precision technical plans, blueprints, drawings, and models. **Engineering and Technology:** The practical application of engineering science and technology. This includes applying principles, techniques, procedures, and equipment to the design and production of various goods and services. **Mechanical Devices:** Machines and tools, including their designs, uses, repair, and maintenance. **Production and Processing:** Raw materials, production processes, quality control, costs, and other techniques for maximizing the effective manufacture and distribution of goods. **Public Safety and Security:** Relevant equipment, policies, procedures, and strategies to promote effective local, state, or national security operations for the protection of people, data, property, and institutions.

WORK ENVIRONMENT—Outdoors; noisy; very hot or cold; contaminants; standing; using hands on objects, tools, or controls.

Secondary School Teachers, Except Special and Vocational Education

- ◎ Education/Training Required: Bachelor's degree
- ◎ Annual Earnings: $46,060
- ◎ Growth: 14.4%
- ◎ Annual Job Openings: 107,000
- ◎ Self-Employed: 0.0%
- ◎ Part-Time: 9.2%

Instruct students in secondary public or private schools in one or more subjects at the secondary level, such as English, mathematics, or social studies. May be designated according to subject matter specialty, such as typing instructors, commercial teachers, or English teachers. Establish and enforce rules for behavior and procedures for maintaining order among the students for whom they are responsible. Instruct through lectures, discussions, and demonstrations in one or more subjects such as English, mathematics, or social studies. Establish clear objectives for all lessons, units, and projects and communicate those objectives to students. Prepare, administer, and grade tests and assignments to evaluate students' progress. Prepare materials and classrooms for class activities. Adapt teaching methods and instructional materials to meet students' varying needs and interests. Assign and grade class work and homework. Maintain accurate and complete student records as required by laws, district policies, and administrative regulations. Enforce all administration policies and rules governing students. Observe and evaluate students' performance, behavior, social development, and physical health. Plan and conduct activities for a balanced program of instruction, demonstration, and work time that provides students with opportunities to observe, question, and investigate. Prepare students for later grades by encouraging them to explore learning opportunities and to persevere with challenging tasks. Guide and counsel students with adjustment and/or academic problems or special academic interests. Instruct and monitor students in the use and care of equipment and materials in order to prevent injuries and damage. Prepare for assigned classes and show written evidence of preparation upon request of immediate supervisors. Meet with parents and guardians to discuss their children's progress and to determine their priorities for their children and their resource needs. Confer with parents or guardians, other teachers, counselors, and administrators in order to resolve students' behavioral and academic problems. Use computers, audiovisual aids, and other equipment and materials to supplement presentations. Prepare objectives and outlines for courses of study, following curriculum guidelines or requirements of states and schools. Meet with other professionals to discuss individual students' needs and progress.

LEVEL OF ACTIVITY (out of 100)—General Physical Activity: 42.6. **Sitting:** 35.1. **Outdoors:** 18.0.

SKILLS—Learning Strategies; Persuasion; Social Perceptiveness; Instructing; Monitoring; Time Management; Service Orientation; Negotiation.

GOE—**Interest Area:** 05. Education and Training. **Work Group:** 05.02. Preschool, Elementary, and Secondary Teaching and Instructing. **Other Jobs in This Work Group:** Elementary School Teachers, Except Special Education; Kindergarten Teachers, Except Special Education; Middle School Teachers, Except Special and Vocational Education; Preschool Teachers, Except Special Education; Special Education Teachers, Middle School; Special Education Teachers, Preschool, Kindergarten, and Elementary School; Special Education Teachers, Secondary School; Teacher Assistants; Vocational Education Teachers, Middle School; Vocational Education Teachers, Secondary School. **PERSONALITY TYPE:** Social. Social occupations frequently involve working with, communicating with, and teaching people. These occupations often involve helping or providing service to others.

EDUCATION/TRAINING PROGRAM(S)— Junior High/Intermediate/Middle School Education and Teaching; Secondary Education and Teaching; Teacher Education, Multiple Levels; Waldorf/Steiner Teacher Education; Agricultural Teacher Education; Art Teacher Education; Business Teacher Education; Driver and Safety Teacher Education; English/Language Arts Teacher Education; Foreign Language Teacher Education; Health Teacher Education; others. **RELATED KNOWLEDGE/COURSES—Education and Training:** Principles and methods for curriculum and training design, teaching and instruction for individuals and groups, and the measurement of training effects. **History and Archeology:** Historical events and their causes, indicators, and effects on civilizations and cultures. **Philosophy and Theology:** Different philosophical systems and religions. This includes their basic principles, values, ethics, ways of thinking, customs, and practices and their impact on human culture. **Sociology and Anthropology:** Group behavior and dynamics, societal trends and influences, human migrations, ethnicity, and cultures and their history and origins. **Geography:** Principles and methods for describing the features of land, sea, and air masses, including their physical characteristics; locations; interrelationships; and distribution of plant, animal, and human life. **Therapy and Counseling:** Principles, methods, and procedures for diagnosis, treatment, and rehabilitation of physical and mental dysfunctions and for career counseling and guidance.

WORK ENVIRONMENT—Indoors; noisy; standing.

Security Guards

- ◎ Education/Training Required: Short-term on-the-job training
- ◎ Annual Earnings: $20,760
- ◎ Growth: 12.6%
- ◎ Annual Job Openings: 230,000
- ◎ Self-Employed: 0.7%
- ◎ Part-Time: 17.1%

Guard, patrol, or monitor premises to prevent theft, violence, or infractions of rules. Patrol industrial or commercial premises to prevent and detect signs of intrusion and ensure security of doors, windows, and gates. Answer alarms and investigate disturbances. Monitor and authorize entrance and departure of employees, visitors, and other persons to guard against theft and maintain security of premises. Write reports of daily activities and irregularities such as equipment or property damage, theft, presence of unauthorized persons, or unusual occurrences. Call police or fire departments in cases of emergency, such as fire or presence of unauthorized persons. Circulate among visitors, patrons, or employees to preserve order and protect property. Answer telephone calls to take messages, answer questions, and provide information during non-business hours or when switchboard is closed. Warn persons of rule infractions or violations and apprehend or evict violators from premises, using force when necessary. Operate detecting devices to screen individuals and prevent passage of prohibited articles into restricted areas. Escort or drive motor vehicle to transport individuals to specified locations or to provide personal protection. Inspect and adjust security systems, equipment, or machinery to ensure operational use and to detect evidence of tampering. Drive or guard armored vehicle to transport money and valuables to prevent theft and ensure safe delivery. Monitor and adjust controls that regulate building systems, such as air conditioning, furnace, or boiler.

LEVEL OF ACTIVITY (out of 100)—General Physical Activity: 54.7. **Sitting:** 46.6. **Outdoors:** 32.8.

SKILLS—Social Perceptiveness; Negotiation; Learning Strategies; Speaking; Equipment Maintenance; Writing; Active Listening; Monitoring.

GOE—Interest Area: 12. Law and Public Safety. **Work Group:** 12.05. Safety and Security. **Other Jobs in This Work Group:** Animal Control Workers; Crossing Guards; Gaming Surveillance Officers and Gaming Investigators; Lifeguards, Ski Patrol, and Other Recreational Protective Service Workers; Private Detectives and Investigators; Transportation Security Screeners. **PERSONALITY TYPE:** Social. Social occupations frequently involve working with, communicating with, and teaching people. These occupations often involve helping or providing service to others.

EDUCATION/TRAINING PROGRAM(S)— Security and Loss Prevention Services; Securities Services Administration/Management. **RELATED KNOWLEDGE/COURSES—Public Safety and Security:** Relevant equipment, policies, procedures, and strategies to promote effective local, state, or national security operations for the protection of people, data, property, and institutions. **Customer and Personal Service:** Principles and processes for providing customer and personal services. This includes customer needs assessment, meeting quality standards for services, and evaluation of customer satisfaction. **Telecommunications:** Transmission, broadcasting, switching, control, and operation of telecommunications systems. **Law and Government:** Laws, legal codes, court procedures, precedents, government regulations, executive orders, agency rules, and the democratic political process. **Clerical Practices:** Administrative and clerical procedures and systems such as word processing, managing files and records, stenography and transcription, designing forms, and other office procedures and terminology. **Transportation:** Principles and methods for moving people or goods by air, rail, sea, or road, including the relative costs and benefits.

WORK ENVIRONMENT—More often outdoors than indoors; noisy; very hot or cold; more often sitting than standing.

Self-Enrichment Education Teachers

- Education/Training Required: Work experience in a related occupation
- Annual Earnings: $32,360
- Growth: 25.3%
- Annual Job Openings: 74,000
- Self-Employed: 31.1%
- Part-Time: 45.6%

Teach or instruct courses other than those that normally lead to an occupational objective or degree. Courses may include self-improvement, nonvocational, and nonacademic subjects. Teaching may or may not take place in a traditional educational institution. Adapt teaching methods and instructional materials to meet students' varying needs and interests. Conduct classes, workshops, and demonstrations and provide individual instruction to teach topics and skills such as cooking, dancing, writing, physical fitness, photography, personal finance, and flying. Monitor students' performance in order to make suggestions for improvement and to ensure that they satisfy course standards, training requirements, and objectives. Observe students to determine qualifications, limitations, abilities, interests, and other individual characteristics. Instruct students individually and in groups, using various teaching methods such as lectures, discussions, and demonstrations. Establish clear objectives for all lessons, units, and projects and communicate those objectives to students. Instruct and monitor students in use and care of equipment and materials in order to prevent injury and damage. Prepare students for further development by encouraging them to explore learning opportunities and to persevere with challenging tasks. Prepare materials and classrooms for class activities. Enforce policies and rules governing students. Plan and conduct activities for a balanced program of instruction, demonstration, and work time that provides students with opportunities to observe, question, and investigate. Prepare instructional program objectives, outlines, and lesson plans. Maintain accurate and complete student records as required by administrative policy. Participate in publicity planning and student recruitment. Plan and supervise class projects, field trips, visits by guest speakers, contests, or other experiential activities and guide students in learning from those activities. Attend professional meetings, conferences, and workshops in order to maintain and improve professional competence. Meet with other instructors to discuss individual students and their progress. Confer with other teachers and professionals to plan and schedule lessons promoting learning and development. Attend staff meetings and serve on committees as required. Prepare and administer written, oral, and performance tests and issue grades in accordance with performance.

LEVEL OF ACTIVITY (out of 100)—General Physical Activity: 52.6. **Sitting:** 41.3. **Outdoors:** 21.6.

SKILLS—Instructing; Learning Strategies; Social Perceptiveness; Service Orientation; Persuasion; Monitoring; Speaking; Time Management.

GOE—Interest Area: 05. Education and Training. **Work Group:** 05.03. Postsecondary and Adult Teaching and Instructing. **Other Jobs in This Work Group:** Adult Literacy, Remedial Education, and GED Teachers and Instructors; Agricultural Sciences Teachers, Postsecondary; Anthropology and Archeology Teachers, Postsecondary; Architecture Teachers, Postsecondary; Area, Ethnic, and Cultural Studies Teachers, Postsecondary; Art, Drama, and Music Teachers, Postsecondary; Atmospheric, Earth, Marine, and Space Sciences Teachers, Postsecondary; Biological Science Teachers, Postsecondary; Business Teachers, Postsecondary; Chemistry Teachers, Postsecondary; Communications Teachers, Postsecondary; Computer Science Teachers, Postsecondary; Criminal Justice and Law Enforcement Teachers, Postsecondary; Economics Teachers, Postsecondary; Education Teachers, Postsecondary; Engineering Teachers, Postsecondary; English Language and Literature Teachers, Postsecondary; Environmental Science Teachers, Postsecondary; Farm and Home Management Advisors; Foreign Language and Literature Teachers, Postsecondary; Forestry and Conservation Science Teachers, Postsecondary; Geography Teachers, Postsecondary; Graduate Teaching Assistants; Health Specialties Teachers, Postsecondary; History Teachers, Postsecondary; Home Economics Teachers, Postsecondary; Law Teachers, Postsecondary; Library Science Teachers, Postsecondary; Mathematical Science Teachers, Postsecondary; Nursing Instructors and Teachers, Postsecondary; Philosophy and Religion Teachers, Postsecondary; Physics Teachers, Postsecondary; Political Science Teachers, Postsecondary; Psychology Teachers, Postsecondary; Recreation and Fitness Studies Teachers, Postsecondary; Social Work Teachers, Postsecondary; Sociology Teachers, Postsecondary; Teachers, Postsecondary; Vocational Education Teachers, Postsecondary. **PERSONALITY TYPE:** Social. Social occupations frequently involve working with, communicating with, and teaching people. These occupations often involve helping or providing service to others.

EDUCATION/TRAINING PROGRAM(S)— Adult and Continuing Education and Teaching. **RELATED KNOWLEDGE/COURSES—Fine Arts:** The theory and techniques required to compose, produce, and perform works of music, dance, visual arts, drama, and sculpture. **Education and Training:** Principles and methods for curriculum and training design, teaching and instruction for individuals and groups, and the measurement of training effects. **Psychology:** Human behavior and performance; individual differences in ability, personality, and interests; learning and motivation; psychological research methods; and the assessment and treatment of behavioral and affective disorders. **Customer and Personal Service:** Principles and processes for providing customer and personal services. This includes customer needs assessment, meeting quality standards for services, and evaluation of customer satisfaction. **Sales and Marketing:** Principles and methods for showing, promoting, and selling products or services. This includes marketing strategy and tactics, product demonstration, sales techniques, and sales control systems. **Administration and Management:** Business and management principles involved in strategic planning, resource allocation, human resources modeling, leadership technique, production methods, and coordination of people and resources.

WORK ENVIRONMENT—Indoors; standing.

Septic Tank Servicers and Sewer Pipe Cleaners

- Education/Training Required: Moderate-term on-the-job training
- Annual Earnings: $30,440
- Growth: 21.8%
- Annual Job Openings: 3,000
- Self-Employed: 12.9%
- Part-Time: 6.2%

Clean and repair septic tanks, sewer lines, or drains. May patch walls and partitions of tank, replace damaged drain tile, or repair breaks in underground piping. Communicate with supervisors and other workers, using equipment such as wireless phones, pagers, or radio telephones. Inspect manholes to locate sewer line stoppages. Break asphalt and other pavement so that pipes can be accessed, using airhammers, picks, and shovels. Cut damaged sections of pipe with cutters; remove broken sections from ditches; and replace pipe sections, using pipe sleeves. Dig out sewer lines manually, using shovels. Drive trucks to transport crews, materials, and equipment. Prepare and keep records of actions taken, including maintenance and repair work. Requisition or order tools and equipment. Service, adjust, and make minor repairs to equipment, machines, and attachments. Locate problems, using specially designed equipment, and mark where digging must occur to reach damaged tanks or pipes. Withdraw cables from pipes and examine them for evidence of mud, roots, grease, and other deposits indicating bro-

ken or clogged sewer lines. Update sewer maps and manhole charts. Cover repaired pipes with dirt and pack backfilled excavations, using air and gasoline tampers. Install rotary knives on flexible cables mounted on machine reels according to the diameters of pipes to be cleaned. Tap mainline sewers to install sewer saddles. Start machines to feed revolving cables or rods into openings, stopping machines and changing knives to conform to pipe sizes. Rotate cleaning rods manually, using turning pins. Operate sewer cleaning equipment, including power rodders, high-velocity water jets, sewer flushers, bucket machines, wayne balls, and vacalls. Measure excavation sites, using plumbers' snakes, tapelines, or lengths of cutting heads within sewers, and mark areas for digging. Ensure that repaired sewer line joints are tightly sealed before backfilling begins. Clean and repair septic tanks; sewer lines; or related structures such as manholes, culverts, and catch basins. Clean and disinfect domestic basements and other areas flooded by sewer stoppages.

LEVEL OF ACTIVITY (out of 100)—General Physical Activity: 61.9. **Sitting:** 37.1. **Outdoors:** 65.7.

SKILLS—Installation; Repairing; Operation and Control; Management of Material Resources; Equipment Maintenance.

GOE—Interest Area: 02. Architecture and Construction. **Work Group:** 02.06. Construction Support/Labor. **Other Jobs in This Work Group:** Construction Laborers; Helpers—Brickmasons, Blockmasons, Stonemasons, and Tile and Marble Setters; Helpers—Carpenters; Helpers—Electricians; Helpers—Installation, Maintenance, and Repair Workers; Helpers—Painters, Paperhangers, Plasterers, and Stucco Masons; Helpers—Pipelayers, Plumbers, Pipefitters, and Steamfitters; Helpers—Roofers; Highway Maintenance Workers. **PERSONALI-**

TY TYPE: Realistic. Realistic occupations frequently involve work activities that include practical, hands-on problems and solutions. They often deal with plants; animals; and real-world materials like wood, tools, and machinery. Many of the occupations require working outside and do not involve a lot of paperwork or working closely with others.

EDUCATION/TRAINING PROGRAM(S)— Plumbing Technology/Plumber. **RELATED KNOWLEDGE/COURSES—Mechanical Devices:** Machines and tools, including their designs, uses, repair, and maintenance. **Building and Construction:** The materials, methods, and tools involved in the construction or repair of houses, buildings, or other structures such as highways and roads. **Engineering and Technology:** The practical application of engineering science and technology. This includes applying principles, techniques, procedures, and equipment to the design and production of various goods and services.

WORK ENVIRONMENT—Outdoors; contaminants; standing; kneeling, crouching, stooping, or crawling; using hands on objects, tools, or controls; bending or twisting the body.

Set and Exhibit Designers

- Education/Training Required: Bachelor's degree
- Annual Earnings: $37,390
- Growth: 9.3%
- Annual Job Openings: 2,000
- Self-Employed: 27.6%
- Part-Time: 21.3%

Design special exhibits and movie, television, and theater sets. May study scripts, confer with directors, and conduct research to determine appropriate architectural styles. Examine objects to be included in exhibits in order to plan where and how to display them. Acquire, or arrange for acquisition of, specimens or graphics required to complete exhibits. Prepare rough drafts and scale working drawings of sets, including floor plans, scenery, and properties to be constructed. Confer with clients and staff in order to gather information about exhibit space, proposed themes and content, timelines, budgets, materials, and promotion requirements. Estimate set- or exhibit-related costs, including materials, construction, and rental of props or locations. Develop set designs based on evaluation of scripts, budgets, research information, and available locations. Direct and coordinate construction, erection, or decoration activities in order to ensure that sets or exhibits meet design, budget, and schedule requirements. Inspect installed exhibits for conformance to specifications and satisfactory operation of special effects components. Plan for location-specific issues

S

such as space limitations, traffic flow patterns, and safety concerns. Submit plans for approval and adapt plans to serve intended purposes or to conform to budget or fabrication restrictions. Prepare preliminary renderings of proposed exhibits, including detailed construction, layout, and material specifications and diagrams relating to aspects such as special effects and lighting. Select and purchase lumber and hardware necessary for set construction. Collaborate with those in charge of lighting and sound so that those production aspects can be coordinated with set designs or exhibit layouts. Research architectural and stylistic elements appropriate to the time period to be depicted, consulting experts for information as necessary. Design and produce displays and materials that can be used to decorate windows, interior displays, or event locations such as streets and fairgrounds. Coordinate the removal of sets, props, and exhibits after productions or events are complete. Select set props such as furniture, pictures, lamps, and rugs. Confer with conservators in order to determine how to handle an exhibit's environmental aspects, such as lighting, temperature, and humidity, so that objects will be protected and exhibits will be enhanced.

LEVEL OF ACTIVITY (out of 100)—General Physical Activity: 66.7. **Sitting:** 46.9. **Outdoors:** 30.1.

SKILLS—Persuasion; Installation; Management of Material Resources; Management of Personnel Resources; Operations Analysis; Negotiation; Coordination; Management of Financial Resources.

GOE—Interest Area: 03. Arts and Communication. **Work Group:** 03.05. Design. **Other Jobs in This Work Group:** Commercial and Industrial Designers; Fashion Designers; Floral Designers; Graphic Designers; Interior Designers; Merchandise Displayers and Window Trimmers. **PERSONALITY TYPE:** Artistic. Artistic occupations frequently involve working with forms, designs, and patterns. They often require self-expression, and the work can be done without following a clear set of rules.

EDUCATION/TRAINING PROGRAM(S)— Design and Visual Communications, General; Illustration; Design and Applied Arts, Other; Technical Theatre/Theatre Design and Technology. **RELATED KNOWLEDGE/ COURSES—Fine Arts:** The theory and techniques required to compose, produce, and perform works of music, dance, visual arts, drama, and sculpture. **Design:** Design techniques, tools, and principles involved in production of precision technical plans, blueprints, drawings, and models. **History and Archeology:** Historical events and their causes, indicators, and effects on civilizations and cultures. **Communications and Media:** Media production, communication, and dissemination techniques and methods. This includes alternative ways to inform and entertain via written, oral, and visual media. **Computers and Electronics:** Circuit boards; processors; chips; electronic equipment; and computer hardware and software, including applications and programming. **Sociology and Anthropology:** Group behavior and dynamics, societal trends and influences, human migrations, ethnicity, and cultures and their history and origins.

WORK ENVIRONMENT—Indoors; sitting; using hands on objects, tools, or controls.

Sheet Metal Workers

- Education/Training Required: Moderate-term on-the-job training
- Annual Earnings: $36,390
- Growth: 12.2%
- Annual Job Openings: 50,000
- Self-Employed: 4.9%
- Part-Time: 5.7%

Fabricate, assemble, install, and repair sheet metal products and equipment, such as ducts, control boxes, drainpipes, and furnace casings. Work may involve any of the following: setting up and operating fabricating machines to cut, bend, and straighten sheet metal; shaping metal over anvils, blocks, or forms, using hammer; operating soldering and welding equipment to join sheet metal parts; and inspecting, assembling, and smoothing seams and joints of burred surfaces. Determine project requirements, including scope, assembly sequences, and required methods and materials, according to blueprints, drawings, and written or verbal instructions. Lay out, measure, and mark dimensions and reference lines on material such as roofing panels, according to drawings or templates, using calculators, scribes, dividers, squares, and rulers. Maneuver completed units into position for installation and anchor the units. Convert blueprints into shop drawings to be followed in the construction and assembly of sheet metal products. Install assemblies, such as flashing, pipes, tubes, heating and air conditioning ducts, furnace casings, rain gutters, and downspouts, in supportive frameworks. Select gauges and types of sheet metal or non-metallic material according to product specifications. Drill and punch holes in metal for screws, bolts, and rivets. Fasten seams and joints together with welds, bolts, cement, rivets, solder, caulks, metal drive clips, and bonds to assemble components into products or to repair sheet metal items. Fabricate or alter parts at construction sites, using shears, hammers, punches, and drills. Finish parts, using hacksaws and hand, rotary, or squaring shears. Trim, file, grind, deburr, buff, and smooth surfaces, seams, and joints of assembled parts, using hand tools and portable power tools. Maintain equipment, making repairs and modifications when necessary. Shape metal material over anvils, blocks, or other forms, using hand tools. Transport prefabricated parts to construction sites for assembly and installation. Develop and lay out patterns that use materials most efficiently, using computerized metalworking equipment to experiment with different layouts. Inspect individual parts, assemblies, and installations for conformance to specifications and building codes, using measuring instruments such as calipers, scales, and micrometers. Secure metal roof panels in place and interlock and fasten grooved panel edges. Fasten roof panel edges and machine-made molding to structures, nailing or welding pieces into place.

LEVEL OF ACTIVITY (out of 100)—General Physical Activity: 76.3. **Sitting:** 22.3. **Outdoors:** 40.5.

SKILLS—Installation; Equipment Maintenance; Repairing; Mathematics; Technology Design; Coordination; Troubleshooting; Equipment Selection.

GOE—Interest Area: 02. Architecture and Construction. **Work Group:** 02.04. Construction Crafts. **Other Jobs in This Work Group:** Boilermakers; Brickmasons and Blockmasons; Carpet Installers; Cement Masons and Concrete

Finishers; Commercial Divers; Construction Carpenters; Crane and Tower Operators; Drywall and Ceiling Tile Installers; Electricians; Fence Erectors; Floor Layers, Except Carpet, Wood, and Hard Tiles; Floor Sanders and Finishers; Glaziers; Hazardous Materials Removal Workers; Insulation Workers, Floor, Ceiling, and Wall; Insulation Workers, Mechanical; Manufactured Building and Mobile Home Installers; Operating Engineers and Other Construction Equipment Operators; Painters, Construction and Maintenance; Paperhangers; Paving, Surfacing, and Tamping Equipment Operators; Pile-Driver Operators; Pipe Fitters and Steamfitters; Pipelayers; Plasterers and Stucco Masons; Plumbers; Plumbers, Pipefitters, and Steamfitters; Rail-Track Laying and Maintenance Equipment Operators; Refractory Materials Repairers, Except Brickmasons; Reinforcing Iron and Rebar Workers; Riggers; Roofers; Rough Carpenters; Security and Fire Alarm Systems Installers; Segmental Pavers; Stone Cutters and Carvers, Manufacturing; Stonemasons; Structural Iron and Steel Workers; Tapers; Terrazzo Workers and Finishers; Tile and Marble Setters. **PERSONALITY TYPE:** Realistic. Realistic occupations frequently involve work activities that include practical, hands-on problems and solutions. They often deal with plants; animals; and real-world materials like wood, tools, and machinery. Many of the occupations require working outside and do not involve a lot of paperwork or working closely with others.

EDUCATION/TRAINING PROGRAM(S)— Sheet Metal Technology/Sheetworking. **RELATED KNOWLEDGE/COURSES**—**Building and Construction:** The materials, methods, and tools involved in the construction or repair of houses, buildings, or other structures such as highways and roads. **Mechanical Devices:** Machines and tools, including their designs,

uses, repair, and maintenance. **Design:** Design techniques, tools, and principles involved in production of precision technical plans, blueprints, drawings, and models. **Physics:** Physical principles and laws and their interrelationships and applications to understanding fluid, material, and atmospheric dynamics and mechanical, electrical, atomic, and subatomic structures and processes. **Production and Processing:** Raw materials, production processes, quality control, costs, and other techniques for maximizing the effective manufacture and distribution of goods. **Mathematics:** Arithmetic, algebra, geometry, calculus, and statistics and their applications.

WORK ENVIRONMENT—Noisy; contaminants; hazardous equipment; minor burns, cuts, bites, or stings; standing; using hands on objects, tools, or controls.

Sheriffs and Deputy Sheriffs

This job can be found in the Part I lists under the title Police and Sheriff's Patrol Officers.

- Education/Training Required: Long-term on-the-job training
- Annual Earnings: $46,290
- Growth: 15.5%
- Annual Job Openings: 47,000
- Self-Employed: 0.0%
- Part-Time: 1.4%

The job openings listed here are shared with Police Patrol Officers.

Enforce law and order in rural or unincorporated districts or serve legal processes of courts. May patrol courthouse, guard court or grand jury, or escort defendants. Drive vehicles or patrol specific areas to detect law violators, issue citations, and make arrests. Investigate illegal or suspicious activities. Verify that the proper legal charges have been made against law offenders. Execute arrest warrants, locating and taking persons into custody. Record daily activities and submit logs and other related reports and paperwork to appropriate authorities. Patrol and guard courthouses, grand jury rooms, or assigned areas in order to provide security, enforce laws, maintain order, and arrest violators. Notify patrol units to take violators into custody or to provide needed assistance or medical aid. Place people in protective custody. Serve statements of claims, subpoenas, summonses, jury summonses, orders to pay alimony, and other court orders. Take control of accident scenes to maintain traffic flow, to assist accident victims, and to investigate causes. Question individuals entering secured areas to determine their business, directing and rerouting individuals as necessary. Transport or escort prisoners and defendants en route to courtrooms, prisons or jails, attorneys' offices, or medical facilities. Locate and confiscate real or personal property as directed by court order. Manage jail operations and tend to jail inmates.

LEVEL OF ACTIVITY (out of 100)—General Physical Activity: 61.7. **Sitting:** 56.0. **Outdoors:** 49.1.

SKILLS—Persuasion; Negotiation; Social Perceptiveness; Service Orientation; Complex Problem Solving; Coordination; Judgment and Decision Making; Equipment Selection.

GOE—Interest Area: 12. Law and Public Safety. **Work Group:** 12.04. Law Enforcement and Public Safety. **Other Jobs in This Work Group:** Bailiffs; Correctional Officers and Jailers; Criminal Investigators and Special Agents; Detectives and Criminal Investigators; Fire Investigators; Forensic Science Technicians; Parking Enforcement Workers; Police and Sheriff's Patrol Officers; Police Detectives; Police Identification and Records Officers; Police Patrol Officers; Transit and Railroad Police. **PERSONALITY TYPE:** Social. Social occupations frequently involve working with, communicating with, and teaching people. These occupations often involve helping or providing service to others.

EDUCATION/TRAINING PROGRAM(S)—Criminal Justice/Police Science; Criminalistics and Criminal Science. **RELATED KNOWLEDGE/COURSES—Public Safety and Security:** Relevant equipment, policies, procedures, and strategies to promote effective local, state, or national security operations for the protection of people, data, property, and institutions. **Law and Government:** Laws, legal codes, court procedures, precedents, government regulations, executive orders, agency rules, and the democratic political process. **Telecommunications:** Transmission, broadcasting, switching, control, and operation of telecommunications systems. **Psychology:** Human behavior and performance; individual differences in ability, personality, and interests; learning and motivation; psychological research methods; and the assessment and treatment of behavioral and affective disorders. **Customer and Personal Service:** Principles and processes for providing customer and personal services. This includes customer needs assessment, meeting quality standards for services, and evaluation of customer satisfaction. **Therapy and Counseling:** Principles, methods, and procedures for diagnosis, treatment, and

S

rehabilitation of physical and mental dysfunctions and for career counseling and guidance.

WORK ENVIRONMENT—More often outdoors than indoors; very hot or cold; contaminants; disease or infections; sitting.

Ship Engineers

- ◉ Education/Training Required: Postsecondary vocational training
- ◉ Annual Earnings: $52,780
- ◉ Growth: 12.7%
- ◉ Annual Job Openings: 1,000
- ◉ Self-Employed: 3.7%
- ◉ Part-Time: 17.4%

Supervise and coordinate activities of crew engaged in operating and maintaining engines; boilers; deck machinery; and electrical, sanitary, and refrigeration equipment aboard ship. Monitor engine, machinery, and equipment indicators when vessels are under way and report abnormalities to appropriate shipboard staff. Record orders for changes in ship speed and direction and note gauge readings and test data, such as revolutions per minute and voltage output, in engineering logs and bellbooks. Perform and participate in emergency drills as required. Fabricate engine replacement parts such as valves, stay rods, and bolts, using metalworking machinery. Install engine controls, propeller shafts, and propellers. Maintain and repair engines, electric motors, pumps, winches, and other mechanical and electrical equipment or assist other crew members with maintenance

and repair duties. Monitor and test operations of engines and other equipment so that malfunctions and their causes can be identified. Operate and maintain off-loading liquid pumps and valves. Perform general marine vessel maintenance and repair work such as repairing leaks, finishing interiors, refueling, and maintaining decks. Start engines to propel ships and regulate engines and power transmissions to control speeds of ships according to directions from captains or bridge computers. Supervise the activities of marine engine technicians engaged in the maintenance and repair of mechanical and electrical marine vessels and inspect their work to ensure that it is performed properly. Act as a liaison between a ship's captain and shore personnel to ensure that schedules and budgets are maintained and that the ship is operated safely and efficiently. Order and receive engine room's stores, such as oil and spare parts; maintain inventories and record usage of supplies. Maintain complete records of engineering department activities, including machine operations. Monitor the availability, use, and condition of lifesaving equipment and pollution preventatives in order to ensure that international regulations are followed. Maintain electrical power, heating, ventilation, refrigeration, water, and sewerage systems. Clean engine parts and keep engine rooms clean.

LEVEL OF ACTIVITY (out of 100)—General Physical Activity: 47.6. **Sitting:** 40.0. **Outdoors:** 40.0.

SKILLS—Operation and Control; Operation Monitoring; Repairing; Equipment Maintenance; Management of Personnel Resources; Systems Evaluation; Troubleshooting; Coordination.

GOE—Interest Area: 13. Manufacturing. **Work Group:** 13.16. Utility Operation and Energy

Distribution. **Other Jobs in This Work Group:** Chemical Plant and System Operators; Gas Compressor and Gas Pumping Station Operators; Gas Plant Operators; Nuclear Power Reactor Operators; Petroleum Pump System Operators, Refinery Operators, and Gaugers; Power Distributors and Dispatchers; Power Plant Operators; Stationary Engineers and Boiler Operators; Water and Liquid Waste Treatment Plant and System Operators. **PERSONALITY TYPE:** Realistic. Realistic occupations frequently involve work activities that include practical, hands-on problems and solutions. They often deal with plants; animals; and real-world materials like wood, tools, and machinery. Many of the occupations require working outside and do not involve a lot of paperwork or working closely with others.

EDUCATION/TRAINING PROGRAM(S)— Marine Maintenance/Fitter and Ship Repair Technology/Technician. **RELATED KNOWLEDGE/COURSES—Mechanical Devices:** Machines and tools, including their designs, uses, repair, and maintenance. **Transportation:** Principles and methods for moving people or goods by air, rail, sea, or road, including the relative costs and benefits. **Engineering and Technology:** The practical application of engineering science and technology. This includes applying principles, techniques, procedures, and equipment to the design and production of various goods and services. **Physics:** Physical principles and laws and their interrelationships and applications to understanding fluid, material, and atmospheric dynamics and mechanical, electrical, atomic, and subatomic structures and processes. **Public Safety and Security:** Relevant equipment, policies, procedures, and strategies to promote effective local, state, or national security operations for the protection of people, data, property, and institutions.

WORK ENVIRONMENT—Indoors; standing; using hands on objects, tools, or controls.

Slaughterers and Meat Packers

- Education/Training Required: Moderate-term on-the-job training
- Annual Earnings: $21,220
- Growth: 13.8%
- Annual Job Openings: 22,000
- Self-Employed: 1.3%
- Part-Time: 10.5%

Work in slaughtering, meat packing, or wholesale establishments performing precision functions involving the preparation of meat. Work may include specialized slaughtering tasks, cutting standard or premium cuts of meat for marketing, making sausage, or wrapping meats. Remove bones and cut meat into standard cuts in preparation for marketing. Slaughter animals in accordance with religious law and determine that carcasses meet specified religious standards. Tend assembly lines, performing a few of the many cuts needed to process a carcass. Saw, split, or scribe carcasses into smaller portions to facilitate handling. Grind meat into hamburger and into trimmings used to prepare sausages, luncheon meats, and other meat products. Cut, trim, skin, sort, and wash viscera of slaughtered animals to separate edible portions from offal. Shave or singe and defeather carcasses and wash them in preparation for further processing or packaging. Slit open, eviscerate, and trim carcasses of slaughtered animals. Stun animals prior to slaughtering. Trim head meat and sever or remove parts of animals' heads or skulls. Trim, clean, and/or cure animal hides. Wrap dressed carcasses and/or meat cuts. Skin sections of animals or whole animals. Sever jugular veins to drain blood and facilitate slaughtering. Shackle hind legs of animals to raise them for slaughtering or skinning.

LEVEL OF ACTIVITY (out of 100)—General Physical Activity: 73.7. **Sitting:** 28.6. **Outdoors:** 31.0.

SKILLS—None met the criteria.

GOE—Interest Area: 13. Manufacturing. **Work Group:** 13.03. Production Work, Assorted Materials Processing. **Other Jobs in This Work Group:** Bakers; Cementing and Gluing Machine Operators and Tenders; Chemical Equipment Operators and Tenders; Cleaning, Washing, and Metal Pickling Equipment Operators and Tenders; Coating, Painting, and Spraying Machine Setters, Operators, and Tenders; Cooling and Freezing Equipment Operators and Tenders; Cutting and Slicing Machine Setters, Operators, and Tenders; Extruding and Forming Machine Setters, Operators, and Tenders, Synthetic and Glass Fibers; Extruding, Forming, Pressing, and Compacting Machine Setters, Operators, and Tenders; Food and Tobacco Roasting, Baking, and Drying Machine Operators and Tenders; Food Batchmakers; Food Cooking Machine Operators and Tenders; Furnace, Kiln, Oven, Drier, and Kettle Operators and Tenders; Heat Treating Equipment Setters, Operators, and Tenders, Metal and Plastic; Helpers—Production Workers; Meat, Poultry, and Fish Cutters and Trimmers; Metal-Refining Furnace Operators and Tenders; Mixing and Blending Machine Setters, Operators, and Tenders; Packaging and Filling Machine Operators and Tenders; Plating and Coating Machine Setters, Operators, and Tenders, Metal and Plastic; Pourers and Casters, Metal; Sawing Machine Setters, Operators, and Tenders, Wood; Separating, Filtering, Clarifying, Precipitating, and Still Machine Setters, Operators, and Tenders; Sewing Machine Operators; Shoe Machine Operators and Tenders; Team Assemblers; Textile Bleaching and Dyeing Machine Operators and Tenders; Tire Builders; Woodworking Machine Setters, Operators, and Tenders, Except Sawing. **PERSONALITY TYPE:** Realistic. Realistic occupations frequently involve work activities that include practical, hands-on problems and solutions. They often deal with plants; animals; and real-world materials like wood, tools, and machinery. Many of the occupations require working outside and do not involve a lot of paperwork or working closely with others.

EDUCATION/TRAINING PROGRAM(S)—Meat Cutting/Meat Cutter. **RELATED KNOWLEDGE/COURSES—Food Production:** Techniques and equipment for planting, growing, and harvesting food products (both plant and animal) for consumption, including storage/handling techniques. **Biology:** Plant and animal organisms and their tissues, cells, functions, interdependencies, and interactions with each other and the environment. **Production and Processing:** Raw materials, production processes, quality control, costs, and other techniques for maximizing the effective manufacture and distribution of goods. **Public Safety and Security:** Relevant equipment, policies, procedures, and strategies to promote effective local, state, or national security operations for the protection of people, data, property, and institutions.

WORK ENVIRONMENT—Indoors; contaminants; minor burns, cuts, bites, or stings; standing; using hands on objects, tools, or controls; repetitive motions.

Soil and Water Conservationists

This job can be found in the Part I lists under the title Conservation Scientists.

- Education/Training Required: Bachelor's degree
- Annual Earnings: $53,350
- Growth: 6.3%
- Annual Job Openings: 2,000
- Self-Employed: 9.0%
- Part-Time: 6.7%

The job openings listed here are shared with Park Naturalists and with Range Managers.

Plan and develop coordinated practices for soil erosion control, soil and water conservation, and sound land use. Develop and maintain working relationships with local government staff and board members. Advise land users such as farmers and ranchers on conservation plans, problems, and alternative solutions and provide technical and planning assistance. Apply principles of specialized fields of science, such as agronomy, soil science, forestry, or agriculture, to achieve conservation objectives. Plan soil management and conservation practices, such as crop rotation, reforestation, permanent vegetation, contour plowing, or terracing, to maintain soil and conserve water. Visit areas affected by erosion problems to seek sources and solutions. Monitor projects during and after construction to ensure projects conform to design specifications. Compute design specifications for implementation of conservation practices, using survey and field information technical guides, engineering manuals, and calculator. Revisit land users to view implemented land use practices and plans. Coordinate and implement technical, financial, and administrative assistance programs for local government units to ensure efficient program implementation and timely responses to requests for assistance. Analyze results of investigations to determine measures needed to maintain or restore proper soil management. Participate on work teams to plan, develop, and implement water and land management programs and policies. Develop, conduct, and/or participate in surveys, studies, and investigations of various land uses, gathering information for use in developing corrective action plans. Survey property to mark locations and measurements, using surveying instruments. Compute cost estimates of different conservation practices based on needs of land users, maintenance requirements, and life expectancy of practices. Provide information, knowledge, expertise, and training to government agencies at all levels to solve water and soil management problems and to assure coordination of resource protection activities. Respond to complaints and questions on wetland jurisdiction, providing information and clarification. Initiate, schedule, and conduct annual audits and compliance checks of program implementation by local government.

LEVEL OF ACTIVITY (out of 100)—General Physical Activity: 73.6. **Sitting:** 46.9. **Outdoors:** 46.2.

SKILLS—Persuasion; Operations Analysis; Science; Quality Control Analysis; Judgment and Decision Making; Active Learning; Installation; Coordination.

GOE—Interest Area: 01. Agriculture and Natural Resources. **Work Group:** 01.02. Resource Science/Engineering for Plants, Animals, and the Environment. **Other Jobs in This Work Group:** Agricultural Engineers; Animal Scientists; Conservation Scientists; Environmental Engineers; Foresters; Mining and Geological Engineers, Including Mining Safety Engineers; Petroleum Engineers; Range Managers; Soil and Plant Scientists; Zoologists and Wildlife Biologists. **PERSONALITY TYPE:** Investigative. Investigative occupations frequently involve working with ideas and require an extensive amount of thinking. These occupations can involve searching for facts and figuring out problems mentally.

EDUCATION/TRAINING PROGRAM(S)— Natural Resources/Conservation, General; Natural Resources Management and Policy; Water, Wetlands, and Marine Resources Management; Land Use Planning and Management/Development; Natural Resources Management and Policy, Other; Forestry, General; Forest Sciences and Biology; Forest Management/Forest Resources Management; Forestry, Other; Wildlife and Wildlands Science and Management; others. **RELATED KNOWLEDGE/COURSES—Geography:** Principles and methods for describing the features of land, sea, and air masses, including their physical characteristics; locations; interrelationships; and distribution of plant, animal, and human life. **Biology:** Plant and animal organisms and their tissues, cells, functions, interdependencies, and interactions with each other and the environment. **Engineering and Technology:** The practical application of engineering science and technology. This includes applying principles, techniques, procedures, and

equipment to the design and production of various goods and services. **Design:** Design techniques, tools, and principles involved in production of precision technical plans, blueprints, drawings, and models. **History and Archeology:** Historical events and their causes, indicators, and effects on civilizations and cultures. **Physics:** Physical principles and laws and their interrelationships and applications to understanding fluid, material, and atmospheric dynamics and mechanical, electrical, atomic, and subatomic structures and processes.

WORK ENVIRONMENT—More often outdoors than indoors; contaminants; sitting.

Solderers and Brazers

This job can be found in the Part I lists under the title Welders, Cutters, Solderers, and Brazers.

◉ **Education/Training Required:** Long-term on-the-job training

◉ **Annual Earnings:** $30,990

◉ **Growth:** 5.0%

◉ **Annual Job Openings:** 52,000

◉ **Self-Employed:** 6.3%

◉ **Part-Time:** 1.7%

The job openings listed here are shared with Welders, Cutters, and Welder Fitters.

Braze or solder together components to assemble fabricated metal parts, using soldering iron, torch, or welding machine and flux. Clean equipment parts, such as tips of soldering irons, using chemical solutions or cleaning compounds. Melt and separate brazed or soldered joints to remove and straighten damaged or mis-aligned components, using hand torches, irons, or furnaces. Place solder bars into containers and turn knobs to specified positions to melt solder and regulate its temperature. Remove work-pieces from fixtures, using tongs, and cool work-pieces, using air or water. Remove workpieces from molten solder and hold parts together until color indicates that solder has set. Select torch tips, flux, and brazing alloys from data charts or work orders. Smooth soldered areas with alter-nate strokes of paddles and torches, leaving sol-dered sections slightly higher than surrounding areas for later filing. Turn valves to start flow of gases and light flames and adjust valves to obtain desired colors and sizes of flames. Melt and apply solder to fill holes, indentations, and seams of fabricated metal products, using solder-ing equipment. Sweat together workpieces coat-ed with solder. Align and clamp workpieces together, using rules, squares, or hand tools, or position items in fixtures, jigs, or vises. Melt and apply solder along adjoining edges of workpieces to solder joints, using soldering irons, gas torch-es, or electric-ultrasonic equipment. Turn dials to set intensity and duration of ultrasonic impulses according to work order specifications. Clean workpieces to remove dirt and excess acid, using chemical solutions, files, wire brushes, or grinders. Adjust electric current and timing cycles of resistance-welding machines to heat metals to bonding temperature. Brush flux onto joints of workpieces or dip braze rods into flux to prevent oxidation of metal. Clean joints of workpieces with wire brushes or by dipping them into cleaning solutions. Connect hoses from torches to regulator valves and cylinders of oxygen and specified gas fuels. Dip workpieces into molten solder, or place solder strips between seams and heat seams with irons, to bond items together. Examine seams for defects and rework defective joints or broken parts.

LEVEL OF ACTIVITY (out of 100)—General Physical Activity: 38.0. **Sitting:** 34.3. **Outdoors:** 27.1.

SKILLS—Operation and Control; Operation Monitoring; Installation; Equipment Selection.

GOE—Interest Area: 13. Manufacturing. **Work Group:** 13.04. Welding, Brazing, and Soldering. **Other Jobs in This Work Group:** Structural Metal Fabricators and Fitters; Welders, Cutters, and Welder Fitters; Welders, Cutters, Solderers, and Brazers; Welding, Soldering, and Brazing Machine Setters, Operators, and Tenders. **PERSONALITY TYPE:** Realistic. Realistic occupa-tions frequently involve work activities that include practical, hands-on problems and solu-tions. They often deal with plants; animals; and real-world materials like wood, tools, and machinery. Many of the occupations require working outside and do not involve a lot of paperwork or working closely with others.

EDUCATION/TRAINING PROGRAM(S)—Welding Technology/Welder. **RELATED KNOWLEDGE/COURSES—Building and Construction:** The materials, methods, and tools involved in the construction or repair of houses, buildings, or other structures such as highways and roads. **Mechanical Devices:** Machines and tools, including their designs, uses, repair, and maintenance. **Engineering and Technology:** The practical application of engi-neering science and technology. This includes applying principles, techniques, procedures, and equipment to the design and production of var-ious goods and services.

WORK ENVIRONMENT—Indoors; contam-inants; hazardous equipment; standing; using hands on objects, tools, or controls; repetitive motions.

Stationary Engineers and Boiler Operators

- ⊚ Education/Training Required: Long-term on-the-job training
- ⊚ Annual Earnings: $44,600
- ⊚ Growth: 3.4%
- ⊚ Annual Job Openings: 5,000
- ⊚ Self-Employed: 1.0%
- ⊚ Part-Time: 3.5%

Operate or maintain stationary engines, boilers, or other mechanical equipment to provide utilities for buildings or industrial processes. Operate equipment such as steam engines, generators, motors, turbines, and steam boilers. Operate or tend stationary engines; boilers; and auxiliary equipment such as pumps, compressors, and air-conditioning equipment in order to supply and maintain steam or heat for buildings, marine vessels, or pneumatic tools. Observe and interpret readings on gauges, meters, and charts registering various aspects of boiler operation in order to ensure that boilers are operating properly. Test boiler water quality or arrange for testing and take any necessary corrective action, such as adding chemicals to prevent corrosion and harmful deposits. Activate valves to maintain required amounts of water in boilers, to adjust supplies of combustion air, and to control the flow of fuel into burners. Monitor boiler water, chemical, and fuel levels and make adjust-

ments to maintain required levels. Fire coal furnaces by hand or with stokers and gas- or oil-fed boilers, using automatic gas feeds or oil pumps. Monitor and inspect equipment, computer terminals, switches, valves, gauges, alarms, safety devices, and meters to detect leaks or malfunctions and to ensure that equipment is operating efficiently and safely. Analyze problems and take appropriate action to ensure continuous and reliable operation of equipment and systems. Maintain daily logs of operation, maintenance, and safety activities, including test results, instrument readings, and details of equipment malfunctions and maintenance work. Adjust controls and/or valves on equipment to provide power and to regulate and set operations of system and/or industrial processes. Switch from automatic controls to manual controls and isolate equipment mechanically and electrically in order to allow for safe inspection and repair work. Clean and lubricate boilers and auxiliary equipment and make minor adjustments as needed, using hand tools. Check the air quality of ventilation systems and make adjustments to ensure compliance with mandated safety codes. Perform or arrange for repairs, such as complete overhauls; replacement of defective valves, gaskets, or bearings; and/or fabrication of new parts. Weigh, measure, and record fuel used.

LEVEL OF ACTIVITY (out of 100)—General Physical Activity: 67.3. **Sitting:** 36.7. **Outdoors:** 41.6.

SKILLS—Repairing; Operation Monitoring; Equipment Maintenance; Installation; Systems Analysis; Operation and Control; Operations Analysis; Troubleshooting.

GOE—Interest Area: 13. Manufacturing. **Work Group:** 13.16. Utility Operation and Energy Distribution. **Other Jobs in This Work Group:** Chemical Plant and System Operators; Gas

Compressor and Gas Pumping Station Operators; Gas Plant Operators; Nuclear Power Reactor Operators; Petroleum Pump System Operators, Refinery Operators, and Gaugers; Power Distributors and Dispatchers; Power Plant Operators; Ship Engineers; Water and Liquid Waste Treatment Plant and System Operators. **PERSONALITY TYPE:** Realistic. Realistic occupations frequently involve work activities that include practical, hands-on problems and solutions. They often deal with plants; animals; and real-world materials like wood, tools, and machinery. Many of the occupations require working outside and do not involve a lot of paperwork or working closely with others.

EDUCATION/TRAINING PROGRAM(S)— Building/Property Maintenance and Management. **RELATED KNOWLEDGE/ COURSES—Mechanical Devices:** Machines and tools, including their designs, uses, repair, and maintenance. **Building and Construction:** The materials, methods, and tools involved in the construction or repair of houses, buildings, or other structures such as highways and roads. **Chemistry:** The chemical composition, structure, and properties of substances and of the chemical processes and transformations that they undergo. This includes uses of chemicals and their danger signs, production techniques, and disposal methods. **Physics:** Physical principles and laws and their interrelationships and applications to understanding fluid, material, and atmospheric dynamics and mechanical, electrical, atomic, and subatomic structures and processes. **Design:** Design techniques, tools, and principles involved in production of precision technical plans, blueprints, drawings, and models. **Engineering and Technology:** The practical application of engineering science and technology. This includes applying principles, techniques, procedures, and equipment to the design and production of various goods and services.

WORK ENVIRONMENT—Noisy; very hot or cold; very bright or dim lighting; contaminants; hazardous conditions; hazardous equipment.

Stonemasons

- Education/Training Required: Long-term on-the-job training
- Annual Earnings: $34,640
- Growth: 13.0%
- Annual Job Openings: 2,000
- Self-Employed: 23.1%
- Part-Time: No data available

Build stone structures, such as piers, walls, and abutments. Lay walks, curbstones, or special types of masonry for vats, tanks, and floors. Lay out wall patterns or foundations, using straight-edge, rule, or staked lines. Shape, trim, face, and cut marble or stone preparatory to setting, using power saws, cutting equipment, and hand tools. Set vertical and horizontal alignment of structures, using plumb bob, gauge line, and level. Mix mortar or grout and pour or spread mortar or grout on marble slabs, stone, or foundation. Remove wedges; fill joints between stones; finish joints between stones, using a trowel; and smooth the mortar to an attractive finish, using a tuck-pointer. Clean excess mortar or grout from surface of marble, stone, or monument, using sponge, brush, water, or acid. Set stone or marble in place according to layout or pattern. Lay brick to build shells of chimneys and smokestacks or to line or reline industrial furnaces, kilns, boilers, and similar installations. Replace broken or missing masonry units in walls or floors. Smooth, polish, and bevel surfaces, using hand tools and power tools. Drill holes in marble or ornamental stone and anchor brackets in holes. Repair cracked or chipped areas of stone or marble, using blowtorch and mastic, and remove rough or defective spots from concrete, using power grinder or chisel and hammer. Remove sections of monument from truck bed and guide stone onto foundation, using skids, hoist, or truck crane. Construct and install prefabricated masonry units. Dig trench for foundation of monument, using pick and shovel. Position mold along guidelines of wall, press mold in place, and remove mold and paper from wall. Line interiors of molds with treated paper and fill molds with composition-stone mixture.

LEVEL OF ACTIVITY (out of 100)—General Physical Activity: 91.0. **Sitting:** 18.9. **Outdoors:** 37.0.

SKILLS—Installation; Management of Personnel Resources; Equipment Maintenance; Repairing; Equipment Selection; Mathematics; Management of Material Resources; Technology Design.

GOE—Interest Area: 02. Architecture and Construction. **Work Group:** 02.04. Construction Crafts. **Other Jobs in This Work Group:** Boilermakers; Brickmasons and Blockmasons; Carpet Installers; Cement Masons and Concrete Finishers; Commercial Divers; Construction Carpenters; Crane and Tower Operators; Drywall and Ceiling Tile Installers; Electricians; Fence Erectors; Floor Layers, Except Carpet, Wood, and Hard Tiles; Floor Sanders and Finishers; Glaziers; Hazardous Materials Removal Workers; Insulation Workers, Floor, Ceiling, and Wall; Insulation Workers, Mechanical; Manufactured Building and Mobile Home Installers; Operating Engineers and Other Construction Equipment Operators; Painters, Construction and Maintenance; Paperhangers; Paving, Surfacing, and Tamping Equipment Operators; Pile-Driver Operators; Pipe Fitters and Steamfitters; Pipelayers; Plasterers and Stucco Masons; Plumbers; Plumbers, Pipefitters, and Steamfitters; Rail-Track Laying and Maintenance Equipment Operators; Refractory Materials Repairers, Except Brickmasons; Reinforcing Iron and Rebar Workers; Riggers; Roofers; Rough Carpenters; Security and Fire Alarm Systems Installers; Segmental Pavers; Sheet Metal Workers; Stone Cutters and Carvers, Manufacturing; Structural Iron and Steel Workers; Tapers; Terrazzo Workers and Finishers; Tile and Marble Setters. **PERSONALITY TYPE:** Realistic. Realistic occupations frequently involve work activities that include practical, hands-on problems and solutions. They often deal with plants; animals; and real-world materials like wood, tools, and machinery. Many of the occupations require working outside and do not involve a lot of paperwork or working closely with others.

EDUCATION/TRAINING PROGRAM(S)—Mason/Masonry. **RELATED KNOWLEDGE/COURSES—Building and Construction:** The materials, methods, and tools involved in the construction or repair of houses, buildings, or other structures such as highways and roads. **Design:** Design techniques, tools, and principles involved in production of precision technical plans, blueprints, drawings, and models. **Mechanical Devices:** Machines and tools, including their designs, uses, repair, and maintenance. **Mathematics:** Arithmetic, algebra, geometry, calculus, and statistics and their applications. **Education and Training:** Principles and methods for curriculum and training design, teaching and instruction for individuals and groups, and the measurement of training effects. **Public Safety and Security:** Relevant equipment, policies, procedures, and strategies to promote effective local, state, or national security operations for the protection of people, data, property, and institutions.

WORK ENVIRONMENT—Outdoors; standing; walking and running; kneeling, crouching, stooping, or crawling; using hands on objects, tools, or controls; bending or twisting the body.

Structural Iron and Steel Workers

- Education/Training Required: Long-term on-the-job training
- Annual Earnings: $40,580
- Growth: 15.0%
- Annual Job Openings: 13,000
- Self-Employed: 2.3%
- Part-Time: 5.8%

Raise, place, and unite iron or steel girders, columns, and other structural members to form completed structures or structural frameworks. May erect metal storage tanks and assemble prefabricated metal buildings. Force structural-steel members into final positions, using turnbuckles, crowbars, jacks, and hand tools. Pull, push, or pry structural-steel members into approximate positions for bolting into place. Ride on girders or other structural-steel members to position them or use rope to guide them into position. Verify vertical and horizontal alignment of structural-steel members, using plumb bobs, laser equipment, transits, and/or levels. Fasten structural-steel members to hoist cables, using chains, cables, or rope. Catch hot rivets in buckets and insert rivets in holes, using tongs. Cut, bend, and weld steel pieces, using metal shears, torches, and welding equipment. Dismantle structures and equipment. Fabricate metal parts such as steel frames, columns, beams, and girders according to blueprints or instructions from supervisors. Hold rivets while riveters use air hammers to form heads on rivets. Insert sealing strips, wiring, insulating material, ladders, flanges, gauges, and valves, depending on types of structures being assembled. Place blocks under reinforcing bars used to reinforce floors. Read specifications and blueprints to determine the locations, quantities, and sizes of materials required. Unload and position prefabricated steel units for hoisting as needed. Drive drift pins through rivet holes in order to align rivet holes in structural-steel members with corresponding holes in previously placed members. Connect columns, beams, and girders with bolts, following blueprints and instructions from supervisors. Bolt aligned structural-steel members in position for permanent riveting, bolting, or welding into place. Assemble hoisting equipment and rigging, such as cables, pulleys, and hooks, to move heavy equipment and materials. Erect metal and precast concrete components for structures such as buildings, bridges, dams, towers, storage tanks, fences, and highway guardrails. Hoist steel beams, girders, and columns into place, using cranes, or signal hoisting equipment operators to lift and position structural-steel members.

LEVEL OF ACTIVITY (out of 100)—General Physical Activity: 85.7. **Sitting:** 31.0. **Outdoors:** 54.7.

SKILLS—Installation; Operation and Control.

GOE—Interest Area: 02. Architecture and Construction. **Work Group:** 02.04. Construction Crafts. **Other Jobs in This Work Group:** Boilermakers; Brickmasons and Blockmasons; Carpet Installers; Cement Masons and Concrete Finishers; Commercial Divers; Construction Carpenters; Crane and Tower Operators; Drywall and Ceiling Tile Installers; Electricians; Fence Erectors; Floor Layers, Except Carpet, Wood, and Hard Tiles; Floor Sanders and Finishers; Glaziers; Hazardous Materials Removal Workers; Insulation Workers, Floor, Ceiling, and Wall; Insulation Workers, Mechanical; Manufactured Building and Mobile Home Installers; Operating Engineers and Other Construction Equipment Operators; Painters, Construction and Maintenance; Paperhangers; Paving, Surfacing, and Tamping Equipment Operators; Pile-Driver Operators; Pipe Fitters and Steamfitters; Pipe-layers; Plasterers and Stucco Masons; Plumbers; Plumbers, Pipefitters, and Steamfitters; Rail-Track Laying and Maintenance Equipment Operators; Refractory Materials Repairers, Except Brickmasons; Reinforcing Iron and Rebar Workers; Riggers; Roofers; Rough Carpenters; Security and Fire Alarm Systems Installers; Segmental Pavers; Sheet Metal Workers; Stone Cutters and Carvers, Manufacturing; Stonemasons; Tapers; Terrazzo Workers and Finishers; Tile and Marble Setters. **PERSONALITY TYPE:** Realistic. Realistic occupations frequently involve work activities that include practical, hands-on problems and solutions. They often deal with plants; animals; and real-world materials like wood, tools, and machinery. Many of the occupations require working outside and do not involve a lot of paperwork or working closely with others.

EDUCATION/TRAINING PROGRAM(S)—Metal Building Assembly/Assembler; Construction Trades, Other. **RELATED KNOWLEDGE/COURSES—Building and Construction:** The materials, methods, and tools involved in the construction or repair of houses, buildings, or other structures such as highways and roads. **Mechanical Devices:** Machines and tools, including their designs, uses, repair, and maintenance. **Engineering and Technology:** The practical application of engineering science and technology. This includes applying principles, techniques, procedures, and equipment to the design and production of various goods and services. **Public Safety and Security:** Relevant equipment, policies, procedures, and strategies to promote effective local, state, or national security operations for the protection of people, data, property, and institutions.

WORK ENVIRONMENT—Outdoors; noisy; very hot or cold; standing; climbing ladders, scaffolds, or poles; using hands on objects, tools, or controls.

Structural Metal Fabricators and Fitters

- Education/Training Required: Moderate-term on-the-job training
- Annual Earnings: $30,290
- Growth: 2.9%
- Annual Job Openings: 18,000
- Self-Employed: 3.1%
- Part-Time: 6.0%

Fabricate, lay out, position, align, and fit parts of structural metal products. Position, align, fit, and weld parts to form complete units or sub-units, following blueprints and layout specifications and using jigs, welding torches, and hand tools. Verify conformance of workpieces to specifications, using squares, rulers, and measuring tapes. Tack-weld fitted parts together. Lay out and examine metal stock or workpieces to be processed in order to ensure that specifications are met. Align and fit parts according to specifications, using jacks, turnbuckles, wedges, drift pins, pry bars, and hammers. Locate and mark workpiece bending and cutting lines, allowing for stock thickness, machine and welding shrinkage, and other component specifications. Position or tighten braces, jacks, clamps, ropes, bolt straps, or bolt parts in position for welding or riveting. Study engineering drawings and blueprints to determine materials requirements and task sequences. Move parts into position manually or by using hoists or cranes. Set up and operate fabricating machines such as brakes, rolls, shears, flame cutters, grinders, and drill presses to bend, cut, form, punch, drill, or otherwise form and assemble metal components. Hammer, chip, and grind workpieces in order to cut, bend, and straighten metal. Smooth workpiece edges and fix taps, tubes, and valves. Design and construct templates and fixtures, using hand tools. Straighten warped or bent parts, using sledges, hand torches, straightening presses, or bulldozers. Mark reference points onto floors or face blocks and transpose them to workpieces, using measuring devices, squares, chalk, and soapstone. Set up face blocks, jigs, and fixtures. Remove high spots and cut bevels, using hand files, portable grinders, and cutting torches. Direct welders to build up low spots or short pieces with weld. Lift or move materials and finished products, using large cranes. Heat-treat parts, using acetylene torches. Preheat workpieces to make them malleable, using hand torches or furnaces. Install boilers, containers, and other structures. Erect ladders and scaffolding to fit together large assemblies.

LEVEL OF ACTIVITY (out of 100)—General Physical Activity: 44.1. **Sitting:** 22.4. **Outdoors:** 29.3.

SKILLS—Quality Control Analysis; Operation Monitoring; Equipment Maintenance; Installation; Repairing; Technology Design; Operation and Control; Management of Personnel Resources.

GOE—Interest Area: 13. Manufacturing. **Work Group:** 13.04. Welding, Brazing, and Soldering. **Other Jobs in This Work Group:** Solderers and

Brazers; Welders, Cutters, and Welder Fitters; Welders, Cutters, Solderers, and Brazers; Welding, Soldering, and Brazing Machine Setters, Operators, and Tenders. **PERSONALITY TYPE:** Realistic. Realistic occupations frequently involve work activities that include practical, hands-on problems and solutions. They often deal with plants; animals; and real-world materials like wood, tools, and machinery. Many of the occupations require working outside and do not involve a lot of paperwork or working closely with others.

EDUCATION/TRAINING PROGRAM(S)— Machine Shop Technology/Assistant. **RELATED KNOWLEDGE/COURSES—Design:** Design techniques, tools, and principles involved in production of precision technical plans, blueprints, drawings, and models. **Building and Construction:** The materials, methods, and tools involved in the construction or repair of houses, buildings, or other structures such as highways and roads. **Mechanical Devices:** Machines and tools, including their designs, uses, repair, and maintenance. **Production and Processing:** Raw materials, production processes, quality control, costs, and other techniques for maximizing the effective manufacture and distribution of goods. **Mathematics:** Arithmetic, algebra, geometry, calculus, and statistics and their applications. **Education and Training:** Principles and methods for curriculum and training design, teaching and instruction for individuals and groups, and the measurement of training effects.

WORK ENVIRONMENT—Noisy; contaminants; hazardous equipment; minor burns, cuts, bites, or stings; standing; using hands on objects, tools, or controls.

Supervisors, Farming, Fishing, and Forestry Workers

See the descriptions of these jobs:

- First-Line Supervisors/Managers of Agricultural Crop and Horticultural Workers
- First-Line Supervisors/Managers of Animal Husbandry and Animal Care Workers
- First-Line Supervisors/Managers of Aquacultural Workers
- First-Line Supervisors/Managers of Logging Workers

Surgical Technologists

- Education/Training Required: Postsecondary vocational training
- Annual Earnings: $34,830
- Growth: 29.5%
- Annual Job Openings: 12,000
- Self-Employed: 0.3%
- Part-Time: 23.2%

Assist in operations under the supervision of surgeons, registered nurses, or other surgical personnel. May help set up operating room;

prepare and transport patients for surgery; adjust lights and equipment; pass instruments and other supplies to surgeons and surgeon's assistants; hold retractors; cut sutures; and help count sponges, needles, supplies, and instruments. Count sponges, needles, and instruments before and after operation. Hand instruments and supplies to surgeons and surgeons' assistants, hold retractors and cut sutures, and perform other tasks as directed by surgeon during operation. Scrub arms and hands and assist the surgical team to scrub and put on gloves, masks, and surgical clothing. Position patients on the operating table and cover them with sterile surgical drapes to prevent exposure. Provide technical assistance to surgeons, surgical nurses, and anesthesiologists. Wash and sterilize equipment, using germicides and sterilizers. Prepare, care for, and dispose of tissue specimens taken for laboratory analysis. Clean and restock the operating room, placing equipment and supplies and arranging instruments according to instruction. Prepare dressings or bandages and apply or assist with their application following surgery. Operate, assemble, adjust, or monitor sterilizers, lights, suction machines, and diagnostic equipment to ensure proper operation. Monitor and continually assess operating room conditions, including patient and surgical team needs. Observe patients' vital signs to assess physical condition. Maintain supply of fluids, such as plasma, saline, blood, and glucose, for use during operations. Maintain files and records of surgical procedures.

LEVEL OF ACTIVITY (out of 100)—General Physical Activity: 54.7. **Sitting:** 22.6. **Outdoors:** 15.0.

SKILLS—Troubleshooting; Instructing; Equipment Selection; Operation Monitoring; Learning Strategies; Science; Reading Comprehension; Active Learning.

GOE—**Interest Area:** 08. Health Science. **Work Group:** 08.02. Medicine and Surgery. **Other Jobs in This Work Group:** Anesthesiologists; Family and General Practitioners; Internists, General; Medical Assistants; Medical Transcriptionists; Obstetricians and Gynecologists; Pediatricians, General; Pharmacists; Pharmacy Aides; Pharmacy Technicians; Physician Assistants; Psychiatrists; Registered Nurses; Surgeons. **PERSONALITY TYPE:** Realistic. Realistic occupations frequently involve work activities that include practical, hands-on problems and solutions. They often deal with plants; animals; and real-world materials like wood, tools, and machinery. Many of the occupations require working outside and do not involve a lot of paperwork or working closely with others.

EDUCATION/TRAINING PROGRAM(S)—Pathology/Pathologist Assistant; Surgical Technology/Technologist. **RELATED KNOWLEDGE/COURSES—Medicine and Dentistry:** The information and techniques needed to diagnose and treat human injuries, diseases, and deformities. This includes symptoms, treatment alternatives, drug properties and interactions, and preventive health-care measures. **Chemistry:** The chemical composition, structure, and properties of substances and of the chemical processes and transformations that they undergo. This includes uses of chemicals and their danger signs, production techniques, and disposal methods. **Customer and Personal Service:** Principles and processes for providing customer and personal services. This includes customer needs assessment, meeting quality standards for services, and evaluation of customer satisfaction. **Psychology:** Human behavior and performance; individual differences in ability, personality, and interests; learning and motivation; psychological research methods; and the assessment and treatment of behavioral and affective disorders. **Philosophy and Theology:** Different philosophical systems and religions. This includes their basic principles, values, ethics, ways of thinking, customs, and practices and their impact on human culture. **Therapy and Counseling:** Principles, methods, and procedures for diagnosis, treatment, and rehabilitation of physical and mental dysfunctions and for career counseling and guidance.

WORK ENVIRONMENT—Indoors; contaminants; disease or infections; hazardous conditions; standing; using hands on objects, tools, or controls.

Surveyors

- Education/Training Required: Bachelor's degree
- Annual Earnings: $45,860
- Growth: 15.9%
- Annual Job Openings: 4,000
- Self-Employed: 3.7%
- Part-Time: 8.1%

Make exact measurements and determine property boundaries. Provide data relevant to the shape, contour, gravitation, location, elevation, or dimension of land or land features on or near the earth's surface for engineering, mapmaking, mining, land evaluation, construction, and other purposes. Prepare and maintain sketches, maps, reports, and legal descriptions of surveys to describe, certify, and assume liability for work performed. Verify the accuracy of survey data, including measure-

ments and calculations conducted at survey sites. Direct or conduct surveys to establish legal boundaries for properties based on legal deeds and titles. Record the results of surveys, including the shape, contour, location, elevation, and dimensions of land or land features. Calculate heights, depths, relative positions, property lines, and other characteristics of terrain. Prepare or supervise preparation of all data, charts, plots, maps, records, and documents related to surveys. Write descriptions of property boundary surveys for use in deeds, leases, or other legal documents. Plan and conduct ground surveys designed to establish baselines, elevations, and other geodetic measurements. Search legal records, survey records, and land titles to obtain information about property boundaries in areas to be surveyed. Coordinate findings with the work of engineering and architectural personnel, clients, and others concerned with projects. Adjust surveying instruments to maintain their accuracy. Establish fixed points for use in making maps, using geodetic and engineering instruments. Determine longitudes and latitudes of important features and boundaries in survey areas, using theodolites, transits, levels, and satellite-based global positioning systems (GPS). Train assistants and helpers and direct their work in such activities as performing surveys or drafting maps. Analyze survey objectives and specifications to prepare survey proposals or to direct others in survey proposal preparation. Compute geodetic measurements and interpret survey data to determine positions, shapes, and elevations of geomorphic and topographic features. Develop criteria for survey methods and procedures. Develop criteria for the design and modification of survey instruments. Conduct research in surveying and mapping methods, using knowledge of techniques of photogrammetric map compilation and electronic data processing.

LEVEL OF ACTIVITY (out of 100)—General Physical Activity: 53.9. **Sitting:** 37.0. **Outdoors:** 42.3.

SKILLS—Mathematics; Management of Personnel Resources; Coordination; Science; Critical Thinking; Equipment Selection; Troubleshooting; Active Listening.

GOE—Interest Area: 02. Architecture and Construction. **Work Group:** 02.03. Architecture/Construction Engineering Technologies. **Other Jobs in This Work Group:** Architectural and Civil Drafters; Architectural Drafters; Civil Drafters. **PERSONALITY TYPE:** Investigative. Investigative occupations frequently involve working with ideas and require an extensive amount of thinking. These occupations can involve searching for facts and figuring out problems mentally.

EDUCATION/TRAINING PROGRAM(S)—Surveying Technology/Surveying. **RELATED KNOWLEDGE/COURSES—Building and Construction:** The materials, methods, and tools involved in the construction or repair of houses, buildings, or other structures such as highways and roads. **Geography:** Principles and methods for describing the features of land, sea, and air masses, including their physical characteristics; locations; interrelationships; and distribution of plant, animal, and human life. **Design:** Design techniques, tools, and principles involved in production of precision technical plans, blueprints, drawings, and models. **Engineering and Technology:** The practical application of engineering science and technology. This includes applying principles, techniques, procedures, and equipment to the design and production of various goods and services. **Mathematics:** Arithmetic, algebra, geometry, calculus, and statistics and their applications. **Computers and Electronics:** Circuit boards; processors; chips; electronic equipment; and computer hardware and software, including applications and programming.

WORK ENVIRONMENT—More often outdoors than indoors; very hot or cold; hazardous equipment; minor burns, cuts, bites, or stings; standing.

Tapers

- Education/Training Required: Moderate-term on-the-job training
- Annual Earnings: $39,870
- Growth: 5.9%
- Annual Job Openings: 5,000
- Self-Employed: 21.0%
- Part-Time: 8.0%

Seal joints between plasterboard or other wallboard to prepare wall surface for painting or papering. Mix sealing compounds by hand or with portable electric mixers. Sand rough spots of dried cement between applications of compounds. Select the correct sealing compound or tape. Apply additional coats to fill in holes and make surfaces smooth. Sand or patch nicks or cracks in plasterboard or wallboard. Spread sealing compound between boards or panels and over cracks, holes, and nail and screw heads, using trowels, broadknives, or spatulas. Seal joints between plasterboard or other wallboard in order to prepare wall surfaces for painting or papering. Spread and smooth cementing material over tape, using trowels or floating machines to blend joints with wall surfaces. Use mechanical applicators that spread compounds and embed tape in one operation. Press paper tape over joints to embed tape into sealing compound and to seal joints. Install metal molding at wall corners to secure wallboard. Countersink nails or screws below surfaces of walls before applying sealing compounds, using hammers or screwdrivers. Check adhesives to ensure that they will work and will remain durable. Apply texturizing compounds and primers to walls and ceilings before final finishing, using trowels, brushes, rollers, or spray guns. Remove extra compound after surfaces have been covered sufficiently.

LEVEL OF ACTIVITY (out of 100)—General Physical Activity: 61.9. Sitting: 28.6. Outdoors: 32.1.

SKILLS—None met the criteria.

GOE—**Interest Area:** 02. Architecture and Construction. **Work Group:** 02.04. Construction Crafts. **Other Jobs in This Work Group:** Boilermakers; Brickmasons and Blockmasons; Carpet Installers; Cement Masons and Concrete Finishers; Commercial Divers; Construction Carpenters; Crane and Tower Operators; Drywall and Ceiling Tile Installers; Electricians; Fence Erectors; Floor Layers, Except Carpet, Wood, and Hard Tiles; Floor Sanders and Finishers; Glaziers; Hazardous Materials Removal Workers; Insulation Workers, Floor, Ceiling, and Wall; Insulation Workers, Mechanical; Manufactured Building and Mobile Home Installers; Operating Engineers and Other Construction Equipment Operators; Painters, Construction and Maintenance; Paperhangers; Paving, Surfacing, and Tamping Equipment Operators; Pile-Driver Operators; Pipe Fitters and Steamfitters; Pipelayers; Plasterers and Stucco Masons; Plumbers; Plumbers, Pipefitters, and Steamfitters; Rail-Track Laying and Maintenance Equipment Operators; Refractory Materials Repairers, Except Brickmasons; Reinforcing Iron and Rebar Workers; Riggers; Roofers; Rough Carpenters; Security and Fire Alarm Systems Installers; Segmental Pavers; Sheet Metal Workers; Stone Cutters and Carvers, Manufacturing; Stonemasons; Structural Iron and Steel Workers; Terrazzo Workers and Finishers; Tile and Marble Setters. **PERSONALITY TYPE:** Realistic. Realistic occupations frequently involve work activities that include practical, hands-on problems and solutions. They often deal with plants; animals; and real-world materials like wood, tools, and machinery. Many of the occupations require working outside and do not involve a lot of paperwork or working closely with others.

EDUCATION/TRAINING PROGRAM(S)—Construction Trades, Other. **RELATED KNOWLEDGE/COURSES—Building and Construction:** The materials, methods, and tools involved in the construction or repair of houses, buildings, or other structures such as highways and roads. **Fine Arts:** The theory and techniques required to compose, produce, and perform works of music, dance, visual arts, drama, and sculpture.

WORK ENVIRONMENT—Indoors; contaminants; minor burns, cuts, bites, or stings; standing; using hands on objects, tools, or controls; bending or twisting the body.

Telecommunications Equipment Installers and Repairers, Except Line Installers

- ⊚ Education/Training Required: Long-term on-the-job training
- ⊚ Annual Earnings: $50,620
- ⊚ Growth: –4.9%
- ⊚ Annual Job Openings: 21,000
- ⊚ Self-Employed: 6.6%
- ⊚ Part-Time: 4.9%

Set up, rearrange, or remove switching and dialing equipment used in central offices. Service or repair telephones and other communication equipment on customers' property. May install equipment in new locations or install wiring and telephone jacks in buildings under construction. Remove and replace plug-in circuit equipment. Collaborate with other workers in order to locate and correct malfunctions. Communicate with bases, using telephones or two-way radios to receive instructions or technical advice or to report equipment status. Demonstrate equipment to customers and explain how it is to be used; respond to any inquiries or complaints. Designate cables available for use. Determine viability of sites through observation and discuss site locations and construction requirements with customers. Drive crew trucks to and from work areas. Install updated software and programs that maintain existing software and/or provide requested features such as time-correlated call routing.

Maintain computer and manual records pertaining to facilities and equipment. Clean and maintain tools, test equipment, and motor vehicles. Program computerized switches and switchboards to provide requested features. Dig holes or trenches as necessary for equipment installation and access. Remove loose wires and other debris after work is completed. Request support from technical service centers when on-site procedures fail to solve installation or maintenance problems. Enter codes needed to correct electronic switching system programming. Measure distances from landmarks to identify exact installation sites for equipment. Perform database verifications, using computers. Provide input into the design and manufacturing of new equipment. Place intercept circuits on terminals to handle vacant lines in central office installations. Diagnose and correct problems from remote locations, using special switchboards to find the sources of problems. Examine telephone transmission facilities to determine requirements for new or additional telephone services. Address special issues or situations, such as illegal or unauthorized use of equipment or cases of electrical or acoustic shock. Adjust or modify equipment to enhance equipment performance or to respond to customer requests. Analyze test readings, computer printouts, and trouble reports to determine equipment repair needs and required repair methods.

LEVEL OF ACTIVITY (out of 100)—General Physical Activity: 63.1. **Sitting:** 38.9. **Outdoors:** 42.9.

SKILLS—Installation; Repairing; Troubleshooting; Quality Control Analysis; Equipment Maintenance; Technology Design; Operation Monitoring.

GOE—Interest Area: 02. Architecture and Construction. **Work Group:** 02.05. Systems and Equipment Installation, Maintenance, and

Repair. **Other Jobs in This Work Group:** Electrical and Electronics Repairers, Powerhouse, Substation, and Relay; Electrical Power-Line Installers and Repairers; Elevator Installers and Repairers; Heating and Air Conditioning Mechanics and Installers; Maintenance and Repair Workers, General; Refrigeration Mechanics and Installers; Telecommunications Line Installers and Repairers. **PERSONALITY TYPE:** Realistic. Realistic occupations frequently involve work activities that include practical, hands-on problems and solutions. They often deal with plants; animals; and real-world materials like wood, tools, and machinery. Many of the occupations require working outside and do not involve a lot of paperwork or working closely with others.

EDUCATION/TRAINING PROGRAM(S)— Communications Systems Installation and Repair Technology. **RELATED KNOWLEDGE/COURSES—Telecommunications:** Transmission, broadcasting, switching, control, and operation of telecommunications systems. **Computers and Electronics:** Circuit boards; processors; chips; electronic equipment; and computer hardware and software, including applications and programming. **Design:** Design techniques, tools, and principles involved in production of precision technical plans, blueprints, drawings, and models. **Mechanical Devices:** Machines and tools, including their designs, uses, repair, and maintenance. **Engineering and Technology:** The practical application of engineering science and technology. This includes applying principles, techniques, procedures, and equipment to the design and production of various goods and services.

WORK ENVIRONMENT—Indoors; standing; using hands on objects, tools, or controls.

Telecommunications Line Installers and Repairers

- Education/Training Required: Long-term on-the-job training
- Annual Earnings: $42,410
- Growth: 10.8%
- Annual Job Openings: 23,000
- Self-Employed: 1.5%
- Part-Time: 2.5%

String and repair telephone and television cable, including fiber optics and other equipment for transmitting messages or television programming. Place insulation over conductors and seal splices with moisture-proof covering. Lay underground cable directly in trenches or string it through conduits running through trenches. Access specific areas to string lines and install terminal boxes, auxiliary equipment, and appliances, using bucket trucks or by climbing poles and ladders or entering tunnels, trenches, or crawl spaces. Inspect and test lines and cables, recording and analyzing test results, to assess transmission characteristics and locate faults and malfunctions. Install equipment such as amplifiers and repeaters in order to maintain the strength of communications transmissions. Compute impedance of wires from poles to houses in order to determine additional resistance needed for reducing signals to desired levels. Measure signal strength at utility poles, using electronic test equipment. Travel to customers' premises to install, maintain, and repair audio and visual electronic reception equipment and accessories. Pull up cable by hand from large reels mounted on trucks; then pull lines through ducts by hand or with winches. Set up service for customers, installing, connecting, testing, and adjusting equipment. Dig trenches for underground wires and cables. String cables between structures and lines from poles, towers, or trenches and pull lines to proper tension. Use a variety of construction equipment to complete installations, including digger derricks, trenchers, and cable plows. Clean and maintain tools and test equipment. Dig holes for power poles, using power augers or shovels; set poles in place with cranes; and hoist poles upright, using winches. Explain cable service to subscribers after installation and collect any installation fees that are due. Fill and tamp holes, using cement, earth, and tamping devices. Participate in the construction and removal of telecommunication towers and associated support structures. Splice cables, using hand tools, epoxy, or mechanical equipment.

LEVEL OF ACTIVITY (out of 100)—General Physical Activity: 76.1. **Sitting:** 28.6. **Outdoors:** 57.1.

SKILLS—Installation; Repairing; Troubleshooting; Equipment Maintenance; Operation Monitoring; Operation and Control.

GOE—Interest Area: 02. Architecture and Construction. **Work Group:** 02.05. Systems and Equipment Installation, Maintenance, and Repair. **Other Jobs in This Work Group:** Electrical and Electronics Repairers, Powerhouse, Substation, and Relay; Electrical Power-Line Installers and Repairers; Elevator Installers and Repairers; Heating and Air Conditioning Mechanics and Installers; Maintenance and Repair Workers, General; Refrigeration Mechanics and Installers; Telecommunications Equipment Installers and

Repairers, Except Line Installers. **PERSONALITY TYPE:** Realistic. Realistic occupations frequently involve work activities that include practical, hands-on problems and solutions. They often deal with plants; animals; and real-world materials like wood, tools, and machinery. Many of the occupations require working outside and do not involve a lot of paperwork or working closely with others.

EDUCATION/TRAINING PROGRAM(S)—Communications Systems Installation and Repair Technology. **RELATED KNOWLEDGE/COURSES—Telecommunications:** Transmission, broadcasting, switching, control, and operation of telecommunications systems. **Mechanical Devices:** Machines and tools, including their designs, uses, repair, and maintenance. **Computers and Electronics:** Circuit boards; processors; chips; electronic equipment; and computer hardware and software, including applications and programming.

WORK ENVIRONMENT—Outdoors; standing; kneeling, crouching, stooping, or crawling; using hands on objects, tools, or controls.

Tile and Marble Setters

- Education/Training Required: Long-term on-the-job training
- Annual Earnings: $36,530
- Growth: 22.9%
- Annual Job Openings: 9,000
- Self-Employed: 24.4%
- Part-Time: 12.3%

Apply hard tile, marble, and wood tile to walls, floors, ceilings, and roof decks. Align and straighten tile, using levels, squares, and straightedges. Determine and implement the best layout to achieve a desired pattern. Cut and shape tile to fit around obstacles and into odd spaces and corners, using hand and power cutting tools. Finish and dress the joints and wipe excess grout from between tiles, using damp sponge. Apply mortar to tile back, position the tile, and press or tap with trowel handle to affix tile to base. Mix, apply, and spread plaster, concrete, mortar, cement, mastic, glue, or other adhesives to form a bed for the tiles, using brush, trowel, and screed. Prepare cost and labor estimates based on calculations of time and materials needed for project. Measure and mark surfaces to be tiled, following blueprints. Level concrete and allow to dry. Build underbeds and install anchor bolts, wires, and brackets. Prepare surfaces for tiling by attaching lath or waterproof paper or by applying a cement mortar coat onto a metal screen. Study blueprints and examine surface to be covered to determine amount of material needed. Cut, surface, polish, and install marble and granite or install pre-cast terrazzo, granite, or marble units. Install and anchor fixtures in designated positions, using hand tools. Cut tile backing to required size, using shears. Remove any old tile, grout, and adhesive, using chisels and scrapers, and clean the surface carefully. Lay and set mosaic tiles to create decorative wall, mural, and floor designs. Assist customers in selection of tile and grout. Remove and replace cracked or damaged tile. Measure and cut metal lath to size for walls and ceilings, using tin snips. Select and order tile and other items to be installed, such as bathroom accessories, walls, panels, and cabinets, according to specifications. Mix and apply mortar or cement to edges and ends of drain tiles to seal halves and joints. Spread mastic or other adhesive base on roof deck to form base for promenade tile, using serrated spreader. Apply a sealer to make grout stain- and water-resistant. Brush glue onto manila paper on which design has been drawn and position tiles, finished side down, onto paper.

LEVEL OF ACTIVITY (out of 100)—General Physical Activity: 81.0. **Sitting:** 24.9. **Outdoors:** 34.5.

SKILLS—Installation; Management of Financial Resources; Mathematics; Social Perceptiveness; Management of Material Resources; Equipment Selection; Technology Design; Complex Problem Solving.

GOE—Interest Area: 02. Architecture and Construction. **Work Group:** 02.04. Construction Crafts. **Other Jobs in This Work Group:** Boilermakers; Brickmasons and Blockmasons; Carpet Installers; Cement Masons and Concrete Finishers; Commercial Divers; Construction Carpenters; Crane and Tower Operators; Drywall and Ceiling Tile Installers; Electricians; Fence Erectors; Floor Layers, Except Carpet, Wood, and Hard Tiles; Floor Sanders and Finishers; Glaziers; Hazardous Materials Removal Workers; Insulation Workers, Floor, Ceiling, and Wall; Insulation Workers, Mechanical; Manufactured Building and Mobile Home Installers; Operating Engineers and Other Construction Equipment Operators; Painters, Construction and Maintenance; Paperhangers; Paving, Surfacing, and Tamping Equipment Operators; Pile-Driver Operators; Pipe Fitters and Steamfitters; Pipelayers; Plasterers and Stucco Masons; Plumbers; Plumbers, Pipefitters, and Steamfitters; Rail-Track Laying and Maintenance Equipment Operators; Refractory Materials Repairers, Except Brickmasons; Reinforcing Iron and Rebar Workers; Riggers; Roofers; Rough Carpenters; Security and Fire Alarm Systems

Installers; Segmental Pavers; Sheet Metal Workers; Stone Cutters and Carvers, Manufacturing; Stonemasons; Structural Iron and Steel Workers; Tapers; Terrazzo Workers and Finishers. **PERSONALITY TYPE:** Realistic. Realistic occupations frequently involve work activities that include practical, hands-on problems and solutions. They often deal with plants; animals; and real-world materials like wood, tools, and machinery. Many of the occupations require working outside and do not involve a lot of paperwork or working closely with others.

EDUCATION/TRAINING PROGRAM(S)— Mason/Masonry. **RELATED KNOWLEDGE/COURSES—Building and Construction:** The materials, methods, and tools involved in the construction or repair of houses, buildings, or other structures such as highways and roads. **Design:** Design techniques, tools, and principles involved in production of precision technical plans, blueprints, drawings, and models. **Production and Processing:** Raw materials, production processes, quality control, costs, and other techniques for maximizing the effective manufacture and distribution of goods. **Economics and Accounting:** Economic and accounting principles and practices, the financial markets, banking, and the analysis and reporting of financial data. **Administration and Management:** Business and management principles involved in strategic planning, resource allocation, human resources modeling, leadership technique, production methods, and coordination of people and resources. **Transportation:** Principles and methods for moving people or goods by air, rail, sea, or road, including the relative costs and benefits.

WORK ENVIRONMENT—Noisy; contaminants; cramped work space, awkward positions; standing; using hands on objects, tools, or controls; bending or twisting the body.

Tool and Die Makers

- Education/Training Required: Long-term on-the-job training
- Annual Earnings: $43,580
- Growth: –2.6%
- Annual Job Openings: 7,000
- Self-Employed: 2.7%
- Part-Time: 4.8%

Analyze specifications; lay out metal stock; set up and operate machine tools; and fit and assemble parts to make and repair dies, cutting tools, jigs, fixtures, gauges, and machinists' hand tools. Study blueprints, sketches, models, or specifications to plan sequences of operations for fabricating tools, dies, or assemblies. Verify dimensions, alignments, and clearances of finished parts for conformance to specifications, using measuring instruments such as calipers, gauge blocks, micrometers, and dial indicators. Visualize and compute dimensions, sizes, shapes, and tolerances of assemblies based on specifications. Set up and operate conventional or computer numerically controlled machine tools such as lathes, milling machines, and grinders to cut, bore, grind, or otherwise shape parts to prescribed dimensions and finishes. File, grind, shim, and adjust different parts to properly fit them together. Fit and assemble parts to make, repair, or modify dies, jigs, gauges, and tools, using machine tools and hand tools. Conduct test runs with completed tools or dies to ensure that parts meet specifications; make adjustments as necessary. Inspect finished dies for smoothness, contour conformity, and defects. Smooth and polish flat and contoured surfaces of parts or tools, using scrapers, abrasive stones, files, emery cloths, or power grinders. Lift, position, and secure machined parts on surface plates or worktables, using hoists, vises, v-blocks, or angle plates. Measure, mark, and scribe metal or plastic stock to lay out machining, using instruments such as protractors, micrometers, scribes, and rulers. Cut, shape, and trim blanks or blocks to specified lengths or shapes, using power saws, power shears, rules, and hand tools. Select metals to be used from a range of metals and alloys, based on properties such as hardness and heat tolerance. Design jigs, fixtures, and templates for use as work aids in the fabrication of parts or products. Set up and operate drill presses to drill and tap holes in parts for assembly. Develop and design new tools and dies, using computer-aided design software. Set pyrometer controls of heat-treating furnaces and feed or place parts, tools, or assemblies into furnaces to harden.

LEVEL OF ACTIVITY (out of 100)—General Physical Activity: 57.9. **Sitting:** 28.4. **Outdoors:** 27.6.

SKILLS—Repairing; Mathematics; Troubleshooting; Technology Design; Equipment Selection; Installation; Equipment Maintenance; Complex Problem Solving.

GOE—Interest Area: 13. Manufacturing. **Work Group:** 13.05. Production Machining Technology. **Other Jobs in This Work Group:** Computer-Controlled Machine Tool Operators, Metal and Plastic; Foundry Mold and Coremakers; Lay-Out Workers, Metal and Plastic; Machinists; Model Makers, Metal and Plastic; Numerical Tool and Process Control Programmers; Patternmakers, Metal and Plastic; Tool Grinders, Filers, and Sharpeners. **PERSONALITY TYPE:** Realistic. Realistic occupations frequently involve work activities that include practical, hands-on problems and solutions. They often deal with plants; animals; and real-world materials like wood, tools, and machinery. Many of the occupations require working outside and do not involve a lot of paperwork or working closely with others.

EDUCATION/TRAINING PROGRAM(S)— Tool and Die Technology/Technician. **RELATED KNOWLEDGE/COURSES—Design:** Design techniques, tools, and principles involved in production of precision technical plans, blueprints, drawings, and models. **Mechanical Devices:** Machines and tools, including their designs, uses, repair, and maintenance. **Engineering and Technology:** The practical application of engineering science and technology. This includes applying principles, techniques, procedures, and equipment to the design and production of various goods and services. **Production and Processing:** Raw materials, production processes, quality control, costs, and other techniques for maximizing the effective manufacture and distribution of goods. **Mathematics:** Arithmetic, algebra, geometry, calculus, and statistics and their applications. **Public Safety and Security:** Relevant equipment, policies, procedures, and strategies to promote effective local, state, or national security operations for the protection of people, data, property, and institutions.

WORK ENVIRONMENT—Noisy; contaminants; hazardous equipment; minor burns, cuts, bites, or stings; standing; using hands on objects, tools, or controls.

Transit and Railroad Police

- ⊚ Education/Training Required: Long-term on-the-job training
- ⊚ Annual Earnings: $48,850
- ⊚ Growth: 9.2%
- ⊚ Annual Job Openings: Fewer than 500
- ⊚ Self-Employed: 0.0%
- ⊚ Part-Time: 1.4%

Protect and police railroad and transit property, employees, or passengers. Patrol railroad yards, cars, stations, and other facilities in order to protect company property and shipments and to maintain order. Examine credentials of unauthorized persons attempting to enter secured areas. Apprehend or remove trespassers or thieves from railroad property or coordinate with law enforcement agencies in apprehensions and removals. Prepare reports documenting investigation activities and results. Investigate or direct investigations of freight theft, suspicious damage or loss of passengers' valuables, and other crimes on railroad property. Direct security activities at derailments, fires, floods, and strikes involving railroad property. Direct and coordinate the daily activities and training of security staff. Interview neighbors, associates, and former employers of job applicants in order to verify personal references and to obtain work history data. Record and verify seal numbers from boxcars containing frequently pilfered items, such as cigarettes and liquor, in order to detect tampering. Plan and implement special safety and preventive programs, such as fire and accident prevention. Seal empty boxcars by twisting nails in door hasps, using nail twisters.

LEVEL OF ACTIVITY (out of 100)—General Physical Activity: 84.1. **Sitting:** 37.9. **Outdoors:** 49.4.

SKILLS—Persuasion; Service Orientation; Social Perceptiveness; Negotiation; Active Listening; Writing; Complex Problem Solving; Speaking.

GOE—**Interest Area:** 12. Law and Public Safety. **Work Group:** 12.04. Law Enforcement and Public Safety. **Other Jobs in This Work Group:** Bailiffs; Correctional Officers and Jailers; Criminal Investigators and Special Agents; Detectives and Criminal Investigators; Fire Investigators; Forensic Science Technicians; Parking Enforcement Workers; Police and Sheriff's Patrol Officers; Police Detectives; Police Identification and Records Officers; Police Patrol Officers; Sheriffs and Deputy Sheriffs. **PERSONALITY TYPE:** Enterprising. Enterprising occupations frequently involve starting up and carrying out projects. These occupations can involve leading people and making many decisions. They sometimes require risk taking and often deal with business.

EDUCATION/TRAINING PROGRAM(S)—Security and Loss Prevention Services; Security and Protective Services, Other. **RELATED KNOWLEDGE/COURSES—Public Safety and Security:** Relevant equipment, policies, procedures, and strategies to promote effective local, state, or national security operations for the protection of people, data, property, and institutions. **Transportation:** Principles and methods for moving people or goods by air, rail, sea, or road, including the relative costs and benefits. **Telecommunications:** Transmission, broadcasting, switching, control, and operation of telecommunications systems. **English Language:** The structure and content of the English language, including the meaning and spelling of words, rules of composition, and grammar. **Law and Government:** Laws, legal codes, court procedures, precedents, government regulations, executive orders, agency rules, and the democratic political process. **Geography:** Principles and methods for describing the features of land, sea, and air masses, including their physical characteristics; locations; interrelationships; and distribution of plant, animal, and human life.

WORK ENVIRONMENT—More often indoors than outdoors; noisy; very hot or cold; very bright or dim lighting; hazardous conditions.

Transportation Inspectors

See the descriptions of these jobs:

- Aviation Inspectors
- Freight and Cargo Inspectors
- Transportation Vehicle, Equipment, and Systems Inspectors, Except Aviation

Transportation Vehicle, Equipment, and Systems Inspectors, Except Aviation

This job can be found in the Part I lists under the title Transportation Inspectors.

- Education/Training Required: Work experience in a related occupation
- Annual Earnings: $49,490
- Growth: 11.4%
- Annual Job Openings: 2,000
- Self-Employed: 1.9%
- Part-Time: 2.3%

The job openings listed here are shared with Aviation Inspectors and with Freight and Cargo Inspectors.

Inspect and monitor transportation equipment, vehicles, or systems to ensure compliance with regulations and safety standards. Investigate and make recommendations on carrier requests for waiver of federal standards. Prepare reports on investigations or inspections and actions taken. Examine carrier operating rules, employee qualification guidelines, and carrier training and testing programs for compliance with regulations or safety standards. Examine transportation vehicles, equipment, or systems to detect damage, wear, or malfunction. Inspect repairs to transportation vehicles and equipment to ensure that repair work was performed properly. Inspect vehicles or equipment to ensure compliance with rules, standards, or regulations. Investigate complaints regarding safety violations. Investigate incidents or violations, such as delays, accidents, and equipment failures. Issue notices and recommend corrective actions when infractions or problems are found. Inspect vehicles and other equipment for evidence of abuse, damage, or mechanical malfunction. Conduct vehicle or transportation equipment tests, using diagnostic equipment.

LEVEL OF ACTIVITY (out of 100)—General Physical Activity: 34.7. **Sitting:** 41.0. **Outdoors:** 53.3.

SKILLS—Operation Monitoring; Quality Control Analysis; Systems Evaluation; Troubleshooting; Equipment Maintenance; Systems Analysis.

GOE—Interest Area: 07. Government and Public Administration. **Work Group:** 07.03. Regulations Enforcement. **Other Jobs in This Work Group:** Agricultural Inspectors; Aviation Inspectors; Compliance Officers, Except Agriculture, Construction, Health and Safety, and Transportation; Construction and Building Inspectors; Environmental Compliance Inspectors; Equal Opportunity Representatives and Officers; Financial Examiners; Fire Inspectors; Fish and Game Wardens; Forest Fire Inspectors and Prevention Specialists; Freight and Cargo Inspectors; Government Property Inspectors and Investigators; Immigration and Customs Inspectors; Licensing Examiners and Inspectors; Nuclear Monitoring Technicians; Occupational Health and Safety Specialists; Occupational Health and Safety Technicians; Tax Examiners, Collectors, and Revenue Agents. **PERSONALITY TYPE:** Realistic. Realistic occupations frequently involve work activities that include practical, hands-on problems and solutions. They often deal with plants; animals;

and real-world materials like wood, tools, and machinery. Many of the occupations require working outside and do not involve a lot of paperwork or working closely with others.

EDUCATION/TRAINING PROGRAM(S)— No related CIP programs; this job is learned through work experience in a related occupation. **RELATED KNOWLEDGE/COURSES—Transportation:** Principles and methods for moving people or goods by air, rail, sea, or road, including the relative costs and benefits. **Public Safety and Security:** Relevant equipment, policies, procedures, and strategies to promote effective local, state, or national security operations for the protection of people, data, property, and institutions. **Mechanical Devices:** Machines and tools, including their designs, uses, repair, and maintenance.

WORK ENVIRONMENT—Outdoors; standing; using hands on objects, tools, or controls.

Tree Trimmers and Pruners

- ◉ Education/Training Required: Short-term on-the-job training
- ◉ Annual Earnings: $27,920
- ◉ Growth: 16.5%
- ◉ Annual Job Openings: 11,000
- ◉ Self-Employed: 22.2%
- ◉ Part-Time: 24.4%

Cut away dead or excess branches from trees or shrubs to maintain right-of-way for roads, side-

walks, or utilities or to improve appearance, health, and value of tree. **Prune or treat trees or shrubs, using handsaws, pruning hooks, shears, and clippers. May use truck-mounted lifts and power pruners. May fill cavities in trees to promote healing and prevent deterioration.** Water, root-feed, and fertilize trees. Apply tar or other protective substances to cut surfaces to seal surfaces and to protect them from fungi and insects. Harvest tanbark by cutting rings and slits in bark and stripping bark from trees, using spuds or axes. Hoist tools and equipment to tree trimmers and lower branches with ropes or block and tackle. Install lightning protection on trees. Plan and develop budgets for tree work and estimate the monetary value of trees. Provide information to the public regarding trees, such as advice on tree care. Scrape decayed matter from cavities in trees and fill holes with cement to promote healing and to prevent further deterioration. Split logs or wooden blocks into bolts, pickets, posts, or stakes, using hand tools such as ax wedges, sledgehammers, and mallets. Supervise others engaged in tree-trimming work and train lower-level employees. Transplant and remove trees and shrubs and prepare trees for moving. Climb trees, using climbing hooks and belts, or climb ladders to gain access to work areas. Operate boom trucks, loaders, stump chippers, brush chippers, tractors, power saws, trucks, sprayers, and other equipment and tools. Clean, sharpen, and lubricate tools and equipment. Trim, top, and reshape trees to achieve attractive shapes or to remove low-hanging branches. Cable, brace, tie, bolt, stake, and guy trees and branches to provide support. Clear sites, streets, and grounds of woody and herbaceous materials, such as tree stumps and fallen trees and limbs. Collect debris and refuse from tree trimming and removal operations into piles, using shovels, rakes, or other tools. Inspect trees to determine if they have diseases or pest problems. Trim jagged stumps, using saws or pruning shears. Operate shredding and chipping equipment and feed limbs and brush into the machines. Spray trees to treat diseased or unhealthy trees, including mixing chemicals and calibrating spray equipment. Prune, cut down, fertilize, and spray trees as directed by tree surgeons. Remove broken limbs from wires, using hooked extension poles. Load debris and refuse onto trucks and haul it away for disposal.

LEVEL OF ACTIVITY (out of 100)—General Physical Activity: 80.9. **Sitting:** 22.9. **Outdoors:** 71.4.

SKILLS—Operation and Control.

GOE—Interest Area: 01. Agriculture and Natural Resources. **Work Group:** 01.05. Nursery, Groundskeeping, and Pest Control. **Other Jobs in This Work Group:** Landscaping and Groundskeeping Workers; Nursery Workers; Pest Control Workers; Pesticide Handlers, Sprayers, and Applicators, Vegetation. **PERSONALITY TYPE:** Realistic. Realistic occupations frequently involve work activities that include practical, hands-on problems and solutions. They often deal with plants; animals; and real-world materials like wood, tools, and machinery. Many of the occupations require working outside and do not involve a lot of paperwork or working closely with others.

EDUCATION/TRAINING PROGRAM(S)— Applied Horticulture/Horicultural Business Services, Other. **RELATED KNOWLEDGE/ COURSES—Biology:** Plant and animal organisms and their tissues, cells, functions, interdependencies, and interactions with each other and the environment. **Chemistry:** The chemical composition, structure, and properties of substances and of the chemical processes and transformations that they undergo. This includes uses of chemicals and their danger signs, production techniques, and disposal methods. **Mechanical Devices:** Machines and tools, including their designs, uses, repair, and maintenance.

WORK ENVIRONMENT—Outdoors; high places; minor burns, cuts, bites, or stings; standing; using hands on objects, tools, or controls; repetitive motions.

Truck Drivers, Heavy and Tractor-Trailer

- Education/Training Required: Moderate-term on-the-job training
- Annual Earnings: $34,280
- Growth: 12.9%
- Annual Job Openings: 274,000
- Self-Employed: 9.3%
- Part-Time: 9.1%

Drive a tractor-trailer combination or a truck with a capacity of at least 26,000 GVW to transport and deliver goods, livestock, or materials in liquid, loose, or packaged form. May be required to unload truck. May require use of automated routing equipment. Requires commercial drivers' license. Follow appropriate safety procedures when transporting dangerous goods. Check vehicles before driving them to ensure that mechanical, safety, and emergency equipment is in good working order. Maintain logs of working hours and of vehicle service and repair status, following applicable state and federal regulations. Obtain receipts or signatures when loads are delivered and collect payment for services when required. Check all load-related documentation to ensure that it is complete and accurate. Maneuver trucks into loading or unloading positions, following signals from loading crew as needed; check that vehicle position is correct and any special loading equipment is properly positioned. Drive trucks with capacities greater than 3 tons, including tractor-trailer combinations, in order to transport and deliver products, livestock, or other materials. Secure cargo for transport, using ropes, blocks, chain, binders, and/or covers. Read bills of lading to determine assignment details. Report vehicle defects, accidents, traffic violations, or damage to the vehicles. Read and interpret maps in order to determine vehicle routes. Couple and uncouple trailers by changing trailer jack positions, connecting or disconnecting air and electrical lines, and manipulating fifth-wheel locks. Collect delivery instructions from appropriate sources, verifying instructions and routes. Drive trucks to weigh stations before and after loading and along routes in order to document weights and to comply with state regulations. Operate equipment such as truck cab computers, CB radios, and telephones to exchange necessary information with bases, supervisors, or other drivers. Check conditions of trailers after contents have been unloaded to ensure that there has been no damage. Crank trailer landing gear up and down to safely secure vehicles. Wrap goods, using pads, packing paper, and containers, and secure loads to trailer walls, using straps. Perform basic vehicle maintenance tasks such as adding oil, fuel, and radiator fluid or performing minor repairs. Load and unload trucks or help others with loading and unloading, operating any special loading-related equipment on vehicles and using other equipment as necessary.

T

LEVEL OF ACTIVITY (out of 100)—General Physical Activity: 65.4. **Sitting:** 57.1. **Outdoors:** 48.8.

SKILLS—Equipment Maintenance; Repairing; Operation Monitoring; Troubleshooting; Operation and Control; Mathematics.

GOE—Interest Area: 16. Transportation, Distribution, and Logistics. **Work Group:** 16.03. Truck Driving. **Other Jobs in This Work Group:** Truck Drivers, Light or Delivery Services. **PERSONALITY TYPE:** Realistic. Realistic occupations frequently involve work activities that include practical, hands-on problems and solutions. They often deal with plants; animals; and real-world materials like wood, tools, and machinery. Many of the occupations require working outside and do not involve a lot of paperwork or working closely with others.

EDUCATION/TRAINING PROGRAM(S)—Truck and Bus Driver/Commercial Vehicle Operation. **RELATED KNOWLEDGE/COURSES—Transportation:** Principles and methods for moving people or goods by air, rail, sea, or road, including the relative costs and benefits. **Geography:** Principles and methods for describing the features of land, sea, and air masses, including their physical characteristics; locations; interrelationships; and distribution of plant, animal, and human life. **Public Safety and Security:** Relevant equipment, policies, procedures, and strategies to promote effective local, state, or national security operations for the protection of people, data, property, and institutions. **Law and Government:** Laws, legal codes, court procedures, precedents, government regulations, executive orders, agency rules, and the democratic political process. **Mechanical Devices:** Machines and tools, including their designs, uses, repair, and maintenance.

WORK ENVIRONMENT—Outdoors; very hot or cold; contaminants; sitting; using hands on objects, tools, or controls; repetitive motions.

Truck Drivers, Light or Delivery Services

- Education/Training Required: Short-term on-the-job training
- Annual Earnings: $24,790
- Growth: 15.7%
- Annual Job Openings: 169,000
- Self-Employed: 8.9%
- Part-Time: 9.1%

Drive a truck or van with a capacity of under 26,000 GVW, primarily to deliver or pick up merchandise or to deliver packages within a specified area. May require use of automatic routing or location software. May load and unload truck. Obey traffic laws and follow established traffic and transportation procedures. Inspect and maintain vehicle supplies and equipment, such as gas, oil, water, tires, lights, and brakes, in order to ensure that vehicles are in proper working condition. Report any mechanical problems encountered with vehicles. Present bills and receipts and collect payments for goods delivered or loaded. Load and unload trucks, vans, or automobiles. Turn in receipts and money received from deliveries. Verify the contents of inventory loads against shipping papers. Maintain records such as vehicle logs, records of cargo, or billing statements in accordance with regulations. Read maps and follow written and verbal geographic directions. Report delays, accidents, or other traffic and transportation situations to bases or other vehicles, using telephones or mobile two-way radios. Sell and keep records of sales for products from truck inventory. Drive vehicles with capacities under three tons in order to transport materials to and from specified destinations such as railroad stations, plants, residences, and offices or within industrial yards. Drive trucks equipped with public address systems through city streets in order to broadcast announcements for advertising or publicity purposes. Use and maintain the tools and equipment found on commercial vehicles, such as weighing and measuring devices. Perform emergency repairs such as changing tires or installing light bulbs, fuses, tire chains, and spark plugs.

LEVEL OF ACTIVITY (out of 100)—General Physical Activity: 66.4. **Sitting:** 42.7. **Outdoors:** 62.9.

SKILLS—Equipment Maintenance; Operation Monitoring; Operation and Control; Social Perceptiveness; Service Orientation; Persuasion; Systems Evaluation; Troubleshooting.

GOE—Interest Area: 16. Transportation, Distribution, and Logistics. **Work Group:** 16.03. Truck Driving. **Other Jobs in This Work Group:** Truck Drivers, Heavy and Tractor-Trailer. **PERSONALITY TYPE:** Realistic. Realistic occupations frequently involve work activities that include practical, hands-on problems and solutions. They often deal with plants; animals; and real-world materials like wood, tools, and machinery. Many of the occupations require working outside and do not involve a lot of paperwork or working closely with others.

EDUCATION/TRAINING PROGRAM(S)—Truck and Bus Driver/Commercial Vehicle Operation. **RELATED KNOWLEDGE/**

COURSES—Transportation: Principles and methods for moving people or goods by air, rail, sea, or road, including the relative costs and benefits. **Production and Processing:** Raw materials, production processes, quality control, costs, and other techniques for maximizing the effective manufacture and distribution of goods.

WORK ENVIRONMENT—Outdoors; very hot or cold; contaminants; cramped work space, awkward positions; minor burns, cuts, bites, or stings; using hands on objects, tools, or controls.

Umpires, Referees, and Other Sports Officials

- Education/Training Required: Long-term on-the-job training
- Annual Earnings: $21,610
- Growth: 19.0%
- Annual Job Openings: 6,000
- Self-Employed: 24.8%
- Part-Time: 47.6%

Officiate at competitive athletic or sporting events. Detect infractions of rules and decide penalties according to established regulations. Officiate at sporting events, games, or competitions to maintain standards of play and to ensure that game rules are observed. Judge performances in sporting competitions in order to award points, impose scoring penalties, and determine results. Signal participants or other officials to make them aware of infractions or to otherwise regulate play or competition. Inspect sporting equipment and/or examine participants in order to ensure compliance with event and safety regulations. Keep track of event times, including race times and elapsed time during game segments, starting or stopping play when necessary. Start races and competitions. Resolve claims of rule infractions or complaints by participants and assess any necessary penalties according to regulations. Verify scoring calculations before competition winners are announced. Direct participants to assigned areas such as starting blocks or penalty areas. Report to regulating organizations regarding sporting activities, complaints made, and actions taken or needed such as fines or other disciplinary actions. Confer with other sporting officials, coaches, players, and facility managers in order to provide information, coordinate activities, and discuss problems. Teach and explain the rules and regulations governing a specific sport. Research and study players and teams in order to anticipate issues that might arise in future engagements. Verify credentials of participants in sporting events and make other qualifying determinations such as starting order or handicap number. Compile scores and other athletic records.

LEVEL OF ACTIVITY (out of 100)—General Physical Activity: 81.6. **Sitting:** 16.7. **Outdoors:** 26.4.

SKILLS—Negotiation; Persuasion; Judgment and Decision Making; Social Perceptiveness; Coordination; Monitoring; Active Listening; Management of Personnel Resources.

GOE—Interest Area: 09. Hospitality, Tourism, and Recreation. **Work Group:** 09.06. Sports. **Other Jobs in This Work Group:** Athletes and Sports Competitors; Coaches and Scouts. **PERSONALITY TYPE:** Enterprising. Enterprising occupations frequently involve starting up and carrying out projects. These occupations can involve leading people and making many decisions. They sometimes require risk taking and often deal with business.

EDUCATION/TRAINING PROGRAM(S)—Personal and Culinary Services, Other. **RELATED KNOWLEDGE/COURSES—Psychology:** Human behavior and performance; individual differences in ability, personality, and interests; learning and motivation; psychological research methods; and the assessment and treatment of behavioral and affective disorders. **Sociology and Anthropology:** Group behavior and dynamics, societal trends and influences, human migrations, ethnicity, and cultures and their history and origins. **Administration and Management:** Business and management principles involved in strategic planning, resource allocation, human resources modeling, leadership technique, production methods, and coordination of people and resources. **Public Safety and Security:** Relevant equipment, policies, procedures, and strategies to promote effective local, state, or national security operations for the protection of people, data, property, and institutions. **Education and Training:** Principles and methods for curriculum and training design, teaching and instruction for individuals and groups, and the measurement of training effects. **Customer and Personal Service:** Principles and processes for providing customer and personal services. This includes customer needs assessment, meeting quality standards for services, and evaluation of customer satisfaction.

WORK ENVIRONMENT—More often outdoors than indoors; noisy; standing; walking and running; repetitive motions.

Veterinarians

- Education/Training Required: First professional degree
- Annual Earnings: $68,910
- Growth: 17.4%
- Annual Job Openings: 8,000
- Self-Employed: 20.7%
- Part-Time: 10.8%

Diagnose and treat diseases and dysfunctions of animals. May engage in a particular function, such as research and development, consultation, administration, technical writing, sale or production of commercial products, or rendering of technical services to commercial firms or other organizations. Includes veterinarians who inspect livestock. Examine animals to detect and determine the nature of diseases or injuries. Treat sick or injured animals by prescribing medication, setting bones, dressing wounds, or performing surgery. Inoculate animals against various diseases such as rabies and distemper. Collect body tissue, feces, blood, urine, or other body fluids for examination and analysis. Operate diagnostic equipment such as radiographic and ultrasound equipment and interpret the resulting images. Advise animal owners regarding sanitary measures, feeding, and general care necessary to promote health of animals. Educate the public about diseases that can be spread from animals to humans. Train and supervise workers who handle and care for animals. Provide care to a wide range of animals or specialize in a particular species, such as horses or exotic birds. Euthanize animals. Establish and conduct quarantine and testing procedures that prevent the spread of diseases to other animals or to humans and that comply with applicable government regulations. Conduct postmortem studies and analyses to determine the causes of animals' deaths. Perform administrative duties such as scheduling appointments, accepting payments from clients, and maintaining business records. Drive mobile clinic vans to farms so that health problems can be treated or prevented. Direct the overall operations of animal hospitals, clinics, or mobile services to farms. Specialize in a particular type of treatment such as dentistry, pathology, nutrition, surgery, microbiology, or internal medicine. Inspect and test horses, sheep, poultry, and other animals to detect the presence of communicable diseases. Research diseases to which animals could be susceptible. Plan and execute animal nutrition and reproduction programs. Inspect animal housing facilities to determine their cleanliness and adequacy. Determine the effects of drug therapies, antibiotics, or new surgical techniques by testing them on animals.

LEVEL OF ACTIVITY (out of 100)—General Physical Activity: 51.0. **Sitting:** 28.7. **Outdoors:** 27.5.

SKILLS—Science; Management of Financial Resources; Judgment and Decision Making; Reading Comprehension; Complex Problem Solving; Management of Personnel Resources; Instructing; Active Learning.

GOE—Interest Area: 08. Health Science. **Work Group:** 08.05. Animal Care. **Other Jobs in This Work Group:** Animal Breeders; Animal Trainers; Nonfarm Animal Caretakers; Veterinary Assistants and Laboratory Animal Caretakers; Veterinary Technologists and Technicians. **PERSONALITY TYPE:**

Investigative. Investigative occupations frequently involve working with ideas and require an extensive amount of thinking. These occupations can involve searching for facts and figuring out problems mentally.

EDUCATION/TRAINING PROGRAM(S)— Veterinary Medicine (DVM); Veterinary Sciences/Veterinary Clinical Sciences, General (Cert, MS, PhD); Veterinary Anatomy (Cert, MS, PhD); Veterinary Physiology (Cert, MS, PhD); Veterinary Microbiology and Immunobiology (Cert, MS, PhD); Veterinary Pathology and Pathobiology (Cert, MS, PhD); Veterinary Toxicology and Pharmacology (Cert, MS, PhD); Large Animal/Food Animal and Equine Surgery and Medicine (Cert, MS, PhD); others. **RELATED KNOWLEDGE/COURSES—Biology:** Plant and animal organisms and their tissues, cells, functions, interdependencies, and interactions with each other and the environment. **Medicine and Dentistry:** The information and techniques needed to diagnose and treat human injuries, diseases, and deformities. This includes symptoms, treatment alternatives, drug properties and interactions, and preventive health-care measures. **Chemistry:** The chemical composition, structure, and properties of substances and of the chemical processes and transformations that they undergo. This includes uses of chemicals and their danger signs, production techniques, and disposal methods. **Therapy and Counseling:** Principles, methods, and procedures for diagnosis, treatment, and rehabilitation of physical and mental dysfunctions and for career counseling and guidance. **Customer and Personal Service:** Principles and processes for providing customer and personal services. This includes customer needs assessment, meeting quality standards for services, and evaluation of customer satisfaction. **Sales and Marketing:** Principles and methods for showing, promoting, and selling products or services. This includes

marketing strategy and tactics, product demonstration, sales techniques, and sales control systems.

WORK ENVIRONMENT—Indoors; noisy; contaminants; disease or infections; standing; using hands on objects, tools, or controls.

Vocational Education Teachers, Secondary School

- ◎ Education/Training Required: Work experience plus degree
- ◎ Annual Earnings: $47,090
- ◎ Growth: 9.1%
- ◎ Annual Job Openings: 10,000
- ◎ Self-Employed: 0.0%
- ◎ Part-Time: 9.2%

Teach or instruct vocational or occupational subjects at the secondary school level. Prepare materials and classroom for class activities. Maintain accurate and complete student records as required by law, district policy, and administrative regulations. Instruct students individually and in groups, using various teaching methods such as lectures, discussions, and demonstrations. Observe and evaluate students' performance, behavior, social development, and physical health. Establish and enforce rules for behavior and procedures for maintaining order among the students for whom they are responsible. Instruct and monitor students in the use and care of equipment and materials in order to prevent injury and damage. Plan and conduct activities for a balanced program of instruction, demonstration, and work time that provides students with opportunities to observe, question, and investigate. Prepare, administer, and grade tests and assignments in order to evaluate students' progress. Enforce all administration policies and rules governing students. Assign and grade class work and homework. Instruct students in the knowledge and skills required in a specific occupation or occupational field, using a systematic plan of lectures; discussions; audiovisual presentations; and laboratory, shop, and field studies. Establish clear objectives for all lessons, units, and projects and communicate those objectives to students. Use computers, audiovisual aids, and other equipment and materials to supplement presentations. Plan and supervise work-experience programs in businesses, industrial shops, and school laboratories. Prepare students for later grades by encouraging them to explore learning opportunities and to persevere with challenging tasks. Confer with parents or guardians, other teachers, counselors, and administrators in order to resolve students' behavioral and academic problems. Guide and counsel students with adjustment and/or academic problems or special academic interests. Prepare objectives and outlines for courses of study, following curriculum guidelines or requirements of states and schools. Keep informed about trends in education and subject matter specialties.

LEVEL OF ACTIVITY (out of 100)—General Physical Activity: 44.1. **Sitting:** 32.4. **Outdoors:** 21.2.

SKILLS—Management of Financial Resources; Learning Strategies; Instructing; Social Perceptiveness; Persuasion; Management of Material Resources; Management of Personnel Resources; Service Orientation.

GOE—Interest Area: 05. Education and Training. **Work Group:** 05.02. Preschool, Elementary, and Secondary Teaching and Instructing. **Other Jobs in This Work Group:** Elementary School Teachers, Except Special Education; Kindergarten Teachers, Except Special Education; Middle School Teachers, Except Special and Vocational Education; Preschool Teachers, Except Special Education; Secondary School Teachers, Except Special and Vocational Education; Special Education Teachers, Middle School; Special Education Teachers, Preschool, Kindergarten, and Elementary School; Special Education Teachers, Secondary School; Teacher Assistants; Vocational Education Teachers, Middle School. **PERSONALITY TYPE:** Social. Social occupations frequently involve working with, communicating with, and teaching people. These occupations often involve helping or providing service to others.

EDUCATION/TRAINING PROGRAM(S)— Technology Teacher Education/Industrial Arts Teacher Education. **RELATED KNOWLEDGE/COURSES—Education and Training:** Principles and methods for curriculum and training design, teaching and instruction for individuals and groups, and the measurement of training effects. **Therapy and Counseling:** Principles, methods, and procedures for diagnosis, treatment, and rehabilitation of physical and mental dysfunctions and for career counseling and guidance. **Psychology:** Human behavior and performance; individual differences in ability, personality, and interests; learning and motivation; psychological research methods; and the assessment and treatment of behavioral and affective disorders. **Design:** Design techniques, tools, and principles involved in production of precision technical plans, blueprints, drawings, and models. **Sociology and Anthropology:**

Group behavior and dynamics, societal trends and influences, human migrations, ethnicity, and cultures and their history and origins. **Clerical Practices:** Administrative and clerical procedures and systems such as word processing, managing files and records, stenography and transcription, designing forms, and other office procedures and terminology.

WORK ENVIRONMENT—Indoors; noisy; standing; using hands on objects, tools, or controls.

Water and Liquid Waste Treatment Plant and System Operators

- ◎ Education/Training Required: Long-term on-the-job training
- ◎ Annual Earnings: $34,930
- ◎ Growth: 16.2%
- ◎ Annual Job Openings: 6,000
- ◎ Self-Employed: 0.0%
- ◎ Part-Time: 5.2%

Operate or control an entire process or system of machines, often through the use of control boards, to transfer or treat water or liquid waste. Add chemicals such as ammonia, chlorine, or lime to disinfect and deodorize water and other liquids. Operate and adjust controls on equipment to purify and clarify water, process or dispose of sewage, and generate power. Inspect equipment or monitor operating conditions, meters, and gauges to determine load requirements and detect malfunctions. Collect and test water and sewage samples, using test equipment and color analysis standards. Record operational data, personnel attendance, or meter and gauge readings on specified forms. Maintain, repair, and lubricate equipment, using hand tools and power tools. Clean and maintain tanks and filter beds, using hand tools and power tools. Direct and coordinate plant workers engaged in routine operations and maintenance activities.

LEVEL OF ACTIVITY (out of 100)—General Physical Activity: 68.0. **Sitting:** 37.3. **Outdoors:** 53.0.

SKILLS—Operation Monitoring; Installation; Operation and Control; Troubleshooting; Management of Material Resources; Operations Analysis; Equipment Maintenance; Management of Personnel Resources.

GOE—Interest Area: 13. Manufacturing. **Work Group:** 13.16. Utility Operation and Energy Distribution. **Other Jobs in This Work Group:** Chemical Plant and System Operators; Gas Compressor and Gas Pumping Station Operators; Gas Plant Operators; Nuclear Power Reactor Operators; Petroleum Pump System Operators, Refinery Operators, and Gaugers; Power Distributors and Dispatchers; Power Plant Operators; Ship Engineers; Stationary Engineers and Boiler Operators. **PERSONALITY TYPE:** Realistic. Realistic occupations frequently involve work activities that include practical, hands-on problems and solutions. They often deal with plants; animals; and real-world materials like wood, tools, and machinery.

Many of the occupations require working outside and do not involve a lot of paperwork or working closely with others.

EDUCATION/TRAINING PROGRAM(S)—Water Quality and Wastewater Treatment Management and Recycling Technology/Technician. **RELATED KNOWLEDGE/COURSES**—Biology: Plant and animal organisms and their tissues, cells, functions, interdependencies, and interactions with each other and the environment. **Chemistry:** The chemical composition, structure, and properties of substances and of the chemical processes and transformations that they undergo. This includes uses of chemicals and their danger signs, production techniques, and disposal methods. **Physics:** Physical principles and laws and their interrelationships and applications to understanding fluid, material, and atmospheric dynamics and mechanical, electrical, atomic, and subatomic structures and processes. **Public Safety and Security:** Relevant equipment, policies, procedures, and strategies to promote effective local, state, or national security operations for the protection of people, data, property, and institutions. **Mechanical Devices:** Machines and tools, including their designs, uses, repair, and maintenance. **Law and Government:** Laws, legal codes, court procedures, precedents, government regulations, executive orders, agency rules, and the democratic political process.

WORK ENVIRONMENT—More often outdoors than indoors; noisy; very hot or cold; contaminants; minor burns, cuts, bites, or stings.

Welders, Cutters, and Welder Fitters

This job can be found in the Part I lists under the title Welders, Cutters, Solderers, and Brazers.

- Education/Training Required: Long-term on-the-job training
- Annual Earnings: $30,990
- Growth: 5.0%
- Annual Job Openings: 52,000
- Self-Employed: 6.3%
- Part-Time: 1.7%

The job openings listed here are shared with Solderers and Brazers.

Use hand-welding or flame-cutting equipment to weld or join metal components or to fill holes, indentations, or seams of fabricated metal products. Operate safety equipment and use safe work habits. Weld components in flat, vertical, or overhead positions. Ignite torches or start power supplies and strike arcs by touching electrodes to metals being welded, completing electrical circuits. Clamp, hold, tack-weld, heat-bend, grind, and/or bolt component parts to obtain required configurations and positions for welding. Detect faulty operation of equipment and/or defective materials and notify supervisors. Operate manual or semi-automatic welding equipment to fuse metal segments, using processes such as gas tungsten arc, gas metal arc, flux-cored arc, plasma arc, shielded metal arc, resistance welding, and submerged arc welding. Monitor the fitting, burning, and welding processes to avoid overheating of parts or warping, shrinking, distortion, or expansion of material. Examine workpieces for defects and measure workpieces with straightedges or templates to ensure conformance with specifications. Recognize, set up, and operate hand and power tools common to the welding trade, such as shielded metal arc and gas metal arc welding equipment. Lay out, position, align, and secure parts and assemblies prior to assembly, using straightedges, combination squares, calipers, and rulers. Chip or grind off excess weld, slag, or spatter, using hand scrapers or power chippers, portable grinders, or arc-cutting equipment. Analyze engineering drawings, blueprints, specifications, sketches, work orders, and material safety data sheets to plan layout, assembly, and welding operations. Connect and turn regulator valves to activate and adjust gas flow and pressure so that desired flames are obtained. Weld separately or in combination, using aluminum, stainless steel, cast iron, and other alloys. Determine required equipment and welding methods, applying knowledge of metallurgy, geometry, and welding techniques. Mark and/or tag material with proper job number, piece marks, and other identifying marks as required. Prepare all material surfaces to be welded, ensuring that there is no loose or thick scale, slag, rust, moisture, grease, or other foreign matter.

LEVEL OF ACTIVITY (out of 100)—General Physical Activity: 62.0. **Sitting:** 27.9. **Outdoors:** 24.7.

SKILLS—Repairing; Equipment Maintenance; Installation; Quality Control Analysis; Equipment Selection; Operation and Control.

GOE—Interest Area: 13. Manufacturing. **Work Group:** 13.04. Welding, Brazing, and Soldering. **Other Jobs in This Work Group:** Solderers and Brazers; Structural Metal Fabricators and Fitters; Welders, Cutters, Solderers, and Brazers; Welding, Soldering, and Brazing Machine Setters, Operators, and Tenders. **PERSONALITY TYPE:** Realistic. Realistic occupations frequently involve work activities that include practical, hands-on problems and solutions. They often deal with plants; animals; and real-world materials like wood, tools, and machinery. Many of the occupations require working outside and do not involve a lot of paperwork or working closely with others.

EDUCATION/TRAINING PROGRAM(S)— Welding Technology/Welder. **RELATED KNOWLEDGE/COURSES—Building and Construction:** The materials, methods, and tools involved in the construction or repair of houses, buildings, or other structures such as highways and roads. **Mechanical Devices:** Machines and tools, including their designs, uses, repair, and maintenance. **Design:** Design techniques, tools, and principles involved in production of precision technical plans, blueprints, drawings, and models. **Engineering and Technology:** The practical application of engineering science and technology. This includes applying principles, techniques, procedures, and equipment to the design and production of various goods and services.

WORK ENVIRONMENT—Noisy; contaminants; minor burns, cuts, bites, or stings; standing; using hands on objects, tools, or controls; repetitive motions.

Welders, Cutters, Solderers, and Brazers

See the descriptions of these jobs:

- ◉ Solderers and Brazers
- ◉ Welders, Cutters, and Welder Fitters

Zoologists and Wildlife Biologists

- ◉ Education/Training Required: Doctoral degree
- ◉ Annual Earnings: $52,050
- ◉ Growth: 13.0%
- ◉ Annual Job Openings: 1,000
- ◉ Self-Employed: 2.5%
- ◉ Part-Time: 8.2%

Study the origins, behavior, diseases, genetics, and life processes of animals and wildlife. May specialize in wildlife research and management, including the collection and analysis of biological data to determine the environmental effects of present and potential use of land and water areas. Study animals in their natural habitats, assessing effects of environment and industry on animals, interpreting findings, and recommending alternative operating conditions for industry. Inventory or estimate plant and wildlife populations. Analyze characteristics of animals to identify and classify them. Make recommendations on management systems and planning for wildlife populations and habitat, consulting with stakeholders and the public at large to explore options. Disseminate information by writing reports and scientific papers or journal articles and by making presentations and giving talks for schools, clubs, interest groups, and park interpretive programs. Study characteristics of animals such as origin, interrelationships, classification, life histories and diseases, development, genetics, and distribution. Perform administrative duties such as fundraising, public relations, budgeting, and supervision of zoo staff. Organize and conduct experimental studies with live animals in controlled or natural surroundings. Oversee the care and distribution of zoo animals, working with curators and zoo directors to determine the best way to contain animals, maintain their habitats, and manage facilities. Coordinate preventive programs to control the outbreak of wildlife diseases. Prepare collections of preserved specimens or microscopic slides for species identification and study of development or disease. Raise specimens for study and observation or for use in experiments. Collect and dissect animal specimens and examine specimens under microscope.

LEVEL OF ACTIVITY (out of 100)—General Physical Activity: 69.1. **Sitting:** 45.6. **Outdoors:** 41.9.

SKILLS—Science; Management of Financial Resources; Coordination; Writing; Persuasion; Management of Personnel Resources; Negotiation; Judgment and Decision Making.

GOE—**Interest Area:** 01. Agriculture and Natural Resources. **Work Group:** 01.02. Resource Science/Engineering for Plants, Animals, and the Environment. **Other Jobs in This Work Group:** Agricultural Engineers;

Animal Scientists; Conservation Scientists; Environmental Engineers; Foresters; Mining and Geological Engineers, Including Mining Safety Engineers; Petroleum Engineers; Range Managers; Soil and Plant Scientists; Soil and Water Conservationists. **PERSONALITY TYPE:** Investigative. Investigative occupations frequently involve working with ideas and require an extensive amount of thinking. These occupations can involve searching for facts and figuring out problems mentally.

EDUCATION/TRAINING PROGRAM(S)— Wildlife and Wildlands Science and Management; Cell/Cellular Biology and Anatomical Sciences, Other; Zoology/Animal Biology; Entomology; Animal Physiology; Animal Behavior and Ethology; Wildlife Biology; Zoology/Animal Biology, Other; Ecology. **RELATED KNOWLEDGE/COURS-ES—Biology:** Plant and animal organisms and their tissues, cells, functions, interdependencies, and interactions with each other and the environment. **Geography:** Principles and methods for describing the features of land, sea, and air masses, including their physical characteristics; locations; interrelationships; and distribution of plant, animal, and human life. **English Language:** The structure and content of the English language, including the meaning and spelling of words, rules of composition, and grammar. **Law and Government:** Laws, legal codes, court procedures, precedents, government regulations, executive orders, agency rules, and the democratic political process. **Administration and Management:** Business and management principles involved in strategic planning, resource allocation, human resources modeling, leadership technique, production methods, and coordination of people and resources. **Computers and Electronics:** Circuit boards; processors; chips; electronic equipment; and computer hardware and software, including applications and programming.

WORK ENVIRONMENT—More often indoors than outdoors; sitting.

APPENDIX A

The GOE Interest Areas and Work Groups

As the introduction explains, the GOE is a way of organizing the world of work into large Interest Areas and more-specific Work Groups containing jobs that have a lot in common.

Interest Areas have two-digit code numbers; Work Groups have four-digit code numbers beginning with the code number for the Interest Area in which they are classified. These are the 16 GOE Interest Areas and their Work Groups:

01 Agriculture and Natural Resources

>   01.01 Managerial Work in Agriculture and Natural Resources

>   01.02 Resource Science/Engineering for Plants, Animals, and the Environment

>   01.03 Resource Technologies for Plants, Animals, and the Environment

>   01.04 General Farming

>   01.05 Nursery, Groundskeeping, and Pest Control

>   01.06 Forestry and Logging

>   01.07 Hunting and Fishing

>   01.08 Mining and Drilling

02 Architecture and Construction

 02.01 Managerial Work in Architecture and Construction

 02.02 Architectural Design

 02.03 Architecture/Construction Engineering Technologies

 02.04 Construction Crafts

 02.05 Systems and Equipment Installation, Maintenance, and Repair

 02.06 Construction Support/Labor

03 Arts and Communication

 03.01 Managerial Work in Arts and Communication

 03.02 Writing and Editing

 03.03 News, Broadcasting, and Public Relations

 03.04 Studio Art

 03.05 Design

 03.06 Drama

 03.07 Music

 03.08 Dance

 03.09 Media Technology

 03.10 Communications Technology

 03.11 Musical Instrument Repair

04 Business and Administration

 04.01 Managerial Work in General Business

 04.02 Managerial Work in Business Detail

 04.03 Human Resources Support

 04.04 Secretarial Support

 04.05 Accounting, Auditing, and Analytical Support

 04.06 Mathematical Clerical Support

 04.07 Records and Materials Processing

 04.08 Clerical Machine Operation

05 Education and Training

    05.01 Managerial Work in Education

    05.02 Preschool, Elementary, and Secondary Teaching and Instructing

    05.03 Postsecondary and Adult Teaching and Instructing

    05.04 Library Services

    05.05 Archival and Museum Services

    05.06 Counseling, Health, and Fitness Education

06 Finance and Insurance

    06.01 Managerial Work in Finance and Insurance

    06.02 Finance/Insurance Investigation and Analysis

    06.03 Finance/Insurance Records Processing

    06.04 Finance/Insurance Customer Service

    06.05 Finance/Insurance Sales and Support

07 Government and Public Administration

    07.01 Managerial Work in Government and Public Administration

    07.02 Public Planning

    07.03 Regulations Enforcement

    07.04 Public Administration Clerical Support

08 Health Science

    08.01 Managerial Work in Medical and Health Services

    08.02 Medicine and Surgery

    08.03 Dentistry

    08.04 Health Specialties

    08.05 Animal Care

    08.06 Medical Technology

    08.07 Medical Therapy

    08.08 Patient Care and Assistance

    08.09 Health Protection and Promotion

09 Hospitality, Tourism, and Recreation

    09.01 Managerial Work in Hospitality and Tourism

    09.02 Recreational Services

    09.03 Hospitality and Travel Services

    09.04 Food and Beverage Preparation

    09.05 Food and Beverage Service

    09.06 Sports

    09.07 Barber and Beauty Services

10 Human Service

    10.01 Counseling and Social Work

    10.02 Religious Work

    10.03 Child/Personal Care and Services

    10.04 Client Interviewing

11 Information Technology

    11.01 Managerial Work in Information Technology

    11.02 Information Technology Specialties

    11.03 Digital Equipment Repair

12 Law and Public Safety

    12.01 Managerial Work in Law and Public Safety

    12.02 Legal Practice and Justice Administration

    12.03 Legal Support

    12.04 Law Enforcement and Public Safety

    12.05 Safety and Security

    12.06 Emergency Responding

    12.07 Military

13 Manufacturing

    13.01 Managerial Work in Manufacturing

    13.02 Machine Setup and Operation

    13.03 Production Work, Assorted Materials Processing

13.04 Welding, Brazing, and Soldering

13.05 Production Machining Technology

13.06 Production Precision Work

13.07 Production Quality Control

13.08 Graphic Arts Production

13.09 Hands-On Work, Assorted Materials

13.10 Woodworking Technology

13.11 Apparel, Shoes, Leather, and Fabric Care

13.12 Electrical and Electronic Repair

13.13 Machinery Repair

13.14 Vehicle and Facility Mechanical Work

13.15 Medical and Technical Equipment Repair

13.16 Utility Operation and Energy Distribution

13.17 Loading, Moving, Hoisting, and Conveying

14 Retail and Wholesale Sales and Service

14.01 Managerial Work in Retail/Wholesale Sales and Service

14.02 Technical Sales

14.03 General Sales

14.04 Personal Soliciting

14.05 Purchasing

14.06 Customer Service

15 Scientific Research, Engineering, and Mathematics

15.01 Managerial Work in Scientific Research, Engineering, and Mathematics

15.02 Physical Sciences

15.03 Life Sciences

15.04 Social Sciences

15.05 Physical Science Laboratory Technology

15.06 Mathematics and Data Analysis

APPENDIX B

Skills Referenced in This Book

In each of the descriptions of the best jobs not behind a desk found in Part II, we've included a listing of skills required for the job. This table contains specific definitions of each skill.

Definitions of Skills

Skill Name	Definition
Active Learning	Understanding the implications of new information for both current and future problem-solving and decision-making
Active Listening	Giving full attention to what other people are saying, taking time to understand the points being made, asking questions as appropriate, and not interrupting at inappropriate times
Complex Problem Solving	Identifying complex problems and reviewing related information to develop and evaluate options and implement solutions
Coordination	Adjusting actions in relation to others' actions
Critical Thinking	Using logic and reasoning to identify the strengths and weaknesses of alternative solutions, conclusions, or approaches to problems
Equipment Maintenance	Performing routine maintenance on equipment and determining when and what kind of maintenance is needed
Equipment Selection	Determining the kind of tools and equipment needed to do a job
Installation	Installing equipment, machines, wiring, or programs to meet specifications
Instructing	Teaching others how to do something
Judgment and Decision Making	Considering the relative costs and benefits of potential actions to choose the most appropriate one
Learning Strategies	Selecting and using training/instructional methods and procedures appropriate for the situation when learning or teaching new things
Management of Financial Resources	Determining how money will be spent to get the work done and accounting for these expenditures

(continued)

(continued)

Definitions of Skills

Skill Name	Definition
Management of Material Resources	Obtaining and seeing to the appropriate use of equipment, facilities, and materials needed to do certain work
Management of Personnel Resources	Motivating, developing, and directing people as they work, identifying the best people for the job
Mathematics	Using mathematics to solve problems
Monitoring	Monitoring or assessing your performance or that of other individuals or organizations to make improvements or take corrective action
Negotiation	Bringing others together and trying to reconcile differences
Operation and Control	Controlling operations of equipment or systems
Operation Monitoring	Watching gauges, dials, or other indicators to make sure a machine is working properly
Operations Analysis	Analyzing needs and product requirements to create a design
Persuasion	Persuading others to change their minds or behavior
Quality Control Analysis	Conducting tests and inspections of products, services, or processes to evaluate quality or performance
Reading Comprehension	Understanding written sentences and paragraphs in work-related documents
Repairing	Repairing machines or systems by using the needed tools
Science	Using scientific rules and methods to solve problems
Service Orientation	Actively looking for ways to help people
Social Perceptiveness	Being aware of others' reactions and understanding why they react as they do
Speaking	Talking to others to convey information effectively
Systems Analysis	Determining how a system should work and how changes in conditions, operations, and the environment will affect outcomes
Systems Evaluation	Identifying measures or indicators of system performance and the actions needed to improve or correct performance relative to the goals of the system
Technology Design	Generating or adapting equipment and technology to serve user needs
Time Management	Managing one's own time and the time of others
Troubleshooting	Determining causes of operating errors and deciding what to do about it
Writing	Communicating effectively in writing as appropriate for the needs of the audience

Index

A

B

G

H

Q–R

T

U–V

W–Z